Basic Skills Curriculum

SPECTRUM SERIES

Reading • Writing • Math
and more basic skills for successful learning

Grade 3

YOU decide when to practice and what to practice!

Advantages of the Basic Skills Curriculum

Quality...as the nation's #1 educational publisher for grades K-12, the skills you practice are the skills taught in school; lessons in this workbook correspond to current classroom curriculums.

Flexibility...you decide what skills to practice and when to practice, allowing you to follow the curriculum used in the classroom.

Price...more pages and more practice for fewer dollars than any other book of its' kind.

Answer Keys...full page answer keys make home learning easier.

This book is dedicated to our children – Alyx, Nathan, Fred S., Dawn, Molly, Ellen, Rashaun, Brianna, Michele, Bradley, BriAnne, Kristie, Caroline, Dominic, Corey, Lindsey, Spencer, Morgan, Brooke, Cody, Sydney – and to all children who deserve a good education and who love to learn.
- McGraw-Hill Consumer Products

TABLE OF CONTENTS

McGraw-Hill
Consumer Products

*A Division of The **McGraw-Hill** Companies*

Published by McGraw-Hill Learning Materials, an imprint of McGraw-Hill Consumer Products.

Send all inquiries to:
McGraw-Hill Consumer Products
8787 Orion Place
Columbus, OH 43240-4027

1-57768-183-5 **2 3 4 5 6 7 8 9 10 DBH 04 03 02 01 00**

No one else

can match the effectiveness, the simplicity, or the appeal of the

SPECTRUM READING SERIES

Students gain meaningful practice—independently

With the SPECTRUM READING SERIES students not only get the practice they need in essential reading skills, they also enjoy being able to do it on their own.

In grades one through six, each lesson features an illustrated story followed by exercises in comprehension and basic reading skills. Because the same format is used consistently throughout, your students will have little trouble doing the lessons independently. And each two-page lesson can be finished easily in one class period.

Students develop and refine key reading skills.

- **Comprehension** exercises help students go beyond understanding of facts and details to drawing conclusions, predicting outcomes, identifying cause and effect, and developing other higher level comprehension skills.
- **Vocabulary development** builds on words from the reading selections. In addition to learning synonyms, antonyms, and words with multiple meanings, students develop sight vocabulary and learn to use context as a clue for meaning.
- **Decoding** exercises refine students' abilities to "attack" and understand new reading words.
- **Study skills** are developed by helping students apply their reading skills to new tasks, such as using reference materials, reading graphs, and applying other everyday life skills.

Reading selections captivate and motivate.

Students get their best reading practice by actually reading. That's why the selections in the SPECTRUM READING SERIES, in addition to offering practice in skills, also motivate students to read–just for fun.

Students quickly become friends with the characters in these entertaining stories. And they enjoy new levels of reading success–thanks in part to carefully controlled vocabulary and readability as well as beautiful illustrations.

The program adapts completely to any teaching situation.

The SPECTRUM READING SERIES can be used in many different ways.

- For the whole class . . . for intensive reinforcement of reading skills or to supplement a basal reading program.
- For reading groups . . . to provide skills practice at the appropriate levels.
- For individual use . . . to help build a completely individualized program.
- For at-home practice . . . to expand on skills learned in the classroom.

Index of Skills for Reading Grade 3

Numerals indicate the exercise pages on which these skills appear.

Knowing the Words

Working with Words

Reading and Thinking

Learning to Study

Editorial Review Board

SPECTRUM READING
Grade 3

Table of Contents

Office Surprise

What would you do with an old, broken robot?

1 "Carlos, would you like to run over to the office with me for a few minutes?" Mrs. Garza asked.

2 Carlos put down the clock he was trying to fix. "Sure, Mom. I like going to your office on Saturdays."

3 Mrs. Garza wrote ads to help people sell things. She used lots of signs and devices in her ads.

4 While his mom worked, Carlos looked around. He wandered into a storeroom filled with old signs. At first he didn't see anything interesting. Then something made him catch his breath. Hidden in a corner was an old, dusty robot. It was nearly as big as Carlos. It had two metal arms with silver fingers. Its head was round and had two green lights for eyes. Carlos pushed some buttons on the robot's chest, but nothing happened.

5 Carlos hurried to his mother's office and said, "Mom, there's a robot . . ." He stopped when he noticed that his mother was talking to her boss, Mrs. Chung.

6 "Oh, that old thing," Mrs. Chung said. "We used it once, but it's just junk now. It's time to get rid of it."

7 "I wish I could buy it," Carlos said dreamily. "I'd love to have a robot."

8 "It isn't worth much," Mrs. Chung said. "I could sell it to you for ten dollars."

9 "Ten dollars?" Carlos asked, grinning. "I already have about six dollars. I could earn the rest. May I, Mom?"

10 "Well, for a person who likes to fix things, I guess a broken robot sounds just right," his mom said, smiling.

11 Carlos ran back to the storeroom. "You won't have to stay here much longer," he said to the robot. "As soon as I save enough money, I'm taking you home with me."

Knowing the Words

Write the words from the story that have the meanings below.

1. announcements of something for sale ________ (Par. 3)
2. equipment ________ (Par. 3)
3. machine that obeys commands ________ (Par. 4)

In each row below, circle the three words that belong together.

4. run walk sleep wander
5. machine snack robot device
6. fingers arms dust chest

Working with Words

A word that means one of something is **singular.** A word that means more than one is **plural.** Most singular words are made plural by adding *s*. Most words that end in *s, ss, x, ch,* and *sh* are made plural by adding *es*. Form the plural of each word below by adding *s* or *es*.

1. button ____
2. boss ____
3. wish ____
4. robot ____
5. clock ____
6. circus ____

Reading and Thinking

1. Check the answer that tells what the story is mainly about.

   ____ finding a robot

   ____ going to the office

   ____ fixing a clock

2. What day of the week is it in this story? ________

3. What do you think will happen when Carlos saves up ten dollars? ________

   ____

4. Some things are real, and some are make-believe. Write **M** next to the two sentences that tell about make-believe things.

   ____ Robots are machines.

   ____ Robots can think for themselves.

   ____ Robots have feelings.

   ____ Robots can obey commands.

Write the best word to complete each sentence below.

5. Andrea had six square ________ on her good coat, but one fell off. (zippers, buttons, dollars)
6. There was a typewriter in each ________. (office, automobile, meadow)
7. The bike was ________ by some bushes. (written, wanted, hidden)

The Ride Home

Would you wave at a robot?

1 Carlos raced to the storeroom where the robot he had just paid for was kept. "In here, Dad," he said, feeling excited.

2 Mr. Garza looked at the dusty piece of metal and tried to smile. "You didn't tell me it was so big."

3 "It's almost as big as I am," Carlos said proudly. He tried to roll the robot, but the wheels were stuck. "Could you grab it under the arms, Dad?" he asked. "I'll carry this end."

4 Together they carried the robot to the van. People stopped to stare. "This is my very own robot," Carlos told them.

5 Mr. Garza opened the back of the van. "Dad, you wouldn't make my new friend ride in there, would you?" Carlos cried.

6 Mr. Garza noticed that people were watching. He slammed the door shut. "Put it in the backseat," he grumbled.

7 Carlos sat in the backseat beside the robot. He moved the robot's arm and made it wave at people on the street. Everyone pointed and laughed. Carlos smiled back. "Isn't it wonderful, Dad?"

8 Mr. Garza frowned at Carlos. "I don't know," his father said. "I feel silly driving around town with a waving robot." Carlos sat back in his seat. Then he made the robot give his father a friendly wave. Mr. Garza laughed. "Well, I must admit this is a ride I'll never forget."

Knowing the Words

Write the words from the story that have the meanings below.

1. said in a low voice ______________________ (Par. 6)

2. say something is true ______________________ (Par. 8)

Working with Words

A **contraction** is a short way to write two words. An apostrophe **(')** shows that one or more letters have been taken out. Write a contraction from the story for each pair of words below.

1. it is ______________________ (Par. 3)

2. I will ______________________ (Par. 3)

3. would not ______________________ (Par. 5)

4. is not ______________________ (Par. 7)

5. do not ______________________ (Par. 8)

Circle the correct letters to complete each word and write them in the blank.

6. Get into the c____ and put on your seat belt.

   or ir ar

7. Did you f____ get to sweep the floor?

   or ir ar

8. Meet us at the corn ____ after the show.

   or ar er

Reading and Thinking

1. Number the sentences to show the order in which things happened.

   ____ Carlos made the robot wave.

   ____ Carlos and his dad went to the storeroom.

   ____ Carlos and his dad took the robot to the van.

   ____ Carlos tried to roll the robot.

2. How big was the robot? ______________________

   ____

3. Carlos and his dad had to carry the robot because ______________________

   ______________________.

4. Tell two ways that a robot is different from a child. ______________________

   ____

   ____

5. What do you think Carlos will do as soon as he gets the robot home? ______

   ____

Robot Commands

What do you think it would take to make a robot move?

1 "It's great," Marie said when she saw her brother's new project.

2 "I'm going to fix it," Carlos said, looking at the robot in the driveway.

3 Marie smiled and said, "I think a robot is harder to fix than a clock."

4 First, Carlos dusted off his new friend. Next, he oiled the wheels and arms. Then Carlos removed the cover from the robot's back. Inside he saw an old battery and some broken wires. Carlos replaced the wires with wires from an old radio. He took the battery from his camping lantern and put it inside the robot. Finally, Carlos was ready to test it. He pressed some buttons on the robot's chest. The robot just sat there.

5 "Why don't you move?" Carlos yelled. Just then the robot's lights flashed on. It started to roll. For a moment, Carlos stood there with his mouth open. Then he saw that the robot was going toward a neighbor's rose bed.

6 Carlos ran after the robot. "Don't go in there," he yelled, but it kept going.

7 Carlos was getting frantic. "Quit! Stop! Don't!" he yelled all at once.

8 The robot halted just before it hit the first rosebush. Carlos rolled the robot back to his own yard. "I'm glad I got you to work," he said, "but I'm going to have to watch what I say around you."

Knowing the Words

Write the words from the story that have the meanings below.

1. something being worked on ______________ (Par. 1)
2. try out ______________ (Par. 4)
3. very upset ______________ (Par. 7)

Check the meaning that fits the underlined word in each sentence.

4. Jane passed her math <u>test</u>.
   ____ something to measure what a person knows
   ____ try out
5. The dog walked through the <u>bed</u> of daisies.
   ____ piece of furniture
   ____ place for flowers
6. I forgot to wear my <u>watch</u>.
   ____ something that keeps time
   ____ look for

Reading and Thinking

1. Check the answer that tells what the story is mainly about.
   ____ bringing the robot home
   ____ stopping the robot
   ____ getting the robot to work
2. How do you think Carlos felt when he tried to get the robot to move?

   ____

   ____
3. How do you think fixing a robot might be like fixing a radio? ________

   ____
4. Carlos pressed buttons on the robot's chest because ______________

   ______________________________.

Learning to Study

Number each list of words below in alphabetical order.

1. ____ dusted
   ____ friend
   ____ camping
   ____ battery
2. ____ wires
   ____ lights
   ____ robot
   ____ yell
3. ____ smile
   ____ fix
   ____ mouth
   ____ removed
4. ____ yard
   ____ watch
   ____ stop
   ____ pressed

A Special Helper

Read to find out what happens when a robot helps with chores.

1 Carlos dashed into the house. "Mom! Dad! Marie! My robot works!"

2 Everyone hurried outside. They clapped as Carlos demonstrated how the robot moved and stopped. Carlos believed he was the luckiest kid in the whole world.

3 After his family had gone back into the house, Carlos patted the robot on the back. "You're good at taking orders. Maybe you can help me with my chores."

4 Carlos went inside and came back with two wastebaskets. He took one of them to the trash can and took off the can's lid. "Empty," Carlos said, pouring the trash into the can. He put the lid back on.

5 "Now it's your turn," Carlos said. He gave the other wastebasket to the robot. "Empty," he commanded. The robot turned the wastebasket over. All the trash landed on the grass. Carlos picked up the trash and stuffed it back into the wastebasket.

6 "Let's try again," Carlos said. He put the wastebasket into the robot's hands and turned it toward the trash can. "Move," he ordered. The robot rolled to the trash can. It stopped when Carlos told it to. "Empty," Carlos said. The robot turned the wastebasket over. The trash landed on the lid of the trash can.

7 "Oh, no, I forgot about the lid," Carlos moaned. "We've both got a lot to learn, robot."

Knowing the Words

Write the words from the story that have the meanings below.

1. showed by example ______ (Par. 2)
2. commands ______ (Par. 3)
3. small jobs ______ (Par. 3)

Words with opposite meanings are called **antonyms.** Match each word from the first list with its antonym from the second list.

4. ____ moved	a. full
5. ____ empty	b. stopped
6. ____ outside	c. inside

Working with Words

Circle the correct word in ( ) and write it in the blank.

1. Chris ______ a beach ball to the lake. (tank, took)
2. Nan lives in a ______ down the street. (hose, house)
3. ______ we will see a full moon tonight. (Merry, Maybe)

Form the plural of each word below by adding *s* or *es*.

4. grass____	7. dish____
5. hand____	8. back____
6. lid____	9. ax____

Reading and Thinking

1. Number the sentences to show the order in which things happened.

   ____ Carlos showed his family what the robot could do.

   ____ The robot dumped the trash on the ground.

   ____ Carlos showed the robot how to empty the trash.

   ____ The robot dumped the trash on the lid of the trash can.

Write **T** if the sentence is true.
Write **F** if the sentence is false.

2. ____ Carlos was excited because his robot followed orders.
3. ____ Carlos kept his robot's tricks a secret.
4. ____ Carlos had to be careful when he gave orders to the robot.
5. ____ The robot could not hear well.

Words such as *he, she, you, it, we,* and *they* are used in place of other words. Read these sentences. *The robot was made of metal. It had green eyes.* In the second sentence, *it* is used in place of *the robot.*

Read each set of sentences below. Fill in each blank.

6. Carlos yelled to his family. He wanted them to see the robot.

   He stands for ______.

7. Marie liked the robot. She liked to see Carlos having fun.

   She stands for ______.

What's your name?

What do you think would be a good name for Carlos's robot?

1 Every day Carlos taught his robot more commands. When he said "Right" the robot turned right, and it turned left when Carlos said "Left." Carlos even taught the robot to shake hands when he said "Shake."

2 "I think you are ready to meet my sister," Carlos said. He held the door open while giving the robot orders. The robot rolled into the kitchen, bumping into things on the way.

3 Marie was preparing supper. "Meet my sister, Marie," Carlos said to the robot. "Shake." Marie had a bowl of ice in her right hand. The robot did not wait for her to set the bowl down. It just grabbed and shook Marie's hand. Ice flew out of the bowl and scattered across the floor.

4 Marie chuckled and said, "I think your robot needs a little more work, Carlos. Have you named it yet?"

5 "Not yet," Carlos answered. "It needs a very special name. Something that tells what a terrific helper it is." Carlos sat down at the table to think. After a while, he said, "I know, I'll name it Mosh, which is short for *my own special helper.* What do you think, Mosh?"

6 Mosh's eyes lit up. "Did you see that, Marie?" Carlos asked, getting excited. "Mosh's eyes lit up, so I guess that means my robot likes that name."

7 "Carlos, that robot is just a machine," his sister said. "It doesn't have feelings. You understand that, don't you?"

8 "That's what she thinks," Carlos whispered to Mosh. Mosh winked back.

Knowing the Words

Write the words from the story that have the meanings below.

1. wonderful ______________________ (Par. 5)

2. things such as happiness, sadness, and anger ______________________ (Par. 7)

3. said with a quiet voice ______________________ (Par. 8)

Some words sound alike but have different spellings and meanings. Write the word with the correct meaning to complete each sentence below.

4. Ann can hardly ______________ for the show to begin. (wait, weight)

5. Please don't ______________ on that paper. (right, write)

6. ______________ will go to the playground. (Eye, I)

Working with Words

Circle the correct word in ( ) and write it in the blank.

1. Phyllis ______________ her puppy a trick. (taught, that)

2. Please ______________ for me while I get my jacket. (want, wait)

3. Do you know where Muffy has hidden her ______________? (boil, bowl)

Reading and Thinking

1. Check the answer that tells what the story is mainly about.

   ____ fixing supper

   ____ talking to Marie

   ____ naming the robot

2. What name was given to the robot?

   ______________ Why was it given that name? ______________

   ____

3. What other commands do you think the robot could be taught? ______________

   ____

Write **T** if the sentence is true.
Write **F** if the sentence is false.

4. ____ The robot did exactly what it was told to do.

5. ____ The robot could talk.

6. ____ The robot knocked the ice out of Marie's hand.

7. ____ Carlos thinks Mosh has feelings.

Write the best word to complete each sentence below.

8. Gilda was ______________ a flat tire on her bike. (bumping, fixing, preparing)

9. Please ______________ off that sand before you come inside. (wait, shake. whisper)

A New Friend

How do you meet new people?

1 "Mosh, I miss my old friends," Carlos said, feeling blue. "I wonder if I'll ever meet any kids in this new neighborhood. At least I have you. Come on, I'll teach you to play tag."

2 Carlos and Mosh went into the backyard. Carlos tapped Mosh on the arm and said, "When I do that, you're 'it.' When I say 'tag,' you have to catch me and touch me." Then Carlos ran away from Mosh and yelled, "Tag!" The robot started rolling.

3 Just then, Mrs. Wilson, a neighbor, came out to pick flowers. Mosh rolled up behind Mrs. Wilson and tagged her.

4 Mrs. Wilson was so startled that her flowers went flying. Carlos ran over to her. "I'm sorry, Mrs. Wilson. I guess my robot thought you were playing tag."

5 "Oh, that's OK. It just surprised me," Mrs. Wilson said, chuckling. Carlos helped her gather the flowers. When he finished, he looked around for Mosh.

6 "Now where's Mosh?" Carlos cried, running to the front yard. Down the street, he could see Mosh chasing a girl. Carlos ran, yelling, "Stop, Mosh!"

7 The girl looked at Carlos and asked, "Is that yours?"

8 "Yes, we were playing tag," Carlos answered.

9 "Gee, I wish I had a robot," the girl said. "Did you just move here?"

10 Carlos nodded and said, "My name is Carlos. What's yours?"

11 "I'm Susan," the girl replied. "May I play tag with you and your robot?"

12 Carlos smiled and ordered, "Mosh, tag." Mosh began chasing the children. The three of them played all afternoon.

13 On the way home, Carlos asked, "Mosh, did you run away intentionally so I could meet a new friend?" Mosh just winked.

Knowing the Words

Write the words from the story that have the meanings below.

1. sad ______________________
(Par. 1)

2. for a reason ______________________
(Par. 13)

In each row below, circle the three words that belong together.

3. girl robot boy child
4. street sidewalk yard driveway
5. chase run ask roll
6. start down behind beside
7. sat yell look cry

Working with Words

A **compound word** is made by combining two smaller words. Write a compound word using the underlined words in each sentence.

1. A house for a dog is a ______________________.
2. A yard in back of a house is a ______________________.
3. A room where you can store things is a ______________________.
4. Days at the end of the week are called the ______________________.
5. A cup used for tea is a ______________________.

Reading and Thinking

1. Number the sentences to show the order in which things happened.

____ Mrs. Wilson picked flowers.

____ Mosh learned to play tag.

____ Carlos met Susan.

____ Mosh chased a girl.

2. Who is Mrs. Wilson? ______________________

____

Write **T** if the sentence is true.
Write **F** if the sentence is false.

3. ____ Mrs. Wilson was angry.
4. ____ Mosh chased the girl away.
5. ____ Carlos was glad Mosh chased the girl.

6. What do you think it meant when Mosh winked at the end of the story?

____

____

7. Write **R** next to the two sentences that tell about real things.

____ Flowers can fly by themselves.

____ Robots can roll.

____ Children can meet new friends.

8. What do you think Carlos and Mosh did after they got home? ______________________

____

Too Much Trash!

Read to find out how being in a hurry gets Carlos into trouble.

1 "Come on, Mosh, we have to put the trash cans next to the curb," Carlos said. "The trash won't be picked up if the cans aren't out in front of our house. Let's hurry because I want to get back to the broken alarm clock my dad gave me."

2 Carlos pulled one big trash can down the driveway. Mosh pulled the other can. Then Carlos hurried back inside to work on the clock. He got so busy he forgot everything else.

3 Suddenly Carlos jumped up. "I forgot Mosh!" he cried. He dashed out the door and came to a quick halt. Carlos couldn't believe his eyes. Every trash can in the neighborhood was out in front of the Garzas' house. He saw Mosh dragging the last can from the end of the block.

4 "Mosh, stop! These cans don't belong here," Carlos said angrily. "Take them back right now!"

5 The robot turned off its lights and stood still. Mosh refused to move. Carlos stopped to think about Mosh's behavior. He thought to himself, "This is no ordinary robot. Could it have feelings?"

6 "I guess it was my fault, too," Carlos said. "I told you the trash wouldn't be picked up if it wasn't in front of our house. I was only talking about our trash, not the neighbors'."

7 Carlos examined each trash can to try and figure out where each one belonged. Then he returned them to the right houses. He was worn out by the time he got home.

8 "I'm sorry I got mad at you, Mosh," Carlos said later. "It's just that sometimes you can be *too* helpful."

Knowing the Words

Write the words from the story that have the meanings below.

1. edge of the street ______________________ (Par. 1)
2. mistake ______________________ (Par. 6)
3. looked at closely ______________________ (Par. 7)

Words that mean the same, or nearly the same, are called **synonyms.** Circle the pair of synonyms in each row.

4. hurried whispered dashed picked
5. guess sorry halt stop
6. busy mad happy angry
7. big small large quick

Write the word with the correct meaning to complete each sentence below.

8. Have you seen ______________________ trash can? (hour, our)
9. I did not ______________________ the phone ring, did you? (here, hear)

Working with Words

An 's at the end of a word may be used to show that something belongs to someone. Add 's to each name in ( ) and write the new word in the blank.

1. ______________________ clock (Dad)
2. ______________________ lights (Mosh)
3. ______________________ room (Marie)

Reading and Thinking

1. Check the answer that tells what the story is mainly about.
   _____ fixing a clock
   _____ moving trash cans
   _____ getting angry
2. Mosh moved all of the neighbors' trash cans because ______________________
   ______________________.
3. Why do you think Mosh turned off its lights and would not move? ______________________
   ____
   ____
4. Was Carlos still angry at the end of the story? Explain your answer.
   ____
   ____
5. What do you think Mosh did after Carlos said he was sorry? ______________________
   ____

Where's my shirt?

What would you do if you went to get dressed and someone else's clothes were in your drawer?

1 "Carlos, are you done putting away the clean clothes so soon?" Marie asked.

2 "I taught Mosh how to do it," Carlos bragged. "I'm teaching Mosh to help me with all my work."

3 "Great, then you can spend your time doing things over when they're done wrong," Marie teased.

4 Carlos woke up the next day to see his dad standing by the bed. "Carlos, you put away the clothes yesterday, didn't you? Do you really expect me to build houses wearing this?" He was holding one of Marie's fancy pink blouses. "I don't think it will fit," he said. He tried to look angry, but there was a twinkle in his eyes.

5 Mrs. Garza came into the room. "Carlos, don't you think I would look silly wearing this to the office?" She had on Carlos's baseball T-shirt with her skirt.

6 Carlos couldn't help laughing at his mother's outfit. "I'm sorry. I taught the robot to put the clothes away. I guess it got mixed up."

7 Just then a cry came from the hallway. Marie stomped into Carlos's room. "I can't go shopping in Dad's work shirt. Where's my . . ." Marie stopped when she saw her mom wearing Carlos's shirt. "What's going on?" she asked.

8 Mr. Garza chuckled and said, "Our clothes are a little mixed up thanks to Mosh." Then Mr. Garza turned to Carlos and said, "Looks like your day will be spent getting our clothes back in the right places."

9 "That will take hours," Carlos moaned. He looked over at Mosh and frowned. He wasn't sure, but the robot looked as if it were almost laughing.

Knowing the Words

Write the words from the story that have the meanings below.

1. women's shirts ____________ (Par. 4)
2. sparkle ____________ (Par. 4)
3. set of clothes ____________ (Par. 6)
4. walked heavily ____________ (Par. 7)

Write the word with the correct meaning to complete each sentence below.

5. We rode our bicycles ____________ an hour this morning. (for, four)
6. Please ____________ the screen door. (clothes, close)
7. This dark ____________ came from a cherry tree. (would, wood)
8. Gina has ____________ sharpened pencils. (two, to)

Working with Words

Say *city*. Circle the words below that have the sound *c* stands for in *city*.

1. fancy can since clothes
2. center expect except force

A word without any ending is a base word. The base word of *asked* is *ask*. Circle each base word below.

3. mixed
4. wearing
5. frowns
6. laughing
7. going
8. looked

Reading and Thinking

Write **T** if the sentence is true.
Write **F** if the sentence is false.

1. _____ Carlos's chore was to put away the clean clothes.
2. _____ Mr. Garza was too big for Marie's blouse.
3. _____ Mr. Garza was very angry.
4. _____ Carlos was not happy at the end of the story.

5. Whose shirt was Mrs. Garza wearing? ____________

6. Marie stomped into Carlos's room because ____________ ____________.

7. What do you think Carlos might do after he puts the clothes away? ____________

The Big Push

Have you ever tried to use a machine that wasn't working quite right?

1 Carlos picked Mosh up off the ground. "I'm sorry, Mosh, I didn't mean to pitch the ball hard enough to knock you over. I guess you're not ready for baseball yet."

2 "I think I would like some lunch now," Susan said. "I'll go make some sandwiches for us while you two wait here."

3 After Susan left, Carlos sat on the swing. "I think it's time I taught you to push me in a swing, Mosh," he said. "Push just a little to get me started. Then, each time I swing back to you, push me away again."

4 Mosh pushed Carlos gently at first, then harder. Carlos thought he was going to fly right out of the swing. "Stop," Carlos told Mosh. But instead of stopping, Mosh pushed harder. Carlos felt dizzy. Again, he ordered the robot to stop, but Mosh kept pushing.

5 Carlos was getting worried. How would he ever get off this swing? Just then Susan came back with the sandwiches. "Can you get Mosh to stop?" Carlos yelled to her.

6 Susan told Mosh to stop, but the robot pushed the swing harder and harder. Then Susan remembered Mosh's battery. She jerked the cover off the robot's back and took out the battery. Mosh stopped instantly. Carlos waited for the swing to stop. His legs trembled as he got off.

7 "There must be something wrong with Mosh," Susan said.

8 When Carlos looked inside Mosh, he found some loose wires. "These wires must have come loose when the baseball hit it," he said.

9 Carlos fixed Mosh. Then he said to the robot, "You are as good as new now. I won't ever ask you to push me in a swing again, though. If you had pushed me any harder, I would have been the first kid in space."

Knowing the Words

Write the words from the story that have the meanings below.

1. right away ______________ (Par. 6)

2. shook ______________ (Par. 6)

Some words are spelled the same but have different meanings. For example, *can* might mean "something that food comes in" or "able to do something."

Look at the list of words below. For each pair of sentences, one word from the list will correctly complete both. Choose the correct word to fill in the blanks for each pair of sentences.

fly left like

3. That kite looks just ______________ mine.

   I really ______________ to watch circus performers.

4. Do you have any money ______________?

   Do you write with your ______________ hand?

5. How do you think birds ______________?

   The ______________ walked on the table.

Working with Words

Fill in each blank with the correct letters to make a word.

kn igh wr ph

1. ______ong
2. r______t
3. ______ee
4. micro______one

Reading and Thinking

1. Number the sentences to show the order in which things happened.

   ____ Susan removed Mosh's battery.

   ____ Carlos taught Mosh to push a swing.

   ____ Mosh was knocked down by a baseball.

   ____ Carlos fixed Mosh's wires.

2. Check two words that tell how Carlos probably felt when Mosh wouldn't obey him.

   ____ frightened ____ amused

   ____ bored ____ confused

3. Mosh wouldn't stop pushing the swing because ______________

   ______________.

4. What did Susan do to get Mosh to stop? ______________

5. Check two sentences that tell how Carlos and Susan are alike.

   ____ They both own a robot.

   ____ They are both children.

   ____ They had trouble with Mosh.

Write the best word to complete each sentence below.

6. Do you ______________ when you are scared? (command, tremble, push)

7. Barb felt ______________ when she got off the ride. (ready, new, dizzy)

More Than Just Worms

How can you tell that seeds have been planted in a certain area?

1 "I'm glad you are going fishing with us today," Carlos said to Susan. "We will be leaving in a couple of hours, so let's dig up some worms now. Mosh can help, and it won't take long."

2 Carlos got a small shovel and a can for the worms. "Do not dig where grass or flowers are growing, Mosh," Carlos explained. He showed the robot how to dig up the worms and put them into the can. "You finish this. Susan and I will get the rest of the stuff ready."

3 The children went into the house and packed a picnic lunch. When they were finished, Susan looked out the window. "I hate to say this, but Mosh is digging up Mrs. Wilson's garden," she said.

4 Carlos dashed outside. "Mosh, stop!" he yelled. He rushed over to Mrs. Wilson's yard. "I know you can't see anything growing, but Mrs. Wilson planted seeds here this morning."

5 Carlos knew he had to tell Mrs. Wilson. He knocked on her door. When Mrs. Wilson opened the door, Carlos said shyly, "My robot accidentally dug up your seeds. Mosh was digging worms for our fishing trip. I'll buy more seeds and stay home to plant them."

6 "Those seeds can wait a day," Mrs. Wilson said. "I wouldn't want you to miss out on a fishing trip. I know how much fun that is." She gave a little sigh. "I haven't been fishing in years."

7 "Would you like to go with us?" Carlos asked.

8 Mrs. Wilson's face lit up. "I would love to. I think I still have my old fishing pole somewhere around here."

9 "Don't worry about worms," Carlos said. "Thanks to Mosh, we have enough to catch every fish in the lake."

Knowing the Words

Write the words from the story that have the meanings below.

1. not done on purpose ______________ (Par. 5)
2. bother ______________ (Par. 9)

Choose the correct word below to fill in the blanks for each pair of sentences.

can   yard

3. This ______________ does not have a label on it.

   I ______________ finish my homework in fifteen minutes.

4. A deer is in the ______________.

   Joan bought a ______________ of ribbon.

Working with Words

A **suffix** is a group of letters added to the end of a word that changes the meaning of the word. The suffix **-ly** helps tell how something was done. *Shyly* means "done in a shy way."

Add **-ly** to the words below. Use the new words to complete the sentences.

accidental   sad   loud

1. Gretchen watched ______________ as her friend rode away.
2. Steve ______________ spilled his apple juice.
3. Agnes laughed ______________.

Reading and Thinking

1. Check the answer that tells what the story is mainly about.

   ____ digging for worms

   ____ going fishing

   ____ talking to Mrs. Wilson

2. Mosh dug up Mrs. Wilson's garden

   because ______________

   ______________.

3. What kind of person do you think Carlos is? Explain your answer.

   ____

   ____

Read each set of sentences below. Fill in each blank.

4. The seeds were planted yesterday. They haven't started growing yet.

   They stands for ______________.

5. Lucy and I are the same age. We go to school together.

   We stands for ______________.

Surprise!

What would you expect to find in a suitcase?

1 "Carlos, would you get my suitcase when you get the fishing poles?" asked Marie. "I'm staying over at Jane's tonight."

2 Carlos got the fishing poles and Marie's suitcase. He gave the suitcase to Mosh and said, "Would you take this to Marie while I take these poles out to the car? Then look for something with a lid to put these worms in. We don't want them to crawl all over the car."

3 After Carlos put the poles in the car, he came back inside to help Mosh with the worms. "OK," he said to the robot, "what did you find to put the worms in?" Mosh didn't move. Carlos looked around, but he didn't see the worms anywhere.

4 Just then a scream came from Marie's room. "Carlos Garza, get in here this second!"

5 Carlos's face turned pale. "Mosh, you didn't put them in Marie's suitcase, did you?" he gasped. Carlos hurried into Marie's bedroom.

6 Marie spoke angrily as she pointed to her suitcase. "This is the worst thing that pile of bolts has ever done!"

7 "I'm sorry," Carlos apologized. "Mosh was just trying to find something with a lid on it."

8 "Those worms have probably ruined my suitcase. What am I going to do?" Marie cried.

9 "Take my suitcase," Carlos offered. "I'll clean this one out. It will be as good as new."

10 Carlos took Marie's suitcase outside and opened it up. He was putting the worms back into the can when Susan came by with her fishing pole. She gave Carlos a strange look. "I've never seen anyone carry their worms in a suitcase before," she said with a chuckle.

11 Carlos grumbled, "Mosh still has a lot to learn."

Knowing the Words

Write the words from the story that have the meanings below.

1. breathed in quickly ______________________ (Par. 5)

2. said you were sorry ______________________ (Par. 7)

Choose the correct word to fill in the blanks for each pair of sentences.

spoke   second

3. The alarm clock will ring any ______________________ now.

   Tracy sits in the ____________ seat in the first row.

4. Donna ____________ in a whisper.

   The wheel on Ann's bike has a broken ______________________.

Working with Words

Words are sometimes easier to read if they are divided into parts called **syllables.** Some words have two consonants between two vowels. These words can be divided into syllables between the consonants, as in *ex/pect.*

In each word below, draw a line to divide the word into syllables.

1.	welcome	5.	temper
2.	perhaps	6.	blossom
3.	forgive	7.	traffic
4.	awful	8.	borrow

Reading and Thinking

Write **T** if the sentence is true.
Write **F** if the sentence is false.

1. _____ Mosh put the worms in Marie's suitcase.

2. _____ Marie was upset when she saw the worms.

3. _____ Susan thought it was funny to see the worms in the suitcase.

4. What two things did Mosh do while Carlos put the fishing poles in the car? ______________________

   ____

5. Why do you think Marie called Mosh a pile of bolts? ______________________

   ____

6. What do you think Carlos will do after he cleans out the suitcase?

   ____

   ____

Write the best word to complete each sentence below.

7. The baby was ______________________ through the grass. (putting, finding, crawling)

8. Jenny ______________________ the can of soup. (opened, grumbled, stayed)

9. Rose wore a ______________________ blue blouse. (round, pale, plenty)

The Fishing Trip

How long do you think it takes to catch a fish?

1 "Dad, can Mosh go fishing with us?" Carlos asked. "After all, Mosh dug up the worms for us."

2 "All right," his dad sighed. "Just try to keep Mosh out of trouble for a few hours."

3 When they got to the lake, Carlos and Susan took Mosh to one side of the dock. Mr. Garza and Mrs. Wilson sat on the other side. Carlos showed Mosh how to throw the line into the water. To Carlos and Susan's surprise, Mosh started making a high-pitched whistling noise. A few seconds later, Mosh's pole was bent over like a rainbow.

4 "You've got a fish, Mosh. Pull it in!" Carlos cried. He helped Mosh pull in the fish. Mosh threw the line back into the lake. The funny whistling noise started again. Soon Mosh, Carlos, and Susan all had fish pulling on their lines.

5 "Hey!" Carlos said excitedly, "Mosh knows how to call the fish."

6 "Carlos, I'm sure there are just more fish on your side of the dock," his dad said.

7 "Can we trade sides to see?" Carlos asked. He, Susan, and Mosh traded places with Mr. Garza. Mrs. Wilson stayed on the side with Mosh just in case Carlos was right.

8 As soon as they had their hooks in the lake, Mosh began to make the noise. "I've got one!" Mrs. Wilson cried.

9 Mr. Garza kept looking back at all the fish the others were catching. He still hadn't caught one fish. Finally, he took his pole and moved next to Mosh. Carlos looked at his father and smiled. Mr. Garza winked.

10 "This is pretty good luck, isn't it?" Carlos said. "Mosh sure is a special robot. Do you think it could've been used in a fishing ad?"

Knowing the Words

Write the word from the story that has the meaning below.

1. high sounding ________________ (Par. 3)

Circle the pair of antonyms (opposites) in each row.

2. pushing crying pulling whistling
3. soon bent side straight
4. later other right wrong
5. started winked finished cried

Working with Words

Write a contraction from the story for each pair of words below.

1. you have ________________ (Par. 4)
2. I am ________________ (Par. 6)
3. I have ________________ (Par. 8)
4. had not ________________ (Par. 9)
5. could have ________________ (Par. 10)

Circle the correct letters to complete each word and write them in the blank.

6. Did Jennifer or Mary go f_____st?

   or ir ar

7. Will you _____der spaghetti?

   or ir ar

8. Let's go ov_____ to my house.

   er ar or

9. Do you h_____ any strange noises?

   are ear ore

Reading and Thinking

1. Number the sentences to show the order in which things happened.

   _____ Mrs. Wilson caught a fish.

   _____ Carlos showed Mosh how to fish.

   _____ Carlos and Susan traded places with Carlos's dad.

   _____ Mr. Garza sat next to Mosh.

2. Write **R** next to the two sentences that tell about real things.

   _____ Worms are used to catch fish.

   _____ Rainbows can be used to catch fish.

   _____ Fish can be on one side of a dock and not the other.

3. The fish were biting because ________________

   ________________.

4. What do you think will happen when Carlos's dad is sitting next to Mosh?

   ____

   ____

   ____

Write the best word to complete each sentence below.

5. The fish on Lin's ________________ was a foot long. (water, hook, lake)
6. Pat put the boat next to the ________________. (dock, noise, rainbow)

Sara and Bill

Read to find out how Mosh teaches a lesson without saying a word.

1 "Dad, Mrs. Wilson's grandchildren are visiting her. Their names are Sara and Bill," Carlos said.

2 "Hmm, those are the names I saw on those papers in our yard," Mr. Garza said. "Will you please go out and clean up the mess?"

3 "Sure," Carlos answered. "Come on, Mosh." Carlos showed the robot how to help pick up the papers and put them in the trash can. Soon the yard was clean.

4 That afternoon Carlos went over to get to know Sara and Bill. Mrs. Wilson served them lemonade at the picnic table. As soon as Sara put her cup down, Mosh picked it up and took it over to the trash can. Mosh did the same when Bill put his cup down.

5 "Mosh doesn't have to do that," Mrs. Wilson said. "Sara and Bill can clean up their own messes."

6 "Yeah, we don't need a dumb robot to pick up our stuff," Sara snapped.

7 "What about all your papers that blew into our yard?" Carlos asked.

8 Sara looked innocently at Carlos. "What papers?" she asked.

9 Before Carlos could answer, Mosh came across the yard with the trash can. The robot turned it over. All the papers went on Sara's lap. "What are you doing?" Sara cried, surprised.

10 Mrs. Wilson looked at the papers. "Why, Sara, aren't these your pictures?

And these papers have your name on them, Bill. It appears that Carlos and Mosh really have been cleaning up after you. Say you're sorry and then clean up this mess," she said, frowning.

11 Sara and Bill were not happy with Carlos when he left, but he didn't care. He put his arm around his one-of-a-kind friend. "Good going, Mosh," he said. "Actions *do* speak louder than words."

Knowing the Words

Write the words from the story that have the meanings below.

1. said in a mean way ______________ (Par. 6)
2. without fault ______________ (Par. 8)
3. looks like ______________ (Par. 10)

Synonyms are words that have the same or nearly the same meaning. Circle the pair of synonyms in each row.

4. paper stuff garbage trash
5. cleaned served put gave

Working with Words

When a word ends with a vowel and a consonant, the consonant is usually doubled before adding **-ed** or **-ing.** For example, *snap + ed = snapped.*

Double the last consonant in the word in ( ). Then add **-ed** or **-ing** to the word to make a word that completes each sentence.

1. Are you ______________ that book on the shelf? (put)
2. Joan ______________ on the ice. (slip)
3. Lou is always ______________ that toy around. (drag)

Fill in each blank with the correct letters to make a word.

wr igh mb

4. du_____ **5.** _____ite **6.** h_____

Reading and Thinking

1. Check the answer that tells what the story is mainly about.
   _____ drinking lemonade
   _____ learning a lesson
   _____ going to Mrs. Wilson's
2. What did Mrs. Wilson serve to the kids? ______________
3. Why did Mosh throw Sara and Bill's cups away as soon as they were finished? ______________
4. What do you think Carlos meant when he called Mosh a "one-of-a-kind friend"? ______________
5. Why do you think Mosh dumped the papers in Sara's lap? ______________

Disappearing Newspapers

People are calling to say they didn't get the newspapers. What do you think happened to the papers?

1 "Let's get these newspapers ready to go, Mosh," Carlos said. "Since we're still new at this, I want to prove that we can do a good job."

2 Carlos rolled up his papers and put rubber bands around them. Mosh put them into the bag. Then Carlos delivered the papers to the people on his route. He did not notice that Mosh had followed him with the trash can. As soon as Carlos finished, he took his bag home and then ran to Susan's house.

3 When Carlos got home, Marie was quite upset. "Why didn't you deliver your papers today?" she asked. "A lot of people have called to complain."

4 "What do you mean?" Carlos asked, puzzled. "I did that before I went to my friend's house."

5 "Well, the phone has not stopped ringing for the last two hours," Marie said. "Everyone says the same thing. They didn't get their papers today."

6 "Gee, fifty papers can't just vanish," Carlos mumbled. He took a walk around his route. He could not find one newspaper. Then he remembered that he had just taught Mosh to put papers in the trash. Carlos raced home. When he looked inside the trash can, he saw a pile of neatly folded newspapers.

7 Carlos found Mosh. "Did you put all of those papers in the trash?" he asked. The robot's green eyes flashed.

8 "Mosh," Carlos said, trying to be patient, "I know I told you that papers belong in the trash, but I meant ones that people don't want anymore. People like to read their newspapers before they throw them away. Now I have to deliver them all again."

9 Carlos put the papers back into his bag. "You stay here, Mosh," he said. "I'm too tired to let you help me right now."

Knowing the Words

Write the words from the story that have the meanings below.

1. talk about things that are wrong ________ (Par. 3)
2. confused ________ (Par. 4)
3. said in a low voice ________ (Par. 6)
4. calm ________ (Par. 8)

In each row below, circle the three words that belong together.

5. taught learned remembered have
6. hour deliver newspaper route
7. phone ring trash talk

Choose the correct word below to fill in the blanks for each pair of sentences.

ring saw

8. I ________ Jill at school.

   This ________ is too dull.

9. We hear the bell ________ every day at noon.

   This ________ does not fit my finger.

Reading and Thinking

1. Where did Carlos find the newspapers? ________
2. The papers had to be delivered twice because ________ ________.

Write **T** if the sentence is true.
Write **F** if the sentence is false.

3. ____ Mosh helped deliver the papers.
4. ____ Carlos had not been delivering papers for very long.
5. ____ Susan told Carlos where he could find the newspapers.
6. What do you think Carlos did after he delivered the papers again? ________ ________

Learning to Study

Number each list of words below in alphabetical order.

1. ____ rush
   ____ remember
   ____ robot
   ____ ring
2. ____ trash
   ____ tell
   ____ too
   ____ that
3. ____ finish
   ____ flash
   ____ friend
   ____ found
4. ____ mumble
   ____ many
   ____ Mosh
   ____ meant

Car Wash

Have you ever been surprised by someone with a hose?

1 "Carlos, if you help me baby-sit for Sara and Bill, I'll share the money with you," Marie said.

2 Carlos paused to think. "Well, I do need money to buy a new battery for Mosh," he said.

3 "Great," Marie said happily. "Let's go!"

4 Marie and Carlos walked over to Mrs. Wilson's. At noon, Marie went inside to fix some lunch. Carlos stayed outside with a book. He wanted to keep an eye on Sara and Bill.

5 "We're going to play car wash," Sara announced. "Do you want to play?"

6 "No, thanks," Carlos said. "I'll just sit here and read my book."

7 Sara and Bill pretended they were washing everything in the yard. They washed the lawn chairs, the picnic table, and the birdbath.

8 Then Sara yelled, "Look at that dirty car!"

9 Carlos looked up and saw Bill pointing the hose at him. "I'm glad that hose isn't turned on," Carlos chuckled. He went back to reading. Then he thought, "I wonder where Sara is?" Carlos looked up just in time to see water shoot out of the hose and spray all over him.

10 Carlos jumped up and tried to run away, but it was already too late. He was soaked. "Turn that off!" Carlos screamed. "Sara, why did you do that?"

11 "I'm sorry," Sara said. "I really didn't think the water would spray that far."

12 "The water did cool me off," Carlos admitted, "but from now on, please wash your pretend cars with pretend water."

Knowing the Words

Write the word from the story that has the meaning below.

1. stopped for a moment ______________ (Par. 2)

Check the meaning that fits the underlined word in each sentence.

2. Sue tried to fix the clock.

   ____ prepare

   ____ repair

3. The wash was hung on the fence.

   ____ clean with water

   ____ clothes being cleaned

Working with Words

Write a compound word using the underlined words in each sentence.

1. A place where a bird can take a bath is a ______________.

2. The time when you eat lunch is called ______________.

An 's at the end of a word is used to show that something belongs to one person or thing. To show that something belongs to more than one person or thing, an apostrophe (') is added to the end of a plural word that ends in *s*.

Circle each group of words below that shows that more than one person or thing owns something.

3.	book's pages	5.	kids' games
4.	cars' wheels	6.	Sara's chair

Reading and Thinking

1. Number the sentences to show the order in which things happened.

   ____ Carlos was sprayed with water.

   ____ Marie and Carlos agreed to baby-sit.

   ____ Marie started to fix lunch.

   ____ Sara apologized.

2. What kind of a person do you think Sara is? Explain your answer. ____

   ____

3. Write two ways in which Sara and Bill's car wash was different from a real car wash. ______________

   ____

4. Who turned the water on when Carlos got sprayed? ______________

5. Did Carlos stay mad at Sara? ____

   How do you know? ______________

   ____

Write the best word to complete each sentence below.

6. Jane ______________ the sponge in the sink. (asked, soaked, pretended)

7. Ruth ______________ when the bee stung her. (cried, chuckled, ate)

Rabbit–Sitting

Read to find out what happens when Mosh becomes jealous of a rabbit.

1 Carlos set the rabbit cage in his room. "I'm glad Susan asked me to watch Fluffy while she is at camp," Carlos said to Mosh.

2 Mosh rolled over to the cage to investigate. The rabbit backed up into a corner and shook. "Get away, Mosh. You are scaring Fluffy," Carlos explained.

3 When Carlos took Fluffy out of the cage, Mosh tried to pet the rabbit. "Don't, Mosh," Carlos said, "you might hurt her." Mosh rolled into a corner and turned off its lights.

4 Carlos played with Fluffy all morning. He locked the rabbit in the cage when he went to eat lunch. When he came back, the cage was empty. Carlos was frantic as he searched all over the house for the missing rabbit. He could not find Fluffy anywhere.

5 Carlos rushed back to his room. "Mosh, did you let that rabbit out of the cage?" he asked. "Why would you do such a thing? Were you trying to play with Fluffy or were you jealous because I was playing with her instead of with you?"

6 Mosh turned around and faced the wall. Carlos thought, "This robot is amazing. It has feelings!" He couldn't help smiling. "So that's it! You are jealous," he said, slightly amused. "Mosh, that rabbit will never take your place. I like her, but I love you. You're my own special helper, remember? Now show me what you did with Fluffy."

7 Mosh rolled over to the closet and opened the door. Inside was a cozy bed made of towels. Fluffy was safely asleep.

8 Carlos grinned. "Let's get her back into the cage," he said. "Or maybe it would be safer to leave Fluffy out and lock you in the cage," he teased.

Knowing the Words

Write the words from the story that have the meanings below.

1. look into ______________ (Par. 2)
2. wanting something that someone else has ______________ (Par. 5)
3. a little bit ______________ (Par. 6)
4. cloths used for drying ______________ (Par. 7)

Working with Words

Some words that have one consonant between two vowels are divided into syllables after the first vowel. The first vowel sound in these words is most often long, as in *bā/by*.

Other words that have one consonant between two vowels are divided after the consonant. In these words, the first vowel is most often short, as in *wăg/on*.

The words below have been divided into syllables. Put a mark above the first vowel in each word to show if the vowel stands for a long or short sound. Mark the long vowels with ¯ over the letter. Mark the short vowels with ˘.

1.	nev/er	**4.**	clos/et	**7.**	si/lent
2.	co/zy	**5.**	sev/en	**8.**	po/ny
3.	pal/ace	**6.**	pi/lot	**9.**	la/dy

Say *gentle*. Circle the words below that have the sound *g* stands for in *gentle*.

10.	cage	get	page	hedge
11.	giant	age	agree	gum
12.	gift	edge	engine	garden

Reading and Thinking

1. Check the answer that tells what the story is mainly about.

   _____ playing with Mosh

   _____ camping out

   _____ taking care of Fluffy

2. Why did Fluffy sit in the corner of her cage and shake? ______________

   ____

3. Mosh put the rabbit in the closet because ______________

   ______________.

4. Did Mosh hurt the rabbit? ______________

   How do you know? ______________

   ____

5. What do you think Carlos and Mosh did after they put Fluffy back in her cage? ______________

   ____

A Pet for Carlos

Have you ever been frightened by something you thought you saw?

1 "I miss Susan's rabbit," Carlos sighed. "I wish I had a soft, furry pet. It's too bad that I'm not allowed to have pets." Suddenly Carlos snapped his fingers and said, "I know, I'll make Mosh my pet."

2 Carlos wrapped Mosh in an old brown rug. Then he put one of Marie's shaggy winter hats over Mosh's head. "You look great, Mosh," Carlos said when he finished. "Let's show Marie."

3 Marie was in the den reading a magazine. She looked up as Carlos and Mosh entered the room and asked, "What are you two doing now?"

4 "Mosh is my new pet," Carlos said proudly.

5 "Pet!" Marie laughed. "It looks more like a monster that you should keep hidden."

6 Carlos decided to call Tommy, a friend from his old neighborhood. He wanted to tell Tommy all about Mosh. "I wish you could move here, too," Carlos said.

7 When Mosh heard the word *move,* he rolled out the door. Carlos heard screaming outside. He looked out and saw kids running in all directions, looking very frightened. "A monster!" he heard one child yell.

8 Carlos quickly said good-bye to Tommy and hung up the phone. He dashed outside and saw Mosh rolling down the sidewalk. The kids were all running away from the disguised robot. "Mosh, stop!" Carlos yelled when he caught up with it. He pulled off Mosh's hat so everyone would see it wasn't really a monster.

9 "I don't know why people were afraid of you," Carlos said. "I think you make a great pet. I guess people just aren't used to seeing pets with wheels."

Knowing the Words

Write the words from the story that have the meanings below.

1. covered with hair ____________ (Par. 1)
2. dressed up so you can't be recognized ____________ (Par. 8)

Circle the pair of antonyms (opposites) in each row.

3.	neighbor	friend	beast	enemy
4.	quickly	loudly	slowly	sadly
5.	shaggy	soft	hard	gentle
6.	great	huge	terrible	old

Learning to Study

The word you look up in a dictionary is called an **entry word.** Many words that have endings are not listed as entry words. To find these words, look up the base word to which the ending is added. To find the word *sighed,* look up *sigh.* Write the word under which each of these words would be listed in a dictionary.

1. wheels ____________
2. reading ____________
3. rolled ____________
4. wanted ____________
5. screaming ____________
6. suddenly ____________
7. directions ____________

Reading and Thinking

1. How was Mosh like a pet when Carlos finished dressing it up?

____

____

2. What did Marie say Mosh looked like? ____________

3. Mosh rolled out the door because ____________.

Write **T** if the sentence is true.
Write **F** if the sentence is false.

4. _____ Mosh was dressed up to look like an animal.
5. _____ Carlos missed his friend.
6. _____ Carlos watched Mosh roll out of the house.
7. _____ The kids were afraid of Mosh's wheels.

The First Day of School

How would you feel about going to a new school?

1 "I'm kind of nervous about going to a new school," Carlos told Susan as they walked to school. "Look, everyone is staring at me."

2 Susan looked around. "They aren't staring at you. Look behind you."

3 Carlos looked back. "Oh, no," he moaned. "Mosh, you can't come to school! What am I going to do? There's no time to take Mosh back home."

4 "We can hide Mosh in the closet where the cleaning supplies are kept," Susan suggested. Susan and Carlos went into the building through the back door so that nobody would see them. They put a rag over the robot and hid it in the back of the closet.

5 Carlos forgot about Mosh once school started. He liked his teacher, Mrs. Bell, and the kids in his class. Everything was fine until Mrs. Bell spilled some paint on the floor. She asked a boy named Chad to get the mop. Carlos felt sick.

6 Soon Chad came rushing back into the room. He was pushing Mosh. "Look what I found!" he said, looking surprised. Carlos wanted to hide.

7 "I wonder if our new principal, Mr. Lee, knows anything about this?" Mrs. Bell said aloud.

8 Carlos didn't want Mrs. Bell to take Mosh to the office. He raised his hand and said, "It's mine. It followed me to school today, so I hid it in the closet."

9 "You have your own robot?" Mrs. Bell asked, sounding pleased. "Tell us about it."

10 Carlos told the class that Mosh was a one-of-a-kind robot. He showed them some of the special things Mosh could do. The children listened with interest while Carlos spoke.

11 On the way home from school, Carlos said to Mosh, "Thanks to you, all the kids in school know me already. But from now on, you stay home and try to keep out of trouble while I go to school."

Knowing the Words

Write the word from the story that has the meaning below.

1. things used to do a job ______________________ (Par. 4)

Synonyms are words that have the same or nearly the same meaning. Circle the pair of synonyms in each row.

2. spill rush start hurry
3. stare hide look push
4. suggest like stay remain

Learning to Study

At the top of each page in a dictionary are two words in dark print called **guide words.** They can help you find other words in the dictionary. The first guide word tells what the first word is on the page. The second guide word tells what the last word is on the page.

The words in a dictionary are listed in alphabetical order. To find a word, decide if it comes in alphabetical order between the guide words on the page. If it docs, the word will be on that page. Check two words that could be found on each page that has these guide words.

1. **mop/nobody**
   - _____ push
   - _____ named
   - _____ nervous
2. **paint/robot**
   - _____ push
   - _____ sound
   - _____ principal
3. **closet/door**
   - _____ cried
   - _____ did
   - _____ back
4. **school/teacher**
   - _____ surprise
   - _____ stare
   - _____ thanks

Reading and Thinking

1. Number the sentences to show the order in which things happened.
   - _____ Mrs. Bell spilled some paint.
   - _____ Carlos showed the class some of the things Mosh could do.
   - _____ Mosh followed Carlos and Susan to school.
   - _____ Chad found Mosh.
2. Where did Carlos and Susan hide Mosh? ______________________
3. The children hid Mosh because ______________________.

Write the best word to complete each sentence below.

4. Alice hung her winter coat in the ______________________. (sink, tent, closet)
5. Do you know the name of the ______________________ at our school? (command, trouble, principal)

Too Cold

Read to find out what Carlos learns about asking Mosh for help.

1 "Carlos, go take your bath and get ready for bed," Marie said. "Hurry! Mom and Dad will be home soon."

2 Carlos was almost finished with a book and didn't want to stop until he knew how the story ended. "Mosh, please go fill the bathtub with water," he said.

3 A few minutes later, Carlos finished the book. He went to check on Mosh. Carlos gasped when he saw the bathtub. "Turn off the water, Mosh! I didn't mean for you to fill it to the top."

4 As he climbed into the bathtub, Carlos scowled. The water was colder than he liked. "Could you get something warm for me to wear when I get out of here?" he asked Mosh.

5 Just as Carlos got out of the tub, Mosh returned with something for Carlos to wear. Carlos looked at it and moaned. "Mosh, I meant something of my own, not my dad's robe."

6 Carlos put on the robe. He hoped he could get to his bedroom without falling. Just as he started down the hall, he heard his parents coming to say good night. Carlos took one step and tripped over the long robe.

7 "Carlos, what are you doing?" his mom asked.

8 Carlos lay on the floor, looking up at his parents. "I asked Mosh to get me something warm to wear. I forgot to say I wanted something of my own."

9 Carlos's mom and dad couldn't help laughing. At last his mom said, "I guess you need to choose your words more carefully when you give Mosh an order."

10 "You can say that again," Carlos said, nodding.

Knowing the Words

Write the words from the story that have the meanings below.

1. investigate ______________ (Par. 3)
2. looked angry ______________ (Par. 4)

Choose the correct word below to fill in the blanks for each pair of sentences.

top check

3. Leah watched the ______________ spin.

   My paper is on ______________.

4. Did you ______________ the spelling of the words in that story?

   Brenda wrote a ______________ to pay for the movie tickets.

Learning to Study

The meanings of words can be found in the dictionary. Some words have more than one meaning. Look at the words and their meanings below. Answer the questions.

trip **1** to fall **2** journey
try to work at
tub container for water

1. Which word means "container for water"? ______________
2. What does the word *try* mean?

   ____
3. What is the first meaning of *trip*?

   ____

Reading and Thinking

Write **T** if the sentence is true.
Write **F** if the sentence is false.

1. _____ Marie was baby-sitting for Carlos.
2. _____ Carlos was happy with the water in the bathtub.
3. _____ Carlos is much shorter than his dad.
4. _____ Carlos's parents were angry with him.
5. What was Carlos doing when Marie told him to go take a bath? ______________

   ____
6. What do you think Carlos did after he spoke to his parents? ______________

   ____

Write the best word to complete each sentence below.

7. Vickie wrote a funny ______________ about a robot. (menu, story, word)
8. Put the shirt in the ______________ when you take it off. (drawer, bathtub, garage)
9. I can't understand you when you ______________. (laugh, mumble, ask)
10. I think I should ______________ my brown pants today. (hurry, hear, wear)

Mosh Speaks

Have you ever tried to fool someone but ended up being sorry you did?

1 "I hope this plan of ours works, Susan," Carlos said as the two of them walked to school with Mosh. "If it does, then Lizzy Wood won't call Mosh a dumb robot any more."

2 "It will work," Susan said. "All you have to do is read the questions from each card in order. The tape player inside Mosh will answer them. Everyone will think Mosh knows how to talk. What could go wrong?"

3 When it was time for sharing, Carlos was chosen to go first. He was so excited that he dropped his cards with the questions on them. Quickly, Carlos picked up the cards and turned on the tape player.

4 "Hi, kids. It's nice to be here today," the voice inside Mosh said. "Carlos, why don't you ask me some questions?"

5 "All right, Mosh, who teaches our class?" Carlos asked.

6 "A kangaroo," answered Mosh. The class roared with laughter. Carlos wished he could stop, but it was too late. The tape was already rolling.

7 "What hops and carries babies in a pouch?" Carlos continued.

8 "Mrs. Bell," Mosh said. The class laughed even harder.

9 "What a dumb robot," Lizzy yelled. Carlos wished he could vanish.

10 "I don't know how he did it, but I think it was clever of Carlos to get Mosh to talk," Mrs. Bell said, smiling.

11 Carlos felt better. But he decided not to play tricks again. He and Mosh got into enough trouble without them.

Knowing the Words

Write the words from the story that have the meanings below.

1. a special way things are arranged ______ (Par. 2)
2. doing with others ______ (Par. 3)
3. small sack ______ (Par. 7)

Working with Words

A **prefix** is a group of letters added to the beginning of a word that changes the meaning of the word. The prefix **re-** means "again." *Rewire* means "wire again."

Read the words below. Write the correct word next to its meaning.

reread reorder reteach rewrap

1. teach again ______
2. order again ______
3. read again ______
4. wrap again ______

Most words that end in a consonant followed by *y* are made plural by changing the *y* to *i* and adding *es*. The plural of *city* is *cities*. Write the plural form of each word below.

5. baby ______
6. company ______
7. penny ______

Reading and Thinking

1. Check the answer that tells what the story is mainly about.

   ____ trying to fool the class

   ____ teaching Mosh to speak

   ____ dropping the question cards

Write **T** if the sentence is true.
Write **F** if the sentence is false.

2. ____ Carlos was trying to teach Lizzy Wood a lesson.
3. ____ When Carlos picked up his cards, they were not in the right order.
4. ____ Something was wrong with the tape player inside Mosh.
5. ____ Carlos's trick taught him a lesson.

Write the best word to complete each sentence below.

6. During the show, Pat made a penny ______. (sing, vanish, wish)
7. Elsa ______ her books on the way to school. (dropped, played, roared)
8. Please write one ______ to ask our guest. (card, answer, question)
9. Jamie gave a ______ answer. (honor, hollow, clever)
10. The children's ______ filled the room. (laughter, book, tape)

Captain Carlos

Have you ever been disappointed? How did you act?

1 "This is the day Mrs. Bell tells who will be the captain of the astronauts in our school play," Susan said to Carlos. "Are you nervous?"

2 "A little," Carlos replied. "I would really like the part, but Lizzy tried out for it, too. She did a very good job."

3 "Well, I'm sure you did a great job, too," Susan said. "And I hope you get to be the captain."

4 That day Mrs. Bell asked if she could talk to Carlos and Lizzy at recess. "I had a hard time deciding who should be the captain in our play," she said. "You were both very good, so I am going to add another part. Carlos, I would like you to be the captain. Lizzy, I would like you to be the first officer."

5 "Will I get to say much?" Lizzy asked as she frowned.

6 "I can tell you're disappointed, Lizzy, but I promise you will have as much to say as Carlos does," Mrs. Bell said calmly. She went on to say, "Carlos, I think Mosh would be good to have in the play, too. What do you think?"

7 "Sure," Carlos agreed. Lizzy sighed and walked away.

8 After school, Carlos walked home with Susan. "I'm so excited about the play!" he said.

9 Just then Lizzy rode up on her bike. "I hope your robot doesn't act up on the night of the play," Lizzy snapped. Then she rode away, leaving Carlos and Susan to wonder what she meant.

Knowing the Words

Write the words from the story that have the meanings below.

1. worried ______________ (Par. 1)

2. what a person in a play says and does ______________ (Par. 2)

3. let down; unhappy ______________ (Par. 6)

Check the meaning that fits the underlined word in each sentence.

4. Carrie went to the park to <u>play</u>.

   ____ have fun

   ____ a show on stage

5. Did Janice eat <u>part</u> of this apple?

   ____ in a play

   ____ a small piece of something

6. Did you hear the limb <u>snap</u>?

   ____ break suddenly

   ____ speak angrily

Working with Words

Write the two words that were used to form each of these contractions.

1. I'm ______________

2. you're ______________

3. we'll ______________

4. isn't ______________

5. don't ______________

6. doesn't ______________

Reading and Thinking

1. Check the answer that tells what the story is mainly about.

   ____ getting a part in the school play

   ____ Lizzy's part in the play

   ____ walking to school

2. Write two words to describe Lizzy.

   ____

3. Carlos wasn't sure he would get to be the captain in the play because

   ____

   ______________.

4. What part was Lizzy asked to play?

   ____

5. Why was Lizzy unhappy? ______________

   ____

Trouble on Stage

Have you ever been in a play? Read to find out how Carlos's school play went.

1 On the night of the school play, the stage looked like the inside of a spaceship. The curtain opened. Captain Carlos walked onto the stage. "Mosh, bring me the space maps," he called clearly.

2 Mosh rolled out onto the stage and turned around in circles. "Mosh, bring me the space maps," Carlos said even louder.

3 Mosh just moved in bigger circles. Carlos didn't know what to do. Something was terribly wrong with Mosh. Carlos guessed right away that Lizzy had something to do with this.

4 "Mosh, I think you have a little space sickness," Carlos said as if it were part of the play. "Go rest." Carlos pushed Mosh behind the curtain. Then he said, "Send in the first officer with my space maps."

5 "Here are the maps, Sir," Lizzy said loudly. She gave Carlos a mean smile.

6 Carlos was angry. It was bad enough that Lizzy was spoiling the play, but she didn't have to hurt Mosh. Just then Mosh rolled back onto the stage. The robot was acting out of control. Mosh chased Lizzy all around the spaceship.

7 "Captain," Lizzy cried, "do something!"

8 At first, Carlos just watched. He thought Lizzy deserved this. Then he felt sorry for her. "Fear not, First Officer," Carlos said dramatically. Then he took out Mosh's battery. Mosh stopped, and Carlos rolled him behind the curtain again. The play went on as it was written.

9 When the play was over, Lizzy apologized to Carlos. She said she would never hurt Mosh again. "Thanks for helping me out," she added.

10 "You're welcome," Carlos replied. "Do you think we could be friends now?"

11 Lizzy smiled and nodded. "I'd like that," she said.

Knowing the Words

Write the words from the story that have the meanings below.

1. awfully ______________________ (Par. 3)
2. earned ______________________ (Par. 8)
3. in an excited way ______________________ (Par. 8)

In each row below, circle the three words that belong together.

4. stage curtain sky play
5. blast-off sick spaceship maps
6. friends Mosh Carlos stage

Working with Words

Write a compound word using the underlined words in each sentence.

1. A ship used to travel in space is a ______________________.
2. Corn that will pop when it is heated is ______________________.
3. A game in which a ball is kicked with the foot is ______________________.

Circle the correct word in ( ) and write it in the blank.

4. Jeanne drew a ______________ on the card. (circle, correct)
5. The ______________ in my glass melted. (act, ice)

Reading and Thinking

1. Number the sentences to show the order in which things happened.

   _____ Mosh chased Lizzy around the stage.

   _____ Carlos pulled out Mosh's battery.

   _____ Lizzy yelled for help.

   _____ Lizzy apologized.

Write **T** if the sentence is true.
Write **F** if the sentence is false.

2. _____ Mosh was disobeying on purpose.
3. _____ Lizzy was frightened when Mosh chased her around the stage.
4. _____ Carlos rescued Lizzy.
5. _____ Carlos planned to take Mosh's battery out during the play.
6. _____ Carlos forgave Lizzy.
7. Write **R** next to the two sentences that tell about real things.

   _____ Robots get sick.

   _____ Robots can be in plays.

   _____ Robots can run on batteries.

Read each sentence and fill in the blank.

8. The people laughed because they enjoyed the play.

   They stands for ______________________.
9. Lizzy screamed when she needed help.

   She stands for ______________________.

Mr. Johnson's Offer

Would you want Mosh to help you in a crowded store?

1 Mr. Johnson owned the small grocery store down the street from where Carlos lived. He had asked if Carlos would like to earn some money by passing out cheese samples for two hours on Saturday. Carlos said that sounded like fun and asked if he could bring Mosh. "Sure, I don't see how it could hurt to have your robot here, too," Mr. Johnson said.

2 Carlos put cheese on crackers and Mosh passed them out. Suddenly Carlos heard a scream. "Oh, that Mosh," he sighed. He found Mosh trying to get a lady to take some cheese. Carlos could see the woman didn't want any cheese and was very angry. He said he was sorry and promised it would not happen again.

3 Carlos went back to his job. Soon he heard a crash, and a voice over the loud speaker said, "We need a cleanup in fruits."

4 "Here we go again," Carlos mumbled. He found Mosh in the middle of hundreds of oranges. Mr. Johnson was standing there with his hands on his hips. "Pick these up, then get that thing out of here," he said, pointing to Mosh.

5 Carlos picked up the oranges, and Mosh put them in a neat pile. A crowd gathered to watch them work. Carlos and Mosh started to leave as soon as they were finished.

6 "Wait, Carlos," Mr. Johnson called. He gave Carlos two dollars. "That's for passing out cheese," he said. "And here's an extra two dollars for attracting a crowd. Crowds are good for my business, and that robot knows how to get a crowd."

7 "Would you like us to come back next Saturday?" Carlos asked hopefully.

8 Mr. Johnson shook his head slowly. "No, Carlos, I'd like to keep my store in one piece a little longer," he said with a laugh.

Knowing the Words

Write the words from the story that have the meanings below.

1. part of the body where legs begin ________ (Par. 4)
2. pulling toward something ________ (Par. 6)
3. wishing for something ________ (Par. 7)

Check the meaning that fits the underlined word in each sentence.

4. Pam ate an <u>orange</u> for lunch.

____ a color

____ fruit

5. Please <u>point</u> to the problem you are working on.

____ show with a finger

____ a dot

6. We bought bread at the <u>store</u>.

____ place to buy food

____ save for later

Reading and Thinking

1. Check the answer that tells what the story is mainly about.

____ hundreds of oranges

____ an angry woman

____ trouble in the grocery store

2. The woman screamed because ________

________.

3. What did Carlos put on the crackers?

____

4. How might this story have ended if Mosh had been left at home? ________

____

5. Was Mr. Johnson angry at the end of the story? Explain your answer.

____

____

____

Learning to Study

Number each list of words below in alphabetical order.

1.		2.	
____	attract	____	hundred
____	ask	____	hand
____	again	____	hip
____	angry	____	hurt
____	ate	____	hush

Lucky Carlos

Carlos thinks he's lucky to have a robot helper. Read to see if you agree.

1 "I'm glad it's Saturday," Carlos said to Marie as he sat at the table. "I've been wanting to work on these walkie-talkies I just bought from Susan. Now I can work all day taking them apart and putting them together again."

2 "No, you can't," Marie replied. "It's your turn to wash the dishes and vacuum the floor. Mom wants it done before she gets home from the office."

3 "Maybe Mosh can help me," Carlos said. "We can be done in fifteen minutes." He showed Mosh how to use the vacuum cleaner. Then Carlos went into the kitchen to wash the dishes. He heard the vacuum roaring in the other room. He felt lucky to have Mosh helping him.

4 Then Carlos heard a loud clattering noise coming from the living room. He rushed in just in time to see Mosh sweeping the table. "Turn it off, Mosh," he yelled. Carlos saw that his walkie-talkies were still on the table, but the tiny screws were gone.

5 "Oh, Mosh, vacuum cleaners are for floors, not tables," Carlos moaned. "I can't put those walkie-talkies back together without the screws. There's only one thing to do."

6 Carlos took the bag full of dirt out of the vacuum cleaner. He took it outside. Carlos dumped the dirt on a newspaper. Then he felt through it with his fingers until he found each tiny screw.

7 Just as he finished, Mrs. Garza drove up. "Carlos, look at your clothes. They are filthy. Why are you going through all that dirt?" his mother asked. "Wait, don't tell me. Mosh is behind this."

8 Carlos nodded and said, "I've just learned the hard way that Mosh doesn't know the best place to use a vacuum cleaner."

Knowing the Words

Write the words from the story that have the meanings below.

1. two-way radios ________________ (Par. 1)

2. very dirty ________________ (Par. 7)

Synonyms are words that have the same or nearly the same meaning. Write **S** after each pair of synonyms. Write **A** after each pair of antonyms (opposites).

3. bought—sold ____
4. yell—whisper ____
5. tiny—little ____
6. glad—happy ____
7. back—front ____
8. filthy—dirty ____
9. loud—soft ____
10. dirt—soil ____

Working with Words

Write the two words that were used to form each of these contractions.

1. it's ________________
2. he's ________________
3. I'll ________________
4. doesn't ________________
5. there's ________________
6. I've ________________
7. let's ________________

Reading and Thinking

1. Number the sentences to show the order in which things happened.

   ____ Mosh swept up the screws to the walkie-talkies.

   ____ Carlos searched through the dirt for the screws.

   ____ Mrs. Garza came home.

   ____ Carlos showed Mosh how to clean the carpet.

2. Where was Mrs. Garza when the story began? ________________

   ____

3. Check one answer that tells how Mrs. Garza probably got to work.

   ____ in a car

   ____ on a bus

4. What chore was Carlos doing? ________

   ____

Write the best word to complete each sentence below.

5. Adam could not find a broom to ________________ the sidewalk. (empty, feel, sweep)

6. There is a blue ________________ in the living room. (dirt, carpet, noise)

7. You cannot ________________ the rug with a broom. (vacuum, find, help)

Mosh to the Rescue

Do you think it is possible that Mosh could do something right?

1 "I fixed those walkie-talkies you sold me," Carlos said to Susan. "I put one inside Mosh. Now I can give orders from far away."

2 "Let's go outside to see how it works," Susan said.

3 Carlos put Mosh on the sidewalk. Then the kids climbed a tree and waited for someone to appear. They spotted Kevin Price bouncing a ball out in front of his house. One time he bounced the ball too hard and could not catch it. The ball bounced toward the street.

4 "Look," Susan cried, "Kevin's going to run into the street."

5 Carlos knew they couldn't get down from the tree fast enough to stop him. "Tag, Mosh," he yelled into the walkie-talkie. Quickly, the robot started to roll toward Kevin. When Kevin saw Mosh, he turned and ran back toward his house. He was so frightened that he started crying. Carlos and Susan climbed down the tree. They got Kevin's ball and took it to his house.

6 Mrs. Price ran out of the house when she heard Kevin crying. "What happened?" she asked the children.

7 "Mosh stopped Kevin from running into the street," Susan explained. "I hope he isn't too frightened."

8 Mrs. Price hugged her son. "I'm sure he will be OK thanks to you."

9 "Mosh, you make a lot of mistakes, but it's nice to know you can be helpful sometimes," Carlos teased.

10 The robot did not like to be teased about its mistakes. So Mosh turned around and rolled home.

Knowing the Words

Write the word from the story that has the meaning below.

1. saw ______________________
(Par. 3)

Write the word with the correct meaning to complete each sentence below.

2. Did you ______________ tigers and elephants at the zoo? (sea, see)

3. Jeannette has a ______________ notebook. (new, knew)

4. We saw a ______________ of cows in the pasture. (heard, herd)

Learning to Study

A **table of contents** is one of the first pages in a book. It shows the chapters that are in the book and on what page each one begins. Use the table of contents below to answer the questions.

How to Build a Robot

Table of Contents

1. How many chapters are in this book? ______________

2. What is the third chapter called?

____

3. On what page does the fourth chapter begin? ______________

Reading and Thinking

1. Check the answer that tells what the story is mainly about.
   ____ saving a child from harm
   ____ bouncing a ball
   ____ climbing a tree

2. Who was Kevin? ______________

____

3. Why did Kevin run back toward his house? ______________

____

4. Check two sentences that tell about both Susan and Kevin.
   ____ They lived near Carlos.
   ____ They were playing outside.
   ____ They cried when they ran away from Mosh.

5. What might have happened if Mosh had not scared Kevin? ______________

____

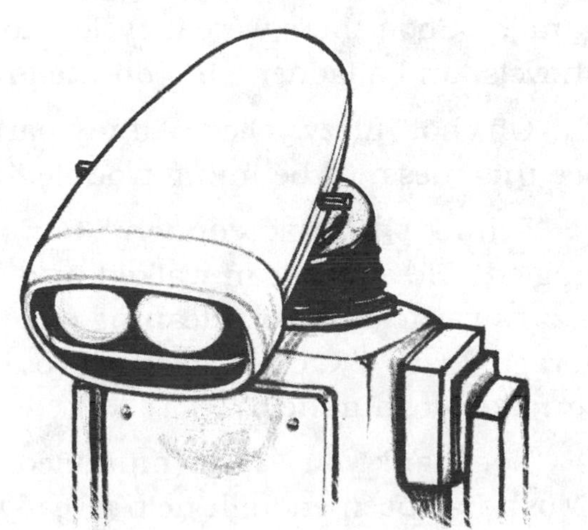

Mosh Is Missing

Read to find out what Carlos does when he can't find Mosh.

1 "Where is Mosh?" Carlos cried when he went outside. He turned to Susan and shrugged as he said, "We were only in the house a short time. What could happen to a robot in a few minutes?"

2 Susan and Carlos searched for Mosh. They walked up and down each street in the neighborhood. When they walked behind Lizzy's house, they heard Lizzy talking. The kids peeked through a crack in the fence. They saw Lizzy in the backyard with Mosh. Carlos and Susan heard Lizzy say, "Carlos has so much fun with you that I want to have some fun, too. Let's play tag." Then Lizzy touched Mosh and said, "You're 'it.' " Mosh just stood still.

3 "So, Lizzy wants to have some fun with Mosh," Carlos whispered to Susan. "I'll show her how much fun Mosh can be." Speaking quietly into his walkie-talkie, he said, "Mosh, clean out the garage."

4 Mosh started taking things out of the garage. Soon there were bicycles, tools, shovels, and a ladder lying on the grass.

5 "Oh, no!" Lizzy yelled. "If my parents see this mess, I'll be in big trouble."

6 "I think she's had enough," Carlos giggled He and Susan walked into Lizzy's yard. "Are you cleaning out the garage, Lizzy?" Carlos asked. "Would you like Mosh to help?"

7 "No, thank you," Lizzy mumbled. "Mosh has been enough help already."

8 "You shouldn't play with things you don't understand. Mosh doesn't take orders from anyone but me," Carlos said. "Let's put these things back in the garage. Then we can play a game of tag."

Knowing the Words

Write the word from the story that has the meaning below.

1. ability to move without slipping ________ (Par. 4)

Check the meaning that fits the underlined word in each sentence.

2. Swing at the baseball with the bat.

____ strike at

____ seat that moves back and forth

3. Don't dump that dirt in the driveway.

____ unload

____ place for trash

4. I ate a roll with my dinner.

____ turn over and over

____ bread

Working with Words

Write a compound word using the underlined words in each sentence.

1. A storm in which snow falls is a ________.

2. A drift made of snow is a ________.

Circle the correct word in ( ) and write it in the blank.

3. Three inches of ________ fell yesterday. (saw, snow)

4. Please ________ out two cups of oatmeal. (scoop, skip)

Reading and Thinking

1. Check the answer that tells what the story is mainly about.

____ drawing in the snow

____ shoveling snow

____ getting too cold

2. Number the sentences to show the order in which things happened.

____ Carlos drew a face in the snow.

____ Carlos put chains on Mosh's wheels.

____ Mosh dumped snow down Carlos's back.

____ Marie's hands got cold.

3. Marie wanted Mosh to help because ________.

4. Why did Carlos put chains on Mosh's wheels? ________

5. Where did Carlos get the chains for Mosh? ________

6. What was Carlos going to draw in the snow after he drew the silly face? ________

7. What do you think Carlos did after Mosh threw the snow on him? ________

A Chilly Experience

What would you do if you had the chance to play in a lot of snow?

1 It had snowed most of the night, so Carlos was listening for school closings on the radio. "There's no school today," he sang as soon as he heard the news.

2 "Before you start playing, I want you and Marie to shovel the snow," Mr. Garza said.

3 Carlos and Marie took turns shoveling. "My hands are cold," Marie said. "Can we get Mosh to help with this?"

4 "We can try," Carlos answered. Mosh came outside, but the robot couldn't move in the snow. Its wheels kept getting stuck. Then Carlos had an idea. "Chains are put on the car tires to get traction," he said. "Maybe chains would work on Mosh's wheels, too."

5 Carlos found two chains from an old swing. He fastened them to Mosh's wheels. The chains kept Mosh from slipping, and the robot had no more trouble moving.

6 "Now I'll teach you how to shovel snow off the sidewalks," Carlos said. He showed Mosh how to scoop up snow with the shovel and dump it off to the side. Mosh learned quickly.

7 "While you're shoveling, I'm going to draw in the snow," Carlos said. He stooped over and drew a picture of a silly face.

8 Carlos stood up and looked at the face. "That looks so good I think I'll draw Mosh now," he said. Just as he stooped over, Mosh rolled by. Before he knew what was happening, Mosh picked up a shovel full of snow and dumped it on Carlos. Most of it landed on Carlos's head. Some slid down his neck and melted inside his coat.

9 Carlos jumped up, looking angry and surprised. Marie laughed and said, "That robot is amazing. This is the first snowstorm, and Mosh already knows how to make a person out of snow."

Knowing the Words

Write the words from the story that have the meanings below.

1. moved shoulders up and down ______________ (Par. 1)

2. looked quickly ______________ (Par. 2)

In each row below, circle the three words that belong together.

3.	garage	car	sky	driveway
4.	curb	concrete	street	grass
5.	ladder	minutes	time	clock
6.	tag	game	fun	mess
7.	shovel	snow	ice	night

Learning to Study

An **index** is a part of a book. It lists a book's topics in alphabetical order. It also lists page numbers so you can find those topics. An index is usually found at the back of a book. Use the index below from a book of games to answer the questions.

rules, 24
tag, 6, 12, 21
tennis, 5, 10–11
volleyball, 2–4, 11, 13

1. On what pages could you find out how to play tag? ______________
2. On what pages could you find out about tennis? ______________
3. On what page could you find rules? ______________

Reading and Thinking

Write **T** if the sentence is true.
Write **F** if the sentence is false.

1. _____ Carlos was upset when Mosh was missing.
2. _____ Lizzy took Mosh to hurt Carlos's feelings.
3. _____ Carlos told Mosh to take things out of Lizzy's garage to help her.
4. _____ Carlos watched Lizzy put everything back in her garage.
5. How do you think Mosh got in Lizzy's yard? ______________
6. What game did Lizzy want to play with Mosh? ______________

Write the best word to complete each sentence below.

7. Agnes ______________ all over the house to find her clay. (heard, touched, searched)
8. We rode our ______________ to the store. (airplanes, bikes, kites)

Snowbot

What do you think a snowbot is?

1 Susan called Carlos on the phone at nine o'clock in the morning. "Guess what I heard on the radio," she said.

2 "You heard that school is closed today," Carlos answered. "That's old news, Susan."

3 "Well, that's not all," Susan said. "I heard Mayor Brown say that the city is having a snow sculpture contest today, too. Let's make something."

4 "Sure," Carlos said, sounding excited. "Come on over."

5 When Susan reached her friend's house, Carlos was ready to build. "Well, what should we make?" he asked.

6 "I don't know," Susan said, "but we better hurry. The mayor is judging the sculptures in two hours."

7 Susan and Carlos thought for a few minutes. Finally Carlos said, "I know, let's make a snow robot."

8 "Yeah," Susan agreed. "We can call it a snowbot."

9 The kids worked in the front yard piling up the snow until it was as high as Mosh. Mosh helped with this part, so it didn't take long. Then Mosh modeled while the kids carved arms, hands, wheels, and a head with their gloved hands.

10 They stepped back to take a look at what they had made. "It looks good, but I think we need to give it eyes," Carlos said. "What could we use?"

11 Mosh rolled toward the garage. Soon the robot returned with two old tennis balls and a green marker. The kids knew what they were supposed to do.

12 By the time Mayor Brown came to judge their snow sculpture, it was finished. "I've looked at all the other snow sculptures. This is the most original one I've seen all day. Those are great eyes. You have earned first place," the mayor said, giving each of them a ribbon.

13 Carlos hung his ribbon on Mosh. "Here, Mosh," he said, "I couldn't have won this without you."

Knowing the Words

Write the words from the story that have the meanings below.

1. leader of a city ________________ (Par. 3)
2. carving; statue ________________ (Par. 3)
3. deciding in a contest ________________ (Par. 6)

Working with Words

Rewrite the following groups of words using *'s* or *s'* to show who owns something. The first one is done for you.

house that belongs to Susan

Susan's house

1. announcement made by the mayor

____

2. sculpture that belongs to the kids

____

3. eyes that belong to the sculpture

____

Circle the correct letters to complete each word and write them in the blank.

4. I felt bett_____ after my nap.

   or ar er

5. Snow fell early this m_____ning.

   or ar er

6. Who will c_____ve this soap?

   or ar er

Reading and Thinking

Write **T** if the sentence is true.
Write **F** if the sentence is false.

1. _____ This story takes place in the winter.
2. _____ The snowstorm knocked down the telephone lines to Carlos's house.
3. _____ Susan made up a new word.
4. _____ The kids took more than two hours to finish their snowbot.
5. Write **M** next to the sentence that tells about something make-believe.

   _____ You could make a robot out of snow.

   _____ Robots can cry like people.

   _____ Tennis balls can be colored green.

Write the best word to complete each sentence below.

6. I made a ________________ of a horse in art class. (mayor, marker, sculpture)
7. What color was the ________________ that you won? (ribbon, sound, yard)

Pine Street Hill

What do you think it would be like to go sledding with a robot?

1 "Get your sled, Carlos," Susan said. "The mayor closed Pine Street so we can slide down that big hill."

2 Carlos got his sled from the garage. "There's just one thing I don't like about sledding. I don't like dragging the sled back up the hill," he said.

3 "Why don't you have Mosh help with that?" Susan suggested.

4 "That's a great idea," Carlos said. Mosh pulled the sleds to Pine Street. Because of the chains, Mosh rolled easily through the snow. "Take the sleds to the top of the hill, Mosh," Carlos ordered.

5 Mosh rolled up the long hill, dragging the sleds behind it. When they reached the top, Carlos and Susan sat down on their sleds. "It's a lot more fun going down the hill," Carlos told Mosh.

6 Hearing that, Mosh started to go back down the hill. "Get out of the way, Mosh!" Carlos yelled. But the sled was moving faster than Mosh was. It bumped into Mosh and knocked the robot into Carlos's lap. When Carlos leaned over to see around Mosh, the sled turned suddenly and ran into a huge snowdrift.

7 Susan ran over to see if Carlos was all right. "You're not hurt, are you?" she asked.

8 "The next time, you stay at the top while I slide down," Carlos told Mosh.

9 "If Mosh stays at the top, who will pull your sled back up the hill for you?" asked Susan.

10 Carlos thought for a moment before he said, "I'll take care of that." When they got to the top of the hill, Carlos sat down near the front of his sled. He asked Susan to put Mosh on the back.

11 "Hold on, Mosh, here we go!" Carlos cried as the sled bounced down the hill. The other sledders stopped to stare at the sled with its unusual passenger. But Carlos didn't mind. He felt sure that Mosh was having fun, too.

Knowing the Words

Write the word from the story that has the meaning below.

1. someone who rides with someone else ________________ (Par. 11)

Circle the pair of antonyms (opposites) in each row.

2. slower faster bigger larger
3. closed dragged ordered opened
4. huge tiny under down

Working with Words

When a word ends with *e*, the *e* is usually dropped before adding **-ed** or **-ing.** For example, *like* + *ed* = *liked*.

Add **-ed** or **-ing** to the word in **( )** to make a word that completes each sentence.

1. My mom ________________ the cat from the tree. (rescue)

2. Why are you ________________ at the wall? (stare)

3. We should start ________________ the doors now. (close)

The prefix **un-** means "not." *Unsure* means "not sure." Add **un-** to the words below. Use the new words to complete the sentences.

even happy

4. Barb was ________________ about losing the game.

5. The top of that table looks

________________.

Reading and Thinking

1. Check the answer that tells what the story is mainly about.

____ rolling through the snow

____ running into a snowdrift

____ sledding down the hill

2. Where did the kids go sledding?

____

3. What helped Mosh roll through the snow? ________________

4. What might have happened if Carlos and Mosh had not run into a snowdrift? ________________

____

5. What do you think Carlos and Susan did when they were done sledding?

____

____

The Nightmare

Have you ever had a bad dream?

1 Carlos tossed and turned because he was having a nightmare. In his dream, Carlos was running away from something. He ran into the house. "Close and block the door," Carlos cried out in his sleep. "Don't let it get in!"

2 But the thing in the dream managed to get through the door, so Carlos escaped through the window and ran through the forest until he came to a cave. He ducked inside, hoping the thing wouldn't find him.

3 It was very cold inside the cave. "I need more clothes," Carlos said, still dreaming. "I'm freezing."

4 Carlos felt he was still being followed. He ran into a dark corner. When Carlos turned around, he saw he was being chased by a huge butterfly. Thinking quickly, Carlos knew what he had to do. He had to catch the butterfly.

5 "I need my net," he cried. Carlos grabbed his butterfly net and swung it at the beast. When Carlos looked in his net, he saw a small, blue butterfly.

6 Then Carlos woke up; his room was dark. Something heavy was on top of him, making him very hot. His head was resting on something hard.

7 Carlos turned on his light and looked around the room. It was such a mess he thought he must still be dreaming. The desk was pushed up against the door. All the clothes from his closet were piled on top of him. His butterfly net was lying on his pillow.

8 "What happened in here, Mosh?" Carlos asked. Then he remembered his dream. He must have talked in his sleep.

9 "Thanks for saving me, Mosh," he said, hugging his robot. "But next time, please don't listen to me unless I'm awake."

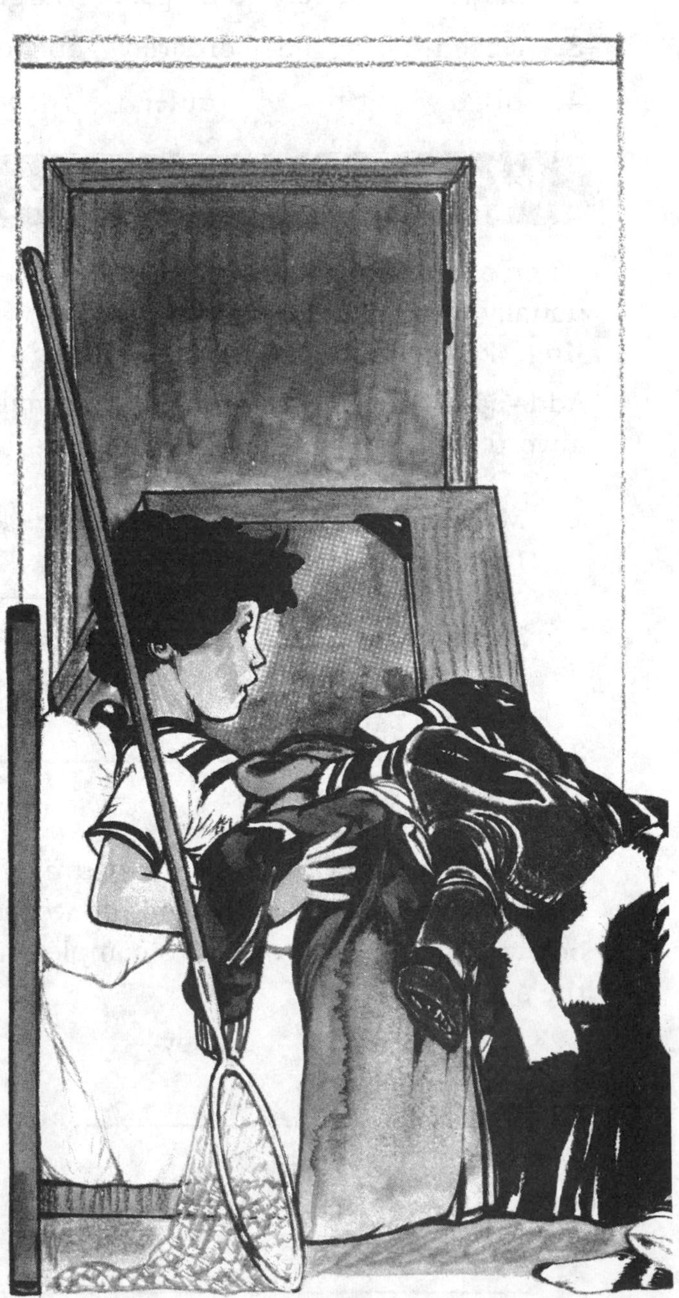

Knowing the Words

Write the words from the story that have the meanings below.

1. was able ______________________
(Par. 2)

2. got out ______________________
(Par. 2)

3. monster ______________________
(Par. 5)

Choose the correct word to fill in the blanks for each pair of sentences.

duck light close

4. Who left the ______________________ on in the garage?

   The canoe was ______________________ enough to carry.

5. The ______________________ flew over the pond.

   Kim needs to ______________________ to get through the opening.

6. Please ______________________ the window.

   Do not get too ______________________ to the parade.

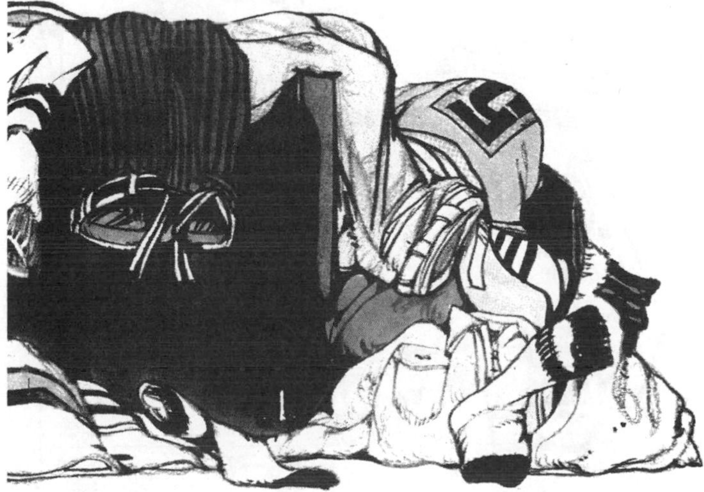

Reading and Thinking

1. Number the sentences to show the order in which things happened.

   _____ Carlos saw the thing that had been chasing him.

   _____ Carlos ran into the house.

   _____ Carlos ran into a cave.

   _____ Carlos woke up.

Write **T** if the sentence is true.
Write **F** if the sentence is false.

2. _____ Carlos was camping out.

3. _____ Carlos woke up during the night.

4. _____ Mosh put the desk in front of the bedroom door.

5. _____ Carlos really caught a butterfly in his net.

Learning to Study

Number each list of words below in alphabetical order.

1. _____ cold
   _____ corner
   _____ cool
   _____ cozy
   _____ comb

2. _____ desk
   _____ deck
   _____ delight
   _____ depend
   _____ deer

3. _____ sleep
   _____ still
   _____ stop
   _____ small
   _____ slip

4. _____ woods
   _____ window
   _____ will
   _____ won
   _____ worry

Birthday Banana Bread

Have you ever tried to follow a recipe?

1 "Today is Dad's birthday, Mosh," Carlos said. "Let's make some of his favorite banana bread and surprise him."

2 Carlos got out a cookbook. "I'll read the recipe, and you follow it. Get out a bowl and spoon while I turn on the oven." Carlos read from the cookbook. "First, mash the bananas in a bowl."

3 The robot threw the bananas into a bowl and was about to mash them with its hands. "Stop!" Carlos yelled. "Let's try this again. Peel the bananas, put them in a bowl, and mash them with the spoon." Carlos watched as Mosh peeled the bananas and put the peeling into the bowl. Again, Carlos told Mosh to stop. Then he showed the robot which part of each banana was supposed to go into the bowl.

4 Then Carlos read, "Add the eggs. No, wait," he said right away. Carlos cracked the eggs open and added them to the mashed bananas. "Now stir that up," he told Mosh.

5 "Last, add flour, milk, and sugar," Carlos said. "Mix everything together. Then pour the batter into the bread pan." Mosh obeyed while Carlos read the rest of the directions to himself.

6 "I'll put this in the oven," Carlos said as he picked up the pan. That is when he saw that Mosh had put the measuring cup in the batter, too. Carlos scooped out the cup and wiped the thick batter off of it.

7 Just then Marie came into the room. "What happened in here?" she gasped.

8 Carlos answered, "Mosh and I made banana bread for Dad's birthday. It was a lot of work, but I think he will be surprised."

9 "If you want it to be a good surprise for Dad," Marie laughed, "you need to give Mosh one more order. Clean up!"

Knowing the Words

Write the words from the story that have the meanings below.

1. directions for preparing food ______________ (Par. 2)
2. mixture ______________ (Par. 5)
3. tool used in cooking ______________ (Par. 6)

In each row below, circle the three words that belong together.

4. cookbook recipe milk directions
5. bowl peel spoon cup
6. flour sugar eggs oven
7. mash batter pan bread
8. mix stir pour eat

Write the word with the correct meaning to complete each sentence below.

9. Who ______________ that ball? (threw, through)
10. Connie tried ______________ of the fresh bread. (sum, some)
11. Please ______________ the milk now. (poor, pour)
12. Can you ______________ ten and twelve? (add, ad)
13. Val ______________ pizza in school today. (made, maid)
14. The ______________ grew through a crack in the street. (flour, flower)

Reading and Thinking

1. Write three things that were needed to make banana bread. ______________
2. How did Carlos know how to make bread? ______________
3. What room do you think Carlos and Mosh were in? ______________

Learning to Study

Use the table of contents below to answer the questions.

Robot Recipes

Table of Contents

1. What is the fourth chapter called? ______________
2. On what page does the chapter about soups begin? ______________
3. In what chapter could you find how to make nut bread? ______________

Birthday Candles

What do you do with birthday candles?

1 Carlos and Mosh had some free time before dinner, so they watched TV. There was a show on about fire safety. Carlos and Mosh listened carefully to what was being said. They learned how to prevent fires and what to do in case of fire. The show had just ended when Mrs. Garza said, "Go wash your hands, Carlos. It's time for dinner."

2 Carlos could hardly wait to surprise his dad with the bread he and Mosh had baked. As soon as dinner was over, Mosh, Carlos, and Marie stood up. "Excuse us," Carlos said. "We'll be right back. Mosh and I made something special for your birthday, Dad."

3 The three of them went into the kitchen. Carlos put lots of candles on the banana bread. After Marie lit the candles, Carlos proudly carried the bread to the table. He set it in front of his dad and said, "Happy birthday, Dad. Make a wish and blow out the candles."

4 Just then Mosh rolled into the room with a glass of water and poured it on the banana bread. The candles went out. Mr. Garza quickly started mopping up the puddle of water.

5 "Mosh, you spoiled Dad's bread," Carlos cried. "Fires on birthday candles are supposed to be blown out, not drowned."

6 "It will be all right," his mom said. "We'll just give it some time to dry out. I'm sure the bread will still taste delicious."

7 "I'm sorry Mosh ruined your surprise," Carlos said.

8 "Mosh gave me a bigger surprise," his dad said, laughing. "Maybe, since my candles went out so fast, my wish will come true sooner."

Knowing the Words

Write the words from the story that have the meanings below.

1. keep from happening ______________ (Par. 1)
2. forgive ______________ (Par. 2)
3. spoiled ______________ (Par. 7)

Synonyms are words that have the same or nearly the same meaning. Circle the pair of synonyms in each row.

4. ended finished begun baked
5. wish wash clean learn
6. laughing crying chuckling sleeping
7. showed cooked baked made

Learning to Study

Use the cookbook index below to answer the questions.

baking, 6–10
banana nut bread, 27
biscuits, 38–40
buns, 28, 31, 33

1. On what page would you look to find out about making banana nut bread? ______________
2. On what pages would you find recipes for buns? ______________
3. On what pages could you find out about how to bake? ______________
4. On what pages could you find out how to make biscuits? ______________

Reading and Thinking

1. Check the answer that tells what the story is mainly about.
   ____ surprising Mr. Garza
   ____ watching TV
   ____ mopping up water
2. Carlos said "Excuse us" when he left the table because ______________
   ______________.
3. Why did Mosh pour water on the candles? ______________
   ____
4. Check three words that tell about Mr. Garza.
   ____ pleasant ____ patient
   ____ frantic ____ kind
5. What kind of person do you think Mrs. Garza is? Explain your answer.
   ____
   ____

Write the best word to complete each sentence below.

6. Sean tries to ______________ accidents by being careful. (watch, prevent, surprise)
7. Joy got muddy when she stepped in the ______________. (candle, pool, puddle)

Aunt Laura's Visit

Have relatives ever come to stay with you? What was it like?

1 Carlos crawled into his sleeping bag. "You know, Mosh," he said, "I like camping out in the den when Aunt Laura comes to stay. But I wish I could still go into my room anytime I want. I would get in a lot of trouble if I bothered Aunt Laura and her spoiled dog, Sweetie."

2 Carlos fluffed up his pillow. "I'm not tired," he complained. "I wish I had my book so I could read, but I left it in my room. I'm sure Aunt Laura is asleep already."

3 Carlos closed his eyes and tried to sleep. Suddenly, he heard a scream coming from his room. Sweetie was barking wildly. Carlos jumped out of his sleeping bag and rushed to his room.

4 "Help!" Aunt Laura yelled.

5 The whole family was there by the time Carlos arrived. Mrs. Garza turned on the light. Aunt Laura stood there looking quite scared. "In there," she whispered, pointing a shaky finger at the closet.

6 Mr. Garza held a baseball bat while he opened the closet door. Everyone gasped. There stood Mosh holding Carlos's book.

7 "I can't believe this," Aunt Laura said, angrily. "You let a machine run around breaking into rooms in the middle of the night?"

8 "I'm sorry," Carlos said quickly. "It won't happen again."

9 "I'll say it won't," his mother said firmly. "If it does, that robot will spend the rest of the week in the garage."

10 Carlos took Mosh back to the den. "Did you hear that, little buddy? You have to be careful while Aunt Laura is here, or you and the car will be sharing the garage." Mosh rolled into a corner and turned off its lights. Carlos felt sad because he knew his friend was upset.

Knowing the Words

Write the words from the story that have the meanings below.

1. upset ______________ (Par. 1)

2. given too much ______________ (Par. 1)

Working with Words

Circle the correct letters to complete each word and write them in the blank.

1. Did the elephants sc______ you?

   ur are ear

2. I forgot to t______n off the radio.

   ur are ear

3. Our dog b______ked all night.

   er or ar

4. Jo cut her fing______ on the broken glass.

   er or ar

5. My shoes are very d______ty.

   or ir ar

The suffix **-ful** means "full of." *Careful* means "full of care." Add **-ful** to the words below. Use the new words to complete the sentences.

help joy fear

6. The team members were ______________ that they won the game.

7. I try to be ______________ by cleaning up my room.

8. Stacy is ______________ of loud noises.

Reading and Thinking

1. Number the sentences to show the order in which things happened.

   _____ Mosh rolled into the corner and turned off its lights.

   _____ Mr. Garza opened the closet door.

   _____ Aunt Laura screamed.

   _____ Carlos tried to go to sleep.

2. What was Mosh getting out of Carlos's room? ______________

3. Who is Sweetie? ______________

4. What do you think Carlos did when he got back to the den after being in Aunt Laura's room? ______________

   ____

5. What do you think Aunt Laura did after everyone left her room? ______________

   ____

Mosh's Friend

Read to find out how a robot can become friends with a dog.

1 On the second day of Aunt Laura's visit, Carlos asked if she had seen Mosh. "Yes," Aunt Laura said. "Mosh is staying in the garage. My poor little Sweetie is afraid of that thing."

2 Carlos went to the garage. "This is just awful, Mosh," he said. "I bet if Sweetie knew what a nice robot you are, he wouldn't be afraid of you anymore. This is going to be a long week."

3 When Carlos went back inside, he saw Aunt Laura getting a leash. Carlos got an idea. "Aunt Laura, would you like me to take Sweetie for a walk?" he asked.

4 "Sure," Aunt Laura replied.

5 Carlos took Sweetie to the garage. "Mosh, this is your chance to prove to Sweetie that you won't hurt him. You can take him for a walk. Stay on the sidewalk and don't cross any streets."

6 About an hour later, Aunt Laura asked Carlos where Sweetie was. "I haven't seen him since his walk," she said.

7 Carlos had forgotten about the dog. He said, "I'll get him for you."

8 Carlos rushed outside and found Mosh standing in the driveway. Sweetie was standing with his front paws up on Mosh. He was licking Mosh's hand. Carlos called Aunt Laura outside to see what was going on.

9 "They're friends," she said, sounding surprised. "How did that happen?"

10 Carlos replied, "I thought if Mosh took Sweetie for a walk the dog would see there is no reason to be afraid of Mosh."

11 "That was a good idea," Aunt Laura said, smiling. "I guess it would be OK to let Mosh come back into the house now."

12 Mosh and Sweetie were together for the rest of the week. Mosh took the dog for a long walk each day. At night, Sweetie slept curled up next to the robot's wheels. Carlos was glad they were friends. Though, he had to admit he missed having Mosh all to himself.

Knowing the Words

Write the words from the story that have the meanings below.

1. chain or rope used to walk a dog ______________ (Par. 3)

2. answered ______________ (Par. 10)

Working with Words

Write the two words that were used to form each of these contractions.

1. wouldn't ______________

2. haven't ______________

3. didn't ______________

Write a compound word using the underlined words in each sentence.

4. A <u>book</u> used to <u>cook</u> with is a

______________.

5. A <u>ball</u> made of <u>snow</u> is a

______________.

Circle the correct word in ( ) and write it in the blank.

6. The ______________ balloon floated over the fairgrounds. (hug, huge)

7. The first ______________ has a picture of a lion on it. (page, pig)

8. A robin's ______________ is a beautiful color of blue. (egg, edge)

Reading and Thinking

Write **T** if the sentence is true.
Write **F** if the sentence is false.

1. _____ Carlos felt sad that Mosh had to stay in the garage.

2. _____ Mosh had hurt Sweetie.

3. _____ Sweetie was licking Mosh because he enjoyed the taste of metal.

4. _____ Mosh and Sweetie spent a lot of time together after the first walk.

5. Check the sentence that tells how Mosh and Sweetie are alike.

_____ They both had wheels.

_____ They both barked.

_____ They both belonged to people.

Circle the name or names that each underlined word stands for.

6. "<u>I</u> want that robot out of here," said Aunt Laura.

Carlos Mosh Aunt Laura

7. "<u>We</u> can go for a walk," Carlos told Mosh.

Mosh and Sweetie Carlos and Mosh
Carlos and Aunt Laura

8. "<u>They</u> are my friends," Carlos said, pointing to Susan and Mosh.

Susan and Mosh Susan and Carlos
Carlos and Mosh

9. "<u>You</u> can ride along," Carlos said to Marie.

Carlos Marie Mosh

Nurse Mosh

Read to find out what happens when Carlos gets sick and thinks Mosh can take care of him.

1 "Mom, I don't feel well," Carlos complained one morning. "My stomach hurts, and I feel hot all over."

2 Mrs. Garza took Carlos's temperature. "You have a fever," she said. "You need to stay home from school today, so I'll ask Mrs. Wilson to stay with you."

3 "You don't need to bother Mrs. Wilson," Carlos said. "Mosh can take care of me."

4 "I would feel better if Mrs. Wilson came over," Mrs. Garza said. "You never know when you might need extra help."

5 Carlos went back to sleep but soon woke up very thirsty. "Mosh, please bring me a glass of juice," he said.

6 Soon Mosh was back with a glass of water. "This isn't juice, but it will stop my thirst," Carlos said.

7 Then Carlos felt hungry. "I think I would like to eat some soup," he told Mosh. "I'm going to fix some now."

8 Carlos got a can of chicken soup and a pan. Suddenly he felt dizzy and thought he might fall. Mrs. Wilson saw Carlos in the kitchen and sent him back to bed. Mosh followed him.

9 Carlos asked Mosh to put the soup in the pan, add water, and bring it to him when it was hot. Soon Mosh came in carrying a hot pan. When Carlos looked in the pan, he saw the soup can in the hot water. "Nice try, Mosh," he said, "but you need to open the can first."

10 Just then Mrs. Wilson came in with a bowl of chicken soup for Carlos. "I saw Mosh fixing your soup," she said, smiling. "I thought you might like this."

11 "Thank you," Carlos said, feeling very hungry. Carlos held the bowl of soup out to Mosh and said, "This is what a bowl of soup should look like." Carlos ate and then lay back to rest some more.

12 Mrs. Garza called later. "How are you and Mosh getting along?" she asked.

13 "Well, I'm glad you asked Mrs. Wilson to come over," Carlos answered. "Mosh is a great friend but a terrible nurse."

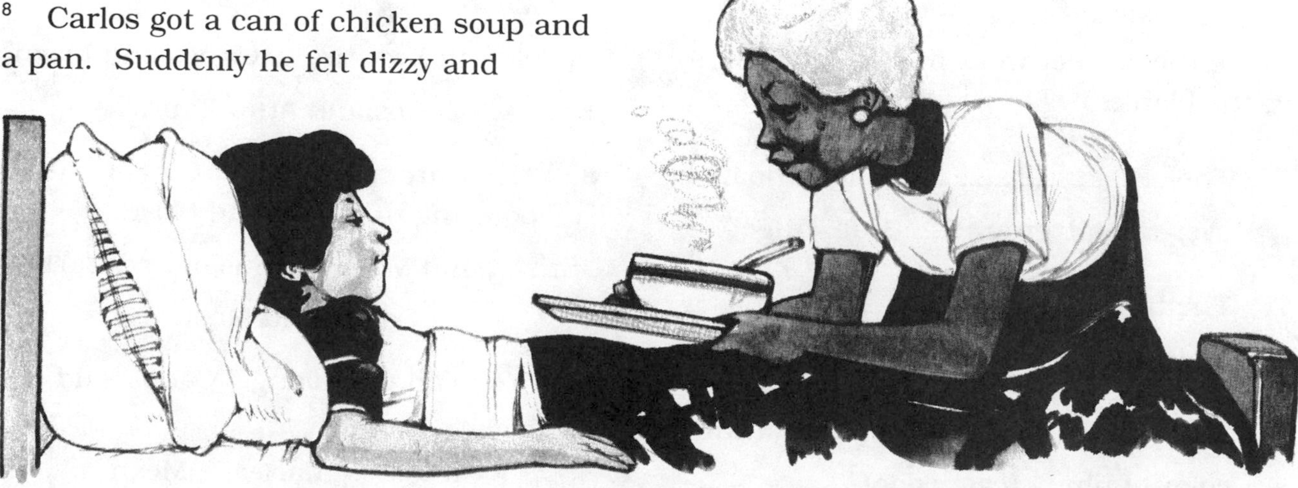

Knowing the Words

Write the word from the story that has the meaning below.

1. in good health ____________________ (Par. 1)

Check the meaning that fits the underlined word in each sentence.

2. Please fill my <u>glass</u> with milk.

   ____ container for holding liquids

   ____ a mirror

3. That is a <u>great</u> idea for a story.

   ____ very large

   ____ excellent

4. <u>Fall</u> begins in September.

   ____ season

   ____ to hit the ground

Working with Words

The ending **-er** sometimes means "more." It may be used to compare two things. The ending **-est** means "most." It is used to compare more than two things.

In each sentence below, add **-er** to the word before the blank if two things are being compared. Add **-est** if more than two things are being compared.

1. That was the great______ movie I have ever seen.
2. An ant is small______ than a bee.
3. Lynne is old______ than I.
4. Heather is the quiet______ person in our class.
5. An orange is sweet______ than a lemon.

Reading and Thinking

1. Check the answer that tells what the story is mainly about.

   ____ eating soup

   ____ having a robot nurse

   ____ staying home from school

2. Carlos had to stay home from school because ____________________

   ____________________.

3. What did Mosh bring instead of juice? ____________________

4. Who was taking care of Carlos?

   ____

Write the best word to complete each sentence below.

5. I have an ____________ pen you may use. (extra, eager, ill)

6. I was so ____________ I drank a large glass of cold milk. (hungry, thirsty, sleepy)

7. The ____________ was made from fruit. (water, juice, milk)

Cleaning Up

Have you ever tried to think of an easy way to wash the dishes? Mosh did.

1 "The house needs to look good for our dinner party tonight," Mrs. Garza told Carlos one Saturday. "Marie is already doing her chores. I want you to clean your room, mop the kitchen floor, and wash the dishes this morning."

2 "OK, Mom," Carlos said. He got the mop and a pail of soapy water. "Guess what, Mosh. You get to clean the kitchen floor today."

3 Carlos taught the robot how to wash the floor. Then Carlos went to clean his messy room. After a little while, he checked up on Mosh.

4 "You're doing a great job, Mosh," Carlos said in surprise. "When you're finished, I'll show you how to wash the dishes." Carlos went back to work on his room.

5 About ten minutes later, Carlos heard Marie calling him, sounding amused. "Carlos, come to the kitchen right now," she sang. "Mosh has made another terrible mess."

6 Carlos sighed, "I knew the clean floor was too good to be true." When he got to the kitchen, he gasped. All the dishes were spread out on the floor, and Mosh was washing them with the mop. Soapy water was splashing everywhere.

7 "Stop!" Carlos cried. "Mosh, you can't wash dishes with a mop. Dishes need to be handled carefully. We're lucky you didn't break these."

8 Carlos put the dishes in the sink. Then he mopped up the water on the floor. Carlos was just finishing the dishes when his parents got home from the store.

9 "Oh, the floor looks marvelous," his mom said.

10 "Thanks to Mosh," Carlos grumbled.

11 "Mosh is getting better at cleaning. Maybe you should let your little friend do more," his dad said.

12 "Believe me, Mosh has done enough today," Carlos said, shaking his head.

Knowing the Words

Write the words from the story that have the meanings below.

1. lying around ____________ (Par. 6)
2. scattering water ____________ (Par. 6)
3. wonderful ____________ (Par. 9)

Circle the pair of antonyms (opposites) in each row.

4.	morning	noon	night	late
5.	soapy	clean	dirty	terrible
6.	messy	lucky	careful	neat

Working with Words

The words below have been divided into syllables. Put a mark above the first vowel to show the sound it stands for. Mark the long vowels with ¯ over the letter. Mark the short vowels with ˘.

1.	min/ute	5.	rap/id	9.	ro/bot
2.	ba/by	6.	fi/nal	10.	man/age
3.	o/ver	7.	pa/per	11.	sec/ond
4.	la/ter	8.	van/ish	12.	fin/ish

Fill in each blank with the correct letters to make a word that completes each sentence below.

mb kn wr

13. Did you see a ______en fly by the window?
14. The plu______er fixed the leaky pipe.
15. The sharp ______ife cut through the meat.

Reading and Thinking

Write **T** if the sentence is true.
Write **F** if the sentence is false.

1. _____ Carlos had not expected Mosh to do such a good job mopping.
2. _____ Mosh tried to wash the dishes and the floor the same way.
3. _____ Marie thought it was funny that Mosh was making a mess.
4. Carlos did not stay to watch Mosh mop the floor because ____________ ____________.
5. Do you think Mosh will ever be asked to wash the dishes again? Explain your answer. ____________ ____________ ____________
6. What do you think Carlos did after he finished washing the dishes? ____________ ____________

The Dinner Party

Do you think it would be a good idea to let Mosh help out at a dinner party?

1 "Mom, can Mosh help at the party?" Carlos asked. "I want Mrs. Chung to see how well Mosh works."

2 "Well, I suppose it wouldn't hurt to let Mosh put the guests' coats away," Mrs. Garza said as she sighed.

3 That evening Carlos took the guests' coats when they arrived. He gave them to Mosh. "Put these away in Mom and Dad's room," he ordered.

4 Mrs. Chung smiled when she saw Mosh. "I'm glad to see that the robot works," she said.

5 When dinner was almost ready, Carlos helped Marie light the candles on the table. Carlos liked the way it looked with the candles and flowers arranged in the middle. Just then Mosh came in with a box of baking soda. Before Carlos could stop the robot, it poured the baking soda on the candles. The flames went out. Carlos felt awful. Marie gasped.

6 "Mosh, you know you aren't supposed to put out candles," Carlos cried.

7 Carlos heard his mom tell the guests to come to the table. Quickly, he and Marie lit the candles before the guests sat down.

8 "The table looks lovely," Mrs. Chung said. "That powder gives the flowers a very soft look."

9 Mrs. Garza's eyes opened wide. "Carlos, what do you know about this?" she asked.

10 "Mosh thought the table was on fire. It put the candles out with baking soda," Carlos said.

11 All the guests laughed. "Now you see what life with a robot is like," Mrs. Garza said, chuckling. Then she whispered to Carlos, "Take Mosh out to the garage. We don't need any more mix-ups tonight."

12 "Mosh, if you don't learn how to behave, you'll never get invited to another dinner party," Carlos warned.

Knowing the Words

Write the words from the story that have the meanings below.

1. used for baking ______________ (Par. 5)

2. mistakes ______________ (Par. 11)

3. told of trouble ahead of time ______________ (Par. 12)

Working with Words

Circle the correct word in ( ) and write it in the blank.

1. Mosh is a robot and not a ________. (toy, today)

2. The bath ____________ made Joyce sneeze. (pour, powder)

3. I forgot to wear my ____________ to school today. (cat, coat)

4. Justin ____________ his lunch. (bought, boat)

To form the plural of a word that ends in *f* or *fe*, the *f* or *fe* is changed to *v*, and *es* is added. Form the plural of each word below.

5. life ______________

6. calf ______________

7. scarf ______________

8. loaf ______________

9. elf ______________

Reading and Thinking

1. Number the sentences to show the order in which things happened.

   _____ Mosh put out the candles.

   _____ Carlos took the guests' coats.

   _____ The guests came to the table.

   _____ The guests arrived.

2. Write the name of one of the Garzas' guests. ______________

3. What two things were in the middle of the dinner table? ______________

   ____

4. The flames on the candles went out because ______________

   ______________.

Write the best word to complete each sentence below.

5. Sara ____________ me to her birthday party. (laughed, poured, invited)

6. Last night we had potatoes for ____________. (breakfast, dinner, lunch)

7. Alice ____________ just when the bell rang. (arrived, liked, lit)

8. The loud horn ____________ us that a tornado was coming. (heard, whispered, warned)

The Missing Coats

Do you remember what happened when Mosh was told to put clothes away?

1 "Carlos, would you please get our guests' coats?" Mr. Garza asked.

2 Carlos went to his parents' room. There were no coats on the bed. He searched the other rooms, but Carlos did not see the coats anywhere.

3 Carlos went to Marie. "I've got a problem," he whispered. "All the guests' coats are gone."

4 "What do you mean?" Marie asked, trying to stay calm. "Where did you tell Mosh to put them?"

5 "In Mom and Dad's room," Carlos answered, "but they aren't there."

6 Marie and Carlos searched for the coats again, but they couldn't find even one.

7 "Exactly what directions did you give Mosh?" Marie asked.

8 "I said to put them away in Mom and Dad's room," Carlos replied. Carlos thought for a few minutes. Then he got an idea. "When Mosh puts our clean clothes away, they go into the drawers. Maybe . . ."

9 Carlos opened a drawer. "Here's one," he said. He opened another drawer and found two more. Carlos had five coats by the time he finished looking in all the drawers.

10 Marie looked in another dresser. "I think I found the rest of the coats," she said. Marie and Carlos took all of the coats to the guests.

11 "Forgive us for taking so long," Marie said to the guests. "When Mosh helps, we never know what to expect. We found your coats in our drawers."

12 Everyone laughed. Mrs. Chung turned to Mrs. Garza and thanked her for a delightful evening. "Mosh made this a party we will never forget," she said, chuckling.

13 "We'll never forget this one either, will we, Carlos?" Mr. Garza said with a wink.

Knowing the Words

Write the words from the story that have the meanings below.

1. missing ______________ (Par. 3)

2. chest of drawers ______________ (Par. 10)

3. pleasant ______________ (Par. 12)

Synonyms are words that have the same or nearly the same meaning. Circle the pair of synonyms in each row.

4. look find discover lose
5. idea problem thought question
6. found forget gone missing

Working with Words

Rewrite the following groups of words using 's or s' to show who owns something.

1. coats that belong to the guests

____

2. bedroom that belongs to Carlos

____

Circle the correct letters to complete each word and write them in the blank.

3. Where is your oth____ glove?

ar er or

4. Will you please f____give me?

ar er or

5. Are you going to the p____ty?

ar er or

Reading and Thinking

1. Check the answer that tells what the story is mainly about.

____ finding the lost coats

____ apologizing to the guests

____ forgetting the party

Write **T** if the sentence is true.
Write **F** if the sentence is false.

2. ____ Carlos did not want the guests to know their coats were lost.
3. ____ Marie thought it was funny that the coats were missing.
4. ____ Marie helped find the coats.
5. ____ Mrs. Chung is a polite person.

6. Where did Carlos and Marie find the coats? ______________

7. What did it mean when Mr. Garza winked? ______________

____

8. What do you think Carlos did after the guests left? ______________

____

9. Do you think the Garzas will have another party? Explain your answer.

____

____

____

Nature Club Camping Trip

Have you ever camped out? What was it like?

1 Carlos's nature club went on a short camping trip. Carlos and Jake, his best friend in the club, were sharing a tent.

2 "Are you sure it was a good idea to bring Mosh?" Jake asked uneasily.

3 "Sure," Carlos answered. "Wasn't it good to have Mosh around when we put up our tent? Besides," he went on, "what could a robot hurt out here in the woods?"

4 "I guess you're right," Jake agreed. "Let's go to the pond till it's time for our five-mile hike."

5 Mosh and the boys went to the pond that was close to camp. The frogs were croaking loudly.

6 "I wonder what those frogs are saying to each other," Jake said.

7 Carlos replied, "They are probably complaining about the cold water."

8 "Mr. Jones is calling us. It must be time for our hike," Jake said.

9 "Stay here, Mosh. Hiking would be hard for you," Carlos said as he left.

10 Carlos was worn out when he got back to the tent after the hike. "I'm going to rest a while," he told Jake. Carlos stopped as soon as he looked inside the tent. "There must be a hundred frogs in here! Mosh!" Carlos screamed.

11 Jake asked, "Why would Mosh put frogs in there?"

12 Carlos thought for a minute before he remembered that he had said the frogs were complaining about the cold water. "Mosh is probably trying to keep them warm," he said. "Come on, let's get them out of here."

13 Jake held back the door of the tent while Carlos crawled around and waved his hands at the frogs to shoo them out toward the pond. "Did you finally get them all?" Jake asked.

14 "I think so," Carlos answered, lying down on his sleeping bag. Just then a frog hopped onto his stomach. Carlos was startled and jumped. "I know one thing about nature," he chuckled. "Frogs belong in ponds, not tents."

Knowing the Words

Write the words from the story that have the meanings below.

1. all things not made by humans ______ (Par. 1)
2. not comfortably ______ (Par. 2)
3. long walk ______ (Par. 4)
4. chase away ______ (Par. 13)

Write the words with the correct meaning to complete each sentence below.

5. Kathy lost a ______ down by the pond. (shoo, shoe)
6. I ______ where to find deer. (know, no)
7. There are ______ pears on the ground. (four, for)
8. I have ______ walk home after school. (too, to, two)
9. We will return in ______ hour. (won, one)
10. The children lost ______ balloons. (there, their)

Reading and Thinking

1. Carlos thought the frogs were croaking loudly because ______ ______.
2. Why wouldn't Carlos let Mosh go on the hike? ______ ______
3. How else might the boys have gotten the frogs out of the tent? ______ ______

Write the best word to complete each sentence below.

4. Roger was ______ at the people on the ship. (waving, complaining, hiking)
5. The ______ hopped off the rock and into the water. (snake, tent, frog)

Learning to Study

A dictionary entry shows the words divided into syllables. A space or a dot shows where the word can be divided at the end of a line of writing.

Read the words below. Next to each, write the number of syllables it has.

1. na ture ____
2. un eas y ____
3. wa ter ____
4. stom ach ____
5. min ute ____
6. grum ble ____

Creature in the Night

Are you ever afraid of the dark?

1 "Let's tell scary stories," Jake said from his sleeping bag.

2 "OK," Carlos agreed, "you go first."

3 "Once there was a group of kids camping out in the woods," Jake began. "At night, a creature with glowing eyes found them, but one of the campers woke up just in time and screamed. The scream scared the creature away. The creature has never been caught, and some say it still roams through the forest today."

4 After the story was finished, Carlos just lay there with his eyes opened wide.

5 "Come on, Carlos," Jake said. "It's your turn now."

6 "I've changed my mind," Carlos said. "One scary story is enough for me."

7 "OK," Jake said, laughing, "let's go to sleep."

8 Jake fell asleep quickly, but Carlos couldn't stop thinking about the story. He was getting jumpier by the minute. When Carlos heard an owl hoot, he almost jumped right out of his sleeping bag. Then he saw a shadow moving along the side of the tent. It had two glowing green spots.

9 "Wake up," Carlos whispered to Jake. "The creature is here."

10 "Go back to sleep," Jake mumbled. "That was only a story."

11 "There is a strange shadow outside our tent!" Carlos said.

12 Jake yelled, "Help, Mr. Jones!" The boys tried to escape, but they were so upset they couldn't even get out of their sleeping bags.

13 "What's going on in there?" Mr. Jones yelled from outside their tent.

14 "Watch out for the creature!" Jake warned Mr. Jones.

15 Mr. Jones laughed. "You mean this robot?" he said, holding the tent door open. There was Mosh with its green eyes glowing.

Knowing the Words

Write the words from the story that have the meanings below.

1. wanders ________________ (Par. 3)

2. more nervous ________________ (Par. 8)

Working with Words

When a word ends in a consonant followed by *y*, the *y* is changed to *i* before **-er** and **-est** is added. Change the *y* to *i* in each word in **( )**. Add **-er** or **-est** to make a word that completes the sentence. The first one is done for you.

Hope's tale was scarier than Jeff's. (scary)

1. I am ________________ now than I was an hour ago. (hungry)

2. That is the ________________ bug of all. (ugly)

3. A rose is the ________________ flower I've ever seen. (pretty)

The suffix **-less** means "without." *Joyless* means "without joy." Add **-less** to the following words. Use the new words to complete the sentences.

sleep care home

4. The ________________ kitten looked hungry and cold.

5. I had a ________________ night because of a barking dog.

6. Because Donna was ________________, she got paint on her clothes.

Reading and Thinking

1. Number the sentences to show the order in which things happened.

   _____ Carlos saw glowing green spots.

   _____ Jake told a scary story.

   _____ Jake fell asleep.

   _____ The boys found out that the creature was Mosh.

2. Carlos was afraid because ________________

   ________________.

3. Who was camping with the boys?

   ____

4. What did Carlos hear that frightened him? ________________

5. How did Carlos feel when he saw the shadow? Explain your answer.

   ____

   ____

6. How do you think Carlos felt when he found out that the creature was Mosh? Explain your answer. ________

   ____

A Mosh Special

What kind of sandwich might Mosh make?

1 "Wake up!" Carlos heard Marie say. "Your alarm clock didn't go off."

2 Carlos slowly opened his eyes. Usually, he was not happy about getting up early, but this morning was different. It was the last day of school, and his class was going on a field trip to the zoo. It was already eight o'clock, so he had only ten minutes to get dressed and pack a lunch. "I don't want to be late!" he said as he leapt out of bed. "I sure wish Mosh knew how to make a sandwich," Carlos said. Then he went to wash his face. He did not notice Mosh rolling out of the bedroom and into the kitchen.

3 By the time Carlos finished dressing, he only had five minutes to pack his lunch and get to school. When he walked into the kitchen, he stopped and smiled. There stood Mosh with a delicious-looking sandwich. "Thanks, Mosh," Carlos said. He quickly put the sandwich in a bag and grabbed a can of juice. Then he raced out the door.

4 For two hours, the children walked around the zoo looking at all kinds of animals from geese to lions. At last, the class sat down to eat lunch. Carlos was hungry. He was looking forward to the sandwich Mosh had fixed.

5 He eagerly took a large bite of the sandwich and started chewing. He stopped suddenly because it tasted a little odd. He looked between the two pieces of bread and started laughing.

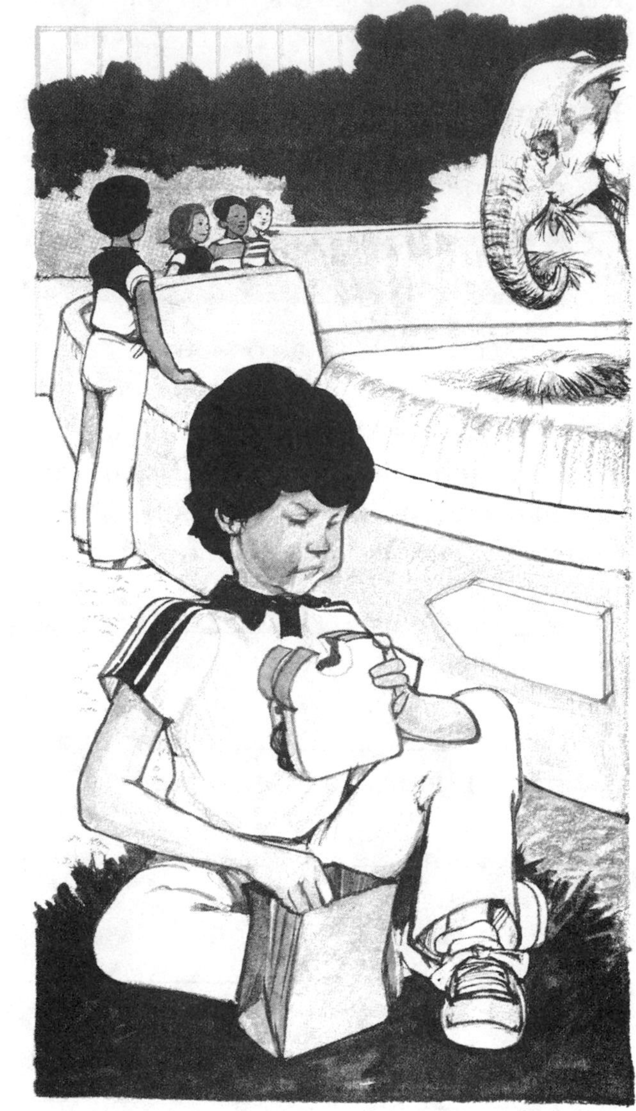

6 "What are you laughing about?" Susan asked.

7 Carlos showed her the sandwich. "Tuna fish, peanut butter, bananas, mustard, and pickles," Susan said, wrinkling up her nose. "What kind of a sandwich is that?"

8 "It is a Mosh special," Carlos said. "It's strange tasting, but I'm hungry." Susan laughed as Carlos took another big bite of the sandwich.

Knowing the Words

Write the words from the story that have the meanings below.

1. visit to someplace with a group ______ (Par. 2)
2. jumped ______ (Par. 2)
3. tasty ______ (Par. 3)

Working with Words

Sometimes the plural form of a word is made by changing the spelling of the word. The plural form of *goose* is *geese*.

Use the plural words below to complete the sentences.

mice women feet children

1. Two ______ live in a cage in our classroom.
2. These tennis shoes are too small for Kay's ______.
3. Twenty ______ rode on a bus to the zoo.
4. My older sister and my mother are ______.

Fill in each blank with the correct letters to make a word that completes each sentence below.

ph wr

5. There is a ____inkle in my shirt.
6. Can you say the al____abet backwards?

Reading and Thinking

Write **T** if the sentence is true.
Write **F** if the sentence is false.

1. ____ Carlos had overslept.
2. ____ It took Carlos five minutes to get dressed.
3. ____ The class might have seen an ostrich at the zoo.
4. ____ Susan thought a Mosh special looked delicious.
5. ____ Carlos thought the sandwich would be tasty.
6. What did Mosh put in the sandwich?

______

______

7. What do you think the class did when they finished eating? ______

______

8. Do you think Mosh will be allowed to make another sandwich? Explain your answer. ______

______

______

Good–bye, Mosh?

How do you think it feels when you have to say good-bye to a good friend?

1 "Mrs. Chung was quite impressed with Mosh when she was here the other night," Mrs. Garza told Carlos. "She mentioned something about how nice it would be to buy the robot back."

2 "Mom, I don't want to sell Mosh," Carlos said, feeling sad. "Do I have to?"

3 "You have had Mosh for almost a year now," his mom said. "Don't you think you'll be getting tired of it soon?"

4 "No, Mosh is my best friend," Carlos answered. "But since Mrs. Chung is your boss, I'll think about it."

5 Carlos felt terrible. He could not imagine life without Mosh. The next day he went to Susan's house, hoping that his friend could cheer him up.

6 When Carlos got home, his house was dark and quiet. As soon as he opened the door, all the lights went on. "Surprise!" his parents and Marie yelled.

7 "What's going on?" Carlos asked, feeling confused.

8 "Did you forget Mosh's birthday?" Marie teased. "It was one year ago today that you brought that robot home."

9 Carlos tried to act happy as he and Mosh opened presents together. Marie gave Carlos some new lights for Mosh's eyes. His father's gift was a new can of oil.

10 "This one is from Mom," Carlos told Mosh. He opened the package and found a large battery. There was also a note that said "This will help Mosh give us another exciting year."

11 "But what about selling Mosh back to Mrs. Chung?" Carlos asked.

12 "Well, I told Mrs. Chung how important Mosh was to you," Mrs. Garza said. "She said she would never want you to sell your friend. But she did say she might like you and Mosh to be in an ad some day."

13 Carlos gave a cheer and hugged Mosh. Mosh's eyes lit up. Then the robot spun around in circles, which was its way of saying "Hooray!"

Knowing the Words

Write the word from the story that has the meaning below.

1. pleased ______________________________ (Par. 1)

Synonyms are words that have the same or nearly the same meaning. Circle the pair of synonyms in each row.

2. box gift paper present
3. terrible awful sad brave
4. hope imagine tease think

Working with Words

Write a compound word using the underlined words in each sentence.

1. The day of your birth is your

______________________________.

2. A fish the color of gold is a

______________________________.

3. Paper with sand on it is called

______________________________.

4. An ache in your head is a

______________________________.

5. Light from the moon is called

______________________________.

In each word below, draw a line to divide the word into syllables.

6. confuse
7. ribbon
8. almost
9. pillow
10. journey
11. lesson

Reading and Thinking

1. Check the answer that tells what the story is mainly about.

_____ saying good-bye to Mosh

_____ selling Mosh to Mrs. Chung

_____ having a party for Mosh

2. What did Marie give to Carlos for Mosh? ______________________________

3. What was Mrs. Garza's gift? ______________________________

4. What do you think Carlos and Mosh did after the party? ______________________________

Write the best word to complete each sentence.

5. The crowd ______________________________ loudly for the team. (teased, thought, cheered)

6. When I close my eyes, it is easy to ______________________________ I am a bird. (imagine, sell, mention)

7. A small ______________________________ came in the mail today. (hug, cheer, package)

8. Can you ______________________________ how to wrap a present? (explain, want, open)

9. After the long walk, Marge was very ______________________________. (nice, tired, brave)

Cat Bath

Why would a cat hide from its owner?

1 "Rick, how would you like to help your good friend give Herbie a bath?" Tracy said. "That dumb cat ran into a skunk, and he smells awful!"

2 "I'll be right there," Rick answered and hung up the phone.

3 When Rick arrived, Tracy said, "Use one hand to hold your nose. You can help me wash Herbie with the other one." Then she called, "Here, Herbie!" and a green-eyed cat came bounding out from the den.

4 "We'd better do this in the basement," Tracy said, "because Herbie just hates **W-A-T-E-R.**" She carried him down the steps and put him on the floor. Then she dumped some cat shampoo in the sink. As soon as Tracy turned the faucet handle, Herbie scrambled across the floor. He jumped into a pile of dirty clothes.

5 When Tracy reached in to get him, Herbie ran out the other side. He dashed up the stairs. "Help me catch him, Rick!" Tracy cried.

6 Rick whirled around and ran up the stairs behind Tracy. Rick and Tracy found Herbie hiding next to the refrigerator. Then they chased him into the broom closet.

7 "Gotcha!" Tracy said as she caught Herbie. They all headed for the basement.

8 "We won't forget to close the door this time," Rick said, pulling it shut behind him.

9 "Oh, no!" Tracy shouted as she started downstairs. "We forgot something even worse than that!"

10 There at the foot of the stairs was a huge soap puddle. A stream of water flowed over the sink.

11 "We forgot to turn off the water!" Rick cried, his eyes wide with surprise.

12 "We've got two messes to clean up now," Tracy moaned. "Let's get busy!"

Knowing the Words

Write the words from the story that have the meanings below.

1. jumping ______________ (Par. 3)
2. pipe that water comes out of ______________ (Par. 4)
3. ran quickly ______________ (Par. 4)
4. turned quickly ______________ (Par. 6)

Some words sound alike but have different spellings and meanings. Write the word with the correct meaning to complete each sentence below.

5. Those ______________ lead to the attic. (stares, stairs)
6. Please ______________ the garage door. (close, clothes)

Working with Words

Circle the correct word in ( ) and write it in the blank.

1. Do not get ______________ in your eyes when you wash. (soup, soap)
2. They ______________ the butterfly in a net. (caught, cat)
3. I'll need a ______________ to clean up this powder. (broom, brim)
4. Can you ______________ that bottle of shampoo? (rich, reach)

Reading and Thinking

1. Check the answer that tells what the story is mainly about.

   _____ a pile of dirty clothes

   _____ a bath for Herbie

   _____ two messes

2. Herbie ran away because

   ______________________________.

3. Put a check beside something that was probably in Tracy's basement.

   _____ a car

   _____ a washing machine

   _____ a mailbox

4. Put a check beside the two answers that tell where Herbie hid.

   _____ in the living room

   _____ in the pile of dirty clothes

   _____ beside the refrigerator

5. What did Tracy mean when she said that there were two messes to clean?

   ____

   ____

6. How do you think Rick and Tracy will clean the basement floor?

   ____

   ____

Ready to Roll

What could you do with a pair of roller skates that no longer fit?

1 One Saturday afternoon Tracy and her friend Elsa decided to roller skate to City Park. "Come in and put on your skates," Tracy said when Elsa arrived at her house. Elsa took off her sneakers and loosened the laces of her skates.

2 "Oof!" she grunted as she tried to squeeze her foot into a skate. "Either my skates have shrunk, or my feet have grown! What good is a pair of skates if they don't fit?"

3 "Hey, I've got an idea!" Tracy said. "If Mr. Levi will give us a board from his lumber pile, we can take your skate wheels off and . . ."

4 ". . . Build a skateboard!" Elsa broke in. "That's a great idea!"

5 Elsa put on her sneakers, and the two of them hurried down the street to explain their idea to Mr. Levi. Mr. Levi smiled and said, "I've got just what you need." He pulled a board from beneath a pile. "This was part of Skipper's old doghouse," he said.

6 "Thanks, Mr. Levi!" the girls said. Then they raced back to Tracy's house.

7 Elsa removed her skate wheels with a screwdriver. Tracy sanded some splinters off the board. Then they used nails to make holes for the screws. Once the wheels were attached, Elsa was ready to roll. "It fits perfectly," she said as she put one foot on the skateboard.

8 While Tracy put on her skates, Elsa set the skateboard on the sidewalk. Then she placed her left foot on top and pushed with her right. "It works!" Elsa yelled as she traveled down the street.

9 "Wait for me!" Tracy called.

10 "You know what I like best about this skateboard?" Elsa said when Tracy caught up. "It will always be a perfect fit, no matter how much my feet grow!"

Knowing the Words

Write the words from the story that have the meanings below.

1. tennis shoes ____________ (Par. 1)
2. made less tight ____________ (Par. 1)
3. strings used for tying ____________ (Par. 1)
4. tiny pieces of wood ____________ (Par. 7)

Check the meaning that fits the underlined word in each sentence.

5. Roll the ball across the floor.
   ____ bread
   ____ move by turning
6. Did you hurt your foot?
   ____ part of the body
   ____ twelve inches
7. I have sand in my shoe.
   ____ to make smooth
   ____ tiny bits of stone

Working with Words

An 's at the end of a word may be used to show that something belongs to someone. Add 's to each name below and write the new word in the correct blank.

Mr. Levi   Skipper   Elsa

1. ____________ lumber
2. ____________ skateboard
3. ____________ doghouse

Reading and Thinking

1. Number the sentences to show the order in which things happened.
   ____ Elsa rolled down the street on her skateboard.
   ____ Mr. Levi gave the girls a piece of wood.
   ____ Elsa discovered that her skates didn't fit.
   ____ The girls attached the skate wheels to the board.
2. Check the sentence that tells why Elsa couldn't get her skates on.
   ____ Her skates had shrunk.
   ____ Her socks were too thick.
   ____ Her feet had grown.
3. Check two words that tell about Mr. Levi.
   ____ helpful   ____ selfish
   ____ grouchy   ____ friendly
4. Check two sentences that tell how Elsa's skateboard and roller skates were alike.
   ____ They both had laces.
   ____ They both had screws.
   ____ They both had wheels.
   ____ They both were made of wood.

Leave It to Rags

Read to find out how Tracy meets her new neighbors.

1 Tracy watched the moving van turn the corner. "I wonder if the new family will have kids my age," she thought. Tracy sat down in a chair close to the window so she could watch the movers. Suddenly there was a loud crash in the alley. Tracy hurried outside to see what was making all the racket.

2 When she reached the alley, she found an empty garbage can lying on its side. Just then a scared puppy poked its head out from behind the can.

3 "Where'd you come from?" Tracy asked. She reached for the tags attached to the dog's collar. " 'My name is Rags,' " she read, " '10 South Street, Oak Hill.' That's nearly a hundred miles from here!" she exclaimed. "I'll get Mom and Dad to phone your owners," Tracy said. She picked up the garbage can. Then she took the pup into her backyard and gave him a bowl of water.

4 Tracy and Rags were playing with a rubber ball when a boy and girl appeared at the fence. "Hi, my name's Lindsay, and this is my brother, Dale," the girl said. "We've just moved here from Oak Hill. It looks as if you found our dog."

5 "Is Rags your dog? That's great! Now we won't have to try to track down the owners in Oak Hill. I just found him out by the garbage can. He was really scared," Tracy said.

6 "He must have slipped out the door when the movers carried the furniture in, but nobody noticed," Lindsay said.

7 "I guess he couldn't wait to go exploring," Tracy chuckled. "My name is Tracy. I'm your new neighbor."

8 "Well, we had hoped to find some friends our age," Dale said. "Leave it to Rags to find one for us!"

Knowing the Words

Write the words from the story that have the meanings below.

1. large truck ______________________ (Par. 1)
2. noise ______________________ (Par. 1)

Abbreviations are shortened forms of words. The abbreviation for *inch* is *in.* Match each word from the first list with its abbreviation from the second list.

3. _____ street	**a.** mi.
4. _____ Mister	**b.** st.
5. _____ mile	**c.** Mr.

Learning to Study

A **table of contents** is on one of the first pages in a book. It shows the chapters that are in the book and on what page each one begins. Use the table of contents below to answer the questions.

All About Dogs

Table of Contents

Kinds of Dogs	1
Dogs as Pets	21
Caring for Your Dog	30
Feeding Your Dog	45

1. How many chapters are in the book?

____

2. What is the first chapter called?

____

3. On what page does "Dogs as Pets" begin? ______________________

Reading and Thinking

1. Check the answer that tells what the story is mainly about.

_____ meeting new neighbors
_____ watching movers
_____ noises in the alley

2. Check the two sentences that tell about Tracy.

_____ She likes to meet people.
_____ She is a good neighbor.
_____ She does not like dogs.

Write **T** if the sentence is true.
Write **F** if the sentence is false.

3. _____ Dale knocked the garbage can over.
4. _____ Tracy could easily walk to Oak Hill.
5. _____ Tracy thought Rags was lost.
6. _____ Tracy wanted to keep Rags.
7. How far had Lindsay and Dale moved from their old home?

____

Write the best word to complete each sentence below.

8. The ______________ in the kitchen is new. (barn, furniture, noise)
9. The ______________ book is funny. (comic, metal, leftover)
10. We rode in the ______________ to the game. (toast, pup, van)

Dinner for Rags

Have you ever worried about something and then found out things were not as bad as they seemed?

1 Since they had moved, Lindsay and Dale had been quite busy. They had unpacked all of their things and had made lots of new friends.

2 Lindsay and Dale were very happy in their new neighborhood. Only one thing troubled them. Even though he seemed to be healthy, Rags had not been eating the food they put out for him each day. Lindsay and Dale tried everything to get him to eat. They bought a different kind of food. They hid treats in the middle of the food. They even pretended they were going to eat his food if he didn't. But nothing worked.

3 Then Lindsay and Dale went to Tracy about their problem. She listened and thought for a minute. Then she snapped her fingers, smiled, and said, "Follow me. I think I know what is going on." Tracy led Lindsay and Dale to the house on the corner of the block. There, a few feet in front of them, stood a small tan dog and Rags sharing a bowl of dog food.

4 "That is Ruffy," Tracy said, pointing to the tan dog. "He belongs to Mr. and Mrs. Breen." Just then two people came to the back door and started talking to the dogs. Rags wagged his tail and barked as if he were talking to the Breens.

5 When Rags saw Lindsay and Dale, he ran over to them. "He just won't stay in our yard when we tell him to," Lindsay said to Mr. and Mrs. Breen. "I don't know how we'll ever get him to obey us."

6 Tracy said, "The Breens used to train dogs. Maybe they'll give you some helpful advice."

7 "We'll do better than that," Mr. Breen said. "We'll help you train this smart little pup. If you're interested, we can start Monday."

8 "That's great!" Lindsay and Dale said eagerly. "Thanks!" Then they took Rags home to tell their parents the good news.

Knowing the Words

Write the words from the story that have the meanings below.

1. worried ______________ (Par. 2)

2. special things ______________ (Par. 2)

3. teach ______________ (Par. 6)

Some words are spelled the same but have different meanings. For example, *yard* can mean "the land around a building" or "thirty-six inches."

Look at the list of words below. For each pair of sentences, one word from the list will correctly complete both. Choose the correct word to fill in the blank for each pair of sentences.

bark   bowl   can

4. I like to ______________ with my friends.

   I poured cereal and milk into my favorite ______________.

5. Floppy doesn't ________ at peoplc she knows.

   The tree ______________ was bumpy.

6. Kevin ______________ play the piano.

   The soup ______________ was empty.

Match each word from the first list with its abbreviation from the second list.

7.	_____ minute	**a.**	ft.
8.	_____ Monday	**b.**	min.
9.	_____ feet	**c.**	Mon.

Reading and Thinking

Words such as *he, she, you, it, we,* and *they* are used in place of other words. Read these sentences. *Rags is a puppy. He is owned by Lindsay and Dale.* Instead of repeating the name *Rags* in the second sentence, *he* is used in the place of *Rags.*

Read each set of sentences below. Fill in each blank.

1. Lindsay told Rags to sit.
   She used a firm voice.

   She stands for ______________.

2. Lindsay and Dale are training Rags.
   They enjoy the work.

   They stands for ______________.

3. The collar wasn't very heavy.
   It was made for a puppy.

   It stands for ______________.

4. Rags was not eating his food at home

   because ______________.

Learning to Study

Number each list of words below in alphabetical order.

1.	_____ problem	**3.**	_____ treats
	_____ pretend		_____ tried
	_____ pride		_____ train
2.	_____ happy	**4.**	_____ ran
	_____ him		_____ Rags
	_____ house		_____ rain

Training Time

Read to find out about a lesson for Rags.

1 Rags seemed to know that something special was going to happen. He was more playful than usual. As the children walked down the block, they could barely hold on to Rags. One minute he tried to run between Dale's legs. The next minute he was trying to run up the steps of a new house.

2 The Breens were waiting for Lindsay and Dale when they arrived. They began to tell Lindsay and Dale how they could train Rags. The children listened carefully. "First you will give him a command," Mr. Breen told them. "When he obeys, you will reward him with praise and a pat on the head. When he doesn't obey, you must say *no* in a firm voice."

3 Mrs. Breen went on to explain that the first thing they taught the dogs was to sit.

4 "That sounds good," Dale said. "We'd like to start with something simple."

5 Lindsay and Dale found out quickly that no trick was going to be simple. They took turns telling Rags to sit. Every time they showed Rags how, he thought they wanted to play. He would jump up and start to lick them. Then he would bark as if to say "Let's have fun!"

6 The children were very patient and kept trying. After what seemed like hours, Rags finally caught on. Lindsay and Dale patted Rags on the head. They told him what a smart dog he was. By this time the children were very tired, but Rags was still lively. "What would you like to teach him next?" Mrs. Breen asked.

7 "Would it be all right if we went home and rested?" Dale said as he sat down, looking very tired. "I think we're going to need a lot more energy before we begin the next trick."

8 Everyone laughed when Rags jumped into Dale's lap as if begging to play some more.

Knowing the Words

Write the words from the story that have the meanings below.

1. something nice that is said ________________ (Par. 2)
2. strong ________________ (Par. 2)
3. waiting without getting upset ________________ (Par. 6)

Words that mean the same, or nearly the same, are called **synonyms.** Circle the pair of synonyms in each row.

4. command ask know order
5. firm bright shy smart

Learning to Study

At the top of each page in a dictionary are two words in dark print called **guide words.** They can help you find other words in the dictionary. The first guide word tells what the first word is on the page. The second guide word tells what the last word is on the page.

The words in a dictionary are listed in alphabetical order. To find a word, decide if it comes in alphabetical order between the guide words on the page. If it does, the word will be on that page. Check each word that could be found between these guide words.

scatter/scout

1. ____ science
2. ____ scramble
3. ____ scene
4. ____ scratch
5. ____ scissors
6. ____ school
7. ____ scrub
8. ____ scent

Reading and Thinking

1. Check the answer that tells what the story is mainly about.

   ____ getting tired

   ____ a long afternoon

   ____ how to train a dog

2. Did Rags mean to misbehave? ______

   Explain your answer. ________________

   ____

3. What other things might Lindsay and Dale train Rags to do? ________________

   ____

4. What did the children do when Rags obeyed their command? ________________

   ____

5. Write **R** next to the two sentences that tell about real things.

   ____ Puppies can talk.

   ____ Puppies can bark.

   ____ Puppies can be trained.

6. Put a check next to the two answers that tell what a person needs to do when training a puppy.

   ____ praise the puppy

   ____ give up

   ____ give a command

   ____ yell loudly

Afternoon Adventure

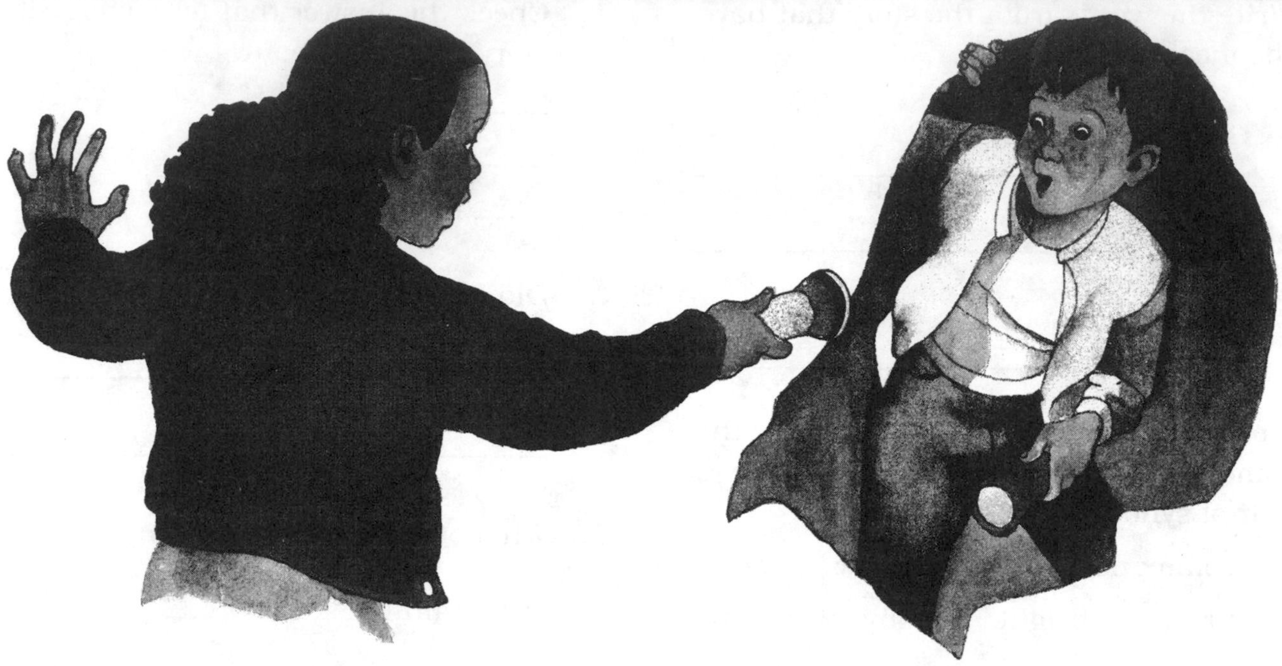

What do you think Rick and Elsa might find in a cave?

1 Elsa and her family had brought a picnic lunch to Rocky Cave State Park. Carmen was still eating. "Hurry up, Carmen," Elsa said to her younger sister. "Rick and I want to see that cave." Elsa loved adventure and was always ready to go exploring.

2 Finally, Carmen was finished. Rick and Elsa grabbed their flashlights. Carmen and her father were close behind. They all started toward a huge opening in the side of the hill. Rick and Elsa went into the cave first and walked along a narrow pathway. It went deep into the cave. They reached a small opening that looked like a doorway. Rick and Elsa stooped down and went through the entrance. They found themselves in a damp, dark room.

3 "It looks like a secret hideout!" Rick exclaimed.

4 "Long ago, people used caves for shelter," Elsa replied.

5 "I hope nobody uses it now. I think this place is spooky!" Rick said as he glanced around.

6 "There's nothing to be scared of," Elsa told Rick. Then suddenly she stopped. "Look!" she said, her feet frozen to the ground and her body stiff with fear. A spot of light moved toward them, and they could hear footsteps.

7 Then in a low, deep voice someone said, "Elsa and Rick, are you in there?"

8 "I'd know that voice anywhere," Elsa said. "It's Dad with Carmen!"

9 Just then Carmen appeared at the entrance to the room and announced, "It's creepy in here!"

10 "You can say that again!" laughed Elsa and Rick.

Knowing the Words

Write the word from the story that has the meaning below.

1. place to go in ____________ (Par. 2)

Words with opposite meanings are called **antonyms.** Circle the pair of antonyms in each row.

2. narrow small wide long
3. door entrance exit tunnel

Working with Words

The endings **-y** or **-ly** can be added to some words. Write the correct word to complete each sentence below.

1. The mountain trail was ____________ and difficult to climb. (rock, rocky)
2. This ____________ is smooth, flat, and round. (rock, rocky)
3. I ____________ grabbed my jacket and ran home. (quick, quickly)
4. ____________ action kept the fire from spreading. (Quick, Quickly)

A word that means one of something is **singular.** A word that means more than one is **plural.** Most singular words are made plural by adding *s.* Most words that end in *s, ss, x, ch,* and *sh* are made plural by adding *es.* Form the plural of each word below by adding *s* or *es.*

5. hammer ______
6. porch ______
7. box ______
8. mess ______
9. bush ______
10. seed ______

Reading and Thinking

1. Check the answer that tells what the story is mainly about.

   _____ a picnic

   _____ frightened explorers

   _____ people who live in caves

Write **T** if the sentence is true.
Write **F** if the sentence is false.

2. _____ Rick was frightened in the cave.
3. _____ Elsa had a picnic in the cave.
4. _____ Someone was living in the cave.
5. Some things are real and some are make-believe. Write **M** next to the sentence that tells about a make-believe thing.

   _____ Caves are dark and damp.

   _____ Animals live in caves.

   _____ Monsters live in caves.

Write the best word to complete each sentence below.

6. I dropped the ____________ and ran. (flashlight, shelter, tunnel)
7. I have a secret ____________ in the attic. (hideout, shadow, cave)
8. We could not sleep outside because the ground was ____________. (green, damp, soft)
9. Stay on the ____________ so you don't get lost. (doorway, entrance, pathway)

Screamer

What would you do if you found a baby bird that had fallen from his nest?

1 Tracy and Dale were playing in Tracy's yard when they discovered a baby blue jay that had fallen from his nest. Tracy filled a shoe box with bits of yarn. Dale gently placed the bird in the box. They set it on the porch step.

2 Just then the baby bird opened his beak and let out a loud scream. "Feed me. I'm hungry!" he seemed to say. Tracy hurried inside to warm some milk while Dale found some birdseed in the garage. They put the seed in a bag. Then they crushed it with a hammer.

3 After mixing the crushed birdseed and milk, Tracy used an eyedropper to squeeze the mixture into the bird's mouth. The blue jay swallowed the food. Then he let out another noisy scream, asking for more. "I think we should name him Screamer," Dale said. Tracy agreed.

4 During the next few weeks, it seemed as if the young bird was hungry all the time. One morning Tracy and Dale fixed some baby cereal for Screamer. When they went outside to feed the bird, the box was empty.

5 They were sure something terrible had happened and that they would never see Screamer again. Heartbroken, they sat in silence beneath an oak tree.

6 Then something drifted down from above. It landed near Dale's foot. "Look!" he said, grabbing it. "It's a piece of yarn from Screamer's shoe box!"

7 Tracy looked high into the tree. Suddenly a loud scream rang out. A blue jay fluttered to the ground. "Hey, it's Screamer!" Dale cried with delight.

8 "We've been so busy taking care of Screamer we didn't notice how much he had grown!" Tracy exclaimed. "But now that Screamer has learned to fly, I guess he will be taking care of himself."

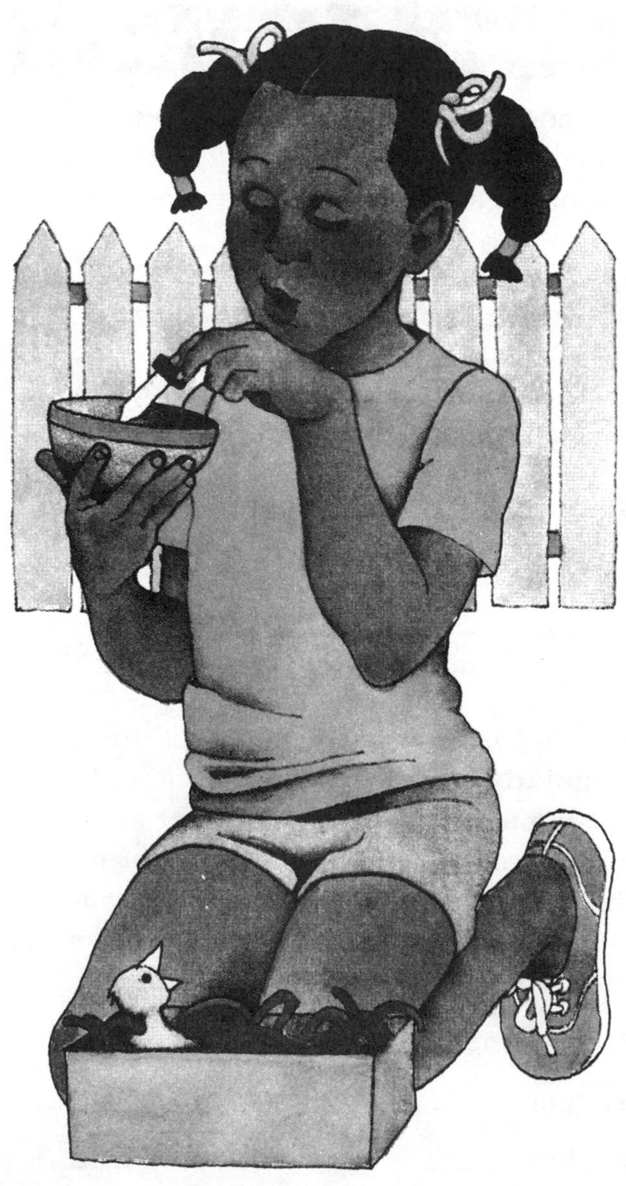

Knowing the Words

Write the words from the story that have the meanings below.

1. bird ____________ (Par. 1)
2. broke into little pieces ____________ (Par. 2)
3. very sad ____________ (Par. 5)
4. flew gently ____________ (Par. 7)

In each row below, circle the three words that belong together.

5. beak feather shoe wing
6. smash flutter crush pound

Working with Words

A **contraction** is a short way to write two words. An apostrophe **(')** shows that one or more letters have been taken out. Write a contraction from the story for each pair of words below.

1. I am ____________ (Par. 2)
2. we have ____________ (Par. 8)
3. did not ____________ (Par. 8)

Most words that end in a consonant followed by *y* are made plural by changing *y* to *i* and adding *es*. Write the plural form of each word below.

4. grocery ____________
5. library ____________
6. city ____________

Reading and Thinking

1. Number the sentences to show the order in which things happened.

   ____ Tracy and Dale fed Screamer.

   ____ Screamer flew to a tree.

   ____ Tracy and Dale found a blue jay.

   ____ Dale put the bird in a shoe box.

2. Tracy and Dale named the blue jay Screamer because ____________ ____________.

3. Tracy and Dale mixed ____________ and ____________ to feed to Screamer.

Write the best word to complete each sentence below.

4. This ____________ will make warm socks. (cereal, yarn, seed)
5. Stir the ____________ till it is smooth. (blue jay, mixture, scream)
6. The kids ____________ that Screamer was young. (agreed, tugged, drifted)

Beginner's Luck

Read to find out how horseshoes is played.

1 One Friday, Tracy and Elsa were watching Mr. Levi trim bushes. "We can't think of anything to do, Mr. Levi," Tracy moaned. "Do you have any ideas?"

2 Mr. Levi stopped and thought for a few seconds. "When I was your age," he said, "I played horseshoes. You could use the ones in my basement if you'd like to learn how to play."

3 "That sounds like fun!" Elsa said. Mr. Levi went inside. He returned with some rusty horseshoes and two steel posts. He laid the posts thirty feet apart. Then he pounded them into the ground.

4 "Each player stands next to this post. Players pitch toward the other post twice," Mr. Levi explained. "A shoe that goes around the post is called a ringer. It's worth three points. If a shoe leans against the post, it earns one point. You can also earn one point if the shoe lands within six inches of the post. The person with the highest score after twenty-five innings wins the game."

5 Tracy, Elsa, and Mr. Levi began playing. By the eighth inning, Mr. Levi and Elsa each had seven points. Tracy had scored only two. "I wish I had beginner's luck," she said as she stepped up to take her turn. She threw the horseshoe. It flew past the post. The shoe landed under the bushes.

6 Tracy looked under a bush for the shoe. After a moment she called, "Is this yours, Mr. Levi?" She dangled a gold chain with something shiny on the end.

7 "My pocket watch!" he exclaimed with surprise. "I lost that a week ago."

8 "Gee, I'm glad I threw that horseshoe crooked," Tracy said. "I guess I do have beginner's luck after all!"

Knowing the Words

Write the words from the story that have the meanings below.

1. covered with a reddish-brown coating ________ (Par. 3)

2. turns to play ________ (Par.4)

3. held something up so that it swung loosely ________ (Par. 6)

4. not straight ________ (Par. 8)

Match each word from the first list with its abbreviation from the second list.

5.	____ seconds	a.	wk.
6.	____ Friday	b.	sec.
7.	____ inch	c.	Fri.
8.	____ week	d.	in.
9.	____ feet	e.	ft.

Learning to Study

Check each word that could be found between the dictionary guide words.

1. colt/crooked

____ crash
____ crept
____ crisp
____ coconut

2. scare/shy

____ slept
____ shore
____ sense
____ scream

3. fiddle/flakes

____ fly
____ finger
____ flow
____ fierce

4. whole/write

____ wrote
____ wink
____ won
____ wheat

Reading and Thinking

1. Check the answer that tells what the story is mainly about.

   ____ trimming the bushes
   ____ looking for a lost watch
   ____ learning to play horseshoes

Write **T** if the sentence is true.
Write **F** if the sentence is false.

2. ____ Mr. Levi's watch fell off his wrist.

3. ____ Horseshoes is a game that could be played indoors.

4. ____ Mr. Levi knew his watch was missing.

5. The number of innings in a game of horseshoes is ________.

6. Write two words from Paragraph 4 that are also used in the game of baseball. ________

   ____

Write the best word to complete each sentence below.

7. A ________ can be used to measure the door. (chain, yardstick, hammer)

8. Brad ________ about the rain. (pounded, whistled, complained)

9. The fence was ________ because it was old. (straight, tall, crooked)

Loud and Clear

How could you stretch a tin can phone between two second-story windows?

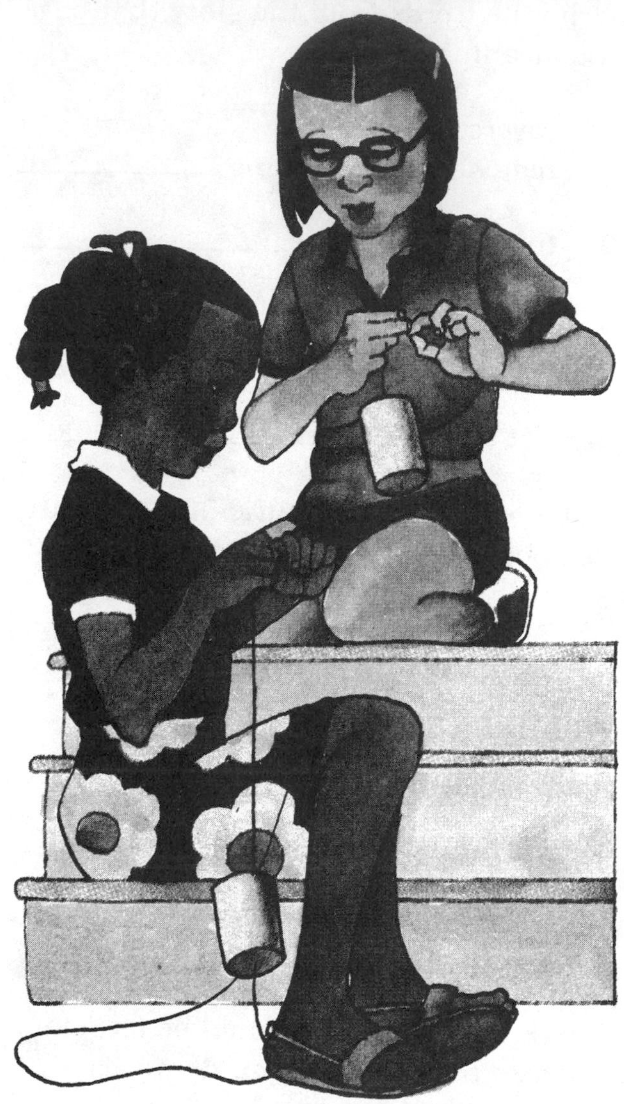

1 Soon after Lindsay moved in, she and Tracy discovered that their upstairs bedroom windows faced each other across the backyards. "Let's make a tin can telephone and stretch it between our windows," Lindsay said.

2 "Then we could have secret talks anytime we like," Tracy added. The girls found two empty soup cans. They washed the cans out. Then they put a hole in the bottom of each one. Finally Lindsay and Tracy threaded a long string through the cans and tied knots at each end.

3 "You take that end up to your room. I'll take this end up to mine," Tracy said with excitement. They each headed for their own houses. Suddenly they realized that it wouldn't work.

4 "If we run the string through our doors and up the stairs," Tracy said, "we won't be able to pull it tight and straight across the yards."

5 "You take both cans up to your room and throw one end over to me in my room," Lindsay suggested. It was a good idea, but every time Tracy tossed the can it landed in Lindsay's yard.

6 The girls met back in the yard. They were ready to give up when Tracy said, "I think I know how to fix it."

7 She grabbed the scissors and cut the string in half. "Take your end to your room. Leave the can on the windowsill. Drop the string out the window," Tracy said. "I'll do the same with this end and meet you back here."

8 Before long a string hung out each window. The girls met outside. "We'll just tie a knot in the string," Tracy explained. Soon the string was connected. Both girls rushed to their rooms. They pulled the string tight.

9 "Can you hear me?" Lindsay asked hopefully.

10 "Loud and clear!" Tracy replied.

Knowing the Words

Write the words from the story that have the meanings below.

1. understood clearly ______________ (Par. 3)

2. gave an idea ______________ (Par. 5)

3. small shelf under a window ______________ (Par. 7)

4. wishing something might happen ______________ (Par. 9)

Check the meaning that fits the underlined word in each sentence.

5. The <u>back</u> door of the house is locked.

   ____ opposite of front

   ____ part of the body

6. I think I have a spot of gravy on my <u>tie</u>.

   ____ to fasten together

   ____ a piece of clothing

Learning to Study

Two pairs of dictionary guide words and their page numbers are shown in dark print. Beside each word below, write the number of the page on which it would be found.

thick/trim p. 302
trouble/try p. 310

1. ______ trumpet
2. ______ tremble
3. ______ truth
4. ______ truck
5. ______ thread
6. ______ trust
7. ______ tight
8. ______ trap

Reading and Thinking

1. Check the answer that tells what the story is mainly about.

   ____ old tin cans

   ____ the secret talk

   ____ making a telephone

2. How is a tin can phone different from a real telephone? ______________

   ____

Write **T** if the sentence is true.
Write **F** if the sentence is false.

3. ____ Sounds can travel through a string.

4. ____ A tin can telephone will not work if the string goes around a corner.

5. ____ Tracy could make a long-distance call on the tin can telephone.

6. ____ A tin can telephone will not work with a knot in the string.

7. What had been in the cans before they were emptied? ______________

Write the best word to complete each sentence below.

8. She ______________ the yarn through the needle. (snatched, threaded, connected)

9. There is a ______________ in this rope. (phone, string, knot)

The Seven–Flavor Favor

What problem did Elsa solve for her music project?

1 All month Elsa had looked forward to the music festival that was to be held at City Park. After much thought, she decided to do a project that would be both musical and colorful.

2 On the day of the festival, Elsa put seven glass jars of the same size into a wagon. She carried a folding table under her arm and pulled the wagon to the park.

3 At the park she set the table up next to a drinking fountain. Then Elsa began to fill a jar. Suddenly she realized she had not brought the dyes to color the water. "I don't have time to run home," she thought.

4 Then she looked across the park. She spied a sign that said "Fresh Fruit Juice." Elsa quickly made her way toward the stand, with the glass jars rattling in the wagon behind her.

5 "I'd like to buy one glass of each flavor you have," Elsa told the man behind the counter.

6 The man smiled as he said, "I've got seven different flavors. Are you sure you want that many glasses?"

7 Elsa explained that she'd planned to put colored water into seven jars. Then she would play a tune by tapping the jars with a wooden spoon. "But I left the dye to color the water at home," she said. "Each flavor of juice is a different color. I'll put juice in the jars in place of dye."

8 "You really know how to solve a problem," the man chuckled as he began to fill some cups with juice.

9 "How much do I owe you?" Elsa asked. The man set the last cup on the counter in front of her.

10 "Nothing," he said. "Anyone who can come up with a good idea like that deserves some help. Let's just call it a seven-flavor favor!"

Knowing the Words

Write the words from the story that have the meanings below.

1. something planned ______ (Par. 1)
2. a place to get water ______ (Par. 3)
3. where things are sold ______ (Par. 4)
4. large shelf ______ (Par. 5)

Synonyms are words that have the same or nearly the same meaning. Circle the pair of synonyms in each row.

5.	dye	orange	coloring	water
6.	radio	tune	song	piano

Working with Words

Use each group of words in a sentence that tells who owns something.

1. Elsa's glass jars ______

______

2. man's fruit juice stand ______

______

Some words are easier to read if they are divided into parts called **syllables.** Some words have two consonants between two vowels. These words can be divided into syllables between the consonants, as in *for/got.*

In each word below, draw a line to divide the word into syllables.

3. forward	**5.** fountain	**7.** carry
4. arrive	**6.** problem	**8.** enjoy

Reading and Thinking

1. Check the answer that tells what the story is mainly about.

   ____ music in City Park

   ____ solving a problem

   ____ a fruit juice stand

2. Why didn't Elsa use plain water in the jars? ______

______

Write **T** if the sentence is true.
Write **F** if the sentence is false.

3. ____ The man thought Elsa's plan was a good one.
4. ____ Elsa could not pay for the fruit juice.
5. ____ Elsa could play eight different notes on the jars.
6. What do you think Elsa will do with the fruit juice after the music festival is over? ______

______

Write the best word to complete each sentence below.

7. The class ______ was finished. (flavor, dye, project)
8. A ______ rainbow appeared after the storm. (fresh, colorful, musical)
9. Would you like ______ with breakfast? (juice, cup, spoon)

Lemonade for Sale

Read to find out about a smart way to run a lemonade stand.

1 All the kids in the neighborhood seemed to be busy on Saturday afternoon except Heather and Michael. "Let's have a lemonade stand!" Michael said to his sister.

2 "Sure!" Heather said. They found some paper cups in the house, but they needed to go to the store on the corner to buy lemons.

3 The children raced back home and made the lemonade. Then they set up a table in the front yard. Michael taped a sign on it and waited for customers.

4 Heather and Michael sat there for thirty minutes. Not one person came by. "I'll bet we'd get some customers if we advertised," Heather said. That gave Michael an idea. He dashed inside to get something.

5 He came back with a pair of walkie-talkies. Michael announced, "I'll go out and find people who look thirsty. I'll let them know we're here! We'll keep in touch with the walkie-talkies."

6 After a few minutes he radioed, "Six kids on bikes should be arriving soon, Heather."

7 "OK, Michael," Heather replied. In the next half hour, Michael sent ten more people to the stand.

8 Soon Heather called to Michael. "I've just run out of cups," she said, "so don't send anybody else."

9 "I just sent a man who said he was awfully thirsty," Michael replied. "See if he'll wait while I buy more cups."

10 "I'll do my best," Heather said, hoping she could convince the man to stay. In a few minutes, Michael came rushing down the street with a new package of cups.

11 "I guess I'm too late," he said when he did not see the man waiting.

12 "It's OK," Heather said, chuckling. "He was so thirsty he drank every last drop—right out of the pitcher!"

Knowing the Words

Write the words from the story that have the meanings below.

1. people who buy ______________ (Par. 3)
2. two-way radios ______________ (Par. 5)
3. make others believe ______________ (Par. 10)
4. a small bit of liquid ______________ (Par. 12)

Choose the correct word below to fill the blanks for each pair of sentences.

pitcher   right

5. Is this the ______________ answer?

   Stomp your ______________ foot.

6. Pour milk into the ______________.

   Who is the team ______________?

Working with Words

Say *city*. Circle the words below that have the sound *c* stands for in *city*.

1.	cave	cent	face	clown
2.	center	dance	calm	twice

When a word ends with *e*, the *e* is usually dropped before adding **-ed** or **-ing.** Add **-ed** or **-ing** to the word in ( ) to make a word that completes each sentence.

3. Mom's plane is ______________ at three o'clock. (leave)

4. Tim ______________ the plants were dry. (notice)

Reading and Thinking

1. Check the answer that tells what the story is mainly about.

   _____ a thirsty man

   _____ Michael's walkie-talkies

   _____ selling lemonade

Write **T** if the sentence is true.
Write **F** if the sentence is false.

2. _____ Heather and Michael washed the used cups.
3. _____ Heather and Michael bought the lemonade at the store.
4. _____ Michael had money to buy more cups.
5. What did the children have to buy to get started? ______________
6. Why did Michael go back to the store? ______________
7. What do you think Heather and Michael will do now that the thirsty man has gone? ______________

____

The Birthday Gift

Why do gifts that you make sometimes mean more than those you buy?

1 Tracy, Rick, and Elsa wanted to give Mr. Levi a special gift for his birthday. They counted their money. They had only two dollars among them. "I think he might like a handmade gift," Tracy said. The three of them tried to think of something they could make that would not cost too much money.

2 After a while, Rick said, "I've got it! In school last year, we made salt jars. We filled jars with green, blue, orange, and white salt to make a picture. All we would need to buy would be salt and colored chalk."

3 Tracy and Elsa agreed that Rick's idea was good. Rick told them what they needed to get started. "We will need a big box of salt, paper towels, chalk, newspapers, and three bowls. We each need a small jar with a lid, too."

4 After all the supplies had been gathered, Tracy covered a table with newspapers. Then Rick poured some salt on a paper towel. He rubbed a piece of blue chalk over the salt. As he rubbed and rubbed the salt turned darker and darker blue. Rick put the blue salt in a bowl. Next he made some orange salt. Finally Rick made some of the salt green.

5 The children took turns pouring the different colors of salt into their jars. They worked on making designs with the salt. Each jar was filled to the top. Then Tracy, Rick, and Elsa put the lids on them.

6 Elsa's jar looked like an orange desert with trees. Rick made a colorful rainbow. Tracy formed snow-covered mountains with a blue sky.

7 They set the jars in a shoe box and put the lid on it. The children wrapped the box carefully. The next morning they gave the gift to Mr. Levi.

8 "They're beautiful!" he exclaimed when he looked at the jars. "I'll put them on a windowsill and look at them every day. They'll remind me of you and how lucky I am to have such thoughtful and inventive friends!"

Knowing the Words

Write the words from the story that have the meanings below.

1. something used for drying ____________ (Par. 3)
2. things needed for a project ____________ (Par. 4)
3. able to make things ____________ (Par. 8)

Write the word with the correct meaning to complete each sentence below.

4. A ____________ of chalk fell to the floor. (peace, piece)
5. The ____________ coat is my favorite one. (blue, blew)

Working with Words

A **suffix** is a group of letters added to the end of a word that changes the meaning of the word. The suffixes **-ful** and **-ous** mean "full of." *Fearful* means "full of fear." *Joyous* means "full of joy."

Add **-ful** or **-ous** to the words below. Use the new words to complete the sentences.

power humor thought

1. It was very ____________ of you to remember my birthday.
2. The ____________ engine pulled the train.
3. The ____________ story made us all laugh.

Reading and Thinking

1. Number the sentences in the order that tells how a salt jar can be made.

   ____ Rub chalk over some salt.

   ____ Pour the salt into the jar.

   ____ Gather supplies.

   ____ Put the lid on the jar.

2. Why did the children give Mr. Levi a present? ____________
3. Write one way in which the three salt jars were alike. ____________
4. Write one way in which the three salt jars were different. ____________
5. Check the word that tells how you think the children felt when Mr. Levi opened the box.

   ____ proud ____ curious ____ sad

6. What did Mr. Levi do with the gifts? ____________

Hocus–Pocus

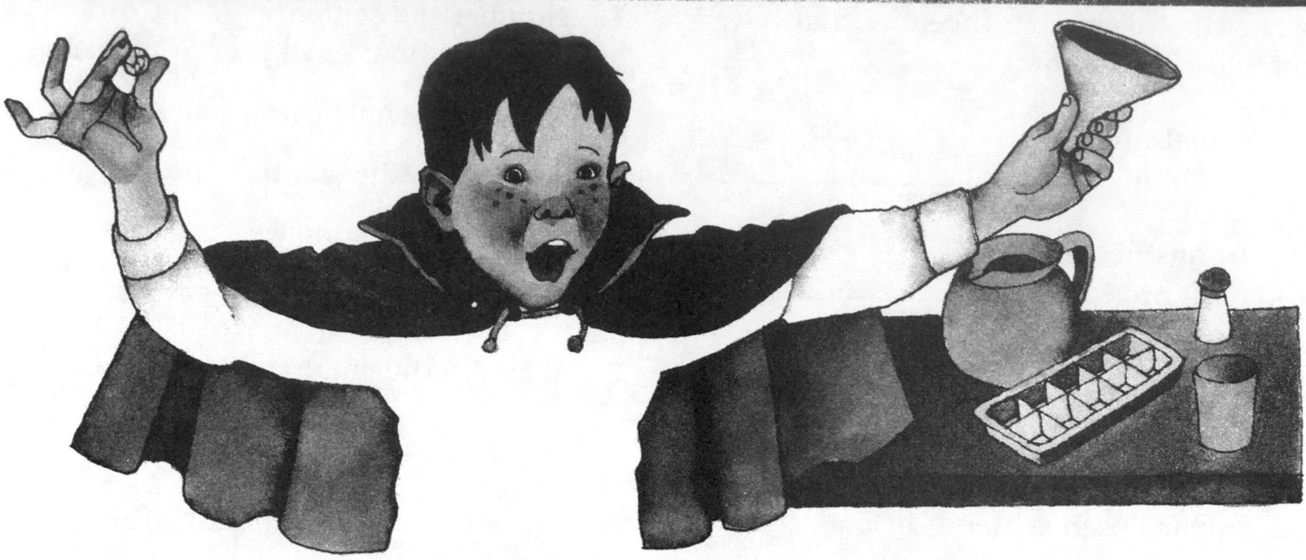

Read to find out about Rick's show.

1 Rick was making a sign one sunny day when Tracy and Elsa skated up to him. He was thinking so hard about what he was doing that he didn't even notice the girls at first. The girls said hello together.

2 Rick was startled. Then he smiled as he saw who it was. "Hi, I didn't hear you come up," Rick said.

3 "You look so busy. What are you making?" Elsa asked.

4 Rick held up a poster with the message "Magic show today. Bring a friend and be amazed. Show time is one o'clock."

5 Tracy and Elsa hurried off to tell their friends. As the girls skated away, they said, "See you at one, Rick."

6 People began arriving a few minutes before one o'clock. Rick had practiced. He knew his show would be a good one, but he was a little nervous anyway. He took a few deep breaths. Then he started the show.

7 "For my first trick," Rick said in a loud, clear voice, "I will pick up this ice cube without ever touching it with my hands." He put the ice cube in a glass of water and sprinkled salt on top of it. Then Rick laid a wet string over the ice. He waved a stick over the glass and slowly said, "Hocus-pocus, ice come up." When Rick picked up the ends of the string, the ice cube came up with it.

8 Then Rick said, "Now I would like a couple of volunteers." Dale and Michael each raised a hand. "Try to blow this ball of aluminum foil out of this funnel," Rick told them. Dale and Michael tried and tried, but neither one was successful. Then Rick took the funnel and said, "Hocus-pocus, ball come out." He blew into the funnel. The ball came out! Rick's audience was amazed. Tracy and Elsa wanted to know his secret. Rick just smiled. He knew that the children would soon learn these same tricks in their science classes.

Knowing the Words

Write the words from the story that have the meanings below.

1. a little frightened ______________ (Par. 6)

2. word said when a trick is being done ______________ (Par. 7)

3. helpers ______________ (Par. 8)

4. thin sheet of metal ______________ (Par. 8)

Working with Words

Say the word *show* and notice the sound *ow* stands for in the word. Circle the words below that have the sound *ow* stands for in *show*.

1.	know	down	blow	cow
2.	slow	arrow	town	throw
3.	hollow	tower	how	glow

A **compound word** is made by combining two smaller words. Write a compound word using the underlined words in each sentence.

4. The yard in the <u>back</u> of a house is a ______________.

5. The time of day <u>after</u> the <u>noon</u> hour is ______________.

6. <u>Seed</u> given to a <u>bird</u> is ______________.

7. A paper that reports the <u>news</u> is a ______________.

Reading and Thinking

1. Number the sentences to show the order in which things happened.

   ____ Kids arrived for Rick's show.

   ____ Rick made a poster.

   ____ Rick did a trick with aluminum foil.

   ____ Rick did his first trick.

2. How were Rick's two tricks alike?

   ____

   ____

3. How were Rick's two tricks different?

   ____

   ____

Write **T** if the sentence is true.
Write **F** if the sentence is false.

4. ____ The word *hocus-pocus* made the tricks happen.

5. ____ The audience enjoyed Rick's performance.

6. ____ Rick's tricks were magic.

7. A **fact** is something that is known to be true. An **opinion** is what someone thinks or feels. Check two sentences that give facts.

   ____ Messages can be put on posters.

   ____ Lifting ice on a string is a good trick.

   ____ Tricks can be learned from books.

Stuck!

Read to find out what happens when Heather and Andy get stuck on a Ferris wheel.

1 Rick's family had planned a trip to the fair. Rick and his brother, Andy, had extra tickets. They invited Michael and Heather to go along. The fairgrounds weren't far from the neighborhood, but the bus ride seemed to take forever.

2 When they arrived, Heather and Andy wanted to go on the rides. Rick and Michael planned to explore the fairgrounds. Mr. and Mrs. Smith had to work at one of the stands. "Let's split into pairs. We'll meet at the bus stop at three o'clock," Mrs. Smith said.

3 The others agreed. They set their watches on the same time. Then each pair hurried off in a different direction. At 2:45, Heather and Andy each had a ticket for one more ride. They chose the Ferris wheel. They were at the top of the first turn when it quit moving.

4 "I'll bet there's something wrong with the motor," Heather guessed.

5 Suddenly Andy pointed in the distance. He cried, "Look, the others are waiting at the bus stop! Somehow we've got to let them know what has happened!"

6 Heather thought a moment. Then she leaned forward to explain the problem to a man in the next car. He told the couple in front of him. They passed the word to the people ahead of them. Before long the message reached a man on the ground. He rushed off to tell Rick, Rick's parents, and Michael not to leave.

7 Finally the Ferris wheel was fixed. Rick and Michael were waiting at the bottom.

8 "What a great way to see the fair!" Heather exclaimed when she got off.

9 "Well, I hope it never happens again," Andy sighed with relief.

10 "I thought you weren't afraid of heights," Rick teased.

11 "I'm not," Andy replied, "but you have my bus fare!"

Knowing the Words

Write the words from the story that have the meanings below.

1. a ride at a fair ______________ (Par. 3)
2. feeling better ______________ (Par. 9)
3. high places ______________ (Par. 10)
4. money that people pay to ride somewhere ______________ (Par. 11)

Write the word with the correct meaning to complete each sentence below.

5. The city bus ______________ is sixty cents. (fair, fare)
6. I'll ______________ you downtown this evening. (meet, meat)
7. I had ______________ tickets for rides. (for, four)

Learning to Study

The word you look up in a dictionary is called an **entry word.** Many words with endings are not listed as entry words. To find these words, look up the word to which the ending was added. To find the word *teased*, look up *tease*.

Write the word you would look under to find each of these words in a dictionary.

1. tickets ______________
2. arrived ______________
3. waiting ______________
4. completely ______________

Reading and Thinking

1. Check the answer that tells what the story is mainly about.

   _____ a long bus ride

   _____ a visit to the fair

   _____ how a Ferris wheel works

2. Andy didn't want Rick to leave the fair without him because ______________

   ______________.

3. How were Heather and Andy alike?

   ____

Write **F** if the sentence gives a fact.
Write **O** if the sentence gives an opinion.

4. _____ Riding a bus is one way to travel.
5. _____ It is scary at the top of a Ferris wheel.
6. _____ Ferris wheels are fun to ride.
7. _____ Ferris wheels have seats.
8. If Heather and Andy had been left behind, how might they have gotten home? ______________

   ____

Confusion

What kinds of things do you need a good memory for?

1 Tracy and Elsa were fixing lunch when Rick came over to introduce his new friends. "This is Lin," he said, motioning to the dark-haired girl. "She will be in our class at school." Then he nodded toward the boy in the striped shirt. "This is her brother, Tat," he said. "They've just taught me a great game. It's called *Confusion.*"

2 "Why don't you explain it? We'll make ham and cheese sandwiches for everyone," Tracy said to Lin.

3 "In this game, each player has a sign," Lin began. "I'll scratch my ear, and that will be my sign. Then I'll wiggle my thumbs, and that could be Rick's sign. Rick must repeat what I've done and add another player's sign. That person repeats the entire thing and adds someone else's sign."

4 "It goes on and on till someone gets confused and forgets the order of the signs," Tat added. "Any questions?"

5 No one had any questions, so Elsa said, "OK, let's play." She set the sandwiches on the table. Each child chose a sign. Soon they were all wiggling, scratching, waving, and giggling. Then Tracy's third turn came. She tried to repeat eleven signs, but she got very confused. Tracy started to laugh. Then she patted her stomach and pointed to her mouth.

6 "Hey, that isn't anybody's sign," Rick broke in.

7 "Yeah, what's that supposed to mean?" asked Tat.

8 "It means," Tracy explained with a chuckle, "that my stomach is growling. That's a sign that it's time for me to eat! Would anyone care to join me?"

9 "Sure," they all answered.

10 "After lunch we can start the game over. We'll use all new signs," Tat suggested. Everyone groaned, but Tat could tell by the smiles on their faces that they thought it was a good idea.

Knowing the Words

Write the words from the story that have the meanings below.

1. mistaking one thing for another ______________ (Par. 1)
2. parts of your hands ______________ (Par. 3)
3. whole ______________ (Par. 3)

In each row below, circle the three words that belong together.

4. thumb stomach ear shirt
5. wave stripe pat wiggle
6. ham cheese plate bread

Working with Words

Write the two words that were used to form each of these contractions.

1. they've ______________
2. I'll ______________
3. that's ______________

Say *children.* Circle the words below that have the sound *ch* stands for in *children.*

4. chose handkerchief ache
5. sandwich chuckle stomach

Reading and Thinking

1. Check the answer that tells what the story is mainly about.

    ____ meeting new neighbors

    ____ playing a game

    ____ making sandwiches

2. What was Lin's sign? ______________

    ____

3. What were the children having for lunch? ______________

    ____

4. Rick came over to Tracy's house because ______________

    ______________.

5. What do you think the children did after Tracy explained why she pointed to her mouth? ______________

    ____

Write the best word to complete each sentence below.

6. The zebra is a ______________ animal. (confused, striped, tiny)
7. Please ______________ this word. (repeat, motion, scratch)
8. Don fixed a ______________ for lunch. (sign, shirt, sandwich)
9. The bear was ______________. (chuckling, reading, growling)

The Contest

Read to find out what happens when Tat and Lin enter the Crunchy Munchies contest.

1 Tat and Lin loved to enter contests. It did not matter what the prize was. Once they wrote a poem for a magazine contest. They won free copies of the magazine for a year. Another time they guessed how many marbles were in a glass jar. They won all the marbles.

2 One morning Tat was reading the Crunchy Munchies cereal box as he ate breakfast. "Lin," he said, "here's another contest to enter. The first-place winner gets a bike. Second prize is a tent."

3 "Those are great prizes," Lin said. "How do we enter?"

4 "Just print our names and address on the back of a Crunchy Munchies box top. Then we send it to the company for a drawing. We've got four weeks to collect all the box tops we can."

5 Starting right then, they ate Crunchy Munchies for breakfast every day. They also asked everyone they knew to save the box tops for them. By the end of the four weeks, Tat and Lin had sixteen box tops to send to the company. "I'm glad that's over," Tat laughed. "I'm tired of eating Crunchy Munchies!"

6 "If I have to look at another box of that stuff, I don't know what I'll do," Lin added.

7 A few weeks passed. One day the mail carrier brought a letter and a large package. "We've won third prize in the Crunchy Munchies contest!" Lin exclaimed as she read the letter.

8 "I didn't even know there was a third-place prize," Tat said as he ripped the carton open. Then Tat and Lin got a surprise. There were two dozen boxes of Crunchy Munchies cereal in the carton.

Knowing the Words

Write the words from the story that have the meanings below.

1. gather ______________ (Par. 4)
2. person who delivers mail ______________ (Par. 7)
3. cardboard box ______________ (Par. 8)

Synonyms are words that have the same or nearly the same meaning. Circle the pair of synonyms in each row.

4. delivered came brought went
5. win collect buy gather
6. eleven some dozen twelve
7. frown chuckle sneeze laugh

Working with Words

The ending **-er** sometimes means "more." It may be used to compare two things. The ending **-est** means "most." It is used to compare more than two things.

In each sentence below, add **-er** to the word before the blank if two things are being compared. Add **-est** if more than two things are being compared.

1. Apple juice is sweet ________ than lemonade.
2. Ken is the young ________ of three sons.
3. The lamp is bright ________ than the flashlight.
4. Kay is the fast ________ swimmer on the team.

Reading and Thinking

1. Write **O** next to two sentences that give opinions.

    _____ Cereal tastes best for breakfast.

    _____ Cereal is in the bread food group.

    _____ A ten-speed bicycle is a good prize.

2. Why did Tat and Lin eat so much cereal? ______________

    ____

3. How many box tops did Tat and Lin send in? ______________
4. How many boxes of cereal did Tat and Lin win? ______________
5. How do you think the children felt when they saw what they had won?

    ____

Write **T** if the sentence is true.
Write **F** if the sentence is false.

6. _____ Tat and Lin won even more cereal than they had eaten.
7. _____ Crunchy Munchies was like oatmeal.
8. What do you think Lin and Tat will do with the cereal they won?

    ____

    ____

Wee Willie Goes Walking

Look at the picture. Is Michael walking the dog? Or is the dog walking Michael?

1 Michael wanted to earn some money. He had started a dog-walking business. So far that day he had walked a bulldog, a poodle, and a beagle. Now he was going to walk Ms. Silva's dog, Wee Willie.

2 Wee Willie was a Saint Bernard puppy who already weighed more than Michael. "Willie is very friendly, but he has lots of spirit. He gets excited easily," Ms. Silva warned. "If you can handle him, I'll let you walk him every day."

3 "I could use the extra money," said Michael. He fastened a chain to Willie's collar. He opened the screen door. Wee Willie scrambled for the sidewalk. He was dragging Michael behind him.

4 Suddenly a robin flew down from a treetop. It landed in their path. Before Michael could say, "No, Willie," the dog had jerked the chain out of Michael's hand. Wee Willie went speeding after the bird.

5 Michael dashed down the alley after Willie, but soon he ran out of breath. He stopped near City Park. He wondered how he'd explain this to Ms. Silva. Just then he heard splashing and barking. It seemed to be coming from the park.

6 Michael ran through the park to the fountain. There he found Wee Willie jumping and biting at the water. Michael leaped into the fountain. The excited dog gave him a messy, wet kiss. Michael coaxed Wee Willie out of the fountain with a soggy dog biscuit.

7 "Ms. Silva," Michael began when he finally got the dog home, "you may not believe this, but . . ."

8 "How thoughtful of you to give Willie a bath as well as a walk!" Ms. Silva said in a pleased voice. "You're hired to walk Wee Willie *every* day!"

Knowing the Words

Write the words from the story that have the meanings below.

1. kind of dog ________________ (Par. 2)
2. gently talked into doing something ________________ (Par. 6)
3. very wet ________________ (Par. 6)
4. gave a job for pay ________________ (Par. 8)

Check the meaning that fits the underlined word in each sentence.

5. The <u>collar</u> was too big for the poodle.
   ____ part of a shirt
   ____ something a dog wears
6. <u>Park</u> the car in that empty space.
   ____ stop for a time
   ____ a place to play
7. Bootsie hid my brother's <u>block</u> under the couch.
   ____ a toy
   ____ area bordered by four streets

Learning to Study

Write the word you would look under to find each of these words in a dictionary.

1. spending ________________
2. businesses ________________
3. weighed ________________
4. copies ________________

Reading and Thinking

1. Check the answer that tells what the story is mainly about.
   ____ jumping in a fountain
   ____ walking a Saint Bernard
   ____ seeing a robin

Write **T** if the sentence is true.
Write **F** if the sentence is false.

2. ____ Wee Willie is a lazy dog.
3. ____ Wee Willie likes water.
4. ____ Michael could carry Wee Willie in his arms.
5. What three kinds of dogs did Michael walk before he walked Wee Willie?

   ____

6. What do you think Michael said when Ms. Silva offered to hire him to walk Willie every day?

   ____

   ____

Write the best word to complete each sentence below.

7. Ann has a ________________ named Puff. (collar, screen, poodle)
8. Ms. Kay ________________ a gift shop in town. (spends, hires, manages)
9. A bird was ________________ in the birdbath. (splashing, leaping, laughing)

Heather's Quarters

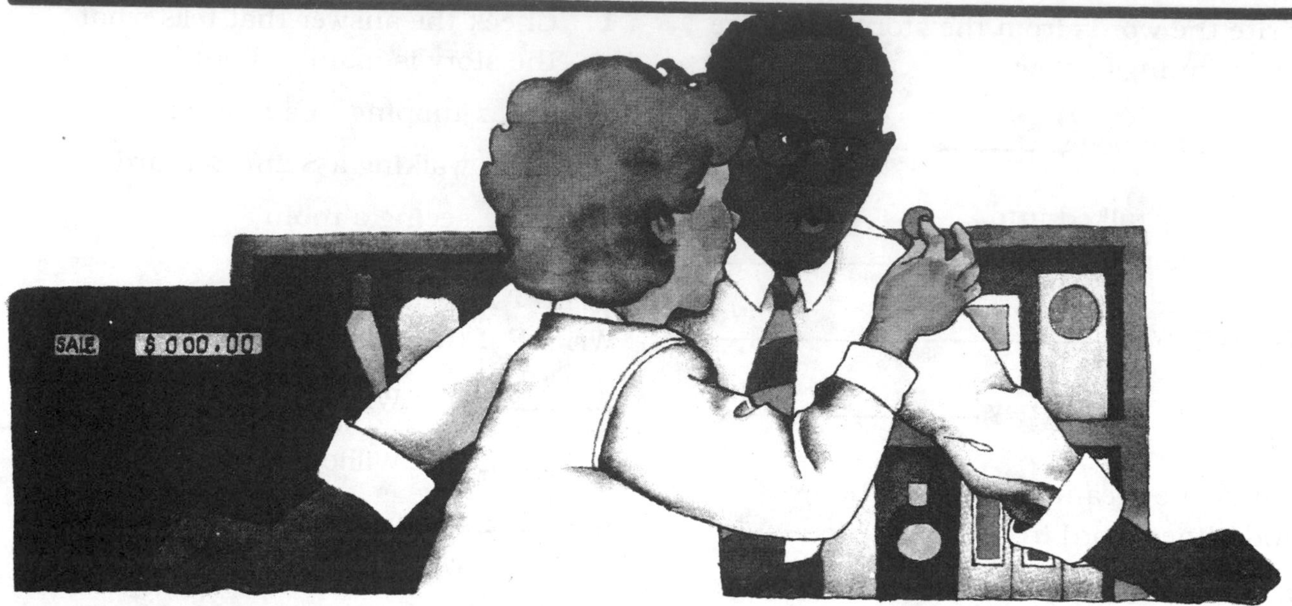

Heather loses something and finds something. Read to find what happened.

1 "Hi, Heather!" Mr. Taylor said as Heather entered the store. "What can I do for you today?"

2 "I have two quarters to spend. I'd like to look around awhile before I decide," Heather said.

3 "Take your time," Mr. Taylor said. Heather was heading for the comic books when she bumped into a rack of birthday cards. She dropped one of her quarters. As she stooped to look for it, she heard another coin drop. A man wearing a green sweatshirt kneeled near her. He looked under a toy shelf.

4 Just as Heather spied her quarter beneath the shelf, the man snatched it. He thought it was his. The man dropped the quarter into his pocket and left.

5 Upset and disappointed, Heather began searching again when suddenly a flash of gold caught her eye. "Look, Mr. Taylor! I'll bet this belongs to the man who found my quarter," she said as she held up a shiny coin.

6 Mr. Taylor looked at the coin. He said in surprise, "That's a twenty-dollar gold piece!"

7 Just then the door flew open. The man in the green sweatshirt burst in. "I've lost my lucky gold piece!" he shouted.

8 "This little girl just found an unusual coin," Mr. Taylor said pointing to the coin in Heather's hand. "Perhaps she'd trade it for the quarter you found."

9 "Make it two quarters!" the man offered quickly and he dropped two quarters into Heather's palm. "I'm sorry. I didn't notice which coin I'd dropped when I picked up your quarter. Thank you so much. I've had that lucky gold piece for years."

10 Heather jingled her three coins. She grinned from ear to ear. "Mr. Taylor," she chuckled, "I think it'll take me even longer to make up my mind now."

Knowing the Words

Write the words from the story that have the meanings below.

1. a piece of clothing ______________________ (Par. 3)

2. rushed in suddenly ______________________ (Par. 7)

Circle the pair of antonyms (opposites) in each row.

3.	buy	spend	sell	trade
4.	door	enter	agree	exit
5.	open	drop	loose	close
6.	found	rolled	lost	heard
7.	now	near	later	gold

Working with Words

Some words that have one consonant between two vowels are divided into syllables after the first vowel. The first vowel sound in these words is most often long, as in *tī/ger.*

Other words that have one consonant between two vowels are divided after the consonant. In these words, the first vowel sound is most often short, as in *trăv/el.*

The words below have been divided into syllables. Put a mark above the first vowel in each word to show if the vowel stands for a long or short sound. Mark the long vowels with ¯ over the letter. Mark the short vowels with

1. lem/on	4. si/lence	7. clos/et
2. wag/on	5. fro/zen	8. sto/len
3. mo/tor	6. cop/y	9. cab/in

Reading and Thinking

1. Number the sentences to show the order in which things happened.

   _____ Heather dropped a quarter.

   _____ The man dropped a coin.

   _____ The man grabbed the quarter.

   _____ The man returned the quarter.

Write **T** if the sentence is true.
Write **F** if the sentence is false.

2. _____ Heather had been in Mr. Taylor's store before.

3. _____ Heather had one dollar to spend in Mr. Taylor's store.

4. _____ Mr. Taylor had never seen a gold piece before.

5. How much was the gold piece worth?

   ____

6. What might Heather buy with her money? ______________________

7. How do you think Heather felt when the man gave her two quarters?

   ____

Write the best word to complete each sentence below.

8. Jim found a ______________ in his pocket. (shirt, shelf, coin)

9. Three ______________ equal seventy-five cents. (quarters, pieces, cards)

Down the Middle

What is the quickest way to get a difficult job done?

1 Rick and Andy shared a bedroom. Each Saturday they were responsible for cleaning it. Most of the time this was not a problem, but they had been especially careless during one week. The room was an awful mess. Clothes and toys were all over the floor. Books and papers were stacked high on the desk. Notes were falling off the overcrowded bulletin board.

2 The boys spent quite a bit of time arguing about who would clean what. Finally they agreed that each of them would take care of his own bed, but the desk, the floor, and the bulletin board would be divided in half. They could tape them down the middle so each boy could see his part.

3 "We can't even see the top of the desk to put tape on it yet," Rick said. "I'll put these books on the shelf. You put those papers in the drawers." With that done, they were able to tape the desk down the middle.

4 They decided to divide the floor next. Once again, they had to move things. They put clothes in the dirty laundry and toys in the toy box before they could even begin to divide the floor.

5 Last, they did the bulletin board. "Here, these are yours, so put them on that side," Andy said to Rick. "These are mine, so I'll put them over here. These notes are old, so I'll throw them away." Now they could see the bulletin board to put tape on it.

6 After they had the room divided they stood back. They looked to see what still needed to be done. Both boys were amazed by what they saw. The room was completely cleaned! Rick and Andy started laughing. Andy said, "I guess we make a pretty good team after all. Next week, let's not waste all this time arguing and taping."

7 "Good idea," Rick said. "Think of the things we can do with the time we'll save."

Knowing the Words

Write the words from the story that have the meanings below.

1. in charge of ______________________ (Par. 1)

2. more than usually ______________________ (Par. 1)

3. holding too much ______________________ (Par. 1)

In each row, circle the three words that belong together.

4. desk clothes bed chair
5. stood said stooped bent
6. laugh agree argue talk

Working with Words

Circle the correct word in ( ) and write it in the blank.

1. The ______________________ talked for a long time. (buys, boys)

2. Did you ______________________ out the garage alone? (clean, clothes)

3. Rick ______________________ in line for thirty minutes. (stand, stood)

4. When Andy went ______________________, Rick was lonely. (away, awake)

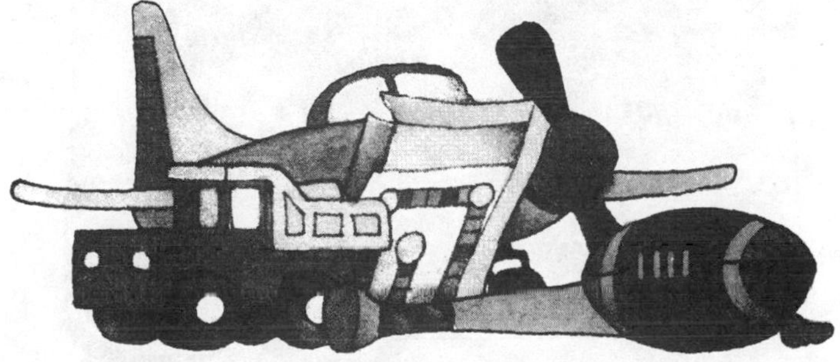

Reading and Thinking

1. Check the answer that tells what the story is mainly about.

   ____ clothes on the floor

   ____ a divided room

   ____ cleaning a room together

2. Rick and Andy divided the room because ______________________________________.

3. Check three words that tell what Rick and Andy divided in half.

   ____ desk ____ bulletin board

   ____ floor ____ toy box

Write **F** if the sentence gives a fact.
Write **O** if the sentence gives an opinion.

4. ____ Cleaning is difficult work.

5. ____ Vacuum cleaners can be used to sweep rugs.

6. ____ A bed is a piece of furniture.

7. ____ Cleaning should be done once a week.

8. Were Rick and Andy still arguing at the end of the story? Explain your answer. ______________________________________

9. What might Rick and Andy do after they clean their room? ______________________________________

Where's Herbie?

Why do you think Herbie is hiding, and where do you think he is?

1 Tracy was so thrilled she could hardly sit still long enough to eat her cereal and toast. Today was Monday, and she was leaving to spend a few weeks with Aunt Ruth and Uncle Stan. She would stay at their home in the country. "I'll be ready in a few minutes, Dad," she said, gulping down the rest of her orange juice. She brushed her teeth. Then she finished packing a few things in her blue canvas bag.

2 Tracy set the bag in the kitchen and went to say good-bye to Herbie. The cat usually napped beneath the couch, but when Tracy glanced under it he was not there. She looked behind the drapes and under the rocking chair, but Herbie was nowhere in sight.

3 "We have to leave in ten minutes, Tracy," her father called. "We've got to get to the bus station in time to pick up your ticket."

4 "I can't find Herbie to say good-bye," Tracy said. "Have you seen him, Dad?"

5 "No, I haven't. Why don't you look in your bedroom?" he suggested. Tracy raced upstairs. She expected to find Herbie asleep on her pillow. He wasn't there either.

6 "Herbie must not care that I'm going away," Tracy said as she came downstairs. She was wearing a long, sad face.

7 "He just doesn't understand that you're leaving," her father said. "I wish there were more time to search for him, but we really need to leave soon."

8 Tracy's sadness now turned to anger. "If Herbie doesn't care, then neither do I!" she grumbled.

9 "Don't forget this," her father said. He handed her a jacket. Tracy unzipped her bag. She was stuffing her jacket inside when she felt something soft and furry. Then two gray ears poked out of the bag.

10 "That's why Herbie didn't say good-bye," she laughed. "He packed himself to come along with me!"

Knowing the Words

Write the words from the story that have the meanings below.

1. a strong cloth ______________ (Par. 1)
2. a long seat with cushions ______________ (Par. 2)
3. said unhappily ______________ (Par. 8)
4. covered with hair ______________ (Par. 9)

Synonyms are words that have the same or nearly the same meaning. Circle the pair of synonyms in each row.

5. shades curtains windows drapes
6. swallow chew lick gulp

Learning to Study

Some words have more than one meaning. In a dictionary, the different meanings of a word are numbered. Read each word in dark print and the dictionary meanings that follow. Then read each sentence below and decide the meaning of the underlined words. Write the number of the correct meaning in the blank.

coun try 1 nation **2** land outside a city

1. _____ Dave works on a farm in the country.
2. _____ Each country has its own flag.

room 1 area with walls inside a building **2** space

3. _____ We have room for one more.
4. _____ The girls gave the room a new coat of paint.

Reading and Thinking

1. Check the answer that tells what the story is mainly about.

   _____ looking for a pet

   _____ a visit to the country

   _____ the blue canvas bag

2. Do you think Tracy meant it when she said she did not care about Herbie? Explain your answer.

   ____

   ____

   ____

Write **T** if the sentence is true.
Write **F** if the sentence is false.

3. _____ Tracy's aunt and uncle live down the street from her.
4. _____ Tracy knew she would miss Herbie while she was gone.
5. _____ Aunt Ruth and Uncle Stan probably met Tracy at the airport.
6. What do you think Tracy did with Herbie after she found him? ______________

   ____

The Fall

What is sometimes the best way to get over being afraid of something?

1 Tracy and Aunt Ruth had saddled up their horses. They were ready to ride when Aunt Ruth said, "Tracy, would you like to ride Big Gabe today?"

2 Tracy had dreamed of the day she would be allowed to ride Big Gabe. He was a huge, tan horse. Tracy was thrilled. Her knees started shaking, and she nearly shouted, "I'd love to!"

3 Tracy managed to get up on Big Gabe. She sat there for a minute feeling proud and tall as she held the reins. Then she gave the horse a gentle kick. Big Gabe started off at an easy trot. Tracy was just beginning to relax when something ran in front of Big Gabe. It frightened him so that he reared up on his hind legs.

4 Tracy was thrown to the ground. Although she was not hurt, she was scared. "I hate that horse. I'm never going to ride him again!" she cried in anger as Aunt Ruth helped her up.

5 "I once knew a girl your age who had been thrown from her horse," Aunt Ruth said. "Afterwards, she was terribly afraid to ride. She wouldn't even go near the horse. But one day there was an emergency at home. A doctor was needed. The girl had to ride the horse into town to get a doctor.

6 "After that," Aunt Ruth went on, "the girl realized that her bravery had helped save someone's life. She made up her mind to practice riding again. After a while she wasn't afraid any more. That girl went on to become a fine rider. She's now grown and sitting next to you."

7 "You, Aunt Ruth?" Tracy inquired, looking surprised.

8 "That's right," she replied. "Now let's walk the horses back to the stalls."

9 "You can walk Ginger if you like," Tracy said as she climbed onto her horse. "I'll ride Big Gabe back home!"

Knowing the Words

Write the words from the story that have the meanings below.

1. something used to control a horse ______________ (Par. 3)
2. awfully ______________ (Par. 5)

Write the word with the correct meaning to complete each sentence below.

3. Spring ______________ help flowers to grow. (reins, rains)
4. ______________ are horses out in the pasture. (Their, There)
5. Who ________ the race? (one, won)

Working with Words

Write a compound word using the underlined words in each sentence.

1. A bowl in which a fish lives is

   a ______________.

2. A knob used to close a door is

   a ______________.

The words below have been divided into syllables. Put a mark above the first vowel in each word to show if the vowel stands for a long or short sound. Mark the long vowels with ¯ over the letter. Mark the short vowels with ˘.

3.	na/tion	**6.**	min/ute	**9.**	nev/er
4.	re/cess	**7.**	fin/ish	**10.**	sta/tion
5.	vis/it	**8.**	pi/lot	**11.**	fi/nal

Reading and Thinking

1. Check the answer that tells what the story is mainly about.

   ____ riding to town on a horse

   ____ a riding accident

   ____ how to ride a horse

2. Check three answers that tell about both Tracy and Aunt Ruth.

   ____ had a scary accident

   ____ lives in the city

   ____ rides horses

   ____ is no longer afraid of horses

   ____ is an adult

3. Check two words that tell how Tracy felt when Big Gabe threw her.

   ____ scared ____ pretty

   ____ hungry ____ angry

   ____ sleepy ____ proud

4. Do you think Tracy will ride Big Gabe after today? Explain your answer.

   ____

   ____

Write the best word to complete each sentence below.

5. Pull the ______________ to make the horse stop. (saddle, reins, rider)

6. Because of her ______________, the woman was given a medal. (fear, bravery, stable)

The Bean Thief

How do you think Tracy will catch whoever is stealing beans from the garden?

1 Tracy liked to work in her aunt and uncle's garden. Each morning she hooked the hose up to the faucet in the stable. Then she watered the young plants. If she saw a weed popping up, she would pull it out by the roots. Tracy was proud of the results of her daily care.

2 One morning she noticed that a row of bean sprouts had been chewed off. She did not think much about it. But more sprouts were missing the following day. It was then she decided to catch the thief. That night Tracy planned to sit on the porch. She thought she would watch the garden all night, but she fell asleep. She didn't wake up till the sun rose. Tracy felt awful when she saw more beans were missing.

3 Then Tracy had a great idea. She put a stake at each corner of the garden. She tied string from one corner to the next until the garden was surrounded. Then she hung aluminum pie pans from the string. "When the thief bumps the string, the pans will rattle. I'll wake up and catch whoever is responsible," she said to herself proudly.

4 Tracy hadn't been asleep long that night when she was awakened by the sound of the pans clattering. She grabbed her flashlight and shined it toward the garden. Sure enough, there was the thief. He was chewing a tasty bean sprout!

5 "Clyde, you naughty goat!" Tracy shouted as she ran toward the garden. "How did you get out of your pen?"

6 Tracy took Clyde back to the pen. She was walking away when Clyde came up to her. She realized that the goat had learned to jump over the side of the pen. "Well, Clyde, I guess you'll just have to be tied up at night. I promise that I will share the beans with you when they are ready," Tracy said, patting Clyde on the head.

Knowing the Words

Write the words from the story that have the meanings below.

1. something that happens because of something else ______________ (Par. 1)
2. a post ______________ (Par. 3)
3. closed in on all sides ______________ (Par. 3)

Circle the pair of antonyms (opposites) in each row.

4. pull push drop fall
5. month night year day
6. race watch asleep awake
7. found planned missed lost

Choose the correct word to fill in the blank for each pair of sentences.

rose felt row

8. David's costume was made from yellow and purple ______________.

   The sidewalk ______________ hot under my feet.

9. Ty helped ______________ the boat yesterday.

   The ______________ of beans is straight.

10. The sun ______________ in the East.

    Kevin found a ______________ near the edge of the garden.

Reading and Thinking

1. Number the sentences to show the order in which things happened.

   _____ Tracy hung aluminum pans around the garden.

   _____ The thief was caught.

   _____ Tracy noticed that some beans were missing.

   _____ Clyde rattled the pie pans.

2. Why did Tracy hang aluminum pans from a string? ______________

   ____

3. How do you think Tracy felt when she saw who the thief was? ______________

   ____

4. Why did Tracy say she would share the ripe beans with Clyde?

   ____

5. What do you think will happen to Clyde now? ______________

   ____

Learning to Study

Number each list of words below in alphabetical order.

1. _____ flavor
   _____ fresh
   _____ friend

2. _____ caught
   _____ catch
   _____ corner

A Helping Hand

Read to find out what Tracy did when she got bored.

1 It was raining for the third day in a row. Tracy was getting bored. She had already read two books. She had finished a paint-by-number picture. She had also written a letter to her parents.

2 She wandered out to the garage where Uncle Stan was busy at the workbench. Tracy gazed out the window and murmured, "Will this rain ever stop?"

3 Just then she saw a little wren sitting on the windowsill. It was trying to stay dry. "I wonder if it is hard for birds to find food in all this rain," Tracy said.

4 Then the idea came to Tracy that she could help this wren and other birds, too. She asked Uncle Stan if he would help her build a bird feeder out of wood. She found some plans in one of her uncle's books. Uncle Stan cut out the pieces she needed. Tracy nailed them together. She sanded the bird feeder to make it smooth. Then she painted it white. As she finished the project, the rain stopped, and the sun came out from behind the clouds. Tracy was happy because she could hang her feeder outside. She would fill it with seeds and wait for her feathered friends to visit.

5 For the rest of her visit, Tracy spent some time each day watching the birds at the bird feeder. They would sit on the fence after they ate. They sang songs for her. Tracy imagined they were saying thank you.

6 Uncle Stan and Aunt Ruth suggested that Tracy take the bird feeder home with her. They said the birds in the city might need help to find food during the winter. Tracy knew she would always remember this vacation. She would have the bird feeder to remind her.

Knowing the Words

Write the words from the story that have the meanings below.

1. a high table used for work ______________ (Par. 2)

2. said in a low voice ______________ (Par. 2)

Synonyms are words that have the same or nearly the same meaning. Circle the pair of synonyms in each row.

3.	gazed	laughed	cried	stared
4.	called	finished	completed	tripped
5.	wrote	murmured	read	said
6.	garage	city	town	window

Working with Words

A **prefix** is a group of letters added to the beginning of a word that changes the meaning of the word. The prefixes **un-** and **dis-** mean "not" or "the opposite of." *Distrust* means "the opposite of trust." *Unfair* means "not fair."

Complete each sentence by writing **un-** or **dis-** in the blank.

1. It is ________ safe to climb on that rock.

2. Sean's wool socks were causing him some ________ comfort.

3. Dan and I ________ agree.

4. I was ________ able to go to the movies because I was sick.

Reading and Thinking

1. Check the answer that tells what the story is mainly about.

 ____ how birds fly

 ____ Tracy's project

 ____ talking with Uncle Stan

Write **T** if the sentence is true.
Write **F** if the sentence is false.

2. ____ Uncle Stan has no hobbies.

3. ____ Tracy likes to help.

4. ____ Tracy is tired of the rain.

5. Write three things Tracy had done to keep herself busy. ______________

 ____

6. Write **R** next to two sentences that tell about real things.

 ____ A girl could fly in a plane.

 ____ A boy could fly like a bird.

 ____ A bird could fly through the clouds.

Write the best word to complete each sentence below.

7. Bob ______________ he was on a ship. (pleased, imagined, sang)

8. The ______________ is big enough for two cars. (skate, garage, workbench)

9. The plant on the ______________ gets lots of sunshine. (closet, river, windowsill)

Vegetable Soup

Look at the picture. Can you tell where this story takes place?

1 Rick's father was a cook. One day when Rick didn't have to go to school, he went to work with his father. They had to get up very early. Rick and his father were on the job before it was light outside. They had to get the food prepared by noon.

2 Rick filled a large pot with water. He set it on the stove. Rick's father cleaned and chopped carrots, potatoes,

tomatoes, and green beans. He was cutting some beef into small chunks when someone came to the back door.

3 "You're a little earlier than usual this morning, Mr. Hastings," Rick's father said. "If you will stop by after your rounds, I'll have some beef scraps for your dog."

4 "Great," Mr. Hastings said. "Just leave them in the refrigerator." Then he emptied the trash bins onto his truck.

5 Rick's father finished cutting up the meat. He added all the vegetables and pieces of beef to the boiling water. He put the beef scraps into a white plastic jar. Then he set the jar inside the refrigerator.

6 When the soup was done cooking, Rick's father poured it into jars. They looked just like the one with the beef scraps. After he put the jars inside the refrigerator, Rick's dad began to fix some salads.

7 By twelve o'clock all the food was prepared, and it was time to go home. "Take some of this soup home for lunch," the chef said. He handed Rick a jar from the refrigerator.

8 "I can't wait to taste your soup, Dad," Rick said when they got home. But when Rick took the lid off of the jar, he could not believe his eyes. "Dad," he cried with amazement, "we've got the jar with the beef scraps!"

9 "Oh, they must have got mixed up in the refrigerator," his father moaned. "Well, I sure hope Mr. Hastings's dog likes my vegetable soup!"

Knowing the Words

Write the words from the story that have the meanings below.

1. leftover pieces ______________ (Par. 3)

2. cook who is in charge ______________ (Par. 7)

Synonyms are words that have the same or nearly the same meaning. Circle the pair of synonyms in each row.

3. garbage collect trash truck

4. jar bucket water pail

5. hope ready prepared leave

6. begin clean stay start

Working with Words

Write a compound word using the underlined words in each sentence.

1. A <u>room</u> with a <u>bed</u> in it is a

______________________.

2. A <u>bench</u> at which to <u>work</u> is a

______________________.

The suffix **-ment** means "the act of." *Enjoyment* means "the act of enjoying." Add **-ment** to the following words. Use the new words to complete the sentences.

amuse agree

3. Joel has an ______________ with his brother about sharing toys.

4. The joke was told for our

______________________.

Reading and Thinking

1. Check the answer that tells what the story is mainly about.

____ making vegetable soup

____ Mr. Hastings's dog

____ eating in a restaurant

2. The soup and beef scraps got mixed up because ______________

______________________.

3. What did Mr. Hastings plan to do with the beef scraps? ______________

____

Write **T** if the sentence is true.
Write **F** if the sentence is false.

4. ____ Mr. Hastings is a cab driver.

5. ____ It was evening when Rick went to work with his father.

6. ____ Rick's dad made a lot of soup.

7. What was in the soup besides vegetables? ______________

8. Number the sentences in the order that tells how the soup was made.

____ The mixture was cooked.

____ Water was boiled.

____ Vegetables and beef were put in the pot.

____ Vegetables and beef were cut up.

____ The soup was put into jars.

It's Alive!

Look closely at the picture. Do you see anything strange that gives a hint about what will "come alive" in the story?

1 Andy liked to play harmless tricks on Rick. Usually Rick didn't mind. But then Andy hid in the bedroom closet and scared Rick. That was just too much. "I guess you'd be scared of just about anything!" Andy had teased.

2 The next day Rick thought of a plan and explained it to Heather. She agreed to help. They gathered leafy twigs and branches from the yard and put them in the basement.

3 That evening Rick quietly crept downstairs. He tied branches to his legs and arms. He stuffed his pockets with twigs and taped leaves to his forehead.

4 It was getting dark outside when the phone rang. Rick knew it was Heather calling for Andy. While Andy talked to her, Rick tiptoed upstairs. He sneaked out the front door. Then he hid next to some bushes.

5 Heather said she was coming over and asked Andy to wait for her outside. He was sitting on the porch step when a strange noise startled him. "Is that you, Heather?" Andy called nervously. There was no reply. "It's just my imagination," he thought. Then he heard the noise again. Andy was glad when he saw Heather coming across the front lawn.

6 "There's something spooky going on, Heather," he whispered. Suddenly something brushed against Andy's arm. He jumped back, shouting, "What was that?" Then a bush began to shake and moan. "It's alive!" Andy yelled. His whole body was shaking with fear.

7 All at once the bush reached out. It gently tapped Andy on the shoulder. The bush, with a voice exactly like Rick's, laughed. Then it said, "Would you like to make a deal with your brother?"

Knowing the Words

Write the words from the story that have the meanings below.

1. having many leaves ______________ (Par. 2)
2. moved slowly and quietly ______________ (Par. 3)
3. moved without anyone knowing ______________ (Par. 4)
4. picturing in one's mind ______________ (Par. 5)

In each row below, circle the three words that belong together.

5. forehead closet elbow shoulder
6. sneaked crept tiptoed stuffed
7. tease moan shout whisper

Working with Words

To write the plural of a word that ends in *f* or *fe*, the *f* or *fe* is changed to *v*, and *es* is added. Write the plural form of each word below.

1. leaf ______________
2. wife ______________
3. half ______________
4. shelf ______________

Say *large*. Circle the words below that have the same sound *g* stands for in *large*.

5. danger gathered grab engine
6. sponge ginger giant dragon

Reading and Thinking

1. Number the sentences to show the order in which things happened.

   _____ Andy waited for Heather.

   _____ Heather telephoned Andy.

   _____ Rick hid beside some bushes.

   _____ Rick scared Andy.

   _____ Rick tied branches to himself.

2. Check the sentence that tells about Rick.

   _____ He was always mean to Andy.

   _____ He wanted to hurt Andy.

   _____ He wanted to teach Andy a lesson.

3. Do you think Rick and Andy will make a deal? What kind? ______________

   ____

4. Write **R** next to two sentences that tell about real things.

   _____ Bushes can talk and moan.

   _____ Fear can make people tremble.

   _____ People can imagine scary things.

Camping Out

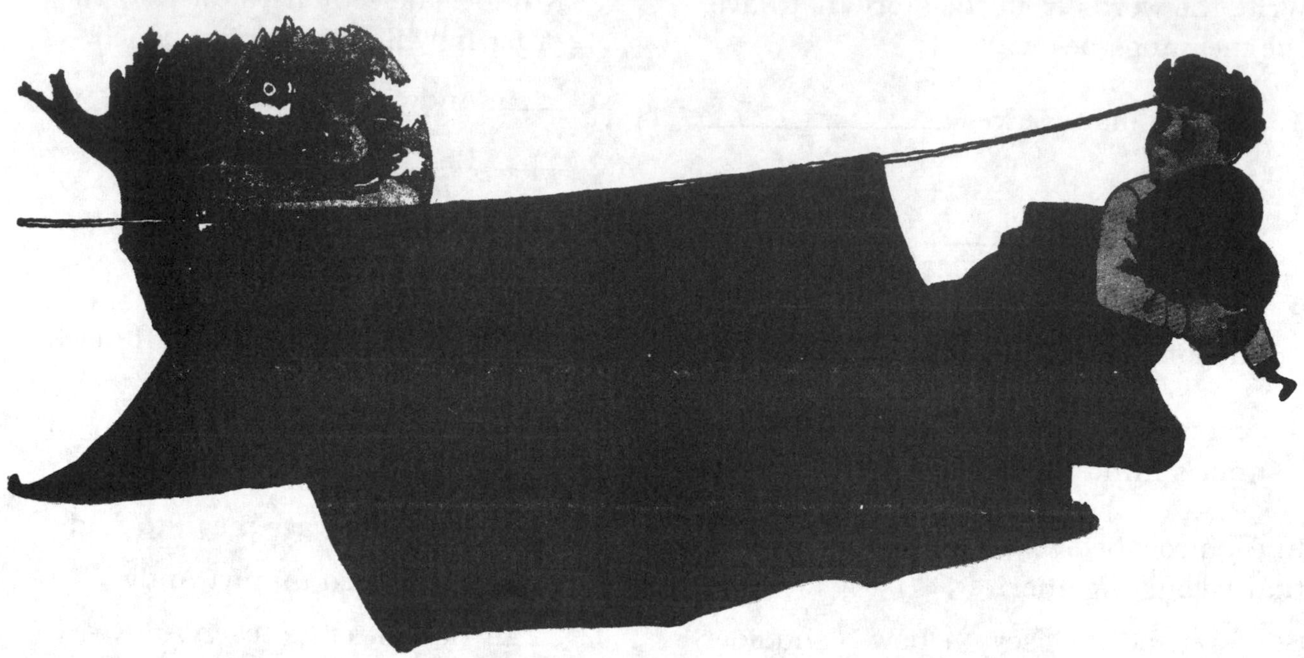

What sort of noises would you expect to hear if you camped out?

1 Andy and Michael got permission to camp out in Andy's yard one night. They used an old blanket for a tent. "Hey, this is great!" Michael said. He sat inside the homemade tent and shined his flashlight on the ceiling. He made a shadow with his hands. The shadow looked like a dog. He asked Andy to guess what it was.

2 Then Andy formed a shadow of a giraffe, but Michael couldn't guess what it was supposed to be. "Giraffes have long necks, but your shadow doesn't have a long neck," Michael said.

3 "It's a baby giraffe," Andy chuckled. Then he unzipped his sleeping bag and snuggled inside. The boys talked for a long time. They told each other their favorite jokes and funniest stories.

4 Just then there was a howling noise from somewhere nearby. Michael sat up, saying, "What's that?"

5 "It's probably a dog," Andy said. "There's no reason to be scared." Soon there was another noise. It sounded like someone tapping on the windows of the house. "It's just the acorns falling off the oak tree. They're hitting the roof of the house," Andy said. "Stop worrying about the noises. Go to sleep," he said as he yawned and turned over. Before long, Andy was sleeping soundly. Michael still wasn't the least bit tired.

6 The next morning Andy woke up early. Michael was gone. Later that day Andy teased Michael, "I didn't think you'd let those noises scare you away."

7 "Did you know you sound like a bulldozer when you're sleeping?" Michael said. "I went home because your snoring was keeping me awake!"

Knowing the Words

Write the words from the story that have the meanings below.

1. the OK to do something ________ (Par. 1)
2. got comfortable ________ (Par. 3)
3. breathing loudly while sleeping ________ (Par. 7)

Synonyms are words that have the same or nearly the same meaning. Write **S** after each pair of synonyms. Write **A** after each pair of antonyms (opposites).

4. zip-unzip ____
5. old-new ____
6. early-late ____
7. tired-sleepy ____
8. better-worse ____
9. nearby-close ____

Learning to Study

A dictionary shows words divided into syllables. A space or a dot shows where the word can be divided at the end of a line of writing.

Read the words below. Next to each write the number of syllables it has.

1. let ter ____
2. ac ci dent ____
3. an oth er ____
4. chuck le ____
5. gi raffe ____
6. morn ing ____
7. ceil ing ____
8. prob a bly ____

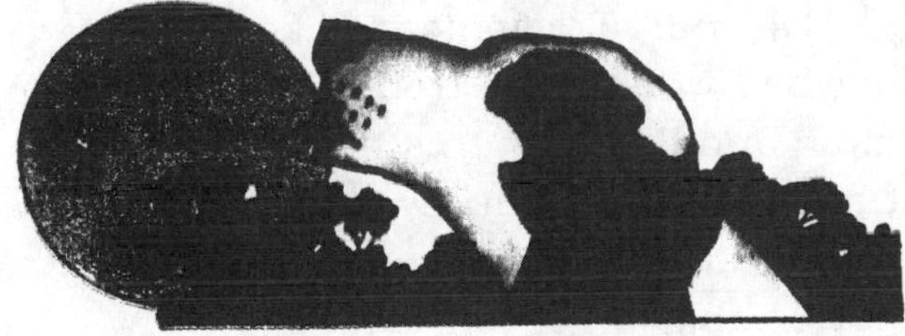

Reading and Thinking

1. Check the answer that tells what the story is mainly about.

 ____ shadows on the roof

 ____ the howling dog

 ____ camping out

2. Andy thought Michael's reason for going home was ________

 ________.

3. Did Andy own a real tent? Explain your answer. ________

 ____

4. Was Michael used to sleeping outdoors? Explain your answer.

 ____

5. Write two things Andy and Michael did before they went to sleep.

 ____

 ____

Write the best word to complete each sentence below.

6. A ________ was used to clear the land. (alligator, bulldozer, yawn)

7. The ________ ate leaves. (beagle, giraffe, shadow)

8. You will need a ________ on your bed. (tent, blanket, story)

Accidents Will Happen

Read to find out how Herbie makes Tracy pay.

1 Tracy had saved her allowance for a long time. She bought a radio-controlled model car. Tracy was outdoors showing all of her friends how it worked. They were excited, but after a while they got bored just watching.

2 Tat suggested that they all play a game of tag. Rick was fast and liked to run, so he volunteered to be "it" first.

3 Tracy yelled, "Hey, wait for me. I need to put my car in the house. I'll just take a minute." She rushed inside and put the car on a table. This was a careless mistake because Herbie was inside the house.

4 Herbie was a very curious cat. It was not long before he saw the new toy. He circled the car. Then he walked around the control box. Soon he batted at the strange-looking machine. When he stepped on top of the control box, the toy came to life and started to roll. Herbie was afraid, so he stepped back. Then the car started coming straight at him. This frightened poor Herbie so much that he jumped from the table onto a rocking chair. The chair started moving back and forth. It bumped against a lamp table. With a loud crash, the lamp fell over and broke.

5 Tracy and the others heard the noise. They scrambled inside to see what had happened. First Tracy noticed the broken lamp. Then she saw Herbie in the rocking chair. Finally she saw that the car was on the floor.

6 "Oh, no," Tracy moaned. "Well, maybe I won't be in trouble if I tell my mom and dad how this happened. Next time, I think I'll put my toys away. Then there will be one curious cat that will not be able to get to them."

Knowing the Words

Write the words from the story that have the meanings below.

1. part where power is ______________ (Par. 4)
2. moving back and forth ______________ (Par. 4)

Circle the pair of antonyms (opposites) in each row.

3. long   large   short   huge
4. whispered   yelled   laughed   sang
5. new   tall   fast   slow

Working with Words

Write the two words that were used to form each of these contractions.

1. wasn't ______________
2. you're ______________
3. it'll ______________
4. it's ______________

The suffix **-less** means "without." *Hopeless* means "without hope." Add **-less** to the following words. Use the new words to complete the sentences.

breath   cloud   spot

5. The windows were ______________ after Jeff washed them.
6. The ______________ sky was a beautiful color of blue.
7. Adam was ______________ after running the race.

Reading and Thinking

1. Check the answer that tells what the story is mainly about.

    ____ a pet cat

    ____ playing tag

    ____ a result of carelessness

2. Why didn't Tracy put the car in a safe place? ______________

    ____

3. How did Herbie make the car move?

    ____

4. Check two words that tell how Tracy might have felt when she saw the broken lamp.

    ____ angry   ____ tired

    ____ sorry   ____ thrilled

Write **T** if the sentence is true.
Write **F** if the sentence is false.

5. ____ Tracy bought the car with her allowance money.
6. ____ Herbie broke the car.
7. ____ Tracy didn't know how the lamp got broken.
8. Write **O** next to three sentences that give opinions.

    ____ Cats are too curious.

    ____ A toy car could be put on a table.

    ____ Toys should always be put in a toy box.

    ____ Cats should not be left alone.

Carmen's Penny

Elsa isn't very happy about taking Carmen to the store with her. Read to find out why she changes her mind.

1 Elsa's dad was folding clothes. He asked Elsa to run an errand for him. He gave her a list and some money. As Elsa was leaving, Carmen ran up to her. She begged to join Elsa. Elsa had planned to ride her bike, but she couldn't if Carmen was tagging along. Since Carmen loved to go to the store, Elsa agreed to take her.

2 Elsa muttered all the way to the store about not being able to ride her bike. Carmen asked Elsa to give her a piggy-back ride. Elsa replied unkindly, "No, you wanted to come along, so you can just walk." They walked the rest of the way in silence.

3 At the store the girls gathered all of the items on the list. They stood in the checkout line for a long time because the store was quite busy. Finally, their turn came. When Elsa saw the total she nearly panicked. It was three cents more than she had! Elsa felt nervous. Her mind started racing as she tried to think of a solution to her problem. She checked all of her pockets twice. When she didn't find any more money, she told the clerk, "I'm sorry, but I don't have enough money. Could we put something back on the shelf?"

4 Just then Carmen reached into her pocket and calmly pulled out a coin. "Do you want this penny?" Carmen asked Elsa, holding a nickel out to her. Elsa glanced down at the money. She smiled in relief. Then she handed the money to the clerk.

5 After the girls left the store, Elsa gave Carmen a big hug. Elsa said, "Do you know you saved the day? Dad will be so proud when I tell him how you helped me out. How would you like it if we spent some time doing what you want to do?"

Knowing the Words

Write the words from the story that have the meanings below.

1. following closely ______________ (Par. 1)

2. said in a low voice ______________ (Par. 2)

3. things ______________ (Par. 3)

4. answer ______________ (Par. 3)

Working with Words

When a word ends in a consonant followed by *y*, the *y* is changed to *i* before an ending is added. Change the *y* to *i* in each word in **( )**. Add **-ly** to make a word that completes the sentence.

1. Mark spoke ______________ to the naughty pup. (angry)

2. Max ______________ won the race. (easy)

3. Jan walked ______________ through the field. (lazy)

Rewrite the following groups of words using *'s* or *s'* to show who owns something. The first one is done for you.

the nickel that Carmen owns

Carmen's nickel

4. the coins that belong to the girls

____

5. the vacuum cleaner that Bill owns

____

Reading and Thinking

1. Number the sentences to show the order in which things happened.

____ Elsa realized she didn't have enough money.

____ Carmen asked to go to the store.

____ Carmen gave Elsa a coin.

____ The girls stood in line.

____ Elsa gave Carmen a hug.

2. Why did Carmen say she had a penny when she really had a nickel?

____

____

____

Write **T** if the sentence is true.
Write **F** if the sentence is false.

3. ____ The store the girls went to was close by.

4. ____ The girls were both upset when they left the house.

5. ____ Elsa was angry with Carmen on the way home.

Write the best word to complete each sentence below.

6. The ______________ was twelve cents. (errand, clerk, total)

7. Mark ______________ to the bank. (laughed, skipped, stopped)

The Clubhouse

What would you put inside a clubhouse to make it seem cozy?

1 Tracy, Rick, and Elsa thought their clubhouse was the finest ever built. "We need some stuff to make it feel cozy inside," Elsa suggested. Rick brought some wooden crates for stools. Elsa hung a poster on the wall. Tracy wanted to do something special for the clubhouse, too. But she couldn't think of anything to add.

2 Then one Saturday while she was doing her chores, she thought of what the clubhouse needed. She told the plan to her dad. Together they went to work. They carried some things to the club. Tracy taped a sign on the door that said "Keep Out—Working in Clubhouse!"

3 When Rick and Elsa came over, Tracy would not allow them in the clubhouse. "You'll have to wait till we're through working," she said. Rick and Elsa tried to peek through the windows, but Tracy had covered each one.

4 As Rick and Elsa sat patiently waiting, they heard the pounding of nails. They were so curious that they could hardly wait to go inside.

5 At last the clubhouse door opened. Tracy announced, "Welcome to the best clubhouse in town!" When Rick and Elsa stepped inside, their feet touched something soft. Pieces of red, blue, and green carpet covered the floor. It made a colorful design. "We've made a patchwork rug!" Tracy said proudly.

6 "I knew these old carpet scraps would be useful sometime," Tracy's father said, smiling.

7 "This is wonderful!" Elsa said. She ran her palms across the soft, shaggy floor.

8 "Now our clubhouse really feels like home!" Rick added.

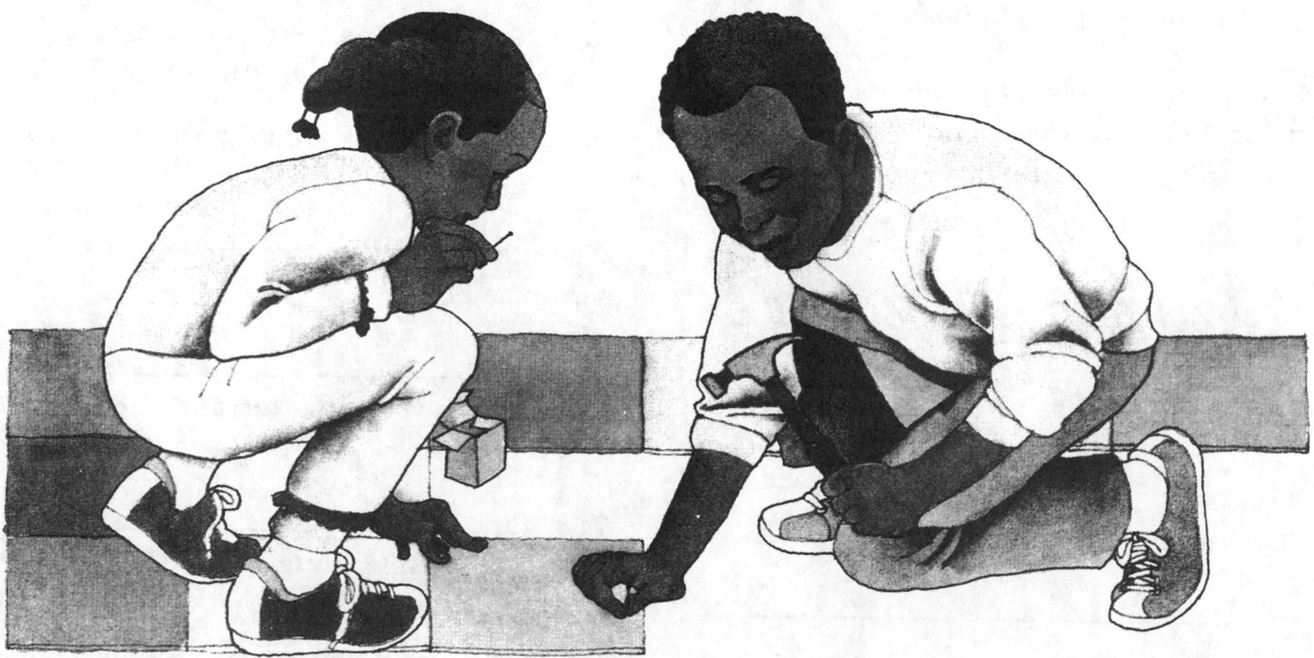

Knowing the Words

Write the words from the story that have the meanings below.

1. boxes ______________ (Par. 1)

2. small jobs ______________ (Par. 2)

3. without making trouble ______________ (Par. 4)

In each row, circle the three words that belong together.

4.	finger	thumb	arm	palm
5.	job	stool	chore	work
6.	wall	rug	carpet	mat
7.	scraps	chunks	pieces	chores

Learning to Study

Write the word you would look under to find each of these words in a dictionary.

1. patiently ______________

2. smiling ______________

3. stepped ______________

4. finest ______________

Number each list of words below in alphabetical order.

5. ____ blue
____ club
____ angry
____ crate
____ animal

6. ____ cat
____ door
____ floor
____ can
____ camp

Reading and Thinking

1. Check the answer that tells what the story is mainly about.

____ Tracy's chores

____ Tracy's idea

____ a sign that said "Keep Out!"

2. Why had Tracy's dad saved the carpet scraps? ______________

____

3. Check the answer that tells what Tracy was probably doing when she thought of making a patchwork rug.

____ washing the dishes

____ making her bed

____ sweeping the carpet

4. Tracy put up a sign and covered the windows because ______________

____

______________.

5. Check two sentences that tell how the clubhouse was like a house.

____ A poster hung on the wall.

____ The floor was carpeted.

____ The sign on the door said "Keep Out!"

Vote for Tat

Have you ever run for class president? Read to find out how Tat ran his campaign.

1 At the end of the week, Tat's class would vote for class president. Tat was running for president even though he had tried last year and lost. He was certain he could do a good job. His task was to convince the rest of his classmates. That would take a bit of work.

2 To begin his campaign, Tat spent three hours making a poster. It showed his picture and a list of promises that he would keep if elected. Tat got permission first thing Monday morning to put the poster near the door of his classroom. That way the students would see it each time they left the room.

3 Next, Tat made a campaign shirt out of one of his father's old T-shirts. He painted "Vote for Tat" on it. All day Tuesday he wore the shirt.

4 The next day Tat used his whole recess to talk to every student from his class. He told them why he would make a good president. Then Tat asked for their votes on Friday.

5 He spent all of Thursday evening writing a speech for election day. After two tries, Tat had a speech that he liked. Tat forgot part of his speech when he practiced it in front of Lin, his parents, and his stuffed animals. He was so worried that he would forget the speech the next day that he practiced it two more times. When he finished, his family praised him for a fine speech.

6 On Friday morning, Tat felt a little nervous as he dressed for school. He put on his favorite shirt, his lucky socks, and a new pair of pants. "Well, what do you think, Lin?" Tat said.

7 "You look like a winner to me," Lin replied. "Good luck today."

8 "Thanks," Tat said as he left for school.

9 Tat's speech had gone well, but he held his breath as the name of the new president was read. It took Tat a minute to realize that his hard work had finally paid off. He had won!

Knowing the Words

Write the words from the story that have the meanings below.

1. the project of getting votes ________ (Par. 2)
2. filled with something ________ (Par. 5)

Write the word with the correct meaning to complete each sentence below.

3. ________ poster is the most colorful. (Hour, Our)
4. Jake has a ________ of tickets for the movie. (pair, pear)
5. Dan has a ________ red wagon. (new, knew)
6. Jo gets a letter in the mail every ________. (weak, week)

Working with Words

Fill in each blank with the correct pair of letters to make a word.

wr kn mb ph

1. co ____
2. ____ ob
3. ____ ote
4. ele ____ ant

Circle the correct word in ( ) and write it in the blank.

5. She ________ for the scarf with quarters. (pad, paid)
6. Will you ________ me for lunch? (join, junk)

Reading and Thinking

1. Check the answer that tells what the story is mainly about.
   ____ being president
   ____ making a poster
   ____ running for president
2. Tell two things Tat did to get votes.
   ____
   ____
3. Write **O** next to the sentence that gives an opinion.
   ____ There are usually five days in a school week.
   ____ A poster is important to a campaign.

Learning to Study

Use the table of contents below to answer the questions.

How to Win an Election

Table of Contents

1. How many chapters are in this book?
   ____
2. On what page does "Nearing Elections" begin? ________
3. What chapter tells how to give a speech? ________

Superskater

Have you ever dreamed of being famous? Could such a dream come true?

1 When Rick awoke, his nose was stopped up, and his throat felt scratchy. "You'll have to stay indoors today," his mother said. Rick had planned to go ice skating at City Park. Now, though, he didn't really feel like going. He just felt like resting. Rick lay his head back on the pillow and fell asleep again.

2 Rick dreamed he was a famous skater who performed all over the world. He would glide smoothly across the ice. Then he would spin so fast his skate blades would flash in the spotlight. After his performance, the audience would clap and cheer until he came back to do one more act. Later, people would crowd around him to take pictures. They would ask for his autograph. They would say nice things about his skating.

3 Rick had not been sleeping long when his father knocked on the bedroom door. "Come in," Rick said sleepily. He rolled over and sat up in bed.

4 "I picked up something for you at the store," his father said. He handed him a brown paper bag.

5 "Orange juice!" Rick exclaimed as he looked inside the package. "Thanks, Dad!"

6 "I've also been to the library," his father said. He handed Rick a book. "Since you're stuck indoors, I thought you'd enjoy reading this story. It's about a champion ice skater who won a gold medal at the Olympics."

7 "Dad," Rick exclaimed with surprise, "I was just dreaming that I was a famous skater! Do you suppose it means something special?"

8 "Who knows?" his father replied with a wink and a smile. "Perhaps it means that someday your dream will come true."

Knowing the Words

Write the words from the story that have the meanings below.

1. a bright light ______ (Par. 2)

2. best at something ______ (Par. 6)

3. a reward ______ (Par. 6)

4. world sports contests ______ (Par. 6)

Working with Words

Circle the prefix or suffix in each word. Then use the words to complete the sentences.

reread useful

unzip sleepless

1. Old rags are ______ for cleaning dirty windows.

2. ______ your coat and hang it on a hanger.

3. Les will ______ the book because he likes it.

4. Tom had a ______ night because a storm kept him awake.

Write the singular form of each word.

5. patches ______

6. cities ______

7. shelves ______

8. boxes ______

9. blueberries ______

Reading and Thinking

1. Check the answer that tells what the story is mainly about.

   ___ a famous Olympic ice skater

   ___ a trip to the library

   ___ a dream that could come true

2. Write two places Rick's father went.

   ______

3. Why do you think Rick's dad brought Rick a book about a skater?

   ______

   ______

4. Dreams are not real, but sometimes they can come true. Check two sentences that tell about dreams that could come true.

   ___ Jim dreamed he was a famous artist.

   ___ Jeff dreamed he lived in a pumpkin.

   ___ Kate dreamed she was an astronaut.

Write the best word to complete each sentence below.

5. The knife ______ is sharp. (handle, blade, cover)

6. "May I have your ______ on this card?" the man asked the singer. (pillow, medal, autograph)

7. The small ______ was on the desk. (package, smile, ice)

Tracy's Storm Delights

Do you like to cook? Read to find out what happens when Tracy makes muffins.

1 Even though it was Saturday, Tracy rolled out of bed early. She looked out the window. A thick blanket of snow covered the ground.

2 "It's a good day for a warm breakfast," Tracy thought. "I'll surprise Mom and Dad with some muffins." She found the recipe in a cookbook. Then she measured the things she needed:

1 egg
2 tablespoons sugar
3/4 cup milk
2 cups baking mix
1/2 cup brown sugar
1 1/2 teaspoons cinnamon

3 She set the oven at 400°F so it would have time to heat. Then she put twelve paper baking cups into a muffin pan. She mixed the egg, sugar, milk, and baking mix in a large bowl. She poured the lumpy batter into the baking cups so each was about two-thirds full. Next she stirred the brown sugar and cinnamon together. Last, she sprinkled the mixture on the muffins.

4 Tracy put the muffins into the oven to bake for fifteen minutes. After ten minutes she checked on the muffins because she hadn't smelled them. They were still a soupy batter. She felt the oven door with her hand. It was not even warm.

5 As she leaned against the wall to think about the problem, her arm bumped the light switch. The light did not come on. "So that's the trouble!" she said. "The storm last night must have knocked a power line down, so there is no electricity."

6 Tracy read a book while she waited for the lines to be fixed. A half hour later, the light flickered. The oven began to heat. As soon as the muffins were done, she sat down to eat. "Mmm, these were worth waiting for," she said as she bit into a warm buttered muffin. "From now on, I think I'll call these Tracy's Storm Delights!"

Knowing the Words

Write the words from the story that have the meanings below.

1. cooking directions ______________ (Par. 2)
2. a spice ______________ (Par. 3)
3. covered lightly with drops ______________ (Par. 3)
4. flashed off and on ______________ (Par. 6)

Match each word in the first list with its abbreviation from the second list.

5. _____ minutes   a. tsp.
6. _____ teaspoon   b. Sat.
7. _____ Saturday   c. min.

Working with Words

Use the following words to form compound words. Then use the compound to complete the sentences.

snow cook flake book

1. This ______________ has a recipe for bean soup.
2. A ______________ landed on my mitten and melted.

Circle the correct word in ( ) and write it in the blank.

3. Add ______________ to the brown sugar. (campaign, cinnamon)
4. The fruit ______________ spilled. (juice, jack)

Reading and Thinking

1. Number the sentences in the order that shows how Tracy's muffins are made.

   _____ Pour the batter into baking cups.

   _____ Combine brown sugar and cinnamon.

   _____ Mix the egg, sugar, milk, and baking mix.

   _____ Put the topping on the muffins.

   _____ Bake the muffins for fifteen minutes.

2. Why didn't the muffins bake?

   ____

Write **T** if the sentence is true.
Write **F** if the sentence is false.

3. _____ Tracy made twelve muffins.
4. _____ Tracy baked the muffins in a gas oven.
5. _____ Tracy would need two eggs to make two dozen muffins.
6. _____ Tracy made the muffins for Tat.
7. _____ The muffins had fruit in them.

Write the best word to complete each sentence below.

8. The blue flame ______________ in the breeze. (flickered, bumped, leaned)
9. They ______________ the muffins turn brown. (watched, decorated, baked)

Crazy Sleds

If you wanted to go sledding but had no sled, what might you use instead?

1 Neither Tracy, Rick, nor Elsa owned a sled, but that didn't stop them from entering the sled races at City Park. They searched their homes for things that would glide on snow. Then they met at the park to practice.

2 Tracy arrived first. She was carrying a blown-up inner tube. Soon Rick came trudging through the snow. He had a garbage can lid that was missing its handle. Finally Elsa appeared. She was dragging a rope with a plastic laundry basket attached.

3 "These are the craziest looking sleds I've ever seen!" Tracy laughed.

4 "Do you think they'll really work?" Rick asked, sounding doubtful.

5 "There's only one way to find out," Elsa said as she climbed into her laundry basket. She grabbed the handles and asked Rick to give her a shove. "It's sort of hard to steer, but it works!" Elsa shouted when she reached the bottom of the hill.

6 Tracy sat on her rubber inner tube and said, "I hope I don't get a flat!" She kicked off with her foot and slid down the slope. "It's not bad except for a few bumps and bounces!" she called.

7 "Here comes the trash can racer!" Rick shouted. He sat cross-legged on the metal lid. Then he gave himself a spin. "I'm a little dizzy, but it got me where I wanted to go!" Rick said when he stopped whirling.

8 "I'm not sure we'll win any races with these," Elsa said as they climbed back to the top of the hill.

9 "Yeah, the kids with regular sleds will probably have the most speed," Rick agreed.

10 "But," Tracy added, "the kids with the crazy sleds will probably have the most fun!"

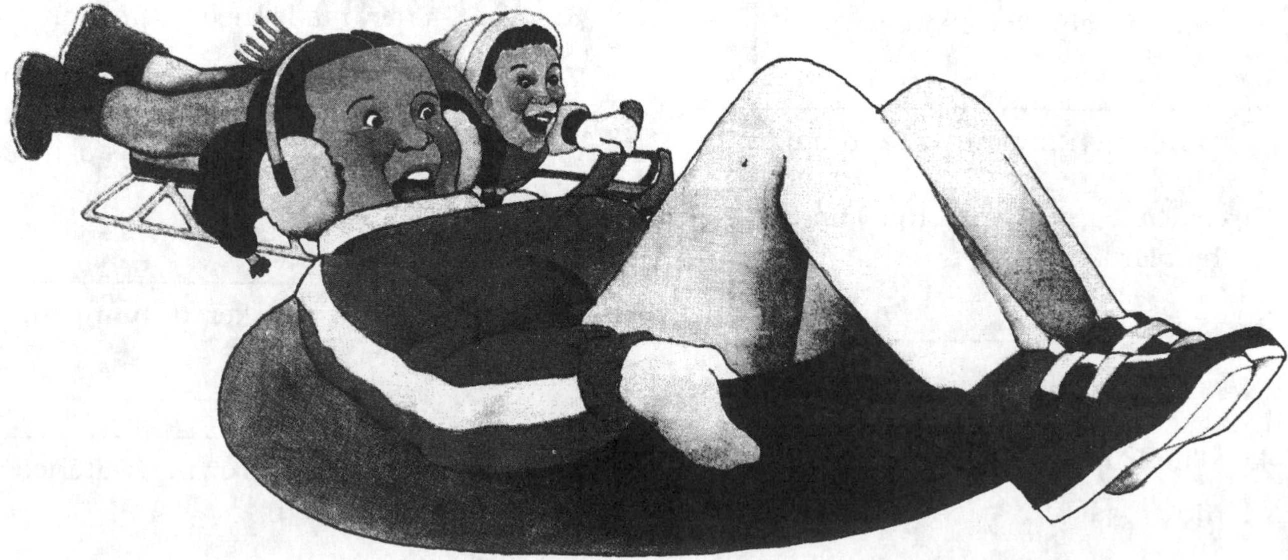

Knowing the Words

Write the words from the story that have the meanings below.

1. filled with air ________ (Par. 2)
2. walking heavily ________ (Par. 2)
3. not sure ________ (Par. 4)

Circle the pair of antonyms (opposites) in each row.

4. tube inner rubber outer
5. doubtful answer certain guess
6. beside top bottom near

Working with Words

Use each group of words in a sentence that tells who owns something.

1. children's ideas ________
____
2. Elsa's basket ________
____
3. friend's sled ________
____
4. kids' races ________
____

In each word below, draw a line to divide the word into syllables.

5. dizzy 7. minus 9. pencil
6. metal 8. garbage 10. crazy

Reading and Thinking

1. Check the answer that tells what the story is mainly about.
   ____ winning a race
   ____ building a sled
   ____ practicing for a race
2. Where were the sled races to be held?
   ____
3. Tracy, Rick, and Elsa had crazy sleds because ________
   ________.
4. Do you think the kids with the crazy sleds will win the race? Explain your answer. ________
   ____
5. Check the answer that tells what Tracy thinks is most important about sledding.
   ____ being the first-place winner
   ____ having a good time
   ____ having the best-looking sleds

In each sentence below, a word is underlined. Circle the name or names that the underlined words stand for.

6. "<u>I</u> will go first," said Elsa to Tracy.
   Tracy Rick Elsa
7. "<u>You</u> look cold," Tracy said to Rick.
   Rick Elsa Tracy
8. "<u>We</u> should leave," Rick said to Tracy.
   Rick Rick and Tracy Tracy

Secret Codes

Have you ever shared a secret code with someone?

1 Heather and Michael had a favorite game. They played it quite often. They made up mysteries for each other to solve. One day when it was just too cold to go outdoors, Heather thought that a mystery was needed.

2 She got a small piece of paper. On it she wrote RM GSV UILMG XOLHVG. Then she quietly dropped it on the floor near the chair where Michael was reading a book. Soon afterwards, Michael got up to get a glass of milk. He found the note.

3 When he first looked at it, he was quite confused. Then he remembered a code he and Heather had used once. They used a backward alphabet so that *a* was written as *z*, *b* as *y*, *c* as *x*, and so on. Michael decoded the message. It said "In the front closet."

4 He didn't know what that meant, but when he looked in the front closet he found another note. This one said LM BLFI WVHP. When he got to his desk, he found a third note! He saw that note number three said "In the den." Michael hurried to the den where he thought he'd find another note. Sure enough he did. But this one looked a little different from the rest. This is what it looked like:

In the kitchen you
will see the answer
to this mystery.

5 When Michael held this note up to a mirror, he could read it with no trouble at all. He followed the instructions on the note and found Heather sitting in the kitchen. "What's up?" he asked.

6 Heather said, "Well, I thought you might like some hot cider on a chilly day. I just wanted to make you curious first."

Knowing the Words

Write the words from the story that have the meanings below.

1. special way of writing ________________ (Par. 3)

2. figured out a secret code ________________ (Par. 3)

3. directions ________________ (Par. 5)

In each row, circle the three words that belong together.

4. message note drop code
5. paper read pen pencil
6. yard den kitchen bedroom
7. chair lamp coat table
8. read fold solve think

Learning to Study

Read each word in dark print and the dictionary meanings that follow. Then read the sentences below and decide the meaning of each underlined word. Write the number of the correct meaning in the blank.

den **1** small room in a house
2 an animal's home

1. _____ The fox was asleep in its den.

2. _____ Is the TV in the den?

glass **1** something that holds liquid
2 material that can break

3. _____ I spilled the glass of water.

4. _____ A piece of glass was in the tire.

Reading and Thinking

1. Number the sentences to show the order in which things happened.

_____ Heather dropped a note near Michael's chair.

_____ Michael decoded the message.

_____ Michael met Heather in the kitchen.

_____ Michael went to the den.

_____ Michael found the first note.

Write **T** if the sentence is true.
Write **F** if the sentence is false.

2. _____ Michael had never seen this code before.

3. _____ It was the middle of summer.

4. _____ All of the notes were inside the house.

5. How many notes did Heather write in all? ________________

6. How were all the notes alike?

____

7. How was one note different from the others? ________________

____

Cocoon Surprise

Have you ever felt sure of something but then found out you were wrong?

1 A white rat, a turtle, and three goldfish all lived in Tracy's classroom. The class took turns caring for the pets. Tracy was glad her teacher, Ms. Carr, liked animals because Tracy did, too.

2 Tracy had a cocoon in a jar that she kept in the garage. She had found the cocoon on a bush. When her dad cleaned the garage on Saturday, he asked her if she still wanted the cocoon.

"Yes, may I take it to school?" Tracy asked. "I don't think Ms. Carr would mind."

3 "OK," her father answered. "Just make sure you take it on Monday."

4 Tracy took the cocoon to school that Monday. She asked her teacher if she could put it beside the pets. Ms. Carr said that was fine with her. "Great!" Tracy said, smiling. "The class will get to see the butterfly come out."

5 "Are you certain that a butterfly will come out of the cocoon, Tracy?" asked Ms. Carr.

6 "Oh, yes, I'm sure," Tracy answered. "And I think it will hatch any day now."

7 "We'll see," Ms. Carr told Tracy.

8 Tracy did not have to wait long to find out what was in the cocoon. Two days later she got quite a surprise. She was the first child in the room that day. As she walked into the room, Ms. Carr pointed toward the corner where the pets were kept. "Look, Tracy!" she said.

9 Tracy saw a large insect in the jar. "What is it?" she asked, wrinkling up her nose.

10 "It's a moth," her teacher told her. "See how its wings are open while it is resting."

11 "Gee, its body looks furry," Tracy said as she pressed her face against the jar.

12 Ms. Carr laughed and said, "Now let's get your moth outside where it can try its wings."

Knowing the Words

Write the words from the story that have the meanings below.

1. a place where some insects grow ______ (Par. 2)

2. insect ______ (Par. 10)

Choose the correct word below to fill the blanks for each pair of sentences.

rest fine

3. That is ______ with me.

   The thread was too ______ to see.

4. Roger needs to ______.

   Did you get the ______ of the programs?

Working with Words

Fill in each blank with the correct pair of letters to make a word. Then use each of the words in a sentence below.

sh ch wr ph

1. bu ____
2. stoma ____
3. hand ____ iting
4. autogra ____
5. My ______ hurts.
6. Leo has beautiful ______.
7. May I have your ______?
8. Look at the cocoon on that ______.

Reading and Thinking

Write **F** if the sentence gives a fact.
Write **O** if the sentence gives an opinion.

1. ____ A moth is a pretty insect.
2. ____ The body of a moth looks furry.
3. ____ Some insects come out of cocoons.
4. ____ A moth is an insect.
5. Why do you think Tracy and Ms. Carr took the moth outside?

   ______

   ______

6. What kind of person do you think Ms. Carr is? Explain your answer.

   ______

Learning to Study

You can look in an **encyclopedia** to find facts about different topics. You may need to look under more than one topic to find the facts you need. To learn more about cocoons, Tracy could have looked under *cocoon*. Also, she could have looked under *moth* or *insect*.

Read each sentence below. Write the names of two topics you might look under.

1. You want to know about blue jays. ______

2. You want to learn about forest animals. ______

A Trip into the Past

What will Michael learn on his class trip?

1 "All right," Michael said to himself, "I've got my lunch. I have my permission note. I guess I'm ready to go."

2 Michael's class was taking a short trip. They were going to Castle Dugan. Michael's grandparents told him he'd have fun. "History is interesting," they said. Michael was not so sure.

3 At the castle, the class was met by a tour guide. "Welcome to Castle Dugan," he said. "This castle was built in the early 1800's. Here, you won't find some of the things you have in your homes. For example, you will not see electric lights. You will not see any closets. Please come this way."

4 The guide led them through several huge rooms. Michael did not see what was so special about the castle. Then the class went into the library. The guide said, "Here's something I think you'll like." He pressed a button on the wall. A hidden door opened, and a secret stairway appeared. The guide explained why the stairway was built. Michael started to pay attention.

5 The guide led the class down the steps to an underground pathway. The only light was from candles. Just as they reached the bottom, the candle closest to them went out. They stopped for a minute to let their eyes get used to the dark. The pathway was cold and damp. When Michael talked, the sound echoed. "I wonder if children used to play here," he thought. The guide led them forward.

6 The pathway led to the stables on the other side of the street. Six old carriages were kept there. Michael dreamed of what it would have been like to drive one of them.

7 As the class ate lunch in the garden, Michael gazed at the castle. His grandparents had been right. History can be interesting.

Knowing the Words

Write the word from the story that has the meaning below.

1. a trip to see something special __________________
(Par. 3)

Check the meaning that fits the underlined word in each sentence.

2. My new shirt is light blue.

_____ pale

_____ not heavy

3. We are planning a trip to England.

_____ vacation

_____ to stumble

4. I left a note on the table.

_____ a musical sound

_____ a short letter

Working with Words

Write the contraction for each pair of words below.

1. you have __________________

2. would not __________________

3. what is __________________

4. you will __________________

5. we are __________________

6. I will __________________

7. do not __________________

8. I have __________________

Reading and Thinking

1. Check the answer that tells what the story is mainly about.

_____ cold, damp walls

_____ a secret stairway

_____ visiting a castle

2. Write **R** next to two sentences that tell about real things.

_____ A person can drive to a castle.

_____ A person can drive into the past.

_____ Castles have walls.

_____ Castles have dragons.

Learning to Study

Each book of an encyclopedia is called a **volume.** Write the number of the volume you could use to find the topics below.

1. castles _____

2. bicycle _____

3. history _____

4. cotton _____

5. fish _____

6. carriages _____

7. gardening _____

8. horses _____

9. dolls _____

10. England _____

WTLR News

Read to learn about a special kind of report.

1 Rick, Tracy, and Lindsay were painting letters on a large box in Tracy's garage. Elsa came by and asked what they were doing.

2 "You'll see," Rick said, smiling.

3 "I think I know," Elsa bragged. "I saw you in the library. Are you working on your project for Monday?"

4 Tracy said, "You'll see."

5 On Monday, Elsa told all the kids in their class that Tracy, Rick, and Lindsay had a surprise for their report. The whole class was eager to see what the three of them had done. When it was time for the reports, Rick, Tracy, and Lindsay were asked to go first.

6 Tracy dragged the box to the front of the room. She and Lindsay sat behind it. Rick stood off to the side and told the class, "You will need to pretend the year is 1903. If there had been TVs then, this interview might have been on the news."

7 Tracy began by saying, "Good evening. This is WTLR news. Tonight we will talk with Mary Anderson about her recent invention. It is a device for wiping rain and snow off of a windshield." Tracy turned to Lindsay. She said, "Hello, Mary. Tell us about your invention."

8 "Well," Lindsay began, "the purpose of this device is to keep the windshield clear on the outside. It helps people drive safely."

9 Then Rick stepped up to the news desk. Tracy turned to him and said, "You have used this device. Can you tell us what you think of it?"

10 "Yes, it has helped my driving quite a bit. I used to have to stop every once in a while to clean off my windshield. But now Mary's invention does it for me."

11 "So, there you have it, folks," Tracy concluded. "Someday we may wonder how we ever got along without this device."

12 The class applauded. They had been surprised.

Knowing the Words

Write the words from the story that have the meanings below.

1. invention ____________ (Par. 7)

2. ended ____________ (Par. 11)

Choose the correct word to fill in the blank for each pair of sentences.

drive saw

3. Ed is too young to ____________.

____________ the nail into the wood.

4. We ____________ you at the game.

Where did you put the ____________?

Learning to Study

Names of people are listed in an encyclopedia by the person's last name. Write the number of the volume you could use to find the topics below.

1. invention ____
2. computers ____
3. Mary Anderson ____
4. Thomas Edison ____

Reading and Thinking

Write **T** if the sentence is true.
Write **F** if the sentence is false.

1. ____ Tracy, Lindsay, and Rick had been to the library.
2. ____ Tracy pretended she was a news reporter.
3. ____ The class was not interested in the project.
4. Did Tracy really talk to Mary Anderson? Explain your answer.

____

5. Why did Mary Anderson make a device for cleaning a windshield?

____

____

Read each set of sentences below. Fill in each blank.

6. Lindsay pretended she was Mary Anderson.

She stands for ____________.

7. Rick said he liked the new invention.

He stands for ____________.

8. The inventor thought she had a good idea.

She stands for ____________.

9. The class was surprised when it saw the report.

It stands for ____________.

Elephant Disappearance

How do you feel when you lose something you need?

1 "Now where is that stuffed elephant?" Dale muttered as he searched through the toy box. "I know it was here yesterday because I was playing with it."

2 Dale was getting upset. A few of his friends in the neighborhood were going to put on a puppet show, and they asked Dale to join them. Dale told them he'd like to, but he didn't have a puppet. Tracy said, "That's OK. Just bring a stuffed animal." So that is just what Dale planned to do.

3 "Lindsay, have you seen my stuffed elephant?" Dale asked hopefully.

4 "No, I haven't, Dale. When and where did you have it last?" Lindsay asked. "It might help to think about that."

5 "Rags and I played with it in my room yesterday. It couldn't have walked out on its own," Dale grumbled. "And I think I've looked everywhere in my room."

6 Dale went on searching. He asked his parents if they had seen the toy. Neither one had. He even talked to Rags about his problem.

7 Finally, Dale began to cry. He was so disappointed and angry! He petted Rags as he said, "Without that elephant, I won't be able to help put on the show."

8 Dale went to his room and lay on his bed. He was not at all happy. After thinking, he said to himself, "Well, I guess I could make a sock puppet." He began to gather everything he needed. Just as he sat down to make the puppet, Rags came into the room. The dog had something in his mouth. He was growling and shaking it. When Dale looked down, he realized that Rags had the lost elephant. Dale was so excited! He raced right outside to find his friends.

9 Lindsay had seen Rags go into Dale's room with the toy. As she watched Dale rush out, she just shook her head. "I don't think he even stopped to wonder why Rags had that elephant or how he got it," she said to herself.

Knowing the Words

Write the word from the story that has the meaning below.

1. moved from side to side ____________ (Par. 9)

Circle the pair of antonyms (opposites) in each row.

2. sing cry laugh applaud
3. lost helped looked won
4. answered said inquired grumbled

Working with Words

The suffix **-ly** helps tell how something was done. *Smoothly* means "done in a smooth way."

Add **-ly** to the words below. Use the new words to complete the sentences.

silent friend loose clear

1. When he was in the library, Robert read a book ____________.
2. Amy tied the knot ____________.
3. Pat was happy to see the ____________ puppy.
4. The announcer spoke ____________.

Say *gather.* Circle the words below that have the sound *g* stands for in *gather.*

5. began edge giant against
6. get goldfish message charge
7. forget eager magic bridge
8. cage goose give together

Reading and Thinking

Write **T** if the sentence is true.
Write **F** if the sentence is false.

1. _____ Dale wanted to help with the puppet show.
2. _____ Dale did not try very hard to find his stuffed elephant.
3. _____ Dale thought of a new way to solve his problem.
4. _____ Dale finally found the toy himself.
5. Dale was going to make a sock puppet because ____________ ____________.
6. What do you think Dale will do now that his elephant has been found? ____________ ____________

Write the best word to complete each sentence below.

7. James ____________ why the tire was flat. (wondered, jumped, searched)
8. The ____________ was bigger than a car. (mouse, robin, elephant)

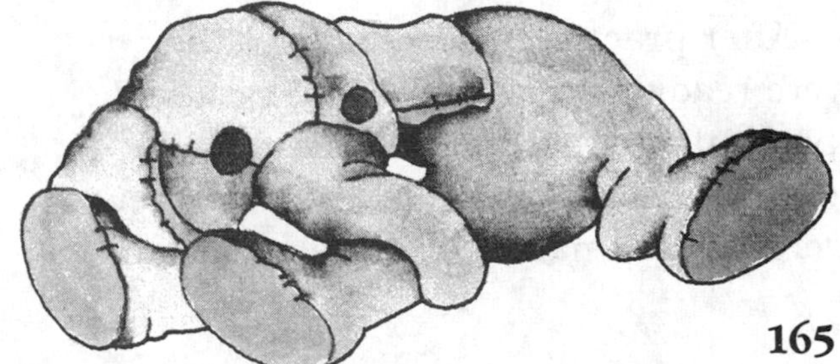

Just for Carmen

How could you cheer up a friend who is ill?

1 Andy and Elsa were already at Tracy's house when Dale arrived. "Sorry it took me so long," he apologized. "I could not find my elephant for a while."

2 "Why are we doing this show anyway?" Dale asked.

3 Elsa answered, "Well, Carmen has a bad cold, so she had to stay inside today. Tracy and I thought a puppet show would cheer her up."

4 "What can we have our puppets do?" Andy asked.

5 "Let's act as if our puppets are circus performers," Elsa suggested. The others agreed that Elsa had a good idea. They began to practice.

6 After practicing several acts, they were ready to perform. They gathered their things and took off running towards Elsa's house. In no time they were inside, making a stage curtain.

7 The children stood behind the curtain. Carmen sat up in bed. The show was about to start. "Attention, please, Carmen!" Tracy said. "You are about to see the best circus show ever! For our first act, the trapeze artists will perform amazing stunts with no net. As a matter of fact, the stunts will be done with no trapeze!"

8 Elsa and Andy made the puppets look as if they were swinging back and forth on a make-believe trapeze. Then they made their puppets look as though they were flipping from one trapeze to another. Carmen giggled and clapped.

9 "Great!" Tracy broke in. "Now sit back and enjoy our elephant act."

10 Dale made his elephant stand on its head. Then he made it walk on its hind legs. Carmen was pleased.

11 Carmen watched the rest of the acts eagerly. She clapped loudly after each one. Tracy, Elsa, Dale, and Andy felt good. They enjoyed helping Carmen forget about her cold.

Knowing the Words

Write the words from the story that have the meanings below.

1. asked forgiveness ________ (Par. 1)

2. common sickness ________ (Par. 3)

Check the meaning that fits the underlined word in each sentence.

3. It is very <u>cold</u> outside.

   ____ low temperature

   ____ sickness

4. This is the third <u>act</u>.

   ____ to behave in a certain way

   ____ part of a show

Learning to Study

An **index** is a part of a book. It lists a book's topics in alphabetical order. It also lists page numbers so you can find those topics. An index is usually at the back of a book. Use the index below to answer the questions.

performances, 1–5
plays, 4, 21
puppets, 4, 8–10
stages, 11–15

1. What topic would you find on pages 1–5? ________

2. What could you learn from pages 11–15?

   ____

3. On what pages would you look if you wanted to make a puppet? ________

Reading and Thinking

1. Number the sentences to show the order in which things happened.

   ____ The puppets did a trapeze act.

   ____ The elephant performed.

   ____ Tracy announced the first act.

   ____ The children went to Elsa's house.

   ____ Dale went to Tracy's house.

Write **F** if the sentence gives a fact.
Write **O** if the sentence gives an opinion.

2. ____ An elephant's skin has wrinkles.

3. ____ The trapeze acts are the most thrilling to watch.

4. ____ An elephant can be trained to stand on its hind legs.

5. ____ Many circuses have elephants.

6. ____ A circus isn't exciting.

Read each sentence below. Fill in the blank.

7. The children knew they had made Carmen happy.

   They stands for ________.

8. Dale believed he had done a good job.

   He stands for ________.

9. Carmen applauded as she watched the performance.

   She stands for ________.

Spring Concert

How much do you believe in yourself?

1 Elsa and Rick were going to sing a song together at the spring concert. They had practiced hard for weeks.

2 The day before the concert Rick told Mr. Barnes, the music teacher, that he did not think he could perform. "Let me ask you a few questions," Mr. Barnes said. "Do you feel as if you know the song?"

3 "Yes, I have it memorized," Rick said.

4 Then Mr. Barnes asked, "Do you like to sing?"

5 "Very much," replied Rick.

6 "Are you nervous?" Mr. Barnes said, going on with his questions.

7 "Well, maybe a little," Rick admitted.

8 Then Mr. Barnes said, "Do you believe me when I say you are a very good singer?"

9 Rick answered, "Sure."

10 Mr. Barnes smiled and said, "Well, now all you have to do is believe in yourself. If you believe in yourself, you won't get so nervous."

11 "OK, I'll try," Rick said as he shrugged his shoulders.

12 Rick was quite nervous on the night of the concert. He said to Elsa, "What if I don't start singing at the right time? What if I forget the words? What if. . ."

13 "Relax," Elsa said, "you'll do fine."

14 Finally, Rick heard Mr. Barnes introduce them to the audience. Elsa walked onto the stage with Rick close behind her. The piano started to play. When Rick started to sing, his voice came out a squeak. Then he quickly thought, "Mr. Barnes thinks I can do it. Elsa thinks I can do it. I must think I can do it." Soon he was singing the song just the way he had practiced it. Before he knew it, the song was over.

15 The crowd applauded, and Rick spotted his parents. He could see by their smiles that they were really proud of him. Rick said to himself, "After I thought I could do it, I did it!"

Knowing the Words

Write the words from the story that have the meanings below.

1. a season ____________ (Par. 1)
2. said something was true ____________ (Par. 7)
3. moved up and down ____________ (Par. 11)
4. saw ____________ (Par. 15)

Choose the correct word below to fill the blank for each pair of sentences.

close spring

5. ____________ begins in March.

   The ____________ in my pen is broken.

6. Please ____________ the window.

   Do not stand too ____________ to the fire.

Learning to Study

Number each list of words below in alphabetical order.

1. ____ shrug
   ____ sing
   ____ shoulders
   ____ piano
   ____ smile
   ____ memorize
   ____ question

2. ____ crowd
   ____ cry
   ____ cute
   ____ concert
   ____ crawl
   ____ believe
   ____ beg

Reading and Thinking

Write **T** if the sentence is true.
Write **F** if the sentence is false.

1. ____ Elsa was very nervous.
2. ____ Rick and Elsa had practiced the song more than once.
3. ____ The concert took place at the beginning of the school year.
4. Rick did not want to sing in the concert because ____________ ____________.
5. Who was Mr. Barnes? ____________ ____________
6. Why did Mr. Barnes tell Rick he needed to believe in himself? ____________
7. How do you think Rick felt about himself after he sang the song? ____________
8. Do you think Rick will ever sing in a concert again? Explain your answer. ____________ ____________

Tracy's First Job

Read to find out what Tracy learned.

1 Tracy told Rick about the bike she had seen for sale down the street. "It needs a new seat and some paint, but I think it's a bargain for twenty dollars," she said. "It will probably be sold before I can save that much money though."

2 "I'm giving up my paper route," Rick said. "You could have that twenty dollars in no time if you took my route. Why don't we talk to Mr. Wise and see if it's OK?"

3 "Great!" Tracy said. "I can almost feel myself riding that bike now."

4 Mr. Wise said it would be fine with him if Tracy took Rick's route. Then he asked Rick to show Tracy the route and explain the job.

5 That afternoon Rick showed Tracy how to fold papers. He gave her hints about how to throw a paper so it landed right in front of the door. As they went through the route, Rick told her the name of each customer as he pointed out the houses on the route. "Maybe you should write down these names and addresses, Tracy," Rick said.

6 "No, I don't need to. I have a good memory," Tracy said.

7 The next day Tracy did the paper route alone. She started at three o'clock. At 3:30 she was at the last house. "That was easy," she thought. "And I still have time to play before supper." But when she looked in her bag there was one more paper. Tracy had no idea where it belonged. How could she find out? Finally, she decided to call Rick to get addresses of all the customers. This time she wrote them down.

8 Tracy found that she had forgotten to give a paper to the Blair family. After the paper was delivered, she looked at her watch. It was time for supper.

9 "Well, I learned two things today," Tracy thought. "One, my memory is not as good as I thought. Two, I will save time if I do my route right the first time."

Knowing the Words

Write the words from the story that have the meanings below.

1. good price ____________ (Par. 1)
2. might be ____________ (Par. 1)

Check the meaning that fits the underlined word in each sentence.

3. Did you see the <u>play</u> Michael was in?
   ____ a show
   ____ to have fun
4. Did Ken <u>watch</u> TV yesterday?
   ____ something that keeps time
   ____ to look at

Working with Words

Circle the correct word in ( ) and write it in the blank.

1. I hope I ____________ two inches this year. (group, grow)
2. The ____________ of his scream frightened me. (sound, sand)
3. Has Sam ____________ of a name for his kitten? (thought, that)
4. The ____________ begins at 8:30. (shoe, show)
5. Did you write ____________ the correct address? (dawn, down)
6. Jenny ____________ us how to tie a knot. (should, showed)

Reading and Thinking

1. Why was Tracy saving money?
   ____
2. Tracy had to call Rick because
   ____
   ____________.
3. How do you think Tracy felt about asking Rick for the addresses?
   ____
4. What do you think Tracy did after she delivered her last paper?
   ____

Learning to Study

Read each question below. Write **dictionary** or **encyclopedia** to answer each one.

1. Where would you find the meaning of the word *newspaper?*
   ____
2. Where could you find the history of newspapers?
   ____
3. Where could you find facts on how newspapers are made?
   ____
4. Where could you find the word *newspaper* divided into syllables?
   ____

Knowing the Words

Write the words from the story that have the meanings below.

1. announcements of something for sale ads (Par. 3)
2. equipment devices (Par. 3)
3. machine that obeys commands robot (Par. 4)

In each row below, circle the three words that belong together.

4. (run) (walk) sleep (wander)
5. (machine) snack (robot) (device)
6. (fingers) (arms) dust (chest)

Working with Words

A word that means one of something is **singular.** A word that means more than one is **plural.** Most singular words are made plural by adding *s*. Most words that end in *s, ss, x, ch,* and *sh* are made plural by adding *es*. Form the plural of each word below by adding *s* or *es*.

1. button s
2. boss es
3. wish es
4. robot s
5. clock s
6. circus es

Reading and Thinking

1. Check the answer that tells what the story is mainly about.
   - ✓ finding a robot
   - ___ going to the office
   - ___ fixing a clock
2. What day of the week is it in this story? Saturday
3. What do you think will happen when Carlos saves up ten dollars? He will buy the robot.
4. Some things are real, and some are make-believe. Write **M** next to the two sentences that tell about make-believe things.
   - ___ Robots are machines.
   - M Robots can think for themselves.
   - M Robots have feelings.
   - ___ Robots can obey commands.

Write the best word to complete each sentence below.

5. Andrea had six square buttons on her good coat, but one fell off. (zippers, buttons, dollars)
6. There was a typewriter in each office. (office, automobile, meadow)
7. The bike was hidden by some bushes. (written, wanted, hidden)

Knowing the Words

Write the words from the story that have the meanings below.

1. said in a low voice grumbled (Par. 6)
2. say something is true admit (Par. 8)

Working with Words

A **contraction** is a short way to write two words. An apostrophe (') shows that one or more letters have been taken out. Write a contraction from the story for each pair of words below.

1. it is it's (Par. 3)
2. I will I'll (Par. 3)
3. would not wouldn't (Par. 5)
4. is not isn't (Par. 7)
5. do not don't (Par. 8)

Circle the correct letters to complete each word and write them in the blank.

6. Get into the c ar and put on your seat belt.
   or ir (ar)
7. Did you f or get to sweep the floor?
   (or) ir ar
8. Meet us at the corn er after the show.
   or ar (er)

Reading and Thinking

1. Number the sentences to show the order in which things happened.
   - 4 Carlos made the robot wave.
   - 1 Carlos and his dad went to the storeroom.
   - 3 Carlos and his dad took the robot to the van.
   - 2 Carlos tried to roll the robot.
2. How big was the robot? It was almost as big as Carlos.
3. Carlos and his dad had to carry the robot because it would not roll.
4. Tell two ways that a robot is different from a child. (Answers will vary.)
5. What do you think Carlos will do as soon as he gets the robot home? (Answers will vary.)

Knowing the Words

Write the words from the story that have the meanings below.

1. something being worked on project (Par. 1)
2. try out test (Par. 4)
3. very upset frantic (Par. 7)

Check the meaning that fits the underlined word in each sentence.

4. Jane passed her math <u>test</u>.
   - ✓ something to measure what a person knows
   - ___ try out
5. The dog walked through the <u>bed</u> of daisies.
   - ___ piece of furniture
   - ✓ place for flowers
6. I forgot to wear my <u>watch</u>.
   - ✓ something that keeps time
   - ___ look for

Reading and Thinking

1. Check the answer that tells what the story is mainly about.
   - ___ bringing the robot home
   - ___ stopping the robot
   - ✓ getting the robot to work
2. How do you think Carlos felt when he tried to get the robot to move? (Answers will vary.)
3. How do you think fixing a robot might be like fixing a radio? (Answers will vary.)
4. Carlos pressed buttons on the robot's chest because he wanted the robot to move.

Learning to Study

Number each list of words below in alphabetical order.

1. 3 dusted, 4 friend, 2 camping, 1 battery
2. 3 wires, 1 lights, 2 robot, 4 yell
3. 4 smile, 1 fix, 2 mouth, 3 removed
4. 4 yard, 3 watch, 2 stop, 1 pressed

Knowing the Words

Write the words from the story that have the meanings below.

1. showed by example demonstrated (Par. 2)
2. commands orders (Par. 3)
3. small jobs chores (Par. 3)

Words with opposite meanings are called **antonyms.** Match each word from the first list with its antonym from the second list.

4. b moved — a. full
5. a empty — b. stopped
6. c outside — c. inside

Working with Words

Circle the correct word in ( ) and write it in the blank.

1. Chris took a beach ball to the lake. (tank, (took))
2. Nan lives in a house down the street. (hose, (house))
3. Maybe we will see a full moon tonight. (Merry, (Maybe))

Form the plural of each word below by adding *s* or *es*.

4. grass es
5. hand s
6. lid s
7. dish es
8. back s
9. ax es

Reading and Thinking

1. Number the sentences to show the order in which things happened.
   - 1 Carlos showed his family what the robot could do.
   - 3 The robot dumped the trash on the ground.
   - 2 Carlos showed the robot how to empty the trash.
   - 4 The robot dumped the trash on the lid of the trash can.

Write **T** if the sentence is true.
Write **F** if the sentence is false.

2. T Carlos was excited because his robot followed orders.
3. F Carlos kept his robot's tricks a secret.
4. T Carlos had to be careful when he gave orders to the robot.
5. F The robot could not hear well.

Words such as *he, she, you, it, we,* and *they* are used in place of other words. Read these sentences. *The robot was made of metal. It had green eyes.* In the second sentence, *it* is used in place of *the robot.*

Read each set of sentences below. Fill in each blank.

6. Carlos yelled to his family. He wanted them to see the robot.
   He stands for Carlos.
7. Marie liked the robot. She liked to see Carlos having fun.
   She stands for Marie.

Knowing the Words

Write the words from the story that have the meanings below.

1. wonderful terrific (Par. 5)
2. things such as happiness, sadness, and anger feelings (Par. 7)
3. said with a quiet voice whispered (Par. 8)

Some words sound alike but have different spellings and meanings. Write the word with the correct meaning to complete each sentence below.

4. Ann can hardly wait for the show to begin. (wait, weight)
5. Please don't write on that paper. (right, write)
6. I will go to the playground. (Eye, I)

Working with Words

Circle the correct word in ( ) and write it in the blank.

1. Phyllis taught her puppy a trick. (taught, that)
2. Please wait for me while I get my jacket. (want, wait)
3. Do you know where Muffy has hidden her bowl? (boil, bowl)

Reading and Thinking

1. Check the answer that tells what the story is mainly about.
   - ___ fixing supper
   - ___ talking to Marie
   - ✓ naming the robot
2. What name was given to the robot? Mosh Why was it given that name? It stands for *my own special helper.*
3. What other commands do you think the robot could be taught? (Answers will vary.)

Write **T** if the sentence is true.
Write **F** if the sentence is false.

4. T The robot did exactly what it was told to do.
5. F The robot could talk.
6. T The robot knocked the ice out of Marie's hand.
7. T Carlos thinks Mosh has feelings.

Write the best word to complete each sentence below.

8. Gilda was fixing a flat tire on her bike. (bumping, fixing, preparing)
9. Please shake off that sand before you come inside. (wait, shake, whisper)

Knowing the Words

Write the words from the story that have the meanings below.

1. sad blue (Par. 1)
2. for a reason intentionally (Par. 13)

In each row below, circle the three words that belong together.

3. (girl) robot (boy) (child)
4. (street) (sidewalk) yard (driveway)
5. (chase) (run) ask (roll)
6. start (down) (behind) (beside)
7. (sat) (yell) look (cry)

Working with Words

A **compound word** is made by combining two smaller words. Write a compound word using the underlined words in each sentence.

1. A house for a dog is a doghouse.
2. A yard in back of a house is a backyard.
3. A room where you can store things is a storeroom.
4. Days at the end of the week are called the weekend.
5. A cup used for tea is a teacup.

Reading and Thinking

1. Number the sentences to show the order in which things happened.
   - 2 Mrs. Wilson picked flowers.
   - 1 Mosh learned to play tag.
   - 4 Carlos met Susan.
   - 3 Mosh chased a girl.
2. Who is Mrs. Wilson? Carlos's neighbor

Write **T** if the sentence is true.
Write **F** if the sentence is false.

3. F Mrs. Wilson was angry.
4. F Mosh chased the girl away.
5. T Carlos was glad Mosh chased the girl.
6. What do you think it meant when Mosh winked at the end of the story? (Answers will vary.)
7. Write **R** next to the two sentences that tell about real things.
   - ___ Flowers can fly by themselves.
   - R Robots can roll.
   - R Children can meet new friends.
8. What do you think Carlos and Mosh did after they got home? (Answers will vary.)

Knowing the Words

Write the words from the story that have the meanings below.

1. edge of the street curb (Par. 1)
2. mistake fault (Par. 6)
3. looked at closely examined (Par. 7)

Words that mean the same, or nearly the same, are called **synonyms**. Circle the pair of synonyms in each row.

4. (hurried) whispered (dashed) picked
5. guess sorry (halt) (stop)
6. busy (mad) happy (angry)
7. (big) small (large) quick

Write the word with the correct meaning to complete each sentence below.

8. Have you seen our trash can? (hour, our)
9. I did not hear the phone ring, did you? (here, hear)

Working with Words

An 's at the end of a word may be used to show that something belongs to someone. Add 's to each name in ( ) and write the new word in the blank.

1. Dad's clock (Dad)
2. Mosh's lights (Mosh)
3. Marie's room (Marie)

Reading and Thinking

1. Check the answer that tells what the story is mainly about.
   - ___ fixing a clock
   - ✓ moving trash cans
   - ___ getting angry
2. Mosh moved all of the neighbors' trash cans because no one told it to stop.
3. Why do you think Mosh turned off its lights and would not move? Carlos yelled at Mosh. (Answers may vary.)
4. Was Carlos still angry at the end of the story? Explain your answer. No. Carlos said he was sorry. (Answers may vary.)
5. What do you think Mosh did after Carlos said he was sorry? (Answers will vary.)

Knowing the Words

Write the words from the story that have the meanings below.

1. women's shirts blouses (Par. 4)
2. sparkle twinkle (Par. 4)
3. set of clothes outfit (Par. 6)
4. walked heavily stomped (Par. 7)

Write the word with the correct meaning to complete each sentence below.

5. We rode our bicycles for an hour this morning. (for, four)
6. Please close the screen door. (clothes, close)
7. This dark wood came from a cherry tree. (would, wood)
8. Gina has two sharpened pencils. (two, to)

Working with Words

Say *city*. Circle the words below that have the sound *c* stands for in *city*.

1. (fancy) can (since) clothes
2. (center) expect (except) (force)

A word without any ending is a base word. The base word of *asked* is *ask*. Circle each base word below.

3. (mix)ed
4. (wear)ing
5. (frown)s
6. (laugh)ing
7. (go)ing
8. (look)ed

Reading and Thinking

Write **T** if the sentence is true.
Write **F** if the sentence is false.

1. T Carlos's chore was to put away the clean clothes.
2. T Mr. Garza was too big for Marie's blouse.
3. F Mr. Garza was very angry.
4. T Carlos was not happy at the end of the story.
5. Whose shirt was Mrs. Garza wearing? Carlos's
6. Marie stomped into Carlos's room because she was angry about having the wrong clothes.
7. What do you think Carlos might do after he puts the clothes away? (Answers will vary.)

Knowing the Words

Write the words from the story that have the meanings below.

1. right away instantly (Par. 6)
2. shook trembled (Par. 6)

Some words are spelled the same but have different meanings. For example, *can* might mean "something that food comes in" or "able to do something."

Look at the list of words below. For each pair of sentences, one word from the list will correctly complete both. Choose the correct word to fill in the blanks for each pair of sentences.

fly left like

3. That kite looks just like mine.

   I really like to watch circus performers.

4. Do you have any money left?

   Do you write with your left hand?

5. How do you think birds fly?

   The fly walked on the table.

Working with Words

Fill in each blank with the correct letters to make a word.

kn igh wr ph

1. wr ong
2. r igh t
3. kn ee
4. micro ph one

Reading and Thinking

1. Number the sentences to show the order in which things happened.

   3 Susan removed Mosh's battery.

   2 Carlos taught Mosh to push a swing.

   1 Mosh was knocked down by a baseball.

   4 Carlos fixed Mosh's wires.

2. Check two words that tell how Carlos probably felt when Mosh wouldn't obey him.

   ✓ frightened ___ amused

   ___ bored ✓ confused

3. Mosh wouldn't stop pushing the swing because the robot was broken

4. What did Susan do to get Mosh to stop? took out the battery

5. Check two sentences that tell how Carlos and Susan are alike.

   ___ They both own a robot.

   ✓ They are both children.

   ✓ They had trouble with Mosh.

Write the best word to complete each sentence below.

6. Do you tremble when you are scared? (command, tremble, push)
7. Barb felt dizzy when she got off the ride. (ready, new, dizzy)

Knowing the Words

Write the words from the story that have the meanings below.

1. not done on purpose accidentally (Par. 5)
2. bother worry (Par. 9)

Choose the correct word below to fill in the blanks for each pair of sentences.

can yard

3. This can does not have a label on it.

   I can finish my homework in fifteen minutes.

4. A deer is in the yard.

   Joan bought a yard of ribbon.

Working with Words

A **suffix** is a group of letters added to the end of a word that changes the meaning of the word. The suffix **-ly** helps tell how something was done. *Shyly* means "done in a shy way."

Add **-ly** to the words below. Use the new words to complete the sentences.

accidental sad loud

1. Gretchen watched sadly as her friend rode away.
2. Steve accidentally spilled his apple juice.
3. Agnes laughed loudly.

Reading and Thinking

1. Check the answer that tells what the story is mainly about.

   ✓ digging for worms

   ___ going fishing

   ___ talking to Mrs. Wilson

2. Mosh dug up Mrs. Wilson's garden because the robot was looking for worms.

3. What kind of person do you think Carlos is? Explain your answer.

   (Answers will vary.)

Read each set of sentences below. Fill in each blank.

4. The seeds were planted yesterday. They haven't started growing yet.

   They stands for the seeds.

5. Lucy and I are the same age. We go to school together.

   We stands for Lucy and I.

Knowing the Words

Write the words from the story that have the meanings below.

1. breathed in quickly gasped (Par. 5)
2. said you were sorry apologized (Par. 7)

Choose the correct word to fill in the blanks for each pair of sentences.

spoke second

3. The alarm clock will ring any second now.

   Tracy sits in the second seat in the first row.

4. Donna spoke in a whisper.

   The wheel on Ann's bike has a broken spoke.

Working with Words

Words are sometimes easier to read if they are divided into parts called **syllables.** Some words have two consonants between two vowels. These words can be divided into syllables between the consonants, as in *ex/pect.*

In each word below, draw a line to divide the word into syllables.

1. wel|come
2. per|haps
3. for|give
4. aw|ful
5. tem|per
6. blos|som
7. traf|fic
8. bor|row

Reading and Thinking

Write **T** if the sentence is true.
Write **F** if the sentence is false.

1. T Mosh put the worms in Marie's suitcase.
2. T Marie was upset when she saw the worms.
3. T Susan thought it was funny to see the worms in the suitcase.
4. What two things did Mosh do while Carlos put the fishing poles in the car? put the worms in the suitcase, gave the suitcase to Marie
5. Why do you think Marie called Mosh a pile of bolts?

   (Answers will vary.)

6. What do you think Carlos will do after he cleans out the suitcase?

   (Answers will vary.)

Write the best word to complete each sentence below.

7. The baby was crawling through the grass. (putting, finding, crawling)
8. Jenny opened the can of soup. (opened, grumbled, stayed)
9. Rose wore a pale blue blouse. (round, pale, plenty)

Knowing the Words

Write the word from the story that has the meaning below.

1. high sounding high-pitched (Par. 3)

Circle the pair of antonyms (opposites) in each row.

2. (pushing) crying (pulling) whistling
3. soon (bent) side (straight)
4. later other (right) (wrong)
5. (started) winked (finished) cried

Working with Words

Write a contraction from the story for each pair of words below.

1. you have you've (Par. 4)
2. I am I'm (Par. 6)
3. I have I've (Par. 8)
4. had not hadn't (Par. 9)
5. could have could've (Par. 10)

Circle the correct letters to complete each word and write them in the blank.

6. Did Jennifer or Mary go f ir st?

   or (ir) ar

7. Will you or der spaghetti?

   (or) ir ar

8. Let's go ov er to my house.

   (er) ar or

9. Do you h ear any strange noises?

   are (ear) ore

Reading and Thinking

1. Number the sentences to show the order in which things happened.

   3 Mrs. Wilson caught a fish.

   1 Carlos showed Mosh how to fish.

   2 Carlos and Susan traded places with Carlos's dad.

   4 Mr. Garza sat next to Mosh.

2. Write **R** next to the two sentences that tell about real things.

   R Worms are used to catch fish.

   ___ Rainbows can be used to catch fish.

   R Fish can be on one side of a dock and not the other.

3. The fish were biting because Mosh was making a noise.

4. What do you think will happen when Carlos's dad is sitting next to Mosh?

   (Answers will vary.)

Write the best word to complete each sentence below.

5. The fish on Lin's hook was a foot long. (water, hook, lake)
6. Pat put the boat next to the dock. (dock, noise, rainbow)

Knowing the Words

Write the words from the story that have the meanings below.

1. said in a mean way snapped (Par. 6)
2. without fault innocently (Par. 8)
3. looks like appears (Par. 10)

Synonyms are words that have the same or nearly the same meaning. Circle the pair of synonyms in each row.

4. paper stuff (garbage) (trash)
5. cleaned (served) put (gave)

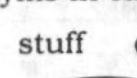
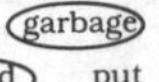

Working with Words

When a word ends with a vowel and a consonant, the consonant is usually doubled before adding **-ed** or **-ing**. For example, *snap + ed = snapped.*

Double the last consonant in the word in ( ). Then add **-ed** or **-ing** to the word to make a word that completes each sentence.

1. Are you putting that book on the shelf? (put)
2. Joan slipped on the ice. (slip)
3. Lou is always dragging that toy around. (drag)

Fill in each blank with the correct letters to make a word.

wr igh mb

4. du mb 5. wr ite 6. h igh

Reading and Thinking

1. Check the answer that tells what the story is mainly about.
   - ___ drinking lemonade
   - ✓ learning a lesson
   - ___ going to Mrs. Wilson's
2. What did Mrs. Wilson serve to the kids? lemonade
3. Why did Mosh throw Sara and Bill's cups away as soon as they were finished? Mosh knew that papers belong in the trash. (Answers may vary.)
4. What do you think Carlos meant when he called Mosh a "one-of-a-kind friend"? Mosh is Carlos's special friend. (Answers may vary.)
5. Why do you think Mosh dumped the papers in Sara's lap? (Answers will vary.)

Knowing the Words

Write the words from the story that have the meanings below.

1. talk about things that are wrong complain (Par. 3)
2. confused puzzled (Par. 4)
3. said in a low voice mumbled (Par. 6)
4. calm patient (Par. 8)

In each row below, circle the three words that belong together.

5. (taught) (learned) (remembered) have
6. hour (deliver) (newspaper) (route)
7. (phone) (ring) trash (talk)

Choose the correct word below to fill in the blanks for each pair of sentences.

ring saw

8. I saw Jill at school.
   This saw is too dull.
9. We hear the bell ring every day at noon.
   This ring does not fit my finger.

Reading and Thinking

1. Where did Carlos find the newspapers? in the trash can
2. The papers had to be delivered twice because Mosh picked them up and threw them away.

Write **T** if the sentence is true.
Write **F** if the sentence is false.

3. F Mosh helped deliver the papers.
4. T Carlos had not been delivering papers for very long.
5. F Susan told Carlos where he could find the newspapers.
6. What do you think Carlos did after he delivered the papers again? (Answers will vary.)

Learning to Study

Number each list of words below in alphabetical order.

1.		3.	
4	rush	1	finish
1	remember	2	flash
3	robot	4	friend
2	ring	3	found
2.		**4.**	
4	trash	4	mumble
1	tell	1	many
3	too	3	Mosh
2	that	2	meant

Knowing the Words

Write the word from the story that has the meaning below.

1. stopped for a moment paused (Par. 2)

Check the meaning that fits the underlined word in each sentence.

2. Sue tried to fix the clock.
   - ___ prepare
   - ✓ repair
3. The wash was hung on the fence.
   - ___ clean with water
   - ✓ clothes being cleaned

Working with Words

Write a compound word using the underlined words in each sentence.

1. A place where a bird can take a bath is a birdbath.
2. The time when you eat lunch is called lunchtime.

An 's at the end of a word is used to show that something belongs to one person or thing. To show that something belongs to more than one person or thing, an apostrophe (') is added to the end of a plural word that ends in s.

Circle each group of words below that shows that more than one person or thing owns something.

3. book's pages
4. (cars' wheels)
5. (kids' games)
6. Sara's chair

Reading and Thinking

1. Number the sentences to show the order in which things happened.
   - 3 Carlos was sprayed with water.
   - 1 Marie and Carlos agreed to baby-sit.
   - 2 Marie started to fix lunch.
   - 4 Sara apologized.
2. What kind of a person do you think Sara is? Explain your answer. (Answers will vary.)
3. Write two ways in which Sara and Bill's car wash was different from a real car wash. There was just one hose. The cars were pretend. (Answers may vary.)
4. Who turned the water on when Carlos got sprayed? Sara
5. Did Carlos stay mad at Sara? No
   How do you know? He said the water cooled him off. (Answers may vary.)

Write the best word to complete each sentence below.

6. Jane soaked the sponge in the sink. (asked, soaked, pretended)
7. Ruth cried when the bee stung her. (cried, chuckled, ate)

Knowing the Words

Write the words from the story that have the meanings below.

1. look into investigate (Par. 2)
2. wanting something that someone else has jealous (Par. 5)
3. a little bit slightly (Par. 6)
4. cloths used for drying towels (Par. 7)

Working with Words

Some words that have one consonant between two vowels are divided into syllables after the first vowel. The first vowel sound in these words is most often long, as in *bā/by*.

Other words that have one consonant between two vowels are divided after the consonant. In these words, the first vowel is most often short, as in *wăg/on*.

The words below have been divided into syllables. Put a mark above the first vowel in each word to show if the vowel stands for a long or short sound. Mark the long vowels with over the letter. Mark the short vowels with .

1. nĕv/er	4. clō/set	7. sī/lent
2. cō/zy	5. sĕv/en	8. pō/ny
3. păl/ace	6. pī/lot	9. lā/dy

Say *gentle*. Circle the words below that have the sound *g* stands for in *gentle*.

10. (cage) get (page) (hedge)
11. (giant) (age) agree gum
12. gift (edge) (engine) garden

Reading and Thinking

1. Check the answer that tells what the story is mainly about.
   - ___ playing with Mosh
   - ___ camping out
   - ✓ taking care of Fluffy
2. Why did Fluffy sit in the corner of her cage and shake? because Mosh scared her
3. Mosh put the rabbit in the closet because Mosh was jealous of Fluffy.
4. Did Mosh hurt the rabbit? No
   How do you know? The story said she was safely asleep.
5. What do you think Carlos and Mosh did after they put Fluffy back in her cage? (Answers will vary.)

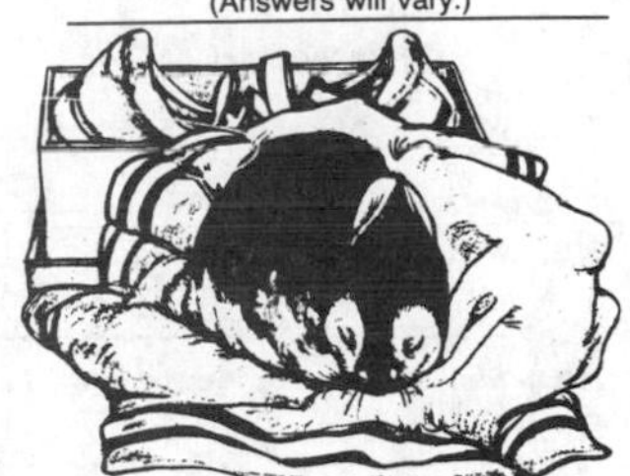

Knowing the Words

Write the words from the story that have the meanings below.

1. covered with hair furry (Par. 1)
2. dressed up so you can't be recognized disguised (Par. 8)

Circle the pair of antonyms (opposites) in each row.

3. neighbor (friend) beast (enemy)
4. (quickly) loudly (slowly) sadly
5. shaggy (soft) (hard) gentle
6. (great) huge (terrible) old

Learning to Study

The word you look up in a dictionary is called an **entry word.** Many words that have endings are not listed as entry words. To find these words, look up the base word to which the ending is added. To find the word *sighed*, look up *sigh*. Write the word under which each of these words would be listed in a dictionary.

1. wheels wheel
2. reading read
3. rolled roll
4. wanted want
5. screaming scream
6. suddenly sudden
7. directions direction

Reading and Thinking

1. How was Mosh like a pet when Carlos finished dressing it up?
   Mosh was brown and furry.
2. What did Marie say Mosh looked like? a monster
3. Mosh rolled out the door because
   Carlos said *move*.

Write **T** if the sentence is true.
Write **F** if the sentence is false.

4. T Mosh was dressed up to look like an animal.
5. T Carlos missed his friend.
6. F Carlos watched Mosh roll out of the house.
7. F The kids were afraid of Mosh's wheels.

Knowing the Words

Write the word from the story that has the meaning below.

1. things used to do a job supplies (Par. 4)

Synonyms are words that have the same or nearly the same meaning. Circle the pair of synonyms in each row.

2. spill (rush) start (hurry)
3. (stare) hide (look) push
4. suggest like (stay) (remain)

Learning to Study

At the top of each page in a dictionary are two words in dark print called **guide words.** They can help you find other words in the dictionary. The first guide word tells what the first word is on the page. The second guide word tells what the last word is on the page.

The words in a dictionary are listed in alphabetical order. To find a word, decide if it comes in alphabetical order between the guide words on the page. If it does, the word will be on that page. Check two words that could be found on each page that has these guide words.

1. **mop/nobody**
   ___ push
   ✓ named
   ✓ nervous
2. **paint/robot**
   ✓ push
   ___ sound
   ✓ principal
3. **closet/door**
   ✓ cried
   ✓ did
   ___ back
4. **school/teacher**
   ✓ surprise
   ✓ stare
   ___ thanks

Reading and Thinking

1. Number the sentences to show the order in which things happened.
   2 Mrs. Bell spilled some paint.
   4 Carlos showed the class some of the things Mosh could do.
   1 Mosh followed Carlos and Susan to school.
   3 Chad found Mosh.
2. Where did Carlos and Susan hide Mosh? in a closet with cleaning supplies
3. The children hid Mosh because there wasn't time to take Mosh home.

Write the best word to complete each sentence below.

4. Alice hung her winter coat in the closet. (sink, tent, closet)
5. Do you know the name of the principal at our school? (command, trouble, principal)

Knowing the Words

Write the words from the story that have the meanings below.

1. investigate check (Par. 3)
2. looked angry scowled (Par. 4)

Choose the correct word below to fill in the blanks for each pair of sentences.

top check

3. Leah watched the top spin.
   My paper is on top.
4. Did you check the spelling of the words in that story?
   Brenda wrote a check to pay for the movie tickets.

Learning to Study

The meanings of words can be found in the dictionary. Some words have more than one meaning. Look at the words and their meanings below. Answer the questions.

trip **1** to fall **2** journey
try to work at
tub container for water

1. Which word means "container for water"? tub
2. What does the word *try* mean? to work at
3. What is the first meaning of *trip*? to fall

Reading and Thinking

Write **T** if the sentence is true.
Write **F** if the sentence is false.

1. T Marie was baby-sitting for Carlos.
2. F Carlos was happy with the water in the bathtub.
3. T Carlos is much shorter than his dad.
4. F Carlos's parents were angry with him.
5. What was Carlos doing when Marie told him to go take a bath?
   reading a book
6. What do you think Carlos did after he spoke to his parents?
   (Answers will vary.)

Write the best word to complete each sentence below.

7. Vickie wrote a funny story about a robot. (menu, story, word)
8. Put the shirt in the drawer when you take it off. (drawer, bathtub, garage)
9. I can't understand when you mumble. (laugh, mumble, ask)
10. I think I should wear my brown pants today. (hurry, hear, wear)

Knowing the Words

Write the words from the story that have the meanings below.

1. a special way things are arranged order (Par. 2)
2. doing with others sharing (Par. 3)
3. small sack pouch (Par. 7)

Working with Words

A **prefix** is a group of letters added to the beginning of a word that changes the meaning of the word. The prefix **re-** means "again." *Rewire* means "wire again."

Read the words below. Write the correct word next to its meaning.

reread reorder reteach rewrap

1. teach again reteach
2. order again reorder
3. read again reread
4. wrap again rewrap

Most words that end in a consonant followed by *y* are made plural by changing the *y* to *i* and adding *es*. The plural of *city* is *cities*. Write the plural form of each word below.

5. baby babies
6. company companies
7. penny pennies

Reading and Thinking

1. Check the answer that tells what the story is mainly about.
   ✓ trying to fool the class
   ___ teaching Mosh to speak
   ___ dropping the question cards

Write **T** if the sentence is true.
Write **F** if the sentence is false.

2. T Carlos was trying to teach Lizzy Wood a lesson.
3. T When Carlos picked up his cards, they were not in the right order.
4. F Something was wrong with the tape player inside Mosh.
5. T Carlos's trick taught him a lesson.

Write the best word to complete each sentence below.

6. During the show, Pat made a penny vanish. (sing, vanish, wish)
7. Elsa dropped her books on the way to school. (dropped, played, roared)
8. Please write one question to ask our guest. (card, answer, question)
9. Jamie gave a clever answer. (honor, hollow, clever)
10. The children's laughter filled the room. (laughter, book, tape)

Knowing the Words

Write the words from the story that have the meanings below.

1. worried ___nervous___ (Par. 1)
2. what a person in a play says and does ___part___ (Par. 2)
3. let down: unhappy ___disappointed___ (Par. 6)

Check the meaning that fits the underlined word in each sentence.

4. Carrie went to the park to play.
   ✓ have fun
   ___ a show on stage
5. Did Janice eat part of this apple?
   ___ in a play
   ✓ a small piece of something
6. Did you hear the limb snap?
   ✓ break suddenly
   ___ speak angrily

Working with Words

Write the two words that were used to form each of these contractions.

1. I'm ___I am___
2. you're ___you are___
3. we'll ___we will *or* we shall___
4. isn't ___is not___
5. don't ___do not___
6. doesn't ___does not___

Reading and Thinking

1. Check the answer that tells what the story is mainly about.
   ✓ getting a part in the school play
   ___ Lizzy's part in the play
   ___ walking to school
2. Write two words to describe Lizzy.
   ___(Answers will vary.)___
3. Carlos wasn't sure he would get to be the captain in the play because ___Lizzy tried out, too, and she was very good___.
4. What part was Lizzy asked to play?
   ___first officer___
5. Why was Lizzy unhappy? ___She wanted to be the captain.___

Knowing the Words

Write the words from the story that have the meanings below.

1. awfully ___terribly___ (Par. 3)
2. earned ___deserved___ (Par. 8)
3. in an excited way ___dramatically___ (Par. 8)

In each row below, circle the three words that belong together.

4. (stage) (curtain) sky (play)
5. (blast-off) sick (spaceship) (maps)
6. (friends) (Mosh) (Carlos) stage

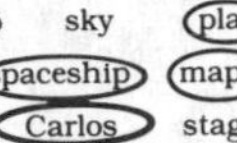

Working with Words

Write a compound word using the underlined words in each sentence.

1. A ship used to travel in space is a ___spaceship___.
2. Corn that will pop when it is heated is ___popcorn___.
3. A game in which a ball is kicked with the foot is ___football___.

Circle the correct word in ( ) and write it in the blank.

4. Jeanne drew a ___circle___ on the card. ((circle) correct)
5. The ___ice___ in my glass melted. (act, (ice))

Reading and Thinking

1. Number the sentences to show the order in which things happened.
   _1_ Mosh chased Lizzy around the stage.
   _3_ Carlos pulled out Mosh's battery.
   _2_ Lizzy yelled for help.
   _4_ Lizzy apologized.

Write **T** if the sentence is true.
Write **F** if the sentence is false.

2. _F_ Mosh was disobeying on purpose.
3. _T_ Lizzy was frightened when Mosh chased her around the stage.
4. _T_ Carlos rescued Lizzy.
5. _F_ Carlos planned to take Mosh's battery out during the play.
6. _T_ Carlos forgave Lizzy.
7. Write **R** next to the two sentences that tell about real things.
   ___ Robots get sick.
   _R_ Robots can be in plays.
   _R_ Robots can run on batteries.

Read each sentence and fill in the blank.

8. The people laughed because they enjoyed the play.
   They stands for ___people___.
9. Lizzy screamed when she needed help.
   She stands for ___Lizzy___.

Knowing the Words

Write the words from the story that have the meanings below.

1. part of the body where legs begin ___hips___ (Par. 4)
2. pulling toward something ___attracting___ (Par. 6)
3. wishing for something ___hopefully___ (Par. 7)

Check the meaning that fits the underlined word in each sentence.

4. Pam ate an orange for lunch.
   ___ a color
   ✓ fruit
5. Please point to the problem you are working on.
   ✓ show with a finger
   ___ a dot
6. We bought bread at the store.
   ✓ place to buy food
   ___ save for later

Reading and Thinking

1. Check the answer that tells what the story is mainly about.
   ___ hundreds of oranges
   ___ an angry woman
   ✓ trouble in the grocery store
2. The woman screamed because ___Mosh was scaring her___.
3. What did Carlos put on the crackers?
   ___cheese___
4. How might this story have ended if Mosh had been left at home?
   ___(Answers will vary.)___
5. Was Mr. Johnson angry at the end of the story? Explain your answer.
   ___(Answers will vary.)___

Learning to Study

Number each list of words below in alphabetical order.

1. _5_ attract
   _3_ ask
   _1_ again
   _2_ angry
   _4_ ate

2. _3_ hundred
   _1_ hand
   _2_ hip
   _4_ hurt
   _5_ hush

Knowing the Words

Write the words from the story that have the meanings below.

1. two-way radios ___walkie-talkies___ (Par. 1)
2. very dirty ___filthy___ (Par. 7)

Synonyms are words that have the same or nearly the same meaning. Write **S** after each pair of synonyms. Write **A** after each pair of antonyms (opposites).

3. bought—sold _A_
4. yell—whisper _A_
5. tiny—little _S_
6. glad—happy _S_
7. back—front _A_
8. filthy—dirty _S_
9. loud—soft _A_
10. dirt—soil _S_

Working with Words

Write the two words that were used to form each of these contractions.

1. it's ___it is *or* it has___
2. he's ___he is *or* he has___
3. I'll ___I will *or* I shall___
4. doesn't ___does not___
5. there's ___there is *or* there has___
6. I've ___I have___
7. let's ___let us___

Reading and Thinking

1. Number the sentences to show the order in which things happened.
   _2_ Mosh swept up the screws to the walkie-talkies.
   _3_ Carlos searched through the dirt for the screws.
   _4_ Mrs. Garza came home.
   _1_ Carlos showed Mosh how to clean the carpet.
2. Where was Mrs. Garza when the story began? ___at the office___
3. Check one answer that tells how Mrs. Garza probably got to work.
   ✓ in a car
   ___ on a bus
4. What chore was Carlos doing? ___washing the dishes___

Write the best word to complete each sentence below.

5. Adam could not find a broom to ___sweep___ the sidewalk. (empty, feel, sweep)
6. There is a blue ___carpet___ in the living room. (dirt, carpet, noise)
7. You cannot ___vacuum___ the rug with a broom. (vacuum, find, help)

Knowing the Words

Write the word from the story that has the meaning below.

1. saw spotted (Par. 3)

Write the word with the correct meaning to complete each sentence below.

2. Did you see tigers and elephants at the zoo? (sea, see)
3. Jeannette has a new notebook. (new, knew)
4. We saw a herd of cows in the pasture. (heard, herd)

Learning to Study

A **table of contents** is one of the first pages in a book. It shows the chapters that are in the book and on what page each one begins. Use the table of contents below to answer the questions.

How to Build a Robot

Table of Contents

1. How many chapters are in this book? five
2. What is the third chapter called? Building the Robot
3. On what page does the fourth chapter begin? 23

Reading and Thinking

1. Check the answer that tells what the story is mainly about.
   - √ saving a child from harm
   - ___ bouncing a ball
   - ___ climbing a tree
2. Who was Kevin? a boy who lived in Carlos's neighborhood
3. Why did Kevin run back toward his house? He was afraid of Mosh.
4. Check two sentences that tell about both Susan and Kevin.
   - √ They lived near Carlos.
   - √ They were playing outside.
   - ___ They cried when they ran away from Mosh.
5. What might have happened if Mosh had not scared Kevin? (Answers will vary.)

Knowing the Words

Write the words from the story that have the meanings below.

1. moved shoulders up and down shrugged (Par. 1)
2. looked quickly peeked (Par. 2)

In each row below, circle the three words that belong together.

3. (garage) (car) sky (driveway)
4. (curb) (concrete) (street) grass
5. ladder (minutes) (time) (clock)
6. (tag) (game) (fun) mess
7. (shovel) (snow) (ice) night

Learning to Study

An **index** is a part of a book. It lists a book's topics in alphabetical order. It also lists page numbers so you can find those topics. An index is usually found at the back of a book. Use the index below from a book of games to answer the questions.

1. On what pages could you find out how to play tag? 6, 12, and 21
2. On what pages could you find out about tennis? 5 and 10–11
3. On what page could you find rules? 24

Reading and Thinking

Write **T** if the sentence is true.
Write **F** if the sentence is false.

1. T Carlos was upset when Mosh was missing.
2. F Lizzy took Mosh to hurt Carlos's feelings.
3. F Carlos told Mosh to take things out of Lizzy's garage to help her.
4. F Carlos watched Lizzy put everything back in her garage.
5. How do you think Mosh got in Lizzy's yard? Lizzy took it there.
6. What game did Lizzy want to play with Mosh? tag

Write the best word to complete each sentence below.

7. Agnes searched all over the house to find her clay. (heard, touched, searched)
8. We rode our bikes to the store. (airplanes, bikes, kites)

Knowing the Words

Write the word from the story that has the meaning below.

1. ability to move without slipping traction (Par. 4)

Check the meaning that fits the underlined word in each sentence.

2. Swing at the baseball with the bat.
   - √ strike at
   - ___ seat that moves back and forth
3. Don't dump that dirt in the driveway.
   - √ unload
   - ___ place for trash
4. I ate a roll with my dinner.
   - ___ turn over and over
   - √ bread

Working with Words

Write a compound word using the underlined words in each sentence.

1. A storm in which snow falls is a snowstorm.
2. A drift made of snow is a snowdrift.

Circle the correct word in ( ) and write it in the blank.

3. Three inches of snow fell yesterday. (saw, (snow))
4. Please scoop out two cups of oatmeal. ((scoop), skip)

Reading and Thinking

1. Check the answer that tells what the story is mainly about.
   - ___ drawing in the snow
   - √ shoveling snow
   - ___ getting too cold
2. Number the sentences to show the order in which things happened.
   - 3 Carlos drew a face in the snow.
   - 2 Carlos put chains on Mosh's wheels.
   - 4 Mosh dumped snow down Carlos's back.
   - 1 Marie's hands got cold.
3. Marie wanted Mosh to help because her hands were cold.
4. Why did Carlos put chains on Mosh's wheels? so Mosh could move in the snow
5. Where did Carlos get the chains for Mosh? from an old swing
6. What was Carlos going to draw in the snow after he drew the silly face? Mosh
7. What do you think Carlos did after Mosh threw the snow on him? (Answers will vary.)

Knowing the Words

Write the words from the story that have the meanings below.

1. leader of a city mayor (Par. 3)
2. carving; statue sculpture (Par. 3)
3. deciding in a contest judging (Par. 6)

Working with Words

Rewrite the following groups of words using 's or s' to show who owns something. The first one is done for you.

house that belongs to Susan
Susan's house

1. announcement made by the mayor mayor's announcement
2. sculpture that belongs to the kids kids' sculpture
3. eyes that belong to the sculpture sculpture's eyes

Circle the correct letters to complete each word and write them in the blank.

4. I felt bett er after my nap.
   or ar (er)
5. Snow fell early this m or ning.
   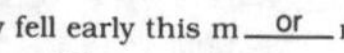
   (or) ar er
6. Who will c ar ve this soap?
   or (ar) er

Reading and Thinking

Write **T** if the sentence is true.
Write **F** if the sentence is false.

1. T This story takes place in the winter.
2. F The snowstorm knocked down the telephone lines to Carlos's house.
3. T Susan made up a new word.
4. F The kids took more than two hours to finish their snowbot.
5. Write **M** next to the sentence that tells about something make-believe.
   - ___ You could make a robot out of snow.
   - M Robots can cry like people.
   - ___ Tennis balls can be colored green.

Write the best word to complete each sentence below.

6. I made a sculpture of a horse in art class. (mayor, marker, sculpture)
7. What color was the ribbon that you won? (ribbon, sound, yard)

Knowing the Words

Write the word from the story that has the meaning below.

1 someone who rides with someone else passenger (Par. 11)

Circle the pair of antonyms (opposites) in each row.

2. slower faster bigger larger
3. closed dragged ordered opened
4. huge tiny under down

Working with Words

When a word ends with *e*, the *e* is usually dropped before adding **-ed** or **-ing**. For example, *like* + *ed* = *liked*.

Add **-ed** or **-ing** to the word in ( ) to make a word that completes each sentence.

1. My mom rescued the cat from the tree. (rescue)
2. Why are you staring at the wall? (stare)
3. We should start closing the doors now. (close)

The prefix **un-** means "not." *Unsure* means "not sure." Add **un-** to the words below. Use the new words to complete the sentences.

even happy

4. Barb was unhappy about losing the game.
5. The top of that table looks uneven.

Reading and Thinking

1. Check the answer that tells what the story is mainly about.
   ___ rolling through the snow
   ___ running into a snowdrift
   ✓ sledding down the hill
2. Where did the kids go sledding? a hill on Pine Street
3. What helped Mosh roll through the snow? chains on its wheels
4. What might have happened if Carlos and Mosh had not run into a snowdrift? (Answers will vary.)
5. What do you think Carlos and Susan did when they were done sledding? (Answers will vary.)

Knowing the Words

Write the words from the story that have the meanings below.

1. was able managed (Par. 2)
2. got out escaped (Par. 2)
3. monster beast (Par. 5)

Choose the correct word to fill in the blanks for each pair of sentences.

duck light close

4. Who left the light on in the garage?
   The canoe was light enough to carry.
5. The duck flew over the pond.
   Kim needs to duck to get through the opening.
6. Please close the window.
   Do not get too close to the parade.

Reading and Thinking

1. Number the sentences to show the order in which things happened.
   3 Carlos saw the thing that had been chasing him.
   1 Carlos ran into the house.
   2 Carlos ran into a cave.
   4 Carlos woke up.

Write **T** if the sentence is true.
Write **F** if the sentence is false.

2. F Carlos was camping out.
3. T Carlos woke up during the night.
4. T Mosh put the desk in front of the bedroom door.
5. F Carlos really caught a butterfly in his net.

Learning to Study

Number each list of words below in alphabetical order.

1. 1 cold, 4 corner, 3 cool, 5 cozy, 2 comb
2. 5 desk, 1 deck, 3 delight, 4 depend, 2 deer
3. 1 sleep, 4 still, 5 stop, 3 small, 2 slip
4. 4 woods, 2 window, 1 will, 3 won, 5 worry

Knowing the Words

Write the words from the story that have the meanings below.

1. directions for preparing food recipe (Par. 2)
2. mixture batter (Par. 5)
3. tool used in cooking measuring cup (Par. 6)

In each row below, circle the three words that belong together.

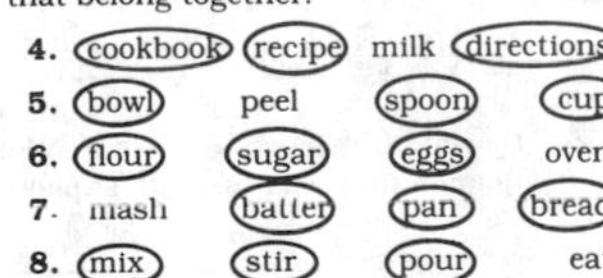

4. cookbook recipe milk directions
5. bowl peel spoon cup
6. flour sugar eggs oven
7. mash batter pan bread
8. mix stir pour eat

Write the word with the correct meaning to complete each sentence below.

9. Who threw that ball? (threw, through)
10. Connie tried some of the fresh bread. (sum, some)
11. Please pour the milk now. (poor, pour)
12. Can you add ten and twelve? (add, ad)
13. Val made pizza in school today. (made, maid)
14. The flower grew through a crack in the street. (flour, flower)

Reading and Thinking

1. Write three things that were needed to make banana bread. bowl, spoon, (Accept any three answers.) recipe, bananas, flour, sugar, milk, eggs, pan, oven, measuring cup
2. How did Carlos know how to make bread? He had a recipe.
3. What room do you think Carlos and Mosh were in? the kitchen

Learning to Study

Use the table of contents below to answer the questions.

Robot Recipes

Table of Contents

1. What is the fourth chapter called? Vegetable Dishes
2. On what page does the chapter about soups begin? 41
3. In what chapter could you find how to make nut bread? Breads or Chapter One

Knowing the Words

Write the words from the story that have the meanings below.

1. keep from happening prevent (Par. 1)
2. forgive excuse (Par. 2)
3. spoiled ruined (Par. 7)

Synonyms are words that have the same or nearly the same meaning. Circle the pair of synonyms in each row.

4. ended finished begun baked
5. wish wash clean learn
6. laughing crying chuckling sleeping
7. showed cooked baked made

Learning to Study

Use the cookbook index below to answer the questions.

1. On what page would you look to find out about making banana nut bread? 27
2. On what pages would you find recipes for buns? 28, 31, and 33
3. On what pages could you find out about how to bake? 6–10
4. On what pages could you find out how to make biscuits? 38–40

Reading and Thinking

1. Check the answer that tells what the story is mainly about.
   ✓ surprising Mr. Garza
   ___ watching TV
   ___ mopping up water
2. Carlos said "Excuse us" when he left the table because he was being polite (Answers may vary.).
3. Why did Mosh pour water on the candles? to put the fire out (Answers may vary.)
4. Check three words that tell about Mr. Garza.
   ✓ pleasant ✓ patient
   ___ frantic ✓ kind
5. What kind of person do you think Mrs. Garza is? Explain your answer. (Answers will vary.)

Write the best word to complete each sentence below.

6. Sean tries to prevent accidents by being careful. (watch, prevent, surprise)
7. Joy got muddy when she stepped in the puddle. (candle, pool, puddle)

Knowing the Words

Write the words from the story that have the meanings below.

1. upset bothered (Par. 1)
2. given too much spoiled (Par. 1)

Working with Words

Circle the correct letters to complete each word and write them in the blank.

1. Did the elephants sc are you?
   ur **are** ear
2. I forgot to t ur n off the radio.
   ur are ear
3. Our dog b ar ked all night.
   er or **ar**
4. Jo cut her fing er on the broken glass.
   er or ar
5. My shoes are very d ir ty.
   or **ir** ar

The suffix **-ful** means "full of." *Careful* means "full of care." Add **-ful** to the words below. Use the new words to complete the sentences.

help joy fear

6. The team members were joyful that they won the game.
7. I try to be helpful by cleaning up my room.
8. Stacy is fearful of loud noises.

Reading and Thinking

1. Number the sentences to show the order in which things happened.
   4 Mosh rolled into the corner and turned off its lights.
   3 Mr. Garza opened the closet door.
   2 Aunt Laura screamed.
   1 Carlos tried to go to sleep.
2. What was Mosh getting out of Carlos's room? a book
3. Who is Sweetie? Aunt Laura's dog
4. What do you think Carlos did when he got back to the den after being in Aunt Laura's room? (Answers will vary.)
5. What do you think Aunt Laura did after everyone left her room? (Answers will vary.)

Knowing the Words

Write the words from the story that have the meanings below.

1. chain or rope used to walk a dog leash (Par. 3)
2. answered replied (Par. 10)

Working with Words

Write the two words that were used to form each of these contractions.

1. wouldn't would not
2. haven't have not
3. didn't did not

Write a compound word using the underlined words in each sentence.

4. A <u>book</u> used to <u>cook</u> with is a cookbook.
5. A <u>ball</u> made of <u>snow</u> is a snowball.

Circle the correct word in ( ) and write it in the blank.

6. The huge balloon floated over the fairgrounds. (hug **huge**)
7. The first page has a picture of a lion on it. (**page** pig)
8. A robin's egg is a beautiful color of blue. (**egg** edge)

Reading and Thinking

Write **T** if the sentence is true.
Write **F** if the sentence is false.

1. T Carlos felt sad that Mosh had to stay in the garage.
2. F Mosh had hurt Sweetie.
3. F Sweetie was licking Mosh because he enjoyed the taste of metal.
4. T Mosh and Sweetie spent a lot of time together after the first walk.
5. Check the sentence that tells how Mosh and Sweetie are alike.
   ___ They both had wheels.
   ___ They both barked.
   √ They both belonged to people.

Circle the name or names that each underlined word stands for.

6. "<u>I</u> want that robot out of here," said Aunt Laura.
   Carlos Mosh **Aunt Laura**
7. "<u>We</u> can go for a walk," Carlos told Mosh.
   Mosh and Sweetie **Carlos and Mosh** Carlos and Aunt Laura
8. "<u>They</u> are my friends," Carlos said, pointing to Susan and Mosh.
   Susan and Mosh Susan and Carlos Carlos and Mosh
9. "<u>You</u> can ride along," Carlos said to Marie.
   Carlos **Marie** Mosh

Knowing the Words

Write the word from the story that has the meaning below.

1. in good health well (Par. 1)

Check the meaning that fits the underlined word in each sentence.

2. Please fill my <u>glass</u> with milk.
   √ container for holding liquids
   ___ a mirror
3. That is a <u>great</u> idea for a story.
   ___ very large
   √ excellent
4. <u>Fall</u> begins in September.
   √ season
   ___ to hit the ground

Working with Words

The ending **-er** sometimes means "more." It may be used to compare two things. The ending **-est** means "most." It is used to compare more than two things.

In each sentence below, add **-er** to the word before the blank if two things are being compared. Add **-est** if more than two things are being compared.

1. That was the great est movie I have ever seen.
2. An ant is small er than a bee.
3. Lynne is old er than I.
4. Heather is the quiet est person in our class.
5. An orange is sweet er than a lemon.

Reading and Thinking

1. Check the answer that tells what the story is mainly about.
   ___ eating soup
   √ having a robot nurse
   ___ staying home from school
2. Carlos had to stay home from school because he was ill (Answers may vary.).
3. What did Mosh bring instead of juice? water
4. Who was taking care of Carlos? Mosh and Mrs. Wilson

Write the best word to complete each sentence below.

5. I have an extra pen you may use. (extra, eager, ill)
6. I was so thirsty I drank a large glass of cold milk. (hungry, thirsty, sleepy)
7. The juice was made from fruit. (water, juice, milk)

Knowing the Words

Write the words from the story that have the meanings below.

1. lying around spread (Par. 6)
2. scattering water splashing (Par. 6)
3. wonderful marvelous (Par. 9)

Circle the pair of antonyms (opposites) in each row.

4. **morning** noon **night** late
5. soapy **clean** **dirty** terrible
6. **messy** lucky careful **neat**

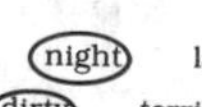

Working with Words

The words below have been divided into syllables. Put a mark above the first vowel to show the sound it stands for. Mark the long vowels with ¯ over the letter. Mark the short vowels with ˘.

1. mĭn/ute	5. răp/id	9. rō/bot
2. bā/by	6. fī/nal	10. măn/age
3. ŏ/ver	7. pā/per	11. sĕc/ond
4. lā/ter	8. văn/ish	12. fĭn/ish

Fill in each blank with the correct letters to make a word that completes each sentence below.

mb kn wr

13. Did you see a wr en fly by the window?
14. The plu mb er fixed the leaky pipe.
15. The sharp kn ife cut through the meat.

Reading and Thinking

Write **T** if the sentence is true.
Write **F** if the sentence is false.

1. T Carlos had not expected Mosh to do such a good job mopping.
2. T Mosh tried to wash the dishes and the floor the same way.
3. T Marie thought it was funny that Mosh was making a mess.
4. Carlos did not stay to watch Mosh mop the floor because he had to clean his room.
5. Do you think Mosh will ever be asked to wash the dishes again? Explain your answer. (Answers will vary.)
6. What do you think Carlos did after he finished washing the dishes? (Answers will vary.)

Knowing the Words

Write the words from the story that have the meanings below.

1. used for baking baking soda *or* soda (Par. 5)
2. mistakes mix-ups (Par. 11)
3. told of trouble ahead of time warned (Par. 12)

Working with Words

Circle the correct word in ( ) and write it in the blank.

1. Mosh is a robot and not a toy. (**toy** today)
2. The bath powder made Joyce sneeze. (pour, **powder**)
3. I forgot to wear my coat to school today. (cat, **coat**)
4. Justin bought his lunch. (**bought** boat)

To form the plural of a word that ends in *f* or *fe*, the *f* or *fe* is changed to *v*, and *es* is added. Form the plural of each word below.

5. life lives
6. calf calves
7. scarf scarves
8. loaf loaves
9. elf elves

Reading and Thinking

1. Number the sentences to show the order in which things happened.
   - 3 Mosh put out the candles.
   - 2 Carlos took the guests' coats.
   - 4 The guests came to the table.
   - 1 The guests arrived.
2. Write the name of one of the Garzas' guests. Mrs. Chung
3. What two things were in the middle of the dinner table? candles and flowers
4. The flames on the candles went out because Mosh put baking soda on them.

Write the best word to complete each sentence below.

5. Sara invited me to her birthday party. (laughed, poured, invited)
6. Last night we had potatoes for dinner. (breakfast, dinner, lunch)
7. Alice arrived just when the bell rang. (arrived, liked, lit)
8. The loud horn warned us that a tornado was coming. (heard, whispered, warned)

Knowing the Words

Write the words from the story that have the meanings below.

1. missing gone (Par. 3)
2. chest of drawers dresser (Par. 10)
3. pleasant delightful (Par. 12)

Synonyms are words that have the same or nearly the same meaning. Circle the pair of synonyms in each row.

4. look **find** **discover** lose
5. **idea** problem **thought** question
6. found forget **gone** **missing**

Working with Words

Rewrite the following groups of words using *'s* or *s'* to show who owns something.

1. coats that belong to the guests guests' coats
2. bedroom that belongs to Carlos Carlos's bedroom

Circle the correct letters to complete each word and write them in the blank.

3. Where is your oth**er** glove? ar **er** or
4. Will you please f**or**give me? ar er **or**
5. Are you going to the p**ar**ty? **ar** er or

Reading and Thinking

1. Check the answer that tells what the story is mainly about.
   - ✓ finding the lost coats
   - ___ apologizing to the guests
   - ___ forgetting the party

Write **T** if the sentence is true.
Write **F** if the sentence is false.

2. T Carlos did not want the guests to know their coats were lost.
3. F Marie thought it was funny that the coats were missing.
4. T Marie helped find the coats.
5. T Mrs. Chung is a polite person.
6. Where did Carlos and Marie find the coats? in drawers
7. What did it mean when Mr. Garza winked? (Answers will vary.)
8. What do you think Carlos did after the guests left? (Answers will vary.)
9. Do you think the Garzas will have another party? Explain your answer. (Answers will vary.)

Knowing the Words

Write the words from the story that have the meanings below.

1. all things not made by humans nature (Par. 1)
2. not comfortably uneasily (Par. 2)
3. long walk hike (Par. 4)
4. chase away shoo (Par. 13)

Write the words with the correct meaning to complete each sentence below.

5. Kathy lost a shoe down by the pond. (shoo, shoe)
6. I know where to find deer. (know, no)
7. There are four pears on the ground. (four, for)
8. I have to walk home after school. (too, to, two)
9. We will return in one hour. (won, one)
10. The children lost their balloons. (there, their)

Reading and Thinking

1. Carlos thought the frogs were croaking loudly because they didn't like the cold water.
2. Why wouldn't Carlos let Mosh go on the hike? It would be too hard for Mosh to move.
3. How else might the boys have gotten the frogs out of the tent? (Answers will vary.)

Write the best word to complete each sentence below.

4. Roger was waving at the people on the ship. (waving, complaining, hiking)
5. The frog hopped off the rock and into the water. (snake, tent, frog)

Learning to Study

A dictionary entry shows the words divided into syllables. A space or a dot shows where the word can be divided at the end of a line of writing.

Read the words below. Next to each, write the number of syllables it has.

1. na ture 2
2. un eas y 3
3. wa ter 2
4. stom ach 2
5. min ute 2
6. grum ble 2

Knowing the Words

Write the words from the story that have the meanings below.

1. wanders roams (Par. 3)
2. more nervous jumpier (Par. 8)

Working with Words

When a word ends in a consonant followed by *y*, the *y* is changed to *i* before **-er** and **-est** is added. Change the *y* to *i* in each word in ( ). Add **-er** or **-est** to make a word that completes the sentence. The first one is done for you.

Hope's tale was *scarier* than Jeff's. (scary)

1. I am hungrier now than I was an hour ago. (hungry)
2. That is the ugliest bug of all. (ugly)
3. A rose is the prettiest flower I've ever seen. (pretty)

The suffix **-less** means "without." *Joyless* means "without joy." Add **-less** to the following words. Use the new words to complete the sentences.

sleep care home

4. The homeless kitten looked hungry and cold.
5. I had a sleepless night because of a barking dog.
6. Because Donna was careless, she got paint on her clothes.

Reading and Thinking

1. Number the sentences to show the order in which things happened.
   - 3 Carlos saw glowing green spots.
   - 1 Jake told a scary story.
   - 2 Jake fell asleep.
   - 4 The boys found out that the creature was Mosh.
2. Carlos was afraid because he had heard a scary story.
3. Who was camping with the boys? Mosh *or* Mr. Jones *or* both
4. What did Carlos hear that frightened him? an owl hoot
5. How did Carlos feel when he saw the shadow? Explain your answer. (Answers will vary.)
6. How do you think Carlos felt when he found out that the creature was Mosh? Explain your answer. (Answers will vary.)

Knowing the Words

Write the words from the story that have the meanings below.

1. visit to someplace with a group ___field trip___ (Par. 2)
2. jumped ___leapt___ (Par. 2)
3. tasty ___delicious___ (Par. 3)

Working with Words

Sometimes the plural form of a word is made by changing the spelling of the word. The plural form of *goose* is *geese*.

Use the plural words below to complete the sentences.

mice women feet children

1. Two ___mice___ live in a cage in our classroom.
2. These tennis shoes are too small for Kay's ___feet___.
3. Twenty ___children___ rode on a bus to the zoo.
4. My older sister and my mother are ___women___.

Fill in each blank with the correct letters to make a word that completes each sentence below.

ph wr

5. There is a ___wr___inkle in my shirt.
6. Can you say the al___ph___abet backwards?

Reading and Thinking

Write **T** if the sentence is true.
Write **F** if the sentence is false.

1. ___T___ Carlos had overslept.
2. ___T___ It took Carlos five minutes to get dressed.
3. ___T___ The class might have seen an ostrich at the zoo.
4. ___F___ Susan thought a Mosh special looked delicious.
5. ___T___ Carlos thought the sandwich would be tasty.
6. What did Mosh put in the sandwich? ___tuna fish, peanut butter, bananas, mustard, and pickles___
7. What do you think the class did when they finished eating? ___(Answers will vary.)___
8. Do you think Mosh will be allowed to make another sandwich? Explain your answer. ___(Answers will vary.)___

Knowing the Words

Write the word from the story that has the meaning below.

1. pleased ___impressed___ (Par. 1)

Synonyms are words that have the same or nearly the same meaning. Circle the pair of synonyms in each row.

2. box (gift) paper (present)
3. (terrible) (awful) sad brave
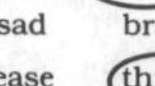
4. hope (imagine) tease (think)

Working with Words

Write a compound word using the underlined words in each sentence.

1. The day of your birth is your ___birthday___.
2. A fish the color of gold is a ___goldfish___.
3. Paper with sand on it is called ___sandpaper___.
4. An ache in your head is a ___headache___.
5. Light from the moon is called ___moonlight___.

In each word below, draw a line to divide the word into syllables.

6. con|fuse
7. rib|bon
8. al|most
9. pil|low
10. jour|ney
11. les|son

Reading and Thinking

1. Check the answer that tells what the story is mainly about.
   - ___ saying good-bye to Mosh
   - ___ selling Mosh to Mrs. Chung
   - ___✓___ having a party for Mosh
2. What did Marie give to Carlos for Mosh? ___lights for eyes___
3. What was Mrs. Garza's gift? ___a battery and a note___
4. What do you think Carlos and Mosh did after the party? ___(Answers will vary.)___

Write the best word to complete each sentence.

5. The crowd ___cheered___ loudly for the team. (teased, thought, cheered)
6. When I close my eyes, it is easy to ___imagine___ I am a bird. (imagine, sell, mention)
7. A small ___package___ came in the mail today. (hug, cheer, package)
8. Can you ___explain___ how to wrap a present? (explain, want, open)
9. After the long walk, Marge was very ___tired___. (nice, tired, brave)

Knowing the Words

Write the words from the story that have the meanings below.

1. jumping ___bounding___ (Par. 3)
2. pipe that water comes out of ___faucet___ (Par. 4)
3. ran quickly ___scrambled___ (Par. 4)
4. turned quickly ___whirled___ (Par. 6)

Some words sound alike but have different spellings and meanings. Write the word with the correct meaning to complete each sentence below.

5. Those ___stairs___ lead to the attic. (stares, stairs)
6. Please ___close___ the garage door. (close, clothes)

Working with Words

Circle the correct word in ( ) and write it in the blank.

1. Do not get ___soap___ in your eyes when you wash. (soup, (soap))
2. They ___caught___ the butterfly in a net. ((caught), cat)
3. I'll need a ___broom___ to clean up this powder. ((broom), brim)
4. Can you ___reach___ that bottle of shampoo? (rich, (reach))

Reading and Thinking

1. Check the answer that tells what the story is mainly about.
   - ___ a pile of dirty clothes
   - ___✓___ a bath for Herbie
   - ___ two messes
2. Herbie ran away because ___he hated water___. (Answers may vary.)
3. Put a check beside something that was probably in Tracy's basement.
   - ___ a car
   - ___✓___ a washing machine
   - ___ a mailbox
4. Put a check beside the two answers that tell where Herbie hid.
   - ___ in the living room
   - ___✓___ in the pile of dirty clothes
   - ___✓___ beside the refrigerator
5. What did Tracy mean when she said that there were two messes to clean? ___They had to clean Herbie and the floor.___
6. How do you think Rick and Tracy will clean the basement floor? ___(Answers will vary.)___

Knowing the Words

Write the words from the story that have the meanings below.

1. tennis shoes ___sneakers___ (Par. 1)
2. made less tight ___loosened___ (Par. 1)
3. strings used for tying ___laces___ (Par. 1)
4. tiny pieces of wood ___splinters___ (Par. 7)

Check the meaning that fits the underlined word in each sentence.

5. Roll the ball across the floor.
   - ___ bread
   - ___✓___ move by turning
6. Did you hurt your foot?
   - ___✓___ part of the body
   - ___ twelve inches
7. I have sand in my shoe.
   - ___ to make smooth
   - ___✓___ tiny bits of stone

Working with Words

An 's at the end of a word may be used to show that something belongs to someone. Add 's to each name below and write the new word in the correct blank.

Mr. Levi Skipper Elsa

1. ___Mr. Levi's___ lumber
2. ___Elsa's___ skateboard
3. ___Skipper's___ doghouse

Reading and Thinking

1. Number the sentences to show the order in which things happened.
   - ___4___ Elsa rolled down the street on her skateboard.
   - ___2___ Mr. Levi gave the girls a piece of wood.
   - ___1___ Elsa discovered that her skates didn't fit.
   - ___3___ The girls attached the skate wheels to the board.
2. Check the sentence that tells why Elsa couldn't get her skates on.
   - ___ Her skates had shrunk.
   - ___ Her socks were too thick.
   - ___✓___ Her feet had grown.
3. Check two words that tell about Mr. Levi.
   - ___✓___ helpful
   - ___ selfish
   - ___ grouchy
   - ___✓___ friendly
4. Check two sentences that tell how Elsa's skateboard and roller skates were alike.
   - ___ They both had laces.
   - ___✓___ They both had screws.
   - ___✓___ They both had wheels.
   - ___ They both were made of wood.

Knowing the Words

Write the words from the story that have the meanings below.

1. large truck __van__ (Par. 1)
2. noise __racket__ (Par. 1)

Abbreviations are shortened forms of words. The abbreviation for *inch* is *in.* Match each word from the first list with its abbreviation from the second list.

3. __b__ street — a. mi.
4. __c__ Mister — b. st.
5. __a__ mile — c. Mr.

Learning to Study

A **table of contents** is on one of the first pages in a book. It shows the chapters that are in the book and on what page each one begins. Use the table of contents below to answer the questions.

All About Dogs

Table of Contents

1. How many chapters are in the book? __four__
2. What is the first chapter called? __Kinds of Dogs__
3. On what page does "Dogs as Pets" begin? __page 21__

Reading and Thinking

1. Check the answer that tells what the story is mainly about.
   - __✓__ meeting new neighbors
   - ____ watching movers
   - ____ noises in the alley
2. Check the two sentences that tell about Tracy.
   - __✓__ She likes to meet people.
   - __✓__ She is a good neighbor.
   - ____ She does not like dogs.

Write **T** if the sentence is true.
Write **F** if the sentence is false.

3. __F__ Dale knocked the garbage can over.
4. __F__ Tracy could easily walk to Oak Hill.
5. __T__ Tracy thought Rags was lost.
6. __F__ Tracy wanted to keep Rags.
7. How far had Lindsay and Dale moved from their old home? __about 100 miles__

Write the best word to complete each sentence below.

8. The __furniture__ in the kitchen is new. (barn, furniture, noise)
9. The __comic__ book is funny. (comic, metal, leftover)
10. We rode in the __van__ to the game. (toast, pup, van)

Knowing the Words

Write the words from the story that have the meanings below.

1. worried __troubled__ (Par. 2)
2. special things __treats__ (Par. 2)
3. teach __train__ (Par. 6)

Some words are spelled the same but have different meanings. For example, *yard* can mean "the land around a building" or "thirty-six inches."

Look at the list of words below. For each pair of sentences, one word from the list will correctly complete both. Choose the correct word to fill in the blank for each pair of sentences.

bark bowl can

4. I like to __bowl__ with my friends.
   I poured cereal and milk into my favorite __bowl__.
5. Floppy doesn't __bark__ at people she knows.
   The tree __bark__ was bumpy.
6. Kevin __can__ play the piano.
   The soup __can__ was empty.

Match each word from the first list with its abbreviation from the second list.

7. __b__ minute — a. ft.
8. __c__ Monday — b. min.
9. __a__ feet — c. Mon.

Reading and Thinking

Words such as *he, she, you, it, we,* and *they* are used in place of other words. Read these sentences. *Rags is a puppy. He is owned by Lindsay and Dale.* Instead of repeating the name *Rags* in the second sentence, *he* is used in the place of *Rags.*

Read each set of sentences below. Fill in each blank.

1. Lindsay told Rags to sit. She used a firm voice.
   She stands for __Lindsay__.
2. Lindsay and Dale are training Rags. They enjoy the work.
   They stands for __Lindsay and Dale__.
3. The collar wasn't very heavy. It was made for a puppy.
   It stands for __the collar__.
4. Rags was not eating his food at home because __he was eating somewhere else__.

Learning to Study

Number each list of words below in alphabetical order.

1. __3__ problem, __1__ pretend, __2__ pride
2. __1__ happy, __2__ him, __3__ house
3. __2__ treats, __3__ tried, __1__ train
4. __3__ ran, __1__ Rags, __2__ rain

Knowing the Words

Write the words from the story that have the meanings below.

1. something nice that is said __praise__ (Par. 2)
2. strong __firm__ (Par. 2)
3. waiting without getting upset __patient__ (Par. 6)

Words that mean the same, or nearly the same, are called **synonyms.** Circle the pair of synonyms in each row.

4. **command** ask know **order** 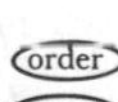
5. firm **bright** shy **smart**

Learning to Study

At the top of each page in a dictionary are two words in dark print called **guide words.** They can help you find other words in the dictionary. The first guide word tells what the first word is on the page. The second guide word tells what the last word is on the page.

The words in a dictionary are listed in alphabetical order. To find a word, decide if it comes in alphabetical order between the guide words on the page. If it does, the word will be on that page. Check each word that could be found between these guide words.

scatter/scout

1. __✓__ science — 5. __✓__ scissors
2. ____ scramble — 6. __✓__ school
3. __✓__ scene — 7. ____ scrub
4. ____ scratch — 8. __✓__ scent

Reading and Thinking

1. Check the answer that tells what the story is mainly about.
   - ____ getting tired
   - ____ a long afternoon
   - __✓__ how to train a dog
2. Did Rags mean to misbehave? ____
   Explain your answer. __(Answers will vary.)__
3. What other things might Lindsay and Dale train Rags to do? __(Answers will vary.)__
4. What did the children do when Rags obeyed their command? __They patted Rags on the head and praised him.__
5. Write **R** next to the two sentences that tell about real things.
   - ____ Puppies can talk.
   - __R__ Puppies can bark.
   - __R__ Puppies can be trained.
6. Put a check next to the two answers that tell what a person needs to do when training a puppy.
   - __✓__ praise the puppy
   - ____ give up
   - __✓__ give a command
   - ____ yell loudly

Knowing the Words

Write the word from the story that has the meaning below.

1. place to go in __entrance__ (Par. 2)

Words with opposite meanings are called **antonyms.** Circle the pair of antonyms in each row.

2. **narrow** small **wide** long
3. door **entrance** 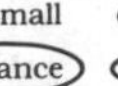 **exit** tunnel

Working with Words

The endings **-y** or **-ly** can be added to some words. Write the correct word to complete each sentence below.

1. The mountain trail was __rocky__ and difficult to climb. (rock, rocky)
2. This __rock__ is smooth, flat, and round. (rock, rocky)
3. I __quickly__ grabbed my jacket and ran home. (quick, quickly)
4. __Quick__ action kept the fire from spreading. (Quick, Quickly)

A word that means one of something is **singular.** A word that means more than one is **plural.** Most singular words are made plural by adding *s.* Most words that end in *s, ss, x, ch,* and *sh* are made plural by adding *es.* Form the plural of each word below by adding *s* or *es.*

5. hammer __s__ — 8. mess __es__
6. porch __es__ — 9. bush __es__
7. box __es__ — 10. seed __s__

Reading and Thinking

1. Check the answer that tells what the story is mainly about.
   - ____ a picnic
   - __✓__ frightened explorers
   - ____ people who live in caves

Write **T** if the sentence is true.
Write **F** if the sentence is false.

2. __T__ Rick was frightened in the cave.
3. __F__ Elsa had a picnic in the cave.
4. __F__ Someone was living in the cave.
5. Some things are real and some are make-believe. Write **M** next to the sentence that tells about a make-believe thing.
   - ____ Caves are dark and damp.
   - ____ Animals live in caves.
   - __M__ Monsters live in caves.

Write the best word to complete each sentence below.

6. I dropped the __flashlight__ and ran. (flashlight, shelter, tunnel)
7. I have a secret __hideout__ in the attic. (hideout, shadow, cave)
8. We could not sleep outside because the ground was __damp__. (green, damp, soft)
9. Stay on the __pathway__ so you don't get lost. (doorway, entrance, pathway)

Knowing the Words

Write the words from the story that have the meanings below.

1. bird blue jay (Par. 1)
2. broke into little pieces crushed (Par. 2)
3. very sad heartbroken (Par. 5)
4. flew gently fluttered (Par. 7)

In each row below, circle the three words that belong together.

5. (beak) (feather) shoe (wing)
6. (smash) flutter (crush) (pound)

Working with Words

A **contraction** is a short way to write two words. An apostrophe (') shows that one or more letters have been taken out. Write a contraction from the story for each pair of words below.

1. I am I'm (Par. 2)
2. we have we've (Par. 8)
3. did not didn't (Par. 8)

Most words that end in a consonant followed by *y* are made plural by changing *y* to *i* and adding *es*. Write the plural form of each word below.

4. grocery groceries
5. library libraries
6. city cities

Reading and Thinking

1. Number the sentences to show the order in which things happened.
   - 3 Tracy and Dale fed Screamer.
   - 4 Screamer flew to a tree.
   - 1 Tracy and Dale found a blue jay.
   - 2 Dale put the bird in a shoe box.
2. Tracy and Dale named the blue jay Screamer because he let out a loud scream.
3. Tracy and Dale mixed milk and birdseed to feed to Screamer.

Write the best word to complete each sentence below.

4. This yarn will make warm socks. (cereal, yarn, seed)
5. Stir the mixture till it is smooth. (blue jay, mixture, scream)
6. The kids agreed that Screamer was young. (agreed, tugged, drifted)

Knowing the Words

Write the words from the story that have the meanings below.

1. covered with a reddish-brown coating rusty (Par. 3)
2. turns to play innings (Par. 4)
3. held something up so that it swung loosely dangled (Par. 6)
4. not straight crooked (Par. 8)

Match each word from the first list with its abbreviation from the second list.

5.	b seconds	a.	wk.
6.	c Friday	b.	sec.
7.	d inch	c.	Fri.
8.	a week	d.	in.
9.	e feet	e.	ft.

Learning to Study

Check each word that could be found between the dictionary guide words.

1. colt/crooked
- ✓ crash
- ✓ crept
- ✓ crisp
- __ coconut

2. scare/shy
- __ slept
- ✓ shore
- ✓ sense
- ✓ scream

3. fiddle/flakes
- __ fly
- ✓ finger
- __ flow
- ✓ fierce

4. whole/write
- __ wrote
- ✓ wink
- ✓ won
- __ wheat

Reading and Thinking

1. Check the answer that tells what the story is mainly about.
   - __ trimming the bushes
   - __ looking for a lost watch
   - ✓ learning to play horseshoes

Write **T** if the sentence is true.
Write **F** if the sentence is false.

2. F Mr. Levi's watch fell off his wrist.
3. F Horseshoes is a game that could be played indoors.
4. T Mr. Levi knew his watch was missing.
5. The number of innings in a game of horseshoes is twenty-five.
6. Write two words from Paragraph 4 that are also used in the game of baseball. (Accept any 2 of these answers.) players, pitch, points, score, innings, game

Write the best word to complete each sentence below.

7. A yardstick can be used to measure the door. (chain, yardstick, hammer)
8. Brad complained about the rain. (pounded, whistled, complained)
9. The fence was crooked because it was old. (straight, tall, crooked)

Knowing the Words

Write the words from the story that have the meanings below.

1. understood clearly realized (Par. 3)
2. gave an idea suggested (Par. 5)
3. small shelf under a window windowsill (Par. 7)
4. wishing something might happen hopefully (Par. 9)

Check the meaning that fits the underlined word in each sentence.

5. The back door of the house is locked.
   - ✓ opposite of front
   - __ part of the body
6. I think I have a spot of gravy on my tie.
   - __ to fasten together
   - ✓ a piece of clothing

Learning to Study

Two pairs of dictionary guide words and their page numbers are shown in dark print. Beside each word below, write the number of the page on which it would be found.

thick/trim p. 302
trouble/try p. 310

1.	p.310 trumpet	5.	p.302 thread
2.	p.302 tremble	6.	p.310 trust
3.	p.310 truth	7.	p.302 tight
4.	p.310 truck	8.	p.302 trap

Reading and Thinking

1. Check the answer that tells what the story is mainly about.
   - __ old tin cans
   - __ the secret talk
   - ✓ making a telephone
2. How is a tin can phone different from a real telephone? (Answers will vary.)

Write **T** if the sentence is true.
Write **F** if the sentence is false.

3. T Sounds can travel through a string.
4. T A tin can telephone will not work if the string goes around a corner.
5. F Tracy could make a long-distance call on the tin can telephone.
6. F A tin can telephone will not work with a knot in the string.
7. What had been in the cans before they were emptied? soup

Write the best word to complete each sentence below.

8. She threaded the yarn through the needle. (snatched, threaded, connected)
9. There is a knot in this rope. (phone, string, knot)

Knowing the Words

Write the words from the story that have the meanings below.

1. something planned project (Par. 1)
2. a place to get water fountain (Par. 3)
3. where things are sold stand (Par. 4)
4. large shelf counter (Par. 5)

Synonyms are words that have the same or nearly the same meaning. Circle the pair of synonyms in each row.

5. (dye) orange (coloring) water
6. radio (tune) (song) piano

Working with Words

Use each group of words in a sentence that tells who owns something.

1. Elsa's glass jars (Answers will vary.)
2. man's fruit juice stand (Answers will vary.)

Some words are easier to read if they are divided into parts called **syllables.** Some words have two consonants between two vowels. These words can be divided into syllables between the consonants, as in *for/got.*

In each word below, draw a line to divide the word into syllables.

3.	for|ward	5.	foun|tain	7.	car|ry
4.	ar|rive	6.	prob|lem	8.	en|joy

Reading and Thinking

1. Check the answer that tells what the story is mainly about.
   - __ music in City Park
   - ✓ solving a problem
   - __ a fruit juice stand
2. Why didn't Elsa use plain water in the jars? She wanted her project to be colorful.

Write **T** if the sentence is true.
Write **F** if the sentence is false.

3. T The man thought Elsa's plan was a good one.
4. F Elsa could not pay for the fruit juice.
5. F Elsa could play eight different notes on the jars.
6. What do you think Elsa will do with the fruit juice after the music festival is over? (Answers will vary.)

Write the best word to complete each sentence below.

7. The class project was finished. (flavor, dye, project)
8. A colorful rainbow appeared after the storm. (fresh, colorful, musical)
9. Would you like juice with breakfast? (juice, cup, spoon)

Knowing the Words

Write the words from the story that have the meanings below.

1. people who buy customers (Par. 3)
2. two-way radios walkie-talkies (Par. 5)
3. make others believe convince (Par. 10)
4. a small bit of liquid drop (Par. 12)

Choose the correct word below to fill the blanks for each pair of sentences.

pitcher right

5. Is this the right answer?
   Stomp your right foot.
6. Pour milk into the pitcher.
   Who is the team pitcher?

Working with Words

Say *city*. Circle the words below that have the sound *c* stands for in *city*.

1. cave (cent) (face) clown
2. (center) (dance) calm (twice)

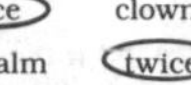

When a word ends with *e*, the *e* is usually dropped before adding **-ed** or **-ing**. Add **-ed** or **-ing** to the word in ( ) to make a word that completes each sentence.

3. Mom's plane is leaving at three o'clock. (leave)
4. Tim noticed the plants were dry. (notice)

Reading and Thinking

1. Check the answer that tells what the story is mainly about.
   ___ a thirsty man
   ___ Michael's walkie-talkies
   ✓ selling lemonade

Write **T** if the sentence is true.
Write **F** if the sentence is false.

2. F Heather and Michael washed the used cups.
3. F Heather and Michael bought the lemonade at the store.
4. T Michael had money to buy more cups.
5. What did the children have to buy to get started? lemons
6. Why did Michael go back to the store? to get more cups
7. What do you think Heather and Michael will do now that the thirsty man has gone? (Answers will vary.)

Knowing the Words

Write the words from the story that have the meanings below.

1. something used for drying towels (Par. 3)
2. things needed for a project supplies (Par. 4)
3. able to make things inventive (Par. 8)

Write the word with the correct meaning to complete each sentence below.

4. A piece of chalk fell to the floor. (peace, piece)
5. The blue coat is my favorite one. (blue, blew)

Working with Words

A **suffix** is a group of letters added to the end of a word that changes the meaning of the word. The suffixes **-ful** and **-ous** mean "full of." *Fearful* means "full of fear." *Joyous* means "full of joy."

Add **-ful** or **-ous** to the words below. Use the new words to complete the sentences.

power humor thought

1. It was very thoughtful of you to remember my birthday.
2. The powerful engine pulled the train.
3. The humorous story made us all laugh.

Reading and Thinking

1. Number the sentences in the order that tells how a salt jar can be made.
   2 Rub chalk over some salt.
   3 Pour the salt into the jar.
   1 Gather supplies.
   4 Put the lid on the jar.
2. Why did the children give Mr. Levi a present? for his birthday
3. Write one way in which the three salt jars were alike. (Answers will vary.)
4. Write one way in which the three salt jars were different. (Answers will vary.)
5. Check the word that tells how you think the children felt when Mr. Levi opened the box.
   ✓ proud ___ curious ___ sad
6. What did Mr. Levi do with the gifts? He put them on a windowsill.

Knowing the Words

Write the words from the story that have the meanings below.

1. a little frightened nervous (Par. 6)
2. word said when a trick is being done hocus-pocus (Par. 7)
3. helpers volunteers (Par. 8)
4. thin sheet of metal aluminum foil (Par. 8)

Working with Words

Say the word *show* and notice the sound *ow* stands for in the word. Circle the words below that have the sound *ow* stands for in *show*.

1. (know) down (blow) cow
2. (slow) (arrow) town (throw)
3. (hollow) tower how (glow)

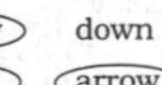
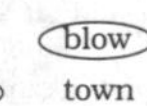
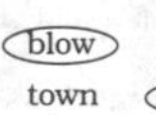
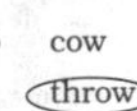

A **compound word** is made by combining two smaller words. Write a compound word using the underlined words in each sentence.

4. The yard in the back of a house is a backyard.
5. The time of day after the noon hour is afternoon.
6. Seed given to a bird is birdseed.
7. A paper that reports the news is a newspaper.

Reading and Thinking

1. Number the sentences to show the order in which things happened.
   2 Kids arrived for Rick's show.
   1 Rick made a poster.
   4 Rick did a trick with aluminum foil.
   3 Rick did his first trick.
2. How were Rick's two tricks alike? (Answers will vary.)
3. How were Rick's two tricks different? (Answers will vary.)

Write **T** if the sentence is true.
Write **F** if the sentence is false.

4. F The word *hocus-pocus* made the tricks happen.
5. T The audience enjoyed Rick's performance.
6. F Rick's tricks were magic.
7. A **fact** is something that is known to be true. An **opinion** is what someone thinks or feels. Check two sentences that give facts.
   ✓ Messages can be put on posters.
   ___ Lifting ice on a string is a good trick.
   ✓ Tricks can be learned from books.

Knowing the Words

Write the words from the story that have the meanings below.

1. a ride at a fair Ferris wheel (Par. 3)
2. feeling better relief (Par. 9)
3. high places heights (Par. 10)
4. money that people pay to ride somewhere fare (Par. 11)

Write the word with the correct meaning to complete each sentence below.

5. The city bus fare is sixty cents. (fair, fare)
6. I'll meet you downtown this evening. (meet, meat)
7. I had four tickets for rides. (for, four)

Learning to Study

The word you look up in a dictionary is called an **entry word.** Many words with endings are not listed as entry words. To find these words, look up the word to which the ending was added. To find the word *teased*, look up *tease*.

Write the word you would look under to find each of these words in a dictionary.

1. tickets ticket
2. arrived arrive
3. waiting wait
4. completely complete

Reading and Thinking

1. Check the answer that tells what the story is mainly about.
   ___ a long bus ride
   ✓ a visit to the fair
   ___ how a Ferris wheel works
2. Andy didn't want Rick to leave the fair without him because Rick had the bus fare.
3. How were Heather and Andy alike? (Answers will vary.)

Write **F** if the sentence gives a fact.
Write **O** if the sentence gives an opinion.

4. F Riding a bus is one way to travel.
5. O It is scary at the top of a Ferris wheel.
6. O Ferris wheels are fun to ride.
7. F Ferris wheels have seats.
8. If Heather and Andy had been left behind, how might they have gotten home? (Answers will vary.)

Knowing the Words

Write the words from the story that have the meanings below.

1. mistaking one thing for another confusion (Par. 1)
2. parts of your hands thumbs (Par. 3)
3. whole entire (Par. 3)

In each row below, circle the three words that belong together.

4. **thumb** **stomach** **ear** shirt

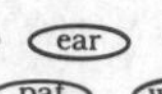

5. **wave** stripe **pat** **wiggle**
6. **ham** **cheese** plate **bread**

Working with Words

Write the two words that were used to form each of these contractions.

1. they've they have
2. I'll I will *or* I shall
3. that's that is *or* that has

Say *children.* Circle the words below that have the sound *ch* stands for in *children.*

4. **chose** **handkerchief** ache

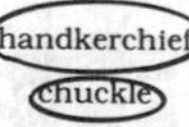

5. **sandwich** **chuckle** stomach

Reading and Thinking

1. Check the answer that tells what the story is mainly about.
   ___ meeting new neighbors
   ✓ playing a game
   ___ making sandwiches
2. What was Lin's sign? scratching her ear
3. What were the children having for lunch? ham and cheese sandwiches
4. Rick came over to Tracy's house because he wanted Tracy to meet Lin and Tat.
5. What do you think the children did after Tracy explained why she pointed to her mouth? (Answers will vary.)

Write the best word to complete each sentence below.

6. The zebra is a striped animal. (confused, striped, tiny)
7. Please repeat this word. (repeat, motion, scratch)
8. Don fixed a sandwich for lunch. (sign, shirt, sandwich)
9. The bear was growling. (chuckling, reading, growling)

Knowing the Words

Write the words from the story that have the meanings below.

1. gather collect (Par. 4)
2. person who delivers mail mail carrier (Par. 7)
3. cardboard box carton (Par. 8)

Synonyms are words that have the same or nearly the same meaning. Circle the pair of synonyms in each row.

4. **delivered** came **brought** went
5. win **collect** buy **gather**
6. eleven some **dozen** **twelve**
7. frown **chuckle** sneeze **laugh**

Working with Words

The ending **-er** sometimes means "more." It may be used to compare two things. The ending **-est** means "most." It is used to compare more than two things.

In each sentence below, add **-er** to the word before the blank if two things are being compared. Add **-est** if more than two things are being compared.

1. Apple juice is sweet er than lemonade.
2. Ken is the young est of three sons.
3. The lamp is bright er than the flashlight.
4. Kay is the fast est swimmer on the team.

Reading and Thinking

1. Write **O** next to two sentences that give opinions.
   O Cereal tastes best for breakfast.
   ___ Cereal is in the bread food group.
   O A ten-speed bicycle is a good prize.
2. Why did Tat and Lin eat so much cereal? to collect box tops *or* to win a contest
3. How many box tops did Tat and Lin send in? sixteen
4. How many boxes of cereal did Tat and Lin win? two dozen *or* 24
5. How do you think the children felt when they saw what they had won? (Answers will vary.)

Write **T** if the sentence is true.
Write **F** if the sentence is false.

6. T Tat and Lin won even more cereal than they had eaten.
7. F Crunchy Munchies was like oatmeal.
8. What do you think Lin and Tat will do with the cereal they won? (Answers will vary.)

Knowing the Words

Write the words from the story that have the meanings below.

1. kind of dog Saint Bernard (Par. 2)
2. gently talked into doing something coaxed (Par. 6)
3. very wet soggy (Par. 6)
4. gave a job for pay hired (Par. 8)

Check the meaning that fits the underlined word in each sentence.

5. The <u>collar</u> was too big for the poodle.
   ___ part of a shirt
   ✓ something a dog wears
6. <u>Park</u> the car in that empty space.
   ✓ stop for a time
   ___ a place to play
7. Bootsie hid my brother's <u>block</u> under the couch.
   ✓ a toy
   ___ area bordered by four streets

Learning to Study

Write the word you would look under to find each of these words in a dictionary.

1. spending spend
2. businesses business
3. weighed weigh
4. copies copy

Reading and Thinking

1. Check the answer that tells what the story is mainly about.
   ___ jumping in a fountain
   ✓ walking a Saint Bernard
   ___ seeing a robin

Write **T** if the sentence is true.
Write **F** if the sentence is false.

2. F Wee Willie is a lazy dog.
3. T Wee Willie likes water.
4. F Michael could carry Wee Willie in his arms.
5. What three kinds of dogs did Michael walk before he walked Wee Willie? bulldog, poodle, beagle
6. What do you think Michael said when Ms. Silva offered to hire him to walk Willie every day? (Answers will vary.)

Write the best word to complete each sentence below.

7. Ann has a poodle named Puff. (collar, screen, poodle)
8. Ms. Kay manages a gift shop in town. (spends, hires, manages)
9. A bird was splashing in the birdbath. (splashing, leaping, laughing)

Knowing the Words

Write the words from the story that have the meanings below.

1. a piece of clothing sweatshirt (Par. 3)
2. rushed in suddenly burst (Par. 7)

Circle the pair of antonyms (opposites) in each row.

3. **buy** spend **sell** trade
4. door **enter** agree **exit**
5. **open** drop loose **close**
6. **found** rolled **lost** heard
7. **now** near **later** gold

Working with Words

Some words that have one consonant between two vowels are divided into syllables after the first vowel. The first vowel sound in these words is most often long, as in *tī/ger.*

Other words that have one consonant between two vowels are divided after the consonant. In these words, the first vowel sound is most often short, as in *trăv/el.*

The words below have been divided into syllables. Put a mark above the first vowel in each word to show if the vowel stands for a long or short sound. Mark the long vowels with ˉ over the letter. Mark the short vowels with ˘.

1. lĕm/on	4. sī/lence	7. clŏs/et
2. wăg/on	5. frō/zen	8. stō/len
3. mō/tor	6. cŏp/y	9. căb/in

Reading and Thinking

1. Number the sentences to show the order in which things happened.
   1 Heather dropped a quarter.
   2 The man dropped a coin.
   3 The man grabbed the quarter.
   4 The man returned the quarter.

Write **T** if the sentence is true.
Write **F** if the sentence is false.

2. T Heather had been in Mr. Taylor's store before.
3. F Heather had one dollar to spend in Mr. Taylor's store.
4. F Mr. Taylor had never seen a gold piece before.
5. How much was the gold piece worth? twenty dollars
6. What might Heather buy with her money? (Answers will vary.)
7. How do you think Heather felt when the man gave her two quarters? (Answers will vary.)

Write the best word to complete each sentence below.

8. Jim found a coin in his pocket. (shirt, shelf, coin)
9. Three quarters equal seventy-five cents. (quarters, pieces, cards)

Knowing the Words

Write the words from the story that have the meanings below.

1. in charge of responsible (Par. 1)
2. more than usually especially (Par. 1)
3. holding too much overcrowded (Par. 1)

In each row, circle the three words that belong together.

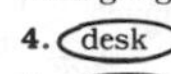 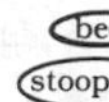 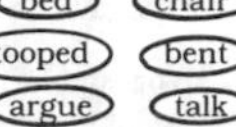

4. (desk) clothes (bed) (chair)
5. (stood) said (stooped) (bent)
6. laugh (agree) (argue) (talk)

Working with Words

Circle the correct word in ( ) and write it in the blank.

1. The boys talked for a long time. (buys, (boys))
2. Did you clean out the garage alone? ((clean), clothes)
3. Rick stood in line for thirty minutes. (stand, (stood))
4. When Andy went away, Rick was lonely. ((away), awake)

Reading and Thinking

1. Check the answer that tells what the story is mainly about.
   ___ clothes on the floor
   ___ a divided room
   √ cleaning a room together
2. Rick and Andy divided the room because neither one wanted to clean more than half.
3. Check three words that tell what Rick and Andy divided in half.
   √ desk √ bulletin board
   √ floor ___ toy box

Write **F** if the sentence gives a fact.
Write **O** if the sentence gives an opinion.

4. O Cleaning is difficult work.
5. F Vacuum cleaners can be used to sweep rugs.
6. F A bed is a piece of furniture.
7. O Cleaning should be done once a week.
8. Were Rick and Andy still arguing at the end of the story? Explain your answer. (Answers will vary.)
9. What might Rick and Andy do after they clean their room? (Answers will vary.)

Knowing the Words

Write the words from the story that have the meanings below.

1. a strong cloth canvas (Par. 1)
2. a long seat with cushions couch (Par. 2)
3. said unhappily grumbled (Par. 8)
4. covered with hair furry (Par. 9)

Synonyms are words that have the same or nearly the same meaning. Circle the pair of synonyms in each row.

5. shades (curtains) windows (drapes)
6. (swallow) chew lick (gulp)

Learning to Study

Some words have more than one meaning. In a dictionary, the different meanings of a word are numbered.

Read each word in dark print and the dictionary meanings that follow. Then read each sentence below and decide the meaning of the underlined words. Write the number of the correct meaning in the blank.

coun try 1 nation **2** land outside a city

1. 2 Dave works on a farm in the country.
2. 1 Each country has its own flag.

room 1 area with walls inside a building **2** space

3. 2 We have room for one more.
4. 1 The girls gave the room a new coat of paint.

Reading and Thinking

1. Check the answer that tells what the story is mainly about.
   √ looking for a pet
   ___ a visit to the country
   ___ the blue canvas bag
2. Do you think Tracy meant it when she said she did not care about Herbie? Explain your answer. (Answers will vary.)

Write **T** if the sentence is true.
Write **F** if the sentence is false.

3. F Tracy's aunt and uncle live down the street from her.
4. T Tracy knew she would miss Herbie while she was gone.
5. F Aunt Ruth and Uncle Stan probably met Tracy at the airport.
6. What do you think Tracy did with Herbie after she found him? (Answers will vary.)

Knowing the Words

Write the words from the story that have the meanings below.

1. something used to control a horse reins (Par. 3)
2. awfully terribly (Par. 5)

Write the word with the correct meaning to complete each sentence below.

3. Spring rains help flowers to grow. (reins, rains)
4. There are horses out in the pasture. (Their, There)
5. Who won the race? (one, won)

Working with Words

Write a compound word using the underlined words in each sentence.

1. A bowl in which a fish lives is a fishbowl.
2. A knob used to close a door is a doorknob.

The words below have been divided into syllables. Put a mark above the first vowel in each word to show if the vowel stands for a long or short sound. Mark the long vowels with ¯ over the letter. Mark the short vowels with ˘.

3. nā/tion	6. mĭn/ute	9. nĕv/er
4. rē/cess	7. fĭn/ish	10. stā/tion
5. vĭs/it	8. pī/lot	11. fī/nal

Reading and Thinking

1. Check the answer that tells what the story is mainly about.
   ___ riding to town on a horse
   √ a riding accident
   ___ how to ride a horse
2. Check three answers that tell about both Tracy and Aunt Ruth.
   √ had a scary accident
   ___ lives in the city
   √ rides horses
   √ is no longer afraid of horses
   ___ is an adult
3. Check two words that tell how Tracy felt when Big Gabe threw her.
   √ scared ___ pretty
   ___ hungry √ angry
   ___ sleepy ___ proud
4. Do you think Tracy will ride Big Gabe after today? Explain your answer. (Answers will vary.)

Write the best word to complete each sentence below.

5. Pull the reins to make the horse stop. (saddle, reins, rider)
6. Because of her bravery, the woman was given a medal. (fear, bravery, stable)

Knowing the Words

Write the words from the story that have the meanings below.

1. something that happens because of something else results (Par. 1)
2. a post stake (Par. 3)
3. closed in on all sides surrounded (Par. 3)

Circle the pair of antonyms (opposites) in each row.

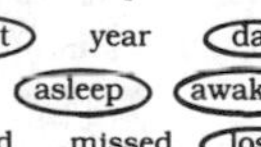

4. (pull) (push) drop fall
5. month (night) year (day)
6. race watch (asleep) (awake)
7. (found) planned missed (lost)

Choose the correct word to fill in the blank for each pair of sentences.

rose felt row

8. David's costume was made from yellow and purple felt.
   The sidewalk felt hot under my feet.
9. Ty helped row the boat yesterday.
   The row of beans is straight.
10. The sun rose in the East.
   Kevin found a rose near the edge of the garden.

Reading and Thinking

1. Number the sentences to show the order in which things happened.
   2 Tracy hung aluminum pans around the garden.
   4 The thief was caught.
   1 Tracy noticed that some beans were missing.
   3 Clyde rattled the pie pans.
2. Why did Tracy hang aluminum pans from a string? to get the thief to make some noise
3. How do you think Tracy felt when she saw who the thief was? (Answers will vary.)
4. Why did Tracy say she would share the ripe beans with Clyde? (Answers will vary.)
5. What do you think will happen to Clyde now? (Answers will vary.)

Learning to Study

Number each list of words below in alphabetical order.

1.		2.	
1	flavor	2	caught
2	fresh	1	catch
3	friend	3	corner

Knowing the Words

Write the words from the story that have the meanings below.

1. a high table used for work ___workbench___ (Par. 2)
2. said in a low voice ___murmured___ (Par. 2)

Synonyms are words that have the same or nearly the same meaning. Circle the pair of synonyms in each row.

3. **gazed** laughed cried **stared**
4. called **finished** **completed** tripped
5. wrote **murmured** read **said**
6. garage **city** **town** window

Working with Words

A **prefix** is a group of letters added to the beginning of a word that changes the meaning of the word. The prefixes **un-** and **dis-** mean "not" or "the opposite of." *Distrust* means "the opposite of trust." *Unfair* means "not fair."

Complete each sentence by writing **un-** or **dis-** in the blank.

1. It is ___un___ safe to climb on that rock.
2. Sean's wool socks were causing him some ___dis___ comfort.
3. Dan and I ___dis___ agree.
4. I was ___un___ able to go to the movies because I was sick.

Reading and Thinking

1. Check the answer that tells what the story is mainly about.
   - ___ how birds fly
   - _✓_ Tracy's project
   - ___ talking with Uncle Stan

Write **T** if the sentence is true.
Write **F** if the sentence is false.

2. _F_ Uncle Stan has no hobbies.
3. _T_ Tracy likes to help.
4. _T_ Tracy is tired of the rain.
5. Write three things Tracy had done to keep herself busy. ___read, painted, wrote a letter___
6. Write **R** next to two sentences that tell about real things.
   - _R_ A girl could fly in a plane.
   - ___ A boy could fly like a bird.
   - _R_ A bird could fly through the clouds.

Write the best word to complete each sentence below.

7. Bob ___imagined___ he was on a ship. (pleased, imagined, sang)
8. The ___garage___ is big enough for two cars. (skate, garage, workbench)
9. The plant on the ___windowsill___ gets lots of sunshine. (closet, river, windowsill)

Knowing the Words

Write the words from the story that have the meanings below.

1. leftover pieces ___scraps___ (Par. 3)
2. cook who is in charge ___chef___ (Par. 7)

Synonyms are words that have the same or nearly the same meaning. Circle the pair of synonyms in each row.

3. **garbage** collect **trash** truck
4. jar **bucket** water **pail**
5. hope **ready** **prepared** leave
6. **begin** clean stay **start**

Working with Words

Write a compound word using the underlined words in each sentence.

1. A room with a bed in it is a ___bedroom___.
2. A bench at which to work is a ___workbench___.

The suffix **-ment** means "the act of." *Enjoyment* means "the act of enjoying." Add **-ment** to the following words. Use the new words to complete the sentences.

amuse agree

3. Joel has an ___agreement___ with his brother about sharing toys.
4. The joke was told for our ___amusement___.

Reading and Thinking

1. Check the answer that tells what the story is mainly about.
   - _✓_ making vegetable soup
   - ___ Mr. Hastings's dog
   - ___ eating in a restaurant
2. The soup and beef scraps got mixed up because ___they were in jars that looked alike___.
3. What did Mr. Hastings plan to do with the beef scraps? ___feed them to his dog___

Write **T** if the sentence is true.
Write **F** if the sentence is false.

4. _F_ Mr. Hastings is a cab driver.
5. _F_ It was evening when Rick went to work with his father.
6. _T_ Rick's dad made a lot of soup.
7. What was in the soup besides vegetables? ___beef___
8. Number the sentences in the order that tells how the soup was made.
   - _4_ The mixture was cooked.
   - _1_ Water was boiled.
   - _3_ Vegetables and beef were put in the pot.
   - _2_ Vegetables and beef were cut up.
   - _5_ The soup was put into jars

Knowing the Words

Write the words from the story that have the meanings below.

1. having many leaves ___leafy___ (Par. 2)
2. moved slowly and quietly ___crept___ (Par. 3)
3. moved without anyone knowing ___sneaked___ (Par. 4)
4. picturing in one's mind ___imagination___ (Par. 5)

In each row below, circle the three words that belong together.

5. **forehead** closet **elbow** **shoulder**
6. **sneaked** **crept** **tiptoed** stuffed
7. tease **moan** **shout** **whisper**

Working with Words

To write the plural of a word that ends in *f* or *fe*, the *f* or *fe* is changed to *v*, and *es* is added. Write the plural form of each word below.

1. leaf ___leaves___
2. wife ___wives___
3. half ___halves___
4. shelf ___shelves___

Say *large*. Circle the words below that have the same sound *g* stands for in *large*.

5. **danger** gathered grab **engine**
6. **sponge** **ginger** **giant** dragon

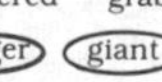
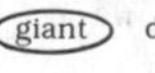
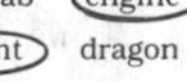

Reading and Thinking

1. Number the sentences to show the order in which things happened.
   - _4_ Andy waited for Heather.
   - _2_ Heather telephoned Andy.
   - _3_ Rick hid beside some bushes.
   - _5_ Rick scared Andy.
   - _1_ Rick tied branches to himself.
2. Check the sentence that tells about Rick.
   - ___ He was always mean to Andy.
   - ___ He wanted to hurt Andy.
   - _✓_ He wanted to teach Andy a lesson.
3. Do you think Rick and Andy will make a deal? What kind? ___(Answers will vary.)___
4. Write **R** next to two sentences that tell about real things.
   - ___ Bushes can talk and moan.
   - _R_ Fear can make people tremble.
   - _R_ People can imagine scary things.

Knowing the Words

Write the words from the story that have the meanings below.

1. the OK to do something ___permission___ (Par. 1)
2. got comfortable ___snuggled___ (Par. 3)
3. breathing loudly while sleeping ___snoring___ (Par. 7)

Synonyms are words that have the same or nearly the same meaning. Write **S** after each pair of synonyms. Write **A** after each pair of antonyms (opposites).

4. zip-unzip _A_
5. old-new _A_
6. early-late _A_
7. tired-sleepy _S_
8. better-worse _A_
9. nearby-close _S_

Learning to Study

A dictionary shows words divided into syllables. A space or a dot shows where the word can be divided at the end of a line of writing.

Read the words below. Next to each write the number of syllables it has.

1. let ter _2_
2. ac ci dent _3_
3. an oth er _3_
4. chuck le _2_
5. gi raffe _2_
6. morn ing _2_
7. ceil ing _2_
8. prob a bly _3_

Reading and Thinking

1. Check the answer that tells what the story is mainly about.
   - ___ shadows on the roof
   - ___ the howling dog
   - _✓_ camping out
2. Andy thought Michael's reason for going home was ___he was frightened by the noises___.
3. Did Andy own a real tent? Explain your answer. ___(Answers will vary.)___
4. Was Michael used to sleeping outdoors? Explain your answer. ___(Answers will vary.)___
5. Write two things Andy and Michael did before they went to sleep. ___made shadows, told jokes and funny stories___

Write the best word to complete each sentence below.

6. A ___bulldozer___ was used to clear the land. (alligator, bulldozer, yawn)
7. The ___giraffe___ ate leaves. (beagle, giraffe, shadow)
8. You will need a ___blanket___ on your bed. (tent, blanket, story)

Knowing the Words

Write the words from the story that have the meanings below.

1. part where power is control (Par. 4)
2. moving back and forth rocking (Par. 4)

Circle the pair of antonyms (opposites) in each row.

3. (long) large (short) huge
4. (whispered) (yelled) laughed sang
5. new tall (fast) (slow)

Working with Words

Write the two words that were used to form each of these contractions.

1. wasn't was not
2. you're you are
3. it'll it will *or* it shall
4. it's it is *or* it has

The suffix **-less** means "without." *Hopeless* means "without hope." Add **-less** to the following words. Use the new words to complete the sentences.

breath cloud spot

5. The windows were spotless after Jeff washed them.
6. The cloudless sky was a beautiful color of blue.
7. Adam was breathless after running the race.

Reading and Thinking

1. Check the answer that tells what the story is mainly about.
   - ___ a pet cat
   - ___ playing tag
   - ✓ a result of carelessness
2. Why didn't Tracy put the car in a safe place? She was in a hurry.
3. How did Herbie make the car move? He stepped on the control box.
4. Check two words that tell how Tracy might have felt when she saw the broken lamp.
   - ✓ angry ___ tired
   - ✓ sorry ___ thrilled

Write **T** if the sentence is true.
Write **F** if the sentence is false.

5. T Tracy bought the car with her allowance money.
6. F Herbie broke the car.
7. F Tracy didn't know how the lamp got broken.
8. Write **O** next to three sentences that give opinions.
   - O Cats are too curious.
   - ___ A toy car could be put on a table.
   - O Toys should always be put in a toy box.
   - O Cats should not be left alone.

Knowing the Words

Write the words from the story that have the meanings below.

1. following closely tagging (Par. 1)
2. said in a low voice muttered (Par. 2)
3. things items (Par. 3)
4. answer solution (Par. 3)

Working with Words

When a word ends in a consonant followed by *y*, the *y* is changed to *i* before an ending is added. Change the *y* to *i* in each word in ( ). Add **-ly** to make a word that completes the sentence.

1. Mark spoke angrily to the naughty pup. (angry)
2. Max easily won the race. (easy)
3. Jan walked lazily through the field. (lazy)

Rewrite the following groups of words using 's or s' to show who owns something. The first one is done for you.

the nickel that Carmen owns

Carmen's nickel

4. the coins that belong to the girls
   girls' coins
5. the vacuum cleaner that Bill owns
   Bill's vacuum cleaner

Reading and Thinking

1. Number the sentences to show the order in which things happened.
   - 3 Elsa realized she didn't have enough money.
   - 1 Carmen asked to go to the store.
   - 4 Carmen gave Elsa a coin.
   - 2 The girls stood in line.
   - 5 Elsa gave Carmen a hug.
2. Why did Carmen say she had a penny when she really had a nickel?
   She didn't know the difference between a nickel and a penny.

Write **T** if the sentence is true.
Write **F** if the sentence is false.

3. T The store the girls went to was close by.
4. F The girls were both upset when they left the house.
5. F Elsa was angry with Carmen on the way home.

Write the best word to complete each sentence below.

6. The total was twelve cents. (errand, clerk, total)
7. Mark skipped to the bank. (laughed, skipped, stopped)

Knowing the Words

Write the words from the story that have the meanings below.

1. boxes crates (Par. 1)
2. small jobs chores (Par. 2)
3. without making trouble patiently (Par. 4)

In each row, circle the three words that belong together.

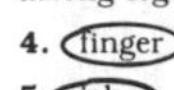
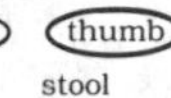
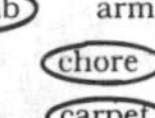
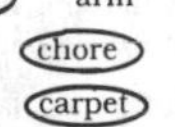
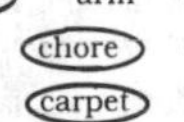
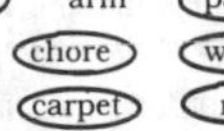
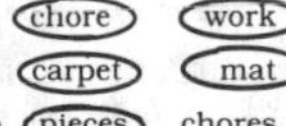

4. (finger) (thumb) arm (palm)
5. (job) stool (chore) (work)
6. wall (rug) (carpet) (mat)
7. (scraps) (chunks) (pieces) chores

Learning to Study

Write the word you would look under to find each of these words in a dictionary.

1. patiently patient
2. smiling smile
3. stepped step
4. finest fine

Number each list of words below in alphabetical order.

5.		6.	
3	blue	3	cat
4	club	4	door
1	angry	5	floor
5	crate	2	can
2	animal	1	camp

Reading and Thinking

1. Check the answer that tells what the story is mainly about.
   - ___ Tracy's chores
   - ✓ Tracy's idea
   - ___ a sign that said "Keep Out!"
2. Why had Tracy's dad saved the carpet scraps? He knew they would be useful.
3. Check the answer that tells what Tracy was probably doing when she thought of making a patchwork rug.
   - ___ washing the dishes
   - ___ making her bed
   - ✓ sweeping the carpet
4. Tracy put up a sign and covered the windows because she wanted to keep what she was doing a secret.
5. Check two sentences that tell how the clubhouse was like a house.
   - ✓ A poster hung on the wall.
   - ✓ The floor was carpeted.
   - ___ The sign on the door said "Keep Out!"

KEEP OUT
RKING IN CLUBHOUSE!

Knowing the Words

Write the words from the story that have the meanings below.

1. the project of getting votes campaign (Par. 2)
2. filled with something stuffed (Par. 5)

Write the word with the correct meaning to complete each sentence below.

3. Our poster is the most colorful. (Hour, Our)
4. Jake has a pair of tickets for the movie. (pair, pear)
5. Dan has a new red wagon. (new, knew)
6. Jo gets a letter in the mail every week. (weak, week)

Working with Words

Fill in each blank with the correct pair of letters to make a word.

wr kn mb ph

1. co mb
2. kn ob
3. wr ote
4. ele ph ant

Circle the correct word in ( ) and write it in the blank.

5. She paid for the scarf with quarters. (pad, (paid))
6. Will you join me for lunch? ((join), junk)

Reading and Thinking

1. Check the answer that tells what the story is mainly about.
   - ___ being president
   - ___ making a poster
   - ✓ running for president
2. Tell two things Tat did to get votes. (Accept any 2 of these answers.) made a poster, made a campaign shirt, talked to classmates, gave a speech
3. Write **O** next to the sentence that gives an opinion.
   - ___ There are usually five days in a school week.
   - O A poster is important to a campaign.

Learning to Study

Use the table of contents below to answer the questions.

How to Win an Election
Table of Contents

1. How many chapters are in this book? four
2. On what page does "Nearing Elections" begin? page 12
3. What chapter tells how to give a speech? Victory Speeches

Knowing the Words

Write the words from the story that have the meanings below.

1. a bright light spotlight (Par. 2)
2. best at something champion (Par. 6)
3. a reward medal (Par. 6)
4. world sports contests Olympics (Par. 6)

Working with Words

Circle the prefix or suffix in each word. Then use the words to complete the sentences.

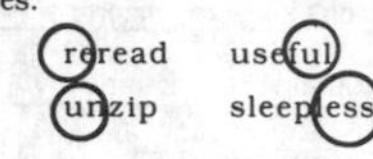

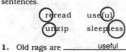

reread useful
unzip sleepless

1. Old rags are useful for cleaning dirty windows.
2. Unzip your coat and hang it on a hanger.
3. Les will reread the book because he likes it.
4. Tom had a sleepless night because a storm kept him awake.

Write the singular form of each word.

5. patches patch
6. cities city
7. shelves shelf
8. boxes box
9. blueberries blueberry

Reading and Thinking

1. Check the answer that tells what the story is mainly about.
   ___ a famous Olympic ice skater
   ___ a trip to the library
   _✓_ a dream that could come true
2. Write two places Rick's father went.
   grocery store and library
3. Why do you think Rick's dad brought Rick a book about a skater?
   (Answers will vary.)
4. Dreams are not real, but sometimes they can come true. Check two sentences that tell about dreams that could come true.
   _✓_ Jim dreamed he was a famous artist.
   ___ Jeff dreamed he lived in a pumpkin.
   _✓_ Kate dreamed she was an astronaut.

Write the best word to complete each sentence below.

5. The knife blade is sharp. (handle, blade, cover)
6. "May I have your autograph on this card?" the man asked the singer. (pillow, medal, autograph)
7. The small package was on the desk. (package, smile, ice)

Knowing the Words

Write the words from the story that have the meanings below.

1. cooking directions recipe (Par. 2)
2. a spice cinnamon (Par. 3)
3. covered lightly with drops sprinkled (Par. 3)
4. flashed off and on flickered (Par. 6)

Match each word in the first list with its abbreviation from the second list.

5. _c_ minutes a. tsp.
6. _a_ teaspoon b. Sat.
7. _b_ Saturday c. min.

Working with Words

Use the following words to form compound words. Then use the compound to complete the sentences.

snow cook flake book

1. This cookbook has a recipe for bean soup.
2. A snowflake landed on my mitten and melted.

Circle the correct word in ( ) and write it in the blank.

3. Add cinnamon to the brown sugar. (campaign, cinnamon)
4. The fruit juice spilled. (juice, jack)

Reading and Thinking

1. Number the sentences in the order that shows how Tracy's muffins are made.
   _2_ Pour the batter into baking cups.
   _3_ Combine brown sugar and cinnamon.
   _1_ Mix the egg, sugar, milk, and baking mix.
   _4_ Put the topping on the muffins.
   _5_ Bake the muffins for fifteen minutes.
2. Why didn't the muffins bake?
   The electricity was off.

Write **T** if the sentence is true.
Write **F** if the sentence is false.

3. _T_ Tracy made twelve muffins.
4. _F_ Tracy baked the muffins in a gas oven.
5. _T_ Tracy would need two eggs to make two dozen muffins.
6. _F_ Tracy made the muffins for Tat.
7. _F_ The muffins had fruit in them.

Write the best word to complete each sentence below.

8. The blue flame flickered in the breeze. (flickered, bumped, leaned)
9. They watched the muffins turn brown. (watched, decorated, baked)

Knowing the Words

Write the words from the story that have the meanings below.

1. filled with air blown-up (Par. 2)
2. walking heavily trudging (Par. 2)
3. not sure doubtful (Par. 4)

Circle the pair of antonyms (opposites) in each row.

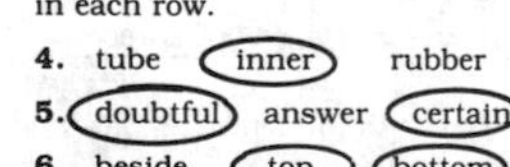

4. tube inner rubber outer
5. doubtful answer certain guess
6. beside top bottom near

Working with Words

Use each group of words in a sentence that tells who owns something.

1. children's ideas (Answers will vary.)
2. Elsa's basket (Answers will vary.)
3. friend's sled (Answers will vary.)
4. kids' races (Answers will vary.)

In each word below, draw a line to divide the word into syllables.

5. diz|zy 7. mi|nus 9. pen|cil
6. met|al 8. gar|bage 10. cra|zy

Reading and Thinking

1. Check the answer that tells what the story is mainly about.
   ___ winning a race
   ___ building a sled
   _✓_ practicing for a race
2. Where were the sled races to be held?
   at City Park
3. Tracy, Rick, and Elsa had crazy sleds because they didn't own regular sleds.
4. Do you think the kids with the crazy sleds will win the race? Explain your answer.
   (Answers will vary.)
5. Check the answer that tells what Tracy thinks is most important about sledding.
   ___ being the first-place winner
   _✓_ having a good time
   ___ having the best-looking sleds

In each sentence below, a word is underlined. Circle the name or names that the underlined words stand for.

6. "I will go first," said Elsa to Tracy.
   Tracy Rick Elsa
7. "You look cold," Tracy said to Rick.
   Rick Elsa Tracy
8. "We should leave," Rick said to Tracy.
   Rick Rick and Tracy Tracy

Knowing the Words

Write the words from the story that have the meanings below.

1. special way of writing code (Par. 3)
2. figured out a secret code decoded (Par. 3)
3. directions instructions (Par. 5)

In each row, circle the three words that belong together.

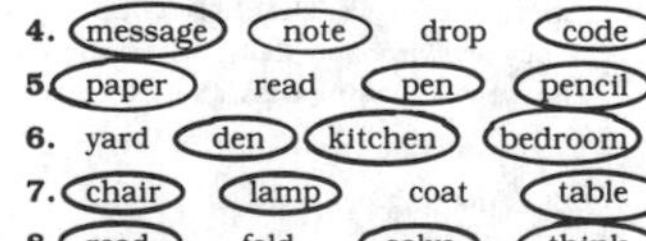

4. message note drop code
5. paper read pen pencil
6. yard den kitchen bedroom
7. chair lamp coat table
8. read fold solve think

Learning to Study

Read each word in dark print and the dictionary meanings that follow. Then read the sentences below and decide the meaning of each underlined word. Write the number of the correct meaning in the blank.

den **1** small room in a house
2 an animal's home

1. _2_ The fox was asleep in its den.
2. _1_ Is the TV in the den?

glass **1** something that holds liquid
2 material that can break

3. _1_ I spilled the glass of water.
4. _2_ A piece of glass was in the tire.

Reading and Thinking

1. Number the sentences to show the order in which things happened.
   _1_ Heather dropped a note near Michael's chair.
   _3_ Michael decoded the message.
   _5_ Michael met Heather in the kitchen.
   _4_ Michael went to the den.
   _2_ Michael found the first note.

Write **T** if the sentence is true.
Write **F** if the sentence is false.

2. _F_ Michael had never seen this code before.
3. _F_ It was the middle of summer.
4. _T_ All of the notes were inside the house.
5. How many notes did Heather write in all? four
6. How were all the notes alike?
   (Answers will vary.)
7. How was one note different from the others?
   (Answers will vary.)

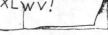

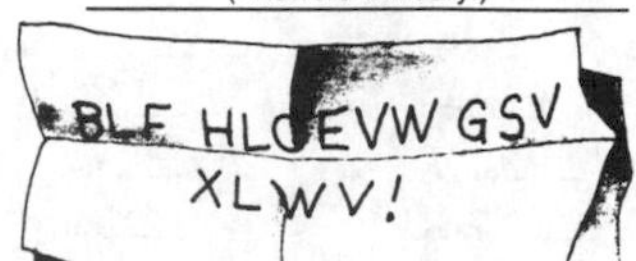

Knowing the Words

Write the words from the story that have the meanings below.

1. a place where some insects grow cocoon (Par. 2)
2. insect moth (Par. 10)

Choose the correct word below to fill the blanks for each pair of sentences.

rest fine

3. That is fine with me.

   The thread was too fine to see.

4. Roger needs to rest.

   Did you get the rest of the programs?

Working with Words

Fill in each blank with the correct pair of letters to make a word. Then use each of the words in a sentence below.

sh ch wr ph

1. bu sh
2. stoma ch
3. hand wr iting
4. autogra ph
5. My stomach hurts.
6. Leo has beautiful handwriting.
7. May I have your autograph?
8. Look at the cocoon on that bush.

Reading and Thinking

Write **F** if the sentence gives a fact.
Write **O** if the sentence gives an opinion.

1. O A moth is a pretty insect.
2. F The body of a moth looks furry.
3. F Some insects come out of cocoons.
4. F A moth is an insect.
5. Why do you think Tracy and Ms. Carr took the moth outside?

   (Answers will vary.)
6. What kind of person do you think Ms. Carr is? Explain your answer.

   (Answers will vary.)

Learning to Study

You can look in an **encyclopedia** to find facts about different topics. You may need to look under more than one topic to find the facts you need. To learn more about cocoons, Tracy could have looked under *cocoon*. Also, she could have looked under *moth* or *insect*.

Read each sentence below. Write the names of two topics you might look under.

1. You want to know about blue jays. (Answers will vary.)
2. You want to learn about forest animals. (Answers will vary.)

Knowing the Words

Write the word from the story that has the meaning below.

1. a trip to see something special tour (Par. 3)

Check the meaning that fits the underlined word in each sentence.

2. My new shirt is light blue.
   - ✓ pale
   - ___ not heavy
3. We are planning a trip to England.
   - ✓ vacation
   - ___ to stumble
4. I left a note on the table.
   - ___ a musical sound
   - ✓ a short letter

Working with Words

Write the contraction for each pair of words below.

1. you have you've
2. would not wouldn't
3. what is what's
4. you will you'll
5. we are we're
6. I will I'll
7. do not don't
8. I have I've

Reading and Thinking

1. Check the answer that tells what the story is mainly about.
   - ___ cold, damp walls
   - ___ a secret stairway
   - ✓ visiting a castle
2. Write **R** next to two sentences that tell about real things.
   - R A person can drive to a castle.
   - ___ A person can drive into the past.
   - R Castles have walls.
   - ___ Castles have dragons.

Learning to Study

Each book of an encyclopedia is called a **volume.** Write the number of the volume you could use to find the topics below.

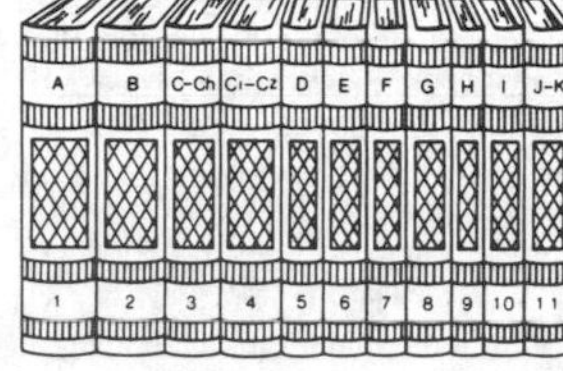

1. castles 3
2. bicycle 2
3. history 9
4. cotton 4
5. fish 7
6. carriages 3
7. gardening 8
8. horses 9
9. dolls 5
10. England 6

Knowing the Words

Write the words from the story that have the meanings below.

1. invention device (Par. 7)
2. ended concluded (Par. 11)

Choose the correct word to fill in the blank for each pair of sentences.

drive saw

3. Ed is too young to drive.

   Drive the nail into the wood.
4. We saw you at the game.

   Where did you put the saw?

Learning to Study

Names of people are listed in an encyclopedia by the person's last name. Write the number of the volume you could use to find the topics below.

A B C-Ch Ci-Cz D E F G H I J-K
1 2 3 4 5 6 7 8 9 10 11

1. invention 10
2. computers 4
3. Mary Anderson 1
4. Thomas Edison 6

Reading and Thinking

Write **T** if the sentence is true.
Write **F** if the sentence is false.

1. T Tracy, Lindsay, and Rick had been to the library.
2. T Tracy pretended she was a news reporter.
3. F The class was not interested in the project.
4. Did Tracy really talk to Mary Anderson? Explain your answer.

   No, she just pretended to.
5. Why did Mary Anderson make a device for cleaning a windshield?

   She wanted to make driving safer.

Read each set of sentences below. Fill in each blank.

6. Lindsay pretended she was Mary Anderson.

   She stands for Lindsay.
7. Rick said he liked the new invention.

   He stands for Rick.
8. The inventor thought she had a good idea.

   She stands for the inventor.
9. The class was surprised when it saw the report.

   It stands for the class.

Knowing the Words

Write the word from the story that has the meaning below.

1. moved from side to side shook (Par. 9)

Circle the pair of antonyms (opposites) in each row.

2. sing (cry) (laugh) applaud
3. (lost) helped looked (won)
4. (answered) said (inquired) grumbled

Working with Words

The suffix **-ly** helps tell how something was done. *Smoothly* means "done in a smooth way."

Add **-ly** to the words below. Use the new words to complete the sentences.

silent friend loose clear

1. When he was in the library, Robert read a book silently.
2. Amy tied the knot loosely.
3. Pat was happy to see the friendly puppy.
4. The announcer spoke clearly.

Say *gather.* Circle the words below that have the sound *g* stands for in *gather.*

5. (began) edge giant (against)
6. (get) (goldfish) message charge
7. (forget) (eager) magic bridge
8. cage (goose) (give) (together)

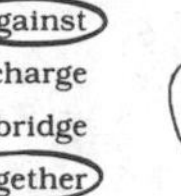

Reading and Thinking

Write **T** if the sentence is true.
Write **F** if the sentence is false.

1. T Dale wanted to help with the puppet show.
2. F Dale did not try very hard to find his stuffed elephant.
3. T Dale thought of a new way to solve his problem.
4. F Dale finally found the toy himself.
5. Dale was going to make a sock puppet because he couldn't find his stuffed elephant.
6. What do you think Dale will do now that his elephant has been found?

   (Answers will vary.)

Write the best word to complete each sentence below.

7. James wondered why the tire was flat. (wondered, jumped, searched)
8. The elephant was bigger than a car. (mouse, robin, elephant)

Knowing the Words

Write the words from the story that have the meanings below.

1. asked forgiveness apologized (Par. 1)
2. common sickness cold (Par. 3)

Check the meaning that fits the underlined word in each sentence.

3. It is very cold outside.
   ✓ low temperature
   ___ sickness
4. This is the third act.
   ___ to behave in a certain way
   ✓ part of a show

Learning to Study

An **index** is a part of a book. It lists a book's topics in alphabetical order. It also lists page numbers so you can find those topics. An index is usually at the back of a book. Use the index below to answer the questions.

performances, 1–5
plays, 4, 21
puppets, 4, 8–10
stages, 11–15

1. What topic would you find on pages 1–5? performances
2. What could you learn from pages 11–15? about stages
3. On what pages would you look if you wanted to make a puppet? 4, 8–10

Reading and Thinking

1. Number the sentences to show the order in which things happened.
   4 The puppets did a trapeze act.
   5 The elephant performed.
   3 Tracy announced the first act.
   2 The children went to Elsa's house.
   1 Dale went to Tracy's house.

Write **F** if the sentence gives a fact. Write **O** if the sentence gives an opinion.

2. F An elephant's skin has wrinkles.
3. O The trapeze acts are the most thrilling to watch.
4. F An elephant can be trained to stand on its hind legs.
5. F Many circuses have elephants.
6. O A circus isn't exciting.

Read each sentence below. Fill in the blank.

7. The children knew they had made Carmen happy.
   They stands for children.
8. Dale believed he had done a good job.
   He stands for Dale.
9. Carmen applauded as she watched the performance.
   She stands for Carmen.

Knowing the Words

Write the words from the story that have the meanings below.

1. a season spring (Par. 1)
2. said something was true admitted (Par. 7)
3. moved up and down shrugged (Par. 11)
4. saw spotted (Par. 15)

Choose the correct word below to fill the blank for each pair of sentences.

close spring

5. Spring begins in March.
   The spring in my pen is broken.
6. Please close the window.
   Do not stand too close to the fire.

Learning to Study

Number each list of words below in alphabetical order.

1. 5 shrug
   6 sing
   4 shoulders
   2 piano
   7 smile
   1 memorize
   3 question
2. 5 crowd
   6 cry
   7 cute
   3 concert
   4 crawl
   2 believe
   1 beg

Reading and Thinking

Write **T** if the sentence is true.
Write **F** if the sentence is false.

1. F Elsa was very nervous.
2. T Rick and Elsa had practiced the song more than once.
3. F The concert took place at the beginning of the school year.
4. Rick did not want to sing in the concert because he was nervous.
5. Who was Mr. Barnes? the music teacher
6. Why did Mr. Barnes tell Rick he needed to believe in himself?
   so Rick wouldn't be nervous
7. How do you think Rick felt about himself after he sang the song?
   (Answers will vary.)
8. Do you think Rick will ever sing in a concert again? Explain your answer.
   (Answers will vary.)

Knowing the Words

Write the words from the story that have the meanings below.

1. good price bargain (Par. 1)
2. might be probably (Par. 1)

Check the meaning that fits the underlined word in each sentence.

3. Did you see the play Michael was in?
   ✓ a show
   ___ to have fun
4. Did Ken watch TV yesterday?
   ___ something that keeps time
   ✓ to look at

Working with Words

Circle the correct word in ( ) and write it in the blank.

1. I hope I grow two inches this year. (group, grow)
2. The sound of his scream frightened me. (sound, sand)
3. Has Sam thought of a name for his kitten? (thought, that)
4. The show begins at 8:30. (shoe, show)
5. Did you write down the correct address? (dawn, down)
6. Jenny showed us how to tie a knot. (should, showed)

Reading and Thinking

1. Why was Tracy saving money?
   for a bike
2. Tracy had to call Rick because
   she needed the customers' addresses.
3. How do you think Tracy felt about asking Rick for the addresses?
   (Answers will vary.)
4. What do you think Tracy did after she delivered her last paper?
   (Answers will vary.)

Learning to Study

Read each question below. Write **dictionary** or **encyclopedia** to answer each one.

1. Where would you find the meaning of the word *newspaper?*
   dictionary
2. Where could you find the history of newspapers?
   encyclopedia
3. Where could you find facts on how newspapers are made?
   encyclopedia
4. Where could you find the word *newspaper* divided into syllables?
   dictionary

SPECTRUM WRITING

CONTENTS

Project Editor: Sandra Kelley
Text: Written Mary Waugh
Design and Production by A Good Thing, Inc.
Illustrated by Karen Pietrobono, Claudia Fouse, Anne Stockwell, Teresa Delgado, Doug Cushman

Things To Remember About Writing

WRITING

- Use sentences in a paragraph only if they tell about the main idea of the paragraph.
- Use words like *next* and *yesterday* to tell when something happens.
- Write directions for doing something in proper order.
- Use *er* or *est, more* or *most* to compare things.
- Use details to tell how something looks, sounds, smells, tastes, or feels.
- Use names, places, and dates when writing facts. Use words like *think* and *should* when stating an opinion.
- Use words like *since* and *because* to join cause and effect parts of sentences.
- Think about your purpose before you start writing.
- Try writing about something from different points of view.

REVISING

- Use words that are exact to make your sentences clear.
- Be sure every sentence has a subject and a verb.
- Combine sentences to make your writing smoother.
- Make all verbs in a story tell about the same time.

PROOFREADING

Check to see that
- you used capital letters correctly
- you put in correct punctuation marks
- all words are spelled correctly
- you used correct verb forms

unit 1
Writing Main Ideas

Things to Remember About Using Main Ideas in Your Writing

The **main idea** of a paragraph is what the paragraph is about.

Writing

- Use sentences in a paragraph only if they tell about the main idea of the paragraph.
- Use a title as a short way to tell the main idea.

Revising

- Use more exact nouns to say just what you want.

Proofreading

Check to see that

- every sentence begins with a capital letter
- every sentence ends with a period
- all the words are spelled correctly
- every sentence has all the words it needs

lesson

1 Finding the right group

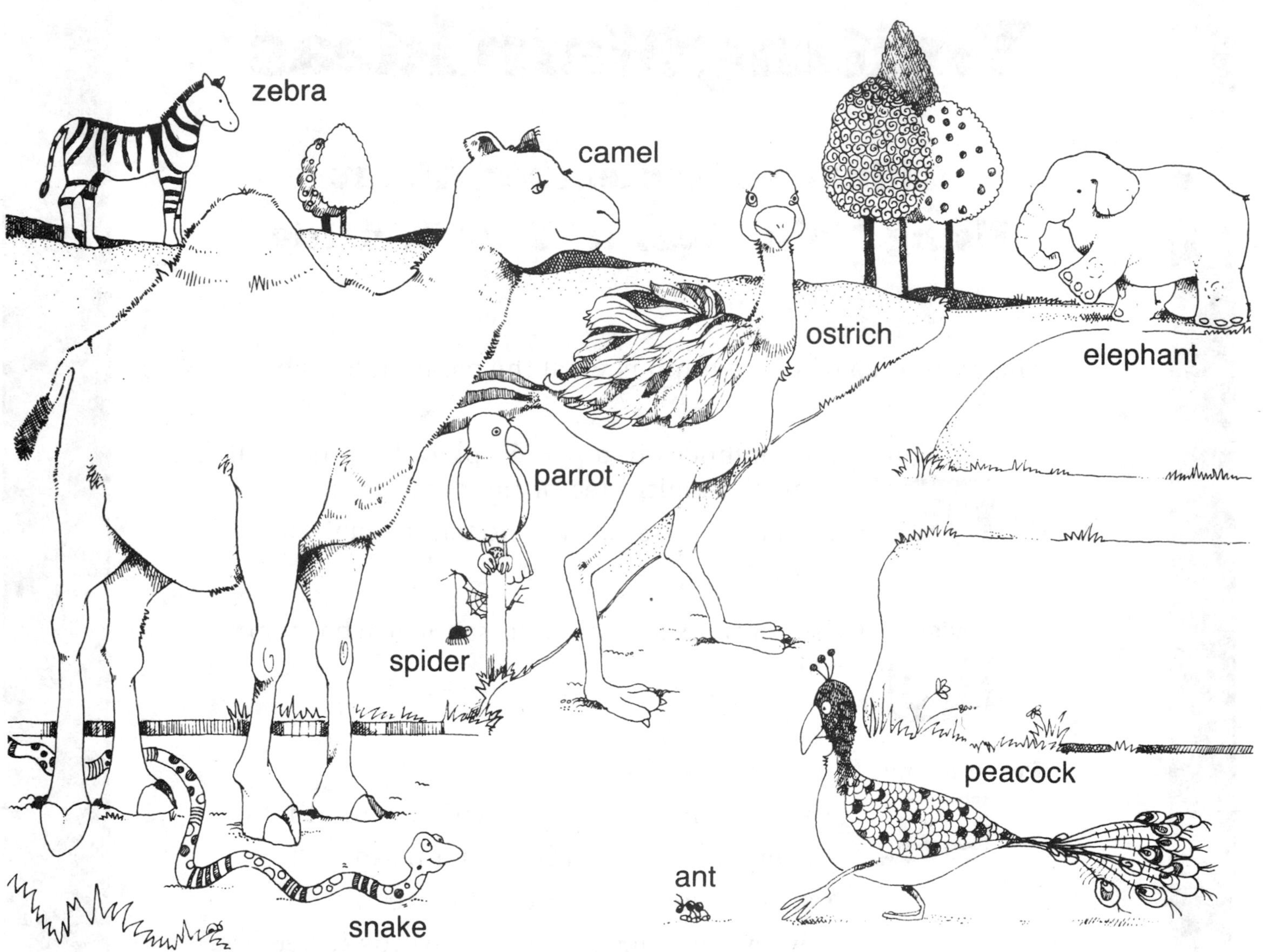

Pretend that you are a zoo keeper. You find your animals running all over. They are all mixed-up. How will you group them? Well, you can put each one in a **category.** A category is a group of things that are alike.

A. Read the category names below. Then write the name of each animal under the correct category name.

Animals with Four Legs	Animals That Crawl	Animals with Feathers
____________	____________	____________
____________	____________	____________
____________	____________	____________

B. The words in each list below belong to a category. Their category names are: Holidays, Fruits, Colors. Write the correct category name above each list.

____________	____________	____________
grape	blue	Halloween
apple	yellow	Columbus Day
banana	red	Memorial Day
pear	green	Thanksgiving Day

C. Read each list of words below. Then draw a line through the word that does *not* belong in each category. Finally, write a correct category name above each list.

____________	____________	____________
sister	lemonade	cheek
mother	cake	nose
brother	milk	foot
car	water	ear

Read the category names below. On a separate sheet of paper, copy the three category names. Then write two words or draw two pictures that belong under each category name.

Things with Wings   People   Things to Read

A category is a group of things that are alike.

lesson

2 Writing the main idea of a picture

Look at the picture. What is the picture about?

A picture can tell us many things. But most pictures tell us *one* **main idea.** The main idea is what the picture is all about. The main idea is what the whole picture means.

A. Which sentence below tells the main idea of the whole picture? Circle your answer.

1. Some girls and boys are playing volleyball.
2. Some girls have curly hair.
3. Some boys are playing volleyball.

B. Which sentence below tells the main idea of this picture?

1. Fred has a new job.
2. Fred's apron is white.
3. Fred is cooking hamburgers.

C. Draw a picture in the space below. Then write the main idea of your picture on the line.

The main idea of my picture is: ______________________________

____

On another sheet of paper, draw three more pictures. Then under each picture, write its main idea. You might want to use the ideas below. Or think up your own ideas for the pictures.

Something that happens at school	Something that happens at home	Something that happens at play

The main idea of a picture is what the picture is all about.

lesson

3 Writing the main idea of a paragraph

Read the paragraph below.

Fish sleep in different ways. Some sleep in the sand. Some sleep on their sides. Others sleep on their tails. One fish sleeps while standing on its head!

You know that pictures have main ideas. Well, paragraphs have main ideas, too. The main idea of a paragraph is what the paragraph is all about.

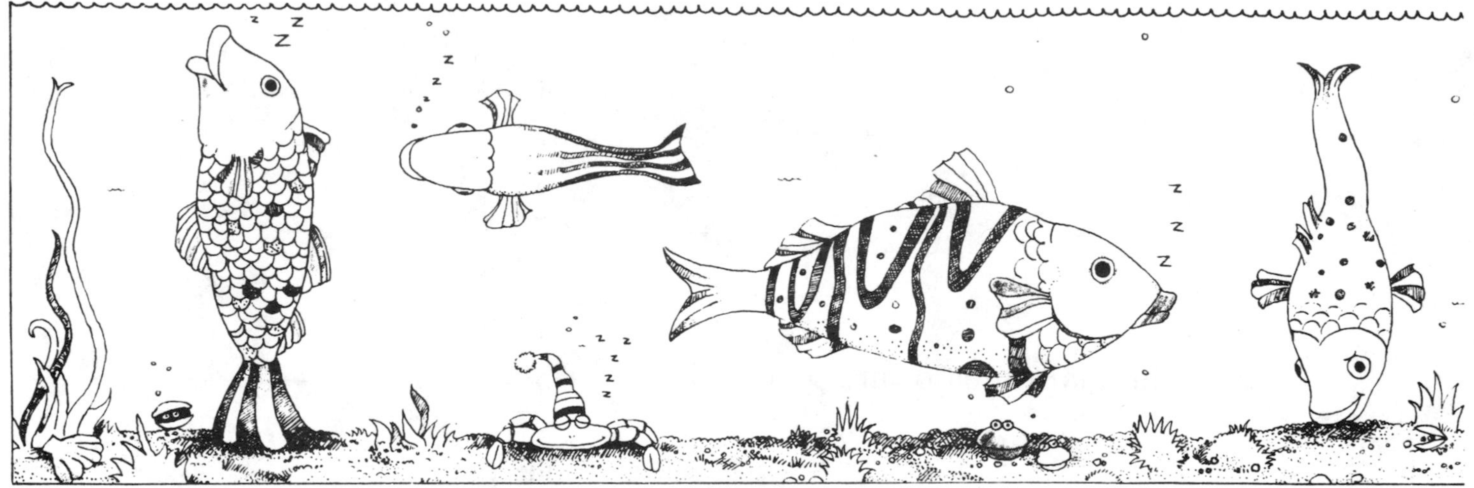

A. Read the paragraph about fish again. Then underline the sentence below that tells its main idea.

1. Fish are lazy.
2. Fish sleep differently.
3. Some fish sleep in the sand.

Read the next paragraph.

I got up early. I jumped out of bed. Quickly, I washed and dressed. Then I ran down the stairs. I gulped down my breakfast. I couldn't wait to go on my first camping trip.

B. What is the main idea of the paragraph? Circle the best answer.

1. I rushed to go camping.
2. I ate a big breakfast.
3. I ran down the stairs.

C. Write your own paragraph on the lines below. Make your paragraph at least four sentences long. You can choose one of the ideas below. Or you can think up your own idea.

I love to go skiing.
One day, I got lost while shopping.

____

____

____

____

Now write a sentence on the line below that tells the main idea of your paragraph.

____

On another sheet of paper, write two paragraphs. Write one paragraph about something that truly happened. Write the other paragraph about something you can imagine might happen. Write "I imagine" above the make-believe paragraph. Write "This really happened" above the paragraph that is true. Then write the main idea of each paragraph below it. Here are some ideas you may want to use. Or you can think up your own ideas.

The last day of school
The day I went sky diving
Building a tree house
Finding a million dollars

The main idea of a paragraph is what the paragraph is all about.

lesson 4 Writing paragraphs that make sense

What doesn't make sense in this picture?

Did you ever read something that didn't make sense? Something that doesn't make sense can juggle your mind. It can mix you up. A picture should make sense. A paragraph should make sense, too. A paragraph makes sense if all its sentences tell about the main idea.

Read the next paragraph. Think about the main idea as you read.

Tulips are my favorite flowers. I love to see the red, yellow, pink, and orange flowers in rows. Tulips tell me that spring is here. We have to stand in rows at school.

A. Answer the following questions about the paragraph. Write your answers on the lines.

1. What is the main idea of the paragraph? ______________

____

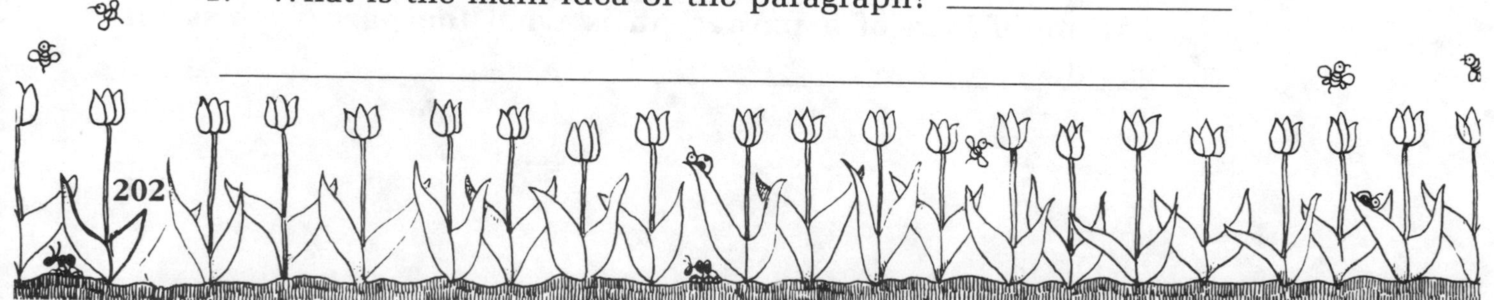

2. Which sentence doesn't make sense in the paragraph?

____

3. Why doesn't one sentence make sense in the paragraph?

____

B. Read the next two paragraphs. Then write your answers on the lines below each one.

Our neighbor told us about her trip into space. She built a spaceship. Last night, she flew in it. She zoomed out of the garage. I took a trip to Disney World. She climbed into space. She flew past many planets. She landed home this morning.

1. The main idea is: ______________________________
2. The sentence that doesn't make sense in the paragraph is:

____

Tugboats are small boats used to move large ships. I'd like to sail a ship someday. A tugboat's engine is very powerful. The small boat can pull or push. It's fun to see tugboats moving big ships around.

3. The main idea is: ______________________________
4. The sentence that doesn't make sense in this paragraph is:

____

Write On

Use this main idea: "One day I put my shoes on the wrong feet." Or use your own main idea. Then, on a separate sheet of paper, write a paragraph using the main idea you have chosen. Remember: Use only sentences that belong with the main idea.

Sentences belong in a paragraph only if they tell about the main idea of the paragraph.

lesson

5 Writing a title

Look at the picture below.

A **title** is a name for a picture or story. It tells what the picture or story is all about. A title is a short way to tell the main idea of a picture or story.

A. Look at the picture again. Then read the titles below. Underline the title that best tells about the picture.

1. Monkey Is Star of Bike Day
2. Playing in the Park
3. Some People Don't Ride Bicycles

Read the next story.

First, Charlotte hit her toe when she jumped out of bed. Then she had no clean socks to wear. At breakfast she burned her toast. Then she spilled her juice on her homework. It was not a good beginning to Charlotte's day.

B. What title below best tells about the whole story? Underline your answer.

1. Charlotte's Day
2. The Burned Toast
3. A Bad Beginning for Charlotte

C. Read the next story. Think about its main idea. Then write a title for the story on the line below.

Have you ever seen a UFO? Some people think UFOs fly around. But nobody knows what they are. Nobody knows if they are real. Some people say they have seen UFOs. Other people say UFOs are a trick.

A good title for this story is: ____________________

On a separate sheet of paper, write your own story. Make it four or more sentences long. Then write a title for your story on the top line of your paper. You can use one of the ideas below. Or you can think up your own idea.

Man Wins Flapjack Contest
Girl Invents New Glue
Elephant Escapes from Zoo

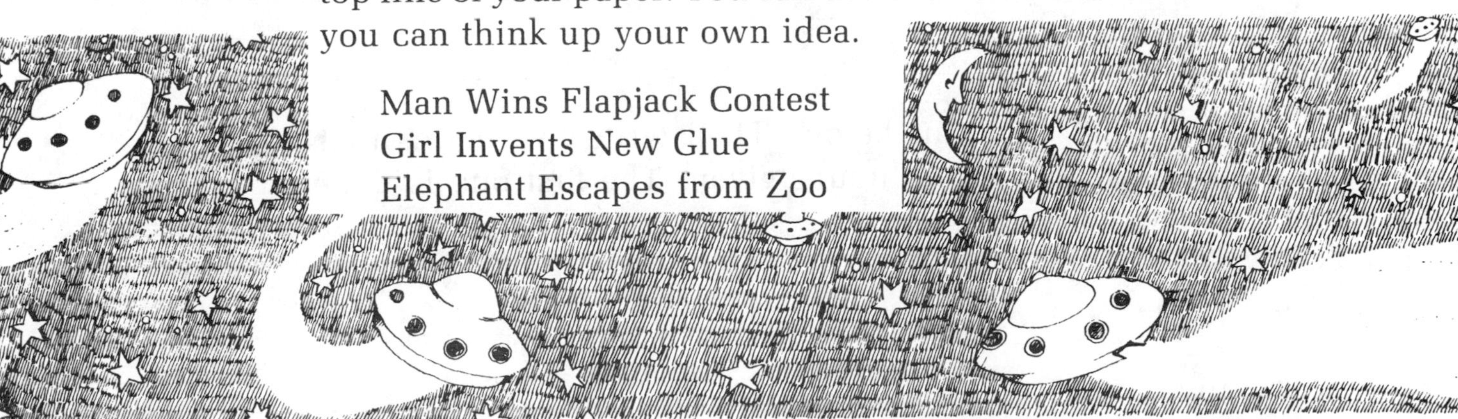

A title is a short way to tell the main idea.

lesson

Revising

Writing nouns that are more exact

The person fed the animal.

The sentence above tells about both pictures. But it doesn't tell enough. The nouns person and animal aren't very exact. The next sentence uses more exact nouns to tell about picture 1.

The queen fed the lion.

A. What more exact nouns would tell about picture 2? Write a sentence with more exact nouns for picture 2 on the line.

____

B. Read the list of nouns below. Then write *two* nouns that are more exact next to the nouns given. The first one is done.

1. building barn house
2. food __________ __________
3. toy __________ __________
4. flower __________ __________

C. Look at the picture. Read the nouns by each person, place or thing. Think of more exact nouns for each one. Using your more exact nouns, write three or more sentences about the picture on the lines below.

____

____

____

____

Look back at the sentences you've written for the **Write On** sections in this unit. Choose three sentences to rewrite. On another sheet of paper, rewrite the three sentences using more exact nouns.

Choose nouns carefully and they will say just what you want them to say.

Proofreading

Correcting your work

Study the story below.

> Sidney Hart   November 21, 19__
>
> Our Class Trip
>
> Our class trip was yesterday. We went to the museum. We saw whale bones. We saw model dinosaurs. We even saw footprints of a very old monster. We had a great day.

The story has been **proofread.** Proofreading means reading over something you have written and then making corrections.

A. Write answers to the questions about the story on the lines below.

1. What mark is used to cross out one letter at a time? ______
2. What mark is used to cross out a whole word? ______
3. What mark is used to add a word? ______

B. Read the next story. Then, using the proofreading marks you have learned, write in the corrections that are needed. Think about capital letters, spelling, and missing words.

bert loves to rune. He sometimes all day long.

this yer he will on the school rack team.

C. Now write a paragraph on the lines below about a trip you took. The trip you write about can be one you took with your class or with your family or even by yourself. After you finish your paragraph, proofread it. Be sure to use the proofreading marks you have learned in this lesson.

____

____

____

____

____

____

____

____

Ask yourself these questions when proofreading your writing:

Does every sentence begin with a capital letter?
Does every sentence end with a period?
Are all the words spelled correctly?
Does every sentence have all the words it needs?

Post-Test

1. Cross out the words that do not belong under each category name.

Animals	Tools	Buildings
bear	hammer	tree
dog	butter	house
duck	saw	school
car	rake	barn

2. Read the next paragraph. Then underline the sentence below it that tells the paragraph's main idea.

   The last snows melted, and the buds on the trees became leaves. Songbirds returned just in time to see the first daffodils bloom. The whole world seemed new again.

   a. It takes a long time for snow to melt.
   b. Spring had begun.
   c. Birds fly south in winter.

3. Write a title for the next paragraph on the line below.

   ____

   The first bicycle had wooden wheels. Imagine how uncomfortable that would be! Wooden wheels did not absorb the bumps on roads like rubber wheels do. In fact, bicycles that had these wooden wheels were called "boneshakers."

4. Rewrite the sentence below. Make the underlined nouns more exact. Use your new sentence as the main idea of a paragraph. Write the paragraph on a separate sheet of paper.

   When I grow up, I will be a <u>person</u> and work in a <u>place</u>.

unit 2

Writing in Sequence

Things to Remember About Writing in Sequence

Sequence tells what comes first, next, or last.

Writing

- Use sequence words like *next* and *yesterday* to tell when something happens.
- Give directions in proper sequence when you tell how something is done.
- Write every story so that it has a beginning, a middle, and an end.

Revising

- Use exact verbs to make your sentences clearer and more interesting.

Proofreading

Check to see that you have

- begun special names with capital letters
- used a capital letter to write the word *I*
- begun every sentence with a capital letter

lesson

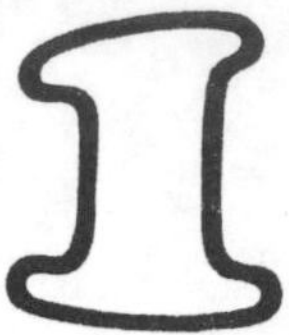

Writing picture stories

A. Look at the groups of pictures below. They can tell a story. Put each group of pictures in correct order so that they do tell a story. Write first, next, or last under each picture to show the correct order.

When you put each group of pictures above in order, you put them in **sequence.** Sequence tells you what comes first, next, or last.

B. The pictures below are in sequence. They tell part of a story. Finish the story by drawing the last picture in the space.

First

Next

Last

C. On each line below, write a sentence that tells about each picture in part **B.** Be sure that your sentences are in sequence.

First: ______________________________

Next: ______________________________

Last: ______________________________

On another sheet of paper, draw your own picture story. Use at least three pictures for your story. Then write a sentence under each picture that tells about the picture. Be sure your pictures and sentences are in sequence. You can use the ideas below. Or you can think up your own idea.

Getting Splashed
Practicing a Music Lesson
Feeding Your Baby Sister

To tell a picture story, draw pictures in sequence.

lesson

2 Writing sequence words

Study the pictures above. The words that are underlined are **sequence words.** Sequence words tell when something happens. *First, then, next,* and *finally* are sequence words. Some other sequence words are *last, second, third, tomorrow, yesterday, before,* and *after.*

A. Read the lists of sequence words below. Then number each word to show which word tells first, second, or last. Use the numbers 1, 2, or 3.

___ middle	___ night
___ beginning	___ morning
___ end	___ noon

B. Find the sequence words in the next paragraph. Underline each one.

First, I gave the crazy monkey a banana. Then she peeled it. Finally, she threw away the banana and ate the peel.

C. There are two groups of sequence words below. For each group, write three sentences in sequence using these words. One is done to show you how.

morning afternoon night

In the morning it was raining. That afternoon it began to hail. At night the snow started to pile up.

1. yesterday today tomorrow

____

____

____

____

2. first then finally

____

____

____

On another sheet of paper, write three sentences using the words <u>morning</u>, <u>noon</u>, and <u>night</u>. Have your sentences tell about something you do at these times of day. Be sure your sentences are written in sequence.

Use sequence words to tell when something happens.

lesson 3

Writing recipes

A **recipe** is a set of directions for making a kind of food. Read the recipe card below.

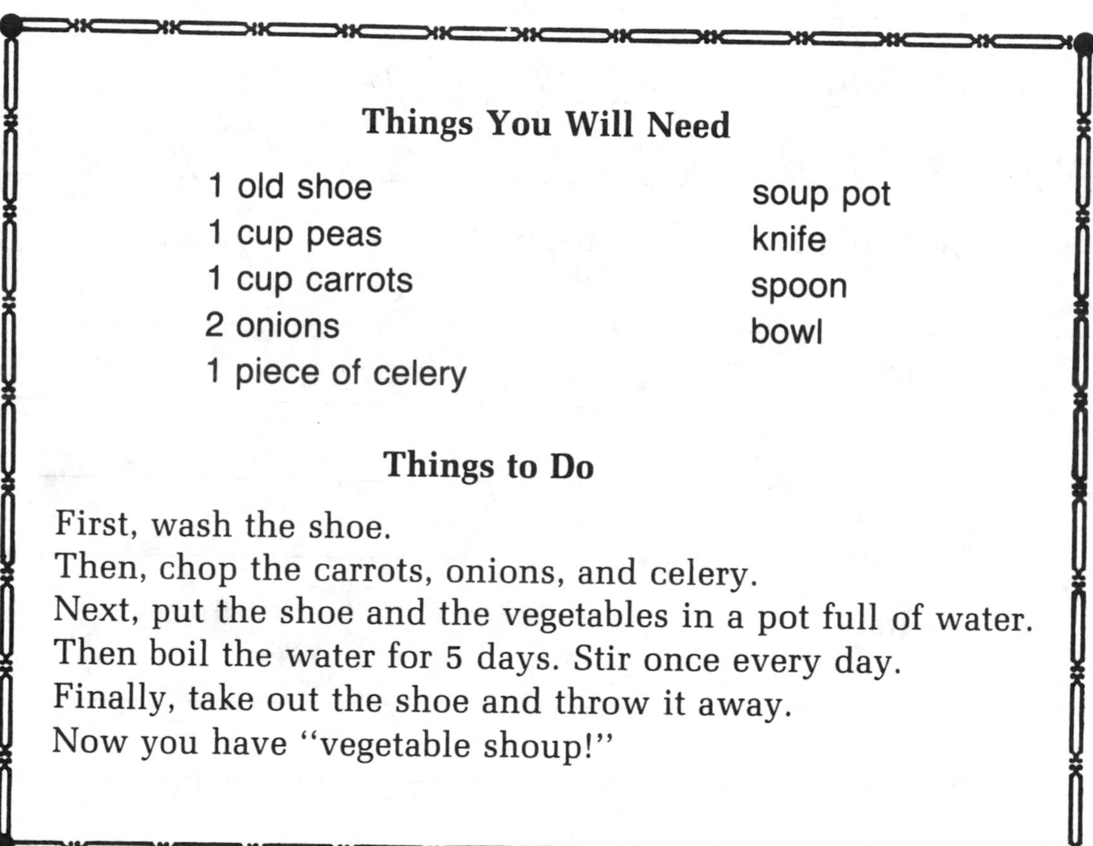

Things You Will Need

1 old shoe	soup pot
1 cup peas	knife
1 cup carrots	spoon
2 onions	bowl
1 piece of celery	

Things to Do

First, wash the shoe.
Then, chop the carrots, onions, and celery.
Next, put the shoe and the vegetables in a pot full of water.
Then boil the water for 5 days. Stir once every day.
Finally, take out the shoe and throw it away.
Now you have "vegetable shoup!"

A. That recipe may not taste very good, but it is written in sequence. What are the sequence words it uses? Write them on the lines below.

B. A recipe usually has two parts. The first part tells the things you will need. The second part tells the things to do. Read the words and sentences below. Then write the words or sentences on the recipe card that follows.

Egg Noodles

2 cups flour
First, break the eggs into the flour.
3 tablespoons water
Finally, roll out the mixture.
Next, add the water and salt and stir.
1 teaspoon salt
2 eggs

Things You Will Need

____

____

____

____

Things to Do

____

____

____

On another sheet of paper, write your own recipe. You can write a recipe for a cake or a stew, a pizza or a meatloaf. Or you may use your own idea. But be sure your directions are written in sequence.

When writing a recipe, give directions in sequence.

Writing "how to" directions

Look at the numbered dots below.

4

1 2

3 5

A. If you follow the directions below carefully, the dots will form a picture.

First, draw a straight line between dots 1 and 2. Then draw a line between dots 2 and 3. Next draw a line between dots 3 and 4. Then between 4 and 5. Finally, draw a line between 5 and 1. What picture have you drawn?

You already know what sequence means. You also know that a recipe is a set of directions that is written in sequence. Now you will learn how to write **how to** directions. "How to" directions tell just that, how to do something.

B. The following directions tell how to wash a car. But they are not in sequence. Put the directions in sequence by numbering each direction. Use the numbers 1, 2, 3, 4, 5, 6.

___ Finally, dry the car with a soft, clean cloth.

___ Second, fill the bucket with water and some soap powder.

___ Fourth, wash the bottom of the car.

___ Fifth, rinse off the soap.

___ Third, wash the top of the car.

___ First, get a bucket, a hose, and a soft cloth.

C. Now, write your own set of directions for making a phone call. Use sequence words and write each step in sequence.

____

____

____

____

On another sheet of paper, write one more set of "how to" directions. Make your directions at least 5 steps long. Remember to use sequence words and to write your directions in sequence. You can use one of the "how to" ideas below. Or you can think up your own.

How to build a skateboard
How to fly a kite
How to play your favorite game

"How to" directions tell how something can be done. Write "how to" directions in sequence.

lesson

5 Writing story parts in order

Some stories are true. For example, most news stories are true. Most stories about real people's lives are true. Can you think of a story about a real person that is true?

Some stories are not true. They are about what a writer has imagined. They are make-believe. For example, *Cinderella* is a make-believe story. Can you think of another make-believe story?

Whether stories are true or make-believe, they all have a **beginning**, a **middle,** and an **end.** The beginning, middle, and end of a story are written in sequence. The beginning comes first, the middle comes second, and the ending comes last.

A. Read each story below. Then write beginning, middle, or end beside the correct part.

1. ______________ Vera found a large egg.

   ______________ A baby dinosaur hopped out of the egg.

   ______________ She broke it.

2. ______________ Next, a snake came out of the man's basket.

   ______________ First, the man began to play his horn.

   ______________ Finally, the snake began to sway to the music.

B. Each group of sentences below can tell a story. But one part of each story is not finished. Write the beginning, middle, or end of each story. Then write the word beginning, middle or end beside the part you have written.

1. It began to snow in the early evening.
   It snowed all night.

   In the morning ______________________________

   ____

2. Jamie and I built a large boat.

   We ____

   ____

   Then we landed on a small island with strange animals.

3. The mailman _________________________________

   ____

   I opened the package as quickly as I could.
   I found a sweater with my name on it.

On another sheet of paper, write a story that tells about the funniest thing that ever happened to you. Be sure your story has a beginning, a middle, and an end. Your story can be make-believe or true.

Write every story so that it has a beginning, a middle, and an end.

lesson

Revising

Writing with interesting verbs

The canoe tipped, and the boy fell into the water.

The words that are underlined in the sentence above are called **verbs.** Verbs tell action or help make a statement in other ways. If you choose exact verbs, they will help you say just what you want to say.

A. Read the sentences below. Then underline each verb.

1. Jan danced on the stage.
2. A frog jumped into my soup.
3. The squirrel scurried up the tree.

B. The most exact verbs make the most interesting sentences. Read the list of verbs below. Then write two verbs that are more exact next to the verbs given. The first one is done to show you how.

1. ran sprinted raced
2. walked ________ ________
3. ate ________ ________
4. talked ________ ________

C. Look at the picture below. There is lots of action. On the lines below it, tell what is happening in the picture. Use exact verbs to make your sentences interesting.

Look back at the sentences you've written for the **Write On** sections in this unit. Choose five sentences to rewrite. On another sheet of paper, rewrite the five sentences using more interesting verbs.

Verbs tell action or help make a statement. Use exact verbs to make your writing interesting.

Proofreading

Using capital letters correctly

Jerry Holmes September 25, 19__

My Green Friend

My friend is a praying mantis. He is mostly green. He sits very still. He loves to eat other insects. His favorite foods are flies and gnats.

Sometimes he eats out of my hand. He also likes to be petted. Often, I tie him to my bed. He looks out for bugs at night. He is a great pet.

Study the model story above.

A. Read the questions below. Then write answers to the questions on the lines.

1. With what kind of letter, a small letter or a capital letter, does each sentence begin? ____________________

2. How is the word I written? ____________________

3. What letters in the person's name who wrote this story are capitals?

   ____

4. How does the date begin? ____________________

Study the box on the next page. It shows you special names that begin with capital letters.

People	Cities
Ms. Carla Jackson	Chicago
Mr. Peter Sanchez	Durham
Days	**Schools**
Tuesday	Washington School
Friday	East Central School
States	**Holidays**
New Mexico	Memorial Day
Pennsylvania	Thanksgiving Day
Streets	**Months**
Green Street	June
Oak Street	February

B. Now, using capital letters correctly, rewrite the paragraph below on the lines. Use the rules below to help you.

michelle myers goes to east windsor school. she jogs down spring street and sprints over to vine street. every wednesday she has soccer practice. on those days, she rides over to stanleyville.

____

____

____

____

____

Begin special names with capital letters.
Use a capital letter to write the word I.
Begin every sentence with a capital letter.

Post-Test

1. Number the following words in sequence. Use the numerals 1–3 for each group.

   a. ____ tomorrow ____ yesterday ____ today

   b. ____ later ____ now ____ before

2. Write three directions that tell how you get to a friend's house from home. Use complete sentences and sequence words.

   a. ______________________________

   b. ______________________________

   c. ______________________________

3. Write a more exact verb for each verb listed below.

   a. move ______________ c. throw ______________

   b. hit ______________ d. laugh ______________

4. Write capital letters where they belong in these sentences.

   a. next monday is columbus day, and lafayette school is closed.

   b. last may ellen gray and i flew to houston, texas.

5. Write a paragraph that tells what you plan to do after school today. Name at least four things you will do. Use sequence words to list these activities in the order you will do them. Try to use exact verbs in your sentences.

unit 3
Writing Comparisons

Things to Remember About Writing Comparisons

A **comparison** tells how things are alike or different.

Writing

- Add *er* or *more* to comparing words when you compare two things.
- Add *est* or *most* to comparing words when you compare more than two things.
- Use *better* and *best* when comparing *good*. Use *worse* and *worst* when comparing *bad*.
- Compare things by using *like* or *as* to make your writing more interesting.

Revising

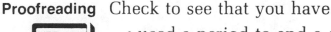

- Use adjectives to make the meaning of your sentences clear.

Proofreading

Check to see that you have

- used a period to end a statement
- used a period to end a command
- used a question mark to end a sentence that asks something
- used an exclamation point after a word or sentence that tells strong feeling

lesson

Writing comparisons of pictures

When we **compare** things, we tell how they are alike or how they are different. The sentences beside the pictures are **comparisons**.

A. Study the pictures. Then read the comparisons. Finally, underline the comparisons that best tell about the pictures.

1.

One player is taller.
One player is thinner.

2.

One animal is longer.
One animal is smarter.

3.

The boy and girl are the same height.
The boy is in the fifth grade.

B. Using the pictures on the right side of the following page, write your own comparisons. Use the words at the top of page 35 for help. Make sure your comparisons are complete sentences. One is done to show you how.

Words used in Comparisons

more	fewer	louder
less	faster	same
bigger	higher	

1. The man on the left has bigger muscles.

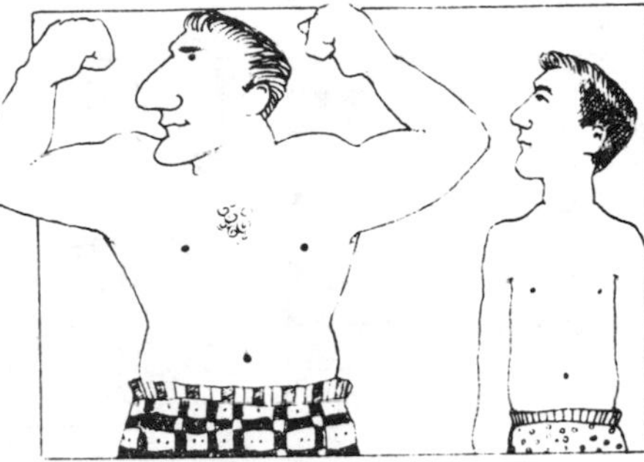

2. ______________________________

____

3. ______________________________

____

On another sheet of paper, draw two sets of pictures. Draw the pictures in each set so that you can write comparisons for them. Then write a comparison for each set. Be sure to write your comparisons in complete sentences.

A comparison tells how things are alike or different.

lesson

2 Writing comparisons with er and more

Miff is smaller than Thor. Thor is larger than Miff.

Both sentences above are comparisons. You already know that comparisons tell how things are alike or different. Well, some comparing words add **er** to their ends to make comparisons. For example: small, smaller—tall, taller—high, higher.

Now read the next sentence.

A feather bed is **more comfortable** than a bed of nails.

What are the words that make the comparison in that sentence? Words like *comfortable* use the word **more** to make comparisons. In fact, most long words use the word more to make certain comparisons. For example: beautiful, more beautiful—important, more important—dangerous, more dangerous.

A. Think about what you have learned. Then, using the list of comparing words, write two comparisons for the picture at the top of page 37. Add er to the correct words.

small fancy new long short

B. This time write two comparisons using the word more. You can use the comparing words below. Or think up your own. Be sure to write complete sentences.

comfortable	dangerous	wonderful
exciting	beautiful	active

On a separate sheet of paper, write a story about a trip you might take. Use comparing words that have er endings or that use the word more.

Below are some comparing words you may want to use in your story. Or you may think up other comparing words.

high	big	large	beautiful
short	fast	tired	dangerous

Add er to short comparing words when you are comparing two things.
Use the word more with longer comparing words when you are comparing two things.

lesson

3 Writing comparisons with est and most

Read the next paragraph.

Flora is the clever**est** magician I know. She can do the **most** wonderful tricks. Her new**est** trick is to make herself disappear. Too bad she hasn't learned how to make herself appear again!

Cleverest, newest, and *most wonderful* are all forms of comparisons. They compare more than two things. When comparing more than two things, add **est** to the ends of short comparing words. But use the word **most** before longer comparing words.

A. Read the following comparing words. Write the word two beside those that can compare two things. Write the words more than two beside those that can compare more than two things.

1. greatest ____________________
2. greater ____________________
3. most wonderful ____________________

B. Write a comparison sentence for each comparing word below. Write each comparison so that it compares more than two things. The two forms are done to show you how.

thoughtful *Harry is the most thoughtful person I know.*

great *That was the greatest time of my life.*

1. old ____________________
2. delicious ____________________
3. tall ____________________

Some comparing words drop, add, or change letters when they change form. For example: funny, funn**ier**, funni**est** – large, larg**er**, larg**est**. If you are not sure of the spelling, check your dictionary.

C. Write three comparisons for the picture below. You may use the following comparing words or think up your own: large, big, small, little. Be sure to check your spelling.

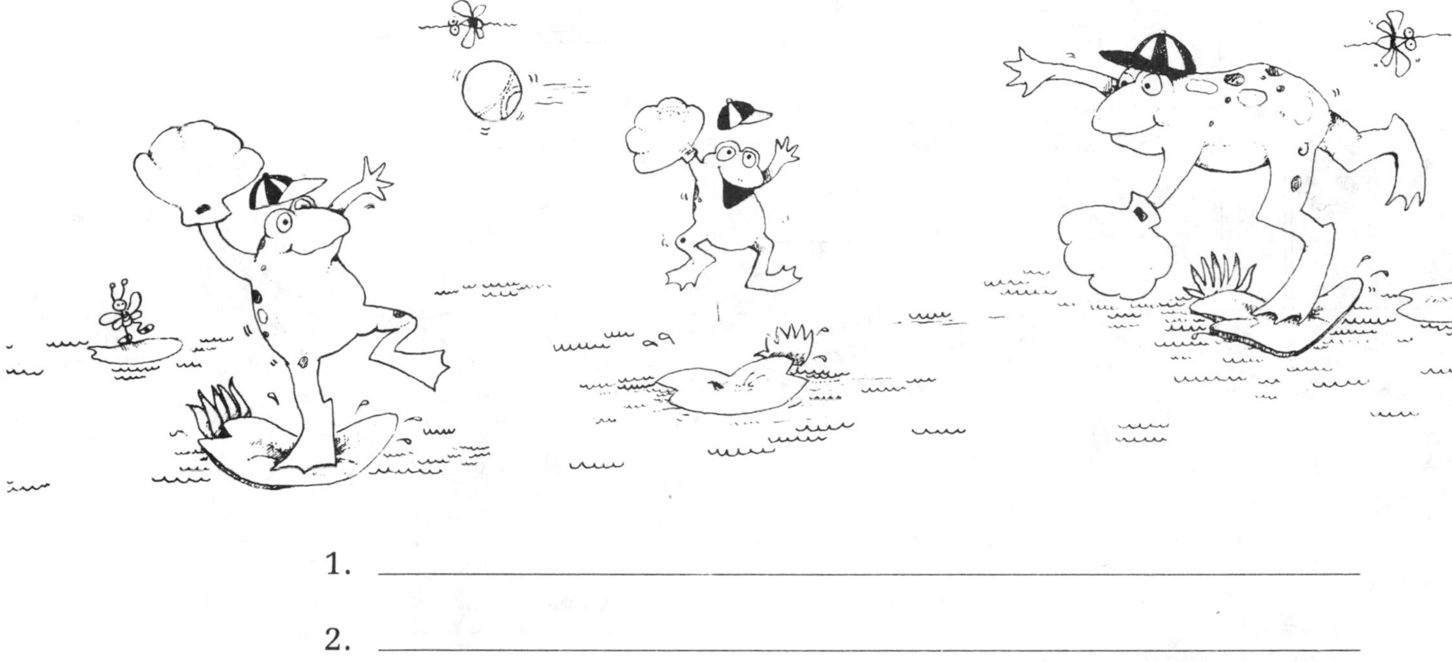

1. ______________________________

2. ______________________________

3. ______________________________

Pretend you are the judge at a costume party. You have to choose the funniest costume, the ugliest costume, and the most unusual costume. On a separate sheet of paper, write a paragraph of five or more sentences that will tell about the costumes. Be sure to use the correct form for each comparison you write.

Add est to short comparing words when you are comparing more than two things.
Use the word most with longer comparing words when you are comparing more than two things.

Writing comparisons with <u>good</u> and <u>bad</u>

Read the sentences below that tell about the picture.

Sam has a **good** seat.
Felicia has a **better** seat than Sam.
Yolanda has the **best** seat of the three.

Now read the sentences below.

Marybeth's bike is in **bad** shape.
Nazir's bike is in **worse** shape than Marybeth's.
Frank's bike is in the **worst** shape of the three.

A. Read the sentences above again. Then answer the following questions. Write your answers on the lines.

1. What word compares two seats? ____________________

2. What word compares more than two seats? ____________

3. What word compares two bikes? ____________________

4. What word compares more than two bikes? ____________

B. Using the two forms of *good* and *bad* that you have learned, write your own comparisons on the lines below. The examples below will show you how.

Good

good	John is a good singer.
better	Manny is a better singer than John.
best	Estella is the best singer of the three.

Bad

bad	Angela has a bad cold.
worse	Glen has a worse cold than Angela.
worst	Melinda has the worst cold of the three.

1. good ____
2. better ____
3. best ____
4. bad ____
5. worse ____
6. worst ____

Write On

Now write about something you saw or something that happened to you. Using a comparison of good or bad, write at least one paragraph. You may use the ideas below or you may think up your own.

The Best Day At School   The Worst Storm

When comparing good, use the words better and best. When comparing bad, use the words worse and worst.

lesson

5 Writing comparisons with like and as

Look at the picture. Then read the sentences below that tell about it.

My horse runs **like the wind.**
My horse runs **as fast as the wind**.

Another way to compare things is to use the words **like** or **as**. When used in comparisons, the words *like* and *as* tell how things compare.

A. Read the sentences about the picture again. Then write answers to the following questions on the lines.

1. To what are the sentences comparing the way the horse runs? ____________________
2. How many things are being compared in the first sentence?

____

3. How many things are being compared in the second sentence? ______________________________

B. Read the following comparisons. Then write your own comparisons by finishing the phrases below.

Daria's smile is like a slice of watermelon.
She is as thin as a wrinkle.

1. Chico laughs like ______________________________

____

2. Our car is like ______________________________

____

3. The pudding looks like ______________________________

____

Write On

Think about a summer day, a party, a friend, or your home. Or you may think about an idea of your own. Then on another sheet of paper, write at least one paragraph that tells about the idea you have chosen. In your paragraph, write comparisons that use the words like and as.

Below are the beginnings of some comparisons you may want to use. Or you may think up your own.

as soft as	the day was like
as lonely as	the food tasted like
as cheerful as	the room was like a

You can compare things by using the words like or as.

lesson

Revising

Writing with interesting adjectives

The plane is taking off.

The sentence above tells something about the picture. But it doesn't tell much. It would tell more if it used comparing words. You already know that comparing words tell how things are alike or different. A shorter name for comparing words is **adjectives.**

A. Now read the two sentences below that use adjectives to tell more about the picture above. Then underline the adjectives in each sentence.

1. The huge, bright, new plane is taking off.
2. The tiny, clumsy, old plane is taking off.

B. Underline each adjective in the next group of sentences.

1. Daisy got a shiny blue bicycle for her birthday.
2. It had a large basket on the handlebars.
3. Last week she took her fluffy kitten for a ride.
4. First, Daisy wrapped the kitten in a soft, green blanket.

C. Now write your own adjectives that tell about each noun below. Two are done for you.

	____old____	house		____new____	socks
1.	__________	rug	6.	__________	magician
2.	__________	hair	7.	__________	elephant
3.	__________	sky	8.	__________	plant
4.	__________	cat	9.	__________	soup
5.	__________	shirt	10.	__________	glass

Write a paragraph using one of the ideas below. Or you may think up your own idea. Make sure that your paragraph has at least one adjective in every sentence. You may use the list of adjectives below for help. Or you may want to think of your own adjectives.

Ideas	Adjectives		
Your favorite TV show	tiny	grumpy	heavy
Moving	old	swift	little
Your favorite person	huge	great	strange
Watching people	chilly	warm	beautiful
Flying in a plane	wonderful	slight	happy

Use adjectives to make your writing interesting.

Proofreading

lesson 7 Writing end punctuation

Read the following sentences. Notice how the **punctuation** is used.

Statement – He gave Erica a bunch of flowers.
Command – Pick up that pile of trash.
Question – How far is it to Okefenokee?
Exclamation – Yipe! That looks like a ghost!

period

•

A. Now write answers to the questions below.

exclamation point

1. What punctuation mark ends the statement?

____

2. What punctuation mark ends the command?

____

question mark

3. What punctuation mark ends the question?

____

4. What punctuation mark ends the exclamation?

____

B. Read the following sentences. Then write the correct punctuation mark for each one.

1. How long is that boat ___
2. Finish painting the fence by tomorrow ___
3. Mr. Hernandez took us to the zoo ___
4. Wow ___ Look at that hit ___
5. Where are you going ___
6. There is a crowd outside the palace ___
7. Don't push ___
8. Will the king give a speech ___

C. Now write the four kinds of sentences yourself. Write two statements, two commands, two questions, and one exclamation. Be sure to punctuate them correctly.

Statement – ________________________________

Statement – ________________________________

Command – ________________________________

Command – ________________________________

Question – ________________________________

Question – ________________________________

Exclamation – ________________________________

Use a period to end a statement.
Use a period to end a command.
Use a question mark to end a sentence that asks something.
Use an exclamation point after a word or sentence that tells strong feeling.

Post-Test

1. Read the adjectives below. For each adjective, write the form that compares two things. Then write the form that compares more than two things.

   a. soft ______________ ______________

   b. sweet ______________ ______________

   c. interesting ______________ ______________

   d. exciting ______________ ______________

2. Write a comparing form of *good* to complete each sentence.

   a. Jeremy is a __________ runner than Kurt.

   b. Sarah is the __________ runner in the school.

   Write a comparing form of *bad* to complete each sentence.

   c. The burnt eggs tasted __________ than the burnt toast.

   d. The burnt oatmeal tasted the __________ of the three foods.

3. Complete the comparisons below.

   a. Dr. Bellows had a voice like a ______________.

   b. The painting was as colorful as ______________.

4. Write an adjective for each noun in the titles below. Then write a story, using one of the titles. Make your story at least four sentences long. Use at least one adjective in each sentence.

   a. The __________ Bear and the __________ Hunter

   b. __________ Children in a __________ House

   c. A __________ Day in the __________ Jungle

unit 4
Writing Details

Things to Remember About Writing with Details

Details are small parts that make a whole.

Writing

- Use details that tell about how something looks, sounds, smells, tastes, and feels.
- Use adjectives to describe objects and people.

Revising

- Use adverbs to tell how, where, or when.

Proofreading

Check to see that you have

- used the s-form of the verb for certain singular subjects
- used the plain form of the verb for certain plural subjects

lesson

1 Writing details from pictures

Look carefully at the pictures.

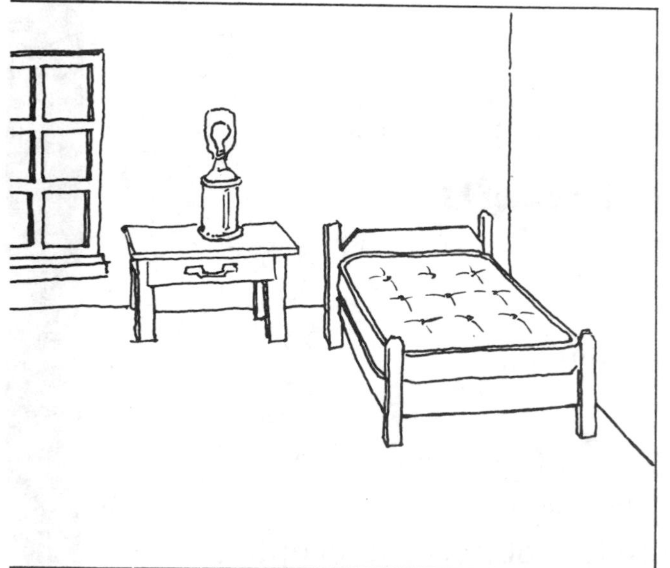

The picture on the right has more **details**. Details are small parts that go together to make a whole. For example, one detail of the picture on the right is the book on the table.

A. Read the sentences below that tell details about the pictures. Then write the letter R beside each sentence that tells about the picture on the right. Write the letter L beside each sentence that tells about the picture on the left.

____ 1. An alarm clock is on the table by the bed.

____ 2. There is no bedspread on the bed.

____ 3. A dog is lying on the rug near the bed.

____ 4. There are curtains on the window.

____ 5. There is no picture on the wall over the bed.

B. A group of sentences that tells details about something is called a **description.** On the lines below, write a description of your classroom or a room in your home.

A B

Write On

Look carefully at both pictures above. Think about all the details. Then, on another sheet of paper, write a detailed description of each clown. Write the letter A above your description of the clown on the left. Write the letter B above your description of the clown on the right.

Details are small parts that go together to make a whole.

lesson

2 Writing with your senses

Study the pictures below.

A. The five **senses** are seeing, hearing, smell, taste, and touch. Write answers to the following questions about the pictures.

1. What sense are the children in picture **A** using mainly?

____

2. What senses are the children in picture **B** using mainly?

____

You know that details are small parts of a larger whole. You know also that a description is a group of sentences that tells details about something. When you gather details, you use your senses. Sometimes you use just one sense or mainly one sense. Other times you may use all of your senses.

B. Below is a description that uses four of the senses. Read the description. Then write the name of the thing being described.

It is round and red. It feels smooth. It tastes sweet. It sounds crunchy when you bite it. It is an ______________________.

Think about a place you like to be. Or you may choose one of the places listed below. Then do the following things: First, write the senses <u>see</u>, <u>hear</u>, <u>smell</u>, <u>touch</u>, and <u>taste</u> across the top of another sheet of paper. Next, write details that tell about the place you chose under each sense. Finally, write your details together in a complete description. Be sure to write your description in complete sentences. If you need help, read the description in part **B** again.

your kitchen at holiday time
a park in the spring
your favorite store

Use your senses when you write a description.

lesson

3 Writing about an object

Some words always describe things. Words like *smooth, soft,* and *loud* are describing words. You already know a word that means a describing word. That word is *adjective.*

A. Look at the picture. Think about the cat. Then circle the adjectives below that describe the cat.

square fluffy soft mad

black wet sad furry

Now think of two more adjectives that describe the cat. Write those adjectives below.

1. ________________ 2. ________________

B. Write one sentence that describes the object in each picture on the next page. Try to use at least two adjectives in each sentence. Then underline your adjectives. One is done to show you how.

A scary, square picture is on the wall.

1. ______________________________

2. ______________________________

On another sheet of paper, write the name of your favorite food, toy, and clothing. Next to each favorite thing, write three adjectives that describe it. Remember to think about your five senses. After you have written your adjectives, choose one of the things to describe. Finally, write four or more sentences that describe your favorite thing. You may use the adjectives below.

Adjectives

playful	speedy	noisy	cold	tasty
furry	quiet	brown	sharp	sweet
colorful	red	bright	soft	yummy

Adjectives can help you to describe objects.

lesson 4 Writing about a person

You know some words that describe objects. There are words that describe people too.

A. Write the word or word group from the list under the picture of the person it describes. Some words may not fit either person.

Words That Can Describe People

tall	curly hair	wearing glasses
short	long hair	flowered dress
thin	dark hair	light hair
freckles	short hair	long pants

B. Write four or more sentences that describe the picture above. Try to describe everything that the picture shows. Tell how the boy looks, how he is dressed, and how he feels.

____

____

____

____

____

Write On

Think about one of your favorite people. Think about how that person looks and how he or she acts. Think about what that person does best. Think about why you like that person. Then, on a sheet of paper, write a paragraph that describes your favorite person. Make your paragraph at least five sentences long. Remember to use words that you learned in this lesson and in the lesson about adjectives.

Adjectives can help you to describe people.

lesson

5 Writing riddles

Read the story above. A story that asks a question in an unusual way and then gives a funny answer is called a **riddle.**

A. Read the following riddles. Notice how they describe things. Then write answers to them on the lines.

1. Once I was a golden ball floating in a clear sea with a white wall around me. But someone broke my wall, and I became breakfast. I am an ______________________________ .
2. We are hard and white. One set of us falls out, but another grows back. We help you to say hello and to enjoy your Thanksgiving turkey. We are ______________________ .

B. Look at the pictures below. Then think of a riddle that would describe each picture with only one detail. Write **X** next to the detail that would best help someone answer the riddle.

1.

___ I have four legs

___ I bark

___ I have a tail.

2.

___ People fly in me.

___ I am silver.

___ I have wings.

Now write some riddles of your own. On another sheet of paper, write at least three riddles. Think of animals, things to eat, things to wear, things in your home or classroom. After you have written your riddles, share them with the class or a friend. If you need help, look back at part **A** of this lesson.

Details are important in riddles.

lesson 6

Revising

Writing with adverbs

Read the next sentence.

The snake is crawling quietly outside now.

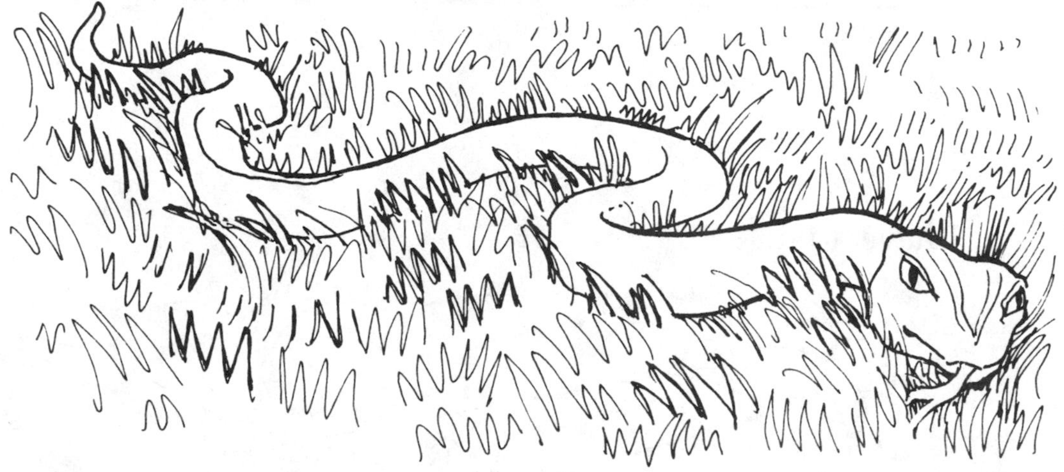

A. Now write answers to the questions below.

1. Which one of the underlined words tells how the snake is crawling? ____________

2. Which word tells where the snake is crawling? ________

3. Which word tells when the snake is crawling? ________

Adverbs are words like those underlined above. Adverbs tell how, where, and when.

B. Find the adverbs in the sentences below. Underline each one.

1. I found my slipper outside today.
2. Rags was chewing it happily.
3. I yelled loudly, and he ran.
4. He ran upstairs and hid.
5. Later, I found him sleeping peacefully.

C. Now write adverbs to complete each sentence below. The words below the lines tell you which kind of adverb to write. One is done to show you how.

Laurie speaks ______softly______.
(how?)

1. Olivia found a skunk ____________________.
(where?)

2. Zeke got to school ____________________.
(when?)

3. The birds sing ____________________.
(how?) (when?)

4. The children ran ____________________
(how?) (where?)

____________________.
(when?)

Write On

Look back over the sentences and paragraphs that you have written for this unit. Choose five sentences or one paragraph to rewrite. Rewrite your sentences or paragraph on another sheet of paper. Use at least one adverb for each sentence that you rewrite.

Adverbs tell how, where, or when.

Proofreading

Using the correct verb form

The pelican gulp**s** the fish. The pelicans gulp the fish.

A. You already know that verbs tell action or help make statements in other ways. Write answers to the questions about the verbs in the sentences.

1. What are the verbs in the sentences below each picture?

   ______________________ ______________________

2. How are the verbs different? ______________________

3. Which verb tells about more than one pelican? __________

Two verb forms are used with certain singular and plural subjects. If the subject is singular, like *pelican*, the verb has an *s* ending. If the subject is plural, like *pelicans*, the verb has no *s*.

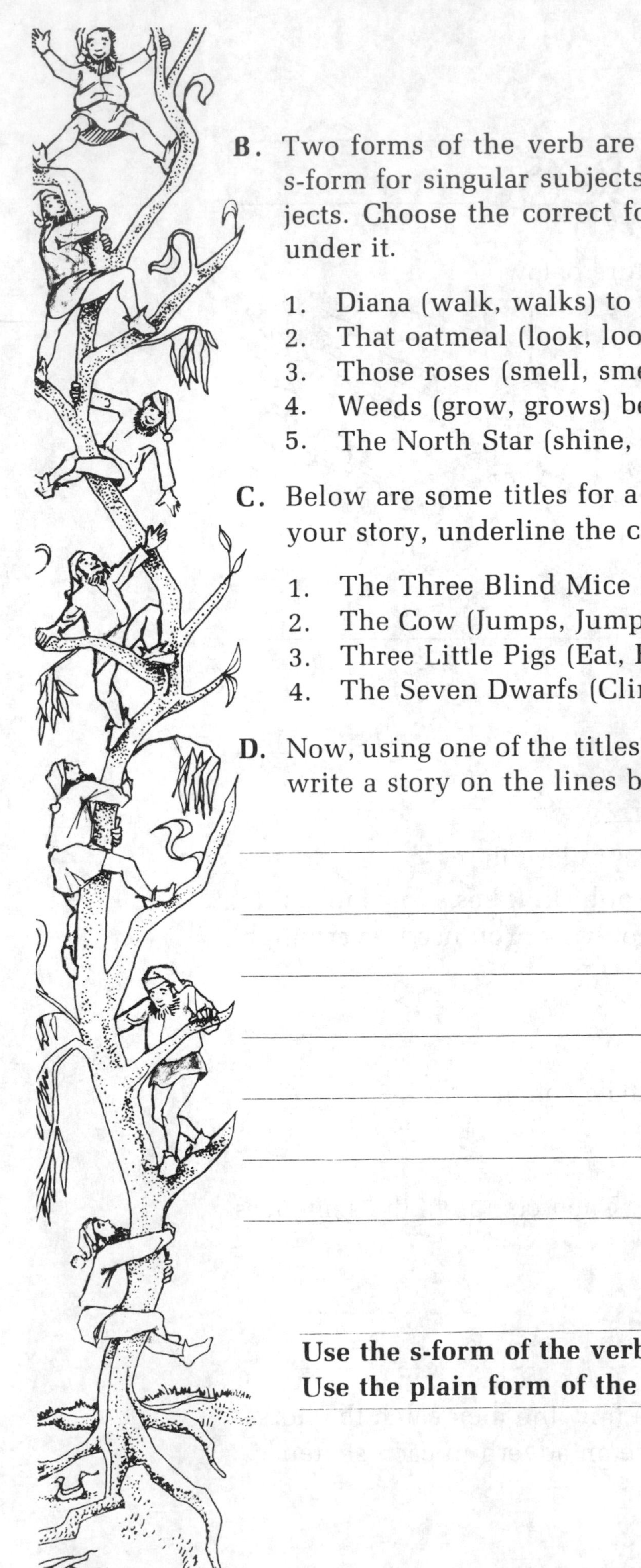

B. Two forms of the verb are given for the sentences below, the s-form for singular subjects and the plain form for plural subjects. Choose the correct form of each verb by drawing a line under it.

1. Diana (walk, walks) to school every day.
2. That oatmeal (look, looks) lumpy.
3. Those roses (smell, smells) sweet.
4. Weeds (grow, grows) best in the garden.
5. The North Star (shine, shines) brightly.

C. Below are some titles for a story you can write. Before writing your story, underline the correct verb form in each title.

1. The Three Blind Mice (Play, Plays) Tag
2. The Cow (Jumps, Jump) over the School
3. Three Little Pigs (Eat, Eats) Lunch
4. The Seven Dwarfs (Climb, Climbs) the Beanstalk

D. Now, using one of the titles from part **C,** or using your own title, write a story on the lines below.

____

____

____

____

____

____

____

Use the s-form of the verb for certain singular subjects.
Use the plain form of the verb for certain plural subjects.

Post-Test

1. Write four details about the picture below.

a. ______________________________

b. ______________________________

c. ______________________________

d. ______________________________

2. What does the following paragraph describe?

It has a head but cannot see or hear. It has a foot but cannot walk. It has many springs but no water. You use it every night and make it every day.

It is a ______________________________.

3. Write two adjectives that describe a banana.

a. ______________ b. ______________

4. Look again at the picture above. Then complete the sentences below with adverbs.

a. The horse runs ______________________.

b. The men chase the horse ______________________.

5. Now write a paragraph that tells how the men catch the horse. Write at least four sentences. Use an adverb in each sentence.

unit 5
Writing Facts and Opinions

Things to Remember About Writing Facts and Opinions

A **fact** is something that is true. An **opinion** is what someone thinks or feels.

Writing

- Use names, places, and dates when writing facts.
- Use words like *think, feel, good,* and *should* when stating an opinion.

Revising

- Give every complete sentence both a subject and a verb.

Proofreading

Check to see that you have

- spelled correctly those verbs that tell about something that has already happened

lesson

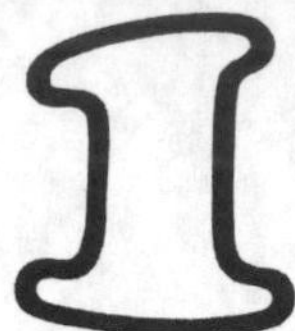

Writing sentences of fact and of opinion

A **fact** is a sentence that is true. An **opinion** is what someone thinks or feels. A sentence that is not true may tell about something that is *make-believe* or *false*.

Read the following sentences.

___ I go to school.

___ I think I would make a good astronaut.

___ I love blueberries.

___ I am an astronaut, and I travel to faraway places.

A. Now write T beside the sentence above that is true about you. Write O beside the sentences that tell what you might think or feel. Write F beside the sentence that is not true.

B. Read the sentences below. Then write fact beside the sentences that are facts. Write opinion beside the sentences that are opinions. Write false beside the sentences that are make-believe or not true.

1. ____________Yesterday, I ate some food.

2. ____________This morning I drove my family's car to school.

3. ____________Some people think that winter is the best time of the year.

4. ____________ The earth moves around the sun.

5. ____________I will have to call a spaceship to get home today.

C. Now write two facts about a good friend. Then write one opinion about that friend. Make each fact and opinion a complete sentence.

Fact: ____

Fact: ____

Opinion: ____

____

Write On

On another sheet of paper, write four sentences that tell about someone in your family. Make two of your sentences facts. Make the other two sentences opinions. Write fact next to the two sentences that tell facts. Write opinion next to the two sentences that tell opinions.

A fact is a sentence that is true.
An opinion tells what someone thinks or feels.

lesson 2

Writing about different topics

Look carefully at the picture below.

You know that facts are true, and opinions are what someone thinks or feels. Certain words are used to write opinions. You can use words like *think*, *better*, *worst*, *like*, and *should* when you write an opinion.

A. On the lines below, write two sentences that tell facts about the picture above. Then write two sentences that tell opinions about the picture. When writing facts, tell exactly what the picture shows. Use words like those above to show your opinion.

1. Fact: ______________________________

2. Fact: ______________________________

3. Opinion: ______________________________

____

4. Opinion: ______________________________

____

B. Now write some facts and opinions about your school. Some facts you might want to write are: where your school is, how many students go to your school, how old your school is, your principal's name, your teacher's name. Some opinions you might want to write are: if you enjoy school, what you like best about your school, what you don't like about your school, how you would change your school. Write your facts and opinions in complete sentences on the lines below.

Facts and Opinions About School:

1. Fact: ______________________________

2. Fact: ______________________________

3. Opinion: ______________________________

____

4. Opinion: ______________________________

____

Write On

Think about your favorite book or story. Then, on a separate sheet of paper, write the name of the book or story. First, write two facts about it. One fact might be where you read or heard the story. Another fact might be the name of the person who wrote the book or told you the story. Next, write your opinion of the book or story. Make your opinion at least three sentences long.

Words like think, feel, best, and should are used to state an opinion.

lesson

3 Writing about yourself in a letter

Read the letter below carefully.

Date →
Greeting →

January 24, 19__

Dear Jane,

I'm glad you just moved into our neighborhood. I sure do enjoy meeting people my own age.

I'm 8 years old. I weigh 65 pounds and I am 4 feet tall. I have green eyes and blond hair. In the summer, I get millions of freckles. Well, maybe I don't get millions, but I do get a lot.

My favorite hobby is spelunking. Have you ever heard of spelunking? That's when you go looking for caves. I think spelunking is a good hobby because it's so exciting.

My favorite school subject is math. I enjoy math because it gives me a chance to figure out problems on my own. I also like math because it is easy for me.

Would you like to come to my house one day after school to play? I would like to know more about you. I'll talk to you about a visit when I see you in school next week. I hope we will become good friends.

Closing →

Best wishes,
Donna

Notice where the **date** of the model letter is placed. Look at the **greeting** and the **closing** of the letter. All letters in good form are set up this way.

A. Now read the letter again. Then underline every sentence in it that tells a fact. Circle every sentence in it that tells an opinion. Remember, opinions are what someone thinks or feels.

B. Write three or more facts about yourself on the lines below the word *Facts*. Write some of your opinions about yourself and other things on the lines below the word *Opinions*. Use complete sentences.

Facts

____

____

____

Opinions

____

____

____

On a separate sheet of paper, write a letter to a person you have not seen in a long time. The person may be real or make-believe. Tell that person facts about yourself. Tell him or her some of your opinions.

Make sure your letter has both facts and opinions. Also, make sure your letter has the date, the greeting, and the closing in the correct form. If you need help, look back at the model letter and at part **B**.

You can write both facts and opinions in a letter.

lesson

Writing facts and opinions about animals

You know what facts and opinions are. Now you will write some facts and opinions about animals.

A. Read the names and look at the pictures of the animals below. Then, on the blank lines, write one or more facts about each animal. Be sure to write your facts in complete sentences.

A Bird

Facts: ______________________________

____

____

____

A Whale

Facts: ______________________________

____

____

____

A Mouse

Facts: ______________________________

____

____

____

B. Look at the picture of each animal below. Then write your opinion of each animal. You will probably use words like *best, think, like, bad,* and *feel* to show your opinion. Make sure your opinions are complete sentences.

A Dog

Opinion: ______________________________

____

____

____

____

A Fish

Opinion: ______________________________

____

____

____

____

Write On

On another sheet of paper, write a paragraph about an animal you would like to have as a pet. Make your paragraph at least five sentences long. Write both facts and opinions. Draw one line under your sentences with facts. Draw two lines under your sentences with opinions.

You can state both facts and opinions in a paragraph.

lesson 5

Writing a make-believe story

You know that some sentences can tell about things that are make-believe or not true. The next sentence tells about something that is make-believe.

Yin Shu chased the dragon.

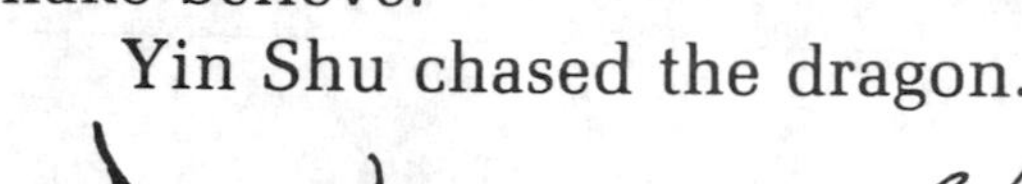

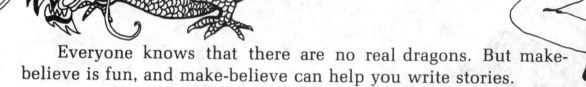

Everyone knows that there are no real dragons. But make-believe is fun, and make-believe can help you write stories.

A. Read the sentences below. Then write **M** beside the sentences that tell about make-believe things. Write **F** beside the sentences that tell facts.

1. ____________Our neighbor's dog told us a story yesterday.
2. ____________Today Viola ate 94 hamburgers and 37 ice cream cones.
3. ____________Once there was a girl who made candy canes out of red pencils.
4. ____________Some people can stand on their heads.

Now read the following make-believe story.

Once there was a boy named Jack who had a cow. Jack lived with his mother way out in the country. They were very poor people.

One day Jack's mother told her son to go to town and sell the cow to get some money. Jack took the cow to town and sold it. But he didn't get any money for his cow. Instead he got *beans* for it. When Jack got home and told his mother what he had done, she became very angry. She snatched the beans out of Jack's hand and threw them out into the yard. Then she sent her son to bed without his dinner.

B. The story about Jack *could* be true. It has sentences that could be facts. But in this lesson you will write stories that tell about make-believe things. Write a make-believe ending to the story about Jack on the lines below. Make your ending at least five sentences long.

____

____

____

____

____

____

____

____

On another sheet of paper, write a complete make-believe story of your own. Be sure that you tell about something that is not real or not true. Make your story at least five sentences long. You may use one of the ideas below for your story or you may think up your own idea.

The Old Cave	Finding a Talking Rock
The Day I Went to Mars	Sleeping for a Hundred Years

You can write stories about things that are make-believe.

Revising

Writing complete sentences

You probably know that a **complete sentence** begins with a capital letter and ends with a period, an exclamation point, or a question mark. But a complete sentence also tells a whole idea. A complete sentence tells at least one whole thought.

Read the complete sentence below.

subject — People walk. — verb

The short sentence above is a complete sentence because it has both a subject and a verb. A *subject* names the person or thing the sentence is about. You already know that a verb tells action. Every complete sentence has both a subject and a verb.

Look at the picture below.

A. Read the word groups on the next page that tell about the picture. Some of the word groups are complete sentences. But some of the word groups are not complete sentences. Decide which word groups are complete sentences and write **CS** next to them. Then write **NS** next to the word groups that are not complete sentences.

1. ___ Mr. Brownstein over there.

2. ___ Mr. Brownstein is funny.

3. ___ Mr. Brownstein dark hair.

4. ___ Mr. Brownstein does tricks.

5. ___ Mr. Brownstein yesterday.

B. Now write complete sentences of your own using the word groups below. Write one complete sentence for each word group that is given. One is done to show you how.

My favorite food is roasted snake skin.

1. The boy ______________________________

2. All of Pam's friends ______________________________

____

3. The greatest trick ______________________________

____

4. The old worn-out car ______________________________

____

Write On Copy the word groups below on another sheet of paper. Then, using each word group, write complete sentences.

1. The sleeping baby
2. Finally, Steve
3. Karen
4. The best thing about school
5. Watch out for
6. Then they
7. All of a sudden
8. Keep the
9. The kangaroo
10. After school we

Every complete sentence has both a subject and a verb.

Proofreading

lesson 7

Writing verbs that tell what already happened

Gillian's tooth ach**es.**
Gillian's tooth ach**ed** yesterday.

A. Read the sentences above. Then write answers to the questions on the lines below.

1. What are the verbs in the sentences?

 ____

2. Which sentence, the first or the second, tells what is happening **now**? ______________________________

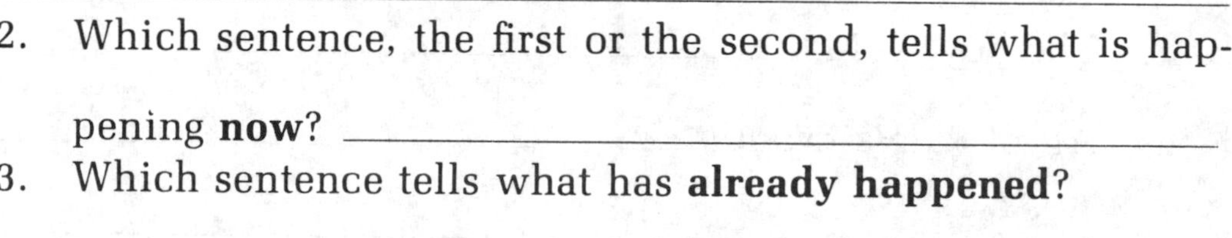

3. Which sentence tells what has **already happened**?

 ____

You know that verbs have different forms to tell about singular subjects or plural subjects. Verbs also have different forms to tell **when** something happens. Most verbs end with **ed** when they tell about something that has *already happened.*

B. Read the pairs of sentences below. Then write the correct form of the verb on each line. One is done to show you how.

The old door squeaks now.

The old door squeaked yesterday.

1. He yells at the cow.

 He __________ at the cow yesterday.

2. She peeks in the door.

 She __________ in the door last night.

Some verbs *don't* add ed to tell about something that has already happened. Instead they change spelling. Read the sentences below. Notice how the verbs change spelling to tell about something that has already happened.

The children eat ice cream.
The children **ate** ice cream.
I see the ball.
I **saw** the ball.

Other verbs that change spelling to tell what already happened are: *feel—felt, run—ran, fly—flew, take—took, catch—caught, drink—drank, throw—threw*. If you are not sure of how a verb is spelled, look it up in your dictionary.

C. Read the sentences below. Then write the correct verb form that tells about what already happened. One is done to show you how.

They take five minutes.

They __took__ five minutes.

1. I feel great.

   I ________ great.
2. We drink ice tea.

   We ________ ice tea.
3. I take a walk in the afternoon.

   I ________ a walk in the afternoon.

Most verbs end with ed to tell if something already happened. Some verbs change spelling to tell if something already happened.

Post-Test

1. Write the word fact beside the sentences that are facts. Write the word false beside the sentences that are not true. Write opinion beside the sentences that are opinions.

   a. ________ Football is the best sport of all.

   b. ________ Each child in my class is 30 feet tall.

   c. ________ Texas is a state of the United States.

   d. ________ You should stand on your head every night.

2. Write **CS** beside each word group that is a complete sentence. Write **NS** beside each word group that is not a complete sentence.

   a. ________ They outside.

   b. ________ Pat came.

   c. ________ Running around.

   d. ________ It was there.

3. Write the word now next to each verb that you would use to tell what is happening now. Write the word past next to each verb that you would use to tell what already happened.

   a. ________ takes

   b. ________ threw

   c. ________ tell

   d. ________ walked

4. On a separate piece of paper, write a paragraph that tells what you like about your own town or neighborhood. Begin with three sentences that give only facts. Then write two sentences that give your opinions.

unit 6
Writing About Cause and Effect

Things to Remember When Writing About Cause and Effect

A **cause** is what makes something happen. An **effect** is what happens.

Writing

- Use words like *since, so,* and *because* to join cause and effect parts of sentences.
- Use causes and effects in paragraphs that explain how things work or how something happens.

Revising

- Combine sentences that have the same subjects or verbs to make your writing smoother.

Proofreading

Check to see that you have

- used an apostrophe to show ownership
- used an apostrophe to join words such as *has* and *not*
- used a comma between names of cities and states
- used a comma between a day and a year
- used a comma after a greeting in a letter
- used a comma after a closing in a letter

lesson

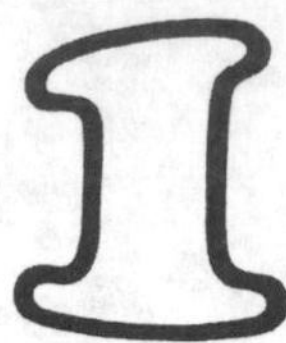

Writing about cause and effect in pictures

Look at the two pictures below.

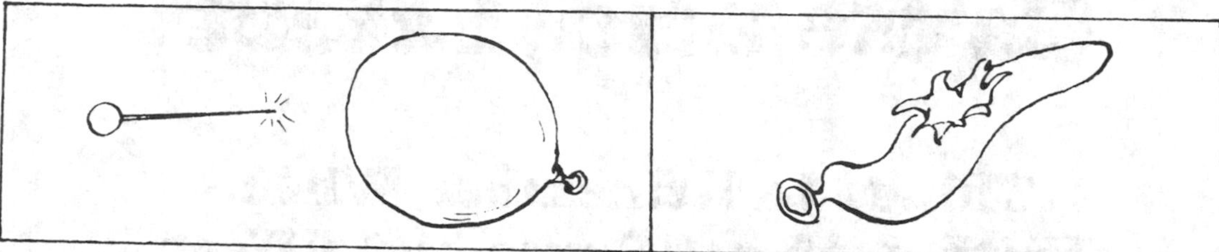

A **cause** is what makes something happen. What is the cause in the pictures? Write your answer on the line. ____________

____

An **effect** is what happens as a result of a cause. What is the effect in the pictures? ____________________

A. Look at the pictures below and on the next page. Match each picture under the word **Cause** with a picture under the word **Effect.** Draw a line between the cause and effect pictures to show which pictures should match.

Cause

1.

2.

Effect

a.

b.

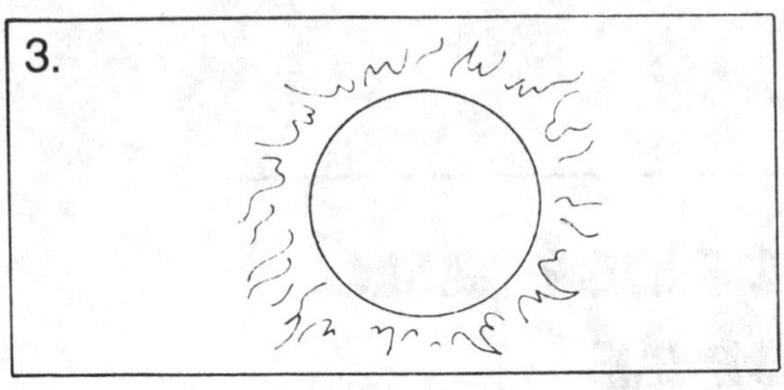

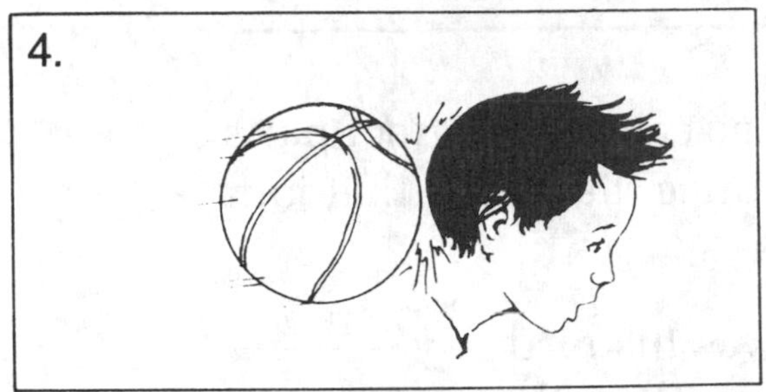

B. Look at the next picture. What is about to happen? Draw a picture of the effect. Or write a sentence that describes the effect. Remember, the effect is what happens after the cause. Write your sentence on the line below. Draw your picture in the space.

The effect is: ______________________________

On a separate sheet of paper write five cause and effect sentences. Just think of things that happen every day. One is done to show you how.

Cause: The <u>cause</u> is pushing the light switch.

Effect: The <u>effect</u> is the light coming on.

A cause is what makes something happen.
An effect is what happens as a result of a cause.

---

lesson 2

Writing with cause and effect words

Certain words or groups of words can join the cause and effect parts of a sentence. Read the sentences below. Notice the words that join the cause and effect parts.

I bought Donald a present **because** it was his birthday.

The tar in the street was melting **as a result of** the hot weather.

A. Write answers to the following questions on the lines.

1. What is the cause in the first sentence?

____

2. What is the effect in the first sentence?

____

3. What is the cause in the second sentence?

____

4. What is the effect in the second sentence?

____

5. What are the words that join the cause and effect parts of both sentences?

_______________ _______________

Some other words and groups of words that can join the cause and effect parts of a sentence are *so, since, on account of, due to the fact that.*

B. Underline the word or words that join the cause and effect parts in the sentences below.

1. I told Ellen to come home because it was time for dinner.
2. My brother and I have saved ten dollars as a result of putting twenty cents in our bank every week.
3. The school was closed yesterday on account of the snowy weather.
4. Sarah could not go to the party due to the fact that she was sick with a bad cold.

C. Write a cause and effect ending for each sentence below. Use a word or word group that will join the cause and effect parts of your sentences.

1. I had to wear boots to school ______________________________

____

2. I like you ______________________________

____

3. Albert had to stay after school ______________________________

____

4. We are going to have a party ______________________________

____

On a separate sheet of paper write four cause and effect sentences of your own. Be sure to use words or word groups that join the cause and effect parts in each of your sentences. If you need help, look back at part **B** of this lesson.

Use words like <u>because</u>, <u>since</u>, and <u>on account of</u> to join cause and effect parts of sentences.

lesson 3

Writing cause and effect sentences

A sentence that tells about a cause is often followed by a sentence that tells about an effect. Or a sentence that tells about an effect may come first. In either case, sentences of cause and effect are related.

A. Read the next two sentences.

The careless elephant stepped on my big toe. I wore a cast on my foot for six months.

Which sentence tells the cause? ______________________

Which sentence tells the effect? ______________________

B. Read the cause and effect sentences below. Then match each cause sentence to an effect. Draw lines between the sentences to show which ones should be matched.

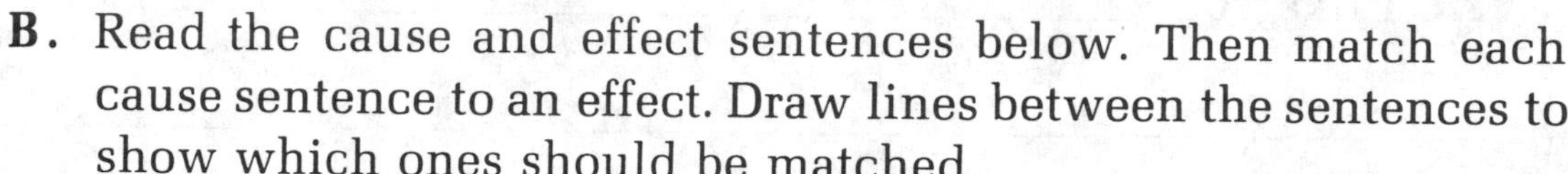

Cause Sentences

1. Oliver stood on his head.
2. It was my ninth birthday.
3. Someone was ringing the doorbell.
4. I wish I were sixteen.
5. It needed a coat of paint.

Effect Sentences

a. Mother painted the kitchen orange.
b. Toni raced to the door.
c. The turkey in the oven was almost done.
d. Suddenly he toppled over.
e. My sister gave me a present.
f. Then I could drive a car.

C. Now read the sentences below that tell causes. Then write sentences below each one to tell a related effect. One is done to show you how.

It was a wonderful program.

We clapped and whistled.

1. Yesterday was my birthday.

2. I slammed the door.

3 Elmo helped his father clean the windows.

D. The following sentences tell effects. Write a sentence above each one to tell a related cause.

1. My dog barked and licked my hand.

2. I could not get up in the morning.

3. So there was an awful noise.

On another sheet of paper, write a paragraph of at least 5 sentences. Write about something you would like to happen. Tell what could *cause* your wish to happen. You may use one of the ideas below or you may think up your own idea.

To live on the moon
To be a great singer
To be in the Olympics
To run for President

Cause and effect sentences often go together in a paragraph.

lesson

Writing paragraphs that explain

Many things that happen can be **explained**. Explaining means telling how something happens or how something works. For example, in the last lesson you explained effects by telling about causes.

Read the next paragraph that explains a computer.

A computer is a machine that solves problems very quickly by counting special numbers. Computers add, subtract, multiply, and divide. An operator "feeds" the computer special information and then tells the computer what to do by writing a program for it. By using a great many small *electronic* machines, computers can do a very large amount of work in a very short time.

A. Paragraphs that explain tell causes and effects. Underline the sentence that tells who causes the computer to work. Then circle one sentence that tells about an effect of a computer.

B. Write sentences that explain each item below. First tell what the item is. Then tell how it works. Use cause and effect sentences.

1. A door ____

____

____

____

2. A bicycle ____

____

____

____

On another sheet of paper, write a paragraph that explains one of the items below. Or you may think up your own item to explain. Make sure your paragraph tells the following things: what the item is or does, what causes the item to work or be, what effects the item has. Make your paragraph at least five sentences long.

A railroad train	A school
Scissors	A pencil

Paragraphs that explain tell how something happens or works.

lesson

Writing story problems and endings

Do you think that Barry and Craig have a problem? They decided to paint the living room of Craig's house. But things got out of hand. The painting job was more difficult than they thought.

The picture can be the beginning of a story. It shows a problem. It can end by **solving** the problem. Solving a problem means telling how a problem is worked out.

A. Look at the picture again. Then choose the ending at the top of page 91 that solves the problem. Write an X beside the ending that you think is the best.

___ Craig's father came home. Then the boys had to spend all day Saturday cleaning the paint off the walls.

___ When Barry saw Craig's father come home, he hid in the closet. Then Craig's father punished Craig, and Barry sneaked out the back door.

___ The boys were given a prize by Craig's father. Then they started their own house painting business.

B. Read the story *ending* below. Then write an X beside the story problem that you think the ending solves.

The men decided to place a board across the pit and walk over it. All but one of them made it. It had been an awful trip.

Story Problem 1. ___ Debby had to practice for two months to get ready for the race. On the day before the race she broke her ankle.

Story Problem 2. ___ There were only two openings out of the cave. One opening was blocked by fallen rock. The other was over a pit of giant spiders.

Story Problem 3. ___ Terry saw her cousin Dena, sleepwalking. Terry was about to wake Dena when suddenly she heard a crash.

Write On

Now write your own story on another sheet of paper. Begin your story with a story problem. Then solve your story problem with an ending. You may use one of the ideas below or you may think up your own idea.

Alone in a Forest The Leaky Roof Earning Money

You can write a story with a problem. Then solve the problem by telling how it is worked out.

Revising

Writing combined sentences

Read the next pair of sentences.

Sheila watched the parade.
Brenda watched the parade.

The sentence below **combines** the pair of sentences. *Combine* means "join."

Sheila **and** Brenda watched the parade.

Read the next pair of sentences.

Pete cooked the dinner.
Pete washed the dishes.

The next sentence combines that pair of sentences.

Pete cooked the dinner **and** washed the dishes.

Sometimes the *subjects* of sentences can be combined, and sometimes the *verbs* of sentences can be combined.

A. Write one combined sentence for each pair of sentences below and on the next page. Two have been done to show you how.

My hands are cold.
My feet are cold. *My hands and feet are cold.*

Ursula went home.
Ursula went to bed. *Ursula went home and went to bed.*

1. Sandy left at noon.
Anne left at noon. ______________________

____

2. Angela hid behind the door.
   Malvia hid behind the door. ______________________________

   ____

3. Seth reads a lot.
   Seth gets good grades. ______________________________

   ____

4. Charles speaks well.
   Charles writes well. ______________________________

   ____

5. The horse ran.
   The rabbit ran. ______________________________

   ____

Now look back at eight or more sentences that you have written for this unit. Combine the eight sentences into *four* sentences. Write your combined sentences on a separate sheet of paper. If you can't find all eight sentences to combine, use the sentences below.

1. Sadie works hard.
   Sadie plays hard.
2. The tables are broken.
   The chairs are broken.
3. His hands are big.
   His feet are big.
4. The basketball team won.
   The hockey team won.

You can combine sentences that have the same subjects or the same verbs. Combined sentences make your writing smoother.

Proofreading

Using commas and apostrophes

Read the letter below.

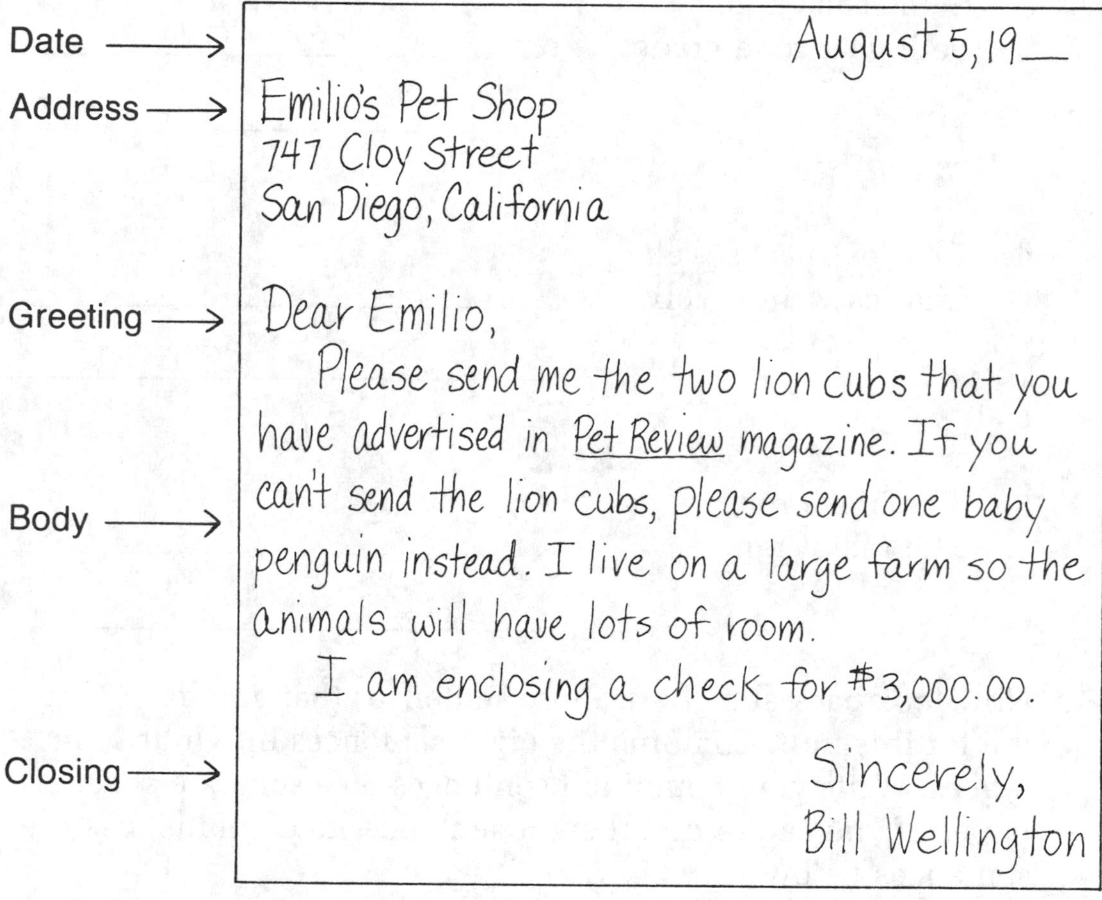

August 5, 19__

Emilio's Pet Shop
747 Cloy Street
San Diego, California

Dear Emilio,

Please send me the two lion cubs that you have advertised in Pet Review magazine. If you can't send the lion cubs, please send one baby penguin instead. I live on a large farm so the animals will have lots of room.

I am enclosing a check for $3,000.00.

Sincerely,
Bill Wellington

Find this mark (,) and this mark (') in the letter. The *lower* mark is a **comma**. The *higher* mark is an **apostrophe**.

A. Now write answers to the following questions.

1. Between which two numerals is the comma placed in the date? ____ ____ This comma separates the day and the month from the year.
2. Between which two letters is an apostrophe placed in the

address? ___ ___ This apostrophe shows *ownership*. It shows that Emilio owns the pet shop.

3. Between which two words is a comma placed in the address? __________ __________ This comma separates the town from the state.

4. The comma in the greeting comes __________________.

5. The comma in the closing comes __________________.

An apostrophe is placed in the body of the letter in the word *can't*. This apostrophe does not show ownership like the apostrophe in the word *Emilio's*. Instead, it shortens two words to make one. The two words it shortens are the words *can* and *not*. Other words that can be shortened with an apostrophe are:

did and *not*—*didn't*
has and *not*—*hasn't*
was and *not*—*wasn't*
could and *not*—*couldn't*

B. Now write commas and apostrophes in the correct places for the sentences or word groups below.

1. We landed on April 5 1902.
2. He fed Arnold s shoes to the gorilla.
3. I can t see from way back here.
4. Dear Cousin Melissa
5. Sincerely yours George Flint

Use an apostrophe to show ownership.
Use an apostrophe to join two words.
Use a comma:
between names of cities and states
between the day and the year
after a greeting
after a closing

Post-Test

1. Circle the word or words that join cause and effect sentences.

very fast	gently	yesterday
because	as a result of	good-bye
so	in the road	since

2. Write the letter of each effect next to its cause.

Causes	Effects
____ The alarm clock rang.	a. The cars stopped.
____ The light turned red.	b. The house got warm.
____ Mom built a fire.	c. Betty woke up.

3. Write one combined sentence for each pair of sentences below.

a. The boy sang. ______________________

The girl sang. ______________________

b. The crowd moaned. ______________________

The crowd groaned. ______________________

4. Write commas and apostrophes where they belong in the sentences or word groups below.

a. I don t live in Bangor Maine.

b. April 12 1976

c. This isn t Roger s book.

d. Dear Uncle Joe

5. On another piece of paper, write a paragraph that explains one of the items below. Use cause and effect sentences to tell how the item works.

a stop sign a window a postage stamp a rubber band

unit 7
Making Your Point in Writing

Things to Remember About Making Your Point in Writing

The **purpose** of a piece of writing may be to make people happy, to give facts, or to get people to do something.

Writing

- Think about your purpose before you start writing.
- Make your writing fit your purpose by adding details and sequence words.
- Tell who, what, when, where, and how much in announcements.
- Use plus or minus words when you write to get people to do something.

Revising

- Make all your verbs tell about the same time in a story.

Proofreading

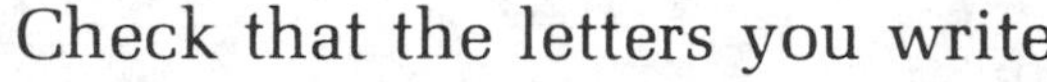

Check that the letters you write

- have capital letters and commas where they are needed
- have a date in the heading
- have commas after the greeting and closing
- have greetings and closings that begin with capital letters

lesson

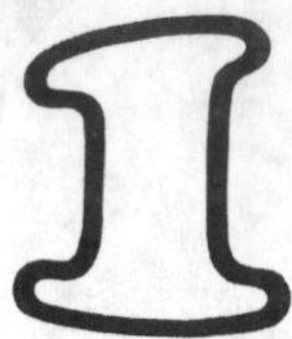

Writing for a purpose

The purpose of a jacket is to keep you warm. The purpose of a street sign is to tell you where you are. Almost everything has a purpose. Things people write usually have a purpose too.

A. Read the three items on the left below. Find each one's purpose on the right. Draw a line from each section of writing to its correct purpose.

1.

Hot Chocolate
1 cup milk
1 tablespoon cocoa
1 marshmallow

Heat milk in a pan. Put cocoa in cup. Pour hot milk into cup and stir. Put marshmallow on top and drink.

- A joke to make you laugh

2.

Al: Why does a cow wear a bell?
Sal: Her horns don't work.

- An ad to make you buy something

3.

Buy Aunt Sue's Moo Juice
It's the blueberry-flavored milk drink that will make you moo for more!

- A recipe telling you how to make something

There are three main purposes for writing. Stories and jokes are for people to enjoy. Recipes and directions give facts. Ads try to get people to do or buy something.

B. Now write something about apples. Choose a purpose for your writing. You may write a joke or story about apples. You may write an apple recipe or tell how to pick an apple. You may write an ad to get people to eat apples. Write your ideas on the lines below. Then write your purpose.

____

____

____

____

____

Purpose: ______________________________

____

On a separate sheet of paper, write three different things. Write a joke or story. Write a recipe or directions. Write an ad. Under each paragraph, write its purpose. Here are three ideas you can use if you wish.

An elephant joke
How to ride an elephant
Why you should buy an elephant for a pet

Most writing is done for a purpose.

lesson 2

Writing to fit the purpose

a. Flasho Toothpaste brightens your smile. It has H3P05 to whiten teeth and freshen breath.
FLASHO
b. I once used Flasho Toothpaste. It was OK.
FLASHO

A. An ad should make you want to buy something. Read the two ads above.

1. Which ad makes you want to buy the toothpaste? ________
2. Which ad uses good-sounding words? ________
3. Can words help to sell things? ________

B. Directions should help you get somewhere. Read the two sets of directions below.

a. Take the Number 3 bus. Get off at Main Street. Walk right on Main for two blocks. The movie is on the corner of Main and Walnut Avenue.

b. Take a green bus. Get off near a park. Walk two blocks. You're at the movie.

1. Which set of directions would help you get to the movie?

______

2. Which set of directions has clear facts? ______

C. Stories should be fun to read. They should tell what happened clearly. Read this story that Tom wrote.

I had a funny dream. I went to a place. It was cold. I woke up without my blanket.

Can you make Tom's story fit the purpose better? Rewrite it, adding details and sequence words.

______

______

______

______

______

______

Write On

Choose two items below. Write them on a separate sheet of paper.

1. Write an ad to sell a new food. Use good-sounding words.
2. Write directions to help someone get to your favorite park. Make your directions clear.
3. Write a story about a trip to the moon. Make it clear and fun to read.

When you write something, think about your purpose. Make your writing fit the purpose.

lesson

3 Writing a thank-you note

It is good to say thank-you when someone does something nice for you or gives you a present. One way to say thank-you is to write a note.

A. Maria liked the birthday present Uncle José gave her. She wrote this note.

July 14, 19__

Dear Uncle José,

The magic set you gave me is great. I practice with it every day after school. Now I can make a coin disappear. Soon I hope to make my brother disappear. Can you come over to see my magic show real soon?

Your niece,
Maria

Check the ways Maria lets her uncle know she likes his gift.

___ She says she likes it.

___ She tells how she uses it.

___ She says it isn't special.

___ She invites him to share the fun.

B. Maria wasn't as careful with the note she wrote to her cousin Reba. Here is her note.

> July 14, 19__
>
> Dear Reba,
>
> I got the book on stars you sent me.
>
> Your cousin,
>
> Maria

How could Maria say thank-you to Reba in a better way? Look at the sentences you checked in **A.** Use some of those ideas to rewrite her note below.

Dear Reba,

____

____

____

____

____

Your cousin,
Maria

Think of someone you'd like to thank. Write that person a note on a separate sheet of paper. Here are some things you might thank someone for: driving you somewhere, making you something good to eat, telling you stories, being your friend.

A thank-you note thanks someone for a gift or favor. Your note should show that you are grateful to that person.

lesson 4

Writing an announcement

The purpose of an **announcement** is to tell about something that has happened or will happen soon. Announcements usually give information about who, what, where, when, and how much.

A. Look at the announcements in the store window above. Then answer the questions about them below.

1. Which announcement gives you more information – the one about the circus or the rodeo? ____________________
2. Fill in the blanks below. Copy the information from the announcement that gives it.

   Who or What? ____________________

   Where? ____________________

   When? ____________________

   How Much? ____________________

B. The picture below is of a movie that will soon open. Look at the picture and the information about the movie. Below the picture, write an announcement of the movie.

What: *Mouse on Mars*
Where: Rialto Theater
When: starts Wednesday, April 13
How Much: $2.50 for adults; $1.25 for children

Write an announcement for your next birthday. Decide if you would like to have a party or go someplace special. Draw a picture if you wish. Remember to tell who or what, when, and where.

Announcements tell who or what, when, where, and how much.

lesson 5

Writing an ad

The purpose of an ad is to get people to buy or do something. Ads do this in different ways. Some ads use **loaded words.** Plus-loaded words, like *wonderful* and *bright,* are good-sounding. Minus-loaded words, like *broken* and *sad,* are bad-sounding.

A. Next to each word below, put a + if it is plus-loaded. Put a − if it is minus-loaded.

___ fresh	___ dull	___ sparkle
___ dirty	___ clean	___ tired

Here is how loaded words can be used in an ad for a new soap.

Tired of dirty, dull skin? Use ZOWIE SOAP.
It will make you feel fresh and clean.
Famous star Marla Moore says,
"When I use ZOWIE, it makes my skin sparkle."

The ad above shows another way to try to make people buy something. An ad can say that a famous person uses the product.

B. Suppose you wanted to sell a new kind of sneaker or running shoe, called Swifty Shoe. Which words below would you use? Draw a circle around each.

tasty	sweet	fast	loser
comfortable	good-fitting	winner	chewy

C. Which person below would you use in your sneaker ad? Put an X next to that person's name.

___ Homer Brown is a third-grader who wears sneakers.

___ Pedro Lopez is a winning runner who wears sneakers.

___ Violet Vocal is a singer who never wears sneakers.

D. Now write your ad for the Swifty Shoe. Use the words you picked in **B** and the person you picked in **C.**

____

____

____

____

____

____

Write On

Pretend you just invented a new kind of toy or food. Think about what makes it special. List the loaded words you will use. Will you use a person in your ad? Then write an ad to sell your invention. Draw a picture if you wish.

Ads use loaded words and famous people to help sell things.

lesson

Revising

Writing verbs that agree

Read the next paragraph. Think about what is wrong with it.

I climb onto the space ship. It takes off. Soon we are streaking toward Planet Ultron. Then we landed with a bump.

What is wrong? The first three verbs tell the story as if it is happening now. They tell about present time. But in the last sentence, the verb is a past form. The last verb tells about past time. But the last verb should agree with the sentences in the rest of the story. The verb should be in present form. The sentence should say, "Then we land with a bump."

When you write a story, you can tell it with present time verbs or past time verbs. But don't change the time of the verbs in the middle of a story.

A. Read each paragraph below. Decide if the sentences tell about present or past time. Then underline the correct verb form to use for the last sentence in each paragraph.

1. The cat chased the mouse. The dog chased the cat. Grandpa (runs, ran) after the dog.
2. The frog raises his magic wand. He taps the princess. Suddenly she (turns, turned) into a frog.
3. Yoko looked out of the window sadly. It was raining again. Then her brother rushed into the room. He (carries, carried) a big box.

B. Now write your own story about a house. You can make it a ghost story or a funny story. The first sentence is started. You must underline the present or past verb form—whichever you want to use. Then write the rest of your story. Keep your verbs all in present or past time.

The old house (stands, stood) at the top of a dark hill.

____

____

____

____

____

____

Look back over the **Write Ons** you've done for this unit. Find a story you wrote. Look at your verbs. Do they tell about the same time? Change any that don't. Then try rewriting the story to change the time. If it tells about present time, make it past. If it tells about past time, make it present.

Don't change the time of your verbs in the middle of a story.

Proofreading

Using good letter form

Here is a letter written in good form.

Heading → June 8, 19__

Greeting → Dear Burt,

Body → Would you like to keep my pet snake for the summer? I can't take him to camp with me. His name is Sneaky. He likes to curl up in my pocket. Please let me know if you want him.

Closing → Your friend,

Signature → Ernie

A. Look carefully at the five parts of the letter above. Then answer these questions.

1. What is in the heading? ______________________

2. Where do you see commas? ______________________

____

3. Besides the first words of sentences, what words begin with capital letters? ______________________

____

4. What part gives the writer's name? ______________

B. On the lines below, write these letter parts in good form. Put them in the right places. Use capital letters and commas.

june 13, 19–
dear ernie
I'd love to take Sneaky. When can I get him?
your friend
burt

____

____

____

____

____

____

Use good form when you write a letter. Use capital letters and commas where they are needed. Remember these rules about writing letters:
The heading gives the date.
Commas come after the greeting and closing.
The greeting and closing begin with capital letters.

Post-Test

1. Write the purpose of each item below: to make you laugh; to make you buy something; to give directions.

   a. For amazing comfort and fun, buy Gilde-Alongs. The tiny jet engines in these sneakers mean you'll never have to walk again!

   ____

   b. Bill: What word is made shorter by adding two letters?
   Jill: Short!

   ____

2. | CAT SHOW AT ECHO PARK. APRIL 15. 2:00 P.M. |
   |---|

   Use the information in the announcement to answer the questions.

   What? ______________________________

   When? ______________________________

   Where? ______________________________

3. Put commas and capital letters in the letter below.

   june 3 19—

   dear uncle max

   Thank you for the records. I play them every day!

   your niece

   justine

4. Think of something that you own but don't ever use. If you wanted to sell it, what special plus-loaded words would you describe it with? List them. Then write a letter to a friend in which you try to persuade him or her to buy the object. Use good letter form.

unit 8
Point of View in Writing

Things to Remember About Point of View in Your Writing

A **point of view** is how someone sees and thinks about something.

Writing

- Think about your point of view before you begin to write.
- Try writing about something from different points of view.
- Use different points of view for different characters in a story.

Revising and Proofreading

Check to see that

- your words are exact and interesting
- your spelling, capital letters, punctuation marks, and verb forms are correct

lesson

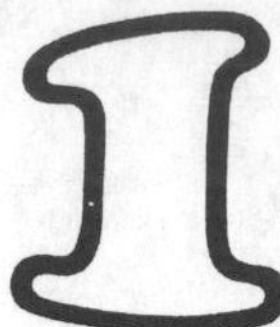

Describing what you view

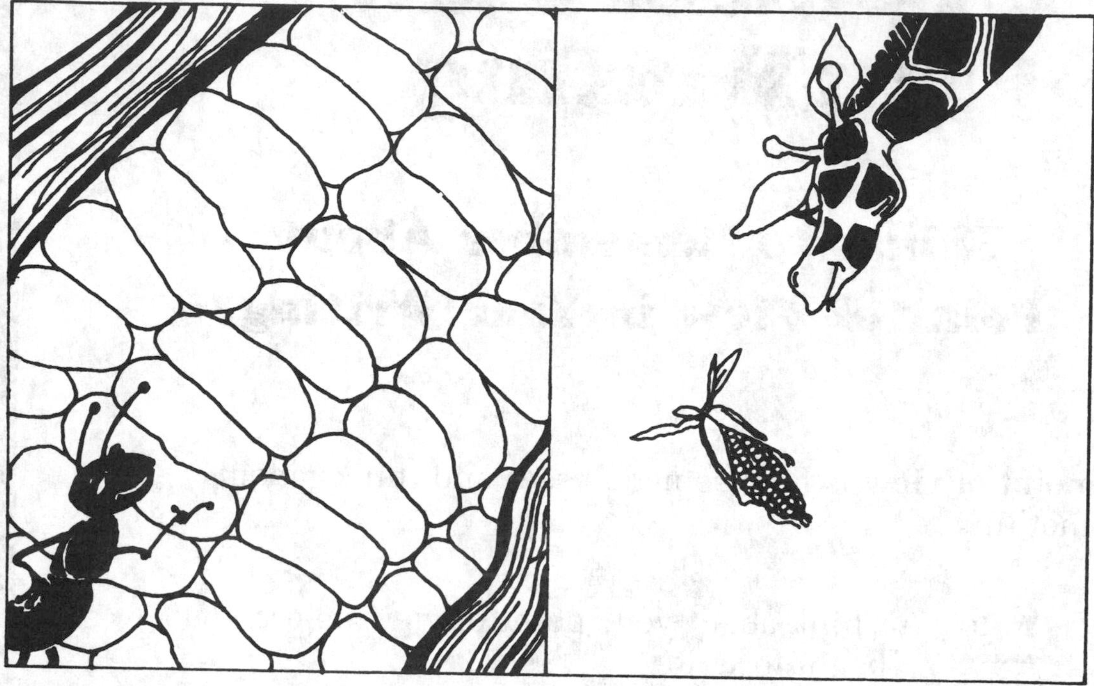

Can you guess what the pictures show? It is an ear of corn. The first picture shows how the corn looks to an ant. The second picture shows how the corn looks to a giraffe.

A. How does an ear of corn look to you? On the lines below, write a description of corn—growing in a field, or on your plate at dinner.

Where you are can change the way you see something and write about it. Is it far away or close? Do you see only the top or the bottom? You can describe something differently, depending on how you view it.

B. Read each paragraph below about clouds. Under each, write who is viewing the clouds – a pilot in a plane or a person lying in the grass.

1. The clouds above look like puffy white animals. They change from elephants to fish to tigers as they march across the sky.

   I am ____.

2. I look down on the clouds. They are like a fluffy white rug under me.

   I am ____.

Try to describe something from two views. First, be yourself and tell how you see it. Then pretend you are an ant looking at it up close – maybe seeing only a small part. Or else pretend you are way up above it, looking down from a plane or a tall building. How does it look from far away? Under each paragraph, tell how you are viewing the thing. Here are some things you might choose to describe:

a flower or tree   a lake   a roller coaster

Where you are can change the way you see something and write about it.

lesson

2 Writing about feelings

A. It is starting to rain. Do all the people in the picture feel the same way about the rain? On the lines below, tell how you think they feel and why.

1. The children feel ______________________

____

____

____

2. The woman feels ______________________

____

____

____

People can look at the same thing, like rain, differently. The way someone looks at, or views, something is called a **point of view.** Your point of view may come from where you stand. It may also come from the way you feel.

B. Have you ever waited on line to see a movie? Imagine that there is a long line waiting to see the latest hit. Write a sentence or two to describe how you think each of these people might be feeling. Use *I* when you write if you wish.

The first person on line: ______________________

____

____

____

The last person on line: ______________________

____

____

____

The ticket-seller: ______________________

____

____

____

Write On

A telephone is something that you see and use every day. But think about it from a different point of view. Choose two of the people below. Write about a telephone as each one might view it. Use *I* when you write.

someone from Mars	a tired person trying to sleep
a telephone repairer	someone with good news to tell

People can have different points of view about the same thing. You can write about something from different points of view.

lesson

3 Writing about different characters

A **character** is a person in a story. The picture shows three characters about to go on a long space trip. They are Amanda, an astronaut; Jimmy, a young boy; and Chris, a news reporter.

A. Read each paragraph that follows. Decide which character is telling about the trip. Write the name of the character after the paragraph that tells how he or she feels.

1. Wow! I've never been away from home before. Now I'm going into space. I hope I don't get homesick.

____

2. What a story this will make! I hope some exciting things happen, so I can write about them.

____

3. I've been training for this trip for a long time. I can't wait to practice what I've learned.

____

B. Now suppose that the three travelers are in space. They see a strange spaceship heading toward them. How would each person act? Write a sentence or two next to each character. Tell what each one says or feels.

Amanda: ______________________

____

____

____

Jimmy: ______________________

____

____

____

Chris: ______________________

____

____

____

Write On

What might happen on the space trip? Will the spaceship crash? Will the travelers get to the moon or a planet? Write a short story about the trip. Tell what each person does and says.

Different characters in a story act differently.

Writing a story from different views

Don is selling cookies to earn some extra money. He comes to the old Miller place, which people say is haunted. His friends dare him to ring the bell.

A. How do you think Don feels? Write the beginning of a story as if you were Don. Use *I* if you wish.

B. Boris, a mean-looking servant, opens the door. What does Don say and do? Write what happens next from Don's point of view.

C. Tell how the story ends. What happens to Don?

Now tell the same story from a different point of view. Choose A or B to do on a separate sheet of paper.

A. Be Boris. How do you feel living in an old house that people are afraid of? What happens when Don rings the bell?

B. Be one of Don's friends. How do you feel when he takes your dare? What do you see and hear from behind the fence? What do you do?

You can write a story from one character's point of view. You can write about the same happenings from another character's point of view.

lesson 5

Revising and Proofreading

Rewriting

Two people went there. They saw some funny things. They enjoy it very much.

The story above doesn't tell very much. But you can make it more interesting when you rewrite it. You can use exact nouns and verbs. You can add adjectives to describe people and things. You can add adverbs to tell where, when, or how. You can combine sentences if you want to. You can check to see that all verbs tell about the same time.

A. Now rewrite the story at the top of the page. Make it as interesting as you can.

____

____

____

____

____

____

Lorna wrote this paragraph about the circus. Her story is interesting, but she didn't proofread it.

Uncle willis and Gina went to the circas on saturday They seen a woman riding on elephant and lien jump through a hoop? One clown put on Ginas hat, but she didnt mind. gina and her uncle enjoyed the day, and they hopes to go again next year.

B. Proofread Lorna's story. Use proofreading marks and write in the corrections needed. Turn to page 14 if you need help.

Write On Look back over the **Write Ons** you've written for this unit. Pick one to rewrite. First, choose words that make your story as interesting as you can. Then, proofread to be sure your spelling, capital letters, punctuation marks, and verb forms are correct. When you are happy with your **Write On,** copy it neatly.

When you finish writing, check to see that your words are exact and interesting. Then proofread your work to be sure that it's correct.

Post-Test

1. What is Raoul describing from his point of view?

   I am on the end of a long board. Terry is on the other end. The middle of the board is on top of a short post. When I touch the ground, Terry goes up in the air.

   Raoul is playing on a ______________ .

2. Read each viewpoint about a spider web. Write the letter of each viewpoint beside the person or insect that would have it.

   a. Look at this beautiful spider web on our gate! ____ a tired old spider

   b. I get so tired spinning this web every night! ____ a person who sees a web

   c. Get me out of this awful web before it's too late! ____ a fly trapped in a web

3. Here are two story characters: Sly, a worm who lives in an apple, and Anna, a girl who starts to eat the apple. Write the name of the character who might say each line below.

   a. "Ugh! What are you doing in my apple!" ______________

   b. "Your apple! I was here first!" ______________

4. Pretend you are from a faraway planet and are visiting Earth for the first time. You do not know what any of the items below are. Write a paragraph that describes one of them for your friends and family back home.

   a traffic jam   a horse race   a football game

Unit 1

Lesson 1

A. **Animals with Four Legs**
camel elephant zebra
Animals That Crawl
ant spider snake
Animals with Feathers
parrot peacock ostrich

B. **Fruits** **Colors** **Holidays**
grape, etc. blue, etc. Halloween, etc.

C. **Family Members**
sister mother brother ~~car~~
Drinks
lemonade ~~cake~~ milk water
Parts of the Face
cheek nose ~~foot~~ ear

Lesson 2

A. 1. Some girls and boys are playing volleyball.
B. 3. Fred is cooking hamburgers.
C. ⇨⇦ When you see this symbol, check with your teacher.

Lesson 3

A. 2. Fish sleep differently.
B. 1. I rushed to go camping.
C. ⇨⇦

Lesson 4

A. 1. Tulips are my favorite flowers.
2. We have to stand in rows at school.
3. It doesn't tell about the main idea.

B. 1. Our neighbor took a trip into space.
2. I took a trip to Disney World.
3. Tugboats move large ships.
4. I'd like to sail a ship someday.

Lesson 5

A. 1. Monkey Is Star of Bike Day
B. 3. A Bad Beginning for Charlotte
C. You might say: UFO's—Real or Not?

Lesson 6

A. The clown fed the elephant.
B. Answers will be different. You might say:
2. eggs banana
3. doll kite
4. rose daisy

C. ⇨⇦

Lesson 7

A. 1. \ 2. ~~go~~ 3. ∧
B. [B]bert loves to runn. He sometimes [runs] all day long. [T]this [year] ~~yer~~ he will be on the school [t]rack team.
C. ⇨⇦

Unit 2

Lesson 1

A. 1. first last next 2. next first last
B. Your picture should show the girl holding her unwrapped present.
C. You might say:
First: Anne gets a present for her birthday.
Next: Anne opens the package.
Last: The (toy elephant, etc.) was just what she wanted!

Lesson 2

A. 2 1 3 3 1 2
B. You should have underlined:
First, Then, Finally
C. ⇨⇦

Lesson 3

A. First Then Next Then Finally Now
B. **Things You Will Need**
2 cups flour 1 teaspoon salt
3 tablespoons water 2 eggs
Things to Do
First, break the eggs into the flour.
Next, add the water and salt and stir.
Finally, roll out the mixture.

Lesson 4

A. The picture should be a star.
B. 6 2 4 5 3 1
C. ⇨⇦

Lesson 5

A. 1. beginning end middle
2. middle beginning end

B. 1. end ⇨⇦ 2. middle ⇨⇦ 3. beginning ⇨⇦

Lesson 6

A. 1. danced 2. jumped 3. scurried
B. Answers will be different. You might say:
2. stepped marched 3. bit chewed
4. yelled whispered

C. ⇨⇦

Lesson 7

A. 1. capital letter 2. capital letter
3. J H 4. capital letter

B. Michelle Myers goes to East Windsor School. She jogs down Spring Street and sprints over to Vine Street. Every Wednesday she has soccer practice. On those days, she rides over to Stanleyville.

Unit 3

Lesson 1

A. 1. One player is thinner.
2. One animal is longer.
3. The boy and girl are the same height.

B. 2. The woman on the left is bigger. (or: The woman on the left is louder.)
3. The two dogs look the same.

Lesson 2

A. You might have said:
The boat on the left is fancier (newer, longer).
The boat on the right is smaller (shorter).

B. ⇨⇦

Lesson 3

A. 1. more than two 2. two
3. more than two

B. ⇨⇦ **C.** ⇨⇦

Lesson 4

A. 1. better 2. best 3. worse
4. worst

B. ⇨⇦

Lesson 5

A. 1. the wind 2. two 3. two

B. ⇨⇦

Lesson 6

A. You should have underlined:
1. huge, bright, new 2. tiny, clumsy, old

B. You should have underlined:
1. shiny blue 2. large 3. fluffy
4. soft, green

C. ⇨⇦

Lesson 7

A. 1. period 2. period
3. question mark 4. exclamation point

B. 1. How long is that boat?
2. Finish painting the fence by tomorrow.
3. Mr. Hernandez took us to the zoo.
4. Wow! Look at that hit!
5. Where are you going?
6. There is a crowd outside the palace. (or !)
7. Don't push! (or .)
8. Will the king give a speech?

C. ⇨⇦

Unit 4

Lesson 1

A. 1. R 2. L 3. R 4. R 5. L

B. ⇨⇦

Lesson 2

A. 1. smell 2. taste, seeing

B. apple

Lesson 3

A. You should have circled: fluffy, soft, furry
You might have written: sleepy, white, or happy

B. ⇨⇦

Lesson 4

A. short, wearing glasses, flowered dress, long hair, light hair
tall, thin, curly hair, dark hair, short hair

B. ⇨⇦

Lesson 5

A. 1. egg 2. teeth

B. 1. I bark. 2. People fly in me.

Lesson 6

A. 1. quietly 2. outside 3. now

B. You should have underlined:
1. outside, today 2. happily
3. loudly 4. upstairs
5. Later, peacefully

C. ⇨⇦

Lesson 7

A. 1. gulps, gulp 2. one ends in s
3. gulp

B. You should have underlined:
1. walks 2. looks 3. smell
4. grow 5. shines

C. You should have underlined:
1. Play 2. Jumps 3. Eat
4. Climb

D. ⇨⇦

Unit 5

Lesson 1

A. T O O F

B. 1. fact 2. false 3. opinion
4. fact 5. false

C. ⇨⇦

Lesson 2

A. **B.**

Lesson 3

A. **You should have underlined these sentences:**
I'm 8 years old.
I weigh 65 pounds and I am 4 feet tall.
I have green eyes and blond hair.
In the summer, I get millions of freckles.
Well, maybe I don't get millions, but I do get a lot.
That's when you go looking for caves.
I'll talk to you about a visit when I see you in school next week.
You should have circled these sentences:
I'm glad you just moved into our neighborhood.
I sure do enjoy meeting people my own age.
My favorite hobby is spelunking.
I think spelunking is a good hobby because it's so exciting.
My favorite school subject is math.
I enjoy math because it gives me a chance to figure out problems on my own.
I also like math because it is easy for me.
I would like to know more about you.
I hope we will become good friends.

B.

Lesson 4

A. **B.**

Lesson 5

A. 1. M 2. M 3. M 4. F
B.

Lesson 6

A. 1. NS 2. CS 3. NS 4. CS 5. NS
B.

Lesson 7

A. 1. aches, ached 2. first 3. second
B. 1. yelled 2. peeked
C. 1. felt 2. drank 3. took

Unit 6

Lesson 1

The pin is the cause. The broken balloon is the effect.

A. 1. b 2. a 3. d 4. c
B. You probably wrote or drew that the waiter slipped and dropped the tray.

Lesson 2

A. 1. Donald's birthday 2. buying a present
3. the hot weather 4. melting tar
5. because as a result of

B. 1. because 2. as a result of
3. on account of 4. due to the fact that
C.

Lesson 3

A. first second
B. 1. d 2. e 3. b 4. f 5. a
C. **D.**

Lesson 4

A. You should have underlined this sentence:
An operator "feeds" the computer special information and then tells the computer what to do by writing a program for it.
You should have circled any of the other sentences.
B.

Lesson 5

A. Craig's father came home. Then the boys had to spend all day Saturday cleaning the paint off the walls.
B. The X belongs next to Story Problem 2.

Lesson 6

A. 1. Sandy and Anne left at noon.
2. Angela and Malvia hid behind the door.
3. Seth reads a lot and gets good grades.
4. Charles speaks well and writes well.
5. The horse and the rabbit ran.

Lesson 7

A. 1. 5, 19— 2. o s
3. San Diego, California
4. After *Emilio* after *Sincerely*
B. 1. We landed on April 5, 1902.
2. He fed Arnold's shoes to the gorilla.
3. I can't see from way back here.
4. Dear Cousin Melissa,
5. Sincerely yours, George Flint

Unit 7

Lesson 1

A. 1. A recipe telling you how to make something
2. A joke to make you laugh
3. An ad to make you buy something
B.

Lesson 2

A. 1. a 2. a 3. yes
B. 1. a 2. a
C.

Lesson 3

A. You should have checked:
She says she likes it.
She tells how she uses it.
She invites him to share the fun.

B. ⇨

Lesson 4

A. 1. the rodeo
2. **Who or What?** Bronco Bill's Rodeo
Where? Civic Center
When? Saturday, May 3 at 2 P.M.
How Much? $3.00 for adults and $1.50 for children

B. ⇨

Lesson 5

A. + fresh − dull + sparkle
− dirty + clean − tired

B. You should have circled: comfortable, good-fitting, fast, winner (You might have circled *loser* if you wanted to use a minus-loaded word.)

C. You would probably choose Pedro Lopez.

D. ⇨

Lesson 6

A. 1. ran 2. turns 3. carried

B. ⇨

Lesson 7

A. 1. the date
2. in the date, after the greeting and closing
3. June, Dear, Burt, Sneaky, Your, Ernie
4. the signature

B. June 13, 19--

Dear Ernie,
I'd love to take Sneaky. When can I get him?
Your friend,
Burt

Unit 8

Lesson 1

A. ⇨

B. 1. a person lying in the grass
2. a pilot in a plane

Lesson 2

A. You might have said something like this:
1. The children feel sad because the rain will spoil their picnic.
2. The woman feels happy because the rain will help her flowers grow and she won't have to water them.

B. ⇨

Lesson 3

A. 1. Jimmy 2. Chris 3. Amanda

B. ⇨

Lesson 4 (pages 120–121)

A. ⇨ B. ⇨ C. ⇨

Lesson 5

A. ⇨

B. Uncle Willis and Gina went to the ~~circas~~ circus on Saturday. They ~~soon~~ saw a woman riding on an elephant and a ~~lion~~ lion jump through a hoop. One clown put on Gina's hat, but she didn't mind. Gina and her uncle enjoyed the day, and they hope~~s~~ to go again next year.

Post-Test Answers; pg 210

1. Animals Tools Buildings
   car butter tree
2. b
3. Answers will vary. Possible titles include: Wooden Bicycle Wheels; The First Bicycle Wheels; Riding on Wood; or some similar title.
4. Be sure the students have replaced the nouns *person* and *place* with more exact nouns. Check that the other sentences in the students' paragraphs support and develop the main idea of students' career plans. Look for any sentences that do not fit with this main idea.

Post-Test Answers; pg 226

1. a. 3 1 2
   b. 3 2 1
2. Answers will vary. Be sure that sequence words are used in proper order.
3. Answers will vary. Possible answers are:
   a. run, hop, walk, jump
   b. tap, pound, beat, strike
   c. pitch, toss, heave, scatter
   d. giggle, howl, chuckle, snicker
4. a. Next, Monday, Columbus Day, Lafayette School
   b. Last, May, Ellen Gray, I, Houston, Texas
5. Answers will vary. Check to see that the students have used sequence words to order the events. You might want to have the students underline the verbs in their sentences and decide whether they are exact enough.

Post-Test Answers; pg 242

1. a. softer softest
   b. sweeter sweetest
   c. more interesting most interesting
   d. more exciting most exciting
2. a. better
   b. best
   c. worse
   d. worst
3. Answers will vary. Be sure that student similes compare unlike things.
4. Answers will vary. Accept any adjectives that sensibly modify the nouns in the titles. Be sure that each sentence develops the idea in the title. You might want to have the students underline the adjective(s) they used in their sentences.

Post-Test Answers; pg 258

1. Answers will vary. Possible details:
   a. A horse is running down the sidewalk.
   b. Two men with a lasso are chasing it.
   c. Four children are watching the horse.
   d. The horse trailer is blocking traffic.

   Accept any detail in the illustration.
2. bed
3. Answers will vary. Some possibilities are *yellow, delicious, soft, tasty, sweet*
4. Answers will vary. Some possibilities are:
   a. *fast, wildly, away, far, there, rapidly*
   b. *quickly, closely, nervously, now*
5. Answers will vary. You may suggest that the students write a title for their paragraph. Also ask them to underline the adverb(s) they have used in their sentences. Besides adverbs, look for adjectives and phrases that add details to the story.

Post-Test Answers; pg 274

1. a. opinion
   b. false
   c. fact
   d. opinion
2. a. NS　c. NS
   b. CS　d. CS
3. a. now　c. now
   b. past　d. past
4. Check to see that each student has written three sentences of fact and two sentences of opinion. Make sure each sentence keeps to the topic of good things about my town. You may want to ask the students to underline the words in the opinion sentences that indicate they are opinions. Students should also check their sentences to make sure they are complete.

Post-Test Answers; pg 290

1. because, so, as a result of, since
2. c, a, b
3. a. The boy and girl sang.
   b. The crowd moaned and groaned.
4. a. I don't live in Bangor, Maine.
   b. April 12, 1976.
   c. This isn't Roger's book.
   d. Dear Uncle Joe,
5. Check to make sure that the students have provided a definition of the item, an explanation of how it works, and a description of how it is used. You might want the students to underline any cause and effect words or phrases they have used.

Post-Test Answers; pg 306

1. a. to make you buy something
   b. to make you laugh
2. What? a cat show
   When? April 15 at 2:00 P.M.
   Where? Echo Park
3. June 3, 19—
   Dear Uncle Max,
   Thank you for the records. I play them every day!
   Your niece,
   Justine
4. Check the students' letters for good letter form. Also check to make sure that students have used plus-loaded words to describe their objects.

Post-Test Answers; pg 318

1. see-saw
2. b, a, c
3. a. Anne
   b. Sly
4. Check to see that the paragraph is written from the point of view of an alien who is unfamiliar with the situations listed in the question. The paragraph should contain no specialized vocabulary associated with these situations, for example. You might want to have the students write a title for their paragraphs.

MATH

Grade 3

Thomas J. Richards
Mathematics Teacher
Lamar Junior-Senior High School
Lamar, Missouri

Photo Credits

Tony Freeman, 464; Glencoe staff photo, 390, 428; Jeff Greenberg, 442; Brent Jones, 342; Dan Witt, 400, 420

Table of Contents

The SPECTRUM
Contents

GRADE ONE

GRADE TWO

GRADE THREE

GRADE FOUR

MATHEMATICS Series of Units

GRADE FIVE

Basic Facts Tests vii–xiv

Addition and Subtraction (2 digit through 6 digit) 1–13

Multiplication (2 digit by 1 digit through 4 digit by 3 digit) 14–25

Division (2, 3, and 4 digit dividends) 26–35

Division (2, 3, and 4 digit dividends) 36–47

Division (4 and 5 digit dividends) 48–57

Metric Measurement 58–69

Measurement (linear, area, capacity, weight) 70–77

Fractional Numbers (fractions, mixed numerals, simplest form) 78–87

Multiplication (fractional numbers) 88–101

Addition (fractional numbers) 102–119

Subtraction (fractional numbers) 120–135

Geometry 136–142

Mid-Book/Final Tests 143–148

Answers 149–157

GRADE SIX

Basic Facts Tests vii–xiv

Addition and Subtraction (whole numbers) 1–11

Multiplication and Division (whole numbers) 12–25

Multiplication (fractions) 26–41

Addition and Subtraction (fractions) 42–53

Division (fractions) 54–65

Addition and Subtraction (decimals) 66–81

Multiplication (decimals) 82–91

Division (decimals) 92–105

Metric Measurement 106–117

Measurement (linear, capacity, weight, time) 118–127

Percent 128–137

Geometry 138–144

Mid-Book/Final Test 142–148

Answers 149–159

GRADE SEVEN

Problem-Solving Strategies (optional) vii–xiv

Addition, Subtraction, Multiplication, and Division (whole numbers) 1–25

Addition, Subtraction, Multiplication, and Division (fractional numbers) 26–49

Addition, Subtraction, Multiplication, and Division (decimals) 50–71

Ratio and Proportion 72–83

Decimals, Fractions, Percent 84–95

Percent 96–107

Interest (simple) 108–117

Metric Measurement 118–125

Geometry 126–135

Perimeter and Area (rectangles, triangles, circles) 136–151

Volume (rectangular solids, triangular prisms, cylinders) 152–159

Statistics and Probability 160–174

Mid-Book/Final Tests 175–180

Answers 179–191

GRADE EIGHT

Problem-Solving Strategies (optional) vii–xiv

Addition, Subtraction, Multiplication, and Division 1–23

Equations 24–37

Using Equations to Solve Problems 38–47

Ratio, Proportion, Percent 48–67

Simple and Compound Interest 68–77

Metric Measurement 78–87

Measurement and Approximation 88–103

Geometry 104–113

Similar Triangles and the Pythagorean Theorem 114–129

Perimeter, Area, and Volume 130–143

Graphs 144–155

Probability 156–172

Mid-Book/Final Tests 173–178

Answers 181–191

Using This Book

SPECTRUM MATHEMATICS is a non-graded, consumable series for students who need special help with the basic skills of computation and problem solving. This successful series emphasizes skill development and practice, without complex terminology or abstract symbolism. Because of the nature of the content and the students for whom the series is intended, readability has been carefully controlled to comply with the mathematics level of each book.

Features:

- A **Pre-Test** at the beginning of each chapter helps determine a student's understanding of the chapter content. The Pre-Test enables students and teachers to identify specific skills that need attention.
- **Developmental exercises** are provided at the top of the page when new skills are introduced. These exercises involve students in learning and serve as an aid for individualized instruction or independent study.
- **Abundant opportunities for practice** follow the developmental exercises.
- **Problem-solving pages** enable students to apply skills to realistic problems they will meet in everyday life.
- A **Test** at the end of each chapter gives students and teachers an opportunity to check understanding. A **Mid-Book Test,** covering Chapters 1–6, and a **Final Test,** covering all chapters, provide for further checks of understanding.
- A **Record of Test Scores** is provided on page xvi of this book so students can chart their progress as they complete each chapter test.
- **Answers** to all problems and test items are included at the back of the book.

This is the third edition of *SPECTRUM MATHEMATICS*. The basic books have remained the same. Some new, useful features have been added.

New Features:

- **Scope and Sequence Charts** for the entire Spectrum Mathematics series are included on pages iv–v.
- **Basic Facts Tests** for addition, subtraction, multiplication, and division are included on pages vii–xiv. There are two forms of each test. These may be given at any time the student or teacher decides they are appropriate.
- An **Assignment Record Sheet** is provided on page xv.

NAME ____________________

Addition Facts (Form A)

	a	b	c	d	e	f	g	h
1.	3 +1	8 +2	1 +6	4 +7	6 +3	2 +8	4 +5	7 +9
2.	6 +4	1 +8	3 +9	2 +1	5 +0	0 +2	9 +1	3 +2
3.	2 +7	6 +9	4 +8	9 +3	2 +2	8 +0	0 +4	7 +1
4.	5 +2	8 +3	1 +5	7 +8	6 +2	4 +6	5 +4	9 +4
5.	2 +3	9 +0	4 +3	2 +9	1 +1	8 +8	3 +5	5 +7
6.	8 +9	3 +3	9 +5	6 +6	3 +8	0 +6	7 +3	2 +6
7.	7 +7	4 +1	3 +6	8 +7	0 +0	9 +8	9 +2	7 +5
8.	2 +4	0 +3	5 +8	2 +5	1 +9	1 +0	5 +9	8 +4
9.	6 +7	3 +4	9 +9	0 +7	8 +5	7 +4	5 +6	3 +7
10.	9 +7	8 +6	5 +5	7 +6	6 +8	6 +5	4 +9	9 +6

Perfect score: 80 My score: __________

NAME ______________________

Addition Facts (Form B)

	a	b	c	d	e	f	g	h
1.	8 +2	7 +0	0 +1	1 +1	6 +4	5 +2	4 +9	2 +7
2.	1 +0	6 +3	3 +0	2 +3	7 +1	8 +1	6 +5	1 +9
3.	0 +5	1 +2	6 +6	3 +5	9 +5	5 +7	7 +6	3 +8
4.	4 +2	6 +8	8 +5	2 +6	5 +8	9 +8	0 +0	4 +4
5.	7 +2	9 +7	0 +8	4 +7	7 +9	5 +9	3 +3	5 +4
6.	1 +3	9 +0	2 +2	5 +1	7 +7	6 +0	8 +6	9 +4
7.	4 +8	9 +3	1 +4	2 +9	9 +2	8 +3	7 +3	0 +9
8.	2 +0	2 +8	8 +4	4 +0	8 +7	9 +1	4 +3	5 +5
9.	8 +9	5 +6	6 +1	1 +7	4 +6	7 +5	9 +9	6 +7
10.	3 +9	9 +6	7 +8	5 +3	6 +9	8 +8	7 +4	3 +7

Perfect score: 80 My score: __________

NAME ____________________

Subtraction Facts (Form A)

	a	*b*	*c*	*d*	*e*	*f*	*g*	*h*
1.	11 −3	8 −4	5 −5	12 −3	2 −1	10 −9	4 −3	11 −9
2.	10 −5	3 −3	6 −3	11 −4	7 −6	10 −6	9 −2	12 −4
3.	16 −7	9 −0	5 −4	13 −7	10 −2	15 −9	8 −8	14 −5
4.	13 −8	4 −2	7 −7	12 −9	2 −0	17 −9	6 −1	11 −7
5.	18 −9	9 −8	6 −4	11 −5	3 −1	15 −7	9 −9	10 −8
6.	12 −6	8 −7	3 −2	13 −9	10 −4	14 −6	7 −5	12 −5
7.	15 −8	8 −3	9 −5	12 −8	8 −6	16 −9	5 −3	12 −7
8.	14 −7	7 −1	6 −5	11 −6	4 −1	10 −7	1 −1	10 −3
9.	13 −4	0 −0	8 −0	16 −8	9 −7	14 −9	6 −6	13 −6
10.	17 −8	9 −6	7 −4	15 −6	11 −2	13 −5	9 −3	14 −8

Perfect score: 80 My score: __________

NAME ______________________

Subtraction Facts (Form B)

	a	*b*	*c*	*d*	*e*	*f*	*g*	*h*
1.	4 − 2	13 − 7	3 − 2	10 − 1	6 − 5	8 − 1	14 − 5	10 − 7
2.	8 − 2	12 − 5	6 − 3	10 − 8	2 − 1	11 − 9	14 − 8	11 − 2
3.	4 − 0	11 − 3	9 − 1	15 − 6	5 − 0	7 − 1	13 − 8	10 − 9
4.	6 − 4	13 − 9	1 − 0	9 − 2	7 − 3	12 − 4	15 − 7	5 − 4
5.	0 − 0	12 − 3	8 − 4	14 − 6	8 − 5	10 − 4	16 − 9	11 − 6
6.	9 − 9	10 − 2	3 − 2	15 − 9	5 − 1	12 − 9	14 − 9	10 − 3
7.	7 − 5	12 − 7	7 − 0	14 − 7	7 − 2	11 − 4	16 − 7	11 − 5
8.	4 − 4	13 − 6	5 − 2	16 − 8	9 − 4	10 − 5	13 − 4	6 − 0
9.	8 − 3	12 − 6	1 − 1	18 − 9	4 − 3	12 − 8	14 − 6	13 − 5
10.	9 − 6	11 − 7	8 − 8	17 − 8	6 − 2	10 − 6	17 − 9	15 − 8

Perfect score: 80   My score: ________

NAME ____________________

Multiplication Facts (Form A)

	a	*b*	*c*	*d*	*e*	*f*	*g*	*h*
1.	2 ×2	6 ×3	0 ×1	3 ×2	8 ×0	1 ×1	7 ×1	8 ×4
2.	7 ×4	3 ×0	8 ×3	2 ×1	5 ×1	3 ×6	2 ×5	6 ×2
3.	3 ×7	5 ×5	8 ×6	6 ×0	4 ×9	9 ×1	7 ×2	4 ×3
4.	8 ×5	2 ×4	7 ×5	4 ×1	8 ×2	6 ×5	7 ×8	1 ×9
5.	4 ×0	8 ×1	9 ×3	5 ×6	3 ×8	2 ×9	5 ×7	9 ×2
6.	7 ×9	6 ×4	4 ×8	7 ×3	6 ×9	9 ×4	2 ×6	8 ×7
7.	1 ×3	9 ×5	5 ×3	8 ×8	4 ×5	0 ×7	3 ×4	7 ×6
8.	3 ×5	9 ×0	2 ×7	7 ×7	5 ×8	9 ×6	2 ×0	6 ×6
9.	9 ×9	1 ×8	6 ×8	0 ×0	9 ×7	0 ×5	3 ×9	8 ×9
10.	4 ×6	9 ×8	2 ×8	4 ×7	1 ×6	6 ×7	3 ×3	5 ×9

Perfect score: 80 My score: ________

NAME ____________________

Multiplication Facts (Form B)

	a	*b*	*c*	*d*	*e*	*f*	*g*	*h*
1.	2 ×2	6 ×4	4 ×1	7 ×7	1 ×0	2 ×9	0 ×2	1 ×4
2.	5 ×0	3 ×1	8 ×3	3 ×9	0 ×9	9 ×6	7 ×3	4 ×8
3.	1 ×2	4 ×9	6 ×3	7 ×2	5 ×7	1 ×5	2 ×8	8 ×2
4.	8 ×4	9 ×5	4 ×2	2 ×3	6 ×9	4 ×7	4 ×3	5 ×6
5.	2 ×4	7 ×1	3 ×3	6 ×2	9 ×4	5 ×1	6 ×8	7 ×6
6.	7 ×4	1 ×1	5 ×8	8 ×5	7 ×0	0 ×8	6 ×1	9 ×3
7.	3 ×8	9 ×7	5 ×2	2 ×6	3 ×4	8 ×9	7 ×5	6 ×7
8.	8 ×6	5 ×4	4 ×6	9 ×2	1 ×7	8 ×1	4 ×4	3 ×5
9.	6 ×5	7 ×8	9 ×9	0 ×0	3 ×7	5 ×5	2 ×5	8 ×8
10.	9 ×1	4 ×5	8 ×7	6 ×6	9 ×8	7 ×9	2 ×7	5 ×9

Perfect score: 80 My score: __________

NAME ______________________________

Division Facts (Form A)

	a	*b*	*c*	*d*	*e*	*f*	*g*
1.	7)7	4)24	9)18	3)18	8)32	6)12	2)8
2.	8)0	1)9	5)15	2)16	7)21	5)0	8)8
3.	3)15	8)40	7)28	4)20	7)63	3)21	9)36
4.	7)14	5)20	6)6	2)18	6)24	1)2	2)10
5.	8)24	5)10	4)28	9)45	1)8	5)45	8)48
6.	5)40	6)30	1)6	5)5	9)0	8)16	4)4
7.	9)54	1)5	7)56	6)18	4)16	6)54	3)6
8.	7)35	3)12	2)0	8)56	2)12	6)0	7)49
9.	4)0	8)64	5)35	4)32	3)24	1)3	6)36
10.	6)42	9)9	4)8	1)0	9)63	4)12	5)25
11.	3)9	2)14	9)72	7)42	2)4	8)72	1)1
12.	9)81	6)48	4)36	2)6	5)30	1)4	3)27

Perfect score: 84 My score: ________

NAME ____________________

Division Facts (Form B)

	a	*b*	*c*	*d*	*e*	*f*	*g*
1.	$2\overline{)2}$	$4\overline{)12}$	$3\overline{)9}$	$6\overline{)24}$	$8\overline{)48}$	$3\overline{)6}$	$8\overline{)0}$
2.	$6\overline{)30}$	$9\overline{)36}$	$7\overline{)14}$	$2\overline{)4}$	$5\overline{)5}$	$5\overline{)40}$	$7\overline{)63}$
3.	$1\overline{)7}$	$5\overline{)0}$	$5\overline{)45}$	$9\overline{)45}$	$4\overline{)8}$	$1\overline{)9}$	$8\overline{)56}$
4.	$3\overline{)3}$	$4\overline{)16}$	$7\overline{)56}$	$5\overline{)35}$	$8\overline{)8}$	$4\overline{)4}$	$9\overline{)54}$
5.	$7\overline{)0}$	$3\overline{)12}$	$8\overline{)64}$	$6\overline{)36}$	$7\overline{)21}$	$2\overline{)6}$	$4\overline{)36}$
6.	$9\overline{)27}$	$2\overline{)8}$	$6\overline{)18}$	$9\overline{)0}$	$6\overline{)54}$	$1\overline{)0}$	$6\overline{)12}$
7.	$6\overline{)0}$	$4\overline{)20}$	$8\overline{)40}$	$1\overline{)1}$	$8\overline{)72}$	$3\overline{)15}$	$5\overline{)30}$
8.	$9\overline{)18}$	$5\overline{)25}$	$7\overline{)49}$	$4\overline{)24}$	$3\overline{)24}$	$9\overline{)63}$	$2\overline{)10}$
9.	$3\overline{)0}$	$9\overline{)9}$	$6\overline{)48}$	$2\overline{)14}$	$6\overline{)6}$	$1\overline{)6}$	$8\overline{)16}$
10.	$3\overline{)18}$	$7\overline{)35}$	$1\overline{)4}$	$9\overline{)72}$	$4\overline{)28}$	$2\overline{)12}$	$7\overline{)42}$
11.	$1\overline{)8}$	$8\overline{)32}$	$5\overline{)20}$	$5\overline{)10}$	$2\overline{)18}$	$6\overline{)42}$	$5\overline{)15}$
12.	$8\overline{)24}$	$3\overline{)21}$	$9\overline{)81}$	$2\overline{)16}$	$7\overline{)28}$	$3\overline{)27}$	$4\overline{)32}$

Perfect score: 84 My score: ________

Assignment Record Sheet

NAME ______________________________

Pages Assigned	Date	Score	Pages Assigned	Date	Score	Pages Assigned	Date	Score

NAME ____________________

SPECTRUM MATHEMATICS

Record of Test Scores

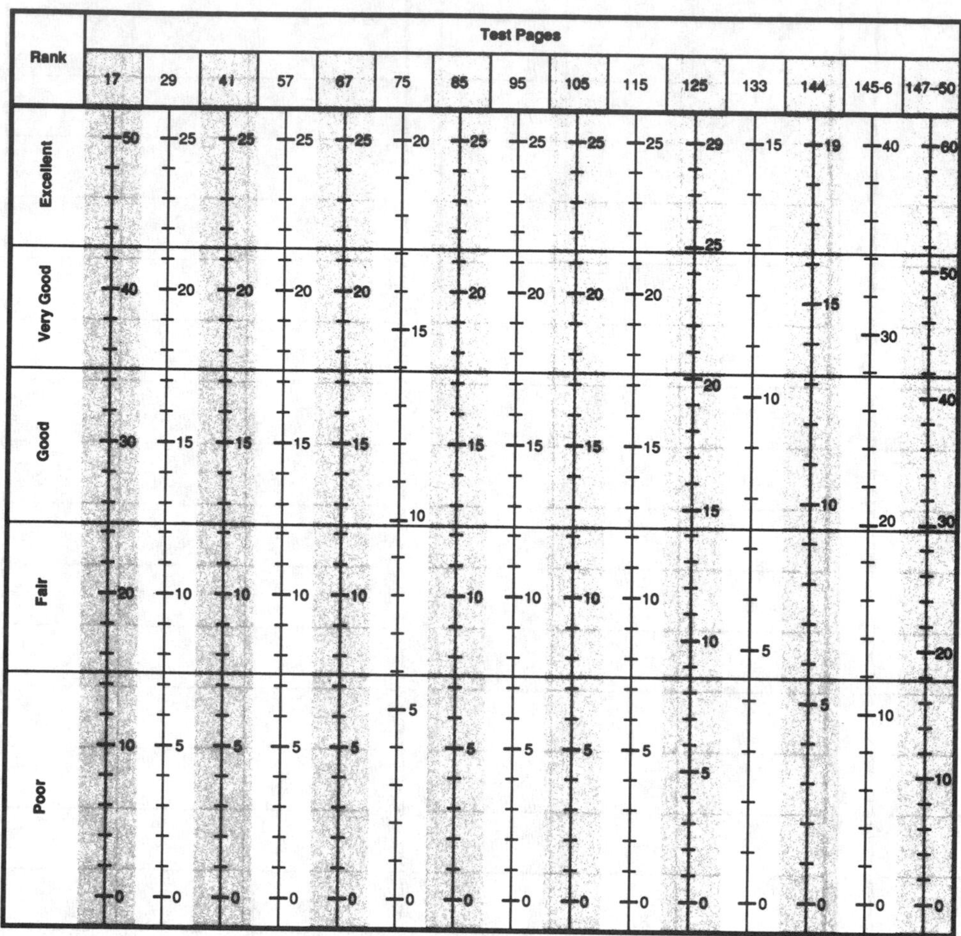

To record the score you receive on a TEST:

(1) Find the vertical scale below the page number of that TEST,
(2) on that vertical scale, draw a ● at the mark which represents your score.

For example, if your score for the TEST on page 17 is "My score: 32," draw a ● at the 32-mark on the first vertical scale. A score of 32 would show that your rank is "Good." You can check your progress from one test to the next by connecting the dots with a line segment.

NAME ________________________

PRE-TEST—Addition and Subtraction

Chapter 1

Add.

	a	b	c	d	e	f
1.	2 +8	7 +5	9 +4	5 +5	6 +8	8 +9
2.	4 +7	8 +5	6 +4	9 +9	1 +9	8 +7
3.	8 +8	9 +5	6 +7	7 +3	4 +8	9 +3
4.	3 +8	6 +6	9 +2	7 +7	9 +7	6 +9

Subtract.

5.	10 − 3	12 − 8	15 − 6	14 − 5	18 − 9	16 − 8
6.	13 − 5	12 − 4	16 − 7	10 − 2	11 − 7	14 − 6
7.	10 − 5	12 − 6	11 − 2	15 − 7	17 − 9	10 − 8
8.	12 − 5	10 − 1	13 − 4	17 − 8	11 − 3	10 − 6
9.	12 − 9	15 − 8	16 − 9	11 − 5	13 − 6	14 − 7

Perfect score: 54 My score: ________

Problem-Solving Pre-Test

Solve each problem.

1. Two adults and two children are playing. How many people are playing?

There are ________ adults.

There are ________ children.

There are ________ people playing.

2. The Durhams played football for 1 hour and then played baseball for 2 hours. How many hours did they play in all?

They played football for ________ hour.

They played baseball for ________ hours.

They played ________ hours in all.

3. The Durhams' house has 5 bedrooms in all. There are 2 bedrooms downstairs. The rest of the bedrooms are upstairs. How many bedrooms are upstairs?

There are ________ bedrooms in all.

There are ________ bedrooms downstairs.

There are ________ bedrooms upstairs.

1.	
2.	
3.	

Perfect score: 9 My score: ________

NAME ______________________

Lesson 1 Addition

2 +6 8	Find the 2 -row. Find the 6 -column. The sum is named where the 2-row and 6-column meet.

6-column

2-row

+	0	1	2	3	4	5	6	7	8	9
0	0	1	2	3	4	5	6	7	8	9
1	1	2	3	4	5	6	7	8	9	
2	2	3	4	5	6	7	(8)	9		
3	3	4	5	6	7	8	9			
4	4	5	6	7	8	9				
5	5	6	7	8	9					
6	6	7	8	9						
7	7	8	9							
8	8	9								
9	9									

Add.

	a	*b*	*c*	*d*	*e*	*f*	*g*	*h*
1.	2 +4	3 +1	1 +2	7 +0	0 +4	1 +4	5 +2	3 +3
2.	2 +0	6 +3	4 +4	3 +0	5 +3	1 +6	0 +5	8 +1
3.	2 +6	1 +0	1 +5	2 +2	3 +2	2 +1	5 +4	1 +7
4.	9 +0	5 +1	0 +3	4 +1	4 +5	1 +8	8 +0	4 +3
5.	0 +0	2 +3	7 +1	0 +9	4 +2	0 +2	0 +7	1 +1
6.	2 +7	0 +1	6 +2	0 +6	1 +3	6 +1	6 +0	7 +2

Perfect score: 48 My score: ________

NAME ____________________

Lesson 2 Subtraction

$$\begin{array}{r} 8 \\ -6 \\ \hline 2 \end{array}$$

Find 8 in the 6 -column.
The difference is named in the at the end of this row.

6-column

−	0	1	2	3	4	5	6	7	8	9
0	0	1	2	3	4	5	6	7	8	9
1	1	2	3	4	5	6	7	8	9	
(2)	2	3	4	5	6	7	8	9		
3	3	4	5	6	7	8	9			
4	4	5	6	7	8	9				
5	5	6	7	8	9					
6	6	7	8	9						
7	7	8	9							
8	8	9								
9	9									

Subtract.

	a	*b*	*c*	*d*	*e*	*f*	*g*	*h*
1.	5 −4	3 −2	7 −7	1 −0	8 −2	9 −7	4 −3	6 −1
2.	7 −2	2 −2	7 −6	8 −7	9 −3	9 −8	4 −1	6 −0
3.	0 −0	7 −1	3 −0	6 −6	4 −2	6 −2	9 −5	8 −6
4.	9 −9	8 −4	9 −1	7 −5	7 −4	6 −5	2 −0	1 −1
5.	3 −1	9 −4	7 −3	5 −2	5 −1	6 −4	4 −4	8 −1
6.	5 −5	2 −1	5 −0	8 −3	9 −0	6 −3	7 −0	5 −3

Perfect score: 48 My score: ________

NAME ______________________________

Lesson 3 Addition

5	→ Find the 5 -row.
+7	→ Find the 7 -column.
	← The sum is named where the 5-row and 7-column meet.

7-column

5-row

+	0	1	2	3	4	5	6	7	8	9
0	0	1	2	3	4	5	6	7	8	9
1	1	2	3	4	5	6	7	8	9	10
2	2	3	4	5	6	7	8	9	10	11
3	3	4	5	6	7	8	9	10	11	12
4	4	5	6	7	8	9	10	11	12	
5	5	6	7	8	9	10	11	(12)		
6	6	7	8	9	10	11	12			
7	7	8	9	10	11	12				
8	8	9	10	11	12					
9	9	10	11	12						

Add.

	a	*b*	*c*	*d*	*e*	*f*
1.	6 +5	7 +3	2 +7	8 +4	9 +2	6 +3
2.	8 +2	3 +9	3 +5	5 +2	6 +4	5 +5
3.	5 +3	9 +3	6 +6	3 +7	4 +7	9 +1
4.	5 +7	8 +1	5 +6	2 +8	2 +5	7 +5
5.	3 +4	4 +5	4 +6	2 +9	8 +3	4 +8
6.	2 +6	1 +9	3 +8	7 +1	7 +4	6 +2

Perfect score: 36 My score: __________

Problem Solving

Solve each problem.

1. Andy played 2 games today. He played 9 games yesterday. How many games did he play in all?

Andy played ________ games today.

Andy played ________ games yesterday.

He played ________ games in all.

2. Jane rode her bicycle 8 kilometers yesterday. She rode 4 kilometers today. How many kilometers did she ride in all?

Jane rode ________ kilometers yesterday.

Jane rode ________ kilometers today.

Jane rode ________ kilometers in all.

3. Paul hit the ball 7 times. He missed 4 times. How many times did he swing at the ball?

Paul hit the ball ________ times.

Paul missed the ball ________ times.

Paul swung at the ball ________ times.

4. There were 4 people in a room. Six more people came in. How many people were in the room then?

________ people were in a room.

________ more people came in.

________ people were in the room then.

5. Paula and Alice each read 6 books. How many books did they read in all?

They read ________ books in all.

1.

2.

3.

4.

5.

Perfect score: 13 My score: ________

NAME ____________________

Lesson 4 Subtraction

$$\begin{array}{r} 11 \\ -4 \\ \hline \end{array}$$

11 → Find 11 in
−4 → the 4 -column.
The difference is named in the
at the end of this row.

4-column

−	0	1	2	3	4	5	6	7	8	9
0	0	1	2	3	4	5	6	7	8	9
1	1	2	3	4	5	6	7	8	9	10
2	2	3	4	5	6	7	8	9	10	11
3	3	4	5	6	7	8	9	10	11	12
4	4	5	6	7	8	9	10	11	12	
5	5	6	7	8	9	10	11	12		
6	6	7	8	9	10	11	12			
(7)	7	8	9	10	11	12				
8	8	9	10	11	12					
9	9	10	11	12						

Subtract.

	a	*b*	*c*	*d*	*e*	*f*
1.	$11 - 7$	$10 - 4$	$10 - 8$	$12 - 9$	$8 - 5$	$11 - 2$
2.	$10 - 1$	$11 - 8$	$7 - 4$	$11 - 6$	$12 - 3$	$9 - 6$
3.	$12 - 7$	$10 - 7$	$9 - 3$	$11 - 9$	$12 - 4$	$10 - 5$
4.	$8 - 6$	$12 - 8$	$9 - 5$	$10 - 6$	$11 - 5$	$8 - 8$
5.	$12 - 6$	$10 - 9$	$9 - 8$	$7 - 6$	$11 - 4$	$9 - 7$
6.	$10 - 2$	$7 - 3$	$10 - 3$	$12 - 5$	$8 - 3$	$11 - 3$

Perfect score: 36 My score: ________

Problem Solving

Solve each problem.

1. There were 12 nails in a box. Willy used 3 of them. How many nails are still in the box?

_________ nails were in a box.

_________ nails were used.

_________ nails are still in the box.

2. There are 11 checkers on a board. Eight of them are black. The rest are red. How many red checkers are on the board?

_________ checkers are on a board.

_________ checkers are black, and the rest are red.

_________ red checkers are on the board.

3. Marty is 10 years old. Her brother Larry is 7. Marty is how many years older than Larry?

Marty's age is _________ years.

Larry's age is _________ years.

Marty is _________ years older than Larry.

4. Joy walked 11 blocks. Ann walked 2 blocks. Joy walked how much farther than Ann?

Joy walked _________ blocks.

Ann walked _________ blocks.

Joy walked _________ blocks farther than Ann.

5. Twelve people are in a room. Five of them are men. How many are women?

_________ women are in the room.

1.

2.

3.

4.

5.

Perfect score: 13 My score: _________

NAME ______________________

Lesson 5 Addition and Subtraction

To check 5+6=11, subtract 6 from 11.

$$\begin{array}{r} 5 \\ +6 \\ \hline 11 \\ -6 \\ \hline 5 \end{array}$$

These should be the same.

To check 13−4=9, add 4 to ______.

$$\begin{array}{r} 13 \\ -4 \\ \hline 9 \\ +4 \\ \hline 13 \end{array}$$

These should be the same.

Add. Check each answer.

	a	*b*	*c*	*d*	*e*	*f*
1.	2 + 9	8 + 4	7 + 3	3 + 8	1 + 9	6 + 6
2.	9 + 3	5 + 6	4 + 8	5 + 5	7 + 4	9 + 1

Subtract. Check each answer.

3.	10 − 8	12 − 7	11 − 3	10 − 4	11 − 7	10 − 7
4.	11 − 9	12 − 8	11 − 8	12 − 5	10 − 6	10 − 3

Perfect score: 24 My score: ______

Problem Solving

Answer each question.

1. Ben had some marbles. He gave 2 of them away and had 9 left. How many marbles did he start with?

   Are you to add or subtract? ______

   How many marbles did he start with? ______

1.

2. A full box has 10 pieces of chalk. This box has only 8 pieces. How many pieces are missing?

   Are you to add or subtract? ______

   How many pieces are missing? ______

2.

3. Jack is 11 years old today. How old was he 4 years ago?

   Are you to add or subtract? ______

   How old was Jack 4 years ago? ______

3.

4. Nine boys were playing ball. Then 3 more boys began to play. How many boys were playing ball then?

   Are you to add or subtract? ______

   How many boys were playing then? ______

4.

5. Millie has as many sisters as brothers. She has 5 brothers. How many brothers and sisters does she have?

   Are you to add or subtract? ______

   How many brothers and sisters does Millie have? ______

5.

6. Tricia invited 12 people to her party. Seven people came. How many people that were invited did not come?

   Are you to add or subtract? ______

   How many people did not come? ______

6.

Perfect score: 12 My score: ______

NAME ______________________

Lesson 6 Addition

6 → Find the 6 -row.
+7 → Find the 7 -column.
The sum is named where the 6-row and 7-column meet.

9 → Find the 9 -row.
+8 → Find the 8 -column.
The sum is named where the 9-row and 8-column meet.

7-column, 8-column, 6-row, 9-row

+	0	1	2	3	4	5	6	7	8	9
0	0	1	2	3	4	5	6	7	8	9
1	1	2	3	4	5	6	7	8	9	10
2	2	3	4	5	6	7	8	9	10	11
3	3	4	5	6	7	8	9	10	11	12
4	4	5	6	7	8	9	10	11	12	13
5	5	6	7	8	9	10	11	12	13	14
6	6	7	8	9	10	11	12	13	14	15
7	7	8	9	10	11	12	13	14	15	16
8	8	9	10	11	12	13	14	15	16	17
9	9	10	11	12	13	14	15	16	17	18

Add.

	a	*b*	*c*	*d*	*e*	*f*
1.	7 +6	8 +7	7 +4	9 +7	4 +9	8 +8
2.	5 +9	6 +4	6 +8	5 +8	8 +4	7 +8
3.	6 +9	5 +5	6 +7	9 +2	8 +6	4 +6
4.	5 +7	8 +9	9 +6	5 +6	9 +4	9 +9
5.	7 +9	8 +2	9 +8	8 +5	9 +1	4 +7
6.	9 +5	6 +6	2 +9	4 +8	7 +7	9 +3

Perfect score: 36 My score: __________

Problem Solving

Solve each problem.

1. Ellen worked 9 hours Monday. She worked 7 hours Tuesday. How many hours did she work in all on those two days?

She worked ________ hours Monday.

She worked ________ hours Tuesday.

She worked ________ hours in all on those two days.

1.

2. Frank has 6 windows to wash. Janet has 9 windows to wash. How many windows do they have to wash in all?

Frank has ________ windows to wash.

Janet has ________ windows to wash.

Together they have ________ windows to wash.

2.

3. Seven cars are in the first row. Six cars are in the second row. How many cars are in the first two rows?

________ cars are in the first two rows.

4. There are 9 men and 8 women at work. How many people are at work?

There are ________ people at work.

3. 4.

5. Phil worked 8 hours. Geraldo worked the same number of hours. How many hours did Phil and Geraldo work in all?

They worked ________ hours in all.

6. There are 6 plants in a box. Seven more are on a table. How many plants are there?

There are ________ plants.

5. 6.

Perfect score: 10 My score: ________

NAME ________________________

Lesson 7 Subtraction

13	Find 13 in
−8	the 8 -column.
	The difference is named in the ______ at the end of that row.

15	Find 15 in
−6	the 6 -column.
	The difference is named in the ______ at the end of that row.

6-column 8-column

−	0	1	2	3	4	5	6	7	8	9
0	0	1	2	3	4	5	6	7		9
1	1	2	3	4	5	6	7	8		10
2	2	3	4	5	6	7	8	9	10	11
3	3	4	5	6	7	8	9	10	11	12
4	4	5	6	7	8	9	10	11	12	13
(5)		6	7	8	9	10	11	12		14
6	6	7	8	9	10	11	12		14	15
7	7	8	9	10	11	12				16
8	8	9	10	11	12					17
9	9	10	11	12						18

Subtract.

	a	b	c	d	e	f
1.	13 − 5	14 − 8	16 − 7	10 − 9	12 − 5	14 − 6
2.	17 − 8	13 − 7	12 − 4	14 − 5	15 − 8	13 − 6
3.	11 − 7	18 − 9	15 − 6	11 − 8	14 − 7	13 − 9
4.	16 − 8	10 − 5	12 − 7	13 − 4	12 − 6	14 − 9
5.	13 − 8	12 − 9	10 − 1	15 − 9	11 − 3	10 − 7
6.	15 − 7	10 − 3	17 − 9	11 − 6	16 − 9	11 − 4

Perfect score: 36 My score: ________

Problem Solving

Solve each problem.

1. Matt wants to collect 13 cars. He now has 5 cars. How many more cars does he need?

Matt wants ________ cars.

He now has ________ cars.

He needs ________ more cars.

2. Susan bought 18 valentines. She mailed 9 of them. How many valentines does she have left?

Susan bought ________ valentines.

She mailed ________ of them.

She has ________ valentines left.

3. Betty had 16 stamps. She used some, and had 7 left. How many stamps did she use?

Betty used ________ stamps.

4. Bret is 14 years old. Sally is 7. Bret is how much older than Sally?

Bret is ________ years older than Sally.

5. Fifteen bolts and nuts were on the table. Seven were bolts. How many were nuts?

There were ________ nuts.

6. There are 17 machine parts in a drawer. Only nine are new parts. How many are not new parts?

________ are not new parts.

1.

2.

3. | **4.**

5. | **6.**

Perfect score: 10   My score: ________

NAME ______________________

Lesson 8 Addition and Subtraction

To check 6+8=14, subtract 8 from 14.

```
   6  ←┐
  +8   │
  14   │ These should
  −8   │ be the same.
   6  ←┘
```

To check 13−6=7, add ______ to 7.

```
  13  ←┐
  −6   │
   7   │ These should
  +6   │ be the same.
  13  ←┘
```

Add. Check each answer.

	a	*b*	*c*	*d*	*e*	*f*
1.	5 + 9	9 + 7	6 + 6	7 + 4	9 + 8	3 + 7
2.	6 + 7	9 + 3	6 + 9	4 + 9	6 + 4	8 + 6

Subtract. Check each answer.

3.	14 − 8	18 − 9	13 − 5	15 − 6	16 − 8	12 − 7
4.	13 − 6	12 − 4	13 − 4	16 − 9	15 − 7	13 − 8

Perfect score: 24 My score: ______

Problem Solving

Answer each question.

1. Penny worked 9 addition problems. She worked 7 subtraction problems. How many problems did she work?

Are you to add or subtract? ____________________

How many problems did she work? ____________________

1.

2. Six people were in the room. Then 8 more people came in. How many people were in the room then?

Are you to add or subtract? ____________________

How many people were in the room then? __________

2.

3. There were 18 chairs in a room. Nine of them were being used. How many were not being used?

Are you to add or subtract? ____________________

How many chairs were not being used? ____________________

3.

4. Mr. Noe and Miss Leikel had 17 pupils absent. Mr. Noe had 9 absent. How many did Miss Leikel have absent?

Are you to add or subtract? ____________________

How many pupils were absent from Miss Leikel's class? __________

4.

5. There were 14 children at the park. Five were boys. How many were girls?

Are you to add or subtract? ____________________

How many girls were at the park? __________

5.

Perfect score: 10 My score: __________

NAME ______________________

CHAPTER 1 TEST

Add.

	a	b	c	d	e	f
1.	7 +8	4 +9	6 +5	2 +8	8 +6	7 +5
2.	9 +1	5 +8	8 +4	9 +2	8 +8	5 +9
3.	5 +7	6 +9	8 +3	8 +9	3 +8	9 +4
4.	9 +6	6 +7	9 +9	6 +6	7 +9	6 +4
5.	8 +5	3 +9	1 +9	7 +4	3 +7	6 +8

Subtract.

	a	b	c	d	e
6.	10 − 6	14 − 7	12 − 3	15 − 7	12 − 8
7.	13 − 4	16 − 7	11 − 9	10 − 5	13 − 6
8.	10 − 2	14 − 6	11 − 6	12 − 7	17 − 9
9.	16 − 8	11 − 7	10 − 3	14 − 8	15 − 8

Perfect score: 50 My score: ________

NAME ______________________

PRE-TEST—Addition and Subtraction

Chapter 2

Add.

	a	b	c	d	e	f
1.	3 +6	43 +6	1 +4	51 +4	2 +5	82 +5
2.	57 +2	26 +1	44 +3	23 +4	42 +3	21 +5
3.	4 +31	5 +43	4 +62	3 +43	5 +12	7 +20
4.	54 +31	26 +12	45 +33	67 +21	42 +33	22 +13
5.	32 +31	24 +24	36 +61	20 +19	45 +23	32 +21

Subtract.

	a	b	c	d	e	f
6.	7 −4	37 −4	5 −2	45 −2	8 −6	38 −6
7.	38 −4	27 −6	54 −3	29 −7	68 −2	26 −3
8.	54 −23	69 −24	37 −21	88 −24	93 −21	87 −37
9.	28 −13	54 −34	87 −26	54 −21	50 −40	37 −10

Perfect score: 54 My score: ________

NAME ____________________

Lesson 1 Addition

	Add the ones.	Add the tens.
36 +2	36 +2 8	36 +2 38

	Add the ones.	Add the tens.
6 +41	6 +41 7	6 +41 47

Add.

	a	*b*	*c*	*d*	*e*	*f*
1.	3 +5	23 +5	2 +3	42 +3	5 +1	25 +1
2.	3 +4	3 +64	4 +5	4 +55	2 +5	2 +85
3.	2 +4	12 +4	22 +4	32 +4	42 +4	52 +4
4.	5 +63	6 +31	24 +3	92 +2	57 +1	2 +41
5.	41 +3	21 +2	3 +63	2 +84	21 +6	4 +14
6.	8 +51	62 +4	25 +3	6 +33	2 +51	5 +43
7.	36 +2	42 +5	2 +51	60 +8	5 +21	34 +2

Perfect score: 42 My score: ________

Problem Solving

Solve each problem.

1. John has 32 red marbles and 5 green marbles. How many red and green marbles does he have? John has ________ red and green marbles.	**1.**
2. Su-Lee had 5 paper cups. She bought 24 more. How many paper cups did she have then? She then had ________ paper cups.	**2.**
3. On the way to work, Billy Joe counted 41 cars and 7 trucks. How many cars and trucks did he count? Billy Joe counted ________ cars and trucks.	**3.**
4. Mark worked all the problems on a test. He had 24 right answers and 4 wrong ones. How many problems were on the test? There were ________ problems on the test.	**4.**
5. Ruth works with 12 women and 6 men. How many people does she work with? She works with ________ people.	**5.**
6. Four men and 11 women are on the bus. How many people are on the bus? ________ people are on the bus.	**6.**
7. Marta weighs 20 kilograms. Her baby brother weighs 4 kilograms. How much do they weigh together? They weigh ________ kilograms together.	**7.**

Perfect score: 7 My score: ________

NAME ____________________

Lesson 2 Addition

	Add the ones.	Add the tens.
36 +43	36 +43 9	36 +43 79

25
+61
86

Add the ones.
Add the tens.

Add.

	a	b	c	d	e	f
1.	23 +45	63 +21	45 +22	61 +30	42 +35	60 +25
2.	48 +41	52 +14	32 +54	63 +20	21 +38	45 +52
3.	34 +22	41 +25	36 +22	51 +40	83 +12	42 +30
4.	63 +24	30 +58	27 +12	44 +23	62 +14	35 +53
5.	24 +31	52 +32	42 +27	51 +33	16 +20	43 +23
6.	34 +25	64 +23	18 +41	54 +24	41 +27	14 +32

Perfect score: 36 My score: ________

Problem Solving

Solve each problem.

1. There are 12 boys and 13 girls in Jean's class. How many pupils are in her class?

There are ________ pupils in that class.

2. Eve scored 32 baskets. She missed 23 times. How many times did she try to score?

Eve tried to score ________ times.

3. One store ordered 52 bicycles. Another store ordered 45 bicycles. How many bicycles did both stores order?

Both stores ordered ________ bicycles.

4. One bear cub weighs 64 kilograms. Another bear cub is 22 kilograms heavier. How much does the heavier cub weigh?

The heavier cub weighs ________ kilograms.

5. Johnny rode the bus 42 blocks east and 25 blocks south. How many blocks did Johnny ride the bus?

Johnny rode the bus ________ blocks.

6. 43 women and 35 men came to the meeting. How many people came to the meeting?

________ people came to the meeting.

7. 68 seats were filled, and 21 were empty. How many seats were there?

There were ________ seats.

1.	
2.	3.
4.	5.
6.	7.

Perfect score: 7 My score: ________

NAME ____________________

Lesson 3 Subtraction

	Subtract the ones.	Subtract the tens.		Subtract the ones.	Subtract the tens.
47 −2	47 −2 5	47 −2 45	64 −23	64 −23 1	64 −23 41

Subtract.

	a	*b*	*c*	*d*	*e*	*f*
1.	9 −3	49 −3	5 −2	35 −2	7 −1	87 −1
2	8 −2	78 −2	4 −3	64 −3	9 −9	89 −9
3.	45 −3	36 −4	78 −5	42 −2	38 −8	65 −4
4.	49 −26	37 −16	58 −23	49 −31	78 −45	73 −20
5.	58 −27	69 −31	42 −21	49 −19	84 −23	78 −64
6.	78 −21	67 −31	40 −20	56 −36	45 −23	92 −21
7.	56 −41	85 −63	94 −32	77 −46	99 −32	86 −23

Perfect score: 42 My score: ________

Problem Solving

Solve each problem.

1. Beth worked 27 problems. She got 6 wrong answers. How many answers did she get right?

Beth got ________ answers right.

2. There were 96 parts in a box. Four parts were broken. How many parts were not broken?

________ parts were not broken.

3. At noon the temperature was 28 degrees Celsius. At nine o'clock in the evening it was 14 degrees Celsius. How many degrees did the temperature drop?

The temperature dropped ________ degrees.

4. Clark had 75 cents. Then he spent 25 cents for some paper. How many cents did he have left?

Clark had ________ cents left.

5. There are 72 houses in Fred's neighborhood. Fred delivers papers to all but 21 of them. How many houses does he deliver papers to?

He delivers papers to ________ houses.

6. Ninety-five pupils were in the gym. Thirty-four were boys. How many were girls?

________ pupils were girls.

7. A rope is 47 inches long. A wire is 17 inches long. How much longer is the rope?

The rope is ________ inches longer.

1.	
2.	**3.**
4.	**5.**
6.	**7.**

Perfect score: 7 My score: ________

NAME ____________________

Lesson 4 Subtraction

To check 37 − 24 = 13, add 24 to ______.

$$\begin{array}{r} 37 \\ -24 \\ \hline 13 \\ +24 \\ \hline 37 \end{array}$$

These should be the same.

To check 59 − 29 = 30, add ______ to 30.

$$\begin{array}{r} 59 \\ -29 \\ \hline 30 \\ +29 \\ \hline 59 \end{array}$$

These should be the same.

Subtract. Check each answer.

	a	*b*	*c*	*d*	*e*	*f*
1.	59 − 34	27 − 14	85 − 23	78 − 23	47 − 24	59 − 26
2.	85 − 25	48 − 32	56 − 24	96 − 35	40 − 30	92 − 81
3.	74 − 23	58 − 26	75 − 24	38 − 23	45 − 35	88 − 35
4.	67 − 24	87 − 24	59 − 36	58 − 24	79 − 54	84 − 23

Perfect score: 24 My score: ______

Problem Solving

Solve each problem.

1. Mr. Ming wants to build a fence 58 meters long. He has 27 meters of fence completed. How much of the fence is left to build? _________ meters of fence is left to build.	**1.**
2. Mr. Boyle is taking an 89-mile trip. He has traveled 64 miles. How much farther must he travel? Mr. Boyle must travel _________ more miles.	**2.**
3. Sean had 95 cents. Then he spent 45 cents. How many cents did he have left? Sean had _________ cents left.	**3.**
4. Beverly scored 62 points and Dorothy scored 78 points. How many more points did Dorothy score than Beverly? Dorothy scored _________ more points.	**4.**
5. Bill lives 38 blocks from the ball park. Joe lives 25 blocks from the park. How much farther from the ball park does Bill live than Joe? Bill lives _________ blocks farther than Joe.	**5.**
6. Eighty-four pupils were in the pool. Fifty of them were boys. How many girls were in the pool? _________ girls were in the pool.	**6.**
7. Larry said that 88 buses stop at Division Street each day. So far, 13 buses have stopped. How many more buses should stop today? _________ more buses should stop.	**7.**

Perfect score: 7 My score: _________

NAME ________________________

Lesson 5 Addition and Subtraction

To check 43 + 14 = 57, subtract 14 from ________.

$$\begin{array}{r} 43 \\ +14 \\ \hline 57 \\ -14 \\ \hline 43 \end{array}$$

These should be the same.

To check 57 − 14 = 43, add ________ to 43.

$$\begin{array}{r} 57 \\ -14 \\ \hline 43 \\ +14 \\ \hline 57 \end{array}$$

These should be the same.

Add. Check each answer.

	a	*b*	*c*	*d*	*e*	*f*
1.	27 + 31	42 + 51	26 + 30	14 + 52	23 + 72	65 + 22
2.	44 + 24	31 + 27	64 + 14	32 + 20	42 + 36	46 + 23

Subtract. Check each answer.

	a	*b*	*c*	*d*	*e*	*f*
3.	78 − 23	48 − 13	27 − 16	58 − 26	67 − 24	38 − 16
4.	75 − 61	46 − 26	39 − 10	45 − 23	67 − 41	38 − 15

Perfect score: 24   My score: ________

Problem Solving

Solve each problem.

1. Mrs. Dial weighs 55 kilograms. Her son weighs 32 kilograms. How much more thar her son does Mrs. Dial weigh?

She weighs ________ kilograms more.

2. Mitzi planted 55 flower seeds. Only 23 of them grew. How many did not grow?

________ seeds did not grow.

3. A city has 48 mail trucks. Twelve are not being used today. How many mail trucks are being used?

________ mail trucks are being used.

4. A mail carrier delivered 38 letters and picked up 15. How many more letters were delivered than were picked up?

The carrier delivered ________ more letters.

5. A city has 89 mail carriers. One day 77 carriers were at work. How many were not at work?

________ carriers were not at work.

6. Our mail carrier walks about 32 miles each week. About how many miles does our carrier walk in two weeks?

Our carrier walks ________ miles in two weeks.

7. Ms. Tottle worked at a store for 23 years. She then worked 26 years at a bank. How many years did she work at these two places?

She worked ________ years at these two places.

1.	
2.	3.
4.	5.
6.	7.

Perfect score: 7 My score: ________

NAME ____________________

CHAPTER 2 TEST

Add or subtract. Check each answer.

	a	*b*	*c*	*d*	*e*	*f*
1.	4 +2	24 +2	36 +3	4 +21	72 +4	9 +30
2.	36 +21	41 +38	65 +22	41 +26	35 +50	66 +21
3.	7 −2	37 −2	45 −4	26 −3	49 −8	27 −5
4.	48 −23	65 −24	45 −22	68 −28	54 −22	67 −30

Solve.

5. Miss Jones has 32 pupils. Mr. Lum has 26 pupils. How many pupils are in the two classes?

There are ________ pupils in the two classes.

Perfect score: 25 My score: ________

NAME ____________________

PRE-TEST—Addition and Subtraction

Chapter 3

Add.

	a	*b*	*c*	*d*	*e*	*f*
1.	53 + 6	24 + 2	2 + 35	8 + 81	64 + 3	25 + 2
2.	36 + 5	54 + 8	8 + 39	2 + 59	48 + 8	26 + 7
3.	42 + 33	72 + 14	54 + 23	61 + 28	19 + 40	26 + 52
4.	54 + 27	35 + 36	59 + 38	54 + 19	27 + 48	39 + 39
5.	49 + 23	62 + 17	43 + 21	48 + 48	26 + 40	56 + 37

Subtract.

	a	*b*	*c*	*d*	*e*	*f*
6.	37 − 3	29 − 4	54 − 4	87 − 2	56 − 5	89 − 6
7.	47 − 9	72 − 5	45 − 7	55 − 9	40 − 5	34 − 7
8.	54 − 12	42 − 30	75 − 64	46 − 23	93 − 81	89 − 41
9.	73 − 25	85 − 49	92 − 24	64 − 56	77 − 48	88 − 38

Perfect score: 54 My score: ________

NAME ____________________

Lesson 1 Addition

	Add the ones. Rename 13 as 10 + 3.		Add the tens.
54 +9	4 +9 = 13 or 10+3	1 over 54, +9, 3	1 over 54, +9, 63

Add.

	a	b	c	d	e	f
1.	27 +5	35 +8	87 +4	38 +9	42 +8	46 +5
2.	45 +9	27 +7	7 +38	20 +65	24 +9	8 +38
3.	27 +3	45 +6	8 +36	9 +29	6 +58	42 +9
4.	76 +7	3 +47	4 +26	27 +4	5 +18	9 +19
5.	6 +15	41 +9	52 +8	65 +9	7 +38	6 +16
6.	9 +28	36 +7	59 +2	7 +36	4 +47	9 +38
7.	46 +8	9 +25	8 +68	4 +59	85 +5	78 +7

Perfect score: 42 My score: ________

Problem Solving

Solve each problem.

1. Last year there were 44 monkeys on an island. There are 8 more monkeys this year. How many monkeys are on the island now?

There were ________ monkeys last year.

There are ________ more monkeys this year.

There are ________ monkeys on the island now.

2. There were 72 children and 9 adults in our group at the zoo. How many people were in our group?

________ children were in our group.

________ adults were in our group.

________ people were in our group.

3. One group of monkeys was fed 6 kilograms of fruit. Another group was fed 19 kilograms. How much fruit was that in all?

That was ________ kilograms of fruit in all.

4. The children drank 68 cartons of milk. There were 8 cartons left. How many cartons of milk were there to start with?

There were ________ cartons of milk to start with.

5. A zoo has 87 kinds of snakes. They are getting 4 new kinds. How many kinds will they have then?

Then they will have ________ kinds of snakes.

1.

2.

3.

4.

5.

Perfect score: 9 My score: ________

NAME ______________________

Lesson 2 Addition

	Add the ones. Rename 15 as 10 + 5.		Add the tens.
48 +27	8 +7 15 or 10 + 5	1 48 +27 5	1 48 + 27 75

Add.

	a	b	c	d	e	f
1.	37 +25	48 +37	26 +54	35 +29	54 +18	62 +29
2.	29 +28	38 +37	47 +25	63 +27	79 +19	64 +17
3.	58 +26	45 +18	27 +57	44 +29	36 +36	77 +17
4.	49 +48	26 +37	73 +19	18 +28	15 +47	29 +27
5.	18 +55	28 +24	38 +37	48 +43	58 +16	68 +28
6.	26 +66	19 +54	57 +29	45 +36	52 +18	33 +29
7.	35 +56	47 +28	31 +39	29 +59	67 +16	55 +28

Perfect score: 42 My score: ______

Problem Solving

Solve each problem.

1. January has 31 days. February has 29 days this year. How many days are in the two months?

There are ________ days in January.

There are ________ days in February this year.

There are ________ days in January and February.

2. Jeff weighs 46 kilograms. His father is 36 kilograms heavier. How much does Jeff's father weigh?

Jeff weighs ________ kilograms.

His father is ________ kilograms heavier.

His father weighs ________ kilograms.

3. Mary had 29 points. She earned 13 more. How many points did she have then?

Mary had ________ points.

She earned ________ more.

She had ________ points then.

4. Hank gained 18 pounds in the last two years. Two years ago he weighed 59 pounds. How much does he weigh today?

Hank weighs ________ pounds today.

5. Kathy read 25 pages of a story. She has 36 more pages to read. How many pages are there in the story?

There are ________ pages in the story.

1.

2.

3.

4.

5.

Perfect score: 11 My score: ________

NAME ____________________

Lesson 3 Subtraction

	To subtract the ones, rename 63 as "5 tens and 13 ones."	Subtract the ones.	Subtract the tens.
$\begin{array}{r} 63 \\ -9 \\ \hline \end{array}$	$\begin{array}{r} {\scriptstyle 5\ 13} \\ \not{6}\ \not{3} \\ -9 \\ \hline \end{array}$	$\begin{array}{r} {\scriptstyle 5\ 13} \\ \not{6}\ \not{3} \\ -9 \\ \hline 4 \end{array}$	$\begin{array}{r} {\scriptstyle 5\ 13} \\ \not{6}\ \not{3} \\ -9 \\ \hline 5\ 4 \end{array}$

Subtract.

	a	*b*	*c*	*d*	*e*	*f*
1.	53 − 8	27 − 9	46 − 9	54 − 5	32 − 6	65 − 7
2.	28 − 9	48 − 9	35 − 6	44 − 7	67 − 8	92 − 9
3.	52 − 6	62 − 4	61 − 6	73 − 5	50 − 9	42 − 5
4.	96 − 8	73 − 6	80 − 7	42 − 3	63 − 4	51 − 9
5.	94 − 8	88 − 9	33 − 4	27 − 9	46 − 8	64 − 7
6.	23 − 9	76 − 8	40 − 4	41 − 6	53 − 7	25 − 7
7.	47 − 8	31 − 7	82 − 8	74 − 6	93 − 9	60 − 5

Perfect score: 42 My score: ________

Problem Solving

Solve each problem.

1. There were 48 words on a spelling test. Sarah missed 9 of them. How many words did she spell correctly?

There were ________ words on the test.

Sarah missed ________ words.

She spelled ________ words correctly.

2. Frank earned 91 points. Mike earned 5 points less than Frank. How many points did Mike earn?

Frank earned ________ points.

Mike earned ________ points less than Frank.

Mike earned ________ points.

3. Sheila lost 7 of the 45 games she played. How many games did she win?

She won ________ games.

4. Ken had 50 tickets to sell. He sold some and had 6 left. How many tickets did he sell?

Ken sold ________ tickets.

5. There were 73 books in the classroom library. Some of the books are checked out. Seven are still there. How many books are checked out?

________ books are checked out.

6. Angela's great-grandfather is 82 years old. How old was he 4 years ago?

Four years ago he was ________ years old.

1.

2.

3.

4.

5.

6.

Perfect score: 10 My score: ________

NAME ______________________

Lesson 4 Subtraction

	To subtract the ones, rename 92 as "8 tens and 12 ones."	Subtract the ones.	Subtract the tens.
92 −38	8 12 ~~9~~ ~~2~~ −3 8	8 12 ~~9~~ ~~2~~ −3 8 4	8 12 ~~9~~ ~~2~~ −3 8 5 4

Subtract.

	a	*b*	*c*	*d*	*e*	*f*
1.	35 − 17	27 − 19	54 − 37	63 − 26	84 − 59	28 − 19
2.	42 − 24	56 − 39	41 − 27	53 − 15	86 − 78	92 − 26
3.	43 − 15	37 − 29	26 − 19	55 − 36	43 − 27	28 − 19
4.	54 − 26	35 − 18	22 − 15	56 − 29	38 − 19	31 − 18
5.	83 − 25	94 − 16	65 − 39	73 − 17	80 − 28	92 − 35
6.	35 − 26	90 − 55	56 − 27	41 − 16	50 − 38	61 − 15
7.	52 − 18	75 − 38	47 − 39	60 − 11	86 − 59	94 − 48

Perfect score: 42 My score: ______

Problem Solving

Solve each problem.

1. Joe weighs 95 pounds. Larry weighs 26 pounds less than Joe. How much does Larry weigh?

Joe weighs ________ pounds.

Larry weighs ________ pounds less than Joe.

Larry weighs ________ pounds.

2. There are 73 children in the gym. Forty-five of them are boys. How many girls are in the gym?

There are ________ children in the gym.

There are ________ boys in the gym.

There are ________ girls in the gym.

3. A store has 84 bicycles. They have 45 girls' bicycles. How many boys' bicycles do they have?

________ bicycles are boy's bicycles.

4. It takes 50 points to win a prize. Penny has 38 points. How many more points does Penny need to win a prize?

Penny needs ________ points.

5. Ann has 19 more pages to read in a book. The book has 46 pages in all. How many pages has Ann already read?

Ann has already read ________ pages.

6. The Tigers scored 33 points. The Bears scored 18 points. How many more points did the Tigers score than the Bears?

The Tigers scored ________ more points.

1.

2.

3. 4.

5. 6.

Perfect score: 10 My score: ________

NAME ________________

Lesson 5 Addition and Subtraction

To check 34 + 19 = 53, subtract 19 from ________.

$$\begin{array}{r} 34 \\ +19 \\ \hline 53 \\ -19 \\ \hline 34 \end{array}$$

These should be the same.

To check 53 − 19 = 34, add ________ to 34.

$$\begin{array}{r} 53 \\ -19 \\ \hline 34 \\ +19 \\ \hline 53 \end{array}$$

These should be the same.

Add. Check each answer.

	a	*b*	*c*	*d*	*e*	*f*
1.	54 + 7	46 + 9	63 + 18	58 + 27	21 + 49	45 + 46
2.	26 + 38	37 + 19	41 + 9	58 + 18	67 + 27	35 + 38

Subtract. Check each answer.

3.	62 − 8	48 − 9	35 − 16	96 − 29	52 − 14	43 − 5
4.	36 − 18	57 − 8	67 − 19	52 − 17	51 − 23	60 − 46

Perfect score: 24 My score: ________

Problem Solving

Answer each question.

1. This morning the temperature was 75 degrees. This afternoon it was 83 degrees. How many degrees did it go up?

Are you to add or subtract? ____________

How many degrees did the temperature go up? ____________

1.

2. There were 45 people at a meeting. After 28 of them left, how many people were still at the meeting?

Are you to add or subtract? ____________

How many people were still at the meeting? ____________

2.

3. Renée drove 67 miles in the morning and 24 miles in the afternoon. How far did she drive?

Are you to add or subtract? ____________

How far did she drive? ____________

3.

4. Harry is 54 inches tall. His sister is 36 inches tall. How much taller is Harry?

Are you to add or subtract? ____________

How much taller is Harry than his sister? ____________

4.

5. A clown has 26 orange balloons and 28 blue balloons. How many balloons is that?

Are you to add or subtract? ____________

How many orange and blue balloons are there? ____________

5.

Perfect score: 10 My score: ________

NAME ____________________

CHAPTER 3 TEST

Add. Check each answer.

	a	*b*	*c*	*d*	*e*	*f*
1.	36 + 7	45 + 9	8 + 23	17 + 7	8 + 44	58 + 6
2.	17 + 25	26 + 48	43 + 38	74 + 19	78 + 18	65 + 16

Subtract. Check each answer.

3.	26 − 8	54 − 9	61 − 3	27 − 9	54 − 6	66 − 9
4.	36 − 17	72 − 44	38 − 19	74 − 26	93 − 89	82 − 57

Solve.

5. Fifty-four girls and 27 boys came to the meeting. How many boys and girls came to the meeting?

________ boys and girls came to the meeting.

Perfect score: 25 My score: ________

NAME ____________________

PRE-TEST—Addition and Subtraction

Chapter 4

Add.

	a	b	c	d	e	f
1.	5 +6	50 +60	7 +8	70 +80	90 +80	70 +70
2.	53 +95	44 +74	82 +96	67 +70	55 +52	73 +86
3.	63 +78	82 +89	97 +27	56 +75	88 +88	97 +44
4.	26 +53	66 +25	74 +65	39 +87	82 +17	76 +72
5.	59 +59	73 +15	83 +67	54 +72	63 +70	35 +45

Subtract.

	a	b	c	d	e	f
6.	16 −7	160 −70	15 −9	150 −90	140 −60	170 −80
7.	136 −53	165 −74	154 −90	186 −93	179 −82	147 −67
8.	146 −97	158 −69	172 −85	163 −77	125 −58	116 −39
9.	176 −53	184 −35	154 −72	153 −74	146 −32	107 −40

Perfect score: 54 My score: ________

NAME ______________________

Lesson 1 Addition and Subtraction

8	8	80	80	14	14	140	140
+6	+6	+60	+60	−6	−6	−60	−60
	14		140		8		80

If 8+6=14, then 80+60=________.

If 14−6=8, then 140−60=________.

Add.

	a	b	c	d	e	f
1.	7 +8	70 +80	6 +9	60 +90	3 +8	30 +80
2.	7 +5	70 +50	8 +9	80 +90	4 +6	40 +60
3.	70 +40	50 +90	30 +90	70 +70	90 +40	80 +40
4.	20 +90	60 +60	70 +60	90 +10	70 +90	80 +80

Subtract.

	a	b	c	d	e	f
5.	13 −5	130 −50	17 −8	170 −80	12 −6	120 −60
6.	15 −6	150 −60	14 −5	140 −50	18 −9	180 −90
7.	140 −80	110 −70	160 −80	130 −60	170 −90	120 −50
8.	130 −90	160 −70	150 −80	120 −80	140 −90	110 −40

Perfect score: 48 My score: ________

Problem Solving

Answer each question.

1. Harold is on a trip of 170 kilometers. So far he has gone 90 kilometers. How many more kilometers must he go?

Are you to add or subtract? ______

How many more kilometers must he go? ______

2. A school has 60 men teachers. It has 60 women teachers. How many teachers are in the school?

Are you to add or subtract? ______

How many teachers are in the school? ______

3. Ken weighs 70 pounds. His older brother weighs 130 pounds. How many more pounds does his older brother weigh?

Are you to add or subtract? ______

How many more pounds does his older brother weigh? ______

4. Joyce has 110 pennies. Emily has 90 pennies. Joyce has how many more pennies than Emily?

Joyce has ______ more pennies than Emily.

5. Vera sold 50 pennants on Monday and 70 on Tuesday. How many pennants did she sell in all?

Vera sold ______ pennants in all.

6. A bag contains 150 red and green marbles. Ninety of them are red. How many marbles are green?

______ marbles are green.

1.	
2.	
3.	4.
5.	6.

Perfect score: 9 My score: ______

NAME ______________

Lesson 2 Addition

	Add the ones.	Add the tens.
43 +86	43 +86 9 ↑ 3+6=9	43 +86 129 ↑ 40+80=120 or 100+20

Add.

	a	*b*	*c*	*d*	*e*	*f*
1.	74 +62	56 +93	49 +60	57 +72	83 +35	94 +24
2.	62 +53	76 +72	34 +95	83 +43	96 +61	72 +41
3.	92 +30	74 +82	93 +92	86 +21	55 +60	34 +82
4.	65 +42	54 +82	83 +93	46 +90	93 +93	62 +64
5.	81 +58	65 +91	42 +84	35 +72	90 +70	80 +85
6.	93 +84	22 +97	45 +72	54 +54	43 +82	61 +81
7.	56 +82	62 +43	70 +76	54 +73	94 +94	85 +92

Perfect score: 42 My score: ______

Problem Solving

Solve each problem.

1. Richard sold 96 tickets. Carmen sold 81. How many tickets did they both sell?

Richard sold ______ tickets.

Carmen sold ______ tickets.

They sold a total of ______ tickets.

2. Fifty-three people live in the first building. Eighty-five people live in the second building. How many people live in both buildings?

______ people live in the first building.

______ people live in the second building.

______ people live in both buildings.

3. A train went 83 kilometers the first hour. The second hour it went 84 kilometers. How far did it go in the two hours?

The first hour the train went ______ kilometers.

The second hour it went ______ kilometers.

In the two hours it went ______ kilometers.

4. Ninety-two train seats are filled. There are 47 empty train seats. How many train seats are there?

There are ______ train seats.

5. Joy collected 72 stamps. Jan collected 76 stamps. How many stamps did they collect in all?

They collected ______ stamps.

1.	
2.	
3.	
4.	5.

Perfect score: 11 My score: ______

NAME ____________________

Lesson 3 Subtraction

	Subtract the ones.	To subtract the tens, rename 1 hundred and 3 tens as "13 tens."	Subtract the tens.
136	136	$\overset{13}{\not{1}\not{3}}6$	$\overset{13}{\not{1}\not{3}}6$
−72	−72	−72	−72
	4	4	64

Subtract.

	a	*b*	*c*	*d*	*e*	*f*
1.	147 − 64	108 − 72	156 − 83	129 − 44	175 − 81	114 − 42
2.	136 − 86	153 − 62	118 − 91	124 − 82	136 − 43	107 − 45
3.	148 − 82	164 − 83	186 − 93	115 − 72	104 − 91	146 − 52
4.	107 − 23	139 − 72	124 − 30	155 − 95	166 − 72	124 − 61
5.	118 − 27	126 − 55	174 − 93	149 − 72	108 − 61	136 − 94
6.	145 − 92	129 − 73	152 − 72	164 − 90	135 − 62	113 − 61
7.	126 − 91	185 − 94	137 − 65	158 − 86	149 − 99	176 − 83

Perfect score: 42 My score: ________

Problem Solving

Solve each problem.

1. Bob had 128 centimeters of string. He used 73 centimeters of it. How much string was left?

The string was ________ centimeters long.

Bob used ________ centimeters of the string.

There were ________ centimeters of string left.

1.

2. Francis and Diane got on a scale. The reading was "145 pounds." Diane got off, and the reading was "75 pounds." How much does Diane weigh?

Together they weighed ________ pounds.

Francis weighs ________ pounds.

Diane weighs ________ pounds.

2.

3. There are 167 pupils in Tony's grade at school. Seventy-one of the pupils are girls. How many of the pupils are boys?

There are ________ pupils in all.

There are ________ girls.

There are ________ boys.

3.

4. Judy counted 156 sheets of paper in the package. Then she used 91 sheets. How many sheets of paper did she have left?

There were ________ sheets of paper left.

5. A jet plane has 184 passenger seats. There are 93 passengers on the plane. How many empty passenger seats are there?

There are ________ empty passenger seats.

4. **5.**

Perfect score: 11 My score: ________

NAME ________________

Lesson 4 Addition and Subtraction

To check 75 + 61 = 136, subtract ________ from 136.

$$\begin{array}{r} 75 \\ +61 \\ \hline 136 \\ -61 \\ \hline 75 \end{array}$$

These should be the same.

To check 157 − 83 = 74, add 83 to ________.

$$\begin{array}{r} 157 \\ -83 \\ \hline 74 \\ +83 \\ \hline 157 \end{array}$$

These should be the same.

Add. Check each answer.

	a	*b*	*c*	*d*	*e*	*f*
1.	74 + 53	85 + 42	96 + 60	43 + 71	61 + 45	32 + 82
2.	91 + 82	53 + 63	96 + 51	45 + 82	32 + 96	53 + 51

Subtract. Check each answer.

3.	175 − 83	156 − 64	162 − 91	189 − 95	144 − 60	128 − 71
4.	136 − 62	165 − 83	157 − 76	128 − 61	147 − 52	104 − 21

Perfect score: 24 My score: ________

Problem Solving

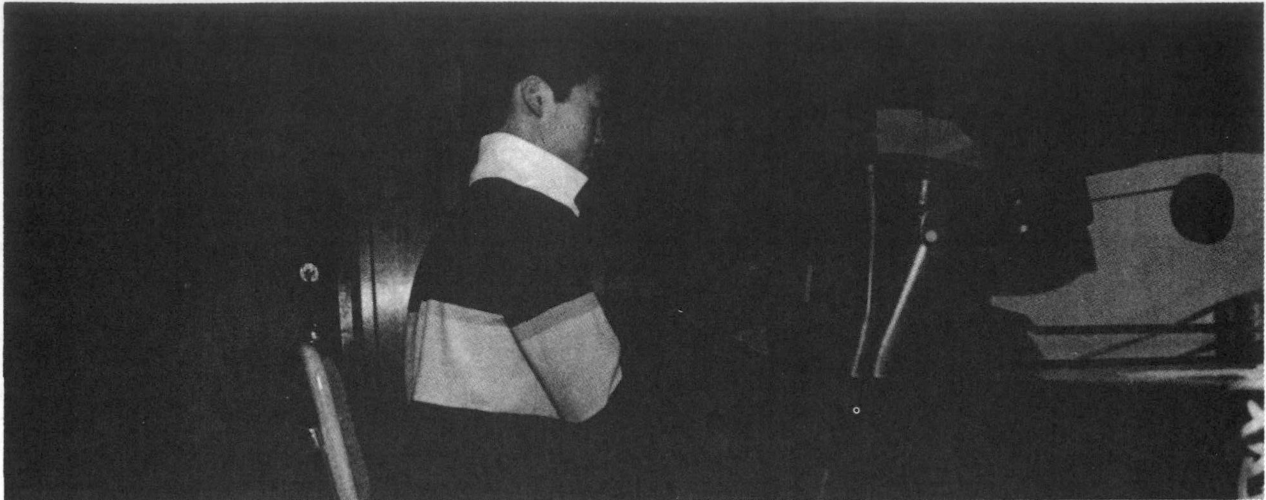

Solve each problem.

1. Derrick worked at the computer for 80 minutes in the morning. That afternoon he worked at it for 40 minutes. How long did he work on the computer that day?

   Are you to add or subtract? ______________

   How long did he work on the computer that day? ______________

   1.

2. Derrick wrote a computer program that has 129 lines. He has put 91 lines in the computer so far. How many more lines does he have to put in the computer?

   Are you to add or subtract? ______________

   How many more lines does he have to put in the computer? ______________

   2.

3. Derrick's mother uses the computer for work. Last month she used it 71 hours. This month she used it for 82 hours. How many hours did she use the computer in the last two months?

   Are you to add or subtract? ______________

   How many hours did she use the computer in the last two months? ______________

   3.

Perfect score: 6 My score: ______

NAME ______________________________

Lesson 5 Addition

	Add the ones.	Add the tens.
58 +76	1 58 +76 4 8+6=14 or 10+4	1 58 +76 134 10+50+70=130 or 100+30

Add.

	a	*b*	*c*	*d*	*e*	*f*
1.	94 +68	77 +46	59 +75	72 +38	43 +99	66 +85
2.	87 +85	39 +92	66 +46	47 +78	75 +55	89 +96
3.	97 +59	89 +59	16 +95	34 +88	63 +98	99 +48
4.	37 +73	94 +28	99 +32	58 +95	67 +75	29 +85
5.	48 +86	69 +57	94 +97	72 +88	89 +64	87 +26
6.	54 +88	76 +76	89 +98	43 +68	96 +29	78 +68

Perfect score: 36 My score: ________

Problem Solving

Solve each problem.

1. A library loaned 74 books on Monday. It loaned 87 books on Tuesday. How many books did it loan on both days?

The library loaned ____________ books on Monday.

The library loaned ____________ books on Tuesday.

The library loaned ____________ books both days.

2. Barbara read 49 pages in the morning. She read 57 pages in the afternoon. How many pages did she read in all?

Barbara read ____________ pages in the morning.

Barbara read ____________ pages in the afternoon.

Barbara read ____________ pages in all.

3. The gym is 48 feet longer than the basketball court. The basketball court is 84 feet long. How long is the gym?

The basketball court is ____________ feet long.

The gym is ____________ feet longer than the basketball court.

The gym is ____________ feet long.

4. At the circus, 84 adult tickets and 96 children's tickets were sold. How many tickets were sold?

__________ tickets were sold.

5. The team scored 66 points in the first half. They scored 68 points the second half. How many points did they score in the game?

They scored ____________ points in the game.

1.

2.

3.

4.

5.

Perfect score: 11 My score: __________

NAME ____________________

Lesson 6 Subtraction

	Rename 1 hundred and 6 ones as "10 tens and 6 ones."	Rename 10 tens and 6 ones as "9 tens and 16 ones."	Subtract the ones.	Subtract the tens.
106 −49	10 ~~10~~6 −49	9 16 ~~106~~ −49	9 16 ~~106~~ −49 7	9 16 ~~106~~ −49 57

Subtract.

	a	b	c	d	e	f
1.	135 −86	108 −19	113 −27	125 −48	142 −59	156 −88
2.	115 −78	122 −78	171 −99	140 −55	107 −18	132 −65
3.	186 −99	153 −65	132 −93	148 −79	115 −57	142 −64
4.	153 −95	104 −37	136 −48	150 −77	162 −95	174 −86
5.	143 −85	154 −96	163 −87	132 −75	120 −61	147 −78
6.	163 −99	174 −87	126 −58	142 −95	133 −58	114 −28
7.	102 −23	175 −97	166 −97	148 −59	133 −74	121 −98

Perfect score: 42 My score: ________

Problem Solving

Solve each problem.

1. Ms. Davis needs 180 meters of fence. She has 95 meters of fence. How many more meters of fence does she need?

Ms. Davis needs ________ meters of fence.

She has ________ meters of fence.

She needs ________ more meters of fence.

2. Eddie knows the names of 128 pupils at school. If 79 are girls, how many are boys?

Eddie knows the names of ________ pupils.

________ are girls.

________ are boys.

3. Margo's family is on a 162-kilometer trip. They have already gone 84 kilometers. How much farther do they have to go?

The trip is ________ kilometers long.

They have gone ________ kilometers.

They have ________ more kilometers to go.

4. Ted's birthday is the 29th day of the year. Karen's birthday is the 126th day. Karen's birthday is how many days after Ted's birthday?

It is ________ days after Ted's birthday?

5. Mr. Darter got 131 trading stamps at two stores. He got 84 stamps at one store. How many did he get at the other store?

Mr. Darter got ________ stamps.

1.

2.

3.

4.

5.

Perfect score: 11 My score: ________

NAME ______________________

Lesson 7 Addition and Subtraction

Add. Check each answer.

	a	*b*	*c*	*d*	*e*	*f*
1.	54 + 38	71 + 56	57 + 86	95 + 24	42 + 37	58 + 26
2.	72 + 96	58 + 74	92 + 37	48 + 22	35 + 43	55 + 55

Subtract. Check each answer.

3.	125 − 92	174 − 33	165 − 87	150 − 90	146 − 76	132 − 84
4.	112 − 47	118 − 33	157 − 26	160 − 45	175 − 76	153 − 83
5.	198 − 39	155 − 97	163 − 84	131 − 71	111 − 24	108 − 39

Perfect score: 30 My score: __________

Problem Solving

Solve each problem.

1. There are 166 people living in my apartment building. If 98 are children, how many are adults?

There are ____________ people in the building.

There are ____________ children.

There are ____________ adults.

2. There were 115 cases on a truck. The driver left 27 cases at the first stop. How many cases are still on the truck?

____________ cases were on a truck.

____________ cases were left at the first stop.

____________ cases are still on the truck.

3. The bus has 84 passenger seats. All the seats are filled and there are 39 passengers standing. How many passengers are on the bus?

The bus has ____________ seats.

There are ____________ passengers standing.

There are ____________ passengers on the bus.

4. Beth counted 63 houses on one side of the street. She counted 89 on the other side. How many houses are on the street?

There are ____________ houses on the street.

5. Martha had 112 balloons. She gave some of them away. She had 35 balloons left. How many balloons did she give away?

She gave away ____________ balloons.

1.
2.
3.
4.
5.

Perfect score: 11 My score: ____________

NAME ______________________

CHAPTER 4 TEST

Add or subtract. Check each answer.

	a	*b*	*c*	*d*	*e*
1.	60 +80	70 +90	85 +63	72 +54	60 +65
2.	84 +57	63 +77	82 +99	78 +78	44 +79
3.	170 −80	160 −80	153 −71	127 −82	175 −91
4.	127 −59	143 −65	166 −89	183 −95	122 −57
5.	147 −36	56 +37	175 −85	57 +89	197 −73

Perfect score: 25 My score: ________

NAME ______________________

PRE-TEST—Addition and Subtraction

Chapter 5

Add.

	a	*b*	*c*	*d*	*e*	*f*
1.	3 4 +7	8 6 +9	9 5 +7	5 6 8 +3	4 9 2 +6	3 7 5 +9
2.	10 30 40 +50	20 30 40 +60	20 40 60 +70	40 30 80 +40	50 50 20 +60	20 60 20 +40
3.	52 41 +30	26 30 +92	33 44 +57	38 46 +69	49 65 +77	27 34 +46
4.	23 23 31 +22	28 17 23 +44	91 22 34 +51	72 54 36 +21	78 52 43 +45	33 25 36 +21
5.	423 101 +324	526 345 +116	123 541 +162	752 348 +150	429 316 541 +302	324 115 462 +115

Subtract.

	a	*b*	*c*	*d*	*e*
6.	752 − 341	673 − 424	583 − 193	765 − 489	605 − 329
7.	4723 − 221	5806 − 447	3924 − 163	7811 − 912	6425 − 587

Perfect score: 40 My score: ________

NAME ______________________

Lesson 1 Addition

		Add the ones.		Add the tens.
67 98 +83	7 8 +3	15 +3 18 or 10 + 8	1 67 98 +83 8	1 67 98 +83 248

Add.

	a	*b*	*c*	*d*	*e*	*f*
1.	4 5 +7	6 8 +9	5 2 +8	9 8 +3	4 6 +5	7 7 +6
2.	10 40 30 +50	20 60 50 +60	10 20 90 +40	20 40 30 +70	10 50 60 +40	20 70 50 +80
3.	44 35 +57	66 58 +59	25 92 +48	49 38 +73	54 66 +45	77 57 +86
4.	25 32 +41	27 35 +42	55 55 +55	32 44 +28	75 16 +58	22 14 +91
5.	57 28 +36	42 54 +78	79 34 +29	68 78 +88	25 36 +42	53 26 +13
6.	45 18 +52	61 29 +58	83 76 +19	49 42 +43	37 67 +26	98 16 +35

Perfect score: 36 My score: ________

Problem Solving

NATIONAL LEAGUE TEAM STANDINGS		
TEAM	WON	LOST
CUBS	72	43
CARDS	69	48
METS	64	52
PIRATES	58	55
PHILLIES	44	68
EXPOS	37	79

Solve each problem.

1. How many games have been won by the first three teams in the National League?

The Cubs have won ____________ games.

The Cards have won ____________ games.

The Mets have won ____________ games.

Together they have won ____________ games.

2. How many games have been lost by the last three teams in the National League?

The Pirates have lost ____________ games.

The Phillies have lost ____________ games.

The Expos have lost ____________ games.

Together they have lost ____________ games.

3. How many games have been won by the Cubs, Mets, Phillies, and Expos?

The Cubs, Mets, Phillies, and Expos have won ____________ games.

4. How many games have the Cubs, Cards, and Pirates lost?

The Cubs, Cards, and Pirates have lost ____________ games.

1.

2.

3.

4.

Perfect score: 10 My score: ________

NAME ______________________

Lesson 2 Addition

	Add the ones.	Add the tens.	Add the hundreds.
642 156 275 +143	[1] 642 156 275 +143 6	[2 1] 642 156 275 +143 16	[2 1] 642 156 275 +143 1216

2+6+5+3=____	10+40+50+70+40=______	200+600+100+200+100=______
16=10+____	210=200+______	1200=1000+______

Add.

	a	*b*	*c*	*d*	*e*	*f*
1.	372 456 +174	382 154 +283	231 336 +136	152 443 +178	321 305 +238	143 116 +212
2.	425 641 +703	443 217 +602	613 247 +138	574 142 +281	382 425 +678	392 456 +731
3.	728 365 +428	639 752 +417	618 304 +120	856 174 +372	564 345 +654	224 305 +406
4.	421 145 162 +231	178 214 103 +407	513 223 641 +412	421 146 273 +154	762 531 444 +258	372 541 635 +413
5.	603 254 316 +222	425 245 542 +254	631 211 431 +222	731 240 635 +214	245 361 524 +113	284 563 711 +245

Perfect score: 30 My score: ______

Problem Solving

Solve each problem.

1. The local theater had a special Saturday movie. They sold 175 tickets to men, 142 to women, and 327 to children. How many tickets did they sell in all?

They sold ______________ tickets to men.

They sold ______________ tickets to women.

They sold ______________ tickets to children.

They sold ______________ tickets in all.

1.

2. In the local high school there are 768 boys, 829 girls, and 107 teachers. How many teachers and pupils are there in all?

There are ______________ boys.

There are ______________ girls.

There are ______________ teachers.

There are ______________ teachers and pupils in all.

2.

3. The number of people living in 4 different apartment buildings is 203, 245, 268, and 275. How many people live in all 4 buildings?

______________ people live in all 4 buildings.

4. A living room floor has 195 tiles. A bedroom floor has 168 tiles. A kitchen floor has 144 tiles. How many tiles are in the 3 rooms?

There are ______________ tiles in these 3 rooms.

3.

4.

Perfect score: 10 My score: ______________

NAME ____________________

Lesson 3 Subtraction

	Rename 40 as "3 tens and 10 ones." Then subtract the ones.	Rename 7 hundreds and 3 tens as "6 hundreds and 13 tens." Then subtract the tens.	Subtract the hundreds.
$\begin{array}{r} 740 \\ -271 \\ \hline \end{array}$	$\begin{array}{r} 7\overset{3}{\not4}\overset{10}{\not0} \\ -271 \\ \hline 9 \end{array}$	$\begin{array}{r} \overset{6}{\not7}\overset{13}{\not3}\overset{10}{\not0} \\ -271 \\ \hline 69 \end{array}$	$\begin{array}{r} \overset{6}{\not7}\overset{13}{\not3}\overset{10}{\not0} \\ -271 \\ \hline 469 \end{array}$

Subtract.

	a	*b*	*c*	*d*	*e*	*f*
1.	534 − 273	263 − 154	758 − 439	450 − 261	536 − 347	274 − 154
2.	463 − 372	782 − 234	594 − 287	681 − 382	384 − 175	806 − 764
3.	764 − 137	635 − 447	492 − 113	780 − 152	444 − 235	562 − 357
4.	836 − 257	944 − 256	758 − 167	504 − 235	672 − 285	892 − 284
5.	945 − 463	378 − 126	564 − 243	839 − 257	245 − 146	776 − 382
6.	805 − 308	900 − 750	764 − 345	840 − 426	955 − 765	436 − 327

Perfect score: 36 My score: ________

Problem Solving

Solve each problem.

1. Babe Ruth hit 714 home runs. Ted Williams hit 521 home runs. How many more home runs did Babe Ruth hit than Ted Williams?

Babe Ruth hit ____________ home runs.

Ted Williams hit ____________ home runs.

Babe Ruth hit ____________ more home runs than Ted Williams.

2. A train has 850 seats. There are 317 empty seats. How many people are seated?

The train has ________ seats.

________ seats are empty.

There are ________ people seated.

3. Hoover Dam is 726 feet high. Folsom Dam is 340 feet high. How much higher is Hoover Dam than Folsom Dam?

Hoover Dam is ____________ feet high.

Folsom Dam is ____________ feet high.

Hoover Dam is ____________ feet higher than Folsom Dam.

4. The quarterback threw 247 passes. Only 138 passes were caught. How many were not caught?

________ passes were not caught.

5. A meeting room can hold 443 people. There are 268 people in the room now. How many more people can it hold?

It can hold ____________ more people.

1.	
2.	
3.	
4.	5.

Perfect score: 11 My score: ________

NAME ______________________

Lesson 4 Subtraction

	Subtract the ones.	Rename 2 hundreds and 5 tens as "1 hundred and 15 tens." Subtract the tens.	Rename 4 thousands and 1 hundred as "3 thousands and 11 hundreds." Subtract the hundreds.	Subtract the thousands.
4253 −281	4253 −281 2	1 15 4~~2~~~~5~~3 −281 72	11 3 ~~1~~ 15 ~~4~~~~2~~~~5~~3 281 972	11 3 ~~1~~ 15 ~~4~~~~2~~~~5~~3 −281 3972

Subtract.

	a	*b*	*c*	*d*	*e*
1.	7543 − 211	6813 − 402	7254 − 132	4936 − 726	2815 − 813
2.	3562 − 235	4253 − 147	6541 − 538	3473 − 255	5496 − 339
3.	3710 − 340	9642 − 271	3817 − 454	5216 − 182	3847 − 377
4.	4295 − 724	4007 − 805	8281 − 470	5554 − 644	6382 − 882
5.	5986 − 537	2413 − 829	4507 − 758	3154 − 205	2640 − 834
6.	8329 − 475	7604 − 829	3987 − 988	4205 − 736	1383 − 529

Perfect score: 30 My score: ________

Problem Solving

Solve each problem.

1. Ms. Ramos bought a car that cost 3,165 dollars. She paid 875 dollars. How much does she still owe?

The new car cost ________ dollars.

Ms. Ramos paid ________ dollars.

She still owes ________ dollars.

2. Mount Whitney is 4,418 meters high. Mount Davis is 979 meters high. How much higher is Mount Whitney?

Mount Whitney is ________ meters high.

Mount Davis is ________ meters high.

Mount Whitney is ________ meters higher.

3. There are 1,156 pupils enrolled in a school. Today 219 pupils are absent. How many are present?

________ pupils are present.

4. There are 5,280 feet in a mile. John walked 895 feet. How many more feet must he go to walk a mile?

He must go ________ more feet to walk a mile.

5. Henry's family went 2,198 kilometers in 5 days. They went 843 kilometers the first 2 days. How many kilometers did they go in the last 3 days?

They went ________ kilometers in the last three days.

6. There are 1,255 people on a police force. If 596 are women, how many are men?

There are ________ men.

1.	
2.	
3.	4.
5.	6.

Perfect score: 10 My score: ________

NAME ____________________

CHAPTER 5 TEST

Add.

	a	*b*	*c*	*d*	*e*
1.	3 2 +5	4 7 +6	8 4 +9	70 30 50 +40	50 70 80 +30
2.	35 24 +20	57 13 +28	74 82 +36	23 32 58 +42	42 53 64 +70
3.	421 312 +148	623 174 +162	473 126 +248	326 112 224 +607	526 381 426 +543

Subtract.

	a	*b*	*c*	*d*
4.	765 − 243	290 − 183	846 − 354	846 − 297
5.	5836 − 314	7542 − 275	6039 − 268	2560 − 764

Solve each problem.

6. Four girls earned the following points in a contest: 145, 387, 245, and 197. What was the total number of points earned?

The total number of points was ____________.

7. Ralph's new car was driven 837 miles. Jo's new car was driven 3275 miles. How many more miles was Jo's new car driven than Ralph's?

Jo's car was driven ____________ more miles.

6.

7.

Perfect score: 25 My score: ________

NAME ____________

PRE-TEST—Measurement

Chapter 6

Complete the following.

	a	*b*
1.	There are ________ days in a year.	4:10 means 10 minutes after ________.
2.	There are ________ days in a leap year.	3:50 means 10 minutes to ________.
3.	There are ________ days in April.	5:45 means ________ minutes after 5.
4.	There are ________ days in March.	5:45 means ________ minutes to 6.

Complete the following as shown.

	a	*b*	*c*
5.	XI = 11	V = ________	IV = ________
6.	XVII = ________	XXVI = ________	XIX = ________
7.	7 = VII	10 = ________	9 = ________
8.	24 = ________	31 = ________	25 = ________

Add or subtract.

	a	*b*	*c*	*d*	*e*
9.	$5.20 +6.89	$12.65 +1.25	46¢ +37¢	29¢ 37¢ +28¢	$ 3.73 .28 +14.50
10.	$16.50 −3.25	$14.75 −2.90	$7.40 −.84	56¢ −38¢	97¢ −50¢

Solve.

11. Ms. Romanez bought a saw for $21.95 and a hammer for $9.49. She paid $1.88 tax. How much was her total bill?

Her total bill was ________________.

Perfect score: 29 My score: ________

NAME ____________________

Lesson 1 Reading Our Calendar

JANUARY

S	M	T	W	T	F	S
						1
2	3	4	5	6	7	8
9	10	11	12	13	14	15
16	17	18	19	20	21	22
23	24	25	26	27	28	29
30	31					

FEBRUARY

S	M	T	W	T	F	S
		1	2	3	4	5
6	7	8	9	10	11	12
13	14	15	16	17	18	19
20	21	22	23	24	25	26
27	28					

MARCH

S	M	T	W	T	F	S
		1	2	3	4	5
6	7	8	9	10	11	12
13	14	15	16	17	18	19
20	21	22	23	24	25	26
27	28	29	30	31		

APRIL

S	M	T	W	T	F	S
					1	2
3	4	5	6	7	8	9
10	11	12	13	14	15	16
17	18	19	20	21	22	23
24	25	26	27	28	29	30

MAY

S	M	T	W	T	F	S
1	2	3	4	5	6	7
8	9	10	11	12	13	14
15	16	17	18	19	20	21
22	23	24	25	26	27	28
29	30	31				

JUNE

S	M	T	W	T	F	S
			1	2	3	4
5	6	7	8	9	10	11
12	13	14	15	16	17	18
19	20	21	22	23	24	25
26	27	28	29	30		

JULY

S	M	T	W	T	F	S
					1	2
3	4	5	6	7	8	9
10	11	12	13	14	15	16
17	18	19	20	21	22	23
24	25	26	27	28	29	30
31						

AUGUST

S	M	T	W	T	F	S
	1	2	3	4	5	6
7	8	9	10	11	12	13
14	15	16	17	18	19	20
21	22	23	24	25	26	27
28	29	30	31			

SEPTEMBER

S	M	T	W	T	F	S
				1	2	3
4	5	6	7	8	9	10
11	12	13	14	15	16	17
18	19	20	21	22	23	24
25	26	27	28	29	30	

OCTOBER

S	M	T	W	T	F	S
						1
2	3	4	5	6	7	8
9	10	11	12	13	14	15
16	17	18	19	20	21	22
23	24	25	26	27	28	29
30	31					

NOVEMBER

S	M	T	W	T	F	S
		1	2	3	4	5
6	7	8	9	10	11	12
13	14	15	16	17	18	19
20	21	22	23	24	25	26
27	28	29	30			

DECEMBER

S	M	T	W	T	F	S
				1	2	3
4	5	6	7	8	9	10
11	12	13	14	15	16	17
18	19	20	21	22	23	24
25	26	27	28	29	30	31

There are 365 days in the calendar year shown. Every four years, there are 366 days in a year. It is called a **leap year.** Only in a leap year is there a February 29.

There are __31__ days in March. There are ______ days in June.

March 1 is on ____Tuesday____. June 1 is on ____________.

On the calendar above, April has __4__ Sundays and ____ Saturdays.

Answer each question. Use the calendar to help you.

	a	*b*
1.	How many days are in July? ____________	On what day is July 1? ____________
2.	How many Tuesdays are in November? ____________	How many Wednesdays are in November? ____________
3.	How many months have 30 days? ____________	How many months have 31 days? ____________
4.	What date is the 3rd Thursday in August? ____________	What date is the 2nd Monday in April? ____________
5.	How many days of the year have passed when we reach May 1? ____________	What date falls forty-five days before December 25? ____________

Perfect score: 10 My score: ________

NAME ____________________

Lesson 2 Telling Time

7:10

7:10 is read "seven ten" and means "10 minutes after 7."

3:40

3:40 is read "three forty" and means "40 minutes after 3" or "20 minutes to 4."

8:55

8:55 is read "eight fifty-five" and means "55 minutes after ____"

or "____ minutes to ____."

Complete the following.

	a	*b*
1.	3:05 means ____ minutes after ____.	6:50 means ____ minutes to ____.
2.	10:20 means ____ minutes after ____.	11:35 means ____ minutes to ____.
3.	8:45 means ____ minutes after ____.	8:45 means ____ minutes to ____.
4.	5:30 means ____ minutes after ____.	5:30 means ____ minutes to ____.
5.	1:10 means ____ minutes after ____.	12:55 means ____ minutes to ____.

For each clockface, write the numerals that name the time.

	a	*b*	*c*	*d*
6.	 ____:____	 ____:____	 ____:____	 ____:____
7.	 ____:____	 ____:____	____:____	____:____

Perfect score: 28 My score: ________

NAME ____________

Lesson 3 Roman Numerals

I means 1. V means 5. X means 10.

II means 1 + 1 or 2.

III means 1 + 1 + 1 or 3.

VI means 5 + 1 or 6.

IV means 5 − 1 or 4.

XXV means 10 + 10 + 5 or 25.

IX means 10 − 1 or 9.

VII means 5 + 1 + ____ or ____.

XXI means 10 + ____ + 1 or ____.

XIV means ____ + 4 or ____.

XIX means ____ + 9 or ____.

Complete the following as shown.

	a	*b*	*c*	*d*
1.	XXIV = 24	XX = ____	XII = ____	VIII = ____
2.	IV = ____	XXVI = ____	XVII = ____	XXXI = ____
3.	XXXVI = ____	XXIX = ____	XI = ____	XXXIII = ____
4.	XVIII = ____	IX = ____	XXXIV = ____	XIII = ____
5.	V = ____	XXV = ____	VI = ____	XXI = ____
6.	XXXVIII = ____	XXXV = ____	XXVII = ____	XVI = ____
7.	XXIII = ____	XXXVII = ____	XIV = ____	XXXII = ____

Write a Roman numeral for each of the following.

	a	*b*	*c*
8.	3 = ____	7 = ____	15 = ____
9.	19 = ____	22 = ____	28 = ____
10.	30 = ____	20 = ____	39 = ____

Perfect score: 36 My score: ____

NAME ______________________

Lesson 4 Money

1 penny	1 nickel	1 dime	1 quarter	1 dollar
1 cent	5 cents	10 cents	25 cents	100 cents
1¢ or $.01	5¢ or $.05	10¢ or $.10	25¢ or $.25	$1.00

25 pennies have a value of ___25___ cents or ___1___ quarter.

5 pennies have a value of ________ cents or ________ nickel.

$2.57 means ___2___ dollars and ___57___ cents.

$3.45 means ______ dollars and ______ cents.

Complete the following.

1. 10 pennies have a value of ________ cents or ____ nickels.
2. 10 pennies have a value of ________ cents or ____ dime.
3. 20 pennies have a value of ________ cents or ____ dimes.
4. 15 pennies have a value of ________ cents or ____ nickels.
5. 20 pennies have a value of ________ cents or ____ nickels.

Complete the following as shown.

6. $14.05 means ______ dollars and ______ cents.
7. $12.70 means ______ dollars and ______ cents.
8. $8.14 means ______ dollars and ______ cents.
9. $.65 means ______ dollars and ______ cents.
10. $10.01 means ______ dollars and ______ cents.

Perfect score: 18 My score: ________

NAME ____________________

Lesson 5 Money

	$12.00				
$9.05	.45	45¢	$ .75	$14.08	$13.00
+6.98	+3.16	+38¢	+.38	−7.25	−6.05
$16.03	$15.61	83¢	$1.13	$6.83	$6.95

Add or subtract as usual.

Put a decimal point (.) and a $ or ¢ in the answer.

Be sure to line up the decimal points.

Add or subtract.

	a	*b*	*c*	*d*	*e*
1.	$ .36 +12.40	$3.75 +1.46	$ 1.36 +40.00	37¢ +58¢	$4.35 +.27
2.	$5.20 −3.18	$12.64 −5.08	$3.00 −.54	88¢ −76¢	$24.42 −1.68
3.	$ 4.23 16.90 +.89	$7.25 .40 +4.42	$ 8.05 12.16 +.58	47¢ 18¢ +25¢	$ .08 3.67 +14.30
4.	$15.40 −3.62	$5.70 −2.08	$11.30 −.86	91¢ −75¢	$17.20 −4.06
5.	$27.00 −13.45	$65.21 +3.80	$ .12 +1.88	47¢ −19¢	$3.00 −1.78
6.	$16.49 +28.98	$40.60 −7.56	$5.00 −2.72	38¢ +35¢	$8.75 +.64

Perfect score: 30   My score: ________

Problem Solving

Solve each problem.

1. Eileen's mother bought a dress for $22.98 and a blouse for $17.64. How much did these items cost altogether?

They cost ________ altogether.

2. Find the total cost of a basketball at $18.69, a baseball at $8.05, and a football at $24.98.

The total cost is ________.

3. Joe has $2.50. Mike has $1.75. Joe has how much more money than Mike?

Joe has ________ more than Mike.

4. In problem 2, how much more does the basketball cost than the baseball? How much more does the football cost than the basketball?

The basketball costs ________ more than the baseball.

The football costs ________ more than the basketball.

5. Charlotte saved $4.20 one week, $.90 the next week, and $2.05 the third week. How much money did she save during these 3 weeks?

Charlotte saved ________ in 3 weeks.

6. Mr. Lewis paid $4.45 for fruit. He paid $.99 for potatoes. The tax was $.33. How much was the total bill?

His total bill was ________.

7. Gary wants to buy a 95¢ whistle. He now has 68¢. How much more money does he need to buy the whistle?

Gary needs ________ more.

1.	2.
3.	
4.	
5.	6.
7.	

Perfect score: 8 My score: ________

NAME ____________________

CHAPTER 6 TEST

Answer each question. Use the calendar to help you.

May

S	M	T	W	T	F	S
		1	2	3	4	5
6	7	8	9	10	11	12
13	14	15	16	17	18	19
20	21	22	23	24	25	26
27	28	29	30	31		

1. How many days are in May? ____________

2. On what day is May 4? ____________

For each clockface, write the numerals that name the time.

3.

a

_____:_____

b

_____:_____

c

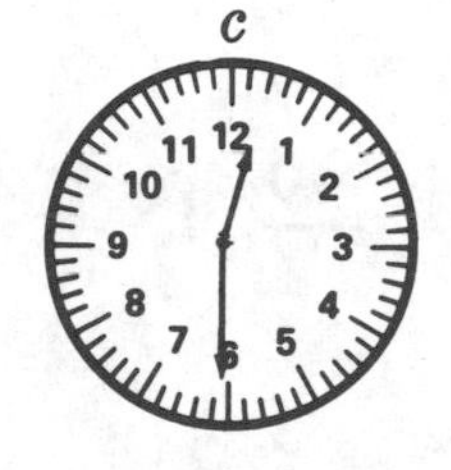

_____:_____

Complete the following as shown.

	a	*b*	*c*
4.	XVI = 16	IX = ______	XXXII = ______
5.	14 = XIV	8 = ______	29 = ______

Add or subtract.

	a	*b*	*c*	*d*	*e*
6.	\$15.32 +16.45	\$3.24 +.73	42¢ +54¢	16¢ 37¢ +20¢	\$ .62 13.40 +1.68
7.	\$3.52 −2.17	\$13.14 −5.33	93¢ −39¢	\$17.50 −1.09	\$5.14 −1.08

Solve.

8. Maria needs \$54.68 to buy a coat she wants. She now has \$50.75. How much more money does she need to buy the coat?

Maria needs ____________________ more.

Perfect score: 20 My score: ________

NAME ______________________

PRE-TEST—Multiplication

Multiply.

	a	*b*	*c*	*d*	*e*	*f*
1.	5×2	7×2	2×2	6×2	4×2	9×2
2.	3×3	5×3	4×3	7×3	9×3	2×3
3.	7×0	5×0	0×4	0×6	3×0	0×8
4.	3×1	7×1	1×4	1×1	5×1	1×8
5.	7×4	3×4	9×4	6×4	5×4	4×4
6.	8×5	6×5	9×5	4×5	3×5	2×5
7.	9×0	8×4	6×3	0×1	5×5	0×3
8.	1×9	2×4	1×2	7×5	8×3	2×1
9.	3×2	1×3	0×7	8×2	1×6	1×5

Perfect score: 54 My score: __________

NAME ______________________

Lesson 1 Multiplication

2×3 is read "two times three." 2×3 means $3+3$.
3×2 is read "three times two." 3×2 means $2+2+2$.
4×5 is read "four times five." 4×5 means $5+5+5+5$.

3×6 is read "three times six." 3×6 means ______________________

2×7 is read "two times seven." 2×7 means ______________________

Complete the following as shown.

1. 2×5 is read "two times five"
2. 3×4 is read ______________________
3. 5×2 is read ______________________
4. 4×8 is read ______________________
5. 4×7 is read ______________________

Complete the following as shown.

	a	*b*
6.	2×4 means ______________	4×2 means ______________
7.	3×5 means ______________	5×3 means ______________
8.	3×7 means ______________	7×3 means ______________
9.	4×6 means ______________	6×4 means ______________
10.	2×8 means ______________	8×2 means ______________
11.	3×9 means ______________	9×3 means ______________

Perfect score: 14 My score: ____________

NAME ____________________

Lesson 2 Multiplication

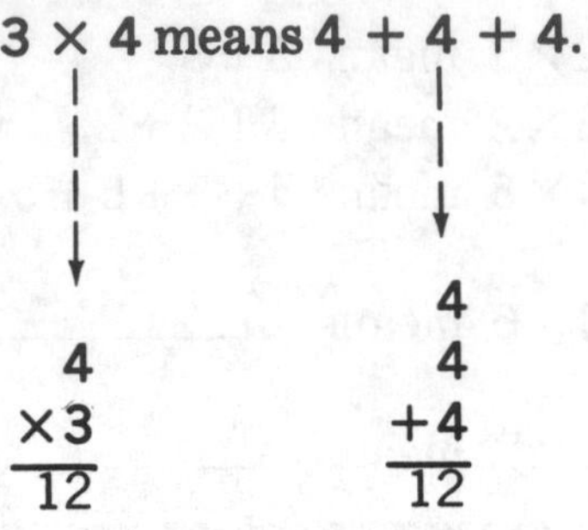

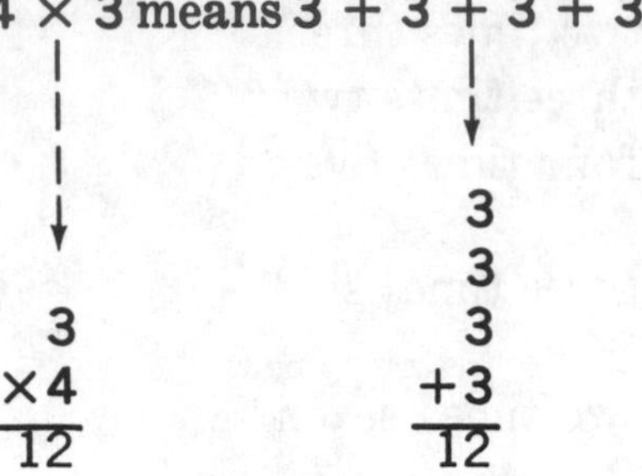

Add or multiply.

	a	*b*	*c*	*d*	*e*	*f*
1.	8 +8	8 ×2	4 +4	4 ×2	5 +5	5 ×2
2.	6 +6	6 ×2	7 +7	7 ×2	2 +2	2 ×2
3.	9 +9	9 ×2	3 +3	3 ×2	1 +1	1 ×2
4.	2 2 +2	2 ×3	3 3 +3	3 ×3	4 4 +4	4 ×3
5.	5 5 +5	5 ×3	6 6 +6	6 ×3	7 7 +7	7 ×3
6.	8 8 +8	8 ×3	9 9 +9	9 ×3	1 1 +1	1 ×3

Perfect score: 36 My score: ________

NAME ____________________

Lesson 3 Multiplication

1	2	0	0	0	1	2	1
×0	×0	×3	×4	×1	×1	×1	×3
0	0	0	0	0	1	2	3

Multiply.

	a	*b*	*c*	*d*	*e*	*f*
1.	0 ×2	9 ×1	1 ×7	6 ×0	1 ×5	0 ×7
2.	4 ×0	8 ×1	1 ×4	0 ×9	7 ×0	6 ×1
3.	5 ×0	0 ×8	5 ×1	1 ×6	1 ×1	8 ×0
4.	1 ×7	0 ×4	3 ×0	9 ×0	7 ×1	1 ×5
5.	0 ×7	1 ×9	1 ×6	0 ×5	1 ×0	2 ×1
6.	1 ×4	1 ×8	4 ×0	8 ×1	0 ×6	0 ×3
7.	0 ×9	6 ×1	0 ×2	9 ×1	0 ×1	3 ×1
8.	1 ×2	6 ×0	7 ×0	1 ×3	4 ×1	0 ×0

Perfect score: 48 My score: ________

Problem Solving

Solve each problem.

1. Molly bought 2 baseball cards. Each baseball card cost 9 cents. How much did Molly pay for the baseball cards?

Molly bought __________ baseball cards.

Each baseball card cost __________ cents.

Molly paid __________ cents for the baseball cards.

2. Bob bought 2 football cards. They cost 6 cents each. How much did Bob pay for the football cards?

Bob bought __________ football cards.

One football card cost __________ cents.

Bob paid __________ cents for the football cards.

3. There are 8 cards in each pack. How many cards are in 3 packs?

__________ cards are in three packs.

4. One basketball card costs 5 cents. How much will 8 basketball cards cost?

Eight basketball cards will cost __________ cents.

1.

2.

3. **4.**

Perfect score: 8 My score: __________

NAME ______________________

Lesson 4 Multiplication

6	→ Find the 6 -row.
×4	→ Find the 4 -column.
24	← The product is named where the 6-row and 4-column meet.

4-column ↓

6-row →

x	0	1	2	3	4	5	6	7	8	9
0	0	0	0	0	[illegible]	0	0	0	0	0
1	0	1	2	3	[illegible]	5	6	7	8	9
2	0	2	4	6	[illegible]	10	12	14	16	18
3	0	3	6	9	[illegible]	15	18	21	24	27
4	0	4	8	12	[illegible]	20	24	28	32	36
5	0	5	10	15	[illegible]	25	30	35	40	45
6	[illegible]	[illegible]	[illegible]	[illegible]	(24)	30				
7	0	7	14	21	28	35				
8	0	8	16	24	32	40				
9	0	9	18	27	36	45				

Multiply.

	a	*b*	*c*	*d*	*e*	*f*
1.	5×4	8×4	7×5	6×5	2×4	4×3
2.	5×5	6×3	9×4	1×4	0×5	4×4
3.	3×5	7×4	2×5	4×2	8×5	9×2
4.	5×3	3×3	8×2	0×4	3×2	5×2
5.	6×4	8×3	4×1	5×0	5×1	6×2
6.	9×5	4×0	3×4	7×2	7×3	1×5

Perfect score: 36 My score: ________

Problem Solving

Solve each problem.

1. Yvonne wants to buy 5 erasers. They cost 9 cents each. How much will she have to pay?

Yvonne wants to buy ________ erasers.

One eraser costs ________ cents.

Yvonne will have to pay ________ cents.

2. There are 5 rows of mailboxes. There are 7 mailboxes in each row. How many mailboxes are there in all?

There are ________ mailboxes in each row.

There are ________ rows of mailboxes.

There are ________ mailboxes in all.

3. Milton, the pet monkey, eats 4 meals every day. How many meals does he eat in a week?

There are ________ days in a week.

Milton eats ________ meals every day.

Milton eats ________ meals in a week.

4. In a baseball game each team gets 3 outs per inning. How many outs does each team get in a 5-inning game?

There are ________ innings in the game.

Each team gets ________ outs per inning.

The team gets ________ outs in the 5-inning game.

5. Howard has gained 4 pounds in each of the past 5 months. How much weight has he gained ?

Howard has gained ________ pounds in 4 months.

1.	
2.	
3.	
4.	5.

Perfect score: 13 My score: ________

NAME ____________________

Lesson 5 Multiplication

Multiply.

	a	*b*	*c*	*d*	*e*	*f*
1.	0×8	4×2	8×5	7×3	6×1	7×0
2.	1×1	9×2	4×4	3×5	6×5	1×4
3.	0×6	1×2	4×0	8×2	9×5	5×5
4.	8×4	6×3	1×5	9×0	2×1	7×2
5.	5×3	7×4	4×5	3×2	9×3	8×1
6.	6×0	3×1	6×2	0×0	2×3	9×4
7.	7×5	8×3	1×0	0×3	4×1	6×4
8.	5×4	2×2	9×1	1×7	2×4	3×3
9.	1×9	2×0	5×2	3×4	2×5	4×3

Perfect score: 54 My score: ________

Problem Solving

Solve each problem.

1. Neal has 6 books. Each book weighs 1 kilogram. What is the weight of all the books?

Neal has ________ books.

Each book weighs ________ kilogram.

The six books weigh ________ kilograms.

2. A baseball game has 4 time periods. Amy's team is to play 8 games. How many periods will her team play?

Amy's team is to play ________ games.

Each game has ________ time periods.

Amy's team will play ________ time periods in all.

3. Ellen works 8 hours every day. How many hours does she work in 5 days?

She works ________ hours in 5 days.

4. Chuck can ride his bicycle 5 miles in an hour. At that speed how far could he ride in 2 hours?

Chuck could ride ________ miles in 2 hours.

5. Calvin bought 5 bags of balloons. Each bag had 6 balloons. How many balloons did he buy?

Calvin bought ________ balloons in all.

6. Eve can build a model car in 3 hours. How long would it take her to build 4 model cars?

Eve could build 4 model cars in ________ hours.

1.	
2.	
3.	4.
5.	6.

Perfect score: 10 My score: ________

NAME ____________________

CHAPTER 7 TEST

Multiply.

	a	*b*	*c*	*d*	*e*
1.	1×6	7×4	9×0	3×4	9×5
2.	4×3	7×3	0×6	1×4	6×2
3.	9×2	8×5	9×3	3×2	4×4
4.	0×1	5×5	9×4	3×0	4×5

Solve each problem.

5. John bought 5 boxes of pencils. There are 6 pencils in each box. How many pencils did he buy?

John bought ________ boxes of pencils.

There are ________ pencils in each box.

He bought ________ pencils in all.

6. Linda is to put 4 apples in each bag. How many apples does she need to fill 8 bags?

Linda needs ________ apples in all.

7. Troy bought 3 boxes of crayons. Each box held 8 crayons. How many crayons did he buy?

Troy bought ________ crayons.

5.	
6.	7.

Perfect score: 25 My score: ________

NAME ____________________

PRE-TEST—Multiplication

Chapter 8

Multiply.

	a	*b*	*c*	*d*	*e*	*f*
1.	7 ×6	6 ×6	4 ×6	8 ×6	5 ×6	9 ×6
2.	8 ×7	4 ×7	9 ×7	7 ×7	6 ×7	5 ×7
3.	9 ×8	5 ×8	7 ×8	8 ×8	6 ×8	4 ×8
4.	6 ×9	9 ×9	5 ×9	8 ×9	4 ×9	7 ×9

Solve each problem.

5. Andrew set up 9 rows of chairs. He put 9 chairs in each row. How many chairs did he use?

Andrew used ________ chairs.

6. Sarah's dad works 7 hours every day. How many hours would he work in 8 days?

He would work ________ hours in 8 days.

7. There are 9 players on a team. How many players are there on 7 teams?

There are ________ players in all.

8. Paul puts 6 apples into each bag. How many apples does he need to fill 7 bags?

He would need ________ apples.

5.	**6.**
7.	**8.**

Perfect score: 28 My score: ________

NAME ______________________________

Lesson 1 Multiplication

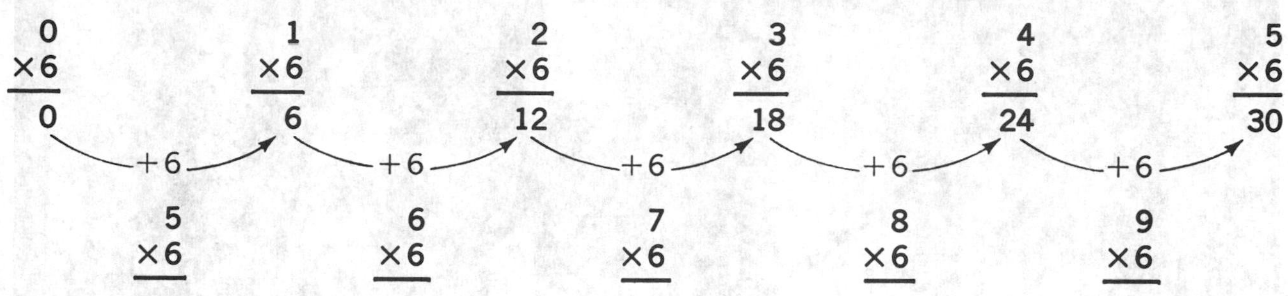

0 ×6 = 0	1 ×6 = 6	2 ×6 = 12	3 ×6 = 18	4 ×6 = 24	5 ×6 = 30

+6 between each product.

5 ×6 = 30	6 ×6 = ____	7 ×6 = ____	8 ×6 = ____	9 ×6 = ____

+6 between each product.

Multiply.

	a	b	c	d	e	f
1.	5 ×6	3 ×3	9 ×6	8 ×4	0 ×5	5 ×3
2.	8 ×5	2 ×6	6 ×4	5 ×5	3 ×4	6 ×1
3.	4 ×3	7 ×4	6 ×5	8 ×6	9 ×4	8 ×3
4.	0 ×3	3 ×6	1 ×5	4 ×4	2 ×3	4 ×5
5.	7 ×6	9 ×5	7 ×5	0 ×4	5 ×2	2 ×4
6.	6 ×6	6 ×2	5 ×4	1 ×3	3 ×5	0 ×6
7.	1 ×4	2 ×5	1 ×6	9 ×3	7 ×3	4 ×6

Perfect score: 42 My score: ________

Problem Solving

Solve each problem.

1. There are 6 rows of cactus plants. Each row has 4 plants. How many cactus plants are there in all?

There are ________ rows of cactus plants.

There are ________ cactus plants in each row.

There are ________ cactus plants in all.

1.

2. There are 8 marigold plants in each row. There are 6 rows. How many marigold plants are there?

There are ________ marigold plants in each row.

There are ________ rows of marigold plants.

There are ________ marigold plants in all.

2.

3. There are 6 rose bushes in each row. There are 9 rows. How many rose bushes are there?

There are ________ rose bushes in each row.

There are ________ rows of rose bushes.

There are ________ rose bushes in all.

3.

Perfect score: 9 My score: ________

NAME ____________________

Lesson 2 Multiplication

4 × 7	5 × 7	6 × 7	7 × 7	8 × 7	9 × 7
____	____	____	____	____	____

+7 +7 +7 +7 +7

4 × 8	5 × 8	6 × 8	7 × 8	8 × 8	9 × 8
____	____	____	____	____	____

+8 +8 +8 +8 +8

Multiply.

	a	*b*	*c*	*d*	*e*	*f*
1.	7 × 7	7 × 6	6 × 8	3 × 7	9 × 8	0 × 7
2.	8 × 8	8 × 5	1 × 8	7 × 3	3 × 8	1 × 7
3.	8 × 0	8 × 6	5 × 8	9 × 7	7 × 1	6 × 7
4.	7 × 8	5 × 7	7 × 0	7 × 2	7 × 5	0 × 8
5.	8 × 7	2 × 8	8 × 4	7 × 4	8 × 3	4 × 8
6.	9 × 4	8 × 1	4 × 7	8 × 2	2 × 7	9 × 6

Perfect score: 36 My score: ________

Problem Solving

Solve each problem.

1. In Rita's building there are 7 floors. There are 9 apartments on each floor. How many apartments are in the building?

There are ________ floors in this building.

There are ________ apartments on each floor.

There are ________ apartments in Rita's building.

2. The science club meets 4 times each month. The club meets for 7 months. How many meetings will the science club have?

The science club meets ________ times each month.

The club meets for ________ months.

The club will have ________ meetings in all.

3. Each bag of corn weighs 8 kilograms. There are 7 bags. How much do the bags weigh in all?

Each bag weighs ________ kilograms.

There are ________ bags.

The bags weigh ________ kilograms in all.

4. There are 7 days in a week. How many days are there in 5 weeks?

There are ________ days in 5 weeks.

5. Brenda walks 6 blocks each day going to and from school. How many blocks does she walk going to and from school in 7 days?

Brenda walks ________ blocks in 7 days.

1.

2.

3.

4.

5.

Perfect score: 11 My score: ________

NAME ____________________

Lesson 3 Multiplication

9 — Find the 9 -row.
×9 — Find the 9 -column.
81 — The product is named where the 9-row and 9-column meet.

9-column

x	0	1	2	3	4	5	6	7	8	9
0	0	0	0	0	0	0	0	0	0	0
1	0	1	2	3	4	5	6	7	8	9
2	0	2	4	6	8	10	12	14	16	18
3	0	3	6	9	12	15	18	21	24	27
4	0	4	8	12	16	20	24	28	32	36
5	0	5	10	15	20	25	30	35	40	45
6	0	6	12	18	24	30	36	42	48	54
7	0	7	14	21	28	35	42	49	56	63
8	0	8	16	24	32	40	48	56	64	72
9	0	9	18	27	36	45	54	63	72	(81)

9-row

Multiply.

	a	*b*	*c*	*d*	*e*	*f*
1.	7 ×9	9 ×6	8 ×8	3 ×7	2 ×9	7 ×3
2.	8 ×5	8 ×7	4 ×9	6 ×8	7 ×0	7 ×7
3.	9 ×9	1 ×8	0 ×9	6 ×9	7 ×8	2 ×8
4.	4 ×8	0 ×7	4 ×7	9 ×2	8 ×4	6 ×7
5.	5 ×8	9 ×7	3 ×8	1 ×9	1 ×7	0 ×8
6.	5 ×9	8 ×0	3 ×9	5 ×7	8 ×9	2 ×7

Perfect score: 36 My score: ________

Problem Solving

Solve each problem.

1. There are 8 chairs around each table. There are 9 tables. How many chairs are around all the tables?

There are ________ chairs around each table.

There are ________ tables.

There are ________ chairs around all the tables.

2. Workers are eating lunch at 9 tables. Each table has 9 workers. How many workers are eating lunch?

There are ________ tables.

________ workers are at each table.

________ workers are eating lunch.

3. The workers drink 9 liters of milk each day. They are at work 5 days each week. How many liters of milk do they drink in 5 days?

They drink ________ liters of milk in 5 days.

4. A bowling league bowls 4 times each month. How many times will the league bowl in 9 months?

The bowling league will bowl ________ times.

5. There are 9 packages of golf balls. Each package has 6 golf balls. How many golf balls are there in all?

There are ________ golf balls.

6. A regular baseball game is 9 innings long. How many innings are in 7 regular games?

There are ________ innings in 7 regular games.

1.	
2.	
3.	4.
5.	6.

Perfect score: 10 My score: ________

NAME ____________________

Lesson 4 Multiplication

Multiply.

	a	b	c	d	e	f
1.	7 ×9	6 ×7	1 ×5	2 ×9	3 ×6	8 ×8
2.	3 ×7	4 ×9	0 ×8	7 ×5	7 ×8	6 ×6
3.	9 ×5	4 ×6	5 ×9	2 ×8	8 ×7	0 ×7
4.	7 ×6	1 ×6	9 ×8	0 ×9	5 ×5	9 ×7
5.	8 ×5	4 ×8	4 ×7	0 ×6	1 ×9	4 ×5
6.	6 ×8	9 ×6	6 ×5	6 ×4	7 ×7	3 ×9
7.	8 ×6	5 ×8	7 ×4	3 ×5	9 ×9	1 ×7
8.	9 ×4	5 ×7	1 ×8	8 ×9	5 ×6	2 ×5
9.	2 ×6	0 ×5	6 ×9	3 ×8	8 ×4	2 ×7

Perfect score: 54 My score: ________

Problem Solving

Solve each problem.

1. Some pupils formed 5 teams. There were 8 pupils on each team. How many pupils were there?

There were ________ teams.

There were ________ pupils on each team.

There were ________ pupils in all.

2. The waiter put 9 napkins on each table. There were 9 tables. How many napkins did the waiter use?

The waiter put ________ napkins on each table.

There were ________ tables.

The waiter used ________ napkins in all.

3. Dr. Mede rides her bicycle 6 kilometers every day. How far would she ride in 9 days?

Dr. Mede rides ________ kilometers every day.

She rides for each of ________ days.

She would ride ________ kilometers in all.

4. Mr. Brown works 7 hours each day. How many hours will he work in 6 days?

Mr. Brown will work ________ hours in 6 days.

5. There are 8 hot dogs in each package. How many hot dogs are there in 9 packages?

There are ________ hot dogs in 9 packages.

6. Suppose you read 8 stories every day. How many stories would you read in 7 days?

You would read ________ stories in 7 days.

1.	
2.	
3.	**4.**
5.	**6.**

Perfect score: 12   My score: ________

NAME ____________________

CHAPTER 8 TEST

Multiply.

	a	*b*	*c*	*d*	*e*
1.	6×7	5×9	8×6	4×7	7×7
2.	9×7	9×9	1×7	4×6	7×9
3.	0×6	7×8	5×8	9×8	7×6
4.	8×9	4×8	9×6	2×7	3×9

Solve each problem.

5. A clerk puts 6 oranges in each package. How many oranges are needed to make 9 packages?

There are ________ oranges in each package.

There are to be ________ packages.

________ oranges are needed in all.

5.

6. A barbershop can handle 8 customers in one hour. How many customers can it handle in 8 hours?

It could handle ________ customers.

6.

7. Mr. Lawkin put 3 pictures in a row. He made 8 rows. How many pictures did he use?

Mr. Lawkin used ________ pictures.

7.

Perfect score: 25 My score: ________

NAME ______________________

PRE-TEST—Multiplication

Chapter 9

Multiply.

	a	*b*	*c*	*d*	*e*	*f*
1.	3 ×2	30 ×2	2 ×4	20 ×4	1 ×7	10 ×7
2.	32 ×3	24 ×2	13 ×3	21 ×4	11 ×5	23 ×3
3.	7 ×4	70 ×4	6 ×3	60 ×3	9 ×4	90 ×4
4.	62 ×3	74 ×2	31 ×8	62 ×4	83 ×2	41 ×5
5.	18 ×4	26 ×3	35 ×2	24 ×3	38 ×2	16 ×5
6.	43 ×4	27 ×5	35 ×3	46 ×6	28 ×6	54 ×5
7.	56 ×7	63 ×2	80 ×5	23 ×2	37 ×2	45 ×5
8.	17 ×4	40 ×8	73 ×3	22 ×3	54 ×3	27 ×6
9.	30 ×9	58 ×4	28 ×4	25 ×3	80 ×4	66 ×2

Perfect score: 54 My score: ______

NAME ______________________

Lesson 1 Multiplication

4	40	2	20	7	70	8	80
×2	×2	×3	×3	×3	×3	×4	×4
8	80	6	60	21	210	32	320

Multiply.

	a	*b*	*c*	*d*	*e*	*f*
1.	3 ×2	30 ×2	2 ×4	20 ×4	6 ×1	60 ×1
2.	10 ×8	40 ×2	10 ×9	10 ×3	30 ×3	70 ×1
3.	9 ×4	90 ×4	6 ×3	60 ×3	5 ×5	50 ×5
4.	70 ×3	60 ×5	40 ×4	50 ×2	80 ×3	90 ×6
5.	20 ×4	30 ×5	40 ×3	20 ×2	30 ×6	40 ×7
6.	70 ×7	30 ×8	10 ×7	80 ×8	90 ×1	60 ×4
7.	40 ×5	20 ×8	60 ×2	50 ×3	10 ×5	40 ×1
8.	60 ×7	50 ×5	80 ×3	20 ×9	70 ×8	90 ×3

Perfect score: 48 My score: __________

Problem Solving

Solve each problem.

1. There are 4 classrooms on the first floor. Each classroom has 30 seats. How many seats are on the first floor?

_______________ seats are in each classroom.

_______________ classrooms are on the first floor.

_______________ seats are on the first floor.

2. Laura placed 2 boxes on a wagon. Each box weighs 20 kilograms. How much do the two boxes weigh?

Each box weighs __________ kilograms.

Laura placed __________ boxes on the wagon.

The two boxes weigh __________ kilograms.

3. Terry bought 3 packages of paper. Each package had 30 sheets. How many sheets of paper did he buy?

Each package contains _______________ sheets of paper.

Terry bought _______________ packages of paper.

Terry bought _______________ sheets of paper.

4. Mrs. Long bought 6 boxes of nails. Each box had 30 nails. How many nails did she buy?

Mrs. Long bought _______________ nails.

5. There are 40 bottles in a case. How many bottles are there in 2 cases?

There are _______________ bottles in 2 cases.

6. A bus has 40 passenger seats. How many passenger seats would there be on 7 such buses?

There are _______________ passenger seats on 7 buses.

1.	
2.	
3.	4.
5.	6.

Perfect score: 12 My score: __________

NAME ________________

Lesson 2 Multiplication

	Multiply 2 ones by 3.	Multiply 7 tens by 3.	
72 ×3	72 ×3 6	72 ×3 6 210	72 ×3 6 210 } Add. 216

Multiply.

	a	b	c	d	e	f
1.	6 2 ×2	7 3 ×3	9 2 ×4	8 4 ×2	5 3 ×2	4 2 ×3
2.	2 3 ×2	3 1 ×3	4 2 ×2	1 2 ×4	3 3 ×3	4 2 ×2
3.	2 1 ×4	6 1 ×3	5 1 ×2	4 3 ×2	8 2 ×4	1 3 ×3
4.	7 2 ×3	3 2 ×3	4 3 ×3	2 3 ×3	3 4 ×2	9 3 ×2

Perfect score: 24 My score: ________

Lesson 3 Multiplication

NAME ______________________________

	Multiply 4 ones by 2.	Multiply. 8 tens by 2.
$\begin{array}{r} 84 \\ \times 2 \\ \hline \end{array}$	$\begin{array}{r} 84 \\ \times 2 \\ \hline 8 \end{array}$	$\begin{array}{r} 84 \\ \times 2 \\ \hline 168 \end{array}$

Multiply.

	a	*b*	*c*	*d*	*e*	*f*
1.	$\begin{array}{r} 62 \\ \times 4 \\ \hline \end{array}$	$\begin{array}{r} 84 \\ \times 2 \\ \hline \end{array}$	$\begin{array}{r} 73 \\ \times 3 \\ \hline \end{array}$	$\begin{array}{r} 82 \\ \times 2 \\ \hline \end{array}$	$\begin{array}{r} 91 \\ \times 2 \\ \hline \end{array}$	$\begin{array}{r} 52 \\ \times 3 \\ \hline \end{array}$
2.	$\begin{array}{r} 43 \\ \times 2 \\ \hline \end{array}$	$\begin{array}{r} 41 \\ \times 4 \\ \hline \end{array}$	$\begin{array}{r} 32 \\ \times 3 \\ \hline \end{array}$	$\begin{array}{r} 61 \\ \times 3 \\ \hline \end{array}$	$\begin{array}{r} 42 \\ \times 4 \\ \hline \end{array}$	$\begin{array}{r} 44 \\ \times 2 \\ \hline \end{array}$
3.	$\begin{array}{r} 72 \\ \times 3 \\ \hline \end{array}$	$\begin{array}{r} 71 \\ \times 3 \\ \hline \end{array}$	$\begin{array}{r} 81 \\ \times 2 \\ \hline \end{array}$	$\begin{array}{r} 43 \\ \times 3 \\ \hline \end{array}$	$\begin{array}{r} 52 \\ \times 4 \\ \hline \end{array}$	$\begin{array}{r} 83 \\ \times 2 \\ \hline \end{array}$
4.	$\begin{array}{r} 62 \\ \times 2 \\ \hline \end{array}$	$\begin{array}{r} 93 \\ \times 3 \\ \hline \end{array}$	$\begin{array}{r} 52 \\ \times 1 \\ \hline \end{array}$	$\begin{array}{r} 74 \\ \times 2 \\ \hline \end{array}$	$\begin{array}{r} 53 \\ \times 2 \\ \hline \end{array}$	$\begin{array}{r} 62 \\ \times 3 \\ \hline \end{array}$
5.	$\begin{array}{r} 72 \\ \times 4 \\ \hline \end{array}$	$\begin{array}{r} 81 \\ \times 5 \\ \hline \end{array}$	$\begin{array}{r} 92 \\ \times 3 \\ \hline \end{array}$	$\begin{array}{r} 63 \\ \times 3 \\ \hline \end{array}$	$\begin{array}{r} 54 \\ \times 2 \\ \hline \end{array}$	$\begin{array}{r} 73 \\ \times 2 \\ \hline \end{array}$
6.	$\begin{array}{r} 61 \\ \times 7 \\ \hline \end{array}$	$\begin{array}{r} 32 \\ \times 4 \\ \hline \end{array}$	$\begin{array}{r} 82 \\ \times 3 \\ \hline \end{array}$	$\begin{array}{r} 81 \\ \times 9 \\ \hline \end{array}$	$\begin{array}{r} 63 \\ \times 2 \\ \hline \end{array}$	$\begin{array}{r} 91 \\ \times 5 \\ \hline \end{array}$
7.	$\begin{array}{r} 53 \\ \times 3 \\ \hline \end{array}$	$\begin{array}{r} 71 \\ \times 6 \\ \hline \end{array}$	$\begin{array}{r} 82 \\ \times 4 \\ \hline \end{array}$	$\begin{array}{r} 91 \\ \times 9 \\ \hline \end{array}$	$\begin{array}{r} 92 \\ \times 4 \\ \hline \end{array}$	$\begin{array}{r} 81 \\ \times 8 \\ \hline \end{array}$

Perfect score: 42 My score: __________

NAME ____________________

Lesson 4 Multiplication

	Multiply 7 ones by 3.	Multiply 1 ten by 3. Add the 2 tens.	
$\begin{array}{r} 17 \\ \times 3 \\ \hline \end{array}$	$\begin{array}{r} \overset{2}{1}7 \\ \times 3 \\ \hline 1 \end{array}$	$\begin{array}{r} \overset{2}{1}7 \\ \times 3 \\ \hline 51 \end{array}$	$\begin{array}{r} 17 \\ \times 3 \\ \hline 51 \end{array}$
	$3 \times 7 = 21 = 20 + 1$	$3 \times 10 = 30$ $30 + 20 = 50$	

Multiply.

	a	b	c	d	e	f
1.	23 × 4	29 × 3	16 × 5	14 × 7	26 × 3	12 × 8
2.	37 × 2	26 × 2	47 × 2	28 × 3	15 × 5	24 × 4
3.	18 × 5	14 × 5	28 × 3	35 × 2	46 × 2	38 × 2
4.	45 × 2	27 × 3	15 × 6	12 × 7	15 × 4	48 × 2
5.	28 × 2	12 × 6	17 × 5	13 × 6	19 × 3	19 × 4
6.	36 × 2	24 × 3	25 × 3	16 × 4	29 × 2	18 × 3

Perfect score: 36 My score: ________

Problem Solving

Solve each problem.

1. Ms. McClean ordered 7 dozen radio antennas. How many antennas did she order? (There are 12 items in a dozen.)

There are ________ items in a dozen.

She ordered ________ dozen antennas.

Ms. McClean ordered ________ radio antennas.

1.

2. There are 14 CB radio units on a shelf. Each unit weighs 5 kilograms. How much do all the units weigh?

There are ________ radio units.

Each unit weighs ________ kilograms.

All the units weigh ________ kilograms.

2.

3. Mr. Tunin bought 2 CB radio units. Each unit cost $49. How much did both units cost?

Both units cost $ ________.

4. Ms. McClean sold 36 radios this week. She sold the same number of radios last week. How many radios did she sell in the two weeks?

She sold ________ radios in the two weeks.

3.

4.

Perfect score: 8 My score: ________

NAME ____________________

Lesson 5 Multiplication

$$\begin{array}{r} 57 \\ \times 5 \\ \hline \end{array}$$

Multiply 7 ones by 5.

$$\begin{array}{r} \overset{3}{5}7 \\ \times 5 \\ \hline 5 \end{array}$$

$5 \times 7 = 35 = 30 + 5$

Multiply 5 tens by 5. Add the 3 tens.

$$\begin{array}{r} \overset{3}{5}7 \\ \times 5 \\ \hline 285 \end{array}$$

$5 \times 50 = 250$

$250 + \mathbf{30} = 280 = 200 + 80$

Multiply.

	a	*b*	*c*	*d*	*e*	*f*
1.	35 × 4	42 × 6	56 × 3	47 × 5	38 × 6	25 × 5
2.	54 × 4	27 × 6	38 × 5	48 × 8	83 × 7	74 × 6
3.	75 × 4	58 × 3	46 × 4	37 × 6	29 × 5	46 × 3
4.	84 × 4	93 × 6	62 × 8	57 × 5	39 × 4	22 × 7
5.	45 × 6	68 × 7	73 × 9	87 × 8	94 × 6	83 × 4
6.	96 × 5	85 × 3	47 × 4	23 × 9	39 × 7	65 × 6

Perfect score: 36 My score: __________

Problem Solving

Solve each problem.

1. Ernest's spelling book has 25 new words on each page. There are 9 pages in the first section. How many new words are there in the first section?

There are ____________________ new spelling words on each page.

There are ___________ pages in the first section.

There are ____________________ new spelling words in the first section.

1.

2. Alan wants to walk up 6 flights of stairs. There are 26 steps in each flight. How many steps will he have to walk up?

There are _______________ steps in each flight.

Alan wants to walk up _______________ flights.

Alan will have to walk up ______________ steps.

2.

3. There are 7 rows of seats in the balcony. There are 36 seats in each row. How many seats are in the balcony?

There are _______________ seats in each row.

There are _______________ rows.

There are _______________ seats in the balcony.

3.

4. There are 25 baseball players on each team. How many players are there on 8 such teams?

There are _______________ players on 8 teams.

5. Bev used 3 rolls of film. She took 36 pictures on each roll. How many pictures did Bev take?

Bev took ________ pictures.

4.

5.

Perfect score: 11 My score: ________

NAME ____________________

CHAPTER 9 TEST

Multiply.

	a	b	c	d	e
1.	30 ×2	42 ×2	23 ×3	60 ×4	80 ×3
2.	84 ×2	73 ×3	21 ×7	14 ×6	27 ×3
3.	57 ×5	38 ×6	42 ×5	29 ×4	36 ×5
4.	15 ×4	73 ×2	58 ×3	40 ×9	28 ×3

Solve each problem.

5. Mary has 4 decks of cards. There are 52 cards in each deck. How many cards does she have?

She has ____________________ decks.

There are ______________ cards in each deck.

Mary has ____________________ cards in all.

6. Tom's father works 37 hours each week. How many hours would he work in 4 weeks?

He would work ______________ hours in 4 weeks.

7. Mr. Richards gave each pupil 3 sheets of paper. There were 28 pupils. How many sheets of paper did he use?

Mr. Richards used ______________ sheets of paper.

5.

6.

7.

Perfect score: 25 My score: __________

NAME ____________________

PRE-TEST—Division

Chapter 10

Divide.

	a	b	c	d	e
1.	$2\overline{)6}$	$2\overline{)12}$	$2\overline{)18}$	$2\overline{)4}$	$2\overline{)10}$
2.	$4\overline{)16}$	$3\overline{)24}$	$3\overline{)9}$	$5\overline{)25}$	$3\overline{)3}$
3.	$1\overline{)4}$	$1\overline{)8}$	$1\overline{)16}$	$4\overline{)36}$	$1\overline{)27}$
4.	$2\overline{)16}$	$1\overline{)1}$	$3\overline{)27}$	$1\overline{)6}$	$1\overline{)21}$
5.	$1\overline{)12}$	$5\overline{)20}$	$2\overline{)14}$	$4\overline{)8}$	$1\overline{)14}$
6.	$1\overline{)5}$	$4\overline{)28}$	$5\overline{)5}$	$1\overline{)2}$	$3\overline{)18}$

Solve each problem.

7. Paula has 18 books. She put them in piles of 3 books each. How many piles of books does she have?

She has ________ piles of books.

7.

8. Jake has 12 pennies. He put 3 pennies in each stack. How many stacks of pennies does he have?

He has ________ stacks of pennies.

8.

9. Dee has 12 pennies. She put 2 pennies in each stack. How many stacks of pennies does she have?

She has ________ stacks of pennies.

9.

Perfect score: 33 My score: ________

NAME ______________________

Lesson 1 Division

$\div$ and $\overline{)\quad}$ mean divide.

$6 \div 2 = 3$ is read "6 divided by 2 is equal to 3."

$8 \div 2 = 4$ is read "____ divided by 2 is equal to ____."

$\begin{array}{r}3\\2\overline{)6}\end{array}$ is read "6 divided by 2 is equal to 3."

$\begin{array}{r}4\\2\overline{)8}\end{array}$ is read "____ divided by 2 is equal to ____."

$\begin{array}{r}3\\2\overline{)6}\end{array}$ — 3: quotient; 2: divisor; 6: dividend

In $\begin{array}{r}4\\2\overline{)8}\end{array}$, the divisor is ____, the dividend is ____, and the quotient is ____.

Complete each sentence.

1. $10 \div 2 = 5$ is read "________ divided by 2 is equal to ________."

2. $21 \div 3 = 7$ is read "________ divided by 3 is equal to ________."

3. $4 \div 2 = 2$ is read "________ divided by 2 is equal to ________."

4. $\begin{array}{r}6\\3\overline{)18}\end{array}$ is read "________ divided by 3 is equal to ________."

5. $\begin{array}{r}9\\2\overline{)18}\end{array}$ is read "________ divided by 2 is equal to ________."

6. $\begin{array}{r}8\\3\overline{)24}\end{array}$ is read "________ divided by 3 is equal to ________."

7. In $\begin{array}{r}7\\3\overline{)21}\end{array}$, the divisor is ________, the dividend is ________, and the quotient is ________.

8. In $\begin{array}{r}2\\2\overline{)4}\end{array}$, the divisor is ________, the dividend is ________, and the quotient is ________.

9. In $\begin{array}{r}5\\2\overline{)10}\end{array}$, the divisor is ________, the dividend is ________, and the quotient is ________.

10. In $\begin{array}{r}6\\3\overline{)18}\end{array}$, the divisor is ________, the dividend is ________, and the quotient is ________.

Perfect score: 24 My score: ________

NAME ____________________

Lesson 2 Division

6 ×'s in all.
2 ×'s in each group.
How many groups?

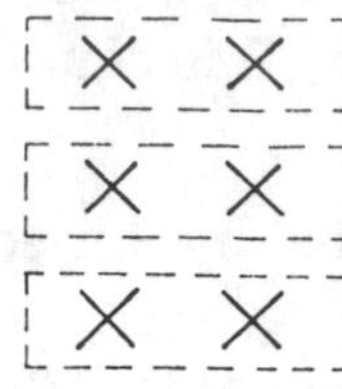

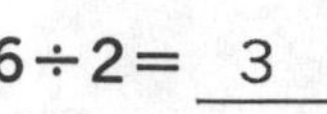

6 ÷ 2 = 3

There are 3 groups.

6 ×'s in all.
3 groups of ×'s.
How many ×'s in each group?

6 ÷ 3 = ____

There are ____ ×'s in each group.

Complete the following.

a

1. 10 ☆'s in all.
2 ☆'s in each group.
How many groups?

10 ÷ 2 = ____

There are ____ groups.

b

10 ☆'s in all.
5 groups of ☆'s.
How many ☆'s in each group?

10 ÷ 5 = ____

There are ____ ☆'s in each group.

2. 8 □'s in all.

____ □'s in each group.
How many groups?

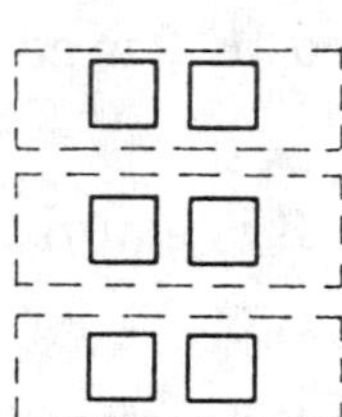

8 ÷ 2 = ____

There are ____ groups.

____ □'s in all.

4 groups of □'s.
How many □'s in each group?

8 ÷ 4 = ____

There are ____ □'s in each group.

3. ____ ○'s in all.

____ ○'s in each group.
How many groups?

4 ÷ 2 = ____

There are ____ groups.

____ ○'s in all.

____ groups of ○'s.
How many ○'s in each group?

4 ÷ 2 = ____

There are ____ ○'s in each group.

Perfect score: 18 My score: ________

Lesson 3 Division

NAME ______________________

$$\begin{array}{r} 3 \\ \times 2 \\ \hline 6 \end{array} \quad \longrightarrow \quad 2\overline{)6}^{\,3}$$

$$\begin{array}{r} 4 \\ \times 3 \\ \hline 12 \end{array} \quad \longrightarrow \quad 3\overline{)12}^{\,4}$$

If $2 \times 3 = 6$, then $6 \div 2 = 3$.

If $3 \times 4 = 12$, then ________ $\div 3 =$ ________.

Divide as shown.

	a		b	
1.	$\begin{array}{r} 5 \\ \times 2 \\ \hline 10 \end{array}$	$2\overline{)10}$ with 5 above	$\begin{array}{r} 6 \\ \times 3 \\ \hline 18 \end{array}$	$3\overline{)18}$
2.	$\begin{array}{r} 7 \\ \times 2 \\ \hline 14 \end{array}$	$2\overline{)14}$	$\begin{array}{r} 8 \\ \times 3 \\ \hline 24 \end{array}$	$3\overline{)24}$
3.	$\begin{array}{r} 1 \\ \times 2 \\ \hline 2 \end{array}$	$2\overline{)2}$	$\begin{array}{r} 3 \\ \times 3 \\ \hline 9 \end{array}$	$3\overline{)9}$
4.	$\begin{array}{r} 8 \\ \times 2 \\ \hline 16 \end{array}$	$2\overline{)16}$	$\begin{array}{r} 9 \\ \times 3 \\ \hline 27 \end{array}$	$3\overline{)27}$

Divide.

	a	b	c	d
5.	$3\overline{)15}$	$2\overline{)6}$	$3\overline{)3}$	$3\overline{)6}$
6.	$3\overline{)21}$	$2\overline{)18}$	$2\overline{)8}$	$2\overline{)12}$

Perfect score: 15 My score: ________

Problem Solving

Solve each problem.

1. Twenty-four people are at work. They work in 3 departments. The same number of people work in each department. How many people work in each department?

There are ________ people.

They work in ________ departments.

There are ________ people in each department.

2. Dan put 8 books into 2 stacks. Each stack had the same number of books. How many books were in each stack?

There were ________ books in all.

They were put into ________ stacks.

There were ________ books in each stack.

3. Janice put 16 liters of water into 2 jars. She put the same number of liters into each jar. How many liters of water did she put into each jar?

Janice put ____________ liters of water into jars.

She used ________ jars.

Janice put ________ liters of water into each jar.

4. Kim has 27 apples. She wants to put the same number of apples in each of 3 boxes. How many apples should she put in each box?

She should put ________ apples in each box.

5. Mr. Green had 18 inches of wire. He cut the wire into 2 pieces. The pieces were the same length. How long was each piece?

Each piece was ________ inches long.

1.

2.

3.

4.

5.

Perfect score: 11 My score: ________

$$\begin{array}{r} 5 \\ \times 4 \\ \hline 20 \end{array} \longrightarrow 4\overline{)20} \text{ quotient } 5$$

$$\begin{array}{r} 9 \\ \times 5 \\ \hline 45 \end{array} \longrightarrow 5\overline{)45} \text{ quotient } 9$$

If 4×5=20, then 20÷4=5. **If 5×9=45, then ________ ÷5= ________.**

Divide as shown.

	a		*b*	
1.	$\begin{array}{r} 7 \\ \times 4 \\ \hline 28 \end{array}$	$4\overline{)28}$	$\begin{array}{r} 6 \\ \times 5 \\ \hline 30 \end{array}$	$5\overline{)30}$
2.	$\begin{array}{r} 4 \\ \times 4 \\ \hline 16 \end{array}$	$4\overline{)16}$	$\begin{array}{r} 3 \\ \times 5 \\ \hline 15 \end{array}$	$5\overline{)15}$
3.	$\begin{array}{r} 6 \\ \times 4 \\ \hline 24 \end{array}$	$4\overline{)24}$	$\begin{array}{r} 4 \\ \times 5 \\ \hline 20 \end{array}$	$5\overline{)20}$
4.	$\begin{array}{r} 9 \\ \times 4 \\ \hline 36 \end{array}$	$4\overline{)36}$	$\begin{array}{r} 8 \\ \times 5 \\ \hline 40 \end{array}$	$5\overline{)40}$

Divide.

	a	*b*	*c*	*d*
5.	$4\overline{)8}$	$5\overline{)10}$	$4\overline{)4}$	$4\overline{)12}$
6.	$5\overline{)25}$	$5\overline{)5}$	$4\overline{)32}$	$5\overline{)35}$

Perfect score: 15 My score: ________

Problem Solving

Solve each problem.

1. A loaf of bread has 24 slices. Mrs. Spencer uses 4 slices each day. How long will a loaf of bread last her?

A loaf of bread has ________ slices.

Mrs. Spencer uses ________ slices a day.

The loaf of bread will last ________ days.

1.

2. A football team played 28 periods. There are 4 periods in a game. How many games did they play?

The football team played ________ periods.

There are ________ periods each game.

The football team played ________ games.

2.

3. A basketball game is 32 minutes long. The game is separated into 4 parts. Each part has the same number of minutes. How long is each part?

A basketball game is ________ minutes long.

The game is separated into ________ parts.

Each part is ________ minutes long.

3.

4. Lilly worked 25 problems. She worked 5 problems on each sheet of paper. How many sheets of paper did she use?

She used ________ sheets of paper.

4.

5. Robert works the same number of hours each week. He worked 45 hours in 5 weeks. How many hours does he work each week?

Robert works ________ hours each week.

5.

Perfect score: 11 My score: ________

NAME ____________________

Lesson 5 Division

$$\begin{array}{r} 8 \\ \times 1 \\ \hline 8 \end{array} \longrightarrow 1\overline{)8}$$

If 1×8=8, then 8÷1=8.

$$\begin{array}{r} 15 \\ \times 1 \\ \hline 15 \end{array} \longrightarrow 1\overline{)15}$$

If 1×15=15, then ________ ÷1=________.

Divide.

	a		*b*	
1.	$\begin{array}{r} 5 \\ \times 1 \\ \hline 5 \end{array}$	$1\overline{)5}$	$\begin{array}{r} 14 \\ \times 1 \\ \hline 14 \end{array}$	$1\overline{)14}$
2.	$\begin{array}{r} 4 \\ \times 1 \\ \hline 4 \end{array}$	$1\overline{)4}$	$\begin{array}{r} 9 \\ \times 1 \\ \hline 9 \end{array}$	$1\overline{)9}$

	a	*b*	*c*	*d*	*e*
3.	$1\overline{)4}$	$1\overline{)3}$	$1\overline{)12}$	$1\overline{)2}$	$1\overline{)16}$
4.	$2\overline{)8}$	$3\overline{)18}$	$2\overline{)18}$	$2\overline{)6}$	$3\overline{)6}$
5.	$4\overline{)16}$	$2\overline{)14}$	$1\overline{)9}$	$5\overline{)5}$	$5\overline{)45}$
6.	$2\overline{)16}$	$4\overline{)12}$	$2\overline{)10}$	$4\overline{)28}$	$1\overline{)18}$
7.	$4\overline{)4}$	$4\overline{)20}$	$5\overline{)10}$	$5\overline{)30}$	$4\overline{)32}$

Perfect score: 29 My score: ________

Problem Solving

Solve each problem.

1. Flo bought 16 rolls. The rolls came in 2 packs. The same number of rolls were in each pack. How many rolls were in each pack?

Flo bought ________ rolls.

These rolls filled ________ packs.

There were ________ rolls in each pack.

1.

2. There are 9 families in an apartment building. There are 3 families on each floor. How many floors are in the building?

There are ________ families in the building.

There are ________ families on each floor.

There are ________ floors in the building.

2.

3. Arlene put 36 oranges in bags. She put 4 oranges in each bag. How many bags did she fill?

Arlene put ________ oranges in bags.

She put ________ oranges in each bag.

Arlene filled ________ bags with oranges.

3.

4. Marcos read 35 pages of science in 5 days. He read the same number of pages each day. How many pages did he read each day?

Marcos read ________ pages each day.

4.

5. Mrs. Allan worked 25 hours in 5 days. She worked the same number of hours each day. How many hours did she work each day?

Mrs. Allan worked ________ hours each day.

5.

Perfect score: 11 My score: ________

NAME ____________________

CHAPTER 10 TEST

Divide.

	a	*b*	*c*	*d*	*e*
1.	$2\overline{)10}$	$1\overline{)4}$	$3\overline{)3}$	$3\overline{)9}$	$2\overline{)16}$
2.	$1\overline{)12}$	$2\overline{)12}$	$3\overline{)12}$	$2\overline{)14}$	$3\overline{)15}$
3.	$3\overline{)6}$	$1\overline{)8}$	$5\overline{)20}$	$1\overline{)9}$	$3\overline{)24}$
4.	$5\overline{)40}$	$5\overline{)5}$	$1\overline{)10}$	$4\overline{)36}$	$4\overline{)24}$

Solve each problem.

5. The 45 pupils in a class separated into 5 groups. Each group has the same number of pupils. How many are in each group? **5.**

There are ________ pupils in all.

The pupils are separated into ________ groups.

There are ________ pupils in each group.

6. Shirley has 28 balloons for a party. She will give each person 4 balloons. How many people will receive balloons? **6.**

________ people will receive balloons.

7. Mr. Graham has 6 birds. How many cages does he need in order to put 2 birds in each cage? **7.**

Mr. Graham needs ________ cages.

Perfect score: 25 My score: ________

NAME ____________________

PRE-TEST—Division

Chapter 11

Divide.

	a	*b*	*c*	*d*	*e*
1.	6)24	6)12	6)18	6)0	6)6
2.	6)42	6)54	6)30	6)36	6)48
3.	7)0	7)28	7)14	7)21	7)7
4.	7)56	7)42	7)63	7)35	7)49
5.	8)8	8)40	8)0	8)32	8)16
6.	8)24	8)48	8)64	8)72	8)56
7.	9)36	9)27	9)45	9)18	9)0
8.	9)72	9)63	9)54	9)9	9)81
9.	5)5	4)28	1)1	5)30	4)12

Perfect score: 45 My score: ________

NAME ____________________

Lesson 1 Division

$$\begin{array}{r} 3 \\ \times 6 \\ \hline 18 \end{array} \quad 6\overline{)18} \to 3$$

If 6×3=18, then 18÷6=3.

$$\begin{array}{r} 4 \\ \times 6 \\ \hline 24 \end{array} \quad 6\overline{)24} \to 4$$

If 6×4=24, then ________ ÷6= ________.

Divide.

	a		*b*	
1.	$\begin{array}{r} 2 \\ \times 6 \\ \hline 12 \end{array}$	$6\overline{)12}$	$\begin{array}{r} 1 \\ \times 6 \\ \hline 6 \end{array}$	$6\overline{)6}$
2.	$\begin{array}{r} 5 \\ \times 6 \\ \hline 30 \end{array}$	$6\overline{)30}$	$\begin{array}{r} 7 \\ \times 6 \\ \hline 42 \end{array}$	$6\overline{)42}$
3.	$\begin{array}{r} 8 \\ \times 6 \\ \hline 48 \end{array}$	$6\overline{)48}$	$\begin{array}{r} 9 \\ \times 6 \\ \hline 54 \end{array}$	$6\overline{)54}$

	a	*b*	*c*	*d*
4.	$6\overline{)6}$	$6\overline{)12}$	$6\overline{)36}$	$6\overline{)18}$
5.	$1\overline{)6}$	$6\overline{)0}$	$6\overline{)24}$	$6\overline{)42}$
6.	$6\overline{)30}$	$6\overline{)54}$	$6\overline{)48}$	$5\overline{)45}$
7.	$4\overline{)32}$	$5\overline{)20}$	$4\overline{)20}$	$5\overline{)30}$

Perfect score: 22 My score: ________

Problem Solving

Solve each problem.

1. There are 6 rows of mailboxes. Each row has the same number of mailboxes. There are 30 mailboxes in all. How many are in each row?

There are _____ mailboxes in all.

The mailboxes are separated into _____ rows.

There are _____ mailboxes in each row.

1.

2. The movie was shown 12 times in 6 days. It was shown the same number of times each day. How many times was it shown each day?

The movie was shown _____ times in all.

The movie was shown for _____ days.

The movie was shown _____ times each day.

2.

3. Jill bought 18 buttons. The buttons were on cards of 6 buttons each. How many cards were there?

Jill bought _________ buttons.

There were _________ buttons on a card.

There were _________ cards.

3.

4. Marvin got 6 hits in 6 games. He got the same number of hits in each game. How many hits did he get in each game?

Marvin got _____ hits in each game.

4.

5. One side of a building has 24 windows. Each floor has 6 windows on that side. How many floors does the building have?

The building has _____ floors.

5.

Perfect score: 11 My score: _________

Lesson 2 Division

NAME ____________

$\begin{array}{r} 3 \\ \times 7 \\ \hline 21 \end{array}$ → $7\overline{)21}$ = 3	$\begin{array}{r} 5 \\ \times 8 \\ \hline 40 \end{array}$ → $8\overline{)40}$ = 5
If 7×3=21, then 21÷7=3.	If 8×5=40, then ________ ÷8= ________.

Divide.

	a		*b*	
1.	$\begin{array}{r} 2 \\ \times 7 \\ \hline 14 \end{array}$	$7\overline{)14}$	$\begin{array}{r} 3 \\ \times 8 \\ \hline 24 \end{array}$	$8\overline{)24}$
2.	$\begin{array}{r} 5 \\ \times 7 \\ \hline 35 \end{array}$	$7\overline{)35}$	$\begin{array}{r} 4 \\ \times 8 \\ \hline 32 \end{array}$	$8\overline{)32}$
3.	$\begin{array}{r} 7 \\ \times 7 \\ \hline 49 \end{array}$	$7\overline{)49}$	$\begin{array}{r} 8 \\ \times 8 \\ \hline 64 \end{array}$	$8\overline{)64}$

	a	*b*	*c*	*d*
4.	$7\overline{)7}$	$8\overline{)0}$	$8\overline{)16}$	$7\overline{)28}$
5.	$8\overline{)48}$	$7\overline{)42}$	$8\overline{)8}$	$7\overline{)56}$
6.	$7\overline{)0}$	$8\overline{)56}$	$1\overline{)7}$	$7\overline{)63}$
7.	$1\overline{)8}$	$8\overline{)40}$	$8\overline{)72}$	$7\overline{)21}$

Perfect score: 22 My score: ________

Problem Solving

Solve each problem.

1. A classroom has 28 chairs in 7 rows. Each row has the same number of chairs. How many chairs are in each row?

There are ________ chairs in the classroom.

The chairs are separated into ________ rows.

There are ________ chairs in each row.

1.

2. There are 48 chairs around the tables in the library. There are 8 chairs for each table. How many tables are in the library?

There are ________ chairs in the library.

There are ________ chairs around each table.

There are ________ tables in the library.

2.

3. David worked the same number of hours each day. He worked 21 hours in 7 days. How many hours did he work each day?

David worked ________ hours each day.

3.

4. There are 16 cars in the parking lot. There are 8 cars in each row. How many rows of cars are there?

There are ________ rows of cars.

4.

5. Mr. Miller sold 7 cars in 7 days. He sold the same number of cars each day. How many did he sell each day?

Mr. Miller sold ________ car each day.

5.

Perfect score: 9 My score: ________

NAME ____________________

Lesson 3 Division

$$\begin{array}{r} 2 \\ \times 9 \\ \hline 18 \end{array} \longrightarrow 9\overline{)18} = 2$$

If $9 \times 2 = 18$, then $18 \div 9 = 2$.

$$\begin{array}{r} 7 \\ \times 9 \\ \hline 63 \end{array} \longrightarrow 9\overline{)63} = 7$$

If $9 \times 7 = 63$, then ________ $\div 9 =$ ________.

Divide.

	a		*b*	
1.	$\begin{array}{r} 5 \\ \times 9 \\ \hline 45 \end{array}$	$9\overline{)45}$	$\begin{array}{r} 3 \\ \times 9 \\ \hline 27 \end{array}$	$9\overline{)27}$
2.	$\begin{array}{r} 8 \\ \times 9 \\ \hline 72 \end{array}$	$9\overline{)72}$	$\begin{array}{r} 4 \\ \times 9 \\ \hline 36 \end{array}$	$9\overline{)36}$
3.	$\begin{array}{r} 6 \\ \times 9 \\ \hline 54 \end{array}$	$9\overline{)54}$	$\begin{array}{r} 9 \\ \times 9 \\ \hline 81 \end{array}$	$9\overline{)81}$

	a	*b*	*c*	*d*
4.	$9\overline{)9}$	$1\overline{)9}$	$9\overline{)18}$	$9\overline{)36}$
5.	$9\overline{)0}$	$9\overline{)72}$	$9\overline{)54}$	$9\overline{)81}$
6.	$8\overline{)72}$	$9\overline{)63}$	$8\overline{)48}$	$9\overline{)45}$
7.	$9\overline{)27}$	$8\overline{)56}$	$7\overline{)63}$	$7\overline{)49}$

Perfect score: 22 My score: ________

Problem Solving

Solve each problem.

1. A farmer planted 54 cherry trees in 9 rows. Each row had the same number of trees. How many trees were in each row?

A farmer planted ________ trees.

There were ________ rows of trees.

There were ________ trees in each row.

1.

2. Ray put 27 tennis balls in 9 cans. He put the same number of balls in each can. How many balls did Ray put in each can?

Ray put ________ tennis balls in cans.

There were ________ cans.

He put ________ balls in each can.

2.

3. There are 9 packs of flashcubes on a shelf. Each pack has the same number of cubes. There are 36 flashcubes in all. How many cubes are in each pack?

There are ________ cubes in each pack.

3.

4. There are 18 cornstalks in a garden. There are 9 stalks in each row. How many rows of cornstalks are there?

There are ________ rows of cornstalks.

4.

5. Kay had 45 pennies. She put the pennies into stacks of 9 pennies each. How many stacks of pennies did she make?

She made ________ stacks of pennies.

5.

Perfect score: 9 My score: ________

NAME ____________________

Lesson 4 Division

Divide.

	a	b	c	d
1.	$2\overline{)10}$	$3\overline{)18}$	$4\overline{)4}$	$1\overline{)8}$
2.	$5\overline{)15}$	$8\overline{)16}$	$6\overline{)24}$	$7\overline{)42}$
3.	$2\overline{)18}$	$3\overline{)24}$	$7\overline{)35}$	$9\overline{)0}$
4.	$5\overline{)25}$	$4\overline{)32}$	$9\overline{)27}$	$6\overline{)36}$
5.	$7\overline{)14}$	$3\overline{)15}$	$8\overline{)8}$	$2\overline{)16}$
6.	$9\overline{)18}$	$6\overline{)12}$	$3\overline{)12}$	$8\overline{)24}$
7.	$5\overline{)20}$	$4\overline{)12}$	$2\overline{)6}$	$5\overline{)10}$
8.	$7\overline{)56}$	$3\overline{)21}$	$8\overline{)40}$	$6\overline{)30}$
9.	$4\overline{)28}$	$9\overline{)45}$	$7\overline{)49}$	$9\overline{)72}$
10.	$8\overline{)64}$	$9\overline{)54}$	$8\overline{)48}$	$9\overline{)81}$

Perfect score: 40 My score: ________

Problem Solving

Solve each problem.

1. Marilyn has 42 apples. She puts 6 apples in a package. How many packages will she have?

Marilyn has ________ apples.

She puts ________ apples in each package.

There will be ________ packages of apples.

2. Marilyn has 63 peaches. She puts 7 peaches in a package. How many packages will she have?

Marilyn has ________ peaches.

Each package will have ________ peaches.

There will be ________ packages of peaches.

3. There are 8 packages of pears. Each package has the same number of pears. There are 64 pears in all. How many pears are in each package?

There are ________ pears in all.

There are ________ packages of pears.

There are ________ pears in each package.

1.
2.
3.

Perfect score: 9 My score: ________

NAME ______________________

CHAPTER 11 TEST

Divide.

	a	b	c	d	e
1.	$6\overline{)12}$	$7\overline{)7}$	$8\overline{)24}$	$6\overline{)36}$	$9\overline{)0}$
2.	$7\overline{)14}$	$9\overline{)45}$	$6\overline{)42}$	$8\overline{)32}$	$1\overline{)9}$
3.	$6\overline{)48}$	$7\overline{)21}$	$8\overline{)40}$	$9\overline{)18}$	$8\overline{)72}$
4.	$8\overline{)64}$	$9\overline{)81}$	$7\overline{)56}$	$6\overline{)54}$	$6\overline{)18}$
5.	$6\overline{)30}$	$7\overline{)28}$	$9\overline{)72}$	$7\overline{)63}$	$8\overline{)48}$

Solve each problem.

6. A classroom has 24 desks. They are in 6 rows. There is the same number of desks in each row. How many desks are in each row?

There are ________ desks in all.

There are ________ rows with the same number of desks in each row.

There are ________ desks in each row.

6.

7. Ted put 24 biscuits on a tray. He put 8 biscuits in each row. How many rows were there?

There were ________ rows.

7.

Perfect score: 29   My score: ________

NAME ____________________

PRE-TEST—Metric Measurement

Chapter 12

Find the length of each object to the nearest centimeter.

1. ______ centimeters 

2. ______ centimeters 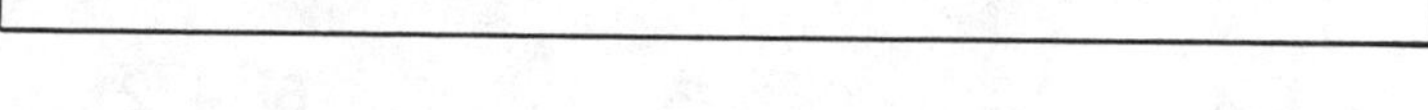

3. ______ centimeters 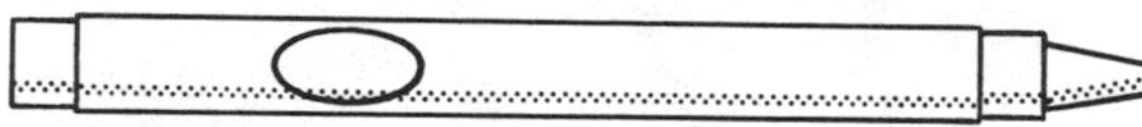

4. ______ centimeters 

5. ______ centimeters

Answer *True* or *False*.

6. A liter is less than 800 milliliters. ____________

7. A liter is more than 1,800 milliliters. ____________

8. A liter is equal to 1,000 milliliters. ____________

Solve.

9. A car can go 6 kilometers on a liter of gasoline. The car has a tank that holds 55 liters. How far can the car go on a full tank of gasoline?

The car can go ________ kilometers.

Perfect score: 9 My score: ________

NAME ____________________

Lesson 1 Centimeter

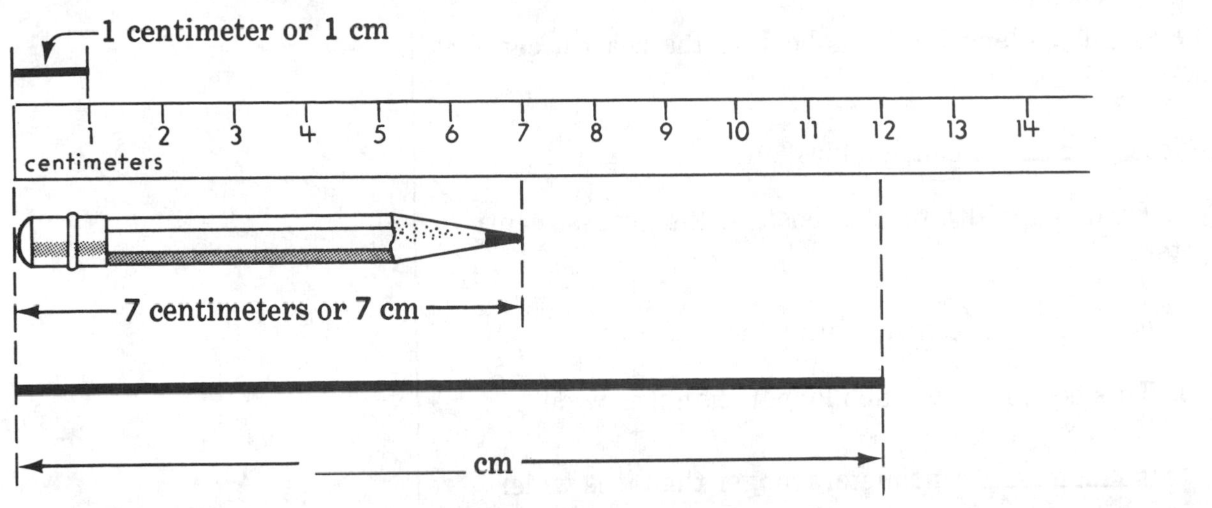

Guess how long each object is in centimeters.
Then find the length of each object to the nearest centimeter.

1. Guess: ________ cm 

Length: ________ cm

2. Guess: ________ cm 

Length: ________ cm

3. Guess: ________ cm 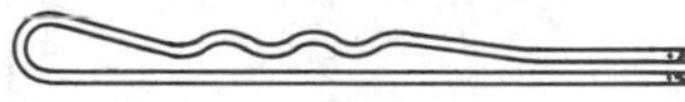

Length: ________ cm

4. Guess: ________ cm 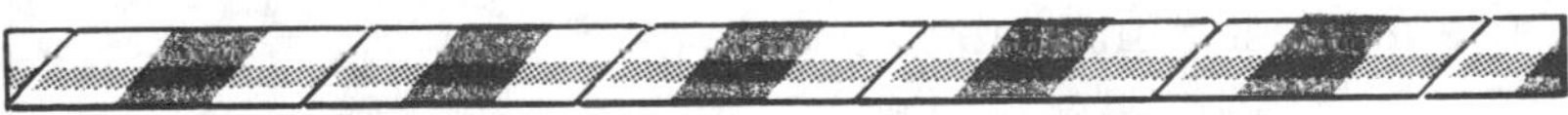

Length: ________ cm

5. Guess: ________ cm 

Length: ________ cm

6. Guess: ________ cm

Length: ________ cm

Perfect score: 6 My score: ________

Problem Solving

Solve each problem.

1. Find the length of this book to the nearest centimeter.

It is ________ centimeters long.

2. Find the width of this book to the nearest centimeter.

It is ________ centimeters wide.

3. This book is how much longer than it is wide?

It is ________ centimeters longer than it is wide.

4. How many centimeters is it across a nickel?

It is ________ centimeters across.

5. How many centimeters would it be across 8 nickels laid in a row?

It would be ________ centimeters across.

6. Find the length of your shoe to the nearest centimeter.

It is ________ centimeters long.

Use a tape measure or string to find the following to the nearest centimeter.

7. the distance around your wrist ________ centimeters

8. the distance around your waist ________ centimeters

9. the distance around your head ________ centimeters

10. the distance around your ankle ________ centimeters

Perfect score: 10 My score: ________

NAME ______________________

Lesson 2 Metric Measurement

From A to B is a length of 12 centimeters.

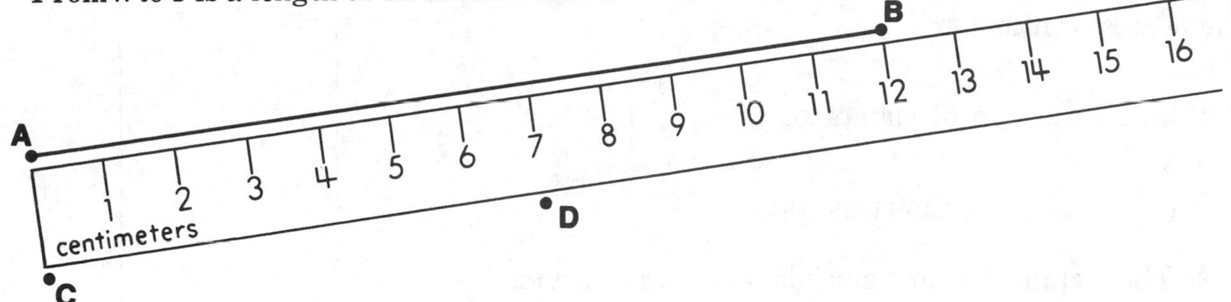

Draw from C to D. It is _______ centimeters long.

---

1. Draw from E to F.

   The length is _______ centimeters.

2. Draw from G to H.

   The length is _______ centimeters.

3. Draw from J to K.

   The length is _______ centimeters.

E H G K J F

Complete the table.

	From	*Length*
4.	A to B	_______ cm
5.	B to C	_______ cm
6.	C to D	_______ cm
7.	D to E	_______ cm
8.	E to A	_______ cm
9.	A to D	_______ cm
10.	C to E	_______ cm

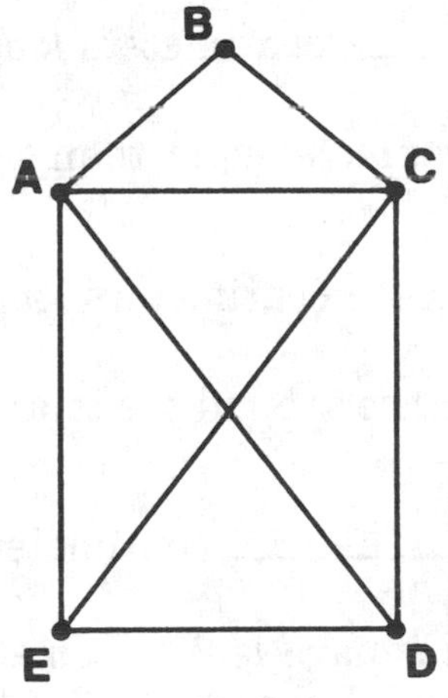

Perfect score: 10 My score: _________

Problem Solving

Solve each problem.

1. Find the length and the width of this rectangle to the nearest centimeter.

It is ________ centimeters long.

It is ________ centimeters wide.

2. The rectangle is how much longer than it is wide?

It is __________ centimeters longer than it is wide.

3. Find the distance around the rectangle.

The distance is ________ centimeters.

4. Draw from A to B, from B to C, and from C to A. Then find the length of each side of the triangle you just drew.

A •

Side AB is ________ centimeters long.

Side BC is ________ centimeters long.

• B

Side CA is ________ centimeters long.

5. Side CA is how much longer than side BC?

Side CA is ________ centimeters longer.

C •

6. Find the distance around the triangle.

The distance is ________ centimeters.

7. One side of a square is 8 centimeters long. What is the distance around the square? (All 4 sides of a square are the same length.)

The distance is ________ centimeters.

Perfect score: 10 My score: ________

NAME ______________________

Lesson 3 Liter

is about the same as

1 liter is a little more than 1 quart.

Answer *Yes* or *No*.

1. You can put 1 quart of water in a 1-liter bottle. __________

2. You can put 3 liters of water in a 3-quart pail. __________

How many liters would each container hold?
Underline the best answer.

3.

1 liter 8 liters 45 liters

4.

2 liters 9 liters 25 liters

5.

1 liter 10 liters 50 liters

6.

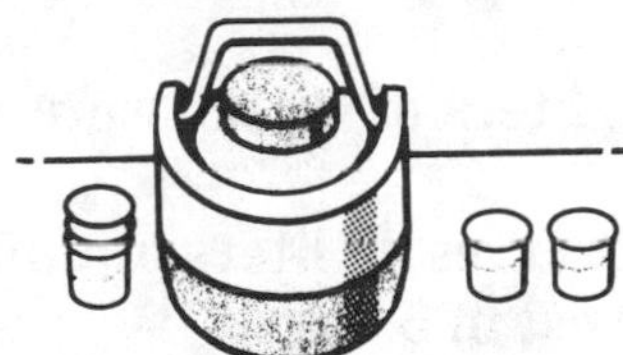

8 liters 28 liters 64 liters

7.

4 liters 16 liters 80 liters

8.

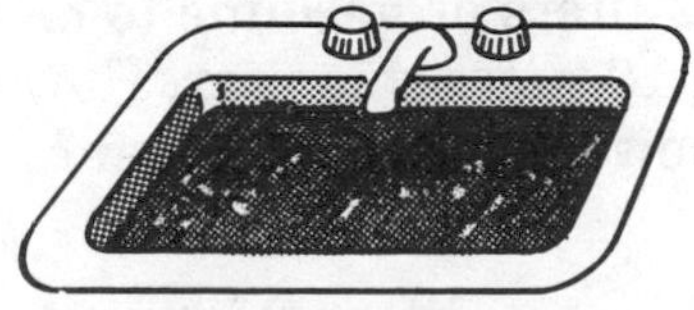

1 liter 4 liters 20 liters

Perfect score: 8 My score: __________

Problem Solving

Solve each problem.

1. The tank in Mr. Sumner's car can hold 85 liters. It took 37 liters of gasoline to fill the tank. How many liters were in the tank before it was filled?

_________ liters were in the tank.

2. Mr. Sumner can drive 5 kilometers on each liter of gasoline. How far could he drive on a full tank (85 liters) of gasoline?

He could drive _________ kilometers on a full tank.

3. Miss Gray uses 17 liters of gasoline to drive to and from work each day. How many liters does she use in 6 days?

She uses _________ liters in 6 days.

4. Paul bought 12 liters of paint. The paint was in 3 cans of the same size. How many liters of paint were in each can?

_________ liters of paint were in each can.

5. Connie used 56 liters of water to fill 8 empty fishbowls. The same amount of water was in each bowl. How many liters were in each fishbowl?

_________ liters of water were in each fishbowl.

6. A cafeteria serves 95 liters of milk each day. How much milk is served in 5 days?

_________ liters of milk is served in 5 days.

7. Rosa uses 2 liters of gasoline to mow a lawn. She mowed the lawn 16 times this year. How much gasoline did she use to mow the lawn this year?

Rosa used _________ liters this year.

1.	**2.**
3.	**4.**
5.	
6.	**7.**

Perfect score: 7 My score: _________

CHAPTER 12 TEST

NAME ____________________

Find each length to the nearest centimeter.

1. ________ cm

2. ________ cm

3. ________ cm

Draw from A to B, from B to C, and from C to A.
Then find each length to the nearest centimeter.

C •

4. From A to B is _____ centimeters.

5. From B to C is _____ centimeters.

6. From C to A is _____ centimeters.

A • • B

How many liters would each container hold? Ring the best answer.

7.

1 liter 10 liters

8.

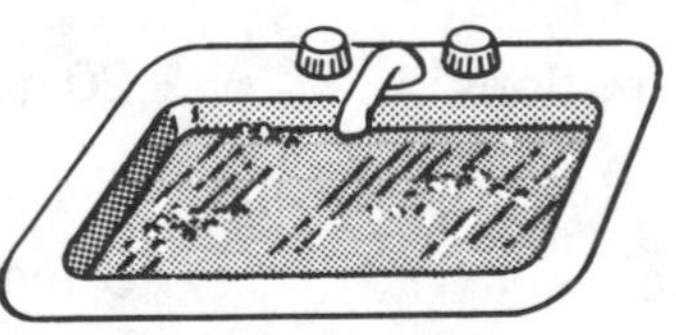

5 liters 500 liters

9.

2 liters 20 liters

Solve each problem.

10. A large carton holds 4 liters of milk. How many liters would 5 of these cartons hold?

Five cartons would hold ________ liters.

11. Karen used an 8-liter sprinkling can to water some plants. She filled the can 4 times. How much water was used?

________ liters of water was used.

12. A car can go 9 kilometers on 1 liter of gasoline. How far could the car go on 50 liters?

The car could go ________ kilometers.

10.	
11.	12.

Perfect score: 15 My score: ________

NAME ____________________

PRE-TEST—Measurement

Chapter 13

Find the length of each object to the nearest inch.

1. ________ inches 

2. ________ inch

3. ________ inches 

Complete the following.

	a	*b*
4.	1 quart = ________ pints	2 quarts = ________ pints
5.	8 pints = ________ quarts	6 pints = ________ quarts
6.	1 gallon = ________ quarts	3 gallons = ________ quarts
7.	8 quarts = ________ gallons	20 quarts = ________ gallons
8.	1 foot = ________ inches	3 feet = ________ inches
9.	1 yard = ________ feet	1 yard = ________ inches
10.	2 weeks = ________ days	1 hour = ________ minutes
11.	4 weeks = ________ days	6 hours = ________ minutes
12.	1 day = ________ hours	2 days = ________ hours

Solve.

13. Annette bought a board that is 6 feet long. What is the length of the board in inches?

It is ________ inches long.

Perfect score: 22 My score: ________

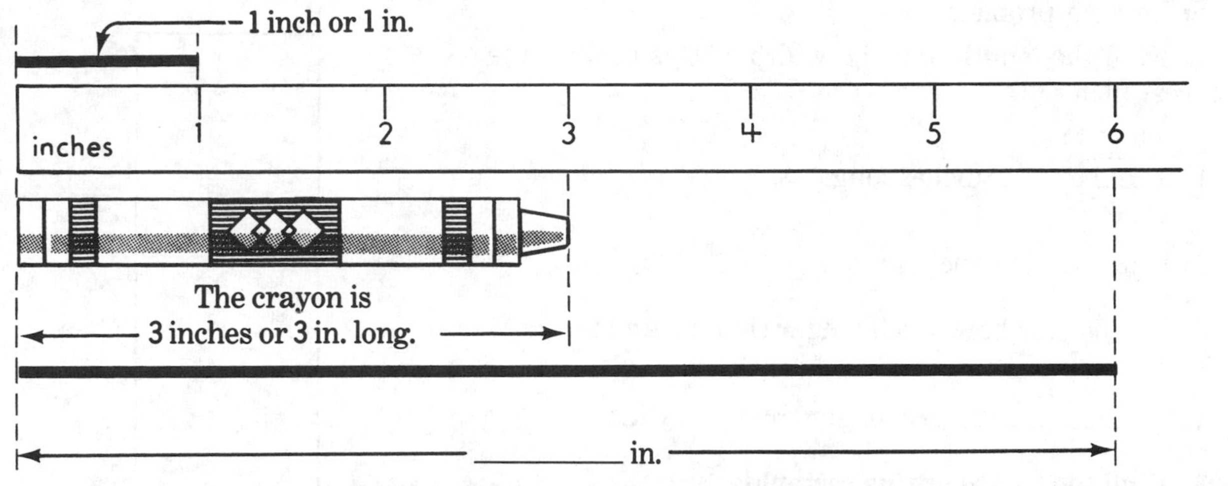

Find the length of each object to the nearest inch.

1. _______ in.

2. _______ in.

3. _______ in.

4. _______ in.

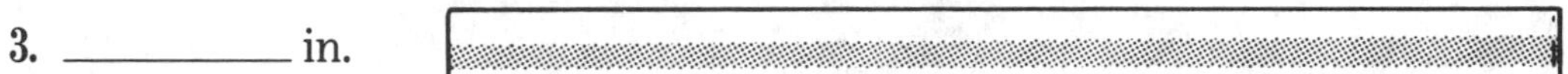

5. _______ in.

Complete the table.

	From	*Length*
6.	A to B	
7.	A to C	
8.	B to D	
9.	B to E	
10.	A to D	

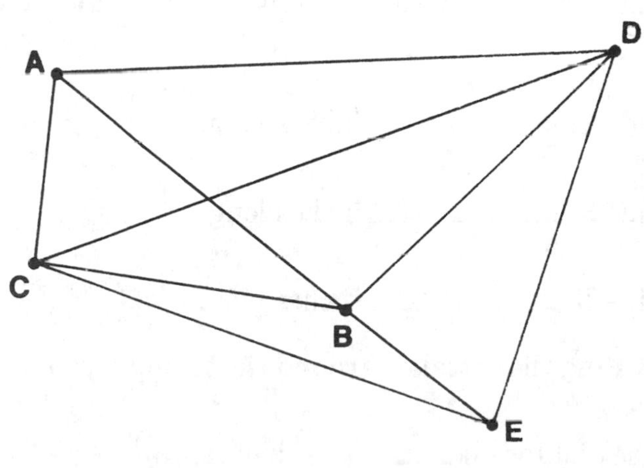

Perfect score: 10 My score: _______

Problem Solving

Solve each problem.

1. Find the length and the width of this book to the nearest inch.

It is ________ inches long.

It is ________ inches wide.

2. The book is how much longer than it is wide?

It is ________ inches longer than it is wide.

3. Find the length of this rectangle.

It is ________ inches long.

4. Find the width of this rectangle.

It is ________ inch wide.

5. The rectangle is how much longer than it is wide?

It is ________ inches longer than it is wide.

6. Find the distance around the rectangle.

The distance is ________ inches.

R

7. Draw from R to S, from S to T, and from T to R. Then find the length of each side of the triangle you just drew.

Side RS is ________ inches long.

Side ST is ________ inches long.

Side TR is ________ inches long.

S • • T

8. Find the distance around the triangle you drew.

The distance is ________ inches.

Perfect score: 11 My score: ________

NAME ____________________

Lesson 2 Measurement

1 foot (ft) = 12 inches (in.)

3 ft = ___?___ in.

Since 1 ft = 12 in., then

$$\begin{array}{r} 1 \\ \times 3 \\ \hline 3 \end{array} \qquad \begin{array}{r} 12 \\ \times 3 \\ \hline 36 \end{array}$$

3 ft = 36 in.

3 feet (ft) = 1 yard (yd)

12 ft = ___?___ yd

Since 3 ft = 1 yd, then

$$3\overline{)12}\ = 4$$

12 ft = 4 yd

Complete the following.

	a	*b*
1.	6 ft = ______ in.	8 ft = ______ in.
2.	3 yd = ______ ft	8 yd = ______ ft
3.	1 yd = ______ in.	2 yd = ______ in.
4.	21 ft = ______ yd	12 ft = ______ yd
5.	5 yd = ______ ft	14 yd = ______ ft
6.	3 ft = ______ in.	3 yd = ______ in.
7.	7 yd = ______ ft	9 ft = ______ in.
8.	18 ft = ______ yd	11 yd = ______ ft
9.	9 yd = ______ ft	5 ft = ______ in.
10.	7 ft = ______ in.	27 ft = ______ yd
11.	6 yd = ______ ft	15 ft = ______ yd
12.	9 ft = ______ yd	10 yd = ______ ft

Perfect score: 24 My score: ______

Problem Solving

Solve each problem.

1. Teresa bought 2 yards of ribbon for a dress. How many feet of ribbon did she buy?

Teresa bought ____________ feet of ribbon.

1.

2. Myron bought a belt that was 2 feet long. How long was the belt in inches?

The belt was ____________ inches long.

2.

3. Mark has a rope that is 3 yards long. How long is the rope in feet?

It is ____________ feet long.

3.

4. In problem 3, how long is the rope in inches?

It is ____________ inches long.

4.

5. Elmer has a piece of wire 5 feet long. How long is the wire in inches?

It is ____________ inches long.

5.

6. The distance between 2 walls is 18 feet. What is this distance in yards?

It is ____________ yards.

6.

7. Pam's driveway is 15 feet wide. How wide is the driveway in yards?

It is ____________ yards wide.

7.

8. A fence post is 4 feet high. How high is the fence post in inches?

It is ____________ inches high.

8.

Perfect score: 8 My score: ____________

NAME ______________________

Lesson 3 Measurement

1 quart (qt) = 2 pints (pt)

5 qt = ? pt

Since 1 qt = 2 pt, then

$$\begin{array}{cc} 1 & 2 \\ \times 5 & \times 5 \\ \hline 5 & 10 \end{array}$$

5 qt = 10 pt

2 pints (pt) = 1 quart (qt)

10 pt = ? qt

Since 2 pt = 1 qt, then

10 pt = 5 qt

1 gallon (gal) = 4 qt or 4 qt = 1 gal

12 qt = ? gal

Since 4 qt = 1 gal, then

12 qt = 3 gal

Complete the following.

	a	*b*
1.	7 qt = ________ pt	3 qt = ________ pt
2.	8 pt = ________ qt	18 pt = ________ qt
3.	5 gal = ________ qt	2 gal = ________ qt
4.	24 qt = ________ gal	36 qt = ________ gal
5.	4 pt = ________ qt	7 gal = ________ qt
6.	8 qt = ________ pt	20 qt = ________ gal
7.	8 gal = ________ qt	12 pt = ________ qt
8.	28 qt = ________ gal	9 qt = ________ pt
9.	14 pt = ________ qt	9 gal = ________ qt

Perfect score: 18 My score: ________

Problem Solving

Solve each problem.

1. Mrs. Collins bought 12 quarts of milk last week. How many pints of milk was this?

   It was ________ pints.

2. In problem 1, how many gallons of milk did Mrs. Collins buy?

   She bought ________ gallons.

3. Mr. Murphy used 24 quarts of paint to paint his house. He bought paint in gallon cans. How many gallons of paint did he use?

   He used ________ gallons of paint.

4. Mr. Johnson sold 18 pints of milk yesterday. How many quarts of milk was this?

   It was ________ quarts of milk.

5. Warren made 8 quarts of lemonade for a party. How many gallons of lemonade did he make?

   He made ________ gallons of lemonade.

6. Maurice drank 10 pints of milk one week. How many quarts of milk did he drink?

   He drank ________ quarts of milk.

7. Ms. Carlow used 4 gallons of paint. How many quarts of paint did she use?

   She used ________ quarts of paint.

8. How many pint glasses could be filled from 8 quarts of juice?

   ________ pint glasses could be filled.

1.
2.
3.
4.
5.
6.
7.
8.

Perfect score: 8 My score: ________

NAME ______________________

Lesson 4 Time

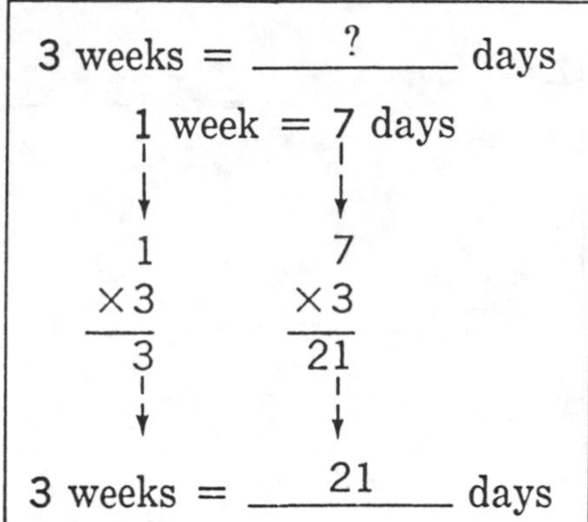

4 hours = ___?___ min
1 hour = 60 min

4 hours = _______ min

2 days = ___?___ hours
1 day = 24 hours

2 days = _______ hours

Complete the following.

	a	*b*
1.	2 weeks = _______ days	8 weeks = _______ days
2.	5 hours = _______ min	7 hours = _______ min
3.	6 days = _______ hours	4 days = _______ hours
4.	6 hours = _______ min	9 weeks = _______ days
5.	6 weeks = _______ days	7 days = _______ hours
6.	9 days = _______ hours	3 hours = _______ min
7.	9 hours = _______ min	5 weeks = _______ days
8.	8 days = _______ hours	7 weeks = _______ days

Perfect score: 16 My score: _______

Problem Solving

Solve each problem.

1. Vernon was at camp for 5 weeks. How many days was he at camp?

There are ______ days in 1 week.

He was at camp ______ weeks.

He was at camp ______ days.

1.

2. Esther attends school 6 hours every school day. How many minutes does she attend every school day?

There are ______ minutes in 1 hour.

She attends school ______ hours.

She attends school ______ minutes.

2.

3. Holly was in the hospital for 4 days. How many hours was she in the hospital?

There are ______ hours in 1 day.

Holly was in the hospital ______ days.

She was in the hospital ______ hours.

3.

4. The Cooke family has lived in their new apartment for 6 weeks. How many days have they lived in their new apartment?

They have lived there ______ days.

4.

5. Nancy was away from home for 1 week. How many hours was she away from home?

Nancy was away from home ______ hours.

5.

Perfect score: 11 My score: ______

NAME ____________________

Lesson 5 Problem Solving

Solve each problem.

1. A piece of wire is 2 feet long. How long is the wire in inches?

The wire is ________ inches long.

2. If you use 14 inches of the wire in 1, how many inches are left?

There will be ________ inches left.

3. On a football field there are 100 yards between goal lines. How many feet is that?

There are ________ feet between goal lines.

4. A container holds 8 quarts of liquid. How many pints does that container hold?

That container holds ________ pints.

5. How many gallons of liquid does the container in 4 hold?

That container holds ________ gallons.

6. A telethon lasted 2 days. How many hours did the telethon last?

The telethon lasted ________ hours.

7. A television mini-series lasted 6 hours. How many minutes did the mini-series last?

The mini-series lasted ________ minutes.

8. The Mohrs spent 3 weeks on their vacation trip. How many days was that?

The vacation trip took ________ days.

1.	2.
3.	4.
5.	6.
7.	8.

Perfect score: 8 My score: ________

NAME ____________________

CHAPTER 13 TEST

Find each length to the nearest inch.

1. ________ in.

2. ________ in.

3. ________ in.

4. ________ in.

Complete the following.

	a	*b*
5.	4 ft = ________ in.	4 pt = ________ qt
6.	6 qt = ________ pt	21 ft = ________ yd
7.	8 gal = ________ qt	9 ft = ________ in.
8.	9 yd = ________ ft	36 qt = ________ gal
9.	6 weeks = ________ days	8 hours = ________ min
10.	3 days = ________ hours	8 weeks = ________ days

Solve each problem.

11. Jill has a rope 8 feet long. How long is the rope in inches?

It is ________ inches long.

11.

12. Jim had a gallon of gasoline. He used 1 quart for the lawn mower. How many quarts did he have left?

He had ________ quarts left.

12.

13. Tonya is 4 feet 11 inches tall. What is her height in inches?

Her height is ________ inches.

13.

Perfect score: 19 My score: ________

NAME ____________________

TEST—Chapters 1–6

Add or subtract.

	a	*b*	*c*	*d*	*e*
1.	6 +5	9 +9	61 +5	35 +43	9 +42
2.	84 +7	64 +18	70 +70	18 +93	85 +89
3.	70 80 +30	478 +596	256 175 +310	$6.98 +7.23	$11.62 3.65 +1.98
4.	16 −7	15 −6	38 −4	87 −15	56 −8
5.	43 −7	80 −17	150 −70	136 −69	181 −93
6.	876 −97	625 −208	8724 −893	$9.85 −6.27	$18.20 −6.75

For each clockface, write the numerals that name the time.

7.

a

_______ : _______

b

_______ : _______

c

_______ : _______

Continued on the next page.

Test—Chapters 1–6 (continued)

Solve each problem.

8. There are 9 bolts in one package. There are 6 bolts in another package. How many bolts are in both packages?

There are ________ bolts in both packages.

9. There are 27 letters to be typed. Only 6 letters have been typed. How many letters still need to be typed?

________ letters still need to be typed.

10. This morning the temperature was 58°. Now it is 18° warmer. What is the temperature now?

Now the temperature is ________°.

11. Dirk read 84 pages in the morning. He read 69 pages in the afternoon. How many pages did he read that day?

He read ________ pages that day.

12. There were 103 plants in the garden. Only 8 were bean plants. How many were not bean plants?

________ were not bean plants.

13. You bought items at a store that cost $1.45, $2.98, and $9.98. How much did these items cost altogether?

These items cost $ ________ altogether.

14. Jennifer wants to buy a purse that costs $18.29. She has $9.55. How much more does she need to buy the purse?

She needs $ ________ more.

8.	9.
10.	**11.**
12.	**13.**
14.	

Perfect score: 40 My score: ________

NAME ______________________________

FINAL TEST—Chapters 1–13

Add or subtract.

	a	b	c	d	e
1.	7 +8	65 +3	82 +16	26 +9	73 +19
2.	20 +90	69 +43	165 +927	36 72 +35	\$21.43 +62.97
3.	12 −4	56 −5	93 −83	62 −7	85 −47
4.	180 −90	125 −76	780 −539	3751 −865	\$25.00 −7.25

Multiply.

	a	b	c	d	e
5.	5 ×3	4 ×4	6 ×5	8 ×3	7 ×2
6.	3 ×9	8 ×7	6 ×8	9 ×7	6 ×6

Continued on the next page.

Final Test (continued)

Multiply.

	a	*b*	*c*	*d*
7.	$\begin{array}{r} 70 \\ \times 5 \\ \hline \end{array}$	$\begin{array}{r} 23 \\ \times 3 \\ \hline \end{array}$	$\begin{array}{r} 18 \\ \times 7 \\ \hline \end{array}$	$\begin{array}{r} 43 \\ \times 7 \\ \hline \end{array}$

Divide.

8.	$2\overline{)12}$	$4\overline{)20}$	$3\overline{)27}$	$1\overline{)8}$
9.	$5\overline{)40}$	$4\overline{)24}$	$7\overline{)0}$	$8\overline{)72}$
10.	$9\overline{)36}$	$7\overline{)49}$	$6\overline{)48}$	$9\overline{)54}$

Answer each question. Use the calendar to help you.

11. How many days are in June? __________

12. On what day is June 17? __________

June

S	M	T	W	T	F	S
				1	2	3
4	5	6	7	8	9	10
11	12	13	14	15	16	17
18	19	20	21	22	23	24
25	26	27	28	29	30	

Continued on the next page.

NAME ______________________

Final Test (continued)

13. Write the numerals that name the time.

______ : ______

Find the length to the nearest centimeter.

14. ______ centimeters

Find the length to the nearest inch.

15. ______ inches

Solve each problem.

16. Juan has 36 inches of wire. How many feet of wire does he have?

Juan has ______ feet of wire.

17. Caryl used 3 liters of gasoline to mow a lawn. She mowed the lawn 12 times this year. How much gasoline did she use to mow the yard this year?

She used ______ liters this year.

16.	17.

Continued on the next page.

Final Test (continued)

Solve each problem.

18. Amanda worked in the automobile factory for 45 days. She worked 5 days each week. How many weeks did she work?

Amanda worked __________ weeks.

19. One store sold 421 radios. Another store sold 294 radios. A third store sold 730 radios. How many radios did all three stores sell?

All three stores sold __________ radios.

20. Ms. O'Connor received 1,439 votes. Mr. Ortega received 810 votes. How many more votes did Ms. O'Connor receive than Mr. Ortega?

Ms. O'Connor received __________ more votes.

21. Jack bought 24 liters of paint. The paint was in 6 cans. All the cans were the same size. How many liters of paint were in each can?

There were __________ liters of paint in each can.

22. A farmer has 6 stacks of bales of hay. Each stack has 36 bales. How many bales of hay does the farmer have?

The farmer has __________ bales of hay.

23. Linda bought items that cost \$3.80, \$2.29, and \$1.75. The sales tax was \$.47. How much did she pay for those items, including tax?

She paid \$ __________.

24. Don had \$27.89. He spent \$11.92. How much did he have left?

Don had \$ __________ left.

18.	19.
20.	21.
22.	23.
24.	

Perfect score: 60 My score: __________

Answers
Math - Grade 3

(Answers for Pre-Tests and Tests are given on pages 497-499.)

Page 343

	a	b	c	d	e	f	g	h
1.	6	4	3	7	4	5	7	6
2.	2	9	8	3	8	7	5	9
3.	8	1	6	4	5	3	9	8
4.	9	6	3	5	9	9	8	7
5.	0	5	8	9	6	2	7	2
6.	9	1	8	6	4	7	6	9

Page 344

	a	b	c	d	e	f	g	h
1.	1	1	0	1	6	2	1	5
2.	5	0	1	1	6	1	3	6
3.	0	6	3	0	2	4	4	2
4.	0	4	8	2	3	1	2	0
5.	2	5	4	3	4	2	0	7
6.	0	1	5	5	9	3	7	2

Page 345

	a	b	c	d	e	f
1.	11	10	9	12	11	9
2.	10	12	8	7	10	10
3.	8	12	12	10	11	10
4.	12	9	11	10	7	12
5.	7	9	10	11	11	12
6.	8	10	11	8	11	8

Page 346

1. 2 ; 9 ; 11
2. 8 ; 4 ; 12
3. 7 ; 4 ; 11
4. 4 ; 6 ; 10
5. 12

Page 347

	a	b	c	d	e	f
1.	4	6	2	3	3	9
2.	9	3	3	5	9	3
3.	5	3	6	2	8	5
4.	2	4	4	4	6	0
5.	6	1	1	1	7	2
6.	8	4	7	7	5	8

Page 348

1. 12 ; 3 ; 9
2. 11 ; 8 ; 3
3. 10 ; 7 ; 3
4. 11 ; 2 ; 9
5. 7

Page 349

	a	b	c	d	e	f
1.	11	12	10	11	10	12
2.	12	11	12	10	11	10
3.	2	5	8	6	4	3
4.	2	4	3	7	4	7

Page 350

1. add ; 11
2. subtract ; 2
3. subtract ; 7
4. add ; 12
5. add ; 10
6. subtract ; 5

Page 351

	a	b	c	d	e	f
1.	13	15	11	16	13	16
2.	14	10	14	13	12	15
3.	15	10	13	11	14	10
4.	12	17	15	11	13	18
5.	16	10	17	13	10	11
6.	14	12	11	12	14	12

Page 352

1. 9 ; 7 ; 16
2. 6 ; 9 ; 15
3. 13
4. 17
5. 16
6. 13

Page 353

	a	b	c	d	e	f
1.	8	6	9	1	7	8
2.	9	6	8	9	7	7
3.	4	9	9	3	7	4
4.	8	5	5	9	6	5
5.	5	3	9	6	8	3
6.	8	7	8	5	7	7

Page 354

1. 13 ; 5 ; 8
2. 18 ; 9 ; 9
3. 9
4. 7
5. 8
6. 8

Page 355

	a	b	c	d	e	f
1.	14	16	12	11	17	10
2.	13	12	15	13	10	14
3.	6	9	8	9	8	5
4.	7	8	9	7	8	5

Page 356

1. add ; 16
2. add ; 14
3. subtract ; 9
4. subtract ; 8
5. subtract ; 9

Page 359

	a	b	c	d	e	f
1.	8	28	5	45	6	26
2.	7	67	9	59	7	87
3.	6	16	26	36	46	56
4.	68	37	27	94	58	43
5.	44	23	66	86	27	18
6.	59	66	28	39	53	48
7.	38	47	53	68	26	36

Page 360

1. 37
2. 29
3. 48
4. 28
5. 18
6. 15
7. 24

Page 361

	a	b	c	d	e	f
1.	68	84	67	91	77	85
2.	89	66	86	83	59	97
3.	56	66	58	91	95	72
4.	87	88	39	67	76	88
5.	55	84	69	84	36	66
6.	59	87	59	78	68	46

Page 362

1. 25
2. 55
3. 97
4. 86
5. 67
6. 78
7. 89

Page 363

	a	b	c	d	e	f
1.	6	46	3	33	6	86
2.	6	76	1	61	0	80
3.	42	32	73	40	30	61
4.	23	21	35	18	33	53
5.	31	38	21	30	61	14
6.	57	36	20	20	22	71
7.	15	22	62	31	67	63

Page 364

1. 21
2. 92
3. 14
4. 50
5. 51
6. 61
7. 30

Page 365

	a	b	c	d	e	f
1.	25	13	62	55	23	33
2.	60	16	32	61	10	11
3.	51	32	51	15	10	53
4.	43	63	23	34	25	61

Page 366

1. 31
2. 25
3. 50
4. 16
5. 13
6. 34
7. 75

Page 367

	a	b	c	d	e	f
1.	58	93	56	66	95	87
2.	68	58	78	52	78	69
3.	55	35	11	32	43	22
4.	14	20	29	22	26	23

Page 368

1. 23
2. 32
3. 36
4. 23
5. 12
6. 64
7. 49

Page 371

	a	b	c	d	e	f
1.	32	43	91	47	50	51
2.	54	34	45	85	33	46
3.	30	51	44	38	64	51
4.	83	50	30	31	23	28
5.	21	50	60	74	45	22
6.	37	43	61	43	51	47
7.	54	34	76	63	90	85

Page 372

1. 44 ; 8 ; 52
2. 72 ; 9 ; 81
3. 25
4. 76
5. 91

Page 373

	a	b	c	d	e	f
1.	62	85	80	64	72	91
2.	57	75	72	90	98	81
3.	84	63	84	73	72	94
4.	97	63	92	46	62	56
5.	73	52	75	91	74	96
6.	92	73	86	81	70	62
7.	91	75	70	88	83	83

Page 374

1. 31 ; 29 ; 60
2. 46 ; 36 ; 82
3. 29 ; 13 ; 42
4. 77
5. 61

Page 375

	a	b	c	d	e	f
1.	45	18	37	49	26	58
2.	19	39	29	37	59	83
3.	46	58	55	68	41	37
4.	88	67	73	39	59	42
5.	86	79	29	18	38	57
6.	14	68	36	35	46	18
7.	39	24	74	68	84	55

Page 376

1. 48 ; 9 ; 39
2. 91 ; 5 ; 86
3. 38
4. 44
5. 66
6. 78

Page 377

	a	b	c	d	e	f
1.	18	8	17	37	25	9
2.	18	17	14	38	8	66
3.	28	8	7	19	16	9
4.	28	17	7	27	19	13
5.	58	78	26	56	52	57
6.	9	35	29	25	12	46
7.	34	37	8	49	27	46

Page 378

1. 95 ; 26 ; 69
2. 73 ; 45 ; 28
3. 39
4. 12
5. 27
6. 15

Page 379

	a	b	c	d	e	f
1.	61	55	81	85	70	91
2.	64	56	50	76	94	73
3.	54	39	19	67	38	38
4.	18	49	48	35	28	14

Page 380

1. subtract ; 8
2. subtract ; 17
3. add ; 91
4. subtract ; 18
5. add ; 54

Page 383

	a	b	c	d	e	f
1.	15	150	15	150	11	110
2.	12	120	17	170	10	100
3.	110	140	120	140	130	120
4.	110	120	130	100	160	160
5.	8	80	9	90	6	60
6.	9	90	9	90	9	90
7.	60	40	80	70	80	70
8.	40	90	70	40	50	70

Page 384

1. subtract ; 80
2. add ; 120
3. subtract ; 60
4. 20
5. 120
6. 60

Page 385

	a	b	c	d	e	f
1.	136	149	109	129	118	118
2.	115	148	129	126	157	113
3.	122	156	185	107	115	116
4.	107	136	176	136	186	126
5.	139	156	126	107	160	165
6.	177	119	117	108	125	142
7.	138	105	146	127	188	177

Page 386

1. 96 ; 81 ; 177
2. 53 ; 85 ; 138
3. 83 ; 84 ; 167
4. 139
5. 148

Page 387

	a	b	c	d	e	f
1.	83	36	73	85	94	72
2.	50	91	27	42	93	62
3.	66	81	93	43	13	94
4.	84	67	94	60	94	63
5.	91	71	81	77	47	42
6.	53	56	80	74	73	52
7.	35	91	72	72	50	93

Page 388

1. 128 ; 73 ; 55
2. 145 ; 75 : 70
3. 167 ; 71 ; 96
4. 65
5. 91

Page 389

	a	b	c	d	e	f
1.	127	127	156	114	106	114
2.	173	116	147	127	128	104
3.	92	92	71	94	84	57
4.	74	82	81	67	95	83

Page 390

1. add ; 120
2. subtract ; 38
3. add ; 153

Answers Grade 3

Page 391

	a	b	c	d	e	f
1.	162	123	134	110	142	151
2.	172	131	112	125	130	185
3.	156	148	111	122	161	147
4.	110	122	131	153	142	114
5.	134	126	191	160	153	113
6.	142	152	187	111	125	146

Page 392

1. 74 ; 87 ; 161
2. 49 ; 57 ; 106
3. 84 ; 48 ; 132
4. 180
5. 134

Page 393

	a	b	c	d	e	f
1.	49	89	86	77	83	68
2.	37	44	72	85	89	67
3.	87	88	39	69	58	78
4.	58	67	88	73	67	88
5.	58	58	76	57	59	69
6.	64	87	68	47	75	86
7.	79	78	69	89	59	23

Page 394

1. 180 ; 95 ; 85
2. 128 ; 79 ; 49
3. 162 ; 84 ; 78
4. 97
5. 47

Page 395

	a	b	c	d	e	f
1.	92	127	143	119	79	84
2.	168	132	129	70	78	110
3.	33	141	78	60	70	48
4.	65	85	131	115	99	70
5.	159	58	79	60	87	69

Page 396

1. 166 ; 98 ; 68
2. 115 ; 27 ; 88
3. 84 ; 39 ; 123
4. 152
5. 77

Page 399

	a	b	c	d	e	f
1.	16	23	15	20	15	20
2.	130	190	160	160	160	220
3.	136	183	165	160	165	220
4.	98	104	165	104	149	127
5.	121	174	142	234	103	92
6.	115	148	178	134	130	149

Page 400

1. 72 ; 69 ; 64 ; 205
2. 55 ; 68 ; 79 ; 202
3. 217
4. 146

Page 401

	a	b	c	d	e	f
1.	1002	819	703	773	864	471
2.	1769	1262	998	997	1485	1579
3.	1521	1808	1042	1402	1563	935
4.	959	902	1789	994	1995	1961
5.	1395	1466	1495	1820	1243	1803

Page 402

1. 175 ; 142 ; 327 ; 644
2. 768 ; 829 ; 107 ; 1704
3. 991
4. 507

Page 403

	a	b	c	d	e	f
1.	261	109	319	189	189	120
2.	91	548	307	299	209	42
3.	627	188	379	628	209	205
4.	579	688	591	269	387	608
5.	482	252	321	582	99	394
6.	497	150	419	414	190	109

Page 404

1. 714 ; 521 ; 193
2. 850 ; 317 ; 533
3. 726 ; 340 ; 386
4. 109
5. 175

Page 405

	a	b	c	d	e
1.	7332	6411	7122	4210	2002
2.	3327	4106	6003	3218	5157
3.	3370	9371	3363	5034	3470
4.	3571	3202	7811	4910	5500
5.	5449	1584	3749	2949	1806
6.	7854	6775	2999	3469	854

Page 406

1. 3165 ; 875 ; 2290
2. 4418; 979 ; 3439
3. 937
4. 4385
5. 1355
6. 659

Page 409

	a	b
1.	31	Friday
2.	5	5
3.	4	7
4.	18th	11th
5.	120	November 10

Page 410

	a		b	
1.	5	3	10	7
2.	20	10	25	12
3.	45	8	15	9
4.	30	5	30	6
5.	10	1	5	1

	a	b	c	d
6.	6:05	2:45	7:20	8:35
7.	3:30	1:25	9:40	10:15

Page 411

	a	b	c	d
1.		20	12	8
2.	4	26	17	31
3.	36	29	11	33
4.	18	9	34	13
5.	5	25	6	21
6.	38	35	27	16
7.	23	37	14	32

	a	b	c
8.	III	VII	XV
9.	XIX	XXII	XXVIII
10.	XXX	XX	XXXIX

Page 412

1. 10 ; 2
2. 10 ; 1
3. 20 ; 2
4. 15 ; 3
5. 20 ; 4
7. 12 ; 70
8. 8 ;14
9. 0 ; 65
10. 10 ; 1

Page 413

	a	b	c	d	e
1.	$12.76	$ 5.21	$41.36	95¢	$ 4.62
2.	$ 2.02	$ 7.56	$ 2.46	12¢	$22.74
3.	$22.02	$12.07	$20.79	90¢	$18.05
4.	$11.78	$ 3.62	$10.44	16¢	$13.14
5.	$13.55	$69.01	$ 2.00	28¢	$ 1.22
6.	$45.47	$33.04	$ 2.28	73¢	$ 9.39

Page 414

1. $40.62
2. $51.72
3. $.75
4. $10.64; $6.29
5. $7.15
6. $5.77
7. 27¢

Page 417

2. three times four
3. five times two
4. four times eight
5. four times seven

	a	b
7.	5+5+5	3+3+3+3+3
8.	7+7+7	3+3+3+3+3+3+3
9.	6+6+6+6	4+4+4+4+4+4
10.	8+8	2+2+2+2+2+2+2+2
11.	9+9+9	3+3+3+3+3+3+3+3+3

Page 418

	a	b	c	d	e	f
1.	16	16	8	8	10	10
2.	12	12	14	14	4	4
3.	18	18	6	6	2	2
4.	6	6	9	9	12	12
5.	15	15	18	18	21	21
6.	24	24	27	27	3	3

Page 419

	a	b	c	d	e	f
1.	0	9	7	0	5	0
2.	0	8	4	0	0	6
3.	0	0	5	6	1	0
4.	7	0	0	0	7	5
5.	0	9	6	0	0	2
6.	4	8	0	8	0	0
7.	0	6	0	9	0	3
8.	2	0	0	3	4	0

Page 420

1. 2 ; 9 ; 18
2. 2 ; 6 ; 12
3. 24
4. 40

Page 421

	a	b	c	d	e	f
1.	20	32	35	30	8	12
2.	25	18	36	4	0	16
3.	15	28	10	8	40	18
4.	15	9	16	0	6	10
5.	24	24	4	0	5	12
6.	45	0	12	14	21	5

Page 422

1. 5 ; 9 ; 45
2. 7 ; 5 ; 35
3. 7 ; 4 ; 28
4. 5 ; 3 ; 15
5. 20

Page 423

	a	b	c	d	e	f
1.	0	8	40	21	6	0
2.	1	18	16	15	30	4
3.	0	2	0	16	45	25
4.	32	18	5	0	2	14
5.	15	28	20	6	27	8
6.	0	3	12	0	6	36
7.	35	24	0	0	4	24
8.	20	4	9	7	8	9
9.	9	0	10	12	10	12

Page 424

1. 6 ; 1 ; 6
2. 8 ; 4 ; 32
3. 40
4. 10
5. 30
6. 12

Page 427

	a	b	c	d	e	f
1.	30	9	54	32	0	15
2.	40	12	24	25	12	6
3.	12	28	30	48	36	24
4.	0	18	5	16	6	20
5.	42	45	35	0	10	8
6.	36	12	20	3	15	0
7.	4	10	6	27	21	24

Page 428

1. 6 ; 4 ; 24
2. 8 ; 6 ; 48
3. 6 ; 9 ; 54

Page 429

	a	b	c	d	e	f
1.	49	42	48	21	72	0
2.	64	40	8	21	24	7
3.	0	48	40	63	7	42
4.	56	35	0	14	35	0
5.	56	16	32	28	24	32
6.	36	8	28	16	14	54

Page 430

1. 7 ; 9 ; 63
2. 4 ; 7 ; 28
3. 8 ; 7 ; 56
4. 35
5. 42

Page 431

	a	b	c	d	e	f
1.	63	54	64	21	18	21
2.	40	56	36	48	0	49
3.	81	8	0	54	56	16
4.	32	0	28	18	32	42
5.	40	63	24	9	7	0
6.	45	0	27	35	72	14

Page 432

1. 8 ; 9 ; 72
2. 9 ; 9 ; 81
3. 45
4. 36
5. 54
6. 63

Page 433

	a	b	c	d	e	f
1.	63	42	5	18	18	64
2.	21	36	0	35	56	36
3.	45	24	45	16	56	0
4.	42	6	72	0	25	63
5.	40	32	28	0	9	20
6.	48	54	30	24	49	27
7.	48	40	28	15	81	7
8.	36	35	8	72	30	10
9.	12	0	54	24	32	14

Page 434

1. 5 ; 8 ; 40
2. 9 ; 9 ; 81
3. 6 ; 9 ; 54
4. 42
5. 72
6. 56

Page 437

	a	b	c	d	e	f
1.	6	60	8	80	6	60
2.	80	80	90	30	90	70
3.	36	360	18	180	25	250
4.	210	300	160	100	240	540
5.	80	150	120	40	180	280
6.	490	240	70	640	90	240
7.	200	160	120	150	50	40
8.	420	250	240	180	560	270

Page 438

1. 30 ; 4 ; 120
2. 20 ; 2 ; 40
3. 30 ; 3 ; 90
4. 180
5. 80
6. 280

Page 439

	a	b	c	d	e	f
1.	124	219	368	168	106	126
2.	46	93	84	48	99	84
3.	84	183	102	86	328	39
4.	216	96	129	69	68	186

Answers Grade 3

Page 440

	a	b	c	d	e	f
1.	248	168	219	164	182	156
2.	86	164	96	183	168	88
3.	216	213	162	129	208	166
4.	124	279	52	148	106	186
5.	288	405	276	189	108	146
6.	427	128	246	729	126	455
7.	159	426	328	819	368	648

Page 441

	a	b	c	d	e	f
1.	92	87	80	98	78	96
2.	74	52	94	84	75	96
3.	90	70	84	70	92	76
4.	90	81	90	84	60	96
5.	56	72	85	78	57	76
6.	72	72	75	64	58	54

Page 442

1. 12; 7 ; 84
2. 14 ; 5 ; 70
3. 98
4. 72

Page 443

	a	b	c	d	e	f
1.	140	252	168	235	228	125
2.	216	162	190	384	581	444
3.	300	174	184	222	145	138
4.	336	558	496	285	156	154
5.	270	476	657	696	564	332
6.	480	255	188	207	273	390

Page 444

1. 25 ; 9 ; 225
2. 26 ; 6 ; 156
3. 36 ; 7 ; 252
4. 200
5. 108

Page 447

1.	10	5
2.	21	7
3.	4	2
4.	18	6
5.	18	9

6.	24	8	
7.	3	21	7
8.	2	4	2
9.	2	10	5
10.	3	18	6

Page 448

	a				b			
1.			5	5			2	2
2.		2	4	4		8	2	2
3.	4	2	2	2	4	2	2	2

Page 449

	a	b
1.		6
2.	7	8
3.	1	3
4.	8	9

	a	b	c	d
5.	5	3	1	2
6.	7	9	4	6

Page 450

1. 24 ; 3 ; 8
2. 8 ; 2 ; 4
3. 16 ; 2 ; 8
4. 9
5. 9

Page 451

	a	b
1.		6
2.	4	3
3.	6	4
4.	9	8

	a	b	c	d
5.	2	2	1	3
6.	5	1	8	7

Page 452

1. 24 ; 4 ; 6
2. 28 ; 4 ; 7
3. 32 ; 4 ; 8
4. 5
5. 9

Page 453

	a	b
1.	5	14
2.	4	9

	a	b	c	d	e
3.	4	3	12	2	16
4.	4	6	9	3	2
5.	4	7	9	1	9
6.	8	3	5	7	18
7.	1	5	2	6	8

Page 454

1. 16 ; 2 ; 8
2. 9 ; 3 ; 3
3. 36 ; 4 ; 9
4. 7
5. 5

Page 457

	a	b
1.	2	1
2.	5	7
3.	8	9

	a	b	c	d
4.	1	2	6	3
5.	6	0	4	7
6.	5	9	8	9
7.	8	4	5	6

Page 458

1. 30 ; 6 ; 5
2. 12 ; 6 ; 2
3. 18 ; 6 ; 3
4. 1
5. 4

Page 459

	a	b
1.	2	3
2.	5	4
3.	7	8

	a	b	c	d
4.	1	0	2	4
5.	6	6	1	8
6.	0	7	7	9
7.	8	5	9	3

Page 460

1. 28 ; 7 ; 4
2. 48 ; 8 ; 6
3. 3
4. 2
5. 1

Page 461

	a	b
1.	5	3
2.	8	4
3.	6	9

	a	b	c	d
4.	1	9	2	4
5.	0	8	6	9
6.	9	7	6	5
7.	3	7	9	7

Page 462

1. 54 ; 9 ; 6
2. 27 ; 9 ; 3
3. 4
4. 2
5. 5

Page 463

	a	b	c	d
1.	5	6	1	8
2.	3	2	4	6
3.	9	8	5	0
4.	5	8	3	6
5.	2	5	1	8
6.	2	2	4	3
7.	4	3	3	2
8.	8	7	5	5
9.	7	5	7	8
10.	8	6	6	9

Page 464

1. 42 ; 6 ; 7
2. 63 ; 7 ; 9
3. 64 ; 8 ; 8

Page 467

1. 1
2. 3
3. 5
4. 11
5. 8
6. 4

Page 468

1. 28 4. 2
2. 21 5. 16
3. 7 6.–10. Answers vary.

Page 469

1. 8 5. 2 8. 4
2. 6 6. 4 9. 5
3. 5 7. 3 10. 5
4. 2

Page 470

1. 7 ; 3 4. 4 ; 5 ; 7 6. 16
2. 4 5. 2 7. 32
3. 20

Page 471

1. Yes 4. 2 liters 7. 4 liters
2. No 5. 10 liters 8. 20 liters
3. 1 liter 6. 8 liters

Page 472

1. 48 4. 4 6. 475
2. 425 5. 7 7. 32
3. 102

Page 475

1. 3 5. 1 8. 2
2. 2 6. 2 9. 1
3. 4 7. 1 10. 3
4. 5

Page 476

1. 11 ; 8 4. 1 7. 2 ; 1 ; 2
2. 3 5. 3 8. 5
3. 4 6. 10

Page 477

	a	*b*		*a*	*b*
1.	72	96	7.	21	108
2.	9	24	8.	6	33
3.	36	72	9.	27	60
4.	7	4	10.	84	9
5.	15	42	11.	18	5
6.	36	108	12.	3	30

Page 478

1. 6 3. 9 5. 60 7. 5
2. 24 4. 108 6. 6 8. 48

Page 479

	a	*b*		*a*	*b*		*a*	*b*
1.	14	6	4.	6	9	7.	32	6
2.	4	9	5.	2	28	8.	7	18
3.	20	8	6.	16	5	9.	7	36

Page 480

1. 24 3. 6 5. 2 7. 16
2. 3 4. 9 6. 5 8. 16

Page 481

	a	*b*		a	b		a	b
1.	14	56	4.	360	63	7.	540	35
2.	300	420	5.	42	168	8.	192	49
3.	144	96	6.	216	180			

Page 482

1. 7 ; 5 ; 35 3. 24 ; 4 ; 96 5. 168
2. 60 ; 6 ; 360 4. 42

Page 483

1. 24 4. 16 7. 360
2. 10 5. 2 8. 21
3. 300 6. 48

Answers for Pre-Tests and Tests for Grade 3

Page 331

	a	b	c	d	e	f	g	h
1.	4	10	7	11	9	10	9	16
2.	10	9	12	3	5	2	10	5
3.	9	15	12	12	4	8	4	8
4.	7	11	6	15	8	10	9	13
5.	5	9	7	11	2	16	8	12
6.	17	6	14	12	11	6	10	8
7.	14	5	9	15	0	17	11	12
8.	6	3	13	7	10	1	14	12
9.	13	7	18	7	13	11	11	10
10.	16	14	10	13	14	11	13	15

Page 332

	a	b	c	d	e	f	g	h
1.	10	7	1	2	10	7	13	9
2.	1	9	3	5	8	9	11	10
3.	5	3	12	8	14	12	13	11
4.	6	14	13	8	13	17	0	8
5.	9	16	8	11	16	14	6	9
6.	4	9	4	6	14	6	14	13
7.	12	12	5	11	11	11	10	9
8.	2	10	12	4	15	10	7	10
9.	17	11	7	8	10	12	18	13
10.	12	15	15	8	15	16	11	10

Page 333

	a	b	c	d	e	f	g	h
1.	8	4	0	9	1	1	1	2
2.	5	0	3	7	1	4	7	8
3.	9	9	1	6	8	6	0	9
4.	5	2	0	3	2	8	5	4
5.	9	1	2	6	2	8	0	2
6.	6	1	1	4	6	8	2	7
7.	7	5	4	4	2	7	2	5
8.	7	6	1	5	3	3	0	7
9.	9	0	8	8	2	5	0	7
10.	9	3	3	9	9	8	6	6

Page 334

	a	b	c	d	e	f	g	h
1.	2	6	1	9	1	7	9	3
2.	6	7	3	2	1	2	6	9
3.	4	8	8	9	5	6	5	1
4.	2	4	1	7	4	8	8	1
5.	0	9	4	8	3	6	7	5
6.	0	8	1	6	4	3	5	7
7.	2	5	7	7	5	7	9	6
8.	0	7	3	8	5	5	9	6
9.	5	6	0	9	1	4	8	8
10.	3	4	0	9	4	4	8	7

Page 335

	a	b	c	d	e	f	g	h
1.	4	18	0	6	0	1	7	32
2.	28	0	24	2	5	18	10	12
3.	21	25	48	0	36	9	14	12
4.	40	8	35	4	16	30	56	9
5.	0	8	27	30	24	18	35	18
6.	63	24	32	21	54	36	12	56
7.	3	45	15	64	20	0	12	42
8.	15	0	14	49	40	54	0	36
9.	81	8	48	0	63	0	27	72
10.	24	72	16	28	6	42	9	45

Page 336

	a	b	c	d	e	f	g	h
1.	4	24	4	49	0	18	0	4
2.	0	3	24	27	0	54	21	32
3.	2	36	18	14	35	5	16	16
4.	32	45	8	6	54	28	12	30
5.	8	7	9	12	36	5	48	42
6.	28	1	40	40	0	0	6	27
7.	24	63	10	12	12	72	35	42
8.	48	20	24	18	7	8	16	15
9.	30	56	81	0	21	25	10	64
10.	9	20	56	36	72	63	14	45

Page 337

	a	b	c	d	e	f	g
1.	1	6	2	6	4	2	4
2.	0	9	3	8	3	0	1
3.	5	5	4	5	9	7	4
4.	2	4	1	9	4	2	5
5.	3	2	7	5	8	9	6
6.	8	5	6	1	0	2	1
7.	6	5	8	3	4	9	2
8.	5	4	0	7	6	0	7
9.	0	8	7	8	8	3	6
10.	7	1	2	0	7	3	5
11.	3	7	8	6	2	9	1
12.	9	8	9	3	6	4	9

Page 338

	a	b	c	d	e	f	g
1.	1	3	3	4	6	2	0
2.	5	4	2	2	1	8	9
3.	7	0	9	5	2	9	7
4.	1	4	8	7	1	1	6
5.	0	4	8	6	3	3	9
6.	3	4	3	0	9	0	2
7.	0	5	5	1	9	5	6
8.	2	5	7	6	8	7	5
9.	0	1	8	7	1	6	2
10.	6	5	4	8	7	6	6
11.	8	4	4	2	9	7	3
12.	3	7	9	8	4	9	8

Page 341

	a	b	c	d	e	f
1.	10	12	13	10	14	17
2.	11	13	10	18	10	15
3.	16	14	13	10	12	12
4.	11	12	11	14	16	15
5.	7	4	9	9	9	8
6.	8	8	9	8	4	8
7.	5	6	9	8	8	2
8.	7	9	9	9	8	4
9.	3	7	7	6	7	7

Page 342

1. 2 ; 2 ; 4   2. 1 ; 2 ; 3   3. 5 ; 2 ; 3

Page 357

	a	b	c	d	e	f
1.	15	13	11	10	14	12
2.	10	13	12	11	16	14
3.	12	15	11	17	11	13
4.	15	13	18	12	16	10
5.	13	12	10	11	10	14

	a	b	c	d	e
6.	4	7	9	8	4
7.	9	9	2	5	7
8.	8	8	5	5	8
9.	8	4	7	6	7

Answers for Pre-Tests and Tests for Grade 3

Page 358

	a	*b*	*c*	*d*	*e*	*f*
1.	9	49	5	55	7	87
2.	59	27	47	27	45	26
3.	35	48	66	46	17	27
4.	85	38	78	88	75	35
5.	63	48	97	39	68	53
6.	3	33	3	43	2	32
7.	34	21	51	22	66	23
8.	31	45	16	64	72	50
9.	15	20	61	33	10	27

Page 369

	a	*b*	*c*	*d*	*e*	*f*
1.	6	26	39	25	76	39
2.	57	79	87	67	85	87
3.	5	35	41	23	41	22
4.	25	41	23	40	32	37
5.	58					

Page 370

	a	*b*	*c*	*d*	*e*	*f*
1.	59	26	37	89	67	27
2.	41	62	47	61	56	33
3.	75	86	77	89	59	78
4.	81	71	97	73	75	78
5.	72	79	64	96	66	93
6.	34	25	50	85	51	83
7.	38	67	38	46	35	27
8.	42	12	11	23	12	48
9.	48	36	68	8	29	50

Page 381

	a	*b*	*c*	*d*	*e*	*f*
1.	43	54	31	24	52	64
2.	42	74	81	93	96	81
3.	18	45	58	18	48	57
4.	19	28	19	48	4	25
5.	81					

Page 382

	a	*b*	*c*	*d*	*e*	*f*
1.	11	110	15	150	170	140
2.	148	118	178	137	107	159
3.	141	171	124	131	176	141
4.	79	91	139	126	99	148
5.	118	88	150	126	133	80
6.	9	90	6	60	80	90
7.	83	91	64	93	97	80
8.	49	89	87	86	67	77
9.	123	149	82	79	114	67

Page 397

	a	*b*	*c*	*d*	*e*
1.	140	160	148	126	125
2.	141	140	181	156	123
3.	90	80	82	45	84
4.	68	78	77	88	65
5.	111	93	90	146	124

Page 398

	a	*b*	*c*	*d*	*e*	*f*
1.	14	23	21	22	21	24
2.	130	150	190	190	180	140
3.	123	148	134	153	191	107
4.	99	112	198	183	218	115
5.	848	987	826	1250	1588	1016

	a	*b*	*c*	*d*	*e*
6.	411	249	390	276	276
7.	4502	5359	3761	6899	5838

Page 407

	a	*b*	*c*	*d*	*e*
1.	10	17	21	190	230
2.	79	98	192	155	229
3.	881	959	847	1269	1876
4.	522	107	492	549	
5.	5522	7267	5771	1796	
6.	974				
7.	2438				

Page 408

	a	*b*	*c*
1.	365	4	
2.	366	4	
3.	30	45	
4.	31	15	
5.		5	4
6.	17	26	19
7.		X	IX
8.	XXIV	XXXI	XXV

	a	*b*	*c*	*d*	*e*
9.	$12.09	$13.90	83¢	94¢	$18.51
10.	$13.25	$11.85	$6.56	18¢	47¢
11.	$33.32				

Page 415

1. 31 2. Friday

	a	*b*	*c*
3.	7:05	10:45	12:30
4.		9	32
5.		VIII	XXIX

	a	*b*	*c*	*d*	*e*
6.	$31.77	$3.97	96¢	73¢	$15.70
7.	$ 1.35	$7.81	54¢	$16.41	$ 4.06
8.	$ 3.93				

Page 416

	a	*b*	*c*	*d*	*e*	*f*
1.	10	14	4	12	8	18
2.	9	15	12	21	27	6
3.	0	0	0	0	0	0
4.	3	7	4	1	5	8
5.	28	12	36	24	20	16
6.	40	30	45	20	15	10
7.	0	32	18	0	25	0
8.	9	8	2	35	24	2
9.	6	3	0	16	6	5

Page 425

	a	*b*	*c*	*d*	*e*
1.	6	28	0	12	45
2.	12	21	0	4	12
3.	18	40	27	6	16
4.	0	25	36	0	20
5.	5 ; 6 ; 30				
6.	32				
7.	24				

Page 426

	a	*b*	*c*	*d*	*e*	*f*
1.	42	36	24	48	30	54
2.	56	28	63	49	42	35
3.	72	40	56	64	48	32
4.	54	81	45	72	36	63
5.	81					
6.	56					
7.	63					
8.	42					

Answers for Pre-Tests and Tests for Grade 3

Page 435

	a	*b*	*c*	*d*	*e*
1.	42	45	48	28	49
2.	63	81	7	24	63
3.	0	56	40	72	42
4.	72	32	54	14	27

5. 6 ; 9 ; 54
6. 64
7. 24

Page 435

	a	*b*	*c*	*d*	*e*	*f*
1.	6	60	8	80	7	70
2.	96	48	39	84	55	69
3.	28	280	18	180	36	360
4.	186	148	248	248	166	205
5.	72	78	70	72	76	80
6.	172	135	105	276	168	270
7.	392	126	400	46	74	225
8.	68	320	219	66	162	162
9.	270	232	112	75	320	132

Page 445

	a	*b*	*c*	*d*	*e*
1.	60	84	69	240	240
2.	168	219	147	84	81
3.	285	228	210	116	180
4.	60	146	174	360	84

5. 4 ; 52 ; 208
6. 148
7. 84

Page 446

	a	*b*	*c*	*d*	*e*
1.	3	6	9	2	5
2.	4	8	3	5	1
3.	4	8	16	9	27
4.	8	1	9	6	21
5.	12	4	7	2	14
6.	5	7	1	2	6

7. 6
8. 4
9. 6

Page 455

	a	*b*	*c*	*d*	*e*
1.	5	4	1	3	8
2.	12	6	4	7	5
3.	2	8	4	9	8
4.	8	1	10	9	6

5. 45 ; 5 ; 9
6. 7
7. 3

Page 456

	a	*b*	*c*	*d*	*e*
1.	4	2	3	0	1
2.	7	9	5	6	8
3.	0	4	2	3	1
4.	8	6	9	5	7
5.	1	5	0	4	2
6.	3	6	8	9	7
7.	4	3	5	2	0
8.	8	7	6	1	9
9.	1	7	1	6	3

Page 465

	a	*b*	*c*	*d*	*e*
1.	2	1	3	6	0
2.	2	5	7	4	9
3.	8	3	5	2	9
4.	8	9	8	9	3
5.	5	4	8	9	6

6. 24 ; 6 ; 4 7. 3

Page 466

1. 4
2. 10
3. 8
4. 3
5. 6
6. False
7. False
8. True
9. 330

Page 473

1. 5
2. 9
3. 3
4. 4
5. 5
6. 3
7. 1 liter
8. 500 liters
9. 2 liters
10. 20
11. 32
12. 450

Page 474

1. 3 2. 1 3. 4

	a	*b*
4.	2	4
5.	4	3
6.	4	12
7.	2	5
8.	12	36
9.	3	36
10.	14	60
11.	28	360
12.	24	48
13.	72	

Page 484

1. 4 2. 1 3. 3 4. 2

	a	*b*
5.	48	2
6.	12	7
7.	32	108
8.	27	9
9.	42	480
10.	72	56

11. 96 12. 3 13. 59

Page 485

	a	*b*	*c*	*d*	*e*
1.	11	18	66	78	51
2.	91	82	140	111	174
3.	180	1074	741	$14.21	$17.25
4.	9	9	34	72	48
5.	36	63	80	67	88
6.	779	417	7831	$ 3.58	$11.45

	a	*b*	*c*
7.	8:00	3:30	6:10

Page 486

8. 15
9. 21
10. 76
11. 153
12. 95
13. 14.41
14. 8.74

Page 487

	a	*b*	*c*	*d*	*e*
1.	15	68	98	35	92
2.	110	112	1092	143	$84.40
3.	8	51	10	55	38
4.	90	49	241	2886	$17.75
5.	15	16	30	24	14
6.	27	56	48	63	36

Page 488

	a	*b*	*c*	*d*
7.	350	69	126	301
8.	6	5	9	8
9.	8	6	0	9
10.	4	7	8	6

11. 30
12. Saturday

Page 489

13. 11:20
14. 9
15. 2
16. 3
17. 36

Page 490

18. 9
19. 1445
20. 629
21. 4
22. 216
23. 8.31
24. 15.97

Student Notes

Spectrum Test Prep

Grade 3
Revised Edition

Test Preparation for:

Reading
Language
Math

Program Authors:
Dale Foreman
Alan C. Cohen
Jerome D. Kaplan
Ruth Mitchell

Table of Contents

Spectrum Test Prep

The Program That Teaches Test-Taking Achievement

For over two decades, McGraw-Hill has helped students perform their best when taking standardized achievement tests. Over the years, we have identified the skills and strategies that students need to master the challenges of taking a standardized test. Becoming familiar with the test-taking experience can help ensure your child's success.

Spectrum Test Prep covers all test skill areas

Spectrum Test Prep contains the subject areas that are represented in the five major standardized tests. *Spectrum Test Prep* will help your child prepare for the following tests:

- California Achievement Tests® (CAT/5)
- Comprehensive Tests of Basic Skills (CTBS/4)
- Iowa Tests of Basic Skills® (ITBS, Form K)
- Metropolitan Achievement Test (MAT/7)
- Stanford Achievement Test(SAT/9)

Spectrum Test Prep provides strategies for success

Many students need special support when preparing to take a standardized test. *Spectrum Test Prep* gives your child the opportunity to practice and become familiar with:

- General test content
- The test format
- Listening and following standard directions
- Working in structured settings
- Maintaining a silent, sustained effort
- Using test-taking strategies

Spectrum Test Prep is comprehensive

Spectrum Test Prep provides a complete presentation of the types of skills covered in standardized tests in a variety of formats. These formats are similar to those your child will encounter when testing. The subject areas covered in this book include:

- Reading
- Language
- Math

Spectrum Test Prep gives students the practice they need

Each student lesson provides several components that help develop test-taking skills:

- An **Example,** with directions and sample test items
- A **Tips** feature, that gives test-taking strategies
- A **Practice** section, that helps students practice answering questions in each test format

Each book gives focused test practice that builds confidence:

- A **Test Yourself** lesson for each unit gives students the opportunity to apply what they have learned in the unit.
- A **Test Practice** section gives students the experience of a longer test-like situation.
- A **Progress Chart** allows students to note and record their own progress.

Spectrum Test Prep is the first and most successful program ever developed to help students become familiar with the test-taking experience. *Spectrum Test Prep* can help to build self-confidence, reduce test anxiety, and provide the opportunity for students to successfully show what they have learned.

A Message to Parents and Teachers:

- **Standardized tests: the yardstick for your child's future**
  Standardized testing is one of the cornerstones of American education. From its beginning in the early part of this century, standardized testing has gradually become the yardstick by which student performance is judged. For better or worse, your child's future will be determined in great part by how well he or she performs on the standardized test used by your school district.

- **Even good students can have trouble with testing**
  In general, standardized tests are well designed and carefully developed to assess students' abilities in a consistent and balanced manner. However, there are many factors that can hinder the performance of an individual student when testing. These might include test anxiety, unfamiliarity with the test's format, or failing to understand the directions.

  In addition, it is rare that students are taught all of the material that appears on a standardized test. This is because the curriculum of most schools does not directly match the content of the standardized test. There will certainly be overlap between what your child learns in school and how he or she is tested, but some materials will probably be unfamiliar.

- **Ready to Test will lend a helping hand**
  It is because of the shortcomings of the standardized testing process that *Spectrum Test Prep* was developed. The lessons in the book were created after a careful analysis of the most popular achievement tests. The items, while different from those on the tests, reflect the types of material that your child will encounter when testing. Students who use *Spectrum Test Prep* will also become familiar with the format of the most popular achievement tests. This learning experience will reduce anxiety and give your child the opportunity to do his or her best on the next standardized test.

We urge you to review with your child the Message to Students and the feature "How to Use This Book" on p.508-509. The information on these pages will help your child to use this book and develop important test-taking skills. We are confident that following the recommendations in this book will help your child to earn a test score that accurately reflects his or her true ability.

A Message to Students:

Frequently in school you will be asked to take a standardized achievement test. This test will show how much you know compared to other students in your grade. Your score on a standardized achievement test will help your teachers plan your education. It will also give you and your parents an idea of what your learning strengths and weaknesses are.

This book will help you do your best on a standardized achievement test. It will show you what to expect on the test and will give you a chance to practice important reading and test-taking skills. Here are some suggestions you can follow to make the best use of *Spectrum Test Prep.*

Plan for success

- You'll do your best if you begin studying and do one or two lessons in this book each week. If you only have a little bit of time before a test is given, you can do one or two lessons each day.
- Study a little bit at a time, no more than 30 minutes a day. If you can, choose the same time each day to study in a quiet place.
- Keep a record of your score on each lesson. The charts on pp. 645-647 of this book will help you do this.

On the day of the test . . .

- Get a good night's sleep the night before the test. Have a light breakfast and lunch to keep from feeling drowsy during the test.
- Use the tips you learned in *Spectrum Test Prep.* The most important tips are to skip difficult items, take the best guess when you're unsure of the answer, and try all the items.
- Don't worry if you are a little nervous when you take an achievement test. This is a natural feeling and may even help you stay alert.

How to Use This Book

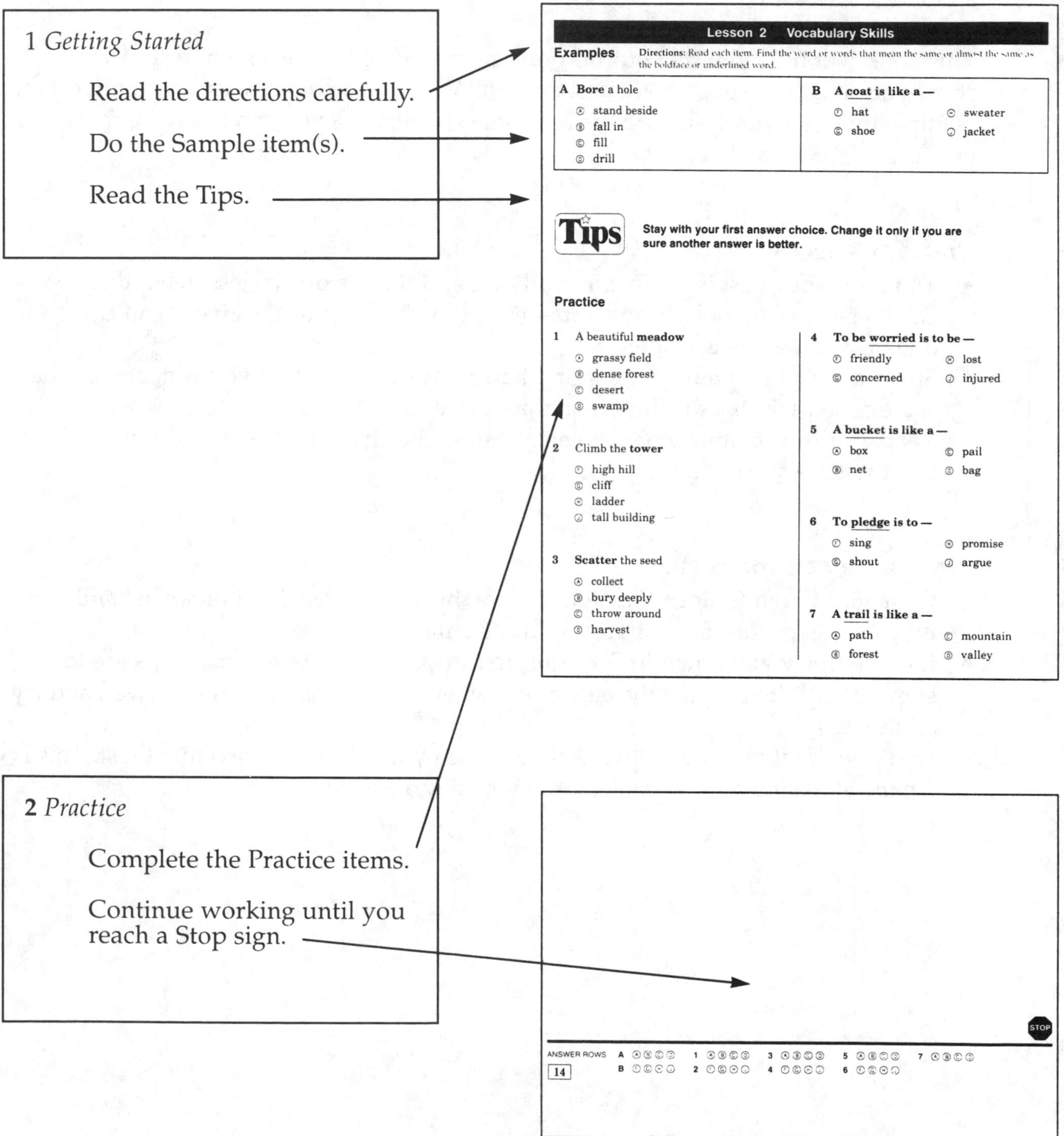

1 *Getting Started*
Read the directions carefully.
Do the Sample item(s).
Read the Tips.
2 *Practice*
Complete the Practice items.
Continue working until you reach a Stop sign.

Lesson 2 Vocabulary Skills

Examples **Directions:** Read each item. Find the word or words that mean the same or almost the same as the boldface or underlined word.

A **Bore** a hole
Ⓐ stand beside
Ⓑ fall in
Ⓒ fill
Ⓓ drill

B **A coat is like a —**
Ⓕ hat
Ⓖ shoe
Ⓗ sweater
Ⓙ jacket

Tips Stay with your first answer choice. Change it only if you are sure another answer is better.

Practice

1 A beautiful **meadow**
Ⓐ grassy field
Ⓑ dense forest
Ⓒ desert
Ⓓ swamp

2 Climb the **tower**
Ⓕ high hill
Ⓖ cliff
Ⓗ ladder
Ⓙ tall building

3 **Scatter** the seed
Ⓐ collect
Ⓑ bury deeply
Ⓒ throw around
Ⓓ harvest

4 **To be worried is to be —**
Ⓕ friendly
Ⓖ concerned
Ⓗ lost
Ⓙ injured

5 **A bucket is like a —**
Ⓐ box
Ⓑ net
Ⓒ pail
Ⓓ bag

6 **To pledge is to —**
Ⓕ sing
Ⓖ shout
Ⓗ promise
Ⓙ argue

7 **A trail is like a —**
Ⓐ path
Ⓑ forest
Ⓒ mountain
Ⓓ valley

STOP

ANSWER ROWS A ⒶⒷⒸⒹ 1 ⒶⒷⒸⒹ 3 ⒶⒷⒸⒹ 5 ⒶⒷⒸⒹ 7 ⒶⒷⒸⒹ
14 B ⒻⒼⒽⒿ 2 ⒻⒼⒽⒿ 4 ⒻⒼⒽⒿ 6 ⒻⒼⒽⒿ

3 *Check It Out*

Check your answers by turning to the Answer Keys at the back of the book.

Keep track of how you're doing by marking the number right on the Progress Charts on pages 645-647.

Mark the lesson you completed on the Table of Contents for each section.

Answer Keys

Reading
Unit1,
Vocabulary
Lesson 1
A C
B J
1 B
2 F
3 D
4 H
5 C
6 J
7 B
Lesson 2
A D
B J
1 A
2 J
3 C
4 G
5 C
6 H
7 A
Lesson 3
A B
B F
1 C
2 J
3 D
4 F
5 C
6 G
7 C
Lesson 4
A B
B H
1 C
2 J
3 B
4 J
5 A
Lesson 5
A C
B G
1 B
2 J
3 C
4 F
5 C
6 J
Lesson 6
E1 C
E2 G
E3 C
1 D
2 F
3 B
4 G
5 D
6 J
7 C
8 J
9 A
10 J
11 B
12 H
13 C
14 F
15 B
16 F
17 D
18 F
19 C
20 F
21 B
22 J
23 A
24 H
25 D
26 G
27 C
28 F
Unit 2, Reading
Comprehension
Lesson 7
A B
1 A
2 H
3 D
Lesson 8
A D
1 B
2 H
3 C
4 J
5 B
6 F
7 D
8 G
Lesson 9
A C
1 B
2 H
3 A
4 J
5 B
6 H
7 C
8 G
9 D
10 H
11 D
12 J
13 D
14 G
15 D
16 G
17 A
18 H
Lesson 10
E1 C
1 C
2 J
3 A
4 F
5 B
6 J
7 A
8 H
9 C
10 G
Test Practice
Part 1
E1 C
E2 G
E3 D
1 A
2 J
3 B
4 F
5 C
6 H
7 B
8 F
9 D
10 J
11 C
12 F
13 C
14 J
15 A
16 J
17 C
18 J
19 C
20 F
21 B
22 J
23 C
14 F
25 B
26 F
27 D
28 G
Test Practice
Part 2
E1 D
1 C
2 G
3 D
4 G
5 D
6 F
7 C
8 G
9 C
10 J
11 D
12 F
13 C
14 H
15 B
16 F
17 B
18 G
19 C
20 F
21 A
22 H
23 D
24 J

140

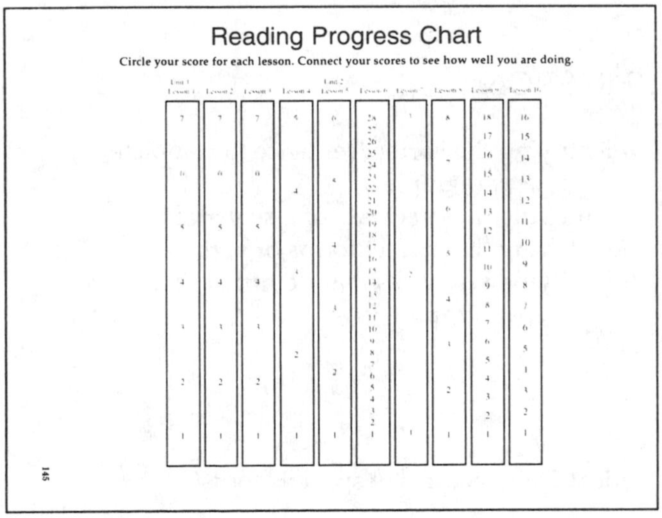

Reading Progress Chart

Circle your score for each lesson. Connect your scores to see how well you are doing.

145

Table of Contents

Language

48

Skills

Reading

VOCABULARY

Identifying synonyms
Identifying words with similar meanings
Identifying antonyms
Identifying multi-meaning words
Identifying words from a defining statement

READING COMPREHENSION

Recognizing story structures
Differentiating between fact and opinion
Making comparisons
Identifying story genres
Recognizing details
Understanding events
Drawing conclusions
Applying story information
Deriving word or phrase meaning
Understanding characters
Recognizing a narrator
Sequencing ideas
Making inferences
Labeling pictures
Generalizing from story information
Predicting from story content
Choosing the best title for a passage
Referring to a graphic
Understanding the author's purpose
Understanding feelings
Understanding the main idea

Language

LANGUAGE MECHANICS

Identifying the need for capital letters (proper nouns, beginning words) in sentences
Identifying the need for capital letters and punctuation marks in printed text
Identifying the need for punctuation marks (period, question mark, apostrophe, comma) in sentences

LANGUAGE EXPRESSION

Identifying the correct forms of nouns and pronouns
Identifying the correct forms of adjectives
Identifying correctly formed sentences
Sequencing sentences within a paragraph
Identifying the subject of a sentence
Combining sentences
Identifying the correct sentence to complete a paragraph
Identifying the predicate of a sentence
Identifying the correct forms of verbs
Identifying sentences that do not fit in a paragraph

SPELLING

Identifying correctly spelled words
Identifying incorrectly spelled words

MATH

CONCEPTS

Recognizing ordinal position
Comparing and ordering whole numbers
Comparing sets
Sequencing numbers
Renaming numerals
Understanding place value
Recognizing fractional parts
Using expanded notation
Using a number line
Grouping by 10s
Recognizing numerals
Skip counting by 10s
Recognizing visual and numeric patterns
Identifying fractions

Comparing and ordering fractions
Using operational symbols, words, and properties
Rounding
Recognizing odd and even numbers
Regrouping
Estimating

COMPUTATION

Adding whole numbers, decimals, and fractions
Dividing whole numbers
Multiplying whole numbers
Subtracting whole numbers, decimals, and fractions

APPLICATIONS

Finding perimeter and area
Solving word problems
Reading a calendar
Reading a thermometer
Recognizing plane and solid figures and their characteristics
Recognizing value of coins, bills, and money notation
Telling time
Identifying information needed to solve a problem
Estimating weight, size, and temperature
Understanding elapsed time
Understanding congruence, symmetry, and line segments
Understanding bar graphs, pictographs, and tables

Strategies

Listening carefully
Following group directions
Utilizing test formats
Locating question and answer choices
Following oral directions
Subvocalizing answer choices
Recalling information about word structure
Skipping difficult items and returning to them later
Identifying and using key words to find the answer
Staying with the first answer
Analyzing answer choices
Trying out answer choices
Eliminating answer choices
Restating a question
Substituting answer choices
Using logic
Using sentence context to find the answer
Referring to a passage to find the correct answer
Indicating that an item has no mistakes
Evaluating answer choices
Recalling the elements of a correctly formed sentence
Converting problems to a workable format
Noting the lettering of answer choices
Taking the best guess when unsure of the answer
Indicating that the correct answer is not given
Identifying the best test-taking strategy
Locating the correct answer
Comparing answer choices
Marking the correct answer as soon as it is found
Adjusting to a structured setting
Maintaining a silent, sustained effort
Managing time effectively
Considering every answer choice
Computing carefully
Working methodically
Using context to find the answer
Locating the correct answer
Understanding unusual item formats
Following complex directions
Inferring word meaning from sentence context
Reasoning from facts and evidence
Encapsulating a passage
Skimming a passage
Avoiding over-analysis of answer choices
Recalling the function of verbs
Noting the differences among answer choices
Referring to a reference source
Recalling the elements of a correctly formed paragraph
Checking answers by the opposite operation
Finding the answer without computing
Performing the correct operation
Understanding oral questions
Identifying and using key words, figures, and numbers
Following written directions
Reworking a problem
Previewing items

Table of Contents
Reading

Unit 1 Vocabulary

Unit 2 Reading Comprehension

Unit 3 Test Practice

UNIT 1 VOCABULARY

Lesson 1 Synonyms

Examples **Directions:** Read each item. Find the word that means the same or almost the same as the underlined word.

A **costly ticket**

Ⓐ distant
Ⓑ ordinary
Ⓒ expensive
Ⓓ winning

B **I felt clumsy when I went skiing.**

Ⓕ tired
Ⓖ graceful
Ⓗ frightened
Ⓙ awkward

If you aren't sure of the answer, replace the underlined word with each answer choice and say the phrase to yourself.

Practice

1 **search beneath**

Ⓐ beside
Ⓑ below
Ⓒ above
Ⓓ along

2 **free the animal**

Ⓕ release
Ⓖ harm
Ⓗ attract
Ⓙ search

3 **sometimes injure**

Ⓐ help
Ⓑ carry
Ⓒ miss
Ⓓ hurt

4 **view the scene**

Ⓕ leave
Ⓖ enjoy
Ⓗ observe
Ⓙ purchase

5 **Ellen's coat was ruined.**

Ⓐ cleaned
Ⓑ repaired
Ⓒ destroyed
Ⓓ lost

6 **The dry leaves were brittle.**

Ⓕ noisy
Ⓖ damp
Ⓗ colorful
Ⓙ fragile

7 **What do you do with stale bread?**

Ⓐ fresh
Ⓑ old
Ⓒ warm
Ⓓ toasted

ANSWER ROWS A Ⓐ Ⓑ Ⓒ Ⓓ 1 Ⓐ Ⓑ Ⓒ Ⓓ 3 Ⓐ Ⓑ Ⓒ Ⓓ 5 Ⓐ Ⓑ Ⓒ Ⓓ 7 Ⓐ Ⓑ Ⓒ Ⓓ
B Ⓕ Ⓖ Ⓗ Ⓙ 2 Ⓕ Ⓖ Ⓗ Ⓙ 4 Ⓕ Ⓖ Ⓗ Ⓙ 6 Ⓕ Ⓖ Ⓗ Ⓙ

Examples

Directions: Read each item. Find the word or words that mean the same or almost the same as the boldface or underlined word.

A **Bore** a hole

Ⓐ stand beside
Ⓑ fall in
Ⓒ fill
Ⓓ drill

B **A coat is like a —**

Ⓕ hat
Ⓖ shoe
Ⓗ sweater
Ⓙ jacket

Stay with your first answer choice. Change it only if you are sure another answer is better.

Practice

1 A beautiful **meadow**

Ⓐ grassy field
Ⓑ dense forest
Ⓒ desert
Ⓓ swamp

2 Climb the **tower**

Ⓕ high hill
Ⓖ cliff
Ⓗ ladder
Ⓙ tall building

3 **Scatter** the seed

Ⓐ collect
Ⓑ bury deeply
Ⓒ throw around
Ⓓ harvest

4 **To be worried is to be —**

Ⓕ friendly
Ⓖ concerned
Ⓗ lost
Ⓙ injured

5 **A bucket is like a —**

Ⓐ box
Ⓑ net
Ⓒ pail
Ⓓ bag

6 **To pledge is to —**

Ⓕ sing
Ⓖ shout
Ⓗ promise
Ⓙ argue

7 **A trail is like a —**

Ⓐ path
Ⓑ forest
Ⓒ mountain
Ⓓ valley

STOP

ANSWER ROWS
A Ⓐ Ⓑ Ⓒ Ⓓ 1 Ⓐ Ⓑ Ⓒ Ⓓ 3 Ⓐ Ⓑ Ⓒ Ⓓ 5 Ⓐ Ⓑ Ⓒ Ⓓ 7 Ⓐ Ⓑ Ⓒ Ⓓ
B Ⓕ Ⓖ Ⓗ Ⓙ 2 Ⓕ Ⓖ Ⓗ Ⓙ 4 Ⓕ Ⓖ Ⓗ Ⓙ 6 Ⓕ Ⓖ Ⓗ Ⓙ

Examples

Directions: Read each item. Choose the word that means the opposite of the underlined word.

A Caitlin will toss the ball first.

Ⓐ hit
Ⓑ catch
Ⓒ throw
Ⓓ find

B buy some

Ⓕ none
Ⓖ several
Ⓗ that
Ⓙ cheap

Remember, you are looking for the answer that means the opposite of the underlined word.

Practice

1 Stony was pleased with his score.

Ⓐ happy
Ⓑ unsure
Ⓒ annoyed
Ⓓ satisfied

2 I stretched my sweater.

Ⓕ lost
Ⓖ washed
Ⓗ found
Ⓙ shrank

3 The train ride was jerky.

Ⓐ long
Ⓑ enjoyable
Ⓒ bumpy
Ⓓ smooth

4 work slowly

Ⓕ rapidly
Ⓖ harshly
Ⓗ kindly
Ⓙ soon

5 recent newspaper

Ⓐ delivered
Ⓑ thick
Ⓒ old
Ⓓ expensive

6 was furious

Ⓕ angry
Ⓖ calm
Ⓗ curious
Ⓙ uncertain

7 except Randy

Ⓐ like
Ⓑ with
Ⓒ including
Ⓓ despite

STOP

ANSWER ROWS
A Ⓐ Ⓑ Ⓒ Ⓓ 1 Ⓐ Ⓑ Ⓒ Ⓓ 3 Ⓐ Ⓑ Ⓒ Ⓓ 5 Ⓐ Ⓑ Ⓒ Ⓓ 7 Ⓐ Ⓑ Ⓒ Ⓓ
B Ⓕ Ⓖ Ⓗ Ⓙ 2 Ⓕ Ⓖ Ⓗ Ⓙ 4 Ⓕ Ⓖ Ⓗ Ⓙ 6 Ⓕ Ⓖ Ⓗ Ⓙ

Examples

Directions: For items A and 1-3, read the two sentences with the blanks. Choose the word that fits both sentences. For items B and 4-5, find the answer in which the underlined word is used the same as in the sentence in the box.

A We looked in both _______ .

What do the _______ say?

Ⓐ paths
Ⓑ directions
Ⓒ words
Ⓓ boxes

B

The park is crowded today.

In which sentence does the word park mean the same thing as in the sentence above?

Ⓕ Where did you park the car?
Ⓖ You will learn to park soon.
Ⓗ The children played in the park.
Ⓙ Park beside the supermarket.

Watch out! Only one answer is correct in both sentences or matches the meaning of the sentence in the box.

Practice

1 Rosa paid a library _______ .

The carpenter did a _______ job.

Ⓐ fee
Ⓑ good
Ⓒ fine
Ⓓ great

2 Let's take a _______ now.

Did Randy _______ his skateboard?

Ⓕ rest
Ⓖ lose
Ⓗ find
Ⓙ break

3 Loren got a _______ for her work.

Be sure to _______ the dog's water.

Ⓐ fee
Ⓑ check
Ⓒ fill
Ⓓ reward

4

Shara hurt her hand yesterday.

In which sentence does the word hand mean the same thing as in the sentence above?

Ⓕ Please hand me that bowl.
Ⓖ The crowd gave the player a hand.
Ⓗ On one hand, they did their best.
Ⓙ Put your hand under the bag.

5

In general, it was a good play.

In which sentence does the word general mean the same thing as in the sentence above?

Ⓐ He made a general comment about the food.
Ⓑ The general will arrive soon.
Ⓒ The small town had a general store.
Ⓓ Lucy's mother is a general.

STOP

ANSWER ROWS A Ⓐ Ⓑ Ⓒ Ⓓ 1 Ⓐ Ⓑ Ⓒ Ⓓ 3 Ⓐ Ⓑ Ⓒ Ⓓ 5 Ⓐ Ⓑ Ⓒ Ⓓ
B Ⓕ Ⓖ Ⓗ Ⓙ 2 Ⓕ Ⓖ Ⓗ Ⓙ 4 Ⓕ Ⓖ Ⓗ Ⓙ

Examples

Directions: For items A and 1-3, read the paragraph or sentence. Find the word below that fits best in the blanks. For items B and 4-6, read the sentence with the underlined word. Find the word below that means the same or almost the same as the underlined word.

A The children helped their parents _______ the family car. They used the garden hose for water.

Ⓐ buy
Ⓑ repair
Ⓒ wash
Ⓓ sell

B **Many people visited the famous museum in our town. Famous means —**

Ⓕ large
Ⓖ well-known
Ⓗ science
Ⓙ old-fashioned

Use the meaning of the sentence to decide which answer choice is correct.

Practice

1 **The test was ______ , but I did well. Find the word that means the test was not easy.**

Ⓐ silent
Ⓑ difficult
Ⓒ short
Ⓓ simple

The rain __(2)__ against the window. The thunder boomed and the __(3)__ flashed.

2
Ⓕ attended
Ⓖ gushed
Ⓗ wet
Ⓙ pounded

3
Ⓐ storm
Ⓑ weather
Ⓒ lightning
Ⓓ wind

4 **The ________ cabin withstood the storm.**

Which word means the cabin was strong?

Ⓕ sturdy
Ⓖ weak
Ⓗ cozy
Ⓙ huge

5 **Are you allowed to go with us? Allowed means —**

Ⓐ happy
Ⓑ excited
Ⓒ permitted
Ⓓ ready

6 **A safety zone surrounded the chemical plant. Zone means —**

Ⓕ fence
Ⓖ road
Ⓗ lake
Ⓙ area

STOP

ANSWER ROWS
A Ⓐ Ⓑ Ⓒ Ⓓ 1 Ⓐ Ⓑ Ⓒ Ⓓ 3 Ⓐ Ⓑ Ⓒ Ⓓ 5 Ⓐ Ⓑ Ⓒ Ⓓ
B Ⓕ Ⓖ Ⓗ Ⓙ 2 Ⓕ Ⓖ Ⓗ Ⓙ 4 Ⓕ Ⓖ Ⓗ Ⓙ 6 Ⓕ Ⓖ Ⓗ Ⓙ

Examples

Directions: Read the phrase with the underlined word. Find the word below that means the same or almost the same as the underlined word.

E1 rely on her

Ⓐ breathe
Ⓑ watch
Ⓒ depend
Ⓓ stand

E2 accept a job

Ⓕ take
Ⓖ reject
Ⓗ seek
Ⓙ realize

E3 Hal broke his ________ .

We'll ________ these boards together.

Ⓐ glasses
Ⓑ glue
Ⓒ nail
Ⓓ pen

1 sunshine is likely

Ⓐ enjoyable
Ⓑ rare
Ⓒ impossible
Ⓓ probable

2 cancel an order

Ⓕ stop
Ⓖ give
Ⓗ make
Ⓙ extend

3 happen frequently

Ⓐ quickly
Ⓑ often
Ⓒ occasionally
Ⓓ now

4 How can we attach this?

Ⓕ separate
Ⓖ connect
Ⓗ repair
Ⓙ examine

5 The house on the lake was lovely.

Ⓐ run-down
Ⓑ lonely
Ⓒ small
Ⓓ charming

6 Rare coins

Ⓕ cheap
Ⓖ beautiful
Ⓗ damaged
Ⓙ unusual

7 Inspect the food

Ⓐ freeze
Ⓑ carry
Ⓒ check carefully
Ⓓ cook well

8 A bundle is a —

Ⓕ friend
Ⓖ mistake
Ⓗ newspaper
Ⓙ package

9 To soar is to —

Ⓐ fly high
Ⓑ sink quickly
Ⓒ run around
Ⓓ follow closely

GO

ANSWER ROWS E1 Ⓐ Ⓑ Ⓒ Ⓓ E3 Ⓐ Ⓑ Ⓒ Ⓓ 2 Ⓕ Ⓖ Ⓗ Ⓙ 4 Ⓕ Ⓖ Ⓗ Ⓙ 6 Ⓕ Ⓖ Ⓗ Ⓙ 8 Ⓕ Ⓖ Ⓗ Ⓙ
E2 Ⓕ Ⓖ Ⓗ Ⓙ 1 Ⓐ Ⓑ Ⓒ Ⓓ 3 Ⓐ Ⓑ Ⓒ Ⓓ 5 Ⓐ Ⓑ Ⓒ Ⓓ 7 Ⓐ Ⓑ Ⓒ Ⓓ 9 Ⓐ Ⓑ Ⓒ Ⓓ

Directions: For numbers 10-14, read the phrase with the underlined word. Find the word below that means the opposite of the underlined word.

10 Those fish are very colorful.

Ⓕ bright
Ⓖ large
Ⓗ strange
Ⓙ dull

11 People often visit this beach.

Ⓐ frequently
Ⓑ rarely
Ⓒ usually
Ⓓ happily

12 The path to the lake is straight for about a mile.

Ⓕ narrow
Ⓖ wide
Ⓗ crooked
Ⓙ dangerous

13 feeling excited

Ⓐ frightened
Ⓑ angry
Ⓒ calm
Ⓓ nervous

14 either road

Ⓕ neither
Ⓖ that
Ⓗ broad
Ⓙ which

Directions: For numbers 15-16, find the word that fits in both sentences. For 17 and 18, find the answer in which the underlined word is used the same as in the sentence in the box.

15 Is _______ meat better for you?

Don't _______ against the paint.

Ⓐ fresh
Ⓑ lean
Ⓒ fall
Ⓓ cheap

16 She got water from the _______ .

Are you feeling _______ ?

Ⓕ well
Ⓖ bottle
Ⓗ sick
Ⓙ hungry

17

Remember to sign your name.

In which sentence does the word sign mean the same thing as in the sentence above?

Ⓐ The sign blew down in the storm.
Ⓑ Robins are a sure sign of spring.
Ⓒ A small sign showed the way to the inn.
Ⓓ Did you sign the form yet?

18

How long will the storm last?

In which sentence does the word last mean the same thing as in the sentence above?

Ⓕ The movie will last until nine o'clock.
Ⓖ Is this the last orange?
Ⓗ The last part of the story is the best.
Ⓙ Rudy moved here last year.

GO

ANSWER ROWS 10 Ⓕ Ⓖ Ⓗ Ⓙ 12 Ⓕ Ⓖ Ⓗ Ⓙ 14 Ⓕ Ⓖ Ⓗ Ⓙ 16 Ⓕ Ⓖ Ⓗ Ⓙ 18 Ⓕ Ⓖ Ⓗ Ⓙ
11 Ⓐ Ⓑ Ⓒ Ⓓ 13 Ⓐ Ⓑ Ⓒ Ⓓ 15 Ⓐ Ⓑ Ⓒ Ⓓ 17 Ⓐ Ⓑ Ⓒ Ⓓ

Directions: For items 19-28, read the sentences, then find the answer that fits best in the blank in the sentence or means the same as an underlined word.

19 Jasmine wanted to ______ the offer.

Find the word that means Jasmine wanted to think about the offer.

Ⓐ exceed Ⓒ consider

Ⓑ dismiss Ⓓ align

20 Thick beams ______ the roof.

Which word means the beams held the roof up?

Ⓕ supported Ⓗ formed

Ⓖ weighed Ⓙ aligned

21 The horse approached the fence.

Approached means —

Ⓐ retreated Ⓒ jumped over

Ⓑ came near Ⓓ beyond

22 Do you recall who said that?

Recall means —

Ⓕ replace Ⓗ forget

Ⓖ dislike Ⓙ remember

The **(23)** ______ of the country went on strike. They wanted the **(24)** ______ to treat them more fairly.

23 Ⓐ citizens Ⓒ enemies

Ⓑ voices Ⓓ creatures

24 Ⓕ friend Ⓗ ruler

Ⓖ manager Ⓙ register

T.J.'s family took a **(25)** ______ vacation. It was a **(26)** ______ trip that lasted a month and included a raft trip down the Colorado River.

25 Ⓐ minor Ⓒ single

Ⓑ plain Ⓓ lengthy

26 Ⓕ certain Ⓗ refunded

Ⓖ wonderful Ⓙ profitable

The price of shoes was **(27)** ______ because of a holiday sale. Marnie **(28)** ______ to buy tennis and running shoes.

27 Ⓐ increased Ⓒ reduced

Ⓑ unchanged Ⓓ lost

28 Ⓕ decided Ⓗ loaded

Ⓖ avoided Ⓙ rested

STOP

ANSWER ROWS
19 Ⓐ Ⓑ Ⓒ Ⓓ 22 Ⓕ Ⓖ Ⓗ Ⓙ 25 Ⓐ Ⓑ Ⓒ Ⓓ 27 Ⓐ Ⓑ Ⓒ Ⓓ
20 Ⓕ Ⓖ Ⓗ Ⓙ 23 Ⓐ Ⓑ Ⓒ Ⓓ 26 Ⓕ Ⓖ Ⓗ Ⓙ 28 Ⓕ Ⓖ Ⓗ Ⓙ
21 Ⓐ Ⓑ Ⓒ Ⓓ 24 Ⓕ Ⓖ Ⓗ Ⓙ

NUMBER RIGHT ______

Lesson 7 Critical Reading

Examples

Directions: Read each item. Choose the answer you think is correct. Mark the space for your answer.

Yesterday morning, the governor signed the bill that will set aside five million dollars to improve state parks and hire school students to work in the parks during the summer.

A This sentence would most likely be found in a —

Ⓐ biography.

Ⓑ newspaper article.

Ⓒ fairy tale.

Ⓓ mystery.

If a question seems confusing, try restating it to yourself in simpler terms.

Practice

1 Arnold is reading a story called "The Dream of Space Travel". Which of these sentences would most likely be at the very end of the story?

Ⓐ The dream has not come true, but it might in the near future.

Ⓑ Before the first plane was invented, people dreamed of space travel.

Ⓒ Rockets were invented by the Chinese almost 1000 years ago.

Ⓓ Stories of travel through the heavens are told in many cultures.

2 Which of these would most likely be found in a mystery story?

Ⓕ The President lives in Washington.

Ⓖ Bears eat many different foods.

Ⓗ Dolores opened the door slowly, but no one was there.

Ⓙ Before you can fix a leaky roof, you must find the leak.

3 A student is reading this story about the West.

The wagon train stopped for the night. Nan and Marty unhitched the horses and tied them to a nearby tree. The horses had fresh grass to eat and cold water to drink from a spring.

Which sentence is most likely to come next?

Ⓐ It was morning, and there was much to do before they could start out.

Ⓑ The first horses were brought to America by Spanish explorers.

Ⓒ The cottonwood tree made a strange shadow in the moonlight.

Ⓓ The two children hurried back to the wagon to help prepare dinner.

STOP

ANSWER ROW A Ⓐ Ⓑ Ⓒ Ⓓ 1 Ⓐ Ⓑ Ⓒ Ⓓ 2 Ⓕ Ⓖ Ⓗ Ⓙ 3 Ⓐ Ⓑ Ⓒ Ⓓ

Lesson 8 Literal Comprehension

Examples

Directions: Read each passage. Choose the best answer for each question that follows the passage.

<table>
<tr>
<td>

"Have you seen my shoes?"

"No. Didn't you leave them on the porch because they were muddy?"

"I guess I did. I'll look there now. Don't leave without me."

</td>
<td>

A These people are probably —

Ⓐ coming home

Ⓑ resting

Ⓒ arguing

Ⓓ going out

</td>
</tr>
</table>

Skim the story and then read the questions. Refer back to the story to answer the questions.

Practice

"Do you hear something, Magda?"

"It sounds like a cat. Where could the noise be coming from?"

Magda and Mr. Howard went outside and looked to see what the noise was. They couldn't find anything. They looked under the car and behind the trash cans.

"Let's go back in, Magda. We can look around later if we hear the sound again."

"I want to look under the bush. Then I'll come in."

Magda crawled way under the bush beside the house. It was dark and she couldn't see very well. Just then, something furry crawled up against her face. Magda almost jumped out of her skin! It was a kitten, and it started licking her.

"Dad! Dad! Remember when you said I could have a kitten? I think my kitten just found me."

1 A bush is a kind of plant. Find another word that is <u>a kind of plant</u>.

Ⓐ rock Ⓑ tree Ⓒ garden

2 What caused Magda to "almost jump out of her skin"?

Ⓕ She heard something under the bush.

Ⓖ She wanted a kitten.

Ⓗ Something furry crawled up against her.

GO

ANSWER ROW A Ⓐ Ⓑ Ⓒ Ⓓ 1 Ⓐ Ⓑ Ⓒ 2 Ⓕ Ⓖ Ⓗ

"Mom, there's nothing to do. I'm bored."

"Why, Reggie, how can that be? We live in one of the biggest cities in the world. There are a million things for you to do. Why don't you walk down to the park?"

"That's really boring. Can I go over to Alida's? Aunt Millie said it's okay."

"That's a good idea. But go right over to the apartment. Don't stop in the video arcade like you usually do. I'll call Aunt Millie in about twenty minutes to check up on you."

Reggie grabbed his coat and hat and ran out the door and down the steps. He waited for the light to change, looked both ways, and crossed the street. There was always a lot of traffic on the street outside his apartment building, and he didn't want to get hit by a car.

He ran into the park and followed the path that went by the lake. Alida and her family lived on the other side of the park. Their apartment was almost a mile away, and he didn't want to waste time and worry his mother.

As Reggie passed the lake, he saw the strangest thing. A crowd of people was gathered around watching pirates row an old-fashioned boat on the lake!

Although he knew he should go right over to Alida's apartment, Reggie couldn't resist joining the crowd of people by the lake. When he got closer, he saw lots of lights, some cameras, and some people shouting orders at the pirates. It was very exciting, especially when the pirates got into a sword fight. None of them got hurt, of course, but one of them fell into the lake. Everyone got a good laugh at that.

After about ten minutes, Reggie suddenly remembered what he was supposed to be doing. He turned away from the crowd and started running down the path. If he hurried, he would still get to Alida's apartment before his mother called.

3 **Where do you think Reggie lives?**

Ⓐ On a quiet street

Ⓑ Near a river

Ⓒ On a busy street

Ⓓ Near the ocean

4 **Which of these statements is probably true about Reggie?**

Ⓕ He never does what his mother says.

Ⓖ His sister's name is Alida.

Ⓗ He often jogs in the park.

Ⓙ He likes to play video games.

5 **What made Reggie stop at the lake on his way to Alida's?**

Ⓐ Students who were practicing for a school play

Ⓑ A crowd watching pirates

Ⓒ Real pirates in the park

Ⓓ Some people getting ready for Halloween

6 **About how long does it usually take to get to Alida's apartment?**

Ⓕ Less than twenty minutes

Ⓖ More than twenty minutes

Ⓗ About five minutes

Ⓙ About thirty minutes

7 **What made Reggie remember what he was supposed to do?**

Ⓐ The sword fight

Ⓑ Seeing someone fall in the lake

Ⓒ Someone in the crowd

Ⓓ The story doesn't say.

8 **When he gets to Alida's house, Reggie will probably —**

Ⓕ make up a story explaining why he was late.

Ⓖ explain what happened in the park.

Ⓗ look for something to eat.

Ⓙ ask Alida what happened in the park that day.

STOP

ANSWER ROWS 3 Ⓐ Ⓑ Ⓒ Ⓓ 5 Ⓐ Ⓑ Ⓒ Ⓓ 7 Ⓐ Ⓑ Ⓒ Ⓓ

4 Ⓕ Ⓖ Ⓗ Ⓙ 6 Ⓕ Ⓖ Ⓗ Ⓙ 8 Ⓕ Ⓖ Ⓗ Ⓙ

Examples **Directions:** Read the passage. Find the best answer to each question that follows the passage.

Robbie got up early without anyone waking him. Today, he and the rest of the family were going fishing at Parker Lake. Robbie loved fishing, and Parker Lake had the best fishing around. They were going to rent a boat and spend the whole day on the lake. He was sure he would catch a big one.	**A How do you think Robbie feels?** Ⓐ Worried Ⓑ Proud Ⓒ Excited Ⓓ Disappointed

Look for key words in the question and the answer choices. They will help you find the correct answer.

Practice

Why should people drink milk?

Humans have probably been drinking milk for as long as they have been on earth. People who study the history of the world have found pictures from long, long ago that show people milking cows and using the milk for food.

Milk is the first food of babies. Animals that produce milk to feed their babies are called mammals. Their mother's milk is usually the best food for all young mammals.

The milk that people in America drink every day comes from cows, although many people prefer to drink the milk of goats. These two animals produce more milk than what their own babies need, and farmers collect the milk to sell it. In other countries, people also drink the milk of camels, horses, yaks, reindeer, sheep, and water buffaloes.

Milk is sometimes called the most nearly perfect food. It contains many of the things that humans need for healthy bodies, such as calcium, phosphorous, and protein. Milk also has several necessary vitamins and is easily digested by most humans. Another reason milk is such a good food is because some of its ingredients are found nowhere else in nature.

The one problem milk has is that it contains a lot of animal fat. This is good for young children, but not for adults. Foods with too much fat cause adults to have heart disease. Sometimes the fatty part of milk, the cream, is removed. This milk is called low-fat milk or skim milk. The cream that is removed from the milk is used to make ice cream and other foods. Milk is also used to make butter, cheese, and other dairy foods that people enjoy.

Besides being an important food, milk also provides chemicals that can be turned into other products. These chemicals are used to make paint, glue, cloth, and plastic.

1 Which phrase from the story describes how good milk is?

Ⓐ ...the first food of babies...

Ⓑ ...the most nearly perfect...

Ⓒ ...easily digested by most humans...

Ⓓ ...other dairy foods...

2 Milk is used for all of these things except—

Ⓕ butter.

Ⓖ fabric for clothing.

Ⓗ paint for a house.

Ⓙ automobile tires.

3 Look at the picture on page 25. The picture shows the children —

Ⓐ drinking milk.

Ⓑ eating something.

Ⓒ waiting for someone.

Ⓓ playing a game.

4 Most of the milk that we drink comes from—

Ⓕ wild animals.

Ⓖ big cities.

Ⓗ yaks and water buffaloes.

Ⓙ farm animals.

5 Which of these would be best for an adult?

Ⓐ Ice cream

Ⓑ Low-fat milk

Ⓒ Butter

Ⓓ Regular milk

6 What is a word from the story that means "something made from other things"?

Ⓕ Ingredient

Ⓖ Necessary

Ⓗ Product

Ⓙ Dairy

GO

ANSWER ROWS A Ⓐ Ⓑ Ⓒ Ⓓ 2 Ⓕ Ⓖ Ⓗ Ⓙ 4 Ⓕ Ⓖ Ⓗ Ⓙ 6 Ⓕ Ⓖ Ⓗ Ⓙ

1 Ⓐ Ⓑ Ⓒ Ⓓ 3 Ⓐ Ⓑ Ⓒ Ⓓ 5 Ⓐ Ⓑ Ⓒ Ⓓ

Graceful and Strong

Maria Tallchief was one of the most famous ballet dancers in the world. When she performed, the people in the audience loved to watch her dance. She was so graceful and so strong that she made the dancing look easy.

Born on an Osage Indian reservation in Oklahoma, Tallchief was given the name Betty Marie. Her mother thought the girl had special talents and tried to encourage them. When she was three, Tallchief began taking piano lessons. The next year, she started dance lessons even though most girls are not ready to start ballet until they are seven or eight years old. The young Tallchief did well in both piano and ballet.

Betty Marie's family moved to California so she and her sister could have more lessons. Betty Marie's teacher told her that a ballet dancer has to train harder than an athlete who plays football or baseball. Dance can be more challenging than any other sport, and Betty Marie worked as hard as she could.

Soon, Betty Marie's teachers told her she had to choose between ballet and piano. It was the only way she could develop her talent. She enjoyed both, but decided that she loved ballet more. When she was a teenager, she joined a Russian ballet group and changed her name. She thought Maria sounded more like a Russian name. She did not give up her Indian name, Tallchief.

Maria loved dancing, and people loved to watch her dance. She became famous all over the world. When Tallchief visited her home state of Oklahoma, the Osage Indian tribe made her a princess and performed Indian dances in her honor.

Tallchief continued to travel and dance, but she did not like being away from her family, especially her child. She stopped dancing to stay at home with her daughter. Later, Maria Tallchief started a ballet school to help other talented youngsters develop their dance skills. She wanted other girls to love ballet as much as she did.

7 Maria Tallchief's two talents in childhood were ___ and ___.

Ⓐ Singing and dancing.

Ⓑ Playing piano and singing.

Ⓒ Dancing and playing piano.

Ⓓ Acting and singing.

8 Which of these is an opinion in the story?

Ⓕ The Osage Indian reservation is in Oklahoma.

Ⓖ People loved to watch Maria Tallchief dance.

Ⓗ Maria Tallchief started a ballet school for young dancers.

Ⓙ Maria Tallchief changed her first name but would not change her last name.

9 You can tell from reading this selection that ballet dancers must be—

Ⓐ beautiful and very smart.

Ⓑ able to play the piano very well.

Ⓒ tall and have long hair.

Ⓓ strong and willing to work hard.

10 At different times in her life, Maria had to make hard choices. She gave up all of these things except one. What did she not give up?

Ⓕ Playing piano

Ⓖ Her family

Ⓗ Ballet

Ⓙ The name Betty Marie

11 Why did the Tallchief family move from Oklahoma to California?

Ⓐ To live with relatives

Ⓑ So Betty Marie's father could get a better job

Ⓒ To give Betty Marie a chance to change her name

Ⓓ So Betty Marie could have better ballet lessons

12 Betty Marie's teacher compares ballet to—

Ⓕ sports that are easy.

Ⓖ games that are fun.

Ⓗ playing a musical instrument.

Ⓙ sports that require hard work.

GO

ANSWER ROWS 7 Ⓐ Ⓑ Ⓒ Ⓓ 9 Ⓐ Ⓑ Ⓒ Ⓓ 11 Ⓐ Ⓑ Ⓒ Ⓓ
8 Ⓕ Ⓖ Ⓗ Ⓙ 10 Ⓕ Ⓖ Ⓗ Ⓙ 12 Ⓕ Ⓖ Ⓗ Ⓙ

An Elephant Grows Up

Sikar was a 7-year-old male elephant. He had lived happily with his mother, aunts, and cousins in their herd in Africa. Sikar ate leaves and grass. He was tall enough to reach tender leaves in the trees.

Sikar's family often traveled as far as fifty miles in a day. They walked to find food and water. Sikar loved to play games with the other elephant children. He liked to put his whole body in the water. The elephants took water in their trunks and sprayed themselves and each other. Then they used their trunks to cover themselves with dust. They didn't do it just to be dirty. The dust helped keep away insects. Sikar was as happy as a young elephant could be.

One day, his mother told him the herd was leaving, but Sikar could not go with them. He would have to stay or go off on his own. "But why, Mama?" cried Sikar. Big tears rolled down his dusty cheeks. His huge ears flapped. His wrinkled, gray face looked even more wrinkled. "I want to stay with you. I love you, Mama."

"I know, dear, but you are almost grown now. I have the other children to care for. You must go with the older males. Our herd has only females and young males. I will always love you, Sikar, but you must grow up now," Sikar's mother explained carefully.

Sikar sadly went to find the other male elephants. He saw two young males who had been in his herd last year. They looked for food together, ate, played in the water, and threw dirt on each other. They even fought a little, but only in play. It was fun not to have his mother watching and calling out to him to be careful. He was lonely at night, though.

Sikar gradually forgot his old herd. He had become a gentle giant, an African elephant who weighed six tons. One day, he passed the herd of mothers and young elephants and saw his mother. She was busy with her children, and he was busy looking for food. Sikar thought about her for a minute, but then went on his way. He enjoyed his new life, and now that he was old enough to want a family, he must find a mate of his own.

13 From this story, you can conclude that elephants —

Ⓐ always stay with the same herd.

Ⓑ stay away from the water.

Ⓒ don't play with one another.

Ⓓ are bothered by insects.

14 Why did Sikar not want to go with the male herd?

Ⓕ He did not like those elephants.

Ⓖ He did not want to leave his mother.

Ⓗ The food they found was not as good.

Ⓙ He was bigger than the other elephants.

15 Sikar became —

Ⓐ too hungry for his first herd.

Ⓑ separated by accident from his mother.

Ⓒ an unfriendly elephant.

Ⓓ too old for his first herd.

16 The boxes show some things that happened in the story.

Sikar's mother said he should leave.		Sikar wanted a family of his own.
1	2	3

Which of these belongs in box 2?

Ⓕ Sikar was lost in the jungle.

Ⓖ Sikar joined a new herd.

Ⓗ Sikar went to live with his mother agai

Ⓙ Sikar was found in the jungle.

17 This story was written to—

Ⓐ tell about how elephants live.

Ⓑ teach a lesson about mothers and children.

Ⓒ explain how elephants find food.

Ⓓ show how large elephants are.

18 By the end of the story, Sikar was —

Ⓕ still sad about leaving his mother.

Ⓖ afraid of the larger elephants.

Ⓗ less interested in his mother.

Ⓙ unhappy with his new life.

STOP

ANSWER ROWS 13 Ⓐ Ⓑ Ⓒ Ⓓ 15 Ⓐ Ⓑ Ⓒ Ⓓ 17 Ⓐ Ⓑ Ⓒ Ⓓ

14 Ⓕ Ⓖ Ⓗ Ⓙ 16 Ⓕ Ⓖ Ⓗ Ⓙ 18 Ⓕ Ⓖ Ⓗ Ⓙ

Examples

Directions: Read the passage. Find the best answer to each question that follows the passage.

E1

The balloon pilot turned on the burner. There was a huge whooshing sound and the balloon began to fill with hot air. Soon it started to rise into the air. In about fifteen minutes, it would be full, and they could take off.

The balloon is being filled with —

Ⓐ helium.

Ⓑ cold air.

Ⓒ hot air.

Ⓓ burning gas.

The way people entertain themselves in America has certainly changed in recent years. It was only about a hundred years ago that reading, singing, dancing, and playing musical instruments were all people had to amuse themselves. Then along came radio, and people didn't have to amuse themselves at all. They could simply listen and someone else would entertain them.

Motion pictures were the next great form of entertainment, and people could see and hear actors performing on the "big screen" in theaters around the country. The "small screen," television, soon made its way into almost every home, and people didn't even have to leave their couch to enjoy themselves. Video games and computers are the latest forms of entertainment technology, and who knows what inventions will be in our living rooms tomorrow.

1 This story is mostly about —

Ⓐ entertainers.

Ⓑ television and radio.

Ⓒ forms of entertainment.

Ⓓ technology.

2 Which of these came first?

Ⓕ Computers

Ⓖ Motion pictures

Ⓗ Television

Ⓙ Radio

For Number 3, choose the best answer to the question.

3 The giant picked up the two children and said, "Gosh, you've been so nice to me. What can I do to thank you?"

This sentence would most likely be found in a —

Ⓐ fairy tale.

Ⓑ biography.

Ⓒ newspaper article.

Ⓓ mystery story.

GO

How did Lilia feel about visiting her grandmother?

Lilia tried hard to keep the tears from filling her large, brown eyes. She felt like a heavy lump was in her chest. School was out, and all her friends were happily planning swimming lessons and family vacations. Lilia's mother had just told her she would have to go far away to spend the summer at Grandmother's. Lilia loved Grandmother, but she would be lonely without her family and friends in the neighborhood.

Lilia's mother put her arms around Lilia and brushed back her long, dark hair. Mrs. McGill had been sick and needed a great deal of rest this summer. Grandmother would take good care of Lilia, and she would come home at the end of summer. Everything would be better then. Lilia sniffed and nodded. She knew her mother was right, but she was still sad.

On the day she arrived, Lilia tried to find something wrong at Grandmother's house, but she couldn't. It had flowers, trees, and a white fence. Grandmother baked bread and cooked the same kind of food that Lilia's mother made at home. Grandmother smiled and told her, "I'm so glad you've come, Lilia."

Grandmother showed Lilia her pet bird, Bitsy, and the dog, Charley. Bitsy chirped at her, and Charley brought his ball for Lilia to throw.

That afternoon, Lilia saw some children next door. She asked Grandmother about them. Grandmother said, "Oh, that's Sally and her brother, Sid. They are twins, and they are the same age as you. I know you'll get along and play together. Their mother and I have lots of things planned for the three of you."

Lilia smiled. She would miss her family and friends back home, but this might be a good summer after all!

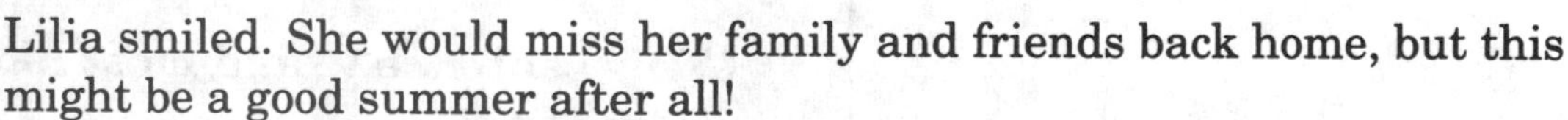

GO

4 In the story, Lilia felt—

Ⓕ sad and then happy.

Ⓖ sad all through the story.

Ⓗ happy and then disappointed.

Ⓙ happy all through the story.

5 This story is written to show—

Ⓐ children have a hard time when their parents are sick.

Ⓑ things often work out better than you think at first.

Ⓒ a child can never be happy away from home for the summer.

Ⓓ grandmothers are not as much fun as mothers.

6 Lilia's grandmother had—

Ⓕ no children as neighbors.

Ⓖ a small house with no yard.

Ⓗ a swimming pool in her back yard.

Ⓙ a bird and a dog for pets.

7 Lilia was a girl who—

Ⓐ tried not to show her mother that she was sad.

Ⓑ did not get along with other children her own age.

Ⓒ was rude to her grandmother when she went to visit.

Ⓓ complained because she was unhappy going to her grandmother's.

8 Why did Lilia smile in the last paragraph?

Ⓕ She knew she would be spending the summer at her own home.

Ⓖ She didn't want Grandmother to see her cry.

Ⓗ She knew she would be happy being away from home.

Ⓙ She loved animals, and Grandmother had two pets.

9 Which words in the story show that Grandmother was trying to make things fun for Lilia?

Ⓐ ...Lilia saw some children next door...

Ⓑ She would miss her family and friends back home...

Ⓒ Their mother and I have lots of things planned...

Ⓓ ... this might be a good summer...

10 Which would be a good title for this story?

Ⓕ My Grandmother

Ⓖ A Surprising Summer

Ⓗ New Friends

Ⓙ Bitsy and Charley

GO

ANSWER ROWS 4 Ⓕ Ⓖ Ⓗ Ⓙ 6 Ⓕ Ⓖ Ⓗ Ⓙ 8 Ⓕ Ⓖ Ⓗ Ⓙ 10 Ⓕ Ⓖ Ⓗ Ⓙ
5 Ⓐ Ⓑ Ⓒ Ⓓ 7 Ⓐ Ⓑ Ⓒ Ⓓ 9 Ⓐ Ⓑ Ⓒ Ⓓ

Lucy sat very still as the plane took off. She liked flying, but always felt a little funny when the plane took off and landed. This plane was smaller than any other she had ever been on, and she didn't know what it would be like.

The take-off was smooth, and in a few minutes, they were flying high above the ground. All around them, Lucy could see the ocean.

The plane headed south from Miami toward Key West. Lucy, her mother, and her two brothers were going there to visit her father. He was in the Coast Guard and was stationed in Key West.

Lucy looked out the window and saw a chain of islands. Her mother said they were the Florida Keys. A road and a series of bridges connected the islands. Key West was the last island in the chain.

"Mom, how come they are called keys?"

"It's from the Spanish word *cayo*, which means island or reef. The first European explorers here were from Spain."

The water below had lots of different colors. The deepest water was dark blue, and along the shore, it was very light. In between, there were many shades of blue. On this background of blue were lots of boats, some with sails and some with motors. As the boats moved across the surface, they left streaks of white in their wake.

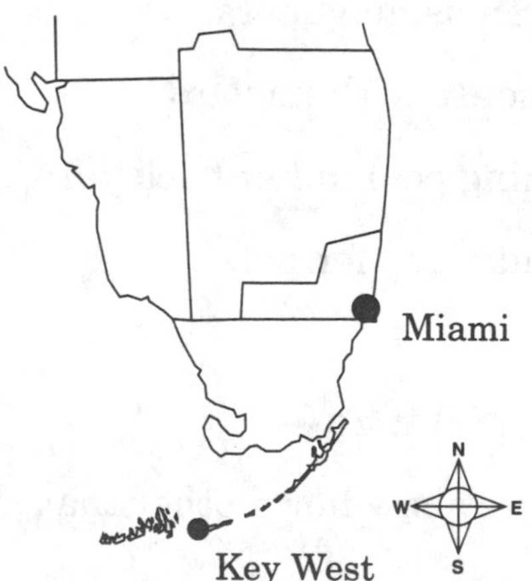

Lucy heard the sound of the engines change and the plane started its descent. In a few minutes, she would see her father for the first time in weeks. It would also be the beginning of a vacation she would remember forever.

11 Which of these is true about Lucy?

Ⓐ She had never flown on a plane before.

Ⓑ She was afraid of flying.

Ⓒ She often flies on small planes.

Ⓓ She had never flown on a plane this small before.

12 When Lucy flies back to Miami, in which direction will she travel?

Ⓕ North

Ⓖ South

Ⓗ East

Ⓙ West

13 How did Lucy first know the plane was about to land?

Ⓐ She saw the airport.

Ⓑ The pilot turned the plane toward the airport.

Ⓒ The sound of the engines changed.

Ⓓ The pilot made an announcement over the intercom.

14 What can you conclude about the water around the Florida Keys?

Ⓕ Deeper water is lighter in color than shallow water.

Ⓖ Deeper water is darker in color than shallow water.

Ⓗ It seems to be very rough.

Ⓙ It seems to be very calm.

15 Why was Lucy going to Key West?

Ⓐ To visit her father

Ⓑ To visit her mother

Ⓒ To move there

Ⓓ To go to school there

16 What kinds of things do you think Lucy will do in Key West?

Ⓕ Climb mountains, ski, and go ice skating

Ⓖ Stay inside and watch television because it is cold

Ⓗ Swim, ride in a boat, and lie on the beach

Ⓙ Visit farms and ride on a tractor

ANSWER ROWS 11 Ⓐ Ⓑ Ⓒ Ⓓ 13 Ⓐ Ⓑ Ⓒ Ⓓ 15 Ⓐ Ⓑ Ⓒ Ⓓ
12 Ⓕ Ⓖ Ⓗ Ⓙ 14 Ⓕ Ⓖ Ⓗ Ⓙ 16 Ⓕ Ⓖ Ⓗ Ⓙ

NUMBER RIGHT ______

Name and Answer Sheet

To the Student:

These tests will give you a chance to put the tips you have learned to work.

A few last reminders…

- Be sure you understand all the directions before you begin each test. You may ask the teacher questions about the directions if you do not understand them.
- Work as quickly as you can during each test.
- When you change an answer, be sure to erase your first mark completely.
- You can guess at an answer or skip difficult items and go back to them later.
- Use the tips you have learned whenever you can.
- It is OK to be a little nervous. You may even do better.

Now that you have completed the lessons in this unit, you are on your way to scoring high!

STUDENT'S NAME

LAST | FIRST | MI

(Each of the 18 name columns: ◯ A B C D E F G H I J K L M N O P Q R S T U V W X Y Z)

SCHOOL

TEACHER

FEMALE ◯ MALE ◯

BIRTH DATE

MONTH	DAY		YEAR	
JAN ◯	0	0		0
FEB ◯	1	1		1
MAR ◯	2	2		2
APR ◯	3	3		3
MAY ◯		4		4
JUN ◯		5	5	5
JUL ◯		6	6	6
AUG ◯		7	7	7
SEP ◯		8	8	8
OCT ◯		9	9	9
NOV ◯				
DEC ◯				

GRADE

② ③ ④

PART 1 VOCABULARY

E1 Ⓐ Ⓑ Ⓒ Ⓓ
E2 Ⓕ Ⓖ Ⓗ Ⓙ
E3 Ⓐ Ⓑ Ⓒ Ⓓ
1 Ⓐ Ⓑ Ⓒ Ⓓ
2 Ⓕ Ⓖ Ⓗ Ⓙ
3 Ⓐ Ⓑ Ⓒ Ⓓ
4 Ⓕ Ⓖ Ⓗ Ⓙ
5 Ⓐ Ⓑ Ⓒ Ⓓ
6 Ⓕ Ⓖ Ⓗ Ⓙ
7 Ⓐ Ⓑ Ⓒ Ⓓ
8 Ⓕ Ⓖ Ⓗ Ⓙ
9 Ⓐ Ⓑ Ⓒ Ⓓ
10 Ⓕ Ⓖ Ⓗ Ⓙ
11 Ⓐ Ⓑ Ⓒ Ⓓ
12 Ⓕ Ⓖ Ⓗ Ⓙ
13 Ⓐ Ⓑ Ⓒ Ⓓ
14 Ⓕ Ⓖ Ⓗ Ⓙ
15 Ⓐ Ⓑ Ⓒ Ⓓ
16 Ⓕ Ⓖ Ⓗ Ⓙ
17 Ⓐ Ⓑ Ⓒ Ⓓ
18 Ⓕ Ⓖ Ⓗ Ⓙ
19 Ⓐ Ⓑ Ⓒ Ⓓ
20 Ⓕ Ⓖ Ⓗ Ⓙ
21 Ⓐ Ⓑ Ⓒ Ⓓ
22 Ⓕ Ⓖ Ⓗ Ⓙ
23 Ⓐ Ⓑ Ⓒ Ⓓ
24 Ⓕ Ⓖ Ⓗ Ⓙ
25 Ⓐ Ⓑ Ⓒ Ⓓ
26 Ⓕ Ⓖ Ⓗ Ⓙ
27 Ⓐ Ⓑ Ⓒ Ⓓ
28 Ⓕ Ⓖ Ⓗ Ⓙ

PART 2 READING COMPREHENSION

E1 Ⓐ Ⓑ Ⓒ Ⓓ
1 Ⓐ Ⓑ Ⓒ Ⓓ
2 Ⓕ Ⓖ Ⓗ Ⓙ
3 Ⓐ Ⓑ Ⓒ Ⓓ
4 Ⓕ Ⓖ Ⓗ Ⓙ
5 Ⓐ Ⓑ Ⓒ Ⓓ
6 Ⓕ Ⓖ Ⓗ Ⓙ
7 Ⓐ Ⓑ Ⓒ Ⓓ
8 Ⓕ Ⓖ Ⓗ Ⓙ
9 Ⓐ Ⓑ Ⓒ Ⓓ
10 Ⓕ Ⓖ Ⓗ Ⓙ
11 Ⓐ Ⓑ Ⓒ Ⓓ
12 Ⓕ Ⓖ Ⓗ Ⓙ
13 Ⓐ Ⓑ Ⓒ Ⓓ
14 Ⓕ Ⓖ Ⓗ Ⓙ
15 Ⓐ Ⓑ Ⓒ Ⓓ
16 Ⓕ Ⓖ Ⓗ Ⓙ
17 Ⓐ Ⓑ Ⓒ Ⓓ
18 Ⓕ Ⓖ Ⓗ Ⓙ
19 Ⓐ Ⓑ Ⓒ Ⓓ
20 Ⓕ Ⓖ Ⓗ Ⓙ
21 Ⓐ Ⓑ Ⓒ Ⓓ
22 Ⓕ Ⓖ Ⓗ Ⓙ
23 Ⓐ Ⓑ Ⓒ Ⓓ
24 Ⓕ Ⓖ Ⓗ Ⓙ

Part 1 Vocabulary

Examples

Directions: For items E1 and 1-9, read the phrase with the underlined word. Find the word that means the same or almost the same. For item E2, mark the answer that is the opposite of the underlined word. For item E3, find the word that best fits in both sentences.

E1 a huge rock

Ⓐ heavy
Ⓑ long
Ⓒ large
Ⓓ small

E2 borrow a pen

Ⓕ steal
Ⓖ lend
Ⓗ lose
Ⓙ find

E3 Do you _______ oranges?

Jim has a bicycle just _______ mine.

Ⓐ enjoy
Ⓑ about
Ⓒ squeeze
Ⓓ like

1 nasty weather

Ⓐ bad
Ⓑ pleasant
Ⓒ normal
Ⓓ acceptable

2 give commands

Ⓕ presents
Ⓖ statements
Ⓗ changes
Ⓙ orders

3 stay home

Ⓐ allow
Ⓑ remain
Ⓒ respond
Ⓓ leave

4 Her business is reliable.

Ⓕ dependable
Ⓖ successful
Ⓗ crowded
Ⓙ new

5 Are you certain about that?

Ⓐ happy
Ⓑ unsure
Ⓒ sure
Ⓓ sad

6 a cautious person

Ⓕ annoying
Ⓖ friendly
Ⓗ careful
Ⓙ healthy

7 to display a picture

Ⓐ paint
Ⓑ show
Ⓒ buy
Ⓓ sell

8 To be frail is to be —

Ⓕ weak
Ⓖ strong
Ⓗ lost
Ⓙ confused

9 To discard is to —

Ⓐ find
Ⓑ trip over
Ⓒ lose
Ⓓ throw away

STOP

Directions: For items 10-14, read the phrase with the underlined word. Find the word that means the opposite of the underlined word.

10 That trail might be dangerous.

Ⓕ expensive
Ⓖ enjoyable
Ⓗ foolish
Ⓙ safe

11 The group stayed together at the zoo.

Ⓐ close
Ⓑ far away
Ⓒ apart
Ⓓ with one another

12 The story about the family of bears made Ted smile.

Ⓕ frown
Ⓖ grin
Ⓗ feel good
Ⓙ feel amused

13 a cool evening

Ⓐ drink
Ⓑ friend
Ⓒ morning
Ⓓ product

14 allow a visit

Ⓕ permit
Ⓖ make
Ⓗ conduct
Ⓙ forbid

Directions: For numbers 15-16, find the word that fits in both sentences. For numbers 17-18, find the answer in which the underlined word is used the same as in the sentence in the box.

15 The swim ______ took place on Saturday morning at nine.

Where did you ______ Sandra?

Ⓐ meet
Ⓑ find
Ⓒ see
Ⓓ match

16 Can you ______ in the ocean?

Our ______ led the parade.

Ⓕ swim
Ⓖ band
Ⓗ dive
Ⓙ float

17

My back was sore after the game.

In which sentence does the word back mean the same thing as in the sentence above?

Ⓐ Come back when you have finished.
Ⓑ The dog is in back of the house.
Ⓒ The pack on her back was heavy.
Ⓓ The light in the back room is on.

18

How much did that stamp cost?

In which sentence does the word stamp mean the same thing as in the sentence above?

Ⓕ Stamp your name on this form.
Ⓖ This machine can stamp metal.
Ⓗ A horse will often stamp its feet.
Ⓙ There's no stamp on the envelope.

GO

Directions: Read the sentences with the blanks. Choose the answer that fits best in the sentence or means the same as the underlined word.

19 We can all ______ the hall.

Find the word that means to make the hall beautiful.

Ⓐ visit Ⓒ decorate

Ⓑ replace Ⓓ attend

20 That light is too ______ for reading.

Which word means the light wasn't very bright?

Ⓕ dim Ⓗ harsh

Ⓖ high Ⓙ shallow

21 The picnic will have to be <u>delayed</u>. <u>Delayed</u> means —

Ⓐ started Ⓒ planned

Ⓑ postponed Ⓓ enjoyed

22 Did Brenda <u>reply</u> to your question? <u>Reply</u> means —

Ⓕ accept Ⓗ startle

Ⓖ harness Ⓙ answer

The dinner you served was **(23)** . We are grateful you remembered us. We'll **(24)** you to our house soon.

23 Ⓐ extended Ⓒ delicious

Ⓑ realized Ⓓ famous

24 Ⓕ invite Ⓗ enjoy

Ⓖ accept Ⓙ frequent

The manager was **(25)** with what the workers did. They finished on time and also saved a great deal of money for the **(26)** .

25 Ⓐ disappointed Ⓒ busy

Ⓑ happy Ⓓ confusing

26 Ⓕ company Ⓗ reasons

Ⓖ benefit Ⓙ acceptance

Be sure to **(27)** Clark Street. There's been an accident and traffic is **(28)** than usual.

27 Ⓐ travel Ⓒ wait

Ⓑ standard Ⓓ avoid

28 Ⓕ almost Ⓗ moving

Ⓖ heavier Ⓙ nearby

STOP

Part 2 Reading Comprehension

Directions: Read each passage, then answer each question. You can look back to the passage to answer the questions.

E1

The cat was curled up in a tiny ball beside the fire. When she heard Martin walk into the room, she opened one eye first and then the other. Domino slowly stood up and stretched. She blinked twice and followed him toward the kitchen.

The cat was probably —

Ⓐ playing.
Ⓑ hunting.
Ⓒ purring.
Ⓓ sleeping.

The travelers found themselves in a forest of talking trees. Just then, all the trees began talking at once. They were so loud that it was impossible to understand what they were saying.

1 Which sentence is most likely to come next in the story?

Ⓐ Once upon a time a group of travelers started on a long journey.
Ⓑ No one knew where they were and they became frightened.
Ⓒ Suddenly, the biggest tree said, "Quiet, everyone!"
Ⓓ The outside of the trunk of a tree is called the bark.

What I remember most about that big old house in Iowa was the kitchen, a room that was always warm and always smelled wonderful.

2 This sentence would most likely be found in —

Ⓕ a newspaper article.
Ⓖ an autobiography.
Ⓗ a fairy tale.
Ⓙ a science book.

3 Which of these would most likely be found in a newspaper article?

Ⓐ "Now hold on there," said the sheriff, "we don't put up with things like that in this town."
Ⓑ It wasn't a star they were looking at, but a spaceship, and it was coming right at them.
Ⓒ Guido said good-bye to his family, picked up his bags, and joined the crowd walking toward the ship.
Ⓓ A recent report from the school board stated that there are more students in school than ever before.

4 Sally is reading a book called *Home Gardening for Young People*. Which of these sentences would most likely be at the beginning of the book?

Ⓕ After you have planted the seeds, you'll have to keep them watered so they don't dry out.
Ⓖ Few things are as rewarding as tending a garden.
Ⓗ Now comes the fun part, eating the vegetables you have raised.
Ⓙ The most difficult part of having a garden is making sure that weeds don't take over.

Last Sunday, my dog Buddy started scratching his face. Pretty soon, it was red and sore. I was really worried.

"Mom, something is wrong with Buddy. Look at his face."

"This doesn't look very good, Lucas. Let's put some medicine on it and see what happens. If it doesn't get any better, we'll have to take him to the doctor."

I rubbed the medicine on Buddy's face and was very careful not to get it into his eyes. He didn't like it very much, but he held still for me.

The next day, he was even worse, so Dad stayed home from work, and he and I took Buddy to the veterinarian. The doctor examined Buddy and gave us some pills. We had to give them to Buddy three times a day. The doctor said it would be easiest if we mixed it into food or a treat. The doctor also gave us a special collar that would keep Buddy from scratching his face. When we put the collar on, Buddy looked like a clown, but I felt bad for him.

I gave Buddy his medicine every day just like the doctor said. For a day or two it didn't seem to help. Then Buddy stopped trying to scratch his face. Pretty soon, his face started to get better.

A week later, my Aunt Janelle and I took Buddy back to the doctor. He examined Buddy again and said he was okay. The veterinarian thought that Buddy had an allergy, kind of like when I start to sneeze when Dad cuts the lawn. He said we should keep an eye on Buddy to see if we could find out what he was allergic to. If we found out, we could avoid it in the future.

GO

5 How do you think Lucas felt at the end of the story?

Ⓐ Worried because Buddy had an allergy

Ⓑ Happy because Buddy had an allergy

Ⓒ Disappointed because the doctor couldn't fix the problem

Ⓓ Relieved because Buddy was getting better

6 Who is telling this story?

Ⓕ Lucas

Ⓖ Buddy

Ⓗ Aunt Janelle

Ⓙ The doctor

7 What made Buddy look like a clown?

Ⓐ Scratches on his nose

Ⓑ The medicine on his face

Ⓒ A special collar

Ⓓ The pills

8 We know that Lucas is a responsible person because he —

Ⓕ rode in the car to the doctor with Aunt Janelle.

Ⓖ gave Buddy his medicine every day.

Ⓗ tried to get to school on time.

Ⓙ felt bad because Lucas had to wear a funny collar.

9 A lesson you can learn from this story is to —

Ⓐ avoid cutting the grass when the wind is blowing.

Ⓑ keep dogs inside as much as possible.

Ⓒ avoid things to which you are allergic.

Ⓓ be careful when you put a new collar on a dog or cat.

He Changed the World

"Chris. Christopher. Chris-to-pher! Come home for dinner!" Chris heard his mother's voice, and walked home slowly. He was watching a ship in the harbor near his home. The sailors were unloading wonderful things that had been brought from far away. There were mysterious bundles and smells that Chris did not recognize. The ship had just come from Asia. The sailors were sunburned and happy. They talked to the young boy on the dock.

When he reached his home, Christopher told his mother, "A ship just came in. It was wonderful. When I grow up, I want to be a sailor. I want to go places and see things."

The boy was Christopher Columbus. He lived in Genoa, Italy, a city by the sea. Genoa was one of the busiest seaports in the world when Chris was born in 1451. He did become a sailor when he was a teenager, and he did see the world.

In the 1400s, ships carried things from Asia to Italy and other places. They brought jewels, ivory, silks, and spices. The ships carried the goods part of the way, and then they had to be unloaded so camels and other animals could carry everything across land. Then the goods would be loaded on another ship to finish the trip.

Christopher Columbus thought he could find a way to go all the way to Asia by water. Many people in his time thought the earth was flat, but he thought it was round. He wanted to sail west to reach Asia. If Columbus could find a new, shorter route to Asia, he would become rich and famous.

Columbus was not poor, but he did not have the money to buy ships for such a trip. He couldn't find any money in his own country. He went to the king and queen of Spain, Ferdinand and Isabella. They first said no, but they changed their minds. They agreed to buy Columbus three ships and give him money to make his trip.

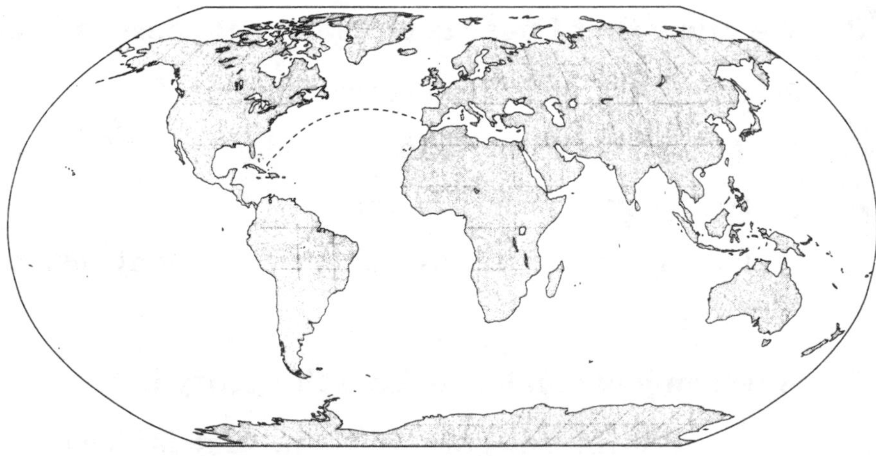

After being at sea for two difficult months and facing many dangers, Columbus saw land. He and his sailors thought they had arrived in Asia and were very excited. They had not found Asia, however. Instead, they had reached the New World, what we now call America. Columbus never got rich, but many others followed. He had changed the world forever.

10 Why didn't Christopher Columbus sail in his own ships?

Ⓕ The king would not let him.

Ⓖ He couldn't find any sailors for his ships.

Ⓗ Only kings and queens could own ships.

Ⓙ He didn't have enough money.

11 This story was written to tell the reader—

Ⓐ how Columbus spent his fortune.

Ⓑ about sailing ships in the 1400s.

Ⓒ about ships going to Asia.

Ⓓ how Columbus achieved his dream.

12 What word in the story means "difficult to explain, strange, unusual"?

Ⓕ Mysterious

Ⓖ Recognize

Ⓗ Explorer

Ⓙ Seaport

13 Christopher became interested in sailing because —

Ⓐ his father was a sailor.

Ⓑ he dreamed about an adventure.

Ⓒ he lived by the sea.

Ⓓ his family owned ships.

14 What mistake did Christopher Columbus and his sailors make?

Ⓕ They sailed in a circle and landed in Europe.

Ⓖ They found Asia instead of America.

Ⓗ They found America instead of Asia.

Ⓙ They had not really found land.

15 Which of these does this story lead you to believe?

Ⓐ Columbus did not know about Asia when he left Spain.

Ⓑ Columbus did not know about the New World when he left Spain.

Ⓒ The king and queen made Columbus a rich man.

Ⓓ Columbus knew the world was flat but tried anyway.

16 Which of these is most like what happened in the story?

Ⓕ Bridgette was looking for her homework and found a ring she had lost a week ago.

Ⓖ Andrew enjoys sailing and hopes to own a boat when he grows up.

Ⓗ Kate and her family planned a vacation carefully and really enjoyed their trip to a national park.

Ⓙ Jake surprised his sister by giving her a party on her birthday.

Schedule for Camp Tonawanabee

Week of July 8 - 13

Eight and nine-year-old campers should check in at camp office between 12 noon and 5 P.M., July 7.

7:00 - 8:30	Wake up, breakfast, clean up
8:30 - 9:30	Boys' swimming Girls' basketball
9:30 - 10:00	Break
10:00 - 11:00	Boys' basketball Girls' swimming
11:00 - 12:30	Lunch, rest
12:30 - 1:30	Crafts for 8-year-olds Ping-pong for 9-year-olds
1:30 - 2:30	Ping-pong for 8-year-olds Crafts for 9-year-olds
2:30 - 3:00	Break
3:00 - 4:00	Horseshoes
4:00 - 5:00	Hiking
5:00 - 6:30	Dinner, rest
6:30 - 7:30	Softball or volleyball
7:30 - 8:30	Movie or group singing
8:30 - 9:00	Cabin meetings, snacks
9:00 - 9:30	Ready for bed, lights out

For more information, call Marissa Johnson at 903-555-1214.

Counselors for 8-year-olds:
Adam Sands, head counselor, boys;
Jack Smithey; Charlie Carlson.
Mary Jones, head counselor, girls;
Sue Martin; Ericka Stevens

Counselors for 9-year-olds:
Joe Johnson, head counselor, boys;
Cedric White; Aaron Lang.
Lisa Gomez, head counselor, girls;
Heather Case; Shalonda Moore

17 At what time do the boys have swimming?

Ⓐ 8:00 - 9:00

Ⓑ 8:30 - 9:30

Ⓒ 10:00 - 11:00

Ⓓ 1:30 - 2:30

18 Which of these activities is <u>not</u> in the morning?

Ⓕ Swimming

Ⓖ Crafts

Ⓗ Breakfast

Ⓙ Basketball

19 Sylvester is a 9-year-old boy. He started a braided leather key chain in crafts class on Tuesday. At what time on Wednesday will he go to crafts again to finish it?

Ⓐ 11:30 - 12:30

Ⓑ 12:30 - 1:30

Ⓒ 1:30 - 2:30

Ⓓ 3:00 - 4:00

20 What are the rest times for all campers?

Ⓕ After lunch and after dinner

Ⓖ Before lunch and after dinner

Ⓗ Before lunch and before dinner

Ⓙ After lunch and before dinner

21 Whom would you call for more information about the camp?

Ⓐ Marissa Johnson

Ⓑ Joe Johnson

Ⓒ Mary Jones

Ⓓ Charlie Carlson

22 Eight-year-old Toby and 9-year-old Tina are a brother and sister going to Camp Tonawanabee this summer. Which activity will they have together?

Ⓕ Crafts

Ⓖ Ping-pong

Ⓗ Hiking

Ⓙ Swimming

23 Who is the head counselor for 9-year-old girls?

Ⓐ Joe Johnson

Ⓑ Mary Jones

Ⓒ Sue Martin

Ⓓ Lisa Gomez

24 Which of these happens last?

Ⓕ Basketball

Ⓖ Boy's swimming

Ⓗ Ping-pong

Ⓙ Softball

STOP

Table of Contents
Language

UNIT 1 LANGUAGE MECHANICS

Lesson 1 Capitalization

Examples **Directions:** Mark the answer that shows the correct capitalization.

A	School Ⓐ	will start Ⓑ	in september. Ⓒ	None Ⓓ

B That dress was worn by ________ .

Ⓕ Queen elizabeth
Ⓖ Queen Elizabeth
Ⓗ queen Elizabeth
Ⓙ queen elizabeth

Sentences and proper nouns begin with capital letters.
If no capital letters are missing, mark the space for "None."

Practice

1	she went Ⓐ	to the beach Ⓑ	last week. Ⓒ	None Ⓓ
2	The name Ⓕ	of the book Ⓖ	is A Terrible Storm. Ⓗ	None Ⓙ
3	Which part Ⓐ	of france Ⓑ	did you like best? Ⓒ	None Ⓓ

4 My ________ came to visit during the holiday.

Ⓕ Best friend
Ⓖ best Friend
Ⓗ Best Friend
Ⓙ best friend

5 Did you walk to school on ________ ?

Ⓐ Friday morning
Ⓑ friday morning
Ⓒ friday Morning
Ⓓ Friday Morning

GO

ANSWER ROWS **A** Ⓐ Ⓑ Ⓒ Ⓓ **1** Ⓐ Ⓑ Ⓒ Ⓓ **3** Ⓐ Ⓑ Ⓒ Ⓓ **5** Ⓐ Ⓑ Ⓒ Ⓓ
B Ⓕ Ⓖ Ⓗ Ⓙ **2** Ⓕ Ⓖ Ⓗ Ⓙ **4** Ⓕ Ⓖ Ⓗ Ⓙ

Lesson 2 Punctuation

Examples

Directions: Mark the answer that shows the correct punctuation.

A Who said it was going to rain today?

Ⓐ . Ⓑ , Ⓒ ! Ⓓ None

B
Ⓕ The gray cat watched
Ⓖ the birds outside Her
Ⓗ tail curled back and forth
Ⓙ *(No mistakes)*

First look for missing punctuation at the end of the sentence. Then look for missing punctuation inside the sentence.

If the punctuation is correct, mark the space for "None" or "No mistakes."

Practice

1 The books are on the shelf

Ⓐ . Ⓑ , Ⓒ ? Ⓓ None

2 Where did you put the bag of groceries?

Ⓕ . Ⓖ , Ⓗ ! Ⓙ None

3 Close the door quickly or the cat will get out

Ⓐ . Ⓑ ! Ⓒ ? Ⓓ None

STOP

4 The pizza ________ ready so we had to wait for a while.

Ⓕ wasn't
Ⓖ wasnt
Ⓗ wasnt'
Ⓙ was'nt

5
Ⓐ The gardener planted
Ⓑ tulips roses and daisies
Ⓒ along the sidewalk.
Ⓓ *(No mistakes)*

STOP

ANSWER ROWS
A Ⓐ Ⓑ Ⓒ Ⓓ 1 Ⓐ Ⓑ Ⓒ Ⓓ 3 Ⓐ Ⓑ Ⓒ Ⓓ 5 Ⓐ Ⓑ Ⓒ Ⓓ
B Ⓕ Ⓖ Ⓗ Ⓙ 2 Ⓕ Ⓖ Ⓗ Ⓙ 4 Ⓕ Ⓖ Ⓗ Ⓙ

Lesson 3 Capitalization and Punctuation

Examples

Directions: Mark the answer that shows the correct capitalization and punctuation. Mark the space "Correct as it is" if the underlined part is correct.

A
Ⓐ Which coat is yours?
Ⓑ Mine is the red one
Ⓒ where did you buy it?
Ⓓ Hang your coat in the closet?

(B) Winning the race won't be easy.

B
Ⓕ Won't
Ⓖ wont'
Ⓗ Wont'
Ⓙ Correct as it is

First think about capitalization errors in the sentence. Then think about punctuation errors.

Remember, choose the answer that is correct.

Practice

1
Ⓐ Which State is the largest?
Ⓑ South carolina has great beaches.
Ⓒ My grandmother spent the night in Chicago Illinois.
Ⓓ The driver knew she was a few hours from Houston, Texas.

2
Ⓕ we can all meet at the park.
Ⓖ Teresa said her brothers want to play with us
Ⓗ Did you remember the basketball?
Ⓙ Randy will be a little late?

---

(3) August 10, 1994

Dear Irma,

The lake is warm enough for swimming. I hope you will come up soon for a visit.

(4) Your Friend
Enrique

3
Ⓐ August 10 1994
Ⓑ August, 10, 1994
Ⓒ august 10, 1994
Ⓓ Correct as it is

4
Ⓕ Your friend,
Ⓖ Your Friend,
Ⓗ your friend,
Ⓙ Correct as it is

GO

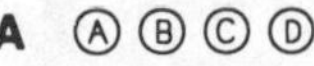

ANSWER ROWS A Ⓐ Ⓑ Ⓒ Ⓓ 1 Ⓐ Ⓑ Ⓒ Ⓓ 3 Ⓐ Ⓑ Ⓒ Ⓓ
B Ⓕ Ⓖ Ⓗ Ⓙ 2 Ⓕ Ⓖ Ⓗ Ⓙ 4 Ⓕ Ⓖ Ⓗ Ⓙ

5 The _______ tail started to wag when we walked into the room.

Ⓐ puppys
Ⓑ puppy's
Ⓒ puppies
Ⓓ puppie's

6 A _______ usually has many traffic problems.

Ⓕ Large City
Ⓖ large City
Ⓗ Large city
Ⓙ large city

Read this diary entry and answer questions 7–10. The diary has groups of underlined words. The questions will ask about them.

Uncle richard did the strangest thing today. **(1)** *He built something that looked like a bird house and said it was for bats.* **(2)** *He is going to put it on the side of the house near the roof.* **(3)** *I never heard of anything called a bat house?* **(4)** *My uncle explained that bats are harmless to people but eat lots of insects like mosquitoes flies, and moths.* **(5)** *If the bat house works, we'll be able to sit on the deck and not be bothered by bugs.* **(6)**

7 In sentence 1, Uncle richard is best written—

Ⓐ uncle richard
Ⓑ Uncle richard
Ⓒ Uncle Richard
Ⓓ as it is

8 **In sentence 4, bat house? is best written—**

Ⓕ bat house.
Ⓖ bat house
Ⓗ bat house,
Ⓙ as it is

9 **In sentence 5, mosquitoes flies, and moths is best written—**

Ⓐ mosquitoes, flies, and moths
Ⓑ mosquitoes flies and moths
Ⓒ mosquitoes, flies, and, moths
Ⓓ as it is

10 **In sentence 6, we'll be able is best written—**

Ⓕ well be able
Ⓖ well' be able
Ⓗ wel'l be able
Ⓙ as it is

STOP

ANSWER ROWS 5 Ⓐ Ⓑ Ⓒ Ⓓ 7 Ⓐ Ⓑ Ⓒ Ⓓ 9 Ⓐ Ⓑ Ⓒ Ⓓ
6 Ⓕ Ⓖ Ⓗ Ⓙ 8 Ⓕ Ⓖ Ⓗ Ⓙ 10 Ⓕ Ⓖ Ⓗ Ⓙ

Lesson 4 Test Yourself

Examples

Directions: Mark the answer that shows incorrect capitalization or punctuation. Mark the space "None" if there are no errors.

E1

the table	in the kitchen	is too small.	None
Ⓐ	Ⓑ	Ⓒ	Ⓓ

E2

- Ⓕ Arizona became a state
- Ⓖ on February 14 1912.
- Ⓗ Its capital is Phoenix.
- Ⓙ *(No mistakes)*

1

The next book	I plan to read	is A dog named Ollie.	None
Ⓐ	Ⓑ	Ⓒ	Ⓓ

2

My friends	are going bowling	on thursday night.	None
Ⓕ	Ⓖ	Ⓗ	Ⓙ

3

how many	pieces of bread	did you eat?	None
Ⓐ	Ⓑ	Ⓒ	Ⓓ

4 The bus arrived at ________ more than three hours late.

- Ⓕ the Station
- Ⓖ The station
- Ⓗ The Station
- Ⓙ the station

5 Can you tell me how to get to ________ ?

- Ⓐ Baker street
- Ⓑ Baker Street
- Ⓒ baker street
- Ⓓ baker Street

6 Lots of squirrels live in the park.

Ⓕ , Ⓖ ! Ⓗ ? Ⓙ None

7 Don't touch that plant

Ⓐ . Ⓑ ! Ⓒ ? Ⓓ None

8 Haven't we been here before

Ⓕ . Ⓖ ! Ⓗ ? Ⓙ None

GO

ANSWER ROWS E1 Ⓐ Ⓑ Ⓒ Ⓓ 1 Ⓐ Ⓑ Ⓒ Ⓓ 3 Ⓐ Ⓑ Ⓒ Ⓓ 5 Ⓐ Ⓑ Ⓒ Ⓓ 7 Ⓐ Ⓑ Ⓒ Ⓓ
E2 Ⓕ Ⓖ Ⓗ Ⓙ 2 Ⓕ Ⓖ Ⓗ Ⓙ 4 Ⓕ Ⓖ Ⓗ Ⓙ 6 Ⓕ Ⓖ Ⓗ Ⓙ 8 Ⓕ Ⓖ Ⓗ Ⓙ

Directions: For items 9-14, mark the answer that shows the correct capitalization and punctuation. Mark the space "No mistakes" if there are no errors.

9 Our coach _______ told us who the captain will be.

- Ⓐ hasnt
- Ⓑ hasnt'
- Ⓒ has'nt
- Ⓓ hasn't

10 What is the correct abbreviation for the word Monday?

- Ⓕ Mon
- Ⓖ Mon.
- Ⓗ Mon,
- Ⓙ Mon;

11
- Ⓐ We helped Mr Phillips
- Ⓑ fix his car. It had
- Ⓒ a flat tire this morning.
- Ⓓ *(No mistakes)*

12
- Ⓕ The box we received had
- Ⓖ gifts from my grandmother for
- Ⓗ my mother my father and me.
- Ⓙ *(No mistakes)*

13
- Ⓐ Will you go to the park with us.
- Ⓑ I drew a picture of the ducks on the pond in the park.
- Ⓒ Many ducks and other birds fly south for the Winter.
- Ⓓ The park is on central avenue.

14
- Ⓕ Is that Carol's house?
- Ⓖ Dont forget to call home if you are going to be late.
- Ⓗ Who wi'll carry the bags?
- Ⓙ Both of them, can go with us.

Directions: For items 15-16, read the letter. Mark the answer that shows the correct punctuation for the underlined phrases. Mark the space "Correct as it is" if there are no errors.

(15) March 5, 1994

Dear Pete,

Thanks for the shirt. All the kids at school wish they had one. They

(16) think Montana is a neat place I hope we can visit you soon.

Your cousin,

Susan

15
- Ⓐ March 5 1994
- Ⓑ March 5 1994,
- Ⓒ March, 5 1994
- Ⓓ Correct as it is

16
- Ⓕ place, I hope
- Ⓖ place I hope.
- Ⓗ place. I hope
- Ⓙ Correct as it is

GO

ANSWER ROWS 9 Ⓐ Ⓑ Ⓒ Ⓓ 11 Ⓐ Ⓑ Ⓒ Ⓓ 13 Ⓐ Ⓑ Ⓒ Ⓓ 15 Ⓐ Ⓑ Ⓒ Ⓓ
10 Ⓕ Ⓖ Ⓗ Ⓙ 12 Ⓕ Ⓖ Ⓗ Ⓙ 14 Ⓕ Ⓖ Ⓗ Ⓙ 16 Ⓕ Ⓖ Ⓗ Ⓙ

17 What is the correct way to begin a letter?

Ⓐ Dear Uncle Mark,
Ⓑ Dear uncle Mark,
Ⓒ dear uncle Mark,
Ⓓ Dear Uncle Mark.

18 The computer in our classroom came from ________ .

Ⓕ Miami. Florida
Ⓖ Miami Florida
Ⓗ miami, florida
Ⓙ Miami, Florida

Read this story and answer questions 19–22. The story has groups of underlined words. The questions will ask about them.

Our neighbors name is Ms. Miller. She is the oldest person in our town. Last
(1) **(2)** **(3)**
year, she had her hundredth birthday. There was a Big Celebration in the
(4)
town hall. Ms. Miller still walks more than a mile every day she also enjoys
(5)
coming to school and visiting our classes. The children like to ask her what
(6)
the town was like when she was a little girl. Her stories are funny and make
(7)
us glad we weren't around then.

19 In sentence 1, Our neighbors name is best written—

Ⓐ our neighbors name
Ⓑ Our neighbors Name
Ⓒ Our neighbor's name
Ⓓ as it is

20 In sentence 4, Big Celebration is best written—

Ⓕ Big celebration
Ⓖ big celebration
Ⓗ big Celebration
Ⓙ as it is

21 In sentence 5, day she also is best written—

Ⓐ day. She also
Ⓑ day, she also
Ⓒ day she also.
Ⓓ as it is

22 In sentence 6, little girl. is best written—

Ⓕ little girl?
Ⓖ little girl!
Ⓗ little girl,
Ⓙ as it is

ANSWER ROWS 17 Ⓐ Ⓑ Ⓒ Ⓓ 19 Ⓐ Ⓑ Ⓒ Ⓓ 21 Ⓐ Ⓑ Ⓒ Ⓓ
18 Ⓕ Ⓖ Ⓗ Ⓙ 20 Ⓕ Ⓖ Ⓗ Ⓙ 22 Ⓕ Ⓖ Ⓗ Ⓙ

NUMBER RIGHT ______

Lesson 5 Nouns and Pronouns

Examples **Directions:** For items 1-3, choose the word that best completes the sentence. For items 4-6, choose the answer that could replace the underlined word in the sentence.

A ________ enjoys playing tennis.

Ⓐ They
Ⓑ He
Ⓒ Him
Ⓓ Them

B Nancy built a bench for the yard.

Ⓕ She
Ⓖ Her
Ⓗ Them
Ⓙ Us

If a question is too difficult, skip it and come back to it later.

Choose the answer that fits best in the sentence.

Practice

1 Mary and ________ went to a concert last Saturday.

Ⓐ her
Ⓑ him
Ⓒ me
Ⓓ I

2 Ask ________ to join us for lunch.

Ⓕ it
Ⓖ them
Ⓗ she
Ⓙ they

3 What did you tell ________ to bring to the party?

Ⓐ her
Ⓑ he
Ⓒ they
Ⓓ I

4 Let Manny have a turn using the computer.

Ⓕ he
Ⓖ his
Ⓗ him
Ⓙ it

5 Joan and Tim built their own house.

Ⓐ They
Ⓑ Him
Ⓒ Her
Ⓓ Them

6 When did you lose your basketball?

Ⓕ him
Ⓖ her
Ⓗ we
Ⓙ it

GO

ANSWER ROWS A Ⓐ Ⓑ Ⓒ Ⓓ 1 Ⓐ Ⓑ Ⓒ Ⓓ 3 Ⓐ Ⓑ Ⓒ Ⓓ 5 Ⓐ Ⓑ Ⓒ Ⓓ
B Ⓕ Ⓖ Ⓗ Ⓙ 2 Ⓕ Ⓖ Ⓗ Ⓙ 4 Ⓕ Ⓖ Ⓗ Ⓙ 6 Ⓕ Ⓖ Ⓗ Ⓙ

Examples

Directions: For items C and 7-8, choose the underlined part of the sentence that is the simple subject. For items D and 9, choose the sentence that contains a complete subject. For items E and 10-11, choose the answer that has a mistake. Mark the space "No mistakes" if there are no errors. For items F-G and 12-15, choose the sentence that is written correctly.

C A dish (A) fell (B) from the kitchen (C) table (D).

D
- Ⓕ Randy began working in an office.
- Ⓖ He has to take the train to work.
- Ⓗ The elevator went quickly.
- Ⓙ Both phones rang at the same time.

E
- Ⓐ That ball is mine.
- Ⓑ I lost them last week
- Ⓒ near the baseball field.
- Ⓓ *(No mistakes)*

F
- Ⓕ Dean planted a tree.
- Ⓖ Visiting a garden store.
- Ⓗ Between the house and the pond.
- Ⓙ A shovel and a pick.

G
- Ⓐ A shopping cart near the door.
- Ⓑ Dropped the milk but not broken.
- Ⓒ The groceries are in the car.
- Ⓓ Forgot the bread for dinner.

7 A large (A) black bear (B) walked (C) nearby (D).

8 Patrick's (F) friend (G) gave him (H) a book (J).

9
- Ⓐ The lawn needs to be mowed.
- Ⓑ Denise and I washed the car.
- Ⓒ Our mailbox was full.
- Ⓓ The vacation was wonderful.

10
- Ⓕ The dogs look thirsty.
- Ⓖ Let's give them water
- Ⓗ before we go outside.
- Ⓙ *(No mistakes)*

11
- Ⓐ Call Andy and Nina.
- Ⓑ Maybe them will want
- Ⓒ to go shopping with us.
- Ⓓ *(No mistakes)*

12
- Ⓕ Him was not happy about losing.
- Ⓖ The game was exciting.
- Ⓗ Me and Tina had good seats.
- Ⓙ The tickets, they were free.

13
- Ⓐ Riding through the muddy field.
- Ⓑ Thought it would be fun.
- Ⓒ Then fell and started laughing.
- Ⓓ The bicycles got very dirty.

14
- Ⓕ The race will start at the park.
- Ⓖ Running for about half an hour.
- Ⓗ Up the hill then down again.
- Ⓙ Started at ten o'clock.

15
- Ⓐ Snowed in summer.
- Ⓑ Surprised by strange weather.
- Ⓒ The date was July 15.
- Ⓓ Remembering it well.

STOP

ANSWER ROWS

C Ⓐ Ⓑ Ⓒ Ⓓ	F Ⓕ Ⓖ Ⓗ Ⓙ	8 Ⓕ Ⓖ Ⓗ Ⓙ	11 Ⓐ Ⓑ Ⓒ Ⓓ	14 Ⓕ Ⓖ Ⓗ Ⓙ
D Ⓕ Ⓖ Ⓗ Ⓙ	G Ⓐ Ⓑ Ⓒ Ⓓ	9 Ⓐ Ⓑ Ⓒ Ⓓ	12 Ⓕ Ⓖ Ⓗ Ⓙ	15 Ⓐ Ⓑ Ⓒ Ⓓ
E Ⓐ Ⓑ Ⓒ Ⓓ	7 Ⓐ Ⓑ Ⓒ Ⓓ	10 Ⓕ Ⓖ Ⓗ Ⓙ	13 Ⓐ Ⓑ Ⓒ Ⓓ	

Examples

Directions: For items A and 1-2, choose the word that best completes the sentence. For items 3-4, choose the sentence that is written correctly. For items B and 5-8, look for the sentence that has a mistake. Mark the circle "No mistakes" if there are no errors. For items 9-10, mark the circle for the part of each sentence that is a simple predicate.

A The package ________ yesterday.

Ⓐ will come
Ⓑ coming
Ⓒ come
Ⓓ came

B
Ⓕ The kittens is playing
Ⓖ with the string. They
Ⓗ are having a good time.
Ⓙ *(No mistakes)*

Remember, a verb is an action word.

If you are not sure which answer is correct, take your best guess.

Practice

1 The fireplace ________ the room warm and cozy.

Ⓐ to keep
Ⓑ keeping
Ⓒ keeps
Ⓓ keep

2 A band ________ in the park next week.

Ⓕ play
Ⓖ will play
Ⓗ played
Ⓙ was playing

3
Ⓐ The plane landed safely.
Ⓑ Our class visit the airport.
Ⓒ We sitted in the pilot's seat.
Ⓓ The lunch we had eat was great.

4
Ⓕ Deena play a computer game.
Ⓖ The weather are too cold.
Ⓗ I carried the box to the attic.
Ⓙ We have did funny things.

5
Ⓐ The money we saved
Ⓑ will be used to buy
Ⓒ a gift for my grandmother.
Ⓓ *(No mistakes)*

6
Ⓕ Stan will hafta wait.
Ⓖ Martha was here earlier
Ⓗ so she will play first.
Ⓙ *(No mistakes)*

7
Ⓐ A room for watching videos.
Ⓑ Books, tapes and magazines.
Ⓒ The library is open tomorrow.
Ⓓ Borrowing books to read for school.

8
Ⓕ Some people tennis all year.
Ⓖ Which sport do you liking?
Ⓗ Watching television not a sport.
Ⓙ Sailing is my favorite sport.

9 The driver (Ⓐ) quickly (Ⓑ) stopped (Ⓒ) the car (Ⓓ).

10 They (Ⓕ) came (Ⓖ) home (Ⓗ) after the movie (Ⓙ).

ANSWER ROWS
A Ⓐ Ⓑ Ⓒ Ⓓ 1 Ⓐ Ⓑ Ⓒ Ⓓ 3 Ⓐ Ⓑ Ⓒ Ⓓ 5 Ⓐ Ⓑ Ⓒ Ⓓ 7 Ⓐ Ⓑ Ⓒ Ⓓ 9 Ⓐ Ⓑ Ⓒ Ⓓ
B Ⓕ Ⓖ Ⓗ Ⓙ 2 Ⓕ Ⓖ Ⓗ Ⓙ 4 Ⓕ Ⓖ Ⓗ Ⓙ 6 Ⓕ Ⓖ Ⓗ Ⓙ 8 Ⓕ Ⓖ Ⓗ Ⓙ 10 Ⓕ Ⓖ Ⓗ Ⓙ

Lesson 7 Adjectives

Examples

Directions: For items A and 1-4, choose the word or words that best completes the sentence. For items 5-7, choose the sentence that is written correctly.

A Who is the ________ runner?

Ⓐ most fast
Ⓑ fastest
Ⓒ more faster
Ⓓ most fastest

B
Ⓕ This is a huge mall.
Ⓖ That was a loudest noise.
Ⓗ I have a worser pain.
Ⓙ This glass is fullest than that one.

If you know which answer is correct, mark it and move on to the next item.

Stay with your first answer choice. It is usually right.

Practice

1 The river is ________ now than it is in the fall.

Ⓐ deep
Ⓑ most deep
Ⓒ deepest
Ⓓ deeper

2 That lamp is ________ .

Ⓕ brightly
Ⓖ bright
Ⓗ most brightest
Ⓙ more brighter

3 Who is ________ , Ann or Ned?

Ⓐ most funnier
Ⓑ funniest
Ⓒ funnier
Ⓓ most funny

4 The ________ gift you can give your grandfather is to visit him.

Ⓕ most wonderful
Ⓖ wonderfully
Ⓗ wonderful
Ⓙ more wonderfuller

5
Ⓐ The trip to the beach took long than we expected.
Ⓑ The wind blew more hard.
Ⓒ This was a most tastier lunch.
Ⓓ Charlene was busy all weekend with her friends.

6
Ⓕ He swims slower than Nora.
Ⓖ The gift is too larger for the box.
Ⓗ A saddest movie is playing now.
Ⓙ It is too lately to go to the lake.

7
Ⓐ A lightest backpack is better than a heaviest one.
Ⓑ The bus was most crowdeder this morning.
Ⓒ This is the widest street in town.
Ⓓ I buy the most ripest fruit.

STOP

ANSWER ROWS
A Ⓐ Ⓑ Ⓒ Ⓓ 1 Ⓐ Ⓑ Ⓒ Ⓓ 3 Ⓐ Ⓑ Ⓒ Ⓓ 5 Ⓐ Ⓑ Ⓒ Ⓓ 7 Ⓐ Ⓑ Ⓒ Ⓓ
B Ⓕ Ⓖ Ⓗ Ⓙ 2 Ⓕ Ⓖ Ⓗ Ⓙ 4 Ⓕ Ⓖ Ⓗ Ⓙ 6 Ⓕ Ⓖ Ⓗ Ⓙ

Lesson 8 Sentences

Examples

Directions: Choose the sentence that is written correctly.

A Ⓐ An apple fell from the tree.

Ⓑ Stopped to buy fruit.

Ⓒ The family on a Sunday ride.

Ⓓ Away from crowded city streets.

B Ⓕ It's time to go we can come again.

Ⓖ Beside the house near the tree.

Ⓗ Our neighbors built a pool.

Ⓙ Your friends called will stop by.

Choose the answer that is the best combination of the underlined sentences.

C <u>Let's go to the zoo.</u>

<u>Let's go tomorrow morning.</u>

Ⓐ Let's go tomorrow to the zoo in the morning.

Ⓑ In the morning, let's go to the zoo tomorrow.

Ⓒ Let's go to the zoo, and let's go tomorrow morning.

Ⓓ Let's go to the zoo tomorrow morning.

Say the answer choices to yourself carefully. Choose the one that sounds the best.

Practice

1 Ⓐ Such a nice day.

Ⓑ The two friends went for a ride on a boat.

Ⓒ To do something that we have never tried before.

Ⓓ A good time all afternoon.

2 Ⓕ The man at the bank helped Kate.

Ⓖ The money she saved from working.

Ⓗ Some in the bank each month for a year.

Ⓙ More than two hundred dollars.

3 Ⓐ Looking for license plates from different states.

Ⓑ A trip to a national park in Idaho.

Ⓒ Finally there for a great visit.

Ⓓ The children were bored because the ride was long.

4 Ⓕ Call before you come we'll be sure to be home.

Ⓖ The bus will stop at our corner you will see our building.

Ⓗ Our apartment is on the second floor of the building.

Ⓙ My mother will drive you home our car will be fixed by then.

GO

ANSWER ROWS **A** Ⓐ Ⓑ Ⓒ Ⓓ **C** Ⓐ Ⓑ Ⓒ Ⓓ **2** Ⓕ Ⓖ Ⓗ Ⓙ **4** Ⓕ Ⓖ Ⓗ Ⓙ

B Ⓕ Ⓖ Ⓗ Ⓙ **1** Ⓐ Ⓑ Ⓒ Ⓓ **3** Ⓐ Ⓑ Ⓒ Ⓓ

Directions: For items 5-6, read the underlined sentences. Choose the answer that is the best combination of the underlined sentences. For items 7-8, choose the word that shows the best way to say the underlined part of each sentence. For items 9-10, choose the sentence that is written correctly.

5 The phone rang four times.

The phone is in the kitchen.

Ⓐ The phone in the kitchen rang four times.

Ⓑ The phone is in the kitchen and it rang four times.

Ⓒ The phone, it rang four times, and it is in the kitchen.

Ⓓ The ringing phone is in the kitchen.

6 Trees surround the lake in the park.

The trees are tall.

Ⓕ Trees surround the lake in the park, and the trees are tall.

Ⓖ The trees that surround the lake in the park are tall trees.

Ⓗ Tall trees surround the lake in the park.

Ⓙ Tall trees that surround the lake are in the park.

---

7 We can go to the movies **after** you finish your homework.

Ⓐ since Ⓑ but Ⓒ and Ⓓ *(No change)*

8 The radio she **buyed** was on sale.

Ⓕ buy Ⓖ bought Ⓗ will buy Ⓙ *(No change)*

9
Ⓐ Next year a bridge across the river.
Ⓑ Across the river, a bridge will be finished.
Ⓒ The bridge across the river will be finished next year.
Ⓓ The bridge next year will be finished across the river.

10
Ⓕ Traffic around the stadium was awful because of the big game.
Ⓖ The big game and awful traffic around the stadium.
Ⓗ Because of the big game, awful traffic around the stadium.
Ⓙ Traffic, which was around the stadium, was awful because of the big game.

ANSWER ROWS 5 Ⓐ Ⓑ Ⓒ Ⓓ 7 Ⓐ Ⓑ Ⓒ Ⓓ 9 Ⓐ Ⓑ Ⓒ Ⓓ
6 Ⓕ Ⓖ Ⓗ Ⓙ 8 Ⓕ Ⓖ Ⓗ Ⓙ 10 Ⓕ Ⓖ Ⓗ Ⓙ

Read this letter. Use it to answer questions 11–14.

Dear Dr. Baker,

Thank you for taking such good care of me last week. **(1)** *I was afraid and sore when I came to the hospital.* **(2)** *You made me feel better and fixed my cut.* **(3)** *It's getting better.* **(4)** *I should be back in school tomorrow.* **(5)** *I did everything you told me to and it helped a lot.* **(6)** *My parents were surprised at how quickly I am improving.* **(7)** *They told me, your daughter, who goes to our school.* **(8)** *When I go back to school I will try to find her.* **(9)** *Maybe can become friends.* **(10)**

11 Sentence 2 is best written—

Ⓐ When I came to the hospital, I was afraid and I was sore.

Ⓑ Afraid and sore, I came to the hospital.

Ⓒ I was afraid when I came to the hospital, and sore.

Ⓓ as it is

12 Sentence 8 is best written—

Ⓕ In our school, they told me you have a daughter.

Ⓖ They told me that your daughter goes to our school.

Ⓗ Your daughter, they told me, who goes to our school.

Ⓙ as it is

13 Which of these is not a sentence?

1	3	5	10
Ⓐ	Ⓑ	Ⓒ	Ⓓ

14 How are sentences 4 and 5 best joined without changing the meaning?

Ⓕ After I get better, I should be back in school tomorrow.

Ⓖ It's getting better, so I should be back in school tomorrow.

Ⓗ Tomorrow, after I am back in school, I should be getting better.

Ⓙ I should, because it's getting better, be back in school tomorrow.

ANSWER ROWS 11 Ⓐ Ⓑ Ⓒ Ⓓ 13 Ⓐ Ⓑ Ⓒ Ⓓ

12 Ⓕ Ⓖ Ⓗ Ⓙ 14 Ⓕ Ⓖ Ⓗ Ⓙ

Lesson 9 Paragraphs

Examples

Directions: Read the paragraph with the blank. Choose the answer that is the best topic sentence for the paragraph.

A _______________ . Although it is very thin, it protects our muscles and internal organs. Skin is flexible and can stretch in every direction. In addition, skin is one of the sense organs and lets us feel temperature, pressure, and other things.

Ⓐ Skin, hair, and fingernails are similar in many ways.

Ⓑ Our skin is truly amazing.

Ⓒ The human skin is thinner than the skin of many other animals.

Ⓓ Skin can be cut or bruised.

Remember, a paragraph should focus on one idea.

Be sure to read all the answer choices.

Practice

1 _______________ . Many people think of art as being paintings or statues. It also includes dancing, music, landscape, buildings, and many other practical things. Some of the most beautiful pieces of art are pots, baskets, and even carpets.

Ⓐ People have enjoyed art for thousands of years.

Ⓑ Painting is a popular form of art.

Ⓒ Art can sometimes be hard to understand.

Ⓓ Art can take many forms.

2 _______________ . Whales swim many thousands of miles to where their calves are born. Some fish return to the same stream where they were born to lay their eggs. Even land animals like elk travel great distances to find places where there is plenty of food.

Ⓕ Birds often fly south for the winter.

Ⓖ Some animals stay in the same place all year.

Ⓗ Many animals other than birds migrate from place to place.

Ⓙ Animals move more than plants.

GO

ANSWER ROWS **A** Ⓐ Ⓑ Ⓒ Ⓓ **1** Ⓐ Ⓑ Ⓒ Ⓓ **2** Ⓕ Ⓖ Ⓗ Ⓙ

Examples

Directions: For items 3-4, read each topic sentence. Choose the answer that best develops the topic sentence.

3 Banks are important for two reasons.

Ⓐ It is easy to open a savings account in a bank. The bank will actually pay you to keep money there.

Ⓑ Money that you put in a bank is very safe. It is protected by the government so you can never lose it.

Ⓒ The money you put in a bank earns interest. This means that your money increases the longer you keep it in a bank.

Ⓓ They give people a safe place to keep their money. Banks also lend money to people for things like buying houses or starting businesses.

4 The Martin family went on a dream vacation. ______________ . The weather was wonderful and they saw many beautiful places.

Ⓕ They live in a small town in Iowa.

Ⓖ They spent a week on a boat sailing from island to island.

Ⓗ The children couldn't wait to tell their friends about it.

Ⓙ When they got on the plane, it was cold and snowy.

Use this paragraph to do numbers 5–7.

[1]It was the first time I had ever gone to a play. [2]After the play, we stopped in a restaurant for dinner. [3]My friends and I took the bus to the theater. [4]We bought our tickets and found our seats. [5]The play was about a pioneer family. [6]I liked the play, but I thought it was too long.

5 Choose the best first sentence for this paragraph.

Ⓐ A play can be exciting, even for children my age.
Ⓑ Have you ever been to a play?
Ⓒ On Saturday we went to a play.
Ⓓ The actors in the play did a wonderful job.

6 Where is the best place for sentence 2?

Ⓕ Where it is now
Ⓖ Between sentences 3 and 4
Ⓗ Between sentences 4 and 5
Ⓙ After sentence 6

7 Choose the best last sentence for this paragraph.

Ⓐ If I have a chance, I think I would like to go to another play.
Ⓑ I was surprised because other children our age were there.
Ⓒ We met our teacher at the theater.
Ⓓ My parents asked me to call when we got to the theater.

GO

ANSWER ROWS 3 Ⓐ Ⓑ Ⓒ Ⓓ 4 Ⓕ Ⓖ Ⓗ Ⓙ 5 Ⓐ Ⓑ Ⓒ Ⓓ 6 Ⓕ Ⓖ Ⓗ Ⓙ 7 Ⓐ Ⓑ Ⓒ Ⓓ

Read this essay. Use it to answer questions 8–11.

Keeping Warm

There are several things you can do to keep warm. **(1)** *The most important thing is to dress in layers.* **(2)** *If you wear long underwear, a sweater, and a coat, you will stay warm in even the coldest weather.* **(3)** *Skiing, hiking, and sledding are good ways to enjoy the outdoors in winter.* **(4)** *Another good idea is to wear a hat.* **(5)** *People lose a lot of body heat through the head.* **(6)** *A hat will prevent this.* **(7)** *Drinking something warm before you go outside or while you are outside will also help.* **(8)**

8 Which sentence would best begin this essay?

- Ⓕ Most people take their vacation in summer rather than winter.
- Ⓖ If you want to enjoy the outdoors in winter, you must keep warm.
- Ⓗ There are many ways to enjoy the outdoors in winter.
- Ⓙ Being cold is not very much fun.

9 Which of these could be added after sentence 7?

- Ⓐ Wool hats that cover your ears are probably the best.
- Ⓑ Hats don't cost a lot.
- Ⓒ A hat can keep the sun out of your eyes in the summer.
- Ⓓ You can buy a hat almost anywhere.

10 Which sentence does not belong in this essay?

1	3	4	6
Ⓕ	Ⓖ	Ⓗ	Ⓙ

11 Which of these could be added at the end of the essay?

- Ⓐ In the end, it is better to be warm than cold.
- Ⓑ You won't have a good time if you stay inside all winter.
- Ⓒ And don't forget, the days are shorter in winter, so be sure to head back while it is light outside.
- Ⓓ Finally, you should keep dry, because getting wet causes you to lose body heat quickly.

Examples

Directions: For items E1 and 1-3, choose the word that best fits the sentence. For item 4, choose the pronoun that could replace the underlined word in the sentence. For items E2 and 5-8, choose the sentence that is written correctly.

E1 The turkey _______ ten pounds.

Ⓐ weigh
Ⓑ weighs
Ⓒ weighing
Ⓓ is weigh

E2 Ⓕ Clothes on hangers neatly.
Ⓖ Keeping toys together in a box.
Ⓗ The door to the closet is open.
Ⓙ The muddy shoes in the garage.

1 This is the _______ dog I have ever met.

Ⓐ friendlier
Ⓑ friendly
Ⓒ friendliest
Ⓓ friend

2 The frogs _______ croaking when we walk by.

Ⓕ will stop
Ⓖ are stopping
Ⓗ stopped
Ⓙ stops

3 This car is _______ than that one.

Ⓐ new
Ⓑ newer
Ⓒ most new
Ⓓ more newer

---

4 Ask <u>Jean and Marcus</u> if they can come tomorrow.

Ⓕ they
Ⓖ her
Ⓗ him
Ⓙ them

5 Ⓐ The door behind you.
Ⓑ The window is open too far.
Ⓒ Wiping feet on the mat.
Ⓓ To come in after playing outside.

6 Ⓕ This computer is more powerful than that one.
Ⓖ My computer is heavy than yours.
Ⓗ The game I bought is the most funner.
Ⓙ My typing is more better because I practice a lot.

7 Ⓐ Nina and José did coming later.
Ⓑ This bicycle have a nice seat.
Ⓒ A truck are coming down the road.
Ⓓ Three planes landed at almost the same time.

8 Ⓕ Thems brought presents for Suki.
Ⓖ Have you told he what time to come?
Ⓗ Ask her to call me tomorrow.
Ⓙ Give they directions to the party.

STOP

ANSWER ROWS
E1 Ⓐ Ⓑ Ⓒ Ⓓ 1 Ⓐ Ⓑ Ⓒ Ⓓ 3 Ⓐ Ⓑ Ⓒ Ⓓ 5 Ⓐ Ⓑ Ⓒ Ⓓ 7 Ⓐ Ⓑ Ⓒ Ⓓ
E2 Ⓕ Ⓖ Ⓗ Ⓙ 2 Ⓕ Ⓖ Ⓗ Ⓙ 4 Ⓕ Ⓖ Ⓗ Ⓙ 6 Ⓕ Ⓖ Ⓗ Ⓙ 8 Ⓕ Ⓖ Ⓗ Ⓙ

Directions: For items 9-13, choose the answer that has a mistake. Mark the space "No mistakes" if there are no errors. For items 14-15, choose the sentence that has the complete subject underlined. For items 16-17, choose the sentence that has the complete predicate underlined. For items 18-19, choose the sentence that has the simple subject underlined. For items 20-21, choose the sentence that has the simple predicate underlined.

9
Ⓐ The flowers you planted
Ⓑ are doing well.
Ⓒ Do you water them often?
Ⓓ *(No mistakes)*

10
Ⓕ Aunt Marcie called.
Ⓖ She wants to know if we
Ⓗ can stay at there house.
Ⓙ *(No mistakes)*

11
Ⓐ I didn't get no sleep.
Ⓑ The bed was too soft
Ⓒ and the wind blew all night long.
Ⓓ *(No mistakes)*

12
Ⓕ The train is late
Ⓖ because an car stopped
Ⓗ on the tracks and got stuck.
Ⓙ *(No mistakes)*

13
Ⓐ A boat will sail
Ⓑ from Miami last week
Ⓒ for a trip to Puerto Rico.
Ⓓ *(No mistakes)*

14
Ⓕ The cereal is on the table.
Ⓖ One sandwich is left in the bag.
Ⓗ You can have the small apple.
Ⓙ The orange juice is finished.

15
Ⓐ People have many different hobbies.
Ⓑ Harvey looks for strange rocks.
Ⓒ An old bottle was found in our attic.
Ⓓ My friend collects stamps.

16
Ⓕ The ice began to melt.
Ⓖ Anita will go to the game.
Ⓗ A letter came for you yesterday.
Ⓙ The boys washed the dishes.

17
Ⓐ A kind woman helped Uri.
Ⓑ It was hard to make a decision.
Ⓒ The train is moving slowly.
Ⓓ Some paint spilled on the floor.

18 The map (Ⓕ) shows (Ⓖ) two ways (Ⓗ) to go home (Ⓙ).

19 A friendly (Ⓐ) cow (Ⓑ) walked (Ⓒ) up to the fence (Ⓓ).

20 They planted (Ⓕ) a tree (Ⓖ) in the back (Ⓗ) yard (Ⓙ).

21 The group (Ⓐ) of hikers (Ⓑ) climbed (Ⓒ) the steep (Ⓓ) trail.

GO

ANSWER ROWS
9 Ⓐ Ⓑ Ⓒ Ⓓ 10 Ⓕ Ⓖ Ⓗ Ⓙ 11 Ⓐ Ⓑ Ⓒ Ⓓ
12 Ⓕ Ⓖ Ⓗ Ⓙ 13 Ⓐ Ⓑ Ⓒ Ⓓ 14 Ⓕ Ⓖ Ⓗ Ⓙ
15 Ⓐ Ⓑ Ⓒ Ⓓ 16 Ⓕ Ⓖ Ⓗ Ⓙ 17 Ⓐ Ⓑ Ⓒ Ⓓ
18 Ⓕ Ⓖ Ⓗ Ⓙ 19 Ⓐ Ⓑ Ⓒ Ⓓ
20 Ⓕ Ⓖ Ⓗ Ⓙ 21 Ⓐ Ⓑ Ⓒ Ⓓ

Read this journal entry. Use it to answer questions 22–25.

My cousins Kevin and Melissa came today they will be staying with us for a week. **(1)** *They are about my age so we do lots of things together.* **(2)** *The last time they were here.* **(3)** *It was in 1992.* **(4)** *This time they brought a camcorder with them.* **(5)** *They want to take videos when we go to the lake.* **(6)** *Water skiing and a boat for it.* **(7)** *They have never gone water skiing before.* **(8)** *I've gone a few times and can get up pretty well.* **(9)** *Mom is a very good water skier.* **(10)** *She will be able to teach them how to do it.* **(11)**

22 Sentence 1 is best written—

Ⓕ My cousins Kevin and Melissa came today. They will be staying with us for a week.

Ⓖ Today my cousins, who are Kevin and Melissa, came for a week to be staying with us.

Ⓗ Kevin and Melissa, my cousins, came today. For a week to be staying with us.

Ⓙ as it is

23 Sentence 5 is best written—

Ⓐ This time a camcorder with them.

Ⓑ This time they brung a camcorder with them.

Ⓒ The camcorder that they brought with them.

Ⓓ as it is

24 Which of these is not a sentence?

2	7	9	10
Ⓕ	Ⓖ	Ⓗ	Ⓙ

25 How are sentences 3 and 4 best joined without changing the meaning?

Ⓐ In 1992 was the last time they were here.

Ⓑ They were here in 1992 for the last time.

Ⓒ The last time they were here was in 1992.

Ⓓ The last time and they were here and it was in 1992.

STOP

ANSWER ROWS 22 Ⓕ Ⓖ Ⓗ Ⓙ 23 Ⓐ Ⓑ Ⓒ Ⓓ 24 Ⓕ Ⓖ Ⓗ Ⓙ 25 Ⓐ Ⓑ Ⓒ Ⓓ

Directions: For items 26-27, choose the answer that is the best combination of the underlined sentences. For items 28-29, choose the word that could replace the underlined word in the sentence. For items 30-31, choose the sentence that is written correctly.

26 The bank is on Fifth Avenue.

The supermarket is on Fifth Avenue.

Ⓕ On Fifth Avenue is the bank and also the supermarket.

Ⓖ The bank is on Fifth Avenue, which is where the supermarket is.

Ⓗ The bank and the supermarket are on Fifth Avenue.

Ⓙ The bank is on Fifth Avenue and the supermarket is on Fifth Avenue.

27 Tina will visit her grandfather next week.

Tina's grandfather is in Georgia.

Ⓐ Tina will visit her grandfather in Georgia next week.

Ⓑ Tina will visit Georgia next week and her grandfather.

Ⓒ In Georgia is Tina's grandfather who she will visit.

Ⓓ Tina's grandfather will be visited by her in Georgia.

---

28 You can go to the mall, **but** you must call when you get there.

Ⓕ since Ⓖ or Ⓗ if Ⓙ *(No change)*

29 The package you were waiting for **coming** yesterday.

Ⓐ will come Ⓑ came Ⓒ comes Ⓓ *(No change)*

---

30 Ⓕ This time of year for which it is warm.
Ⓖ It is very warm for this time of year.
Ⓗ Although it is warm, it is this time of year.
Ⓙ A warm time of year it is for this.

31 Ⓐ Having the tools you need before beginning.
Ⓑ Before you have the tools you should be beginning.
Ⓒ The tools, which you should be having, before you begin.
Ⓓ Before you begin, be sure you have all the tools you will need.

GO

ANSWER ROWS 26 Ⓕ Ⓖ Ⓗ Ⓙ 28 Ⓕ Ⓖ Ⓗ Ⓙ 30 Ⓕ Ⓖ Ⓗ Ⓙ
27 Ⓐ Ⓑ Ⓒ Ⓓ 29 Ⓐ Ⓑ Ⓒ Ⓓ 31 Ⓐ Ⓑ Ⓒ Ⓓ

Directions: For item 32, read the paragraph with the blank. Choose the answer that is the best topic sentence for the paragraph. For item 33, read each topic sentence. Choose the answer that best develops the topic sentence. For items 34-35, read the paragraph with the blank. Choose the sentence that best fits in the paragraph.

32 ________________ . Some people like running or biking, which are very hard work. Others prefer fishing or golf, which are much easier.

Ⓕ Many sports require special equipment.

Ⓖ People enjoy many different kinds of sports.

Ⓗ Sports can be played in all seasons.

Ⓙ Soccer is a popular sport around the world.

33 Traffic was terrible yesterday afternoon.

Ⓐ Cars were backed up from the bridge all the way to the interstate. It took my parents almost an hour to get home from work.

Ⓑ A truck crashed into the bridge over the river. The driver was not injured, but it will take several months to fix the bridge.

Ⓒ Normally it takes my parents about twenty minutes to get home. They work near each other and come home from work together.

Ⓓ The bridge was damaged when a truck crashed into it. The truck was carrying wood and bricks for a new house.

34 We began feeding birds this winter. ________________ . The birds enjoy different kinds of seeds, peanuts, and even apples.

Ⓕ It has snowed more than usual this year.

Ⓖ Our state bird is the cardinal.

Ⓗ You can buy bird food at many different stores.

Ⓙ There isn't much food for them, especially if it snows.

35 My friend Dora lives in the apartment below us. ________________ . Dora's parents opened a restaurant just a few blocks from our building.

Ⓐ Another friend, Seth, lives near school.

Ⓑ Sometimes it is hard to make friends.

Ⓒ Her family moved here a few months ago.

Ⓓ My favorite food is pizza with everything on it.

GO

ANSWER ROWS 32 ⒻⒼⒽⒿ 33 ⒶⒷⒸⒹ 34 ⒻⒼⒽⒿ 35 ⒶⒷⒸⒹ

Read this letter. Use it to answer questions 36–39.

Dear Mr. Howard,

The old library is small and has too few books. **(1)** *We would like to raise enough money to add space and buy more books and some computers.* **(2)**

One way we are raising money is asking business owners to allow us to sell t-shirts outside their stores. **(3)** *We would set up a table near your door and sell our shirts on Saturday.* **(4)** *It won't cost you anything and we promise not to bother your customers.* **(5)** *Our school was named after the woman who was our town's first mayor.* **(6)**

36 Which sentence would best begin this letter?

Ⓕ Many students want to read books but can't find them.

Ⓖ Our school is raising money for a new library.

Ⓗ Our school is one of the oldest in the state.

Ⓙ Last week I visited your store.

37 Which of these could be added after sentence 4?

Ⓐ You can play games on computers.

Ⓑ Friday is a school day.

Ⓒ My teacher is new to our school this year.

Ⓓ The table would be set up from nine to four.

38 Which sentence does not belong in this letter?

1	3	5	6
Ⓕ	Ⓖ	Ⓗ	Ⓙ

39 Which of these could be added at the end of the letter?

Ⓐ We also promise to clean everything up when we are finished.

Ⓑ She was also the owner of the first store in town.

Ⓒ Your store is very busy, and we know a lot of people will come to shop on Saturday.

Ⓓ It doesn't take long to get from our school to your store, so I am sure we will be on time.

ANSWER ROWS 36 Ⓕ Ⓖ Ⓗ Ⓙ 37 Ⓐ Ⓑ Ⓒ Ⓓ 38 Ⓕ Ⓖ Ⓗ Ⓙ 39 Ⓐ Ⓑ Ⓒ Ⓓ NUMBER RIGHT ______

Lesson 11 Spelling Skills

Examples

Directions: For items A and 1-6, find the word that best fits in the sentence and is spelled correctly. For items B-D and 7-10, look for the word that is spelled incorrectly. Mark the circle "No mistakes" if there are no errors.

A Money is the _______ reason we can't go.
- Ⓐ cheif
- Ⓑ cheaf
- Ⓒ chief
- Ⓓ cheef

B
- Ⓕ fix
- Ⓖ time
- Ⓗ rest
- Ⓙ stiff
- Ⓚ *(No mistakes)*

C
- Ⓐ stain
- Ⓑ cogh
- Ⓒ again
- Ⓓ window

D We had a snak (Ⓕ) after (Ⓖ) the band concert. (Ⓗ) No mistake (Ⓙ)

Carefully read the directions! In this lesson you must find both correctly and incorrectly spelled words.

Don't look at the words too long or they all look misspelled.

Practice

1 Don't _______ the cat.
- Ⓐ bothr
- Ⓑ bather
- Ⓒ bothur
- Ⓓ bother

2 My dog's tail has a _______ in it.
- Ⓕ curl
- Ⓖ kurl
- Ⓗ cerl
- Ⓙ kerl

3 A _______ was on the road.
- Ⓐ bolder
- Ⓑ bulder
- Ⓒ boulder
- Ⓓ bouldr

4 That's a good _______ .
- Ⓕ trik
- Ⓖ trick
- Ⓗ terick
- Ⓙ treck

5 We'll arrive home at about _______ .
- Ⓐ nune
- Ⓑ noone
- Ⓒ noon
- Ⓓ noun

6 My phone _______ is in the book.
- Ⓕ number
- Ⓖ nummber
- Ⓗ numbir
- Ⓙ numbber

7
- Ⓐ mask
- Ⓑ feathur
- Ⓒ sorry
- Ⓓ tame
- Ⓔ *(No mistakes)*

8
- Ⓕ catch
- Ⓖ point
- Ⓗ snail
- Ⓙ both
- Ⓚ *(No mistakes)*

9
- Ⓐ pony
- Ⓑ faster
- Ⓒ binch
- Ⓓ seed
- Ⓔ *(No mistakes)*

10
- Ⓕ strange
- Ⓖ fright
- Ⓗ thought
- Ⓙ pound
- Ⓚ *(No mistakes)*

GO

ANSWER ROWS

A	Ⓐ Ⓑ Ⓒ Ⓓ	D	Ⓕ Ⓖ Ⓗ Ⓙ	3	Ⓐ Ⓑ Ⓒ Ⓓ	5	Ⓐ Ⓑ Ⓒ Ⓓ	7	Ⓐ Ⓑ Ⓒ Ⓓ Ⓔ	9	Ⓐ Ⓑ Ⓒ Ⓓ Ⓔ
B	Ⓕ Ⓖ Ⓗ Ⓙ Ⓚ	1	Ⓐ Ⓑ Ⓒ Ⓓ	4	Ⓕ Ⓖ Ⓗ Ⓙ	6	Ⓕ Ⓖ Ⓗ Ⓙ	8	Ⓕ Ⓖ Ⓗ Ⓙ Ⓚ	10	Ⓕ Ⓖ Ⓗ Ⓙ Ⓚ
C	Ⓐ Ⓑ Ⓒ Ⓓ	2	Ⓕ Ⓖ Ⓗ Ⓙ								

Directions: For items 11-19, find the word that is spelled incorrectly. For items 20-24, read the sentence. Look for the word that has a mistake. Mark the circle "No mistakes" if there are no errors.

11
Ⓐ load
Ⓑ October
Ⓒ therteen
Ⓓ myself

12
Ⓕ lettuce
Ⓖ jelly
Ⓗ tries
Ⓙ nobb

13
Ⓐ weke
Ⓑ harder
Ⓒ yesterday
Ⓓ clown

14
Ⓕ earth
Ⓖ pudle
Ⓗ broom
Ⓙ packed

15
Ⓐ baggage
Ⓑ sighte
Ⓒ bucket
Ⓓ basketball

16
Ⓕ root
Ⓖ merry
Ⓗ cage
Ⓙ arive

17
Ⓐ sting
Ⓑ heard
Ⓒ messige
Ⓓ pillow

18
Ⓕ riting
Ⓖ dove
Ⓗ roar
Ⓙ travel

19
Ⓐ pitcher
Ⓑ rained
Ⓒ softly
Ⓓ daily

---

20 The drivers (Ⓕ) were unabel (Ⓖ) to stop on the icy (Ⓗ) road. No mistake (Ⓙ)

21 We picked (Ⓐ) berries (Ⓑ) on a farm near the river. (Ⓒ) No mistake (Ⓓ)

22 I filt (Ⓕ) bad about losing (Ⓖ) my sister's sweater. (Ⓗ) No mistake (Ⓙ)

23 Learning (Ⓐ) about computers (Ⓑ) is a lot (Ⓒ) of fun. No mistake (Ⓓ)

24 The water presure in our house is too low. No mistake

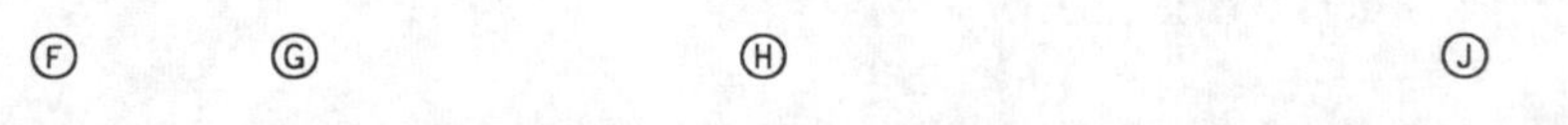

ANSWER ROWS
11 Ⓐ Ⓑ Ⓒ Ⓓ 14 Ⓕ Ⓖ Ⓗ Ⓙ 17 Ⓐ Ⓑ Ⓒ Ⓓ 19 Ⓐ Ⓑ Ⓒ Ⓓ 21 Ⓐ Ⓑ Ⓒ Ⓓ 23 Ⓐ Ⓑ Ⓒ Ⓓ
12 Ⓕ Ⓖ Ⓗ Ⓙ 15 Ⓐ Ⓑ Ⓒ Ⓓ 18 Ⓕ Ⓖ Ⓗ Ⓙ 20 Ⓕ Ⓖ Ⓗ Ⓙ 22 Ⓕ Ⓖ Ⓗ Ⓙ 24 Ⓕ Ⓖ Ⓗ Ⓙ
13 Ⓐ Ⓑ Ⓒ Ⓓ 16 Ⓕ Ⓖ Ⓗ Ⓙ

Examples

Directions: For items E1 and 1-8, find the word that best fits in the sentence and is spelled correctly. For items E2-E4 and 9-13, look for the word that is spelled incorrectly. Mark the circle "No mistakes" if there are no errors.

E1 Can you please make a ________ of this?

Ⓐ copie
Ⓑ copee
Ⓒ kopy
Ⓓ copy

E2
Ⓕ table
Ⓖ strate
Ⓗ touch
Ⓙ crisp
Ⓚ *(No mistakes)*

E3
Ⓐ separaite
Ⓑ speech
Ⓒ frame
Ⓓ cause

E4 We continued (Ⓕ) to drive (Ⓖ) behind a school (Ⓗ) bus for a long time. No mistake (Ⓙ)

1 That is a ________ dress.

Ⓐ kolorful
Ⓑ colorfill
Ⓒ colorful
Ⓓ colorfull

2 This movie is ________ .

Ⓕ boreing
Ⓖ borring
Ⓗ boring
Ⓙ borng

3 Use the ________ spoon.

Ⓐ wooden
Ⓑ woulden
Ⓒ woden
Ⓓ woodden

4 Kanisha has been to the museum ________ .

Ⓕ twoice
Ⓖ twyce
Ⓗ twaice
Ⓙ twice

5 That's a ________ apple.

Ⓐ tastie
Ⓑ tasty
Ⓒ tastey
Ⓓ taisty

6 When did you ________?

Ⓕ retern
Ⓖ retorn
Ⓗ ruturn
Ⓙ return

7 You gave me ________ advice.

Ⓐ useful
Ⓑ usful
Ⓒ usefull
Ⓓ usefill

8 How would you ________ this picture?

Ⓕ describ
Ⓖ discribe
Ⓗ describe
Ⓙ descreib

9
Ⓐ pretty
Ⓑ smart
Ⓒ tough
Ⓓ younger
Ⓔ *(No mistakes)*

10
Ⓕ train
Ⓖ poinnt
Ⓗ certain
Ⓙ decision
Ⓚ *(No mistakes)*

11
Ⓐ finished
Ⓑ manage
Ⓒ saddle
Ⓓ seade
Ⓔ *(No mistakes)*

12
Ⓕ teacher
Ⓖ fraight
Ⓗ mailbox
Ⓙ admire
Ⓚ *(No mistakes)*

13
Ⓐ tower
Ⓑ beyond
Ⓒ planned
Ⓓ pownd
Ⓔ *(No mistakes)*

GO

ANSWER ROWS

E1 Ⓐ Ⓑ Ⓒ Ⓓ
E2 Ⓕ Ⓖ Ⓗ Ⓙ Ⓚ
E3 Ⓐ Ⓑ Ⓒ Ⓓ
E4 Ⓕ Ⓖ Ⓗ Ⓙ
1 Ⓐ Ⓑ Ⓒ Ⓓ
2 Ⓕ Ⓖ Ⓗ Ⓙ
3 Ⓐ Ⓑ Ⓒ Ⓓ
4 Ⓕ Ⓖ Ⓗ Ⓙ
5 Ⓐ Ⓑ Ⓒ Ⓓ
6 Ⓕ Ⓖ Ⓗ Ⓙ
7 Ⓐ Ⓑ Ⓒ Ⓓ
8 Ⓕ Ⓖ Ⓗ Ⓙ
9 Ⓐ Ⓑ Ⓒ Ⓓ Ⓔ
10 Ⓕ Ⓖ Ⓗ Ⓙ Ⓚ
11 Ⓐ Ⓑ Ⓒ Ⓓ Ⓔ
12 Ⓕ Ⓖ Ⓗ Ⓙ Ⓚ
13 Ⓐ Ⓑ Ⓒ Ⓓ Ⓔ

Directions: For items 14-22, find the word that is spelled incorrectly. For items 23-27, look for the word that is spelled incorrectly. Mark the circle "No mistakes" if there are no errors.

14
- (F) donate
- (G) first
- (H) uncle
- (J) thinkt

15
- (A) answer
- (B) adress
- (C) having
- (D) station

16
- (F) tipe
- (G) without
- (H) hidden
- (J) flew

17
- (A) peeceful
- (B) nearly
- (C) kind
- (D) swimmer

18
- (F) report
- (G) steer
- (H) rownd
- (J) child

19
- (A) borrow
- (B) workd
- (C) story
- (D) scrub

20
- (F) morning
- (G) lucky
- (H) guard
- (J) playce

21
- (A) fingur
- (B) puzzle
- (C) right
- (D) crush

22
- (F) sheet
- (G) basemint
- (H) office
- (J) dirty

STOP

---

23 Of cours you can stay for dinner. No mistake

(A) cours (B) stay (C) dinner (D) No mistake

24 The largest tree will be difficult to climb. No mistake

(F) largest (G) tree (H) difficult (J) No mistake

25 Each machene has a special key. No mistake

(A) Each (B) machene (C) special (D) No mistake

26 Did somone try to complete the form? No mistake

(F) somone (G) try (H) complete (J) No mistake

27 Wendy droppded the box before I was ready. No mistake

(A) Wendy (B) droppded (C) before (D) No mistake

ANSWER ROWS
14 (F) (G) (H) (J)
15 (A) (B) (C) (D)
16 (F) (G) (H) (J)
17 (A) (B) (C) (D)
18 (F) (G) (H) (J)
19 (A) (B) (C) (D)
20 (F) (G) (H) (J)
21 (A) (B) (C) (D)
22 (F) (G) (H) (J)
23 (A) (B) (C) (D)
24 (F) (G) (H) (J)
25 (A) (B) (C) (D)
26 (F) (G) (H) (J)
27 (A) (B) (C) (D)

NUMBER RIGHT ______

Lesson 13 Study Skills

Examples **Directions:** Read each question. Fill in the circle for the answer you think is correct.

A Which of these words comes first in alphabetical order?

Ⓐ tin
Ⓑ toy
Ⓒ table
Ⓓ trick

B Where would you look to find the most information about sailing?

Ⓕ in an encyclopedia
Ⓖ in a dictionary
Ⓗ in a history book
Ⓙ in a newspaper

Read each question carefully. Look at any reference materials that are part of the question. Then look at all the answer choices. Choose the one you think is right.

Practice

Marianne was reading a book about art for a group project. Use this Table of Contents and Index to answer numbers 1-3. They are from the art book Marianne is reading.

Table of Contents

Index

1 Marianne can find information about modern art on page—

23	24	49	74
Ⓐ	Ⓑ	Ⓒ	Ⓓ

2 Information about famous statues can be found on all these pages *except*—

23	30	31	32
Ⓕ	Ⓖ	Ⓗ	Ⓙ

3 To find out when people first began to create art, Marianne should read Chapter—

1	3	4	5
Ⓐ	Ⓑ	Ⓒ	Ⓓ

STOP

ANSWER ROWS A Ⓐ Ⓑ Ⓒ Ⓓ 1 Ⓐ Ⓑ Ⓒ Ⓓ 3 Ⓐ Ⓑ Ⓒ Ⓓ
B Ⓕ Ⓖ Ⓗ Ⓙ 2 Ⓕ Ⓖ Ⓗ Ⓙ

Directions: Use the picture dictionary on the left side of the page to do items 4-9.

celebrate

To celebrate is to remember an event with special activities.

currency

Coins and bills used as money are currency.

fox

A fox is a wild animal in the dog family.

hippopotamus

A hippopotamus is a large African animal that lives near water.

karate

Karate is a method of self-defense invented in Japan.

nutrition

The study of the value of different kinds of foods is nutrition.

recover

To recover is to get better after being sick.

4 Which word best fits in the sentence, "Quincy saw a ________ in the river when he visited Africa"?

Ⓕ fox
Ⓖ hippopotamus
Ⓗ currency
Ⓙ celebrate

5 How do you spell the word that means "a method of self-defense"?

Ⓐ karete
Ⓑ kerate
Ⓒ kurate
Ⓓ karate

6 Which word best fits in the sentence, "Carl read a book about ________ so he would know which foods were best"?

Ⓕ recover
Ⓖ celebrate
Ⓗ nutrition
Ⓙ currency

7 How do you spell the word that means "coins and bills used as money"?

Ⓐ currency
Ⓑ curency
Ⓒ currincy
Ⓓ currencie

8 Which of these words go together best?

Ⓕ eat nutrition
Ⓖ recover quickly
Ⓗ angry currency
Ⓙ celebrate against

9 Which word best fits in the sentence, "When will Agnes ________ from her cold"?

Ⓐ nutrition
Ⓑ celebrate
Ⓒ fox
Ⓓ recover

GO

ANSWER ROWS 4 Ⓕ Ⓖ Ⓗ Ⓙ 6 Ⓕ Ⓖ Ⓗ Ⓙ 8 Ⓕ Ⓖ Ⓗ Ⓙ
5 Ⓐ Ⓑ Ⓒ Ⓓ 7 Ⓐ Ⓑ Ⓒ Ⓓ 9 Ⓐ Ⓑ Ⓒ Ⓓ

In numbers 10-14, which word comes first in alphabetical order?

10 Ⓕ hurry Ⓖ help Ⓗ house Ⓙ high

11 Ⓐ again Ⓑ another Ⓒ action Ⓓ asleep

12 Ⓕ this Ⓖ touch Ⓗ trip Ⓙ toast

13 Ⓐ bread Ⓑ best Ⓒ boat Ⓓ blink

14 Ⓕ open Ⓖ owe Ⓗ oven Ⓙ old

---

15 Look at these guide words from a dictionary page.

nice—note

Which word would be found on the page?

Ⓐ noise Ⓑ nap Ⓒ now Ⓓ neither

16 Look at these guide words from a dictionary page.

count—crisp

Which word would be found on the page?

Ⓕ collect Ⓖ celebrate Ⓗ crane Ⓙ crow

Use the sample dictionary entries and the Pronunciation Guide below to answer numbers 17-19.

heal [hēl] *v.* 1. to make whole; restore to health 2. to bring to an end 3. to purify 4. to cure
health [helth] *n.* 1. the condition of the body or mind 2. freedom from disease
heap [hēp] 1. *n.* a group of things lying on one another 2. *v.* to put things in a pile

---

Pronunciation Guide:
act, w**ā**y, d**â**re, **ä**rt, s**e**t, **ē**qual, b**i**g, **ī**ce, b**o**x, **ō**ver, h**ô**rse, b**o͝o**k, t**o͞o**l, **u**s, t**û**rn; **ə** = a in *alone*, e in *mitten*, o in *actor*, u in *circus*

17 The word health sounds most like the word—

Ⓐ here Ⓑ learn Ⓒ set Ⓓ beach

18 Which definition best fits the word heal as it is used in the sentence below?

A bridge will heal the traffic problem.

1	2	3	4
Ⓕ	Ⓖ	Ⓗ	Ⓙ

19 The word heap sounds most like the word—

Ⓐ let
Ⓑ date
Ⓒ help
Ⓓ deep

STOP

ANSWER ROWS 10 Ⓕ Ⓖ Ⓗ Ⓙ 11 Ⓐ Ⓑ Ⓒ Ⓓ 12 Ⓕ Ⓖ Ⓗ Ⓙ 13 Ⓐ Ⓑ Ⓒ Ⓓ 14 Ⓕ Ⓖ Ⓗ Ⓙ 15 Ⓐ Ⓑ Ⓒ Ⓓ 16 Ⓕ Ⓖ Ⓗ Ⓙ 17 Ⓐ Ⓑ Ⓒ Ⓓ 18 Ⓕ Ⓖ Ⓗ Ⓙ 19 Ⓐ Ⓑ Ⓒ Ⓓ

Examples

Directions: Read each question. Fill in the circle for the answer you think is correct.

E1 Which of these words comes <u>first</u> in alphabetical order?

Ⓐ bend
Ⓑ bush
Ⓒ brick
Ⓓ boat

E2 Which one of these is a main heading that includes the other three words?

Ⓕ Apple
Ⓖ Peach
Ⓗ Fruit
Ⓙ Orange

Directions: For items 1-4, carefully read the question in each item in order to choose the correct answer.

1 Which of these would tell you the page on which the chapters of a book start?

Ⓐ the index
Ⓑ the table of contents
Ⓒ the bibliography
Ⓓ the title page

2 Which of these would tell you how to break the word <u>tomorrow</u> into syllables?

Ⓕ an atlas
Ⓖ an encyclopedia
Ⓗ a mathematics book
Ⓙ a dictionary

3 Which of these would tell you the name, address, and telephone number of the restaurants in your town?

Ⓐ a dictionary
Ⓑ a cookbook
Ⓒ a telephone book
Ⓓ an atlas

4 Which one of these is a main heading that includes the other three words?

Ⓕ Clothes
Ⓖ Hat
Ⓗ Coat
Ⓙ Shirt

The table of contents below is from a book called *Homes for Americans*. Use it to answer numbers 5 and 6.

Homes for Americans

Table of Contents

5 Which chapter might tell you about the homes of people near the North Pole?

Ⓐ 1 Ⓑ 3 Ⓒ 6 Ⓓ 8

6 Chapter 8 might tell us about

Ⓕ the weather tomorrow.
Ⓖ houses in the desert.
Ⓗ Civil War homes.
Ⓙ future ways to build homes.

GO

ANSWER ROWS
E1 Ⓐ Ⓑ Ⓒ Ⓓ 1 Ⓐ Ⓑ Ⓒ Ⓓ 3 Ⓐ Ⓑ Ⓒ Ⓓ 5 Ⓐ Ⓑ Ⓒ Ⓓ
E2 Ⓕ Ⓖ Ⓗ Ⓙ 2 Ⓕ Ⓖ Ⓗ Ⓙ 4 Ⓕ Ⓖ Ⓗ Ⓙ 6 Ⓕ Ⓖ Ⓗ Ⓙ

In numbers 7-11, which word comes first in alphabetical order?

7 Ⓐ much Ⓑ most Ⓒ mouse Ⓓ merry

8 Ⓕ vest Ⓖ vote Ⓗ valley Ⓙ village

9 Ⓐ deep Ⓑ dial Ⓒ dull Ⓓ dove

10 Ⓕ send Ⓖ soon Ⓗ shore Ⓙ scratch

11 Ⓐ north Ⓑ need Ⓒ nine Ⓓ numb

---

12 Look at these guide words from a dictionary page.

letter—line

Which word would be found on the page?

Ⓕ like
Ⓖ lead
Ⓗ lunch
Ⓙ list

13 Look at these guide words from a dictionary page.

bath—brick

Which word would be found on the page?

Ⓐ bad
Ⓑ brand
Ⓒ brush
Ⓓ by

Use the sample dictionary entries and the Pronunciation Guide below to answer numbers 14-15.

ex • press [ik spres′] *v.* 1. to put into words 2. to show or reveal 3. to send quickly *adj.* 4. clear or easily understood 5. quick *n.* 6. a direct train
ex • pres • sion [ik spresh′ ən] *n.* 1. the act of saying something 2. a special way of saying something

---

Pronunciation Guide:
act, wā̄y, dâre, ärt, set, ēqual, big, īce, box, ōver, hôrse, bo͝ok, to͞ol, us, tûrn; ə = a in *alone*, e in *mitten*, o in *actor*, u in *circus*

14 What is the correct way to divide expression into syllables?

Ⓕ exp—res—sion
Ⓖ expres—sion
Ⓗ ex—pres—sion
Ⓙ express—ion

15 Which definition best fits the word express as it is used in the sentence below?

The express will get us home quickly.

1	2	5	6
Ⓐ	Ⓑ	Ⓒ	Ⓓ

STOP

ANSWER ROWS 7 Ⓐ Ⓑ Ⓒ Ⓓ 10 Ⓕ Ⓖ Ⓗ Ⓙ 13 Ⓐ Ⓑ Ⓒ Ⓓ
8 Ⓕ Ⓖ Ⓗ Ⓙ 11 Ⓐ Ⓑ Ⓒ Ⓓ 14 Ⓕ Ⓖ Ⓗ Ⓙ
9 Ⓐ Ⓑ Ⓒ Ⓓ 12 Ⓕ Ⓖ Ⓗ Ⓙ 15 Ⓐ Ⓑ Ⓒ Ⓓ

NUMBER RIGHT ______

Name and Answer Sheet

To the Student:

These tests will give you a chance to put the tips you have learned to work.

A few last reminders...

- Be sure you understand all the directions before you begin each test. You may ask the teacher questions about the directions if you do not understand them.
- Work as quickly as you can during each test.
- When you change an answer, be sure to erase your first mark completely.
- You can guess at an answer or skip difficult items and go back to them later.
- Use the tips you have learned whenever you can.
- It is OK to be a little nervous. You may even do better.

Now that you have completed the lessons in this unit, you are on your way to scoring high!

STUDENT'S NAME

LAST | FIRST | MI

Ⓐ Ⓑ Ⓒ Ⓓ Ⓔ Ⓕ Ⓖ Ⓗ Ⓘ Ⓙ Ⓚ Ⓛ Ⓜ Ⓝ Ⓞ Ⓟ Ⓠ Ⓡ Ⓢ Ⓣ Ⓤ Ⓥ Ⓦ Ⓧ Ⓨ Ⓩ

SCHOOL

TEACHER

FEMALE ◯ MALE ◯

BIRTHDATE

MONTH	DAY		YEAR	
JAN ◯	0	0		0
FEB ◯	1	1		1
MAR ◯	2	2		2
APR ◯	3	3		3
MAY ◯		4		4
JUN ◯		5	5	5
JUL ◯		6	6	6
AUG ◯		7	7	7
SEP ◯		8	8	8
OCT ◯		9	9	9
NOV ◯				
DEC ◯				

GRADE

② ③ ④

PART 1 LANGUAGE MECHANICS

E1 Ⓐ Ⓑ Ⓒ Ⓓ	3 Ⓐ Ⓑ Ⓒ Ⓓ	7 Ⓐ Ⓑ Ⓒ Ⓓ	11 Ⓐ Ⓑ Ⓒ Ⓓ	15 Ⓐ Ⓑ Ⓒ Ⓓ	19 Ⓐ Ⓑ Ⓒ Ⓓ
E2 Ⓕ Ⓖ Ⓗ Ⓙ	4 Ⓕ Ⓖ Ⓗ Ⓙ	8 Ⓕ Ⓖ Ⓗ Ⓙ	12 Ⓕ Ⓖ Ⓗ Ⓙ	16 Ⓕ Ⓖ Ⓗ Ⓙ	20 Ⓕ Ⓖ Ⓗ Ⓙ
1 Ⓐ Ⓑ Ⓒ Ⓓ	5 Ⓐ Ⓑ Ⓒ Ⓓ	9 Ⓐ Ⓑ Ⓒ Ⓓ	13 Ⓐ Ⓑ Ⓒ Ⓓ	17 Ⓐ Ⓑ Ⓒ Ⓓ	21 Ⓐ Ⓑ Ⓒ Ⓓ
2 Ⓕ Ⓖ Ⓗ Ⓙ	6 Ⓕ Ⓖ Ⓗ Ⓙ	10 Ⓕ Ⓖ Ⓗ Ⓙ	14 Ⓕ Ⓖ Ⓗ Ⓙ	18 Ⓕ Ⓖ Ⓗ Ⓙ	22 Ⓕ Ⓖ Ⓗ Ⓙ

PART 2 LANGUAGE EXPRESSION

E1 Ⓐ Ⓑ Ⓒ Ⓓ	5 Ⓐ Ⓑ Ⓒ Ⓓ	11 Ⓐ Ⓑ Ⓒ Ⓓ	17 Ⓐ Ⓑ Ⓒ Ⓓ	23 Ⓐ Ⓑ Ⓒ Ⓓ	27 Ⓐ Ⓑ Ⓒ Ⓓ
E2 Ⓕ Ⓖ Ⓗ Ⓙ	6 Ⓕ Ⓖ Ⓗ Ⓙ	12 Ⓕ Ⓖ Ⓗ Ⓙ	18 Ⓕ Ⓖ Ⓗ Ⓙ	24 Ⓕ Ⓖ Ⓗ Ⓙ	28 Ⓕ Ⓖ Ⓗ Ⓙ
1 Ⓐ Ⓑ Ⓒ Ⓓ	7 Ⓐ Ⓑ Ⓒ Ⓓ	13 Ⓐ Ⓑ Ⓒ Ⓓ	19 Ⓐ Ⓑ Ⓒ Ⓓ	25 Ⓐ Ⓑ Ⓒ Ⓓ	29 Ⓐ Ⓑ Ⓒ Ⓓ
2 Ⓕ Ⓖ Ⓗ Ⓙ	8 Ⓕ Ⓖ Ⓗ Ⓙ	14 Ⓕ Ⓖ Ⓗ Ⓙ	20 Ⓕ Ⓖ Ⓗ Ⓙ	26 Ⓕ Ⓖ Ⓗ Ⓙ	30 Ⓕ Ⓖ Ⓗ Ⓙ
3 Ⓐ Ⓑ Ⓒ Ⓓ	9 Ⓐ Ⓑ Ⓒ Ⓓ	15 Ⓐ Ⓑ Ⓒ Ⓓ	21 Ⓐ Ⓑ Ⓒ Ⓓ		
4 Ⓕ Ⓖ Ⓗ Ⓙ	10 Ⓕ Ⓖ Ⓗ Ⓙ	16 Ⓕ Ⓖ Ⓗ Ⓙ	22 Ⓕ Ⓖ Ⓗ Ⓙ		

PART 3 SPELLING

E1 Ⓐ Ⓑ Ⓒ Ⓓ Ⓔ	3 Ⓐ Ⓑ Ⓒ Ⓓ	9 Ⓐ Ⓑ Ⓒ Ⓓ Ⓔ	15 Ⓐ Ⓑ Ⓒ Ⓓ	20 Ⓕ Ⓖ Ⓗ Ⓙ	24 Ⓕ Ⓖ Ⓗ Ⓙ
E2 Ⓕ Ⓖ Ⓗ Ⓙ Ⓚ	4 Ⓕ Ⓖ Ⓗ Ⓙ	10 Ⓕ Ⓖ Ⓗ Ⓙ Ⓚ	16 Ⓕ Ⓖ Ⓗ Ⓙ	21 Ⓐ Ⓑ Ⓒ Ⓓ	25 Ⓐ Ⓑ Ⓒ Ⓓ
E3 Ⓐ Ⓑ Ⓒ Ⓓ Ⓔ	5 Ⓐ Ⓑ Ⓒ Ⓓ	11 Ⓐ Ⓑ Ⓒ Ⓓ Ⓔ	17 Ⓐ Ⓑ Ⓒ Ⓓ	22 Ⓕ Ⓖ Ⓗ Ⓙ	26 Ⓕ Ⓖ Ⓗ Ⓙ
E4 Ⓕ Ⓖ Ⓗ Ⓙ Ⓚ	6 Ⓕ Ⓖ Ⓗ Ⓙ	12 Ⓕ Ⓖ Ⓗ Ⓙ Ⓚ	18 Ⓕ Ⓖ Ⓗ Ⓙ	23 Ⓐ Ⓑ Ⓒ Ⓓ	27 Ⓐ Ⓑ Ⓒ Ⓓ
1 Ⓐ Ⓑ Ⓒ Ⓓ	7 Ⓐ Ⓑ Ⓒ Ⓓ	13 Ⓐ Ⓑ Ⓒ Ⓓ Ⓔ	19 Ⓐ Ⓑ Ⓒ Ⓓ		
2 Ⓕ Ⓖ Ⓗ Ⓙ	8 Ⓕ Ⓖ Ⓗ Ⓙ	14 Ⓕ Ⓖ Ⓗ Ⓙ			

PART 4 STUDY SKILLS

E1 Ⓐ Ⓑ Ⓒ Ⓓ	2 Ⓕ Ⓖ Ⓗ Ⓙ	5 Ⓐ Ⓑ Ⓒ Ⓓ	8 Ⓕ Ⓖ Ⓗ Ⓙ	11 Ⓐ Ⓑ Ⓒ Ⓓ	14 Ⓕ Ⓖ Ⓗ Ⓙ
E2 Ⓕ Ⓖ Ⓗ Ⓙ	3 Ⓐ Ⓑ Ⓒ Ⓓ	6 Ⓕ Ⓖ Ⓗ Ⓙ	9 Ⓐ Ⓑ Ⓒ Ⓓ	12 Ⓕ Ⓖ Ⓗ Ⓙ	15 Ⓐ Ⓑ Ⓒ Ⓓ
1 Ⓐ Ⓑ Ⓒ Ⓓ	4 Ⓕ Ⓖ Ⓗ Ⓙ	7 Ⓐ Ⓑ Ⓒ Ⓓ	10 Ⓕ Ⓖ Ⓗ Ⓙ	13 Ⓐ Ⓑ Ⓒ Ⓓ	16 Ⓕ Ⓖ Ⓗ Ⓙ

Part 1 Language Mechanics

Directions: For items E1 and 1-3, read the sentences that are divided into parts. Fill in the circle for the part that has a word that should begin with a capital letter. For items 4-5, choose the answer that fits best in the blank and has the correct capitalization. For items E2 and 6-8, fill in the circle for the punctuation mark that is needed in the sentence. Choose "None" if no punctuation is needed.

E1 When will (A) | you move (B) | to your new house? (C) | None (D)

E2
- (F) The cars trucks and buses
- (G) moved slowly because
- (H) the fog was heavy.
- (J) *(No mistakes)*

1 In oregon (A) | there are (B) | many forests. (C) | None (D)

2 Both of my sisters (F) | played basketball (G) | in high school. (H) | None (J)

3 The weather (A) | last april (B) | was warmer than usual. (C) | None (D)

---

4 A flock of birds landed in ________ .

- (F) the Tall tree
- (G) the tall Tree
- (H) the tall tree
- (J) the Tall Tree

5 Turn right ________ and drive for three more miles.

- (A) at Riverside Park
- (B) at riverside park
- (C) at Riverside park
- (D) at riverside Park

---

6 Have you finished your homework yet?

(F) ! (G) . (H) , (J) None

7 Is that your friend's bicycle

(A) . (B) ! (C) ? (D) None

8 Ruth jumped into a pile of leaves

(F) . (G) ! (H) ? (J) None

STOP

Directions: For item 9, choose the answer that you think is correct. For item 10, choose the answer that fits best in the blank and has the correct punctuation.

9 **Which is the correct way to begin a letter to a friend of your parents?**

Ⓐ Dear Mr Morris,
Ⓑ Dear Mr. Morris
Ⓒ Dear Mr Morris
Ⓓ Dear Mr. Morris,

10 **The children ________ able to eat all the pizza.**

Ⓕ werent
Ⓖ were'nt
Ⓗ weren't
Ⓙ werent'

Directions: For items 11-12, find the answer choice that has a punctuation mistake. Mark the circle "No mistakes" if there are no errors.

11
Ⓐ "Will you be able
Ⓑ to find one for me?" Nancy
Ⓒ asked the store clerk.
Ⓓ *(No mistakes)*

12
Ⓕ Which of these colors
Ⓖ do you think
Ⓗ is the prettiest
Ⓙ *(No mistakes)*

Directions: For items 13-14, find the answer choice that has a correct punctuation. Mark the circle "No mistakes" if there are no errors.

13
Ⓐ We can build a tree house.
Ⓑ The children asked their parents if they could borrow some tools
Ⓒ it took them a few days to finish the tree house.
Ⓓ How can i help?

14
Ⓕ Have you read Better Health
Ⓖ The book Space Adventure will become a movie.
Ⓗ The Biggest river is a great book.
Ⓙ Judy Harlan wrote Only Child

Directions: For items 15-16, read the letter. Find the answer choice that shows the correct capitalization and punctuation for the underlined parts.

(15) October 29 1994,

Dear Aunt Millie,

(16) I'm sorry to hear you have been sick. I hope you get well soon so we can play tennis again.

Your nephew,

Bruce

15
Ⓐ October 29 1994
Ⓑ October 29, 1994
Ⓒ October, 29, 1994
Ⓓ correct as it is

16
Ⓕ sick I
Ⓖ sick, I
Ⓗ sick. i
Ⓙ correct as it is

STOP

17 The factory was first opened on ________.

Ⓐ january 4, 1908
Ⓑ January, 4, 1908
Ⓒ january, 4, 1908
Ⓓ January 4, 1908

18 The house on the corner was bought by ________.

Ⓕ A. N. Wise
Ⓖ A N Wise
Ⓗ a n wise
Ⓙ a. n. wise

Read this story and answer questions 19–22. The story has groups of underlined words. The questions will ask about them.

Our fishing trip started out fine. **(1)** *We got to the boat around* *six oclock* *in the morning and headed from* *shore about* **(2)** *30 minutes later, we stopped the boat and began to fish.* *We caught a few fish and were having a* *Good Time.* **(3)** *Then the wind started to blow, and it got cloudy.* **(4)** *Soon it began to rain.* **(5)** *We headed back to the dock, but the rain got worse.* **(6)** *By the time we reached the dock, we were* *cold, wet, and tired.* **(7)**

19 In sentence 2, six oclock is best written—

Ⓐ Six Oclock
Ⓑ six o'clock
Ⓒ Six O'clock
Ⓓ as it is

20 In sentence 2, shore about is best written—

Ⓕ shore. About
Ⓖ shore. about
Ⓗ shore, about
Ⓙ as it is

21 In sentence 3, Good Time is best written—

Ⓐ good Time
Ⓑ Good time
Ⓒ good time
Ⓓ as it is

22 In sentence 7, cold, wet, and tired is best written—

Ⓕ cold wet and tired
Ⓖ cold, wet, and, tired
Ⓗ cold, wet and tired
Ⓙ as it is

Part 2 Language Expression

Directions: For items E1 and 1-3, find the word that fits best in the blank. For item 4, read the sentence. Find the pronoun that can replace the underlined word. For items E2 and 5-8, fill in the circle for the answer choice that is a complete and correctly written sentence.

E1

It is too ________ to walk to the store.

- Ⓐ farther
- Ⓑ farthest
- Ⓒ more farther
- Ⓓ far

E2

- Ⓕ Lynne lost her gloves.
- Ⓖ Dwayne and me will be late.
- Ⓗ Them are not my friends.
- Ⓙ This is you seat.

1 The children ________ the steps to the top of the tower.

- Ⓐ climbs
- Ⓑ is climbing
- Ⓒ climbed
- Ⓓ was climbing

2 The ________ flowers are on the plant near the wall.

- Ⓕ prettiest
- Ⓖ prettier
- Ⓗ more pretty
- Ⓙ most prettiest

3 You can lend ________ your hat.

- Ⓐ she
- Ⓑ her
- Ⓒ he
- Ⓓ its

---

4 Is Emmet going to meet us at the picnic?

- Ⓕ he
- Ⓖ him
- Ⓗ his
- Ⓙ them

5

- Ⓐ Garage door opening slowly.
- Ⓑ Packing things in the trunk.
- Ⓒ Mia and her father this afternoon.
- Ⓓ The car ran out of gas.

6

- Ⓕ An owl flew fastly from a tree.
- Ⓖ The woods seem quiet tonight.
- Ⓗ We walked more slower because it was so dark.
- Ⓙ This is a very brightest flashlight.

7

- Ⓐ Give we a good map.
- Ⓑ We can borrow hims paddles.
- Ⓒ He and I are planning a canoe trip.
- Ⓓ Them will not be able to find us tomorrow.

8

- Ⓕ Our town is growed this year.
- Ⓖ My mother working on Hill Street.
- Ⓗ The parade always start at the park.
- Ⓙ This new store opened last week.

GO

Directions: For items 9-13, find the answer choice that has a mistake. Mark the circle "No mistakes" if there are no errors. For items 14-15, find the sentence that has the complete subject underlined. For items 16-17, mark the sentence that has the complete predicate underlined. For items 18-19, find the simple subject of the sentence. For items 20-21, find the simple predicate of the sentence.

9
- Ⓐ There ain't no way
- Ⓑ we can get to the post office
- Ⓒ before it closes.
- Ⓓ *(No mistakes)*

10
- Ⓕ Cassie called. She wants
- Ⓖ to know if you can
- Ⓗ meet her at the pool.
- Ⓙ *(No mistakes)*

11
- Ⓐ School will be closed
- Ⓑ next week. My family will
- Ⓒ go camping near an lake.
- Ⓓ *(No mistakes)*

12
- Ⓕ The box you have is
- Ⓖ largest than the ones
- Ⓗ Warren and I brought.
- Ⓙ *(No mistakes)*

13
- Ⓐ The boots she bought
- Ⓑ wasn't the right size.
- Ⓒ She had to return them.
- Ⓓ *(No mistakes)*

14
- Ⓕ A truck delivered our new stove.
- Ⓖ Many cars are built in Michigan.
- Ⓗ A large rock fell on the road.
- Ⓙ Four vans are in the lot.

15
- Ⓐ The blue towel is still wet.
- Ⓑ The clothes are drying on the line.
- Ⓒ We should wash the sheets today.
- Ⓓ The soap spilled on the floor.

16
- Ⓕ The farmer plowed the field.
- Ⓖ The barn door swung open.
- Ⓗ The corn grew quickly.
- Ⓙ Her father bought a farm.

17
- Ⓐ Your letter arrived yesterday.
- Ⓑ They will come tomorrow.
- Ⓒ The boat sank quickly.
- Ⓓ We walked on the beach.

---

18 The picture of a lake was hanging on the wall.

Ⓕ picture Ⓖ lake Ⓗ hanging Ⓙ wall

19 Two large men carried the sofa into the house.

Ⓐ Two Ⓑ men Ⓒ sofa Ⓓ house

---

20 Lightning hit the tree by the barn.

Ⓕ Lightning Ⓖ hit Ⓗ tree Ⓙ barn

21 My sister's team won the championship.

Ⓐ sister's Ⓑ team Ⓒ won Ⓓ championship

GO

Read this essay. Use it to answer questions 22–25.

The earth is part of the solar system. **(1)** *The sun is in the center of the solar system the planets revolve around it.* **(2)** *There are nine planets.* **(3)** *Mercury is the closest planet to the sun.* **(4)** *The earth is the third planet from the sun.* **(5)** *Saturn is different from the other planets.* **(6)** *It has visible rings.* **(7)** *The rings of dust and small rocks.* **(8)** *You can see the rings if you use a telescope or even good binoculars.* **(9)** *Many of the planets have moons.* **(10)** *The earth has one moon, but some other planets may have as many as twenty moons.* **(11)**

22 Sentence 2 is best written—

Ⓕ The sun is in the center, the planets revolve around it.

Ⓖ The planets, revolving around the sun, which is at the center of the solar system.

Ⓗ The sun is in the center of the solar system. The planets revolve around it.

Ⓙ as it is

23 Which of these could be added after sentence 4?

Ⓐ Pluto is farthest from the sun.

Ⓑ Planets are made up of different substances.

Ⓒ A moon is not a planet.

Ⓓ The sun is a star.

24 Which of these is not a sentence?

3	5	8	10
Ⓕ	Ⓖ	Ⓗ	Ⓙ

25 How are sentences 6 and 7 best joined without changing the meaning?

Ⓐ Saturn is different from the other planets, and it has visible rings.

Ⓑ Saturn is different from the other planets because it has visible rings.

Ⓒ The visible rings it has, which make Saturn different from the other planets.

Ⓓ The visible rings of Saturn, which it has, make it different from the other planets.

GO

Directions: Read the underlined sentences. Choose the answer that is the best combination of the sentences.

26 <u>**A group of children went to the park.**</u>

<u>**A group of children had a picnic.**</u>

Ⓕ **A group of children, going to the park, had a picnic.**

Ⓖ **A group of children went to the park and had a picnic.**

Ⓗ **A group of children, who had a picnic, went to the park.**

Ⓙ **A group of children going to the park and having a picnic.**

Directions: Read the sentence. Choose the answer that shows the best way to write the underlined part. Mark the circle "No change" if the part is correct.

27 **Next summer, I <u>was visit</u> my friend in Ohio.**

Ⓐ **will visit** Ⓑ **visits** Ⓒ **to visit** Ⓓ ***(No change)***

Directions: Mark the circle for the sentence that is correctly formed.

28 Ⓕ We couldn't find the brushes, so we painted the porch.

Ⓖ It was the porch we wanted to paint, if we could find the brushes.

Ⓗ We wanted to paint the porch, but we couldn't find the brushes.

Ⓙ Although we couldn't find the brushes, we painted the porch.

Directions: Find the answer choice that is the best topic sentence for the story.

29 **______________. When my sister practices the piano, Molly sings along. Molly sits beside the piano and howls until Elena chases her away.**

Ⓐ **My dog Molly is four years old.**

Ⓑ **My dog Molly does something very funny.**

Ⓒ **My sister plays the piano.**

Ⓓ **Dogs can learn many interesting tricks.**

Directions: Find the answer choice that best fits the paragraph.

30 **The roof of our house started leaking yesterday. ______________. He and my mother will try to fix it today.**

Ⓕ **Our house is over a hundred years old.**

Ⓖ **The weather has been cold and snowy for weeks.**

Ⓗ **My father thinks it was caused by ice.**

Ⓙ **My father often repairs our car.**

Part 3 Spelling

Examples

Directions: For items E1 and 1-8, find the word that is spelled correctly. For items E2-E3 and 9-13, mark the space for the misspelled word.

E1

Don't make any _______ movements.

Ⓐ suddin
Ⓑ sudden
Ⓒ suden
Ⓓ suddinn

E2

Ⓕ thick
Ⓖ lunch
Ⓗ nobody
Ⓙ ladder
Ⓚ *(No mistakes)*

E3

Ⓐ main
Ⓑ sign
Ⓒ partey
Ⓓ trunk

1 You can play _______ this afternoon.

Ⓐ toogether
Ⓑ togethir
Ⓒ togather
Ⓓ together

2 Your socks don't _______ .

Ⓕ mach
Ⓖ match
Ⓗ madch
Ⓙ madtch

3 Practice will _______ your swimming.

Ⓐ improve
Ⓑ improv
Ⓒ impruv
Ⓓ impruve

4 _______ way did the rabbit run?

Ⓕ Wich
Ⓖ Whitch
Ⓗ Widch
Ⓙ Which

5 Her horse is _______ .

Ⓐ gentl
Ⓑ gentle
Ⓒ gentel
Ⓓ gentul

6 Mark gave a _______ answer.

Ⓕ polite
Ⓖ polit
Ⓗ polyte
Ⓙ poleite

7 This is my _______ restaurant.

Ⓐ favrit
Ⓑ favrite
Ⓒ favorite
Ⓓ favorit

8 The new bank looks very _______ .

Ⓕ modrn
Ⓖ moddern
Ⓗ modern
Ⓙ modren

9
Ⓐ chickin
Ⓑ pattern
Ⓒ honest
Ⓓ waste
Ⓔ *(No mistakes)*

10
Ⓕ silly
Ⓖ oposite
Ⓗ bunch
Ⓙ worn
Ⓚ *(No mistakes)*

11
Ⓐ stretch
Ⓑ leave
Ⓒ beside
Ⓓ readey
Ⓔ *(No mistakes)*

12
Ⓕ pitch
Ⓖ dull
Ⓗ airrport
Ⓙ large
Ⓚ *(No mistakes)*

13
Ⓐ build
Ⓑ making
Ⓒ windy
Ⓓ respect
Ⓔ *(No mistakes)*

GO

Part 3 Spelling

Directions: For items 14-22, find the word that is spelled incorrectly. For items 23-27, read the sentence. Mark the space for the word that is spelled incorrectly. Mark the space for "No mistakes" if there are no errors.

14
Ⓕ clevir
Ⓖ unfair
Ⓗ lived
Ⓙ rain

15
Ⓐ heart
Ⓑ oldist
Ⓒ funny
Ⓓ attach

16
Ⓕ easy
Ⓖ cover
Ⓗ happy
Ⓙ repare

17
Ⓐ rocky
Ⓑ control
Ⓒ defind
Ⓓ bridge

18
Ⓕ several
Ⓖ huge
Ⓗ mountin
Ⓙ fault

19
Ⓐ trace
Ⓑ frend
Ⓒ loud
Ⓓ every

20
Ⓕ again
Ⓖ welcome
Ⓗ lettr
Ⓙ disobey

21
Ⓐ parrtly
Ⓑ float
Ⓒ visitor
Ⓓ cheek

22
Ⓕ everybody
Ⓖ unless
Ⓗ smooth
Ⓙ choyce

---

23 My sister (Ⓐ) had to rush (Ⓑ) aftr (Ⓒ) the bus. No mistake (Ⓓ)

24 How many (Ⓕ) poeple (Ⓖ) will the pot of soup serve? (Ⓗ) No mistake (Ⓙ)

25 Be caerful (Ⓐ) and drive a little (Ⓑ) slower. (Ⓒ) No mistake (Ⓓ)

26 We had to laugh (Ⓕ) at the kitten (Ⓖ) under the chair. (Ⓗ) No mistake (Ⓙ)

27 You got the highist (Ⓐ) grade (Ⓑ) in the class. (Ⓒ) No mistake (Ⓓ)

STOP

Examples

Directions: Read each question. Fill in the circle for the answer you think is correct.

E1

Which of these words comes first in alphabetical order?

Ⓐ after
Ⓑ against
Ⓒ among
Ⓓ about

E2

Which one of these is a main heading that includes the other three words?

Ⓕ Lunch
Ⓖ Meal
Ⓗ Dinner
Ⓙ Breakfast

On this page there are pictures and words from a picture dictionary. Use them to answer the questions below.

assist

To assist is to give help or aid.

employee

An employee is a person who works for a company.

imitate

To imitate is to act like another person.

pelican

A pelican is a bird that has a large bill and eats fish.

spiny

To be spiny is to be covered with sharp spines.

talented

To be talented is to be able to do things well.

1 Which word best fits in the sentence, "Teena ________ the way her mother played tennis"?

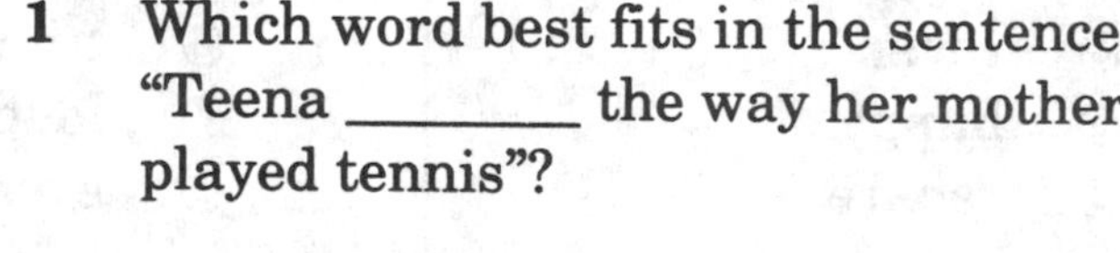

Ⓐ arrived
Ⓑ talented
Ⓒ imitated
Ⓓ assisted

2 How do you spell the word that means "to help someone"?

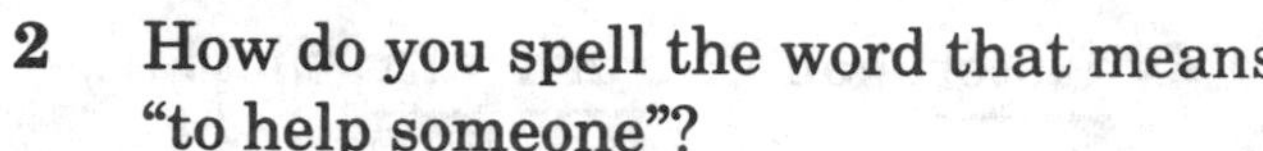

Ⓕ assist
Ⓖ asist
Ⓗ assisst
Ⓙ asisst

3 Which of these words go together best?

Ⓐ spiny pelican
Ⓑ assisted spiny
Ⓒ pelican imitated
Ⓓ talented employee

4 How do you spell the word that means "someone who works for a company"?

Ⓕ empleyee
Ⓖ employye
Ⓗ employ
Ⓙ employee

GO

Directions: For items 12-16, carefully read the question in each item in order to choose the correct answer.

In numbers 5-9, which word comes first in alphabetical order?

5 Ⓐ crash Ⓑ cent Ⓒ chicken Ⓓ care

6 Ⓕ west Ⓖ write Ⓗ wore Ⓙ wind

7 Ⓐ friend Ⓑ fourth Ⓒ flint Ⓓ float

8 Ⓕ roast Ⓖ risk Ⓗ rust Ⓙ rope

9 Ⓐ north Ⓑ need Ⓒ nine Ⓓ near

---

10 Look at these guide words from a dictionary page.

very—vote

Which word would be found on the page?

Ⓕ voice Ⓖ van Ⓗ vow Ⓙ vulture

11 Look at these guide words from a dictionary page.

lime—lose

Which word would be found on the page?

Ⓐ like Ⓑ luck Ⓒ list Ⓓ leak

12 Which of these would you use to find the date of Thanksgiving this year?

Ⓕ a dictionary
Ⓖ a catalog
Ⓗ a calendar
Ⓙ a telephone book

13 Which of these books would give you ideas about where you could take a camping vacation?

Ⓐ *Making A Campfire*
Ⓑ *Inexpensive Vacations*
Ⓒ *Fishing and Hunting*
Ⓓ *Campgrounds in America*

14 Suppose your teacher asked you to write about your favorite person. Which of these would be most helpful before you begin to write?

Ⓕ Think about some people you like
Ⓖ Think about your favorite pet
Ⓗ Draw a picture of someone
Ⓙ Write a note to a friend

15 Which one of these is a main heading that includes the other three words?

Ⓐ Fish
Ⓑ Pet
Ⓒ Cats
Ⓓ Birds

16 Which one of these is a main heading that includes the other three words?

Ⓕ Flower
Ⓖ Rose
Ⓗ Daisy
Ⓙ Tulip

STOP

Table of Contents
Math

UNIT 1 CONCEPTS

Lesson 1 Numeration

Example

Directions: Read and work each problem. Find the correct answer. Mark the space for your choice.

A Which of these is greater than 4?

Ⓐ 2
Ⓑ 3
Ⓒ 4
Ⓓ 5

B What is another name for 68?

Ⓕ 8 tens and 6 ones
Ⓖ 6 tens and 8 ones
Ⓗ 7 tens and 8 ones
Ⓙ 5 tens and 18 ones

Read each question carefully. Look for key words and numbers that will help you find the answers.

Practice

1 What number goes in the box on this number line?

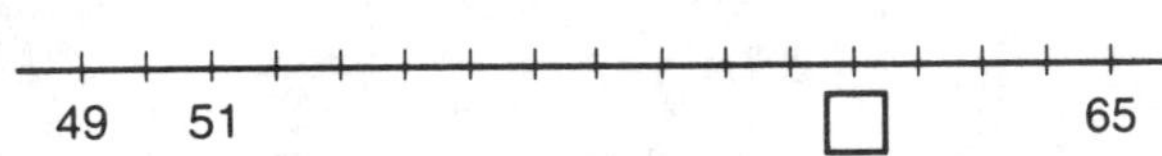

Ⓐ 58
Ⓑ 60
Ⓒ 61
Ⓓ 63

2 A group of students were recording the amount of rain that fell during each day in April. All their measurements were between 0.15 and 1.28 inches. Which of the measurements below might they have taken?

Ⓕ 0.58
Ⓖ 0.08
Ⓗ 2.26
Ⓙ 1.51

3 Your friend is twelfth in line for a roller coaster ride. Exactly how many people are ahead of your friend?

Ⓐ 10
Ⓑ 11
Ⓒ 14
Ⓓ 17

4 Which of these groups has five more bananas than monkeys?

Ⓕ 

Ⓖ

Ⓗ

Ⓙ

GO

ANSWER ROWS A Ⓐ Ⓑ Ⓒ Ⓓ 1 Ⓐ Ⓑ Ⓒ Ⓓ 3 Ⓐ Ⓑ Ⓒ Ⓓ
B Ⓕ Ⓖ Ⓗ Ⓙ 2 Ⓕ Ⓖ Ⓗ Ⓙ 4 Ⓕ Ⓖ Ⓗ Ⓙ

5 Which of these shows numerals in the correct counting order?

Ⓐ 27, 29, 38, 30

Ⓑ 26, 27, 28, 29

Ⓒ 25, 28, 29, 30

Ⓓ 24, 23, 22, 21

6 How many of these numbers are greater than 128?

182	104	127	227	119	132

Ⓕ 2

Ⓖ 3

Ⓗ 4

Ⓙ 5

7 Another name for 4 hundreds, 7 tens and 9 ones is

Ⓐ 479

Ⓑ 40,079

Ⓒ 4709

Ⓓ 4791

8 The number 978 is less than

Ⓕ 878

Ⓖ 966

Ⓗ 789

Ⓙ 998

9 Which of these shows the same number of carrots and pears?

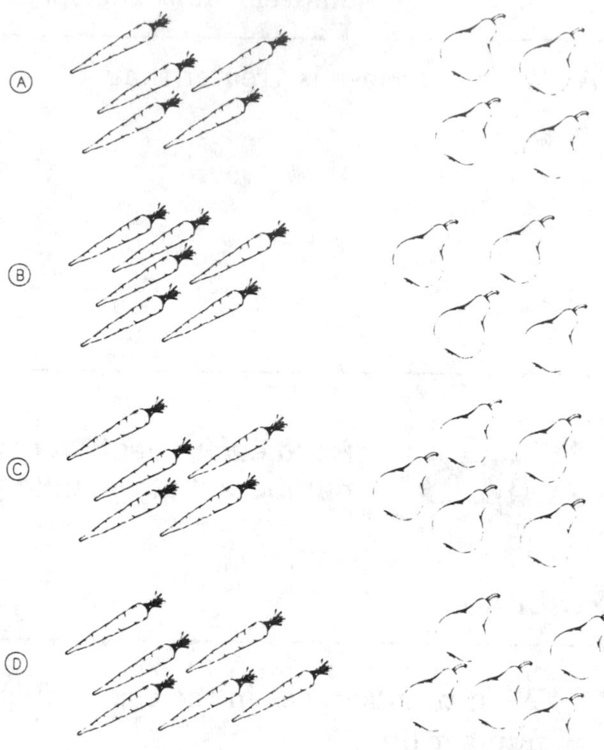

10 If you arranged these numbers from least to greatest, which would be last?

1038	1084	1308	1208	1803

Ⓕ 1803

Ⓖ 1208

Ⓗ 1084

Ⓙ 1308

11 How many tens are in 47?

Ⓐ 47

Ⓑ 10

Ⓒ 7

Ⓓ 4

STOP

ANSWER ROWS 5 Ⓐ Ⓑ Ⓒ Ⓓ 7 Ⓐ Ⓑ Ⓒ Ⓓ 9 Ⓐ Ⓑ Ⓒ Ⓓ 11 Ⓐ Ⓑ Ⓒ Ⓓ

6 Ⓕ Ⓖ Ⓗ Ⓙ 8 Ⓕ Ⓖ Ⓗ Ⓙ 10 Ⓕ Ⓖ Ⓗ Ⓙ

Example

Directions: Read and work each problem. Find the correct answer. Mark the space for your choice.

A Which of these is fifty-seven?

Ⓐ 50
Ⓑ 57
Ⓒ 75
Ⓓ 507

B Which of these is an even number?

Ⓕ 11
Ⓖ 9
Ⓗ 8
Ⓙ 5

Key words, numbers, pictures, and figures will help you find the answers.

When you are not sure of an answer, take your best guess.

Practice

1 What number do you think is represented by this chart?

100's	10's	1's
///	/////	///////

Ⓐ 15
Ⓑ 357
Ⓒ 3570
Ⓓ 30,507

2 What number is missing from the sequence below?

7, 16, 25, 34, ____ , 52

Ⓕ 38
Ⓖ 39
Ⓗ 42
Ⓙ 43

3 8 hundreds and 6 thousands =

Ⓐ 8600
Ⓑ 8606
Ⓒ 6800
Ⓓ 806

4 From the figures below, you know that

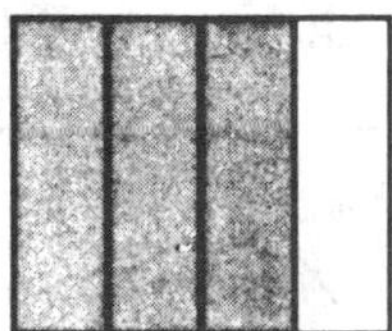

Ⓕ $\frac{3}{4}$ is greater than $\frac{1}{2}$.
Ⓖ $\frac{1}{3}$ is greater than $\frac{1}{2}$.
Ⓗ $\frac{3}{4}$ is less than $\frac{1}{2}$.
Ⓙ $\frac{3}{4}$ is less than $\frac{1}{3}$.

GO

ANSWER ROWS A Ⓐ Ⓑ Ⓒ Ⓓ 1 Ⓐ Ⓑ Ⓒ Ⓓ 3 Ⓐ Ⓑ Ⓒ Ⓓ
B Ⓕ Ⓖ Ⓗ Ⓙ 2 Ⓕ Ⓖ Ⓗ Ⓙ 4 Ⓕ Ⓖ Ⓗ Ⓙ

5 Counting by tens, which number comes after 50 and before 70?

Ⓐ 60

Ⓑ 80

Ⓒ 90

Ⓓ 160

6 Which of the numbers below has a 5 in the hundreds place?

Ⓕ 2395

Ⓖ 3259

Ⓗ 5932

Ⓙ 9532

7 Which group of numbers has three even numbers?

Ⓐ 8, 9, 16, 20, 44, 90, 97

Ⓑ 4, 9, 15, 27, 46, 68, 71

Ⓒ 3, 21, 44, 66, 75, 83, 93

Ⓓ 7, 24, 32, 56, 71, 82,95

8 How much of this figure is shaded?

Ⓕ $\frac{3}{4}$

Ⓖ $\frac{2}{3}$

Ⓗ $\frac{1}{3}$

Ⓙ $\frac{3}{10}$

9 Which of these numbers is even and can be divided by 5?

Ⓐ 58

Ⓑ 21

Ⓒ 15

Ⓓ 10

10 Which of these fractions is the smallest?

Ⓕ $\frac{1}{2}$

Ⓖ $\frac{2}{3}$

Ⓗ $\frac{1}{9}$

Ⓙ $\frac{3}{4}$

11 Look at the pattern below. Which shape is missing from the pattern?

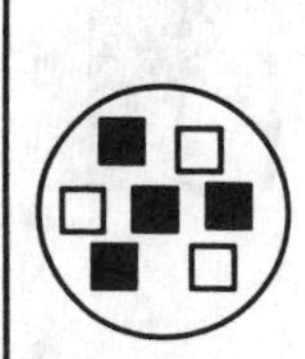
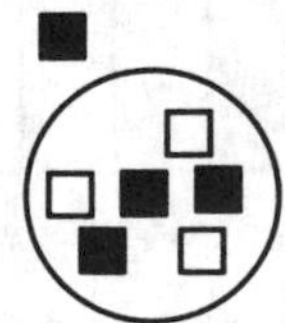
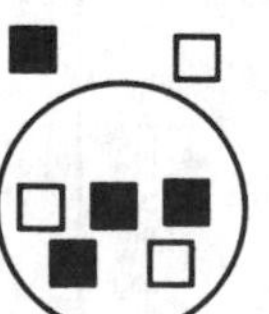
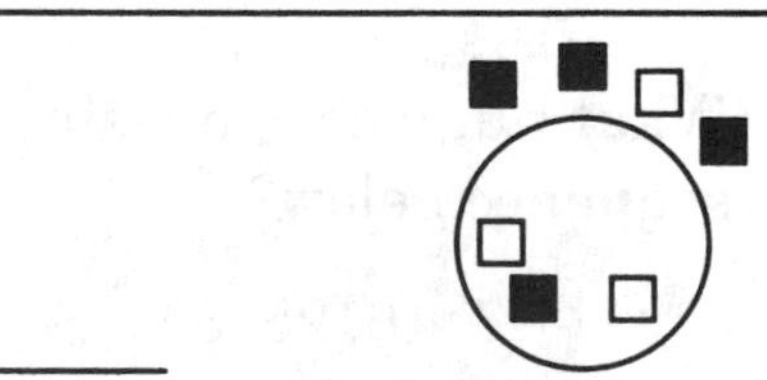

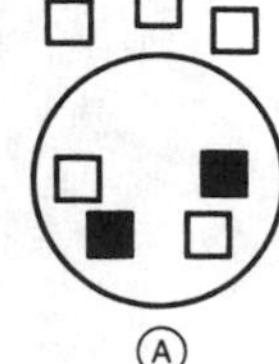
Ⓐ

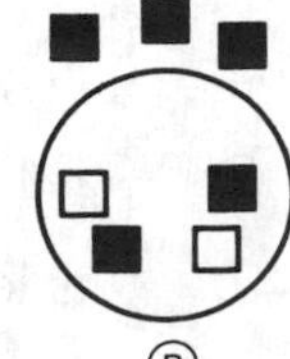
Ⓑ

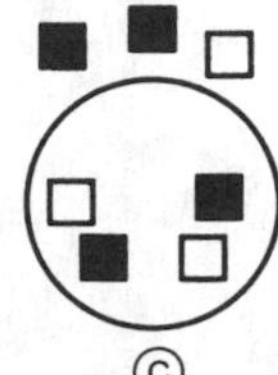
Ⓒ

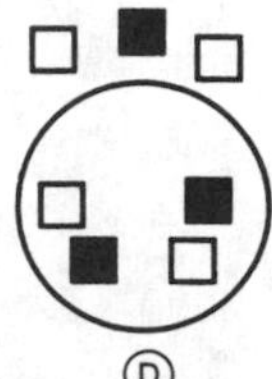
Ⓓ

ANSWER ROWS 5 Ⓐ Ⓑ Ⓒ Ⓓ 7 Ⓐ Ⓑ Ⓒ Ⓓ 9 Ⓐ Ⓑ Ⓒ Ⓓ 11 Ⓐ Ⓑ Ⓒ Ⓓ

6 Ⓕ Ⓖ Ⓗ Ⓙ 8 Ⓕ Ⓖ Ⓗ Ⓙ 10 Ⓕ Ⓖ Ⓗ Ⓙ

Lesson 3 Properties

Example

Directions: Read and work each problem. Find the correct answer. Mark the space for your choice.

A What number completes the number sentence □ + 0 = 5?

- Ⓐ 0
- Ⓑ 5
- Ⓒ 10
- Ⓓ 50

B What is 285 rounded to the nearest hundred?

- Ⓕ 200
- Ⓖ 280
- Ⓗ 290
- Ⓙ 300

Read the question carefully. Think about what the question is asking before you choose an answer.

If you work on scratch paper, be sure you transfer numbers correctly.

Practice

1 What number completes both of the number sentences below?

21 – □ = 17

8 + □ = 12

- Ⓐ 4
- Ⓑ 5
- Ⓒ 9
- Ⓓ 13

2 Which of the number sentences below is true?

- Ⓕ 299 < 290
- Ⓖ 299 > 390
- Ⓗ 390 = 290
- Ⓙ 390 > 299

3 Which of these answer choices is closest in value to 140?

- Ⓐ 39
- Ⓑ 129
- Ⓒ 136
- Ⓓ 148

4 What symbol correctly completes the number sentence below?

7 □ 3 = 21

- Ⓕ ÷
- Ⓖ x
- Ⓗ –
- Ⓙ +

GO

ANSWER ROWS A Ⓐ Ⓑ Ⓒ Ⓓ 1 Ⓐ Ⓑ Ⓒ Ⓓ 3 Ⓐ Ⓑ Ⓒ Ⓓ
B Ⓕ Ⓖ Ⓗ Ⓙ 2 Ⓕ Ⓖ Ⓗ Ⓙ 4 Ⓕ Ⓖ Ⓗ Ⓙ

5 Another way to write 3 x 7 is

Ⓐ 7 x 3 x 3

Ⓑ 3 + 7

Ⓒ 7 x 7 x 7

Ⓓ 7 + 7 + 7

6 If you round the numbers below to the nearest hundred, how many of them would be 300?

321, 233, 402, 287, 430, 294

Ⓕ 2

Ⓖ 3

Ⓗ 4

Ⓙ 6

7 $\frac{1}{4} = \frac{3}{\square}$ $\square =$

Ⓐ 3

Ⓑ 6

Ⓒ 12

Ⓓ 24

8 0.7 =

Ⓕ $\frac{7}{10}$

Ⓖ $\frac{7}{100}$

Ⓗ $\frac{7}{70}$

Ⓙ $\frac{70}{10}$

9 What symbol belongs in the circle in the number sentence below?

10 – 1 = 7 ○ 2

Ⓐ –

Ⓑ +

Ⓒ x

Ⓓ ÷

10 Suppose you wanted to estimate how to find 73 x 48 to the nearest 10. Which of these would you use?

Ⓕ 100 x 40

Ⓖ 100 x 50

Ⓗ 70 x 50

Ⓙ 70 x 40

11 Which number sentence shows how to find the total number of chairs in the box?

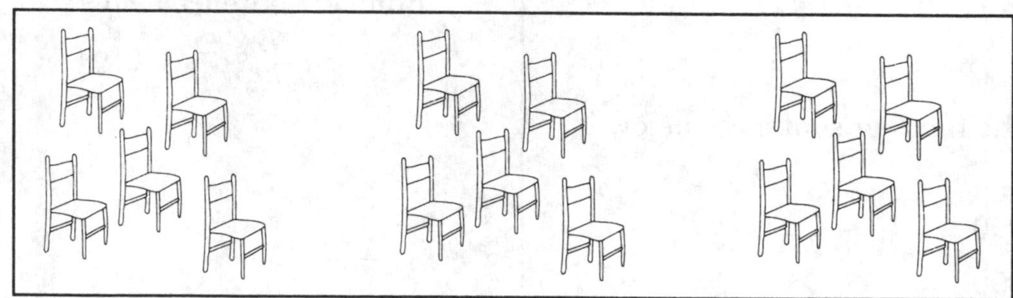

3 + 5 = ☐ Ⓐ

3 – 5 = ☐ Ⓑ

3 x 5 = ☐ Ⓒ

3 ÷ 5 = ☐ Ⓓ

STOP

ANSWER ROWS 5 Ⓐ Ⓑ Ⓒ Ⓓ 7 Ⓐ Ⓑ Ⓒ Ⓓ 9 Ⓐ Ⓑ Ⓒ Ⓓ 11 Ⓐ Ⓑ Ⓒ Ⓓ

6 Ⓕ Ⓖ Ⓗ Ⓙ 8 Ⓕ Ⓖ Ⓗ Ⓙ 10 Ⓕ Ⓖ Ⓗ Ⓙ

Lesson 4 Test Yourself

Examples

Directions: Read and work each problem. Find the correct answer. Mark the space for your choice.

E1

Twenty apples were on a tree. Six fell off. How can you find the number left?

Ⓐ add
Ⓑ subtract
Ⓒ multiply
Ⓓ divide

E2

Which letter of the alphabet comes immediately after the tenth letter?

Ⓕ J
Ⓖ K
Ⓗ M
Ⓙ P

1 Which of these means three thousand, nine hundred forty-six?

Ⓐ 3006
Ⓑ 3046
Ⓒ 3900
Ⓓ 3946

2 Look at the counting pattern below. What number comes next?

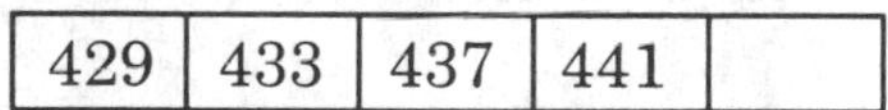

Ⓕ 443
Ⓖ 444
Ⓗ 445
Ⓙ 447

3 Which point on the number line below is closest to 7.1?

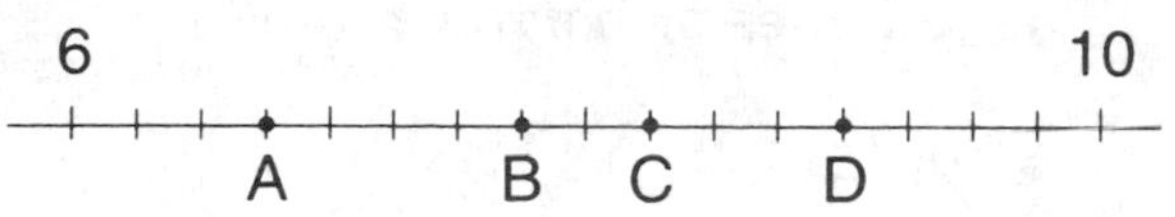

Ⓐ A
Ⓑ B
Ⓒ C
Ⓓ D

4 Counting by ones, what number comes before 249?

Ⓕ 248
Ⓖ 250
Ⓗ 251
Ⓙ 348

5 Which of these numbers has a 1 in the tens place and a 7 in the ones place?

Ⓐ 710
Ⓑ 701
Ⓒ 517
Ⓓ 471

6 If one more block in this figure were shaded, what fraction of the figure would be shaded?

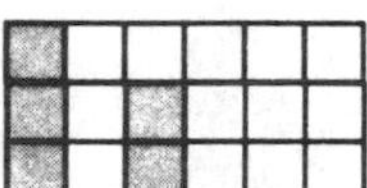

Ⓕ $\frac{1}{6}$
Ⓖ $\frac{1}{3}$
Ⓗ $\frac{1}{2}$
Ⓙ $\frac{2}{3}$

GO

ANSWER ROWS E1 Ⓐ Ⓑ Ⓒ Ⓓ 1 Ⓐ Ⓑ Ⓒ Ⓓ 3 Ⓐ Ⓑ Ⓒ Ⓓ 5 Ⓐ Ⓑ Ⓒ Ⓓ
E2 Ⓕ Ⓖ Ⓗ Ⓙ 2 Ⓕ Ⓖ Ⓗ Ⓙ 4 Ⓕ Ⓖ Ⓗ Ⓙ 6 Ⓕ Ⓖ Ⓗ Ⓙ

7 Look at the number below. Suppose you increased the value of the digit in the hundreds place by 2. What would the new number be?

1429

Ⓐ 3429
Ⓑ 1449
Ⓒ 1629
Ⓓ 1431

8 What is 3,297,495 rounded to the nearest hundred thousand?

Ⓕ 3,330,300
Ⓖ 3,300,300
Ⓗ 3,030,000
Ⓙ 3,300,000

9 Which of these patterns shows counting by threes?

Ⓐ 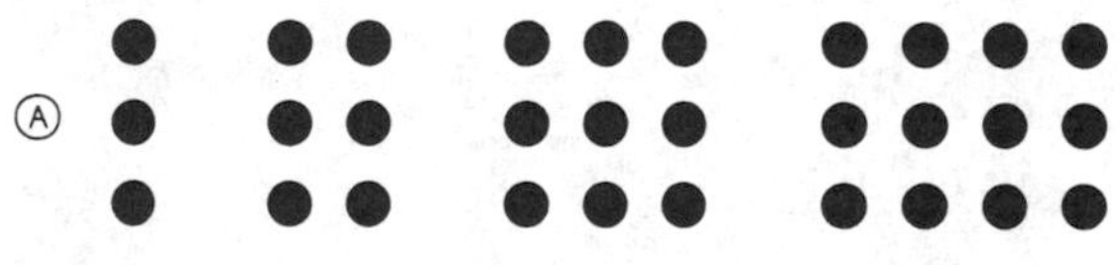

Ⓑ 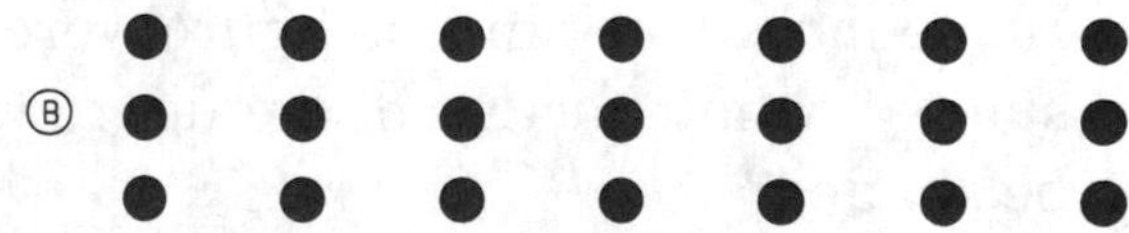

Ⓒ 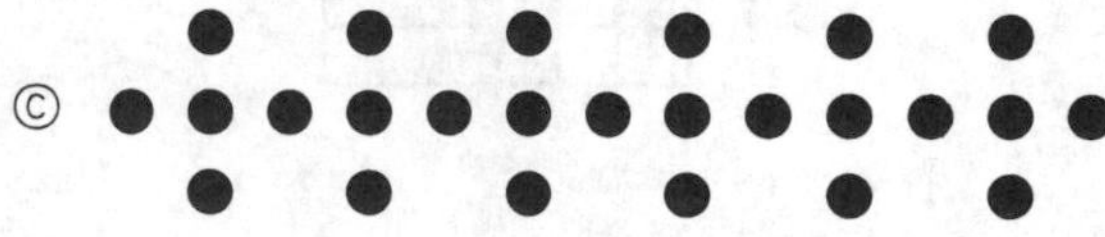

Ⓓ 

10 If you arranged these numbers from least to greatest, which would be in the middle?

934 199 560 237 248

Ⓕ 237
Ⓖ 248
Ⓗ 199
Ⓙ 560

11 Which of these is the same as $\frac{43}{100}$?

Ⓐ 4.3
Ⓑ 0.043
Ⓒ 0.43
Ⓓ 43

12 What should replace the □ in the number sentence below?

20 + □ = 20

Ⓕ 0
Ⓖ 1
Ⓗ 20
Ⓙ 100

13 In which of these must you rename a ten as ten ones or borrow a ten?

Ⓐ 29 – 6 =
Ⓑ 36 – 0 =
Ⓒ 19 – 5 =
Ⓓ 15 – 9 =

GO

ANSWER ROWS 7 Ⓐ Ⓑ Ⓒ Ⓓ 9 Ⓐ Ⓑ Ⓒ Ⓓ 11 Ⓐ Ⓑ Ⓒ Ⓓ 13 Ⓐ Ⓑ Ⓒ Ⓓ
8 Ⓕ Ⓖ Ⓗ Ⓙ 10 Ⓕ Ⓖ Ⓗ Ⓙ 12 Ⓕ Ⓖ Ⓗ Ⓙ

14 What should replace the circle in this multiplication problem?

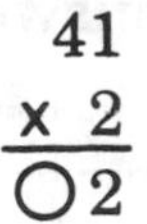

Ⓕ 0

Ⓖ 6

Ⓗ 8

Ⓙ 9

15 Counting by fours, what comes after 28?

Ⓐ 32

Ⓑ 30

Ⓒ 24

Ⓓ 8

16 Which of these shows a shaded area that is greater than one half?

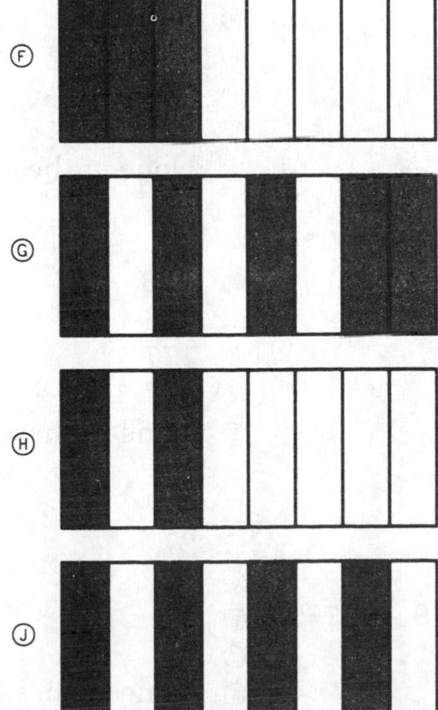

17 Which of these is greater than 35 and can be divided by 7?

Ⓐ 14

Ⓑ 35

Ⓒ 41

Ⓓ 42

18 What will make the number sentence below true?

8 + □ + □ = 30

Ⓕ 9

Ⓖ 11

Ⓗ 22

Ⓙ 38

19 Which numeral means thirty one thousand, fifty six?

Ⓐ 310,056

Ⓑ 31,560

Ⓒ 31,056

Ⓓ 30,156

20 Which of these is the best way to estimate the answer to this problem?

286 x 109 = □

Ⓕ 300 x 100 = □

Ⓖ 200 x 100 = □

Ⓗ 300 x 200 = □

Ⓙ 100 x 100 = □

ANSWER ROWS 14 Ⓕ Ⓖ Ⓗ Ⓙ 16 Ⓕ Ⓖ Ⓗ Ⓙ 18 Ⓕ Ⓖ Ⓗ Ⓙ 20 Ⓕ Ⓖ Ⓗ Ⓙ
15 Ⓐ Ⓑ Ⓒ Ⓓ 17 Ⓐ Ⓑ Ⓒ Ⓓ 19 Ⓐ Ⓑ Ⓒ Ⓓ

NUMBER RIGHT______

Lesson 5 Addition

Example

Directions: Mark the space for the correct answer to each addition problem. Choose "None of these" if the right answer is not given.

A

4
+ 7

Ⓐ 3
Ⓑ 11
Ⓒ 12
Ⓓ 47
Ⓔ None of these

B

27 + 3 =

Ⓕ 20
Ⓖ 29
Ⓗ 32
Ⓙ 33
Ⓚ None of these

Be sure to add carefully.

If the right answer is not given, mark the space for "None of these."

Practice

1

26 + 6 =

Ⓐ 32
Ⓑ 31
Ⓒ 30
Ⓓ 20
Ⓔ None of these

2

1368
+ 5121

Ⓕ 5489
Ⓖ 6487
Ⓗ 6489
Ⓙ 6589
Ⓚ None of these

3

32 + 81 =

Ⓐ 111
Ⓑ 113
Ⓒ 123
Ⓓ 124
Ⓔ None of these

4

22
11
+ 43

Ⓕ 33
Ⓖ 54
Ⓗ 66
Ⓙ 76
Ⓚ None of these

5

841
+ 66

Ⓐ 807
Ⓑ 1007
Ⓒ 1447
Ⓓ 1507
Ⓔ None of these

6

402
+ 183

Ⓕ 585
Ⓖ 595
Ⓗ 603
Ⓙ 782
Ⓚ None of these

7

104
21
+ 52

Ⓐ 73
Ⓑ 156
Ⓒ 177
Ⓓ 357
Ⓔ None of these

8

14 + 19 + 4 =

Ⓕ 27
Ⓖ 37
Ⓗ 44
Ⓙ 73
Ⓚ None of these

GO

ANSWER ROWS
A Ⓐ Ⓑ Ⓒ Ⓓ Ⓔ 1 Ⓐ Ⓑ Ⓒ Ⓓ Ⓔ 3 Ⓐ Ⓑ Ⓒ Ⓓ Ⓔ 5 Ⓐ Ⓑ Ⓒ Ⓓ Ⓔ 7 Ⓐ Ⓑ Ⓒ Ⓓ Ⓔ
B Ⓕ Ⓖ Ⓗ Ⓙ Ⓚ 2 Ⓕ Ⓖ Ⓗ Ⓙ Ⓚ 4 Ⓕ Ⓖ Ⓗ Ⓙ Ⓚ 6 Ⓕ Ⓖ Ⓗ Ⓙ Ⓚ 8 Ⓕ Ⓖ Ⓗ Ⓙ Ⓚ

9

$\frac{1}{7} + \frac{3}{7} =$

Ⓐ $\frac{2}{7}$
Ⓑ $\frac{4}{14}$
Ⓒ $\frac{3}{7}$
Ⓓ $\frac{4}{7}$
Ⓔ None of these

10

41 + 29 + 7 + 2 =

Ⓕ 70
Ⓖ 76
Ⓗ 78
Ⓙ 81
Ⓚ None of these

11

$$\begin{array}{r} 700 \\ +\ 700 \\ \hline \end{array}$$

Ⓐ 770
Ⓑ 1400
Ⓒ 1700
Ⓓ 7700
Ⓔ None of these

12

$$\begin{array}{r} 7288 \\ +\ 932 \\ \hline \end{array}$$

Ⓕ 8220
Ⓖ 7220
Ⓗ 6426
Ⓙ 6356
Ⓚ None of these

13

\$6.37 + \$5.94 =

Ⓐ \$0.43
Ⓑ \$11.23
Ⓒ \$11.31
Ⓓ \$12.31
Ⓔ None of these

14

$$\begin{array}{r} 7.6 \\ +\ 0.25 \\ \hline \end{array}$$

Ⓕ 7.35
Ⓖ 7.41
Ⓗ 7.75
Ⓙ 7.85
Ⓚ None of these

15

25 + 28 =

Ⓐ 53
Ⓑ 54
Ⓒ 63
Ⓓ 107
Ⓔ None of these

16

$$\begin{array}{r} 261 \\ 17 \\ +\ 503 \\ \hline \end{array}$$

Ⓕ 520
Ⓖ 771
Ⓗ 776
Ⓙ 781
Ⓚ None of these

17

$$\begin{array}{r} 489 \\ +\ 33 \\ \hline \end{array}$$

Ⓐ 512
Ⓑ 522
Ⓒ 532
Ⓓ 582
Ⓔ None of these

18

2.7 + 4.8 =

Ⓕ 2.1
Ⓖ 6.1
Ⓗ 6.5
Ⓙ 7.6
Ⓚ None of these

19

$$\begin{array}{r} 80 \\ 10 \\ +\ 30 \\ \hline \end{array}$$

Ⓐ 130
Ⓑ 120
Ⓒ 110
Ⓓ 93
Ⓔ None of these

20

$$\begin{array}{r} 199 \\ +\ 222 \\ \hline \end{array}$$

Ⓕ 301
Ⓖ 311
Ⓗ 421
Ⓙ 422
Ⓚ None of these

STOP

ANSWER ROWS
9 Ⓐ Ⓑ Ⓒ Ⓓ Ⓔ 12 Ⓕ Ⓖ Ⓗ Ⓙ Ⓚ 15 Ⓐ Ⓑ Ⓒ Ⓓ Ⓔ 18 Ⓕ Ⓖ Ⓗ Ⓙ Ⓚ
10 Ⓕ Ⓖ Ⓗ Ⓙ Ⓚ 13 Ⓐ Ⓑ Ⓒ Ⓓ Ⓔ 16 Ⓕ Ⓖ Ⓗ Ⓙ Ⓚ 19 Ⓐ Ⓑ Ⓒ Ⓓ Ⓔ
11 Ⓐ Ⓑ Ⓒ Ⓓ Ⓔ 14 Ⓕ Ⓖ Ⓗ Ⓙ Ⓚ 17 Ⓐ Ⓑ Ⓒ Ⓓ Ⓔ 20 Ⓕ Ⓖ Ⓗ Ⓙ Ⓚ

Lesson 6 Subtraction

Example

Directions: Mark the space for the correct answer to each subtraction problem. Choose "NG" if the right answer is not given.

A

13 − 8 =

Ⓐ 3
Ⓑ 4
Ⓒ 5
Ⓓ 21
Ⓔ NG

B

$$\begin{array}{r} 9 \\ -\ 3 \\ \hline \end{array}$$

Ⓕ 5
Ⓖ 7
Ⓗ 11
Ⓙ 12
Ⓚ NG

If the right answer is not given, mark the space for "NG." This means "not given."

When you are not sure of an answer, check it by adding.

Practice

1

$$\begin{array}{r} 27 \\ -\ 4 \\ \hline \end{array}$$

Ⓐ 13
Ⓑ 23
Ⓒ 27
Ⓓ 31
Ⓔ NG

2

$$\begin{array}{r} 59 \\ -\ 17 \\ \hline \end{array}$$

Ⓕ 32
Ⓖ 43
Ⓗ 62
Ⓙ 76
Ⓚ NG

3

$$\begin{array}{r} 42 \\ -\ 19 \\ \hline \end{array}$$

Ⓐ 61
Ⓑ 51
Ⓒ 33
Ⓓ 23
Ⓔ NG

4

96 − 48 =

Ⓕ 48
Ⓖ 49
Ⓗ 54
Ⓙ 58
Ⓚ NG

5

200 − 60 =

Ⓐ 260
Ⓑ 240
Ⓒ 144
Ⓓ 140
Ⓔ NG

6

$$\begin{array}{r} 6.78 \\ -\ 0.6 \\ \hline \end{array}$$

Ⓕ 6.18
Ⓖ 5.72
Ⓗ 5.18
Ⓙ 0.78
Ⓚ NG

7

$$\begin{array}{r} 795 \\ -\ 83 \\ \hline \end{array}$$

Ⓐ 612
Ⓑ 711
Ⓒ 718
Ⓓ 878
Ⓔ NG

8

$$\begin{array}{r} 129 \\ -\ 51 \\ \hline \end{array}$$

Ⓕ 68
Ⓖ 78
Ⓗ 138
Ⓙ 180
Ⓚ NG

GO

ANSWER ROWS
A Ⓐ Ⓑ Ⓒ Ⓓ Ⓔ 1 Ⓐ Ⓑ Ⓒ Ⓓ Ⓔ 3 Ⓐ Ⓑ Ⓒ Ⓓ Ⓔ 5 Ⓐ Ⓑ Ⓒ Ⓓ Ⓔ 7 Ⓐ Ⓑ Ⓒ Ⓓ Ⓔ
B Ⓕ Ⓖ Ⓗ Ⓙ Ⓚ 2 Ⓕ Ⓖ Ⓗ Ⓙ Ⓚ 4 Ⓕ Ⓖ Ⓗ Ⓙ Ⓚ 6 Ⓕ Ⓖ Ⓗ Ⓙ Ⓚ 8 Ⓕ Ⓖ Ⓗ Ⓙ Ⓚ

9

$0.82 – $0.24 =

Ⓐ $0.40
Ⓑ $0.52
Ⓒ $0.58
Ⓓ $1.06
Ⓔ NG

10

$$\begin{array}{r} 418 \\ -\ 232 \\ \hline \end{array}$$

Ⓕ 114
Ⓖ 176
Ⓗ 186
Ⓙ 226
Ⓚ NG

11

$$\begin{array}{r} 52 \\ -\ 27 \\ \hline \end{array}$$

Ⓐ 25
Ⓑ 32
Ⓒ 35
Ⓓ 37
Ⓔ NG

12

$\frac{8}{9} - \frac{4}{9} =$

Ⓕ $\frac{5}{18}$
Ⓖ $\frac{4}{9}$
Ⓗ $\frac{5}{9}$
Ⓙ 5
Ⓚ NG

13

$$\begin{array}{r} 8686 \\ -\ 275 \\ \hline \end{array}$$

Ⓐ 8411
Ⓑ 8409
Ⓒ 8301
Ⓓ 7411
Ⓔ NG

14

$$\begin{array}{r} 6009 \\ -\ 3115 \\ \hline \end{array}$$

Ⓕ 2814
Ⓖ 2893
Ⓗ 3894
Ⓙ 3994
Ⓚ NG

15

66 – 3 =

Ⓐ 36
Ⓑ 52
Ⓒ 59
Ⓓ 63
Ⓔ NG

16

$$\begin{array}{r} 70 \\ -\ 20 \\ \hline \end{array}$$

Ⓕ 40
Ⓖ 48
Ⓗ 68
Ⓙ 90
Ⓚ NG

17

48 – 29 =

Ⓐ 27
Ⓑ 21
Ⓒ 19
Ⓓ 17
Ⓔ NG

18

$$\begin{array}{r} \$6.25 \\ -\ \$0.11 \\ \hline \end{array}$$

Ⓕ $5.11
Ⓖ $5.14
Ⓗ $6.04
Ⓙ $6.14
Ⓚ NG

19

$$\begin{array}{r} 1000 \\ -\ 275 \\ \hline \end{array}$$

Ⓐ 725
Ⓑ 775
Ⓒ 825
Ⓓ 875
Ⓔ NG

20

$$\begin{array}{r} 400 \\ -\ 131 \\ \hline \end{array}$$

Ⓕ 259
Ⓖ 269
Ⓗ 369
Ⓙ 331
Ⓚ NG

STOP

ANSWER ROWS

9 Ⓐ Ⓑ Ⓒ Ⓓ Ⓔ	12 Ⓕ Ⓖ Ⓗ Ⓙ Ⓚ	15 Ⓐ Ⓑ Ⓒ Ⓓ Ⓔ	18 Ⓕ Ⓖ Ⓗ Ⓙ Ⓚ
10 Ⓕ Ⓖ Ⓗ Ⓙ Ⓚ	13 Ⓐ Ⓑ Ⓒ Ⓓ Ⓔ	16 Ⓕ Ⓖ Ⓗ Ⓙ Ⓚ	19 Ⓐ Ⓑ Ⓒ Ⓓ Ⓔ
11 Ⓐ Ⓑ Ⓒ Ⓓ Ⓔ	14 Ⓕ Ⓖ Ⓗ Ⓙ Ⓚ	17 Ⓐ Ⓑ Ⓒ Ⓓ Ⓔ	20 Ⓕ Ⓖ Ⓗ Ⓙ Ⓚ

Example

Directions: Mark the space for the correct answer to each multiplication or division problem. Choose "NH" if the right answer is not given.

A 7×6	Ⓐ 13 Ⓑ 24 Ⓒ 40 Ⓓ 42 Ⓔ NH	**B** 8 ÷ 2 =	Ⓕ 28 Ⓖ 16 Ⓗ 6 Ⓙ 2 Ⓚ NH

Pay careful attention to each problem so you perform the correct operation.

If the right answer is not given, mark the space for "NH." This means "not here."

Practice

1 0 x 4 =

Ⓐ 44
Ⓑ 40
Ⓒ 4
Ⓓ 0
Ⓔ NH

2 3)10

Ⓕ 3
Ⓖ 3 R1
Ⓗ 3 R2
Ⓙ 4
Ⓚ NH

3 44×4

Ⓐ 48
Ⓑ 166
Ⓒ 176
Ⓓ 256
Ⓔ NH

4 4)56

Ⓕ 12
Ⓖ 12 R2
Ⓗ 13 R3
Ⓙ 14
Ⓚ NH

5 7 x 7 =

Ⓐ 49
Ⓑ 48
Ⓒ 39
Ⓓ 14
Ⓔ NH

6 310×5

Ⓕ 1650
Ⓖ 1550
Ⓗ 315
Ⓙ 305
Ⓚ NH

7 2515 ÷ 5 =

Ⓐ 623
Ⓑ 515
Ⓒ 512
Ⓓ 502
Ⓔ NH

8 18 ÷ 3 = □

Ⓕ 15
Ⓖ 9
Ⓗ 8
Ⓙ 6
Ⓚ NH

GO

ANSWER ROWS
A Ⓐ Ⓑ Ⓒ Ⓓ Ⓔ 1 Ⓐ Ⓑ Ⓒ Ⓓ Ⓔ 3 Ⓐ Ⓑ Ⓒ Ⓓ Ⓔ 5 Ⓐ Ⓑ Ⓒ Ⓓ Ⓔ 7 Ⓐ Ⓑ Ⓒ Ⓓ Ⓔ
B Ⓕ Ⓖ Ⓗ Ⓙ Ⓚ 2 Ⓕ Ⓖ Ⓗ Ⓙ Ⓚ 4 Ⓕ Ⓖ Ⓗ Ⓙ Ⓚ 6 Ⓕ Ⓖ Ⓗ Ⓙ Ⓚ 8 Ⓕ Ⓖ Ⓗ Ⓙ Ⓚ

9

$4\overline{)800}$

Ⓐ 20
Ⓑ 80
Ⓒ 100
Ⓓ 200
Ⓔ NH

10

7 ÷ 7 =

Ⓕ 1
Ⓖ 2
Ⓗ 11
Ⓙ 49
Ⓚ NH

11

$\begin{array}{r} 212 \\ \times\ 26 \\ \hline \end{array}$

Ⓐ 5422
Ⓑ 5512
Ⓒ 5522
Ⓓ 5626
Ⓔ NH

12

28 ÷ 4 =

Ⓕ 5
Ⓖ 6
Ⓗ 7
Ⓙ 9
Ⓚ NH

13

$\begin{array}{r} 4 \\ \times\ 2 \\ \hline \end{array}$

Ⓐ 4
Ⓑ 6
Ⓒ 8
Ⓓ 42
Ⓔ NH

14

$8\overline{)0}$

Ⓕ 0
Ⓖ 6
Ⓗ 8
Ⓙ 10
Ⓚ NH

15

$\begin{array}{r} 28 \\ \times\ 3 \\ \hline \end{array}$

Ⓐ 31
Ⓑ 84
Ⓒ 88
Ⓓ 103
Ⓔ NH

16

$6\overline{)64}$

Ⓕ 1 R4
Ⓖ 10 R4
Ⓗ 11
Ⓙ 11 R2
Ⓚ NH

17

$\begin{array}{r} 12 \\ \times\ 12 \\ \hline \end{array}$

Ⓐ 104
Ⓑ 112
Ⓒ 122
Ⓓ 144
Ⓔ NH

18

$7\overline{)49}$

Ⓕ 4
Ⓖ 5
Ⓗ 6
Ⓙ 8
Ⓚ NH

19 In the table below, the numbers in Column II are 4 times larger than those in Column I. Which number belongs in the empty space in the table?

Column I	Column II
2	8
3	12
4	

Ⓐ 1
Ⓑ 8
Ⓒ 14
Ⓓ 16
Ⓔ NH

STOP

ANSWER ROWS
9 Ⓐ Ⓑ Ⓒ Ⓓ Ⓔ 12 Ⓕ Ⓖ Ⓗ Ⓙ Ⓚ 15 Ⓐ Ⓑ Ⓒ Ⓓ Ⓔ 18 Ⓕ Ⓖ Ⓗ Ⓙ Ⓚ
10 Ⓕ Ⓖ Ⓗ Ⓙ Ⓚ 13 Ⓐ Ⓑ Ⓒ Ⓓ Ⓔ 16 Ⓕ Ⓖ Ⓗ Ⓙ Ⓚ 19 Ⓐ Ⓑ Ⓒ Ⓓ Ⓔ
11 Ⓐ Ⓑ Ⓒ Ⓓ Ⓔ 14 Ⓕ Ⓖ Ⓗ Ⓙ Ⓚ 17 Ⓐ Ⓑ Ⓒ Ⓓ Ⓔ

Examples

Directions: Read and work each problem. Mark the space for the correct answer. Choose "N" if the right answer is not given.

E1

12 + 3 =

Ⓐ 16
Ⓑ 15
Ⓒ 11
Ⓓ 9
Ⓔ N

E2

3 x 0 =

Ⓕ 1
Ⓖ 3
Ⓗ 4
Ⓙ 30
Ⓚ N

1

44 − 8 =

Ⓐ 52
Ⓑ 26
Ⓒ 24
Ⓓ 22
Ⓔ N

2

  86
+ 10

Ⓕ 76
Ⓖ 86
Ⓗ 96
Ⓙ 97
Ⓚ N

3

9 x 5 =

Ⓐ 45
Ⓑ 48
Ⓒ 59
Ⓓ 63
Ⓔ N

4

$6.00 – $4.49 =

Ⓕ $2.51
Ⓖ $1.51
Ⓗ $1.49
Ⓙ $1.41
Ⓚ N

5

6 x 400 =

Ⓐ 2600
Ⓑ 2400
Ⓒ 2200
Ⓓ 2000
Ⓔ N

6

  764
− 283

Ⓕ 947
Ⓖ 581
Ⓗ 521
Ⓙ 481
Ⓚ N

7

6) 13

Ⓐ 3
Ⓑ 2 R3
Ⓒ 2 R1
Ⓓ 2
Ⓔ N

8

  22
  84
+ 77

Ⓕ 106
Ⓖ 161
Ⓗ 173
Ⓙ 183
Ⓚ N

9

  903
− 77

Ⓐ 974
Ⓑ 926
Ⓒ 874
Ⓓ 816
Ⓔ N

10

7.8 + 4.1 =

Ⓕ 11.9
Ⓖ 11.81
Ⓗ 11.18
Ⓙ 10.9
Ⓚ N

GO

ANSWER ROWS

E1	Ⓐ Ⓑ Ⓒ Ⓓ Ⓔ	2	Ⓕ Ⓖ Ⓗ Ⓙ Ⓚ	5	Ⓐ Ⓑ Ⓒ Ⓓ Ⓔ	8	Ⓕ Ⓖ Ⓗ Ⓙ Ⓚ
E2	Ⓕ Ⓖ Ⓗ Ⓙ Ⓚ	3	Ⓐ Ⓑ Ⓒ Ⓓ Ⓔ	6	Ⓕ Ⓖ Ⓗ Ⓙ Ⓚ	9	Ⓐ Ⓑ Ⓒ Ⓓ Ⓔ
1	Ⓐ Ⓑ Ⓒ Ⓓ Ⓔ	4	Ⓕ Ⓖ Ⓗ Ⓙ Ⓚ	7	Ⓐ Ⓑ Ⓒ Ⓓ Ⓔ	10	Ⓕ Ⓖ Ⓗ Ⓙ Ⓚ

11

$\frac{4}{5} - \frac{1}{5} =$

Ⓐ $\frac{1}{4}$
Ⓑ $\frac{3}{10}$
Ⓒ $\frac{3}{5}$
Ⓓ 3
Ⓔ N

12

$$\begin{array}{r} 230 \\ \times \quad 4 \\ \hline \end{array}$$

Ⓕ 920
Ⓖ 824
Ⓗ 820
Ⓙ 724
Ⓚ N

13

$$\begin{array}{r} 1.8 \\ +\,0.89 \\ \hline \end{array}$$

Ⓐ 1.89
Ⓑ 1.97
Ⓒ 2.09
Ⓓ 2.89
Ⓔ N

14

\$0.68 + \$0.41 =

Ⓕ \$0.27
Ⓖ \$0.69
Ⓗ \$0.72
Ⓙ \$1.09
Ⓚ N

15

3 x 61 =

Ⓐ 318
Ⓑ 193
Ⓒ 183
Ⓓ 123
Ⓔ N

16

12 ÷ 3 = □

Ⓕ 2
Ⓖ 3
Ⓗ 4
Ⓙ 9
Ⓚ N

17

$$\begin{array}{r} 834 \\ -\,699 \\ \hline \end{array}$$

Ⓐ 134
Ⓑ 135
Ⓒ 265
Ⓓ 335
Ⓔ N

18

51 + 24 + 9 + 8 =

Ⓕ 75
Ⓖ 84
Ⓗ 92
Ⓙ 102
Ⓚ N

19

96 − 30 =

Ⓐ 36
Ⓑ 63
Ⓒ 93
Ⓓ 126
Ⓔ N

20

$$\begin{array}{r} 6945 \\ +\,6336 \\ \hline \end{array}$$

Ⓕ 13,281
Ⓖ 13,271
Ⓗ 12,881
Ⓙ 12,281
Ⓚ N

21

$$\begin{array}{r} 802 \\ \times\ 11 \\ \hline \end{array}$$

Ⓐ 809
Ⓑ 813
Ⓒ 8082
Ⓓ 8822
Ⓔ N

22

$$\begin{array}{r} \$4.99 \\ -\,3.29 \\ \hline \end{array}$$

Ⓕ \$1.67
Ⓖ \$1.70
Ⓗ \$1.90
Ⓙ \$1.99
Ⓚ N

GO

ANSWER ROWS
11 Ⓐ Ⓑ Ⓒ Ⓓ Ⓔ 14 Ⓕ Ⓖ Ⓗ Ⓙ Ⓚ 17 Ⓐ Ⓑ Ⓒ Ⓓ Ⓔ 20 Ⓕ Ⓖ Ⓗ Ⓙ Ⓚ
12 Ⓕ Ⓖ Ⓗ Ⓙ Ⓚ 15 Ⓐ Ⓑ Ⓒ Ⓓ Ⓔ 18 Ⓕ Ⓖ Ⓗ Ⓙ Ⓚ 21 Ⓐ Ⓑ Ⓒ Ⓓ Ⓔ
13 Ⓐ Ⓑ Ⓒ Ⓓ Ⓔ 16 Ⓕ Ⓖ Ⓗ Ⓙ Ⓚ 19 Ⓐ Ⓑ Ⓒ Ⓓ Ⓔ 22 Ⓕ Ⓖ Ⓗ Ⓙ Ⓚ

23

$\frac{1}{3} + \frac{1}{3} =$

Ⓐ $\frac{1}{9}$
Ⓑ $\frac{1}{3}$
Ⓒ $\frac{2}{3}$
Ⓓ 1
Ⓔ N

24

3 x 93 =

Ⓕ 249
Ⓖ 267
Ⓗ 273
Ⓙ 279
Ⓚ N

25

4 + 7 + 6 =

Ⓐ 13
Ⓑ 17
Ⓒ 19
Ⓓ 29
Ⓔ N

26

$4\overline{)80}$

Ⓕ 32
Ⓖ 30
Ⓗ 20 R4
Ⓙ 20
Ⓚ N

27

$$\begin{array}{r} 124 \\ 62 \\ +\,477 \\ \hline \end{array}$$

Ⓐ 549
Ⓑ 562
Ⓒ 563
Ⓓ 653
Ⓔ N

28

$7\overline{)3654}$

Ⓕ 622
Ⓖ 522
Ⓗ 521
Ⓙ 489
Ⓚ N

29

15 + 22 =

Ⓐ 7
Ⓑ 32
Ⓒ 37
Ⓓ 172
Ⓔ N

30

\$1.25 – \$1.19 =

Ⓕ \$1.44
Ⓖ \$1.34
Ⓗ \$0.16
Ⓙ \$0.06
Ⓚ N

31

$$\begin{array}{r} 40 \\ \times\ 11 \\ \hline \end{array}$$

Ⓐ 440
Ⓑ 411
Ⓒ 410
Ⓓ 51
Ⓔ N

32

100 ÷ 10 =

Ⓕ 101
Ⓖ 11
Ⓗ 1
Ⓙ 0
Ⓚ N

33 In the table below, the numbers in Column II are 7 times larger than those in Column I. Which numbers belong in the empty spaces in the table?

Column I	Column II
3	21
4	
5	35
6	

Ⓐ 14, 21
Ⓑ 21, 35
Ⓒ 27, 43
Ⓓ 28, 42
Ⓔ N

STOP

ANSWER ROWS
23 Ⓐ Ⓑ Ⓒ Ⓓ Ⓔ 26 Ⓕ Ⓖ Ⓗ Ⓙ Ⓚ 29 Ⓐ Ⓑ Ⓒ Ⓓ Ⓔ 32 Ⓕ Ⓖ Ⓗ Ⓙ Ⓚ
24 Ⓕ Ⓖ Ⓗ Ⓙ Ⓚ 27 Ⓐ Ⓑ Ⓒ Ⓓ Ⓔ 30 Ⓕ Ⓖ Ⓗ Ⓙ Ⓚ 33 Ⓐ Ⓑ Ⓒ Ⓓ Ⓔ
25 Ⓐ Ⓑ Ⓒ Ⓓ Ⓔ 28 Ⓕ Ⓖ Ⓗ Ⓙ Ⓚ 31 Ⓐ Ⓑ Ⓒ Ⓓ Ⓔ

NUMBER RIGHT______

Example

Directions: Find the correct answer to each geometry problem. Mark the space for your choice.

A What is the area of the shape on the right?

Ⓐ 4 square units
Ⓑ 5 square units
Ⓒ 7 square units
Ⓓ 8 square units

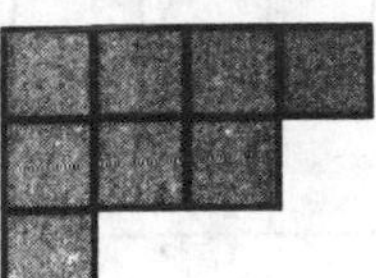

Pay careful attention to key words, numbers, pictures, and figures. They will help you find the answers.

When you are not sure of an answer, eliminate the choices you know are wrong, then take your best guess.

Practice

1 Which of these letters can be folded in half so the parts match exactly?

Ⓐ **J**
Ⓑ **F**
Ⓒ **H**
Ⓓ **L**

2 Look at the shapes below. Which one comes on the left of the largest square?

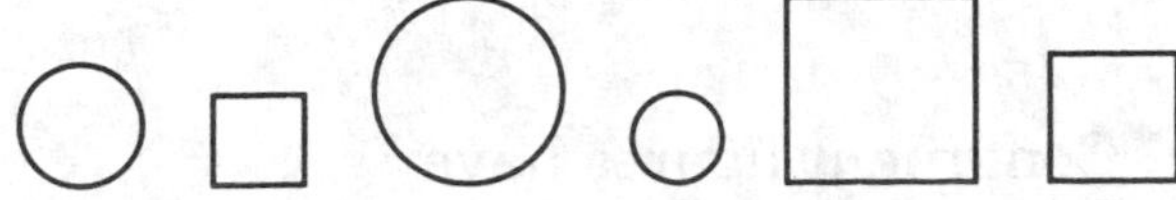

Ⓕ the smallest circle
Ⓖ the largest square
Ⓗ the smallest square
Ⓙ the medium-sized circle

3 This shape is called a —

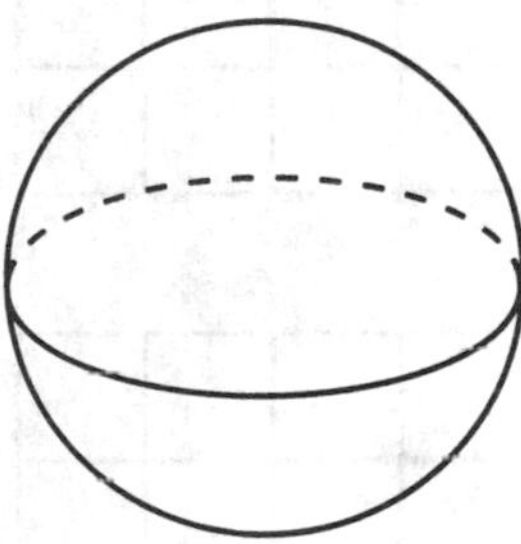

Ⓐ cube
Ⓑ sphere
Ⓒ cylinder
Ⓓ pyramid

4 A three-sided figure is a

Ⓕ rectangle
Ⓖ square
Ⓗ circle
Ⓙ triangle

GO

ANSWER ROWS A Ⓐ Ⓑ Ⓒ Ⓓ 2 Ⓕ Ⓖ Ⓗ Ⓙ 4 Ⓕ Ⓖ Ⓗ Ⓙ
1 Ⓐ Ⓑ Ⓒ Ⓓ 3 Ⓐ Ⓑ Ⓒ Ⓓ

5 Which of these shapes are congruent?

P
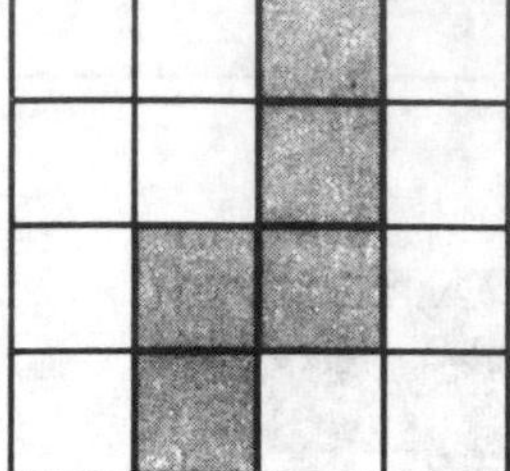

Q
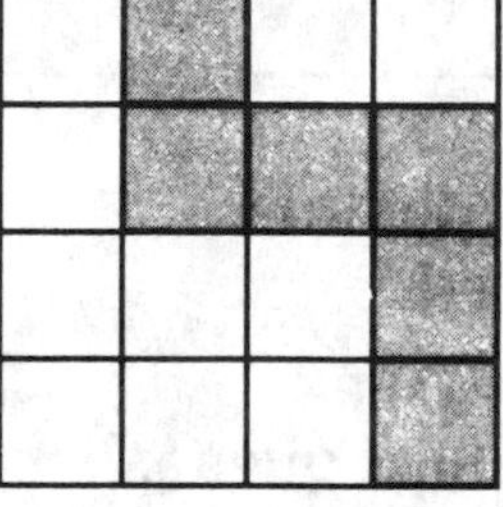

R

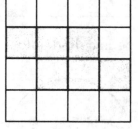

S

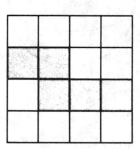

Ⓐ P, R, and S
Ⓑ P and S
Ⓒ Q and R
Ⓓ Q and S

6 Which of these figures has no line segments?

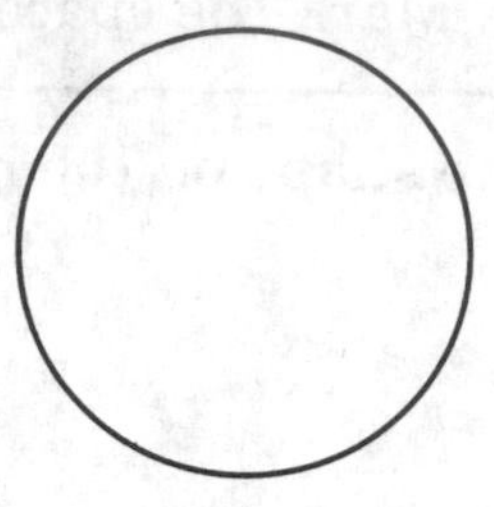
Ⓕ

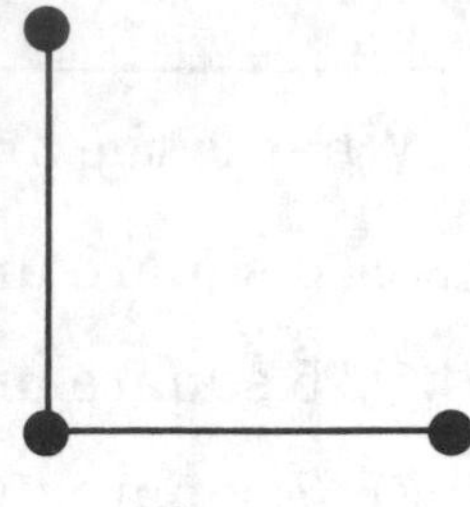
Ⓖ

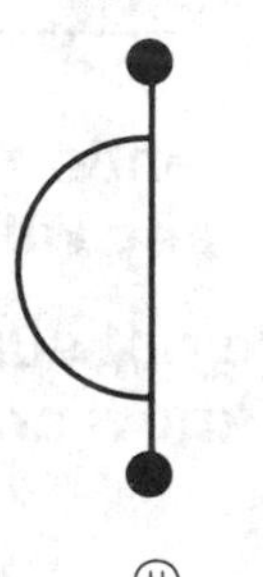
Ⓗ

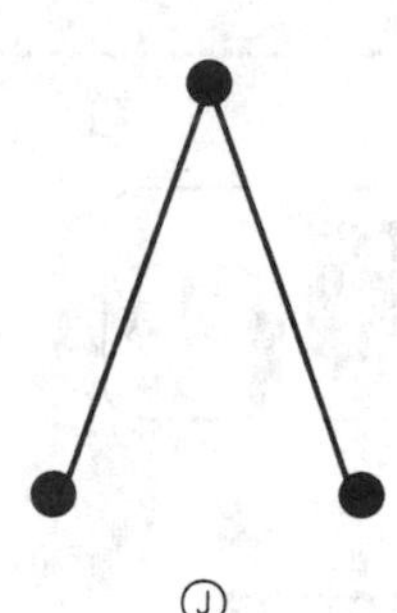
Ⓙ

7 The perimeter of this shape is

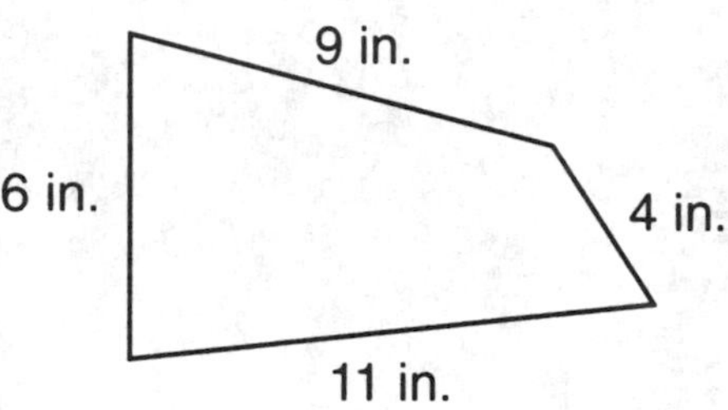

Ⓐ 10 in.
Ⓑ 20 in.
Ⓒ 29 in.
Ⓓ 30 in.

8 Congruent figures have

Ⓕ the same shape but different size
Ⓖ the same size but different shape
Ⓗ the same size and shape
Ⓙ different size and shape

9 Which pair of figures has the same shape but different size?

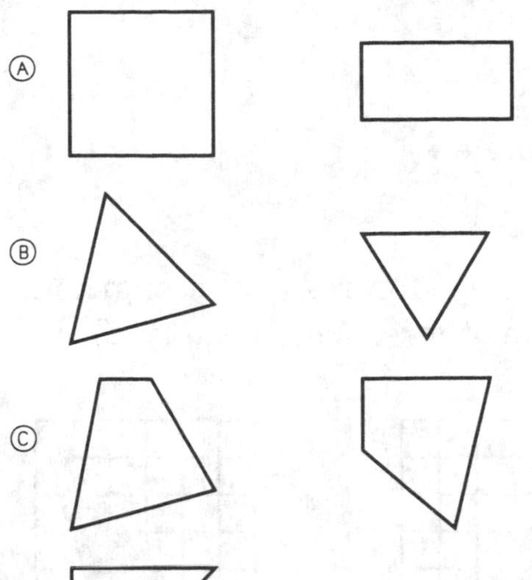

10 The perimeter of this figure is 32 units. How long is the missing side?

12 units

4 units 4 units

?

Ⓕ 12 units

Ⓖ 16 units

Ⓗ 24 units

Ⓙ 30 units

11 The area of the shaded portion of this shape is —

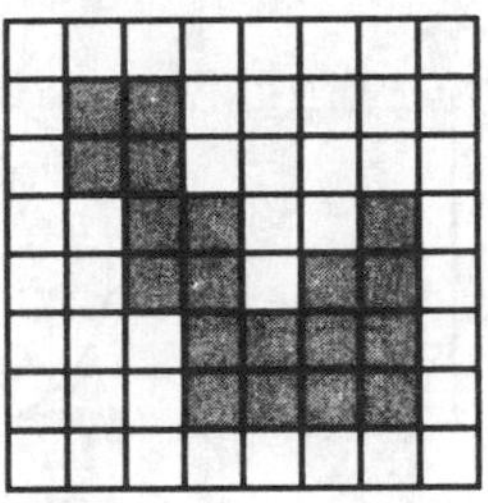

Ⓐ 64 sq. in.

Ⓑ 48 sq. in.

Ⓒ 19 sq. in.

Ⓓ 28 sq. in.

12 Which statement is true about the figure below?

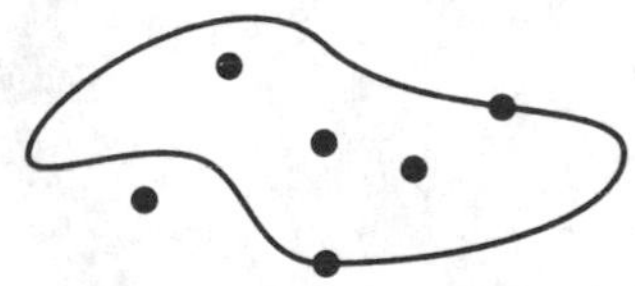

Ⓕ One dot is on the closed curve.

Ⓖ Three dots are inside the closed curve.

Ⓗ Three dots are on the closed curve.

Ⓙ Two dots are outside the closed curve.

13 Which of these figures is divided into three triangles?

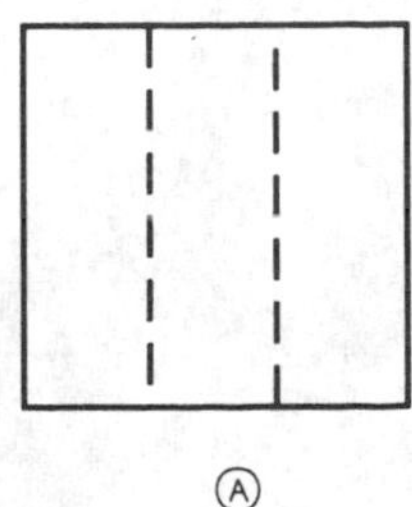

Ⓐ

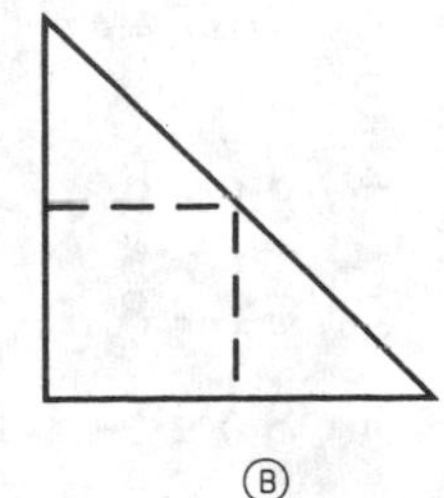

Ⓑ

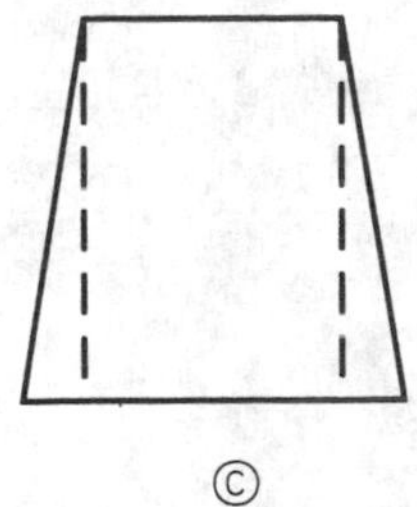

Ⓒ

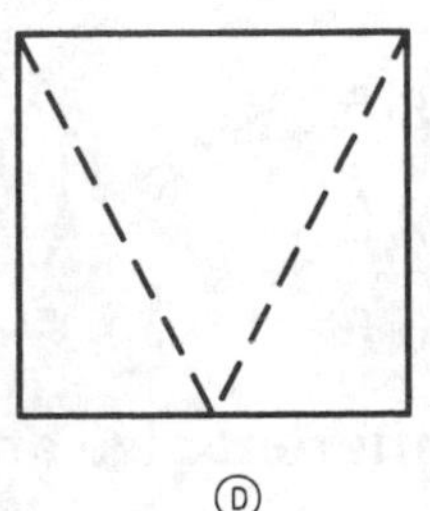

Ⓓ

GO

14 If you cut a sphere in half any way, which of these would be formed?

Ⓕ

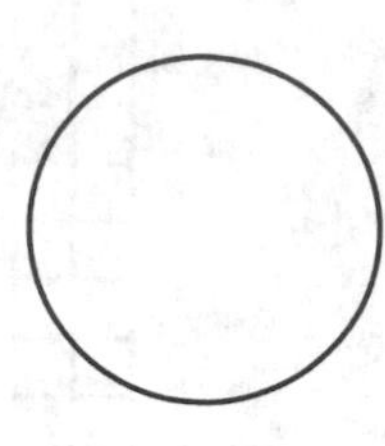

Ⓖ

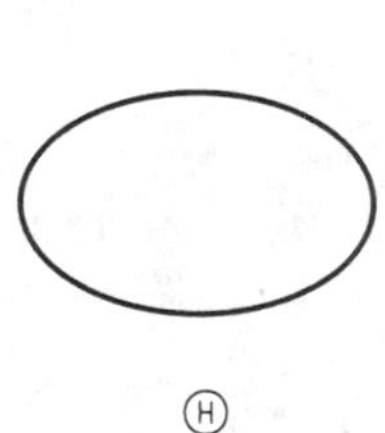

Ⓗ

Ⓙ

15 A can is shaped like a

Ⓐ sphere

Ⓑ cube

Ⓒ cone

Ⓓ cylinder

16 The perimeter of this figure is

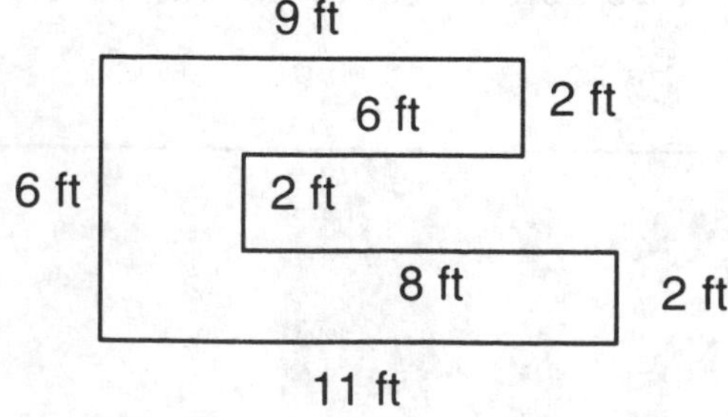

Ⓕ 46 ft

Ⓖ 42 ft

Ⓗ 40 ft

Ⓙ different size and shape

17 I have one more side than a triangle. All of my sides are equal. I am a —

Ⓐ pyramid

Ⓑ circle

Ⓒ square

Ⓓ triangle

18 One of these figures is not congruent with the others. Which one is it?

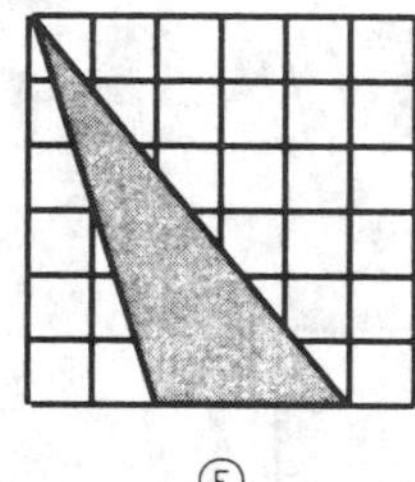

Ⓕ

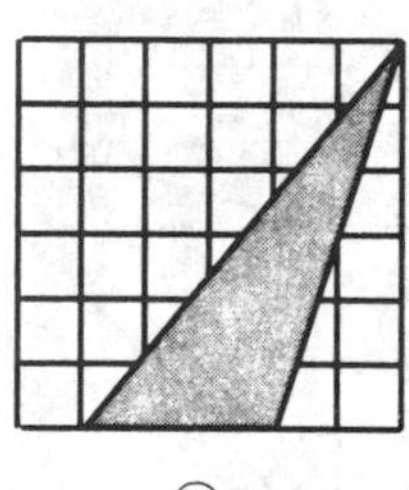

Ⓖ

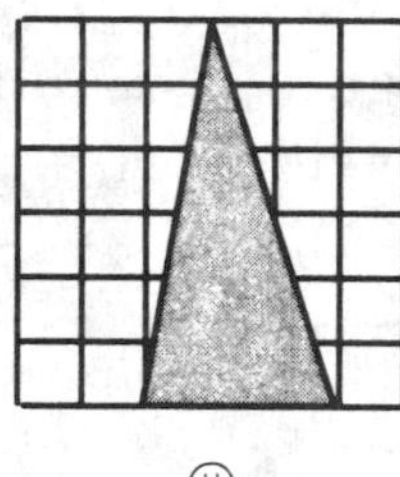

Ⓗ

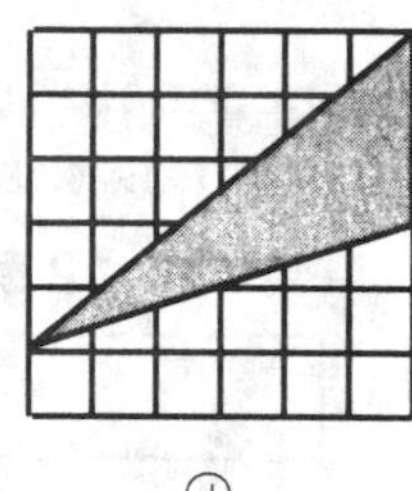

Ⓙ

19 How would you find the area of the unshaded portion of this figure?

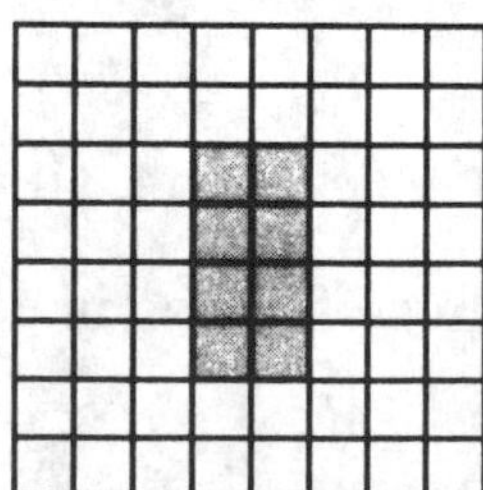

Ⓐ 2 x 4

Ⓑ 64 – 8

Ⓒ 64 + 8

Ⓓ 8 + 8 + 8 + 8

STOP

ANSWER ROWS 14 Ⓕ Ⓖ Ⓗ Ⓙ 16 Ⓕ Ⓖ Ⓗ Ⓙ 18 Ⓕ Ⓖ Ⓗ Ⓙ

15 Ⓐ Ⓑ Ⓒ Ⓓ 17 Ⓐ Ⓑ Ⓒ Ⓓ 19 Ⓐ Ⓑ Ⓒ Ⓓ

Lesson 10 Measurement

Example

Directions: Find the correct answer to each measurement problem. Mark the space for your choice.

A What is the temperature shown on this thermometer?

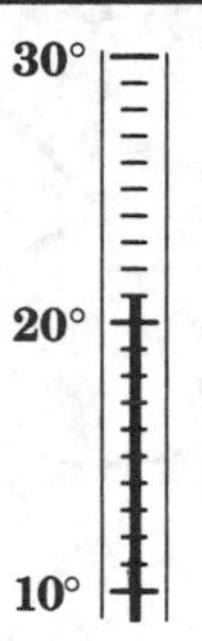

Ⓐ 18°

Ⓑ 19°

Ⓒ 21°

Ⓓ 29°

Read each question carefully. You can answer some questions without computing. If you must compute an answer, use scratch paper and work carefully.

Practice

1 Which of these statements is true?

Ⓐ 1 foot = 21 inches

Ⓑ 1 foot = 3 inches

Ⓒ 1 yard = 36 inches

Ⓓ 1 yard = 39 inches

2 A student bought a pen and received the coins below as change. The pen cost $1.25. How much money did the student give the cashier?

Ⓕ $1.50

Ⓖ $1.25

Ⓗ $1.00

Ⓙ $.25

3 A piece of typing paper is $8\frac{1}{2}$ by 11 inches. If you wanted to measure a piece of typing paper using the metric system, which unit would make the most sense?

Ⓐ meters

Ⓑ centimeters

Ⓒ grams

Ⓓ liters

4 It takes a train 36 hours to travel from Boston to Denver. This is the same as —

Ⓕ half a day

Ⓖ a day

Ⓗ a day and a half

Ⓙ two days

GO

ANSWER ROWS A Ⓐ Ⓑ Ⓒ Ⓓ 2 Ⓕ Ⓖ Ⓗ Ⓙ 4 Ⓕ Ⓖ Ⓗ Ⓙ

1 Ⓐ Ⓑ Ⓒ Ⓓ 3 Ⓐ Ⓑ Ⓒ Ⓓ

5 What time is shown on this clock?

Ⓐ 4:05

Ⓑ 1:20

Ⓒ 1:40

Ⓓ 4:01

6 Milly looked at her watch and saw it was 10:40. Her next class begins in 25 minutes. What time does her next class begin?

Ⓕ 10:55

Ⓖ 11:20

Ⓗ 11:05

Ⓙ 10:45

7 Which of these is 1000 meters?

Ⓐ a kilometer

Ⓑ 0.01 kilometers

Ⓒ a centimeter

Ⓓ 100 centimeters

8 Which answer is the same as $6.28?

Ⓕ six dollar bills, two dimes, three cents

Ⓖ six dollar bills, a quarter, three cents

Ⓗ five dollar bills, five quarters

Ⓙ five dollar bills, five quarters, a dime

Use this calendar to answer questions 9 through 11.

SEPTEMBER						
SUN	MON	TUE	WED	THU	FRI	SAT
				1	2	3
4	5	6	7	8	9	10
11	12	13	14	15	16	17
18	19	20	21	22	23	24
25	26	27	28	29	30	

9 What date is the last Sunday of the month?

Ⓐ September 25

Ⓑ September 31

Ⓒ September 18

Ⓓ September 26

10 What day of the week is September 9?

Ⓕ Wednesday

Ⓖ Thursday

Ⓗ Friday

Ⓙ Monday

11 On Tuesday, September 13, the students in a class were given a homework assignment that was due the following Monday. What date was the homework assignment due?

Ⓐ September 5

Ⓑ September 13

Ⓒ September 12

Ⓓ September 19

GO

ANSWER ROWS 5 Ⓐ Ⓑ Ⓒ Ⓓ 7 Ⓐ Ⓑ Ⓒ Ⓓ 9 Ⓐ Ⓑ Ⓒ Ⓓ 11 Ⓐ Ⓑ Ⓒ Ⓓ
6 Ⓕ Ⓖ Ⓗ Ⓙ 8 Ⓕ Ⓖ Ⓗ Ⓙ 10 Ⓕ Ⓖ Ⓗ Ⓙ

12 About how long is this nail?

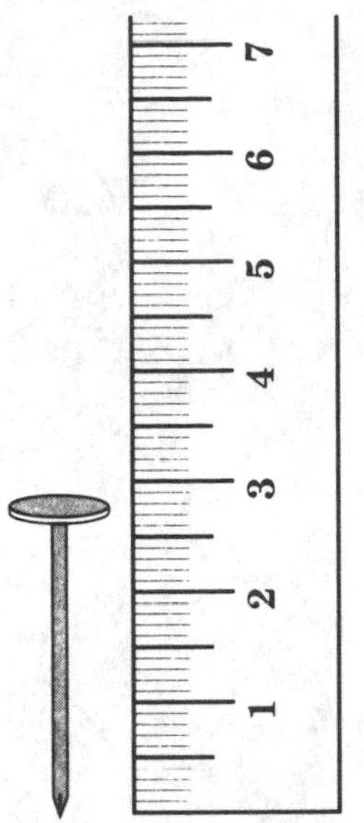

Ⓕ 1 cm

Ⓖ 3 cm

Ⓗ 4 cm

Ⓙ 6 cm

13 This thermometer shows the temperature at 8:00 in the morning. By noon, the temperature has risen by 12°. What is the temperature at noon?

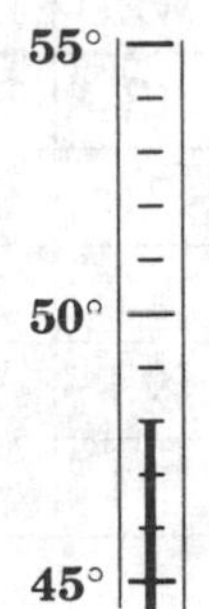

Ⓐ 48°

Ⓑ 58°

Ⓒ 60°

Ⓓ 92°

14 What time is shown on this clock?

Ⓕ 9:45

Ⓖ 8:50

Ⓗ 9:10

Ⓙ 9:50

15 A motorist crossed a bridge that has a toll of $1.50. The motorist paid the toll with a five-dollar bill. How much change did the motorist receive?

Ⓐ $1.50

Ⓑ $3.00

Ⓒ $3.50

Ⓓ $4.50

16 A group of students wants to weigh boxes of cereal to determine if the boxes contain as much cereal as they are supposed to. What unit of measure should the students use to get the most accurate measurement?

Ⓕ centimeters

Ⓖ pounds

Ⓗ kilograms

Ⓙ ounces

GO

ANSWER ROWS 12 Ⓕ Ⓖ Ⓗ Ⓙ 14 Ⓕ Ⓖ Ⓗ Ⓙ 16 Ⓕ Ⓖ Ⓗ Ⓙ
13 Ⓐ Ⓑ Ⓒ Ⓓ 15 Ⓐ Ⓑ Ⓒ Ⓓ

17 What is the diameter of the circle shown below?

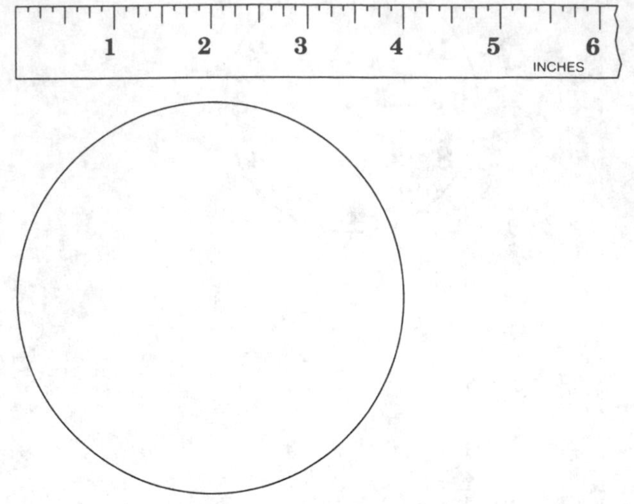

Ⓐ 1 inch

Ⓑ 2 inches

Ⓒ 4 inches

Ⓓ 6 inches

18 Which unit of measurement is longer than a foot but shorter than a meter?

Ⓕ a yard

Ⓖ a meter

Ⓗ a centimeter

Ⓙ a mile

19 On a summer day, you would feel most comfortable at what temperature?

Ⓐ 35°

Ⓑ 30°

Ⓒ 95°

Ⓓ 75°

20 Which of these clocks shows 5:20?

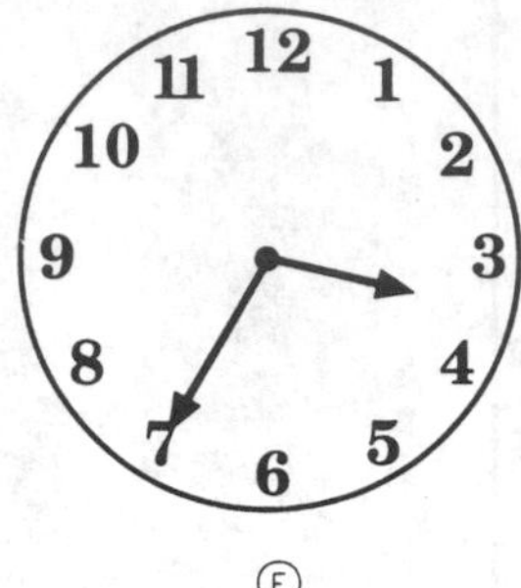

Ⓕ

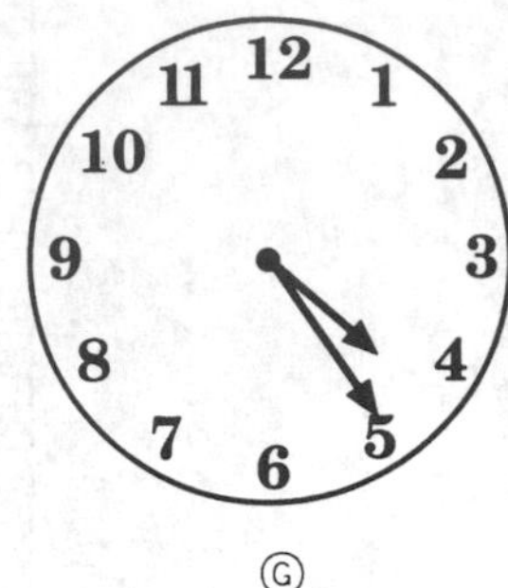

Ⓖ

Ⓗ

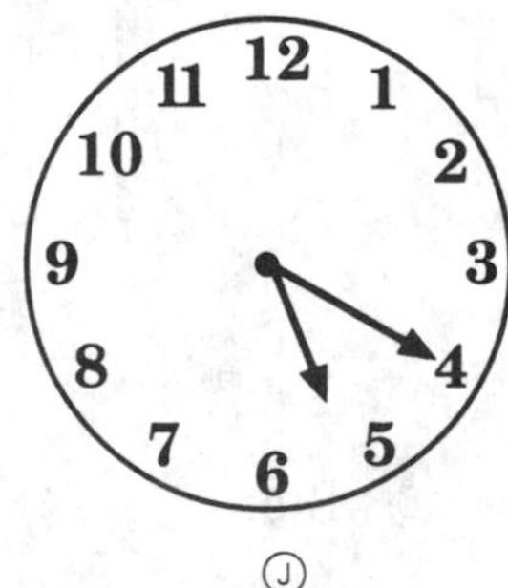

Ⓙ

21 Look at the calendar below. What is the date of the second Sunday of March?

March						
SUN	MON	TUE	WED	THU	FRI	SAT
	1	2	3	4	5	6
7	8	9	10	11	12	13
14	15	16	17	18	19	20
21	22	23	24	25	26	27
28	29	30	31			

Ⓐ March 7

Ⓑ March 14

Ⓒ March 15

Ⓓ March 13

STOP

ANSWER ROWS 17 Ⓐ Ⓑ Ⓒ Ⓓ 19 Ⓐ Ⓑ Ⓒ Ⓓ 21 Ⓐ Ⓑ Ⓒ Ⓓ

18 Ⓕ Ⓖ Ⓗ Ⓙ 20 Ⓕ Ⓖ Ⓗ Ⓙ

Lesson 11 Problem Solving

Examples

Directions: For items A and 1-2, choose the number sentence that shows how to solve the problem. For items B and 3-5, find the correct answer to the problem and mark the space for your choice.

A Athletic shoes normally cost $50. The price was reduced by $10. What is the new price of the shoes?

Ⓐ $50 + $10 = ☐
Ⓑ $10 - $50 = ☐
Ⓒ $50 $10 = ☐
Ⓓ $50 - $10 = ☐

B What is the cost of 6 gallons of gasoline if 1 gallon costs $1.10?

Ⓕ $1.16
Ⓖ $6.06
Ⓗ $6.60
Ⓙ Not Given

Read the question carefully. Look for key words, numbers, pictures, and figures. If necessary, work the problem on scratch paper.

Be sure to consider all the answer choices.

Practice

1 There are 24 students in a class. If they form teams of 6 students each, how many teams can they form?

Ⓐ 24 - 6 = ☐
Ⓑ 24 6 = ☐
Ⓒ 24 + 6 = ☐
Ⓓ 24 64 = ☐

2 A puppy weighed 11 pounds when a family bought it. The puppy gained 5 pounds. How much did the puppy weigh?

Ⓕ 11 + 5 = ☐
Ⓖ 11 x 5 = ☐
Ⓗ 11 - 5 = ☐
Ⓙ 5 - 11 = ☐

3 A postal worker walks 16 miles in a day. How far does the worker walk in 6 days?

Ⓐ 12 miles
Ⓑ 20 miles
Ⓒ 96 miles
Ⓓ 99 miles

4 A researcher studied 17 frogs. Eight of them were leopard frogs. How many of them were not leopard frogs?

Ⓕ 8
Ⓖ 9
Ⓗ 25
Ⓙ Not Given

5 A person earns $480 dollars a week. What else do you need to know to find out how much the person earns in an hour?

Ⓐ How many weeks the person worked in a year
Ⓑ How many hours the person worked in a day
Ⓒ How much money the person earns in a day
Ⓓ Not Given

GO

ANSWER ROWS A Ⓐ Ⓑ Ⓒ Ⓓ 1 Ⓐ Ⓑ Ⓒ Ⓓ 3 Ⓐ Ⓑ Ⓒ Ⓓ 5 Ⓐ Ⓑ Ⓒ Ⓓ
B Ⓕ Ⓖ Ⓗ Ⓙ 2 Ⓕ Ⓖ Ⓗ Ⓙ 4 Ⓕ Ⓖ Ⓗ Ⓙ

Use this menu to answer questions 6 through 8.

KREITNER'S RESTAURANT	
MegaBurger	$2.50
SuperDog	$2.25
MuchoVeggie	$2.50
Fries	$.95
Onion Rings	$1.10
Squash Chips	$.95
Cola	$.75
Lemon-Lime	$.75
Milk	$.50

6 Which of these cost the least?

Ⓕ MegaBurger
Ⓖ MuchoVeggie
Ⓗ SuperDog
Ⓙ Not Given

7 How much would a SuperDog, milk, and fries cost?

Ⓐ $3.70
Ⓑ $3.75
Ⓒ $3.38
Ⓓ Not Given

8 Which combination costs the most?

Ⓕ MuchoVeggie and milk
Ⓖ MuchoVeggie and cola
Ⓗ Fries, onion rings, and milk
Ⓙ Not Given

9 The trip from Homeville to Lincoln usually takes 25 minutes by car. While making the trip, a driver spent 12 minutes getting gas and 5 minutes waiting for a road crew. How long did it take the driver to make the trip?

Ⓐ 32 minutes
Ⓑ 37 minutes
Ⓒ 48 minutes
Ⓓ Not Given

This graph shows the amount of wood burned by several families during a winter. Study the graph, then answer numbers 10 and 11.

AMOUNT OF WOOD BURNED

Family 1	🪵🪵🪵🪵🪵🪵🪵🪵
Family 2	🪵🪵
Family 3	🪵🪵🪵🪵🪵🪵🪵
Family 4	🪵🪵🪵

Each 🪵 = 1 cord of wood

10 Which family used the least wood?

Ⓕ Family 1
Ⓖ Family 2
Ⓗ Family 4
Ⓙ Not Given

11 If wood costs $90 a cord, how much did Family 3 pay for wood?

Ⓐ $270
Ⓑ $620
Ⓒ $630
Ⓓ Not Given

GO

ANSWER ROWS 6 Ⓕ Ⓖ Ⓗ Ⓙ 8 Ⓕ Ⓖ Ⓗ Ⓙ 10 Ⓕ Ⓖ Ⓗ Ⓙ
7 Ⓐ Ⓑ Ⓒ Ⓓ 9 Ⓐ Ⓑ Ⓒ Ⓓ 11 Ⓐ Ⓑ Ⓒ Ⓓ

This graph shows how much weight catfish gained each year when they were fed different diets. Study the graph, then answer numbers 12, 13, and 14.

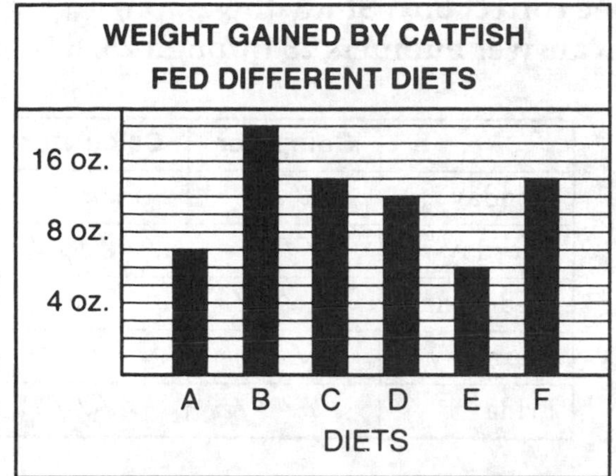

12 Which diet caused fish to gain more than a pound?

- Ⓕ F
- Ⓖ D
- Ⓗ B
- Ⓙ Not Given

13 How much did the fish gain on diet E?

- Ⓐ 6 ounces
- Ⓑ 8 ounces
- Ⓒ 9 ounces
- Ⓓ Not Given

14 Which two diets produced the same weight gains?

- Ⓕ A and D
- Ⓖ A and E
- Ⓗ D and F
- Ⓙ Not Given

15 A group of friends were waiting for a bus to ride to a movie. They knew the bus would arrive in 6 minutes. What else would they have to know to find out what time the bus was due?

- Ⓐ What time the movie started.
- Ⓑ What time it was now.
- Ⓒ Where the bus was now.
- Ⓓ Not Given

16 The price of bread was $1.29 but was increased by 8 cents. What was the new price of the bread?

- Ⓕ $1.21
- Ⓖ $1.36
- Ⓗ $1.37
- Ⓙ Not Given

17 Four families each gave $20 to a local organization for the homeless. How much money did they give all together?

- Ⓐ $24
- Ⓑ $60
- Ⓒ $84
- Ⓓ Not Given

18 The level of a pond dropped 37 inches below normal during a dry spell. It then rose 11 inches because of heavy rains. How far below normal was it?

- Ⓕ 24 inches
- Ⓖ 26 inches
- Ⓗ 48 inches
- Ⓙ Not Given

GO

ANSWER ROWS 12 Ⓕ Ⓖ Ⓗ Ⓙ 14 Ⓕ Ⓖ Ⓗ Ⓙ 16 Ⓕ Ⓖ Ⓗ Ⓙ 18 Ⓕ Ⓖ Ⓗ Ⓙ
13 Ⓐ Ⓑ Ⓒ Ⓓ 15 Ⓐ Ⓑ Ⓒ Ⓓ 17 Ⓐ Ⓑ Ⓒ Ⓓ

19 Sheri, Dan, and Carol each bought a snack cake for $.35. How much did they spend all together for snack cakes?

Ⓐ $.38
Ⓑ $1.05
Ⓒ $1.15
Ⓓ Not Given

20 A bus has 42 seats. Half the seats are by the window. How many seats in the bus are beside the window?

Ⓕ 21
Ⓖ 20
Ⓗ 12
Ⓙ Not Given

21 A farmer planted 18 acres on Monday, 29 on Tuesday, and 27 on Wednesday. How many acres did she plant all together?

Ⓐ 56
Ⓑ 64
Ⓒ 73
Ⓓ Not Given

22 If you knew how far it was from Boston to Phoenix and the speed of an airplane that made the trip, what information could you find?

Ⓕ The time it took off and landed.
Ⓖ The amount of fuel used.
Ⓗ How long it took to fly between the cities.
Ⓙ Not Given

This graph shows how many students used a computer and a calculator in a class each day. Each time a student used a computer or calculator, the student put a check in the correct box. Study the graph, then answer numbers 23 through 25.

	Computer	Calculator
Monday	✓✓✓✓	✓✓
Tuesday	✓✓✓	✓✓✓✓✓✓
Wednesday	✓✓✓✓✓	✓✓✓
Thursday	✓✓	✓✓✓✓✓
Friday	✓✓✓✓✓	✓✓✓✓

23 The greatest number of students who used one of the machines was on —

Ⓐ Tuesday
Ⓑ Wednesday
Ⓒ Thursday
Ⓓ Not Given

24 How many students in all used the computer?

Ⓕ 21
Ⓖ 20
Ⓗ 19
Ⓙ Not Given

25 On Thursday, how many more students used the calculator than the computer?

Ⓐ 2
Ⓑ 3
Ⓒ 8
Ⓓ Not Given

STOP

ANSWER ROWS
19 Ⓐ Ⓑ Ⓒ Ⓓ 21 Ⓐ Ⓑ Ⓒ Ⓓ 23 Ⓐ Ⓑ Ⓒ Ⓓ 25 Ⓐ Ⓑ Ⓒ Ⓓ
20 Ⓕ Ⓖ Ⓗ Ⓙ 22 Ⓕ Ⓖ Ⓗ Ⓙ 24 Ⓕ Ⓖ Ⓗ Ⓙ

Examples

Directions: For items 1-3, choose the number sentence that shows how to solve each problem. For items 4-7, find the correct answer to each problem, and mark the space for your choice.

E1 A pet store owner had 18 fish. He had 3 tanks, and wanted to put the same number of fish in each tank. How many fish would he put in each tank?

Ⓐ 18 + 3 = ☐
Ⓑ 18 - 3 = ☐
Ⓒ 18 ÷ 3 = ☐
Ⓓ 18 x 3 = ☐

E2 A four-sided figure in which all the sides are equal is a ______

Ⓕ rectangle
Ⓖ square
Ⓗ circle
Ⓙ triangle

1 What is the total cost of an item if the price is $4.00 and the tax is $.24?

Ⓐ $4 + $.24 = ☐
Ⓑ $.24 - ☐ = $4
Ⓒ $4 - $.24 = ☐
Ⓓ $4 x $.24 = ☐

2 How much juice will it take to fill 10 glasses if each glass holds 8 ounces?

Ⓕ 10 + 8 = ☐
Ⓖ 10 - 8 = ☐
Ⓗ 10 x 8 = ☐
Ⓙ 10 ÷ 8 = ☐

3 A parking lot normally holds 87 cars. Because of construction, only 63 cars could fit in the lot today. How many fewer cars than normal is this?

Ⓐ 87 + 63 = ☐
Ⓑ 63 + 87 = ☐
Ⓒ 63 - ☐ = 87
Ⓓ 87 - 63 = ☐

4 A square garden is 7 feet long on each side. What is the perimeter of the garden?

Ⓕ 35 feet
Ⓖ 28 feet
Ⓗ 24 feet
Ⓙ 14 feet

5 If a piece of lumber costs $2.10, how much would 4 pieces cost?

Ⓐ $2.14
Ⓑ $4.80
Ⓒ $8.14
Ⓓ $8.40

6 What time is shown on this clock?

Ⓕ 1:55
Ⓖ 2:55
Ⓗ 11:02
Ⓙ 11:10

7 After a spring storm, it took 30 hours for the snow to melt. This is —

Ⓐ the same as a week
Ⓑ about two days
Ⓒ between one and two days
Ⓓ the same as a day

GO

ANSWER ROWS E1 Ⓐ Ⓑ Ⓒ Ⓓ 1 Ⓐ Ⓑ Ⓒ Ⓓ 3 Ⓐ Ⓑ Ⓒ Ⓓ 5 Ⓐ Ⓑ Ⓒ Ⓓ 7 Ⓐ Ⓑ Ⓒ Ⓓ
E2 Ⓕ Ⓖ Ⓗ Ⓙ 2 Ⓕ Ⓖ Ⓗ Ⓙ 4 Ⓕ Ⓖ Ⓗ Ⓙ 6 Ⓕ Ⓖ Ⓗ Ⓙ

8 Which of these objects is shaped like a cube?

Ⓕ Ⓖ Ⓗ Ⓙ

9 Which of these shapes can be folded along the dotted line so the parts match?

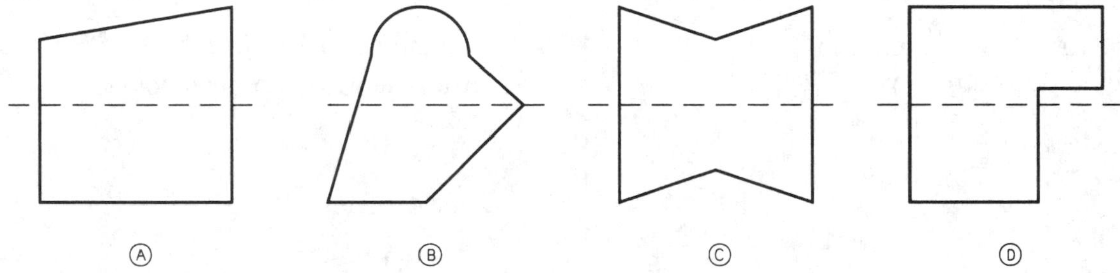

Ⓐ Ⓑ Ⓒ Ⓓ

10 Which statement about this pattern is true?

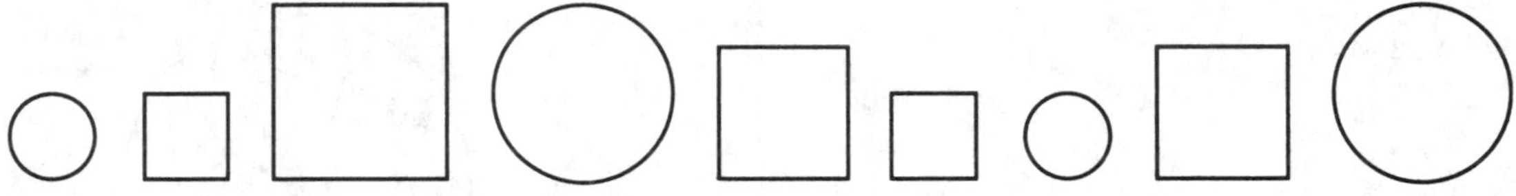

- Ⓕ There are more circles than squares.
- Ⓖ There are the same number of squares and circles.
- Ⓗ The smallest circle is always beside the largest square.
- Ⓙ The smallest circle is always beside the smallest square.

11 Which of these shapes has one more side than a square?

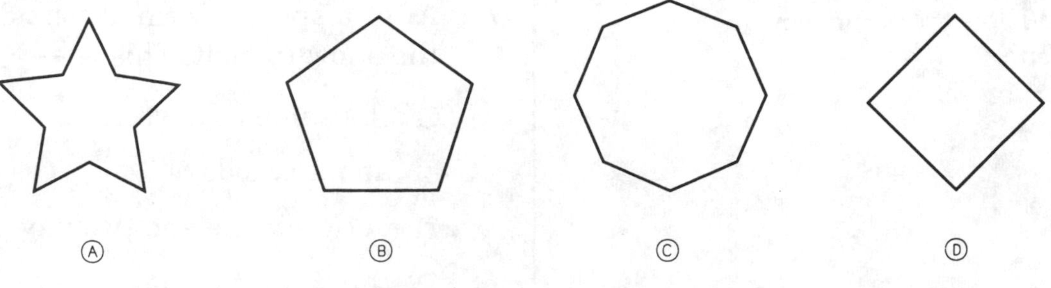

Ⓐ Ⓑ Ⓒ Ⓓ

GO

ANSWER ROWS 8 Ⓕ Ⓖ Ⓗ Ⓙ 9 Ⓐ Ⓑ Ⓒ Ⓓ 10 Ⓕ Ⓖ Ⓗ Ⓙ 11 Ⓐ Ⓑ Ⓒ Ⓓ

Study the figure below, then answer numbers 12 and 13.

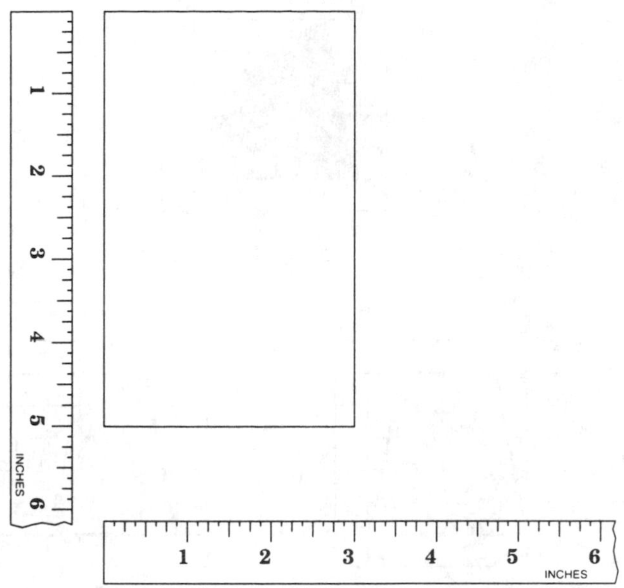

12 What is the length of the longest side of the figure?

Ⓕ 6 inches

Ⓖ 5 inches

Ⓗ 3 inches

Ⓙ 2 inches

13 The perimeter of the figure is —

Ⓐ 16 inches

Ⓑ 12 inches

Ⓒ 8 inches

Ⓓ 5 inches

14 How many quarters are in a dollar?

Ⓕ 1

Ⓖ 2

Ⓗ 3

Ⓙ 4

15 Look at the clock below. What time will it be in 40 minutes?

Ⓐ 6:40

Ⓑ 7:00

Ⓒ 7:20

Ⓓ 7:40

This graph shows the temperature measured at five different times during the day. Study the graph, then answer question 16.

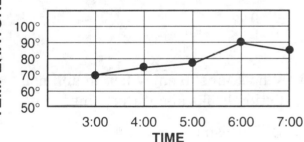

Temperature Measurements

TEMPERATURE

100°
90°
80°
70°
60°
50°

3:00 4:00 5:00 6:00 7:00

TIME

16 Based on the information shown on the graph, which of these questions can you not answer?

Ⓕ The high temperature between 3:00 and 7:00.

Ⓖ The low temperature between 3:00 and 7:00.

Ⓗ The low temperature for the day.

Ⓙ The temperature change from 3:00 to 7:00.

GO

ANSWER ROWS 12 Ⓕ Ⓖ Ⓗ Ⓙ 14 Ⓕ Ⓖ Ⓗ Ⓙ 16 Ⓕ Ⓖ Ⓗ Ⓙ
13 Ⓐ Ⓑ Ⓒ Ⓓ 15 Ⓐ Ⓑ Ⓒ Ⓓ

This graph shows the number of books read by the students in a class during a one-month period. A filled circle ● indicates a fiction book, and an empty circle ○ indicates a non-fiction book. Study the graph, then answer numbers 17 through 19.

	BOOKS READ
Natasha	○○○○○●●●
John	○○○●●●
Christopher	○●●●●●
Albert	○○○○○○●●●
Nancy	○○●●●

○ = Non-Fiction
● = Fiction

17 How many books in all did Nancy read?

Ⓐ 3

Ⓑ 5

Ⓒ 8

Ⓓ 9

18 Who seems to enjoy fiction and non-fiction books about the same?

Ⓕ Natasha

Ⓖ Nancy

Ⓗ John

Ⓙ Christopher

19 How many more non-fiction than fiction books did Albert read?

Ⓐ 6

Ⓑ 5

Ⓒ 4

Ⓓ 3

20 Which of the gray shapes is congruent with the dark shape?

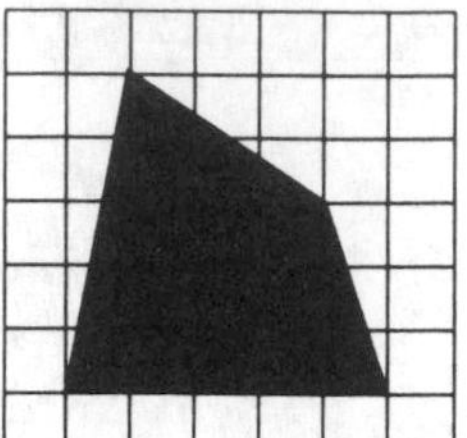

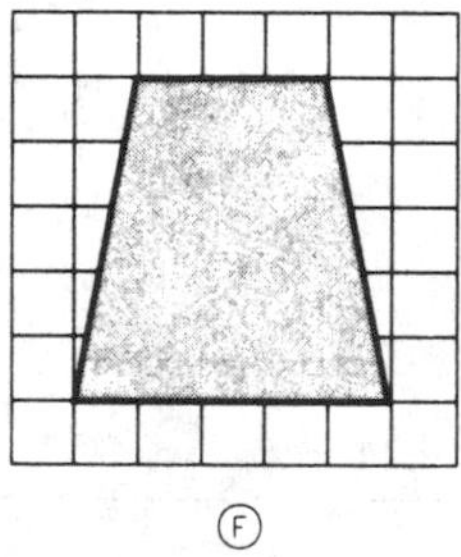

Ⓕ

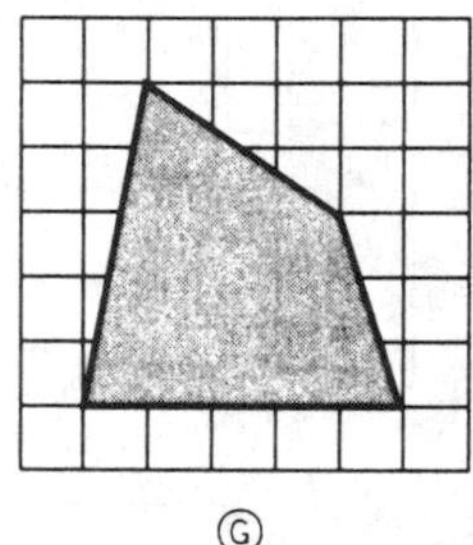

Ⓖ

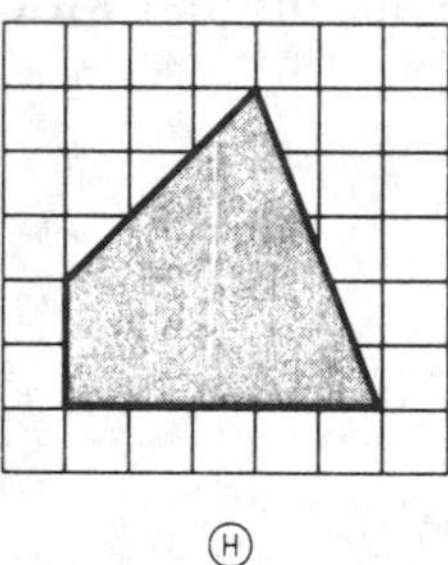

Ⓗ

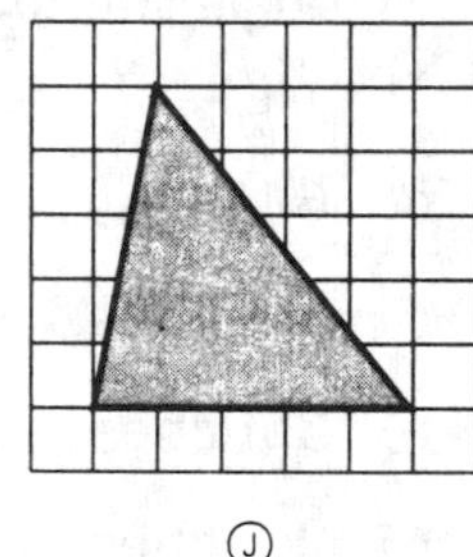

Ⓙ

21 How much money is this?

Ⓐ $.76

Ⓑ $.61

Ⓒ $.31

Ⓓ $26

ANSWER ROWS 17 Ⓐ Ⓑ Ⓒ Ⓓ 19 Ⓐ Ⓑ Ⓒ Ⓓ 21 Ⓐ Ⓑ Ⓒ Ⓓ

18 Ⓕ Ⓖ Ⓗ Ⓙ 20 Ⓕ Ⓖ Ⓗ Ⓙ

NUMBER RIGHT______

Name and Answer Sheet

To the Student:

These tests will give you a chance to put the tips you have learned to work.

A few last reminders…

- Be sure you understand all the directions before you begin each test. You may ask the teacher questions about the directions if you do not understand them.
- Work as quickly as you can during each test.
- When you change an answer, be sure to erase your first mark completely.
- You can guess at an answer or skip difficult items and go back to them later.
- Use the tips you have learned whenever you can.
- It is OK to be a little nervous. You may even do better.

Now that you have completed the lessons in this unit, you are on your way to scoring high!

STUDENT'S NAME

LAST | FIRST | MI

◯ A B C D E F G H I J K L M N O P Q R S T U V W X Y Z

SCHOOL

TEACHER

FEMALE ◯ MALE ◯

BIRTHDATE

MONTH	DAY		YEAR	
JAN ◯	0	0		0
FEB ◯	1	1		1
MAR ◯	2	2		2
APR ◯	3	3		3
MAY ◯		4		4
JUN ◯		5	5	5
JUL ◯		6	6	6
AUG ◯		7	7	7
SEP ◯		8	8	8
OCT ◯		9	9	9
NOV ◯				
DEC ◯				

GRADE

1 2 3 4 5 6

PART 1 CONCEPTS

E1 Ⓐ Ⓑ Ⓒ Ⓓ	**3** Ⓐ Ⓑ Ⓒ Ⓓ	**7** Ⓐ Ⓑ Ⓒ Ⓓ	**11** Ⓐ Ⓑ Ⓒ Ⓓ	**15** Ⓐ Ⓑ Ⓒ Ⓓ	**19** Ⓐ Ⓑ Ⓒ Ⓓ
E2 Ⓕ Ⓖ Ⓗ Ⓙ	**4** Ⓕ Ⓖ Ⓗ Ⓙ	**8** Ⓕ Ⓖ Ⓗ Ⓙ	**12** Ⓕ Ⓖ Ⓗ Ⓙ	**16** Ⓕ Ⓖ Ⓗ Ⓙ	**20** Ⓕ Ⓖ Ⓗ Ⓙ
1 Ⓐ Ⓑ Ⓒ Ⓓ	**5** Ⓐ Ⓑ Ⓒ Ⓓ	**9** Ⓐ Ⓑ Ⓒ Ⓓ	**13** Ⓐ Ⓑ Ⓒ Ⓓ	**17** Ⓐ Ⓑ Ⓒ Ⓓ	**21** Ⓐ Ⓑ Ⓒ Ⓓ
2 Ⓕ Ⓖ Ⓗ Ⓙ	**6** Ⓕ Ⓖ Ⓗ Ⓙ	**10** Ⓕ Ⓖ Ⓗ Ⓙ	**14** Ⓕ Ⓖ Ⓗ Ⓙ	**18** Ⓕ Ⓖ Ⓗ Ⓙ	

PART 2 COMPUTATION

E1 Ⓐ Ⓑ Ⓒ Ⓓ Ⓔ	**3** Ⓐ Ⓑ Ⓒ Ⓓ Ⓔ	**7** Ⓐ Ⓑ Ⓒ Ⓓ Ⓔ	**11** Ⓐ Ⓑ Ⓒ Ⓓ Ⓔ	**15** Ⓐ Ⓑ Ⓒ Ⓓ Ⓔ	**19** Ⓐ Ⓑ Ⓒ Ⓓ Ⓔ
E2 Ⓕ Ⓖ Ⓗ Ⓙ Ⓚ	**4** Ⓕ Ⓖ Ⓗ Ⓙ Ⓚ	**8** Ⓕ Ⓖ Ⓗ Ⓙ Ⓚ	**12** Ⓕ Ⓖ Ⓗ Ⓙ Ⓚ	**16** Ⓕ Ⓖ Ⓗ Ⓙ Ⓚ	**20** Ⓕ Ⓖ Ⓗ Ⓙ Ⓚ
1 Ⓐ Ⓑ Ⓒ Ⓓ Ⓔ	**5** Ⓐ Ⓑ Ⓒ Ⓓ Ⓔ	**9** Ⓐ Ⓑ Ⓒ Ⓓ Ⓔ	**13** Ⓐ Ⓑ Ⓒ Ⓓ Ⓔ	**17** Ⓐ Ⓑ Ⓒ Ⓓ Ⓔ	**21** Ⓐ Ⓑ Ⓒ Ⓓ Ⓔ
2 Ⓕ Ⓖ Ⓗ Ⓙ Ⓚ	**6** Ⓕ Ⓖ Ⓗ Ⓙ Ⓚ	**10** Ⓕ Ⓖ Ⓗ Ⓙ Ⓚ	**14** Ⓕ Ⓖ Ⓗ Ⓙ Ⓚ	**18** Ⓕ Ⓖ Ⓗ Ⓙ Ⓚ	

PART 3 APPLICATIONS

E1 Ⓐ Ⓑ Ⓒ Ⓓ	**4** Ⓕ Ⓖ Ⓗ Ⓙ	**9** Ⓐ Ⓑ Ⓒ Ⓓ	**14** Ⓕ Ⓖ Ⓗ Ⓙ	**19** Ⓐ Ⓑ Ⓒ Ⓓ	**22** Ⓕ Ⓖ Ⓗ Ⓙ
E2 Ⓕ Ⓖ Ⓗ Ⓙ	**5** Ⓐ Ⓑ Ⓒ Ⓓ	**10** Ⓕ Ⓖ Ⓗ Ⓙ	**15** Ⓐ Ⓑ Ⓒ Ⓓ	**20** Ⓕ Ⓖ Ⓗ Ⓙ	**23** Ⓐ Ⓑ Ⓒ Ⓓ
1 Ⓐ Ⓑ Ⓒ Ⓓ	**6** Ⓕ Ⓖ Ⓗ Ⓙ	**11** Ⓐ Ⓑ Ⓒ Ⓓ	**16** Ⓕ Ⓖ Ⓗ Ⓙ	**21** Ⓐ Ⓑ Ⓒ Ⓓ	**24** Ⓕ Ⓖ Ⓗ Ⓙ
2 Ⓕ Ⓖ Ⓗ Ⓙ	**7** Ⓐ Ⓑ Ⓒ Ⓓ	**12** Ⓕ Ⓖ Ⓗ Ⓙ	**17** Ⓐ Ⓑ Ⓒ Ⓓ		
3 Ⓐ Ⓑ Ⓒ Ⓓ	**8** Ⓕ Ⓖ Ⓗ Ⓙ	**13** Ⓐ Ⓑ Ⓒ Ⓓ	**18** Ⓕ Ⓖ Ⓗ Ⓙ		

Part 1 Concepts

Examples **Directions:** Find the correct answer to each problem. Mark the space for your choice.

E1

Counting by ones, what number comes after 321?

Ⓐ 320

Ⓑ 322

Ⓒ 332

Ⓓ 422

E2

How many tens are in 98?

Ⓕ 0

Ⓖ 6

Ⓗ 9

Ⓙ 10

1 How many of these numbers are less than 365?

329	265	429	502	456

Ⓐ 2

Ⓑ 3

Ⓒ 4

Ⓓ 5

2 Suppose you were the sixth person in line to get on a subway. Your friend is the eighth person in line. Which person would be between you?

Ⓕ the ninth person

Ⓖ the fifth person

Ⓗ the eighth person

Ⓙ the seventh person

3 What symbol correctly completes the number sentence below?

15 □ 8 = 7

Ⓐ +

Ⓑ –

Ⓒ x

Ⓓ ÷

4 Another way to write 4 x 9 is

Ⓕ 4 + 4 + 4 + 4

Ⓖ 4 + 9 + 4 + 9

Ⓗ 9 + 9 + 9 + 9

Ⓙ 9 + 4

5 In which of these must you rename a ten as ten ones or borrow a ten?

Ⓐ 22 – 0 =

Ⓑ 23 – 2 =

Ⓒ 28 – 3 =

Ⓓ 23 – 8 =

6 Which of these number lines is correct?

Ⓕ 1 1.5 2 2.5 3 4

Ⓖ 1 2 2.5 3 4 4.5

Ⓗ 1 2 2.5 3 4 4.5

Ⓙ 1 2 3 3.5 4 4.5

7 Counting by threes, what comes before the number 42?

Ⓐ 40

Ⓑ 39

Ⓒ 38

Ⓓ 36

8 Which of these numbers has a 9 in the ones place and a 3 in the hundreds place?

Ⓕ 9388

Ⓖ 9839

Ⓗ 13,903

Ⓙ 19,309

9 Which numeral means forty thousand, nine hundred eight?

Ⓐ 40,908

Ⓑ 49,108

Ⓒ 400,908

Ⓓ 440,980

10 In which answer are $\frac{2}{3}$ of the circles shaded?

Ⓕ 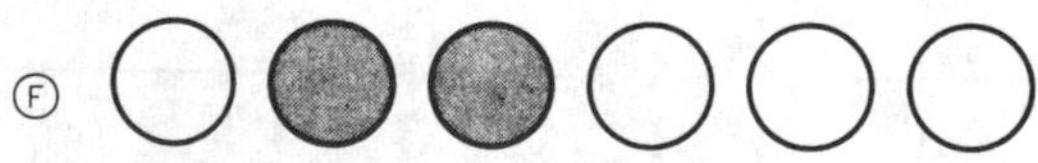

Ⓖ 

Ⓗ 

Ⓙ 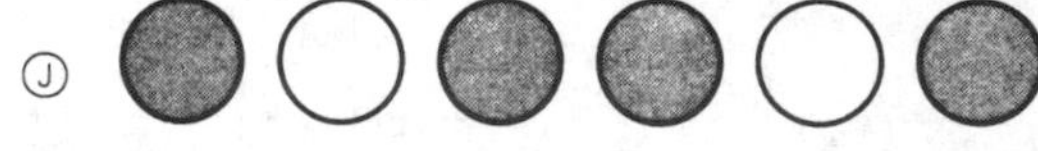

11 What number should come next in the counting pattern below?

223	228	233	238	

Ⓐ 243

Ⓑ 242

Ⓒ 248

Ⓓ 253

12 What will make the number sentences below true?

$$\square + 11 = 19$$

$$22 - \square = 14$$

Ⓕ 12

Ⓖ 11

Ⓗ 9

Ⓙ 8

13 There are 27 students in a class. Each student brought in 5 insects for a science project. How can you find the number of insects they brought in all together?

Ⓐ add

Ⓑ subtract

Ⓒ multiply

Ⓓ divide

14 Which of these should you use to estimate 83 – 38 to the nearest ten?

Ⓕ 80 – 30 =

Ⓖ 80 – 40 =

Ⓗ 90 – 40 =

Ⓙ 90 – 30 =

GO

15 Which of these is the same as $\frac{7}{100}$?

Ⓐ 0.7

Ⓑ 1.7

Ⓒ 0.17

Ⓓ 0.07

16 Which of these shows one more telephone than lock?

Ⓕ 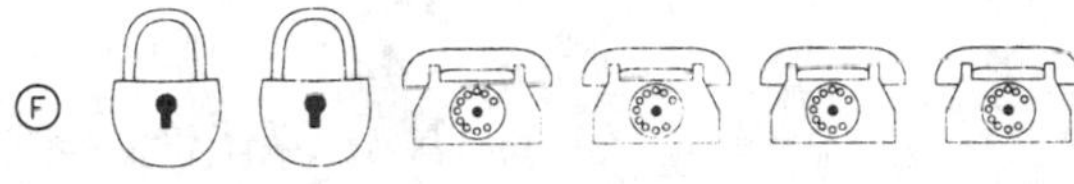

Ⓖ 

Ⓗ 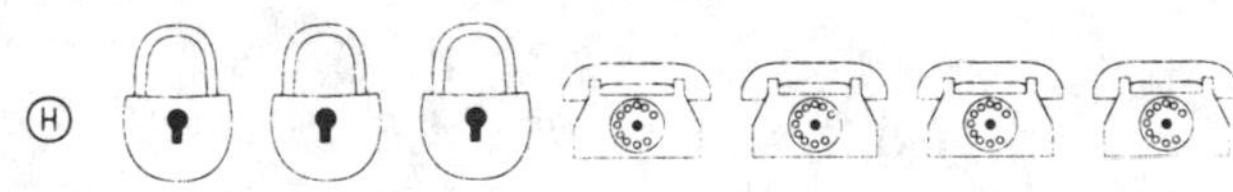

Ⓙ 

17 Which of these is smaller than 56 and can be divided by 6?

Ⓐ 54

Ⓑ 55

Ⓒ 60

Ⓓ 64

18 If you arranged these numbers from least to greatest, which would be last?

506 521 498 152 374

Ⓕ 506

Ⓖ 498

Ⓗ 521

Ⓙ 152

19 The picture below shows a group of dogs. Some have collars, and others do not. Which of these statements is true about the dogs?

Ⓐ Fewer dogs have collars than do not.

Ⓑ More dogs have collars than do not.

Ⓒ There are a total of 8 dogs.

Ⓓ The same number of dogs have collars and do not have collars.

20 Which of these is less than $\frac{1}{6}$?

Ⓕ $\frac{1}{7}$

Ⓖ $\frac{1}{5}$

Ⓗ $\frac{2}{3}$

Ⓙ $\frac{3}{7}$

21 Look at the number sentence below. What number fits in the box to make the sentence correct?

$$1 + 6 + 7 = 10 + \square$$

Ⓐ 10

Ⓑ 9

Ⓒ 7

Ⓓ 4

STOP

Part 2 Computation

Examples

Directions: Mark the space for the correct answer to each problem. Choose "None of these" if the right answer is not given.

E1

3)9

Ⓐ 12
Ⓑ 9
Ⓒ 3
Ⓓ 1
Ⓔ None of these

E2

12 − 8 =

Ⓕ 3
Ⓖ 5
Ⓗ 8
Ⓙ 20
Ⓚ None of these

1

2 x 7 =

Ⓐ 15
Ⓑ 14
Ⓒ 9
Ⓓ 6
Ⓔ None of these

2

$$\begin{array}{r} 51 \\ -\ 9 \\ \hline \end{array}$$

Ⓕ 60
Ⓖ 44
Ⓗ 43
Ⓙ 32
Ⓚ None of these

3

12)100

Ⓐ 8 R4
Ⓑ 10
Ⓒ 10 R4
Ⓓ 12
Ⓔ None of these

4

$$\begin{array}{r} 99 \\ 21 \\ +\ 8 \\ \hline \end{array}$$

Ⓕ 138
Ⓖ 129
Ⓗ 128
Ⓙ 120
Ⓚ None of these

5

27 ÷ 9 =

Ⓐ 3
Ⓑ 9
Ⓒ 18
Ⓓ 24
Ⓔ None of these

6

$$\begin{array}{r} 14 \\ 109 \\ +\ 20 \\ \hline \end{array}$$

Ⓕ 114
Ⓖ 129
Ⓗ 143
Ⓙ 144
Ⓚ None of these

7

11.8 − 8.2 =

Ⓐ 3.6
Ⓑ 3.82
Ⓒ 4.6
Ⓓ 9.0
Ⓔ None of these

8

$$\begin{array}{r} \$6.00 \\ .28 \\ +\ 7.99 \\ \hline \end{array}$$

Ⓕ $12.99
Ⓖ $13.26
Ⓗ $13.27
Ⓙ $13.28
Ⓚ None of these

9

$$\begin{array}{r} 40 \\ \times\ 70 \\ \hline \end{array}$$

Ⓐ 2800
Ⓑ 2400
Ⓒ 2040
Ⓓ 470
Ⓔ None of these

10

$1 - \frac{1}{2} = \square$

Ⓕ 0
Ⓖ $\frac{1}{4}$
Ⓗ $\frac{1}{2}$
Ⓙ 1
Ⓚ None of these

GO

11

$\frac{3}{11} + \frac{4}{11} =$

Ⓐ $\frac{7}{11}$
Ⓑ $\frac{8}{11}$
Ⓒ $\frac{14}{15}$
Ⓓ 11
Ⓔ None of these

12

8) 63

Ⓕ 6 R3
Ⓖ 7 R6
Ⓗ 7 R7
Ⓙ 8
Ⓚ None of these

13

14 x 2 =

Ⓐ 16
Ⓑ 24
Ⓒ 26
Ⓓ 29
Ⓔ None of these

14

19 + 3 + 22 =

Ⓕ 34
Ⓖ 44
Ⓗ 46
Ⓙ 48
Ⓚ None of these

15

9)9009

Ⓐ 100
Ⓑ 101
Ⓒ 563
Ⓓ 1001
Ⓔ None of these

16

1.3
0.22
+ 9.1

Ⓕ 10.62
Ⓖ 10.26
Ⓗ 10.13
Ⓙ 10.06
Ⓚ None of these

17

100 − 39 =

Ⓐ 17
Ⓑ 61
Ⓒ 71
Ⓓ 139
Ⓔ None of these

18

287 + 539 =

Ⓕ 826
Ⓖ 726
Ⓗ 725
Ⓙ 352
Ⓚ None of these

19

21
x 10

Ⓐ 310
Ⓑ 220
Ⓒ 210
Ⓓ 31
Ⓔ None of these

20

99 ÷ 33 =

Ⓕ 132
Ⓖ 123
Ⓗ 66
Ⓙ 3
Ⓚ None of these

21 In the table below, the numbers in Column II are 3 times larger than those in Column I. Which numbers belong in the empty spaces in the table?

Column I	Column II
9	27
10	
11	
12	36

Ⓐ 30, 31
Ⓑ 30, 32
Ⓒ 31, 33
Ⓓ 33, 34
Ⓔ None of these

STOP

Examples

Directions: For items 1-3, choose the number sentence that shows how to solve each problem. For items 4-8, find the correct answer to each problem, and mark the space for your choice.

E1 A square garden is 20 feet on each side. What is the distance around the garden? Ⓐ 20 + 4 = ☐ Ⓑ 20 - 4 = ☐ Ⓒ 20 ÷ 4 = ☐ Ⓓ 20 x 4 = ☐	**E2** About how long is a $1 bill? Ⓕ 6 inches Ⓖ 10 inches Ⓗ 1 foot Ⓙ 10 centimeters

1 A box of popcorn costs $1.25. You pay for it with 2 dollar bills. How much change will you receive?

Ⓐ $2.00 ÷ $1.25 = ☐

Ⓑ $1.25 + $2.00 = ☐

Ⓒ $2.00 x $1.25 = ☐

Ⓓ $2.00 - $1.25 = ☐

2 The temperature at 2:00 is 78° . It rises 6° by 3:00. What is the temperature at 3:00?

Ⓕ 78 + 6 = ☐

Ⓖ 78 -☐ = 6

Ⓗ 6 x☐ = 78

Ⓙ 78 - 6 = ☐

3 A case of juice has 24 cans. Each can holds 12 ounces of juice. How many ounces of juice are in a case?

Ⓐ 24 ÷ 12 = ☐

Ⓑ 24 - 12 = ☐

Ⓒ 24 x 12 = ☐

Ⓓ ☐+ 12 = 24

4 Scotty gets on the bus at 8:05 and arrives at school at 8:20. How long is his bus ride?

Ⓕ 5 minutes

Ⓖ 15 minutes

Ⓗ 20 minutes

Ⓙ 60 minutes

5 Jackie has 20 yards of rope she wants to be cut into 5 pieces. How long will each piece of rope be?

Ⓐ 25 yards

Ⓑ 7 yards

Ⓒ 5 yards

Ⓓ 4 yards

6 What time is shown on this clock?

Ⓕ 8:20

Ⓖ 3:40

Ⓗ 3:08

Ⓙ 8:40

7 How many quarts are in a gallon?

Ⓐ 2

Ⓑ 3

Ⓒ 4

Ⓓ 8

8 What metric unit is best to use to measure the weight of a large dog?

Ⓕ kilometer

Ⓖ meter

Ⓗ gram

Ⓙ kilogram

Use this calendar to answer questions 9 through 11.

January						
SUN	MON	TUE	WED	THU	FRI	SAT
1	2	3	4	5	6	7
8	9	10	11	12	13	14
15	16	17	18	19	20	21
22	23	24	25	26	27	28
29	30	31				

9 This calendar is for January. What day of the week was the last day in December?

Ⓐ Monday

Ⓑ Saturday

Ⓒ Sunday

Ⓓ Tuesday

10 How many Tuesdays are in January?

Ⓕ 3

Ⓖ 4

Ⓗ 5

Ⓙ 6

11 For the class trip this year, the students are going on a ski trip beginning on the third Wednesday in January and ending the following Saturday. What date will the ski trip begin?

Ⓐ January 4

Ⓑ January 25

Ⓒ January 21

Ⓓ January 18

12 A naturalist was watching the birds around a pond. Fifteen ducks were swimming in the pond when he arrived, and 8 geese landed soon afterwards. Seven cranes wandered to the pond from a nearby swamp. How many birds in all did the naturalist see?

Ⓕ 30

Ⓖ 29

Ⓗ 19

Ⓙ 15

This graph shows how long it takes students to ride the bus to school. Study the graph, then answer questions 13 and 14.

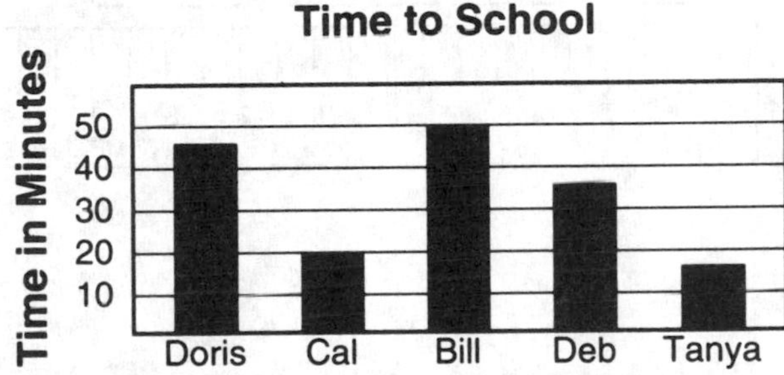

13 Whose trip is less than half an hour?

Ⓐ Deb and Tanya

Ⓑ Doris and Bill

Ⓒ Cal and Deb

Ⓓ Cal and Tanya

14 If Bill's father drives him to school, he saves 15 minutes. How long does it take Bill to get to school if his father drives?

Ⓕ 50 minutes

Ⓖ 35 minutes

Ⓗ 25 minutes

Ⓙ 15 minutes

The figure below shows a calculator and two metric rulers. Study the figure, then answer numbers 15 and 16.

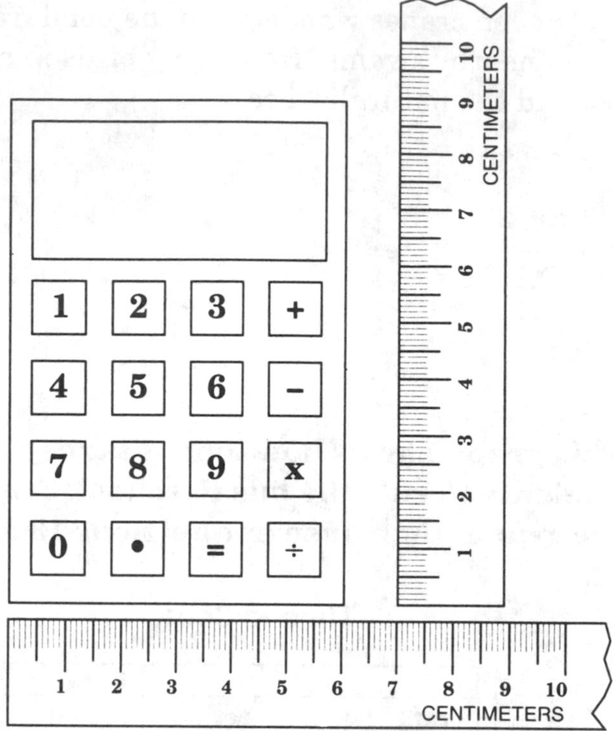

15 What are the width and length of the calculator?

Ⓐ 6 cm wide by 10 cm long

Ⓑ 6 cm wide by 9 cm long

Ⓒ 10 cm wide by 10 cm long

Ⓓ 10 cm wide by 9 cm long

16 Suppose you wanted to put colored tape around the perimeter of the calculator to decorate it. How much tape would you need?

Ⓕ 15 cm

Ⓖ 16 cm

Ⓗ 24 cm

Ⓙ 30 cm

17 Which clock shows 1:50?

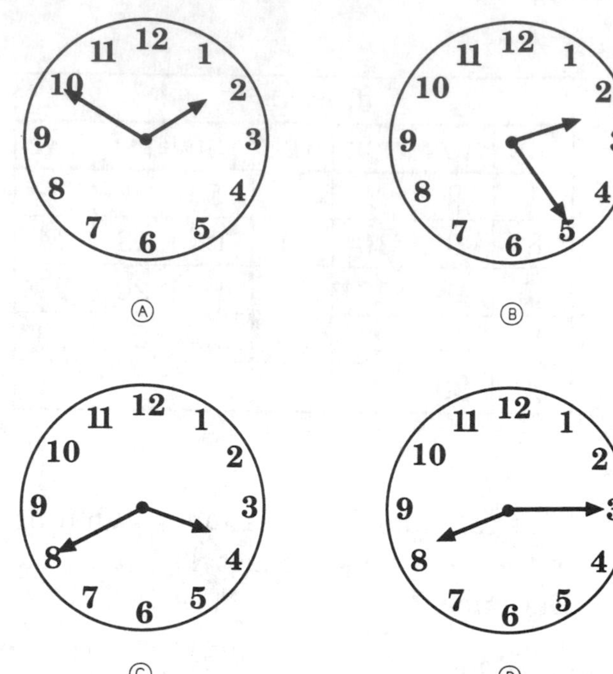

18 A gardener works for 6 hours and earns $48. Which number sentence shows how to find the amount of money the gardener earns in one hour?

Ⓕ 6 x $48 = □

Ⓖ $8 + □ = $48

Ⓗ $48 – □ = 6

Ⓙ 6 x □ = $48

19 A plane has 124 passengers. There are 3 members of the flying crew and 9 cabin attendants. How many people in all are on the plane?

Ⓐ 136

Ⓑ 135

Ⓒ 133

Ⓓ 112

GO

This chart shows the number of students in school. The chart shows how many students were in each grade during two different years. Study the graph, then answer numbers 20 through 22.

	1990	1991
Grade 1	52	61
Grade 2	57	59
Grade 3	54	60
Grade 4	48	55
Grade 5	47	45

20 Which grade in 1990 had the most students?

Ⓕ Grade 1

Ⓖ Grade 2

Ⓗ Grade 3

Ⓙ Grade 4

21 What was the increase in the number of students in grade 4 between 1990 and 1991?

Ⓐ 7

Ⓑ 6

Ⓒ 4

Ⓓ 3

22 What was the total number of students enrolled in grades 1, 2, and 3 in 1991?

Ⓕ 120 students

Ⓖ 173 students

Ⓗ 175 students

Ⓙ 180 students

23 Which two shapes are congruent?

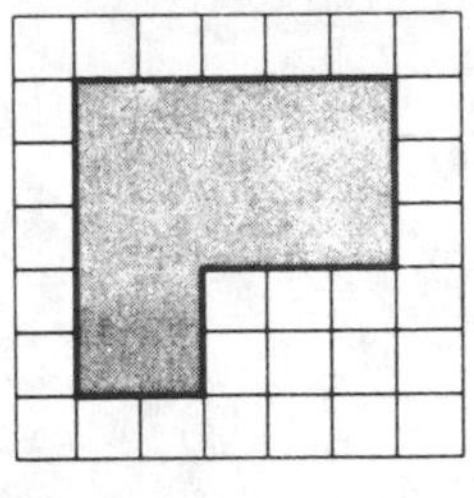

M

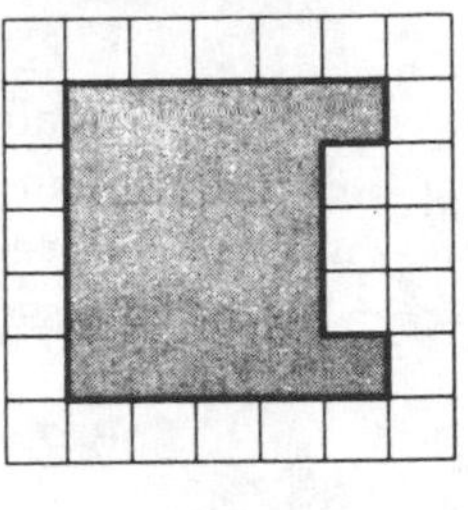

N

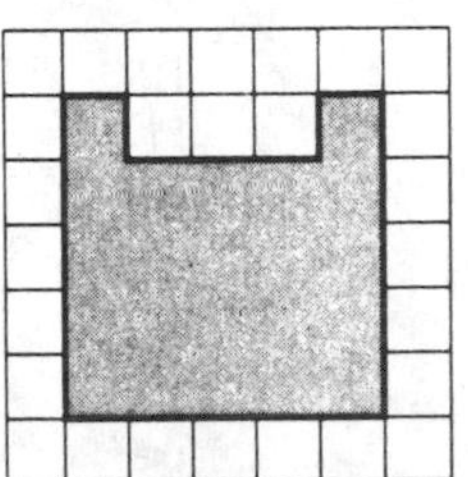

O

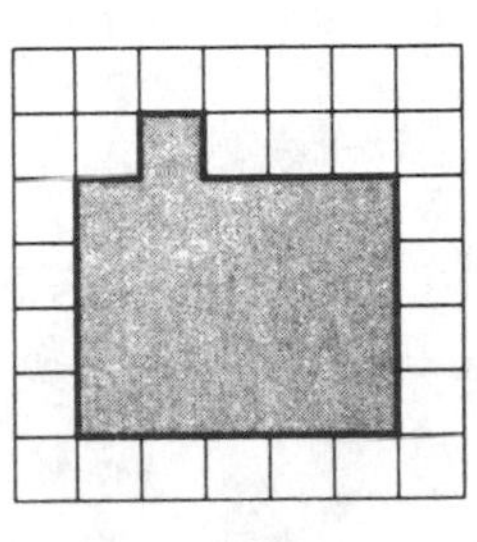

P

Ⓐ M and N

Ⓑ O and M

Ⓒ N and O

Ⓓ P and M

24 How much money is this?

Ⓕ $4.70

Ⓖ $4.87

Ⓗ $4.97

Ⓙ $5.07

STOP

Answer Keys

Reading
Unit 1,
Vocabulary

Lesson 1-pg.513

A	C
B	J
1	B
2	F
3	D
4	H
5	C
6	J
7	B

Lesson 2-pg.514

A	D
B	J
1	A
2	J
3	C
4	G
5	C
6	H
7	A

Lesson 3-pg.515

A	B
B	F
1	C
2	J
3	B
4	J
5	C
6	G
7	C

Lesson 4-pg.516

A	B
B	H
1	C
2	J
3	B
4	J
5	A

Lesson 5-pg.517

A	C
B	G
1	B
2	J
3	C
4	F
5	C
6	J

Lesson 6-pgs. 518-520

E1	C
E2	F
E3	C
1	D
2	F
3	B
4	G
5	D
6	J
7	C
8	J
9	A
10	J
11	B
12	H
13	C
14	F
15	B
16	F
17	D
18	F
19	C
20	F
21	B
22	J
23	A
24	H
25	D
26	G
27	C
28	F

Unit 2, Reading
Comprehension

Lesson 7-pg.521

A	B
1	A
2	H
3	D

Lesson 8-pgs.522-524

A	D
1	B
2	H
3	C
4	J
5	B
6	F
7	D
8	G

Lesson 9-pgs.525-530

A	C
1	B
2	J
3	A
4	J
5	B
6	H
7	C
8	G
9	D
10	H
11	D
12	J
13	D
14	G
15	D
16	G
17	A
18	H

Lesson 10-pgs.531-535

E1	C
1	C
2	J
3	A
4	F
5	B
6	J
7	A
8	H
9	C
10	G
11	D
12	F
13	C
14	G
15	A
16	H

Test Practice
Part 1-pgs.538-540

E1	C
E2	G
E3	D
1	A
2	J
3	B
4	F
5	C
6	H
7	B
8	F
9	D
10	J
11	C
12	F
13	C
14	J
15	A
16	J
17	C
18	J
19	C
20	F
21	B
22	J
23	C
24	F
25	B
26	F
27	D
28	G

Test Practice
Part 2-pgs.541-547

E1	D
1	C
2	G
3	D
4	G
5	D
6	F
7	C
8	G
9	C
10	J
11	D
12	F
13	C
14	H
15	B
16	F
17	B
18	G
19	C
20	F
21	A
22	H
23	D
24	J

Language
Unit 1, Language Mechanics
Lesson 1-pg. 549

A C
B G
1 A
2 J
3 B
4 J
5 A

Lesson 2-pg.550

A D
B G
1 A
2 J
3 B
4 F
5 B

Lesson 3-pgs.551-552

A A
B J
1 D
2 H
3 D
4 F
5 B
6 J
7 C
8 F
9 A
10 J

Lesson 4-pgs.553-555

E1 A
E2 G
1 C
2 H
3 A
4 J
5 B
6 J
7 B
8 H
9 D
10 G
11 A
12 H
13 B
14 F
15 D
16 H
17 A
18 J
19 C
20 G
21 A
22 J

Unit 2, Language Expression
Lesson 5-pgs.556-557

A B
B F
1 D
2 G
3 A
4 H
5 A
6 J
C A
D J
E B
F F
G C
7 B
8 G
9 B
10 J
11 B
12 G
13 D
14 F
15 C

Lesson 6-pg.558

A D
B F
1 C
2 G
3 A
4 H
5 D
6 F
7 C
8 J
9 C
10 G

Lesson 7-pg.559

A B
B F
1 D
2 G
3 C
4 F
5 D
6 F
7 C

Lesson 8-pgs.560-562

A A
B H
C D
1 B
2 F
3 D
4 H
5 A
6 H
7 D
8 G
9 C
10 F
11 D
12 G
13 D
14 G

Lesson 9-pgs.563-565

A B
1 D
2 H
3 D
4 G
5 C
6 J
7 A
8 G
9 A
10 H
11 D

Lesson 10-pgs.566-571

E1 B
E2 H
1 C
2 F
3 B
4 J
5 B
6 F
7 D
8 H
9 D
10 H
11 A
12 G
13 A
14 G
15 D
16 G
17 C
18 F
19 B
20 F
21 C
22 F
23 D
24 G
25 C
26 H
27 A
28 J
29 B
30 G
31 D
32 G
33 A
34 J
35 C
36 G
37 D
38 J
39 A

Unit 3, Spelling
Lesson 11-pgs.572-573

A C
B K
C B
D F
1 D
2 F
3 C
4 G
5 C
6 F
7 B
8 K
9 C
10 K
11 C
12 J
13 A
14 G
15 B
16 J
17 C
18 F
19 D
20 G
21 D
22 F
23 D
24 G

Lesson 12-pgs.574-575

E1 D
E2 G
E3 A
E4 J
1 C
2 H

3 A
4 J
5 B
6 J
7 A
8 H
9 E
10 G
11 D
12 G
13 D
14 J
15 B
16 F
17 A
18 H
19 B
20 J
21 A
22 G
23 A
24 J
25 B
26 F
27 B

Unit 4, Study Skills
Lesson 13-pgs. 576-578

A C
B F
1 B
2 J
3 A
4 G
5 D
6 H
7 A
8 G
9 D
10 G
11 C
12 F
13 B
14 J
15 A
16 H
17 C
18 G
19 D

Lesson 14-pgs. 579-580

E1A
E2H
1B
2J
3C
4 F
5 B
6 J
7 D
8 H
9 A
10 J
11 B
12 F
13 B
14 H
15 D

Unit 5, Test Practice
Part 1-pgs. 583-585

E1 D
E2 F
1 A
2 J
3 B
4 H
5 A
6 J
7 C
8 F
9 D
10 H
11 D
12 H
13 A
14 G
15 B
16 J
17 D
18 F
19 B
20 F
21 C
22 J

Test Practice
Part 2-pgs. 586-589

E1 D
E2 F
1 C
2 F
3 B
4 F
5 D
6 G
7 C
8 J
9 A
10 J
11 C
12 G
13 B
14 J
15 A
16 H
17 B
18 F
19 B
20 G
21 C
22 H
23 A
24 H
25 B
26 G
27 A
28 H
29 B
30 H

Test Practice
Part 3-pgs. 590-591

E1 B
E2 K
E3 C
1 D
2 G
3 A
4 J
5 B
6 F
7 C
8 H
9 A
10 G
11 D
12 H
13 E
14 F
15 B
16 J
17 C
18 H
19 B
20 H
21 A
22 J
23 C
24 G
25 A
26 J
27 A

Test Practice
Part 4-pgs. 592-593

E1 D
E2 G
1 C
2 F
3 D
4 J
5 D
6 F
7 C
8 G
9 D
10 F
11 C
12 H
13 D
14 F
15 B
16 F

Math
Unit 1, Concepts
Lesson 1-pgs. 595-596

A D
B G
1 C
2 F
3 B
4 J
5 B
6 G
7 A
8 J
9 C
10 F
11 D

Lesson 2-pgs. 597-598

A B
B H
1 B
2 J
3 C
4 F
5 A
6 J
7 B
8 G
9 D
10 H
11 C

Lesson 3-pgs. 599-600

A B
B J
1 A

2 J
3 C
4 G
5 D
6 G
7 C
8 F
9 B
10 H
11 C

Lesson 4-pgs. 601-603

E1 B
E2 G
1 D
2 H
3 A
4 F
5 C
6 G
7 C
8 J
9 A
10 G
11 C
12 F
13 D
14 H
15 A
16 G
17 D
18 G
19 C
20 F

Unit 2, Computation

Lesson 5-pgs. 604-605

A B
B K
1 A
2 H
3 B
4 J
5 E
6 F
7 C
8 G
9 D
10 K
11 B
12 F
13 D
14 J
15 A
16 J
17 B
18 K
19 B
20 H

Lesson 6-pgs. 606-607

A C
B K
1 B
2 K
3 D
4 F
5 D
6 F
7 E
8 G
9 C
10 H
11 A
12 G
13 A
14 K
15 D
16 K
17 C
18 J
19 A
20 G

Lesson 7-pgs. 608-609

A D
B K
1 D
2 G
3 C
4 J
5 A
6 G
7 E
8 J
9 D
10 F
11 B
12 H
13 C
14 F
15 B
16 G
17 D
18 K
19 D

Lesson 8-pgs. 610-612

E1 B
E2 K
1 E
2 H
3 A
4 G
5 B
6 J
7 C
8 J
9 E
10 F
11 C
12 F
13 E
14 J
15 C
16 H
17 B
18 H
19 E
20 F
21 D
22 G
23 C
24 J
25 B
26 J
27 E
28 G
29 C
30 J
31 A
32 K
33 D

Unit 3, Applications

Lesson 9-pgs. 613-616

A D
1 C
2 F
3 B
4 J
5 B
6 F
7 D
8 H
9 B
10 F
11 C
12 G
13 D
14 G
15 D
16 F
17 C
18 H
19 B

Lesson 10-pgs. 617-620

A C
1 C
2 F
3 B
4 H
5 B
6 H
7 A
8 G
9 A
10 H
11 D
12 G
13 C
14 F
15 C
16 J
17 C
18 F
19 D
20 J
21 B

Lesson 11-pgs. 621-624

A D
B H
1 B
2 F
3 C
4 G
5 D
6 H
7 A
8 G
9 D
10 G
11 C
12 H
13 A
14 J
15 B
16 H
17 D
18 G
19 B
20 F
21 D
22 H
23 A

24 H
25 B

Lesson 12-pgs.625-628

E1 C
E2 G
1 A
2 H
3 D
4 G
5 D
6 F
7 C
8 F
9 C
10 J
11 B
12 G
13 A
14 J
15 B
16 H
17 B
18 H
19 D
20 G
21 A

Unit 4, Test Practice
Part 1-pgs.631-633

E1 B
E2 H
1 A
2 J
3 B
4 H
5 D
6 H
7 B
8 J
9 A
10 J
11 A
12 J
13 C
14 G
15 D
16 H
17 A
18 H
19 B
20 F
21 D

Test Practice
Part 2-pgs.634-635

E1 C
E2 K
1 B
2 K
3 A
4 H
5 A
6 H
7 A
8 K
9 A
10 H
11 A
12 H
13 E
14 G
15 D
16 F
17 B
18 F
19 C
20 J
21 E

Test Practice
Part 3-pgs.636-639

E1 D
E2 F
1 D
2 F
3 C
4 G
5 D
6 G
7 C
8 J
9 B
10 H
11 D
12 F
13 D
14 G
15 B
16 J
17 A
18 J
19 A
20 G
21 A
22 J
23 C
24 G

Reading Progress Chart

Circle your score for each lesson. Connect your scores to see how well you are doing.

Unit 1 Lesson 1	7, 6, 5, 4, 3, 2, 1
Lesson 2	7, 6, 5, 4, 3, 2, 1
Lesson 3	7, 6, 5, 4, 3, 2, 1
Lesson 4	5, 4, 3, 2, 1
Unit 2 Lesson 5	6, 5, 4, 3, 2, 1
Lesson 6	28, 27, 26, 25, 24, 23, 22, 21, 20, 19, 18, 17, 16, 15, 14, 13, 12, 11, 10, 9, 8, 7, 6, 5, 4, 3, 2, 1
Lesson 7	3, 2, 1
Lesson 8	8, 7, 6, 5, 4, 3, 2, 1
Lesson 9	18, 17, 16, 15, 14, 13, 12, 11, 10, 9, 8, 7, 6, 5, 4, 3, 2, 1
Lesson 10	16, 15, 14, 13, 12, 11, 10, 9, 8, 7, 6, 5, 4, 3, 2, 1

Language Progress Chart

Circle your score for each lesson. Connect your scores to see how well you are doing.

Unit 1 Lesson 1	Lesson 2	Lesson 3	Lesson 4	Lesson 5	Unit 2 Lesson 6	Lesson 7	Lesson 8	Lesson 9	Lesson 10	Unit 3 Lesson 11	Lesson 12	Lesson 13	Lesson 14
5	5	10	22	15	10	7	14	11	39	24	27	19	15
4	4	9	21	14	9	6	13	10	38	23	26	18	14
3	3	8	20	13	8	5	12	9	37	22	25	17	13
2	2	7	19	12	7	4	11	8	36	21	24	16	12
1	1	6	18	11	6	3	10	7	35	20	23	15	11
		5	17	10	5	2	9	6	34	19	22	14	10
		4	16	9	4	1	8	5	33	18	21	13	9
		3	15	8	3		7	4	32	17	20	12	8
		2	14	7	2		6	3	31	16	19	11	7
		1	13	6	1		5	2	30	15	18	10	6
			12	5			4	1	29	14	17	9	5
			11	4			3		28	13	16	8	4
			10	3			2		27	12	15	7	3
			9	2			1		26	11	14	6	2
			8	1					25	10	13	5	1
			7						24	9	12	4	
			6						23	8	11	3	
			5						22	7	10	2	
			4						21	6	9	1	
			3						20	5	8		
			2						19	4	7		
			1						18	3	6		
									17	2	5		
									16	1	4		
									15		3		
									14		2		
									13		1		
									12				
									11				
									10				
									9				
									8				
									7				
									6				
									5				
									4				
									3				
									2				
									1				

Math Progress Chart

Circle your score for each lesson. Connect your scores to see how well you are doing.

Unit 1	Lesson 1	11 10 9 8 7 6 5 4 3 2 1
	Lesson 2	11 10 9 8 7 6 5 4 3 2 1
	Lesson 3	11 10 9 8 7 6 5 4 3 2 1
Unit 2	Lesson 4	20 19 18 17 16 15 14 13 12 11 10 9 8 7 6 5 4 3 2 1
	Lesson 5	20 19 18 17 16 15 14 13 12 11 10 9 8 7 6 5 4 3 2 1
	Lesson 6	20 19 18 17 16 15 14 13 12 11 10 9 8 7 6 5 4 3 2 1
	Lesson 7	19 18 17 16 15 14 13 12 11 10 9 8 7 6 5 4 3 2 1
Unit 3	Lesson 8	33 32 31 30 29 28 27 26 25 24 23 22 21 20 19 18 17 16 15 14 13 12 11 10 9 8 7 6 5 4 3 2 1
	Lesson 9	19 18 17 16 15 14 13 12 11 10 9 8 7 6 5 4 3 2 1
Unit 4	Lesson 10	21 20 19 18 17 16 15 14 13 12 11 10 9 8 7 6 5 4 3 2 1
	Lesson 11	25 24 23 22 21 20 19 18 17 16 15 14 13 12 11 10 9 8 7 6 5 4 3 2 1
	Lesson 12	21 20 19 18 17 16 15 14 13 12 11 10 9 8 7 6 5 4 3 2 1

McGRAW-HILL LEARNING MATERIALS

Offers a selection of workbooks to meet all your needs.

Look for all of these fine educational workbooks
in the McGraw-Hill Learning Materials SPECTRUM Series.
All workbooks meet school curriculum guidelines and correspond to
The McGraw-Hill Companies classroom textbooks.

SPECTRUM GEOGRAPHY – NEW FOR 1998!

Full-color, three-part lessons strengthen geography knowledge and map reading skills. Focusing on five geographic themes including location, place, human/environmental interaction, movement and regions. Over 150 pages. Glossary of geographical terms and answer key included.

TITLE	ISBN	PRICE
Grade 3, Communities	1-57768-153-3	$7.95
Grade 4, Regions	1-57768-154-1	$7.95
Grade 5, USA	1-57768-155-X	$7.95
Grade 6, World	1-57768-156-8	$7.95

SPECTRUM MATH

Features easy-to-follow instructions that give students a clear path to success. This series has comprehensive coverage of the basic skills, helping children to master math fundamentals. Over 150 pages. Answer key included.

TITLE	ISBN	PRICE
Grade 1	1-57768-111-8	$6.95
Grade 2	1-57768-112-6	$6.95
Grade 3	1-57768-113-4	$6.95
Grade 4	1-57768-114-2	$6.95
Grade 5	1-57768-115-0	$6.95
Grade 6	1-57768-116-9	$6.95
Grade 7	1-57768-117-7	$6.95
Grade 8	1-57768-118-5	$6.95

SPECTRUM PHONICS

Provides everything children need to build multiple skills in language. Focusing on phonics, structural analysis, and dictionary skills, this series also offers creative ideas for using phonics and word study skills in other language arts. Over 200 pages. Answer key included.

TITLE	ISBN	PRICE
Grade K	1-57768-120-7	$6.95
Grade 1	1-57768-121-5	$6.95
Grade 2	1-57768-122-3	$6.95
Grade 3	1-57768-123-1	$6.95
Grade 4	1-57768-124-X	$6.95
Grade 5	1-57768-125-8	$6.95
Grade 6	1-57768-126-6	$6.95

SPECTRUM READING

This full-color series creates an enjoyable reading environment, even for below-average readers. Each book contains captivating content, colorful characters, and compelling illustrations, so children are eager to find out what happens next. Over 150 pages. Answer key included.

TITLE	ISBN	PRICE
Grade K	1-57768-130-4	$6.95
Grade 1	1-57768-131-2	$6.95
Grade 2	1-57768-132-0	$6.95
Grade 3	1-57768-133-9	$6.95
Grade 4	1-57768-134-7	$6.95
Grade 5	1-57768-135-5	$6.95
Grade 6	1-57768-136-3	$6.95

SPECTRUM SPELLING – NEW FOR 1998!

This series links spelling to reading and writing and increases skills in words and meanings, consonant and vowel spellings and proofreading practice. Over 200 pages in full color. Speller dictionary and answer key included.

TITLE	ISBN	PRICE
Grade 1	1-57768-161-4	$7.95
Grade 2	1-57768-162-2	$7.95
Grade 3	1-57768-163-0	$7.95
Grade 4	1-57768-164-9	$7.95
Grade 5	1-57768-165-7	$7.95
Grade 6	1-57768-166-5	$7.95

SPECTRUM WRITING

Lessons focus on creative and expository writing using clearly stated objectives and pre-writing exercises. Eight essential reading skills are applied. Activities include main idea, sequence, comparison, detail, fact and opinion, cause and effect, and making a point. Over 130 pages. Answer key included.

TITLE	ISBN	PRICE
Grade 1	1-57768-141-X	$6.95
Grade 2	1-57768-142-8	$6.95
Grade 3	1-57768-143-6	$6.95
Grade 4	1-57768-144-4	$6.95
Grade 5	1-57768-145-2	$6.95
Grade 6	1-57768-146-0	$6.95
Grade 7	1-57768-147-9	$6.95
Grade 8	1-57768-148-7	$6.95

SPECTRUM TEST PREP from the Nation's #1 Testing Company

Prepares children to do their best on current editions of the five major standardized tests. Activities reinforce test-taking skills through examples, tips, practice and timed exercises. Subjects include reading, math and language. 150 pages. Answer key included.

TITLE	ISBN	PRICE
Grade 3	1-57768-103-7	$8.95
Grade 4	1-57768-104-5	$8.95
Grade 5	1-57768-105-3	$8.95
Grade 6	1-57768-106-1	$8.95
Grade 7	1-57768-107-X	$8.95
Grade 8	1-57768-108-8	$8.95

Look for these other fine educational series available from McGRAW-HILL LEARNING MATERIALS.

BASIC SKILLS CURRICULUM
A complete basic skills curriculum, a school year's worth of practice! This series reinforces necessary skills in the following categories: reading comprehension, vocabulary, grammar, writing, math applications, problem solving, test taking and more. Over 700 pages. Answer key included.

TITLE	ISBN	PRICE
Grade 3 – new for 1998!	1-57768-093-6	$19.95
Grade 4 – new for 1998!	1-57768-094-4	$19.95
Grade 5 – new for 1998!	1-57768-095-2	$19.95
Grade 6 – new for 1998!	1-57768-096-0	$19.95
Grade 7	1-57768-097-9	$19.95
Grade 8	1-57768-098-7	$19.95

BUILDING SKILLS MATH
Six basic skills practice books give children the reinforcement they need to master math concepts. Each single-skill lesson consists of a worked example as well as self-directing and self-correcting exercises. 48pages. Answer key included.

TITLE	ISBN	PRICE
Grade 3	1-57768-053-7	$2.49
Grade 4	1-57768-054-5	$2.49
Grade 5	1-57768-055-3	$2.49
Grade 6	1-57768-056-1	$2.49
Grade 7	1-57768-057-X	$2.49
Grade 8	1-57768-058-8	$2.49

BUILDING SKILLS READING
Children master eight crucial reading comprehension skills by working with true stories and exciting adventure tales. 48pages. Answer key included.

TITLE	ISBN	PRICE
Grade 3	1-57768-063-4	$2.49
Grade 4	1-57768-064-2	$2.49
Grade 5	1-57768-065-0	$2.49
Grade 6	1-57768-066-9	$2.49
Grade 7	1-57768-067-7	$2.49
Grade 8	1-57768-068-5	$2.49

BUILDING SKILLS PROBLEM SOLVING
These self-directed practice books help students master the most important step in math – how to think a problem through. Each workbook contains 20 lessons that teach specific problem solving skills including understanding the question, identifying extra information, and multi-step problems. 48pages. Answer key included.

TITLE	ISBN	PRICE
Grade 3	1-57768-073-1	$2.49
Grade 4	1-57768-074-X	$2.49
Grade 5	1-57768-075-8	$2.49
Grade 6	1-57768-076-6	$2.49
Grade 7	1-57768-077-4	$2.49
Grade 8	1-57768-078-2	$2.49

THE McGRAW-HILL
JUNIOR ACADEMIC™ WORKBOOK SERIES

An exciting new partnership between the world's #1 educational publisher and the world's premiere entertainment company brings the respective strengths and reputation of each great media company to the educational publishing arena. McGraw-Hill and Warner Bros. have partnered to provide high-quality educational materials in a fun and entertaining way.

For more than 110 years, school children have been exposed to McGraw-Hill educational products. This new educational workbook series addresses the educational needs of young children, ages three through eight, stimulating their love of learning in an entertaining way that features Warner Bros.' beloved Looney Tunes™ and Animaniacs™ cartoon characters.

The McGraw-Hill Junior Academic™ Workbook Series features twenty books – four books for five age groups including toddler, preschool, kindergarten, first grade and second grade. Each book has up to 80 pages of full-color lessons such as: colors, numbers, shapes and the alphabet for toddlers; and math, reading, phonics, thinking skills, and vocabulary for preschoolers through grade two.

This fun and educational workbook series will be available in bookstores, mass market retail outlets, teacher supply stores and children's specialty stores in summer 1998. Look for them at a store near you, and look for some serious fun!

TODDLER SERIES
32-page workbooks featuring the Baby Looney Tunes™

	ISBN	PRICE
My Colors Go 'Round	1-57768-208-4	$2.25
My 1, 2, 3's	1-57768-218-1	$2.25
My A, B, C's	1-57768-228-9	$2.25
My Ups & Downs	1-57768-238-6	$2.25

PRESCHOOL SERIES
80-page workbooks featuring the Looney Tunes™

	ISBN	PRICE
Math	1-57768-209-2	$2.99
Reading	1-57768-219-X	$2.99
Vowel Sounds	1-57768-229-7	$2.99
Sound Patterns	1-57768-239-4	$2.99

KINDERGARTEN SERIES
80-page workbooks featuring the Looney Tunes™

	ISBN	PRICE
Math	1-57768-200-9	$2.99
Reading	1-57768-210-6	$2.99
Phonics	1-57768-220-3	$2.99
Thinking Skills	1-57768-230-0	$2.99

A McGraw-Hill Workbook

CERTIFICATE OF ACCOMPLISHMENT

THIS CERTIFIES THAT

HAS SUCCESSFULLY COMPLETED

BASIC SKILLS CURRICULUM

Grade 3

Congratulations and keep up the good work!

McGraw-Hill
Consumer Products
A Division of The ***McGraw-Hill*** *Companies*

____

Publisher

Student Notes

Student Notes